CERAMICS AND ARTIFACTS FROM EXCAVATIONS IN

THE COPAN RESIDENTIAL ZONE

Papers of the
PEABODY MUSEUM OF
ARCHAEOLOGY AND ETHNOLOGY
HARVARD UNIVERSITY
CAMBRIDGE, MASSACHUSETTS, U.S.A.

VOLUME 80

BY

Gordon R. Willey
HARVARD UNIVERSITY

Richard M. Leventhal
UNIVERSITY OF CALIFORNIA,
LOS ANGELES

Arthur A. Demarest
VANDERBILT UNIVERSITY

William L. Fash, Jr.
NORTHERN ILLINOIS UNIVERSITY

WITH THE ASSISTANCE OF AND SECTIONS BY

Julia A. Hendon
Daniel R. Potter
Fred Valdez
Kevin H. Baxter
Mary Bane Stevens

APPENDICES BY

Ronald L. Bishop
Marilyn P. Beaudry
Garman Harbottle
Hector Neff
Mary D. Pohl
Lawrence H. Feldman

CERAMICS AND ARTIFACTS FROM EXCAVATIONS IN

The Copan Residential Zone

Peabody Museum of
Archaeology and Ethnology
Harvard University
Cambridge, Massachusetts, U.S.A.

1994

Cover illustration of Copador Polychrome by Barbara Fash

Design by Janis Owens

Composition by Compset Inc.

Prepress by Jay's Publishers Services

Printing and binding by Walsworth Publishing Company

Production coordination by Donna M. Dickerson

Contents

FIGURES

Scale for all drawings is 1:1, unless otherwise noted in figure legend.

TABLES

Preface

The background and history of the Harvard University Copan Valley Settlement Pattern Project of the 1970s are presented in detail in the following introduction. Our work in the Copan Valley in the 1975–77 seasons should be considered a part of an ongoing research effort in Copan archaeology. We are happy to have been the ones to have begun this recent effort.

Although this is the first of two final reports from us on our investigations, we realize that our ceramic and artifact descriptions, analyses, and comparisons are but the beginning of a series of comparable studies that will be forthcoming on the part of our various colleagues who have followed us at Copan in the 1970s, 1980s, and beyond.

G. R. W.
R. M. L.
A. A. D.
W. L. F.
Cambridge, Massachusetts
July 1989

Acknowledgments

Our debt to the people of the municipality of Copan and the Copan Valley is great. They played a major part in our work there over three seasons in the field. Specifically, we would like to thank Oscar Cruz Melgar, the Copan Representative of the Instituto Hondureño de Antropologia e Historia (IHAH), who not only spent hours in the field with us but also provided us with valuable advice on many practical matters. Lysandro Arias was, in effect, our host as he was the owner of most of the land on which our surveys and excavations were carried out. We acknowledge his willingness to let us take over some of this land, which, at the time, was under cultivation as a part of his finca. Raul and Marina Welches provided excellent hospitality at the Hotel Marina on various occasions. It should be noted that Don Raul was also Mayor of the town of Copan during our stay. Copan, as an archaeological site and park, is maintained by a sizable staff of employees of IHAH. These men and women provided us with help and advice on many occasions. Finally, in expressing our gratitude to the people of Copan, we want, especially, to thank the survey and excavation crews who worked long hours with us over the three seasons. Their loyalty and good spirits were as much appreciated then as they are in retrospect.

The initial invitation to come to Copan, and, subsequently, to work there for two additional seasons, was extended by our good friend J. Adan Cueva, of Tegucigalpa, at that time Gerente of IHAH. Dr. Cueva maintained a close interest in our research, visiting us in the field on many occasions and offering throughout his encouragement and good counsel. In addition, we want to thank Vito Veliz, Director of Field Research at IHAH, who aided us in both Tegucigalpa and Copan. We also received frequent help from other staff members of the IHAH office in the capital.

On a more personal note, we would like to remember Sr. and Sra. Nicolas Agurcia of Tegucigalpa, who entertained us while we were in that city.

Barbara Fash served as Project Artist both in the field in Copan and in Cambridge following the period of excavations. Her work is well represented in this volume, along with drawings by Aaron Paul and Mary Jane Westland. We are indebted to all of these artists. Hillel Burger, Staff Photographer of the Peabody Museum, and Louise Krasniewicz took some of the pictures of ceramics and artifacts herein illustrated. Katharine W. Willey restored most of the pottery vessels described and illustrated. Nerisa Russell conducted a technical study of all of our ceramics. Maria von Mering Huggins and Kathy O'Connor typed the manuscript. We thank them for their efforts. The staff of the Peabody Museum and the Directors of that institution during the term of the Harvard Copan Project, Stephen Williams and C. C. Lamberg-Karlovksy, gave us full support throughout, and we hereby express our gratitude.

The major financial support for the Harvard Copan Project came from the National Science Foundation and its Division of Anthropology, headed at the time by Nancie Gonzalez. Important secondary support for the fieldwork came from the funds of the Charles P. Bowditch Endowment for Mexican and Central American Archaeology, including the John G. Owens Fund. Laboratory study of the collections and this publication were paid for by these various Bowditch monies. A special note of thanks goes to George P. Gardner, Jr., who, through his affiliation with the United Fruit Company, arranged for our personnel and equipment to be shipped from the United States to Honduras in the 1976 season.

In shipping our collections from Honduras to the United States for study (in 1977)—and also in returning these collections to IHAH (in 1983)—we depended upon the good services of T. D. Downing, Customs Agents in Boston, and upon our friend Jorge Molanphy, of San Pedro Sula, Honduras. In addition, we express our special thanks to Jorge and Marta Molanphy for many kindnesses shown us in both San Pedro Sula and Copan.

1 Introduction

BACKGROUND TO COPAN ARCHAEOLOGICAL INVESTIGATIONS

Copan, in southwestern Honduras (fig. 1), is the largest and architecturally most impressive site in the southeastern Maya region. Although the terrain of the Copan Valley is not the typical lowland environment of Classic Maya civilization—being of an intermediate elevation between Maya lowlands and highlands—the archaeological material of the Copan site is fully Maya in its architecture, great art, and hieroglyphic and calendric inscriptions.

Intensive archaeological research at Copan dates back to the 1890s, with the first project of Harvard University's Peabody Museum of Archaeology and Ethnology at that great site, which lasted throughout most of the decade (Gordon 1896, 1902). After this, a second period of work at Copan occurred during the 1930s, under the aegis of the Carnegie Institution of Washington (Stromsvik 1938; Longyear 1952). Finally, a third period of research began in the 1970s and is still continuing. We are concerned here with an aspect of this lattermost period of research.

Its inception was in the spring of 1975, when Dr. J. Adan Cueva, then director of the Instituto Hondureño de Antropologia e Historia (IHAH), invited Gordon R. Willey, of Harvard University, to make a preliminary survey of Copan and the Copan Valley and to recommend future lines of archaeological investigation. Willey did this in conjunction with William R. Coe and Robert J. Sharer, of the University of Pennsylvania, who were then excavating at Quirigua in Guatemala. Together, they submitted a set of research recommendations to IHAH (Willey, Coe, and Sharer 1975). Willey followed this up by sending Richard M. Leventhal, at that time a graduate student at Harvard, to Copan during the summer of 1975 with instructions to make a general settlement survey of the valley. This was followed by a Peabody Museum expedition to Copan during the dry seasons of 1976 and 1977. In this expedition, which was supported by a National Science Foundation grant, Leventhal continued to assist Willey. William L. Fash, Jr., another Harvard graduate student, and Vito Veliz, of IHAH, also joined the party.

The objectives of the Harvard Copan Project were those of settlement study, particularly within the "Copan Pocket," or immediate Copan sector, of the Copan Valley, and the excavation of a selected sample of the smaller ruin mounds in this sector, but lying outside of the Copan Main Center. Some preliminary results of these two seasons of work have been published (Willey, Leventhal, and Fash 1978; Willey and Leventhal 1979), and a second final report on settlement mapping and excavations, including detail on architecture, burials, and other special features, is being prepared (Leventhal, in prep.). This report is our final analysis and comparative examination of the ceramics and other artifacts from these surveys and excavations.

A further word is in order here about other investigations in this third period of Copan archaeological research. Following Harvard's field operations of 1976–77, the Honduran government initiated large-scale studies with the aid of funds made available through the Central American Bank. This work was directed by Claude Baudez, on leave from the Musée de l'Homme of Paris. This phase of Copan exploration extended through the two seasons of 1978 and 1979. It continued the Harvard settlement survey of the valley and focused also on major digging in the Copan Main Center (see Baudez 1983). The Honduran government-sponsored research was then continued by William T. Sanders and David Webster, of Pennsylvania State University, from 1980 through 1985. Additional settlement survey was pursued throughout the Copan Valley as well as in some surrounding valleys, and more digging was done in the Copan Main Center, but the primary focus was upon detailed excavation and examination of an elite residential area lying within the "Copan Pocket," which is known as Las Sepulturas (see Sanders 1986). Most recently (from 1986 to the present), research has gone on at Copan under the direction of Fash, now affiliated with Northern Illinois University. Fash's studies are centered upon the excavation of the Temple of the Hieroglyphic Stairway, within the Copan Main Center, and a study of the hieroglyphic texts and monuments of that famous building.

BRIEF DESCRIPTION OF THE HARVARD COPAN PROJECT

Our Copan Valley study involved three lines of investigation: (1) the survey and mapping of the ancient settlement outside of the Copan Main Center; (2) test excavations in a number of these settlement units; and (3) more intensive and detailed excavations of three plaza group units in the Las Sepulturas zone of the valley. All of the ceramics and other artifacts presented and described in this report were derived from the excavations as defined under (2) and (3).

The survey of the valley took two forms. The first was a general walking survey to identify, locate, and describe the ancient settlement throughout the 26 square km of the valley (fig. 2). This was done during the preliminary 1975 surveys and at the beginning of the 1976 season. The second part of the survey was the detailed instrument mapping of the ancient settlement within the approximately 7 square km surrounding the Copan Main Center on the north side of the Copan River (see map, Leventhal, in prep.).

Test excavations, numbering 35, were made in settlement units located within the carefully mapped area of the valley. Each of these consisted of a 3 x 2 meter pit excavated to sterile soil. Pits were placed in the plaza area, or otherwise near the mounds, of settlement units. We hoped to glean some chronological information about the ancient occupation of the valley with minimal effort, expense, and destruction of site unit architecture. We were moderately successful in this, although some of our tests yielded so little in the way of sherd material that ceramic dating and ceramic stratigraphy were precluded.

In our survey of the valley, we devised a rule of thumb for the classification of the settlement units. The criteria of classification were mound size and the number of mounds within a unit. These two criteria tended to correlate positively—larger mounds were most often found in plaza arrangements with several mounds, smaller mounds were found singly or in smaller groups. We rated or classified our units on an ascending scale of 1 to 4, based upon unit size and elaboration of construction. For our more extensive and detailed excavations, we selected three settlement units (fig. 3): CV-16 (Type 1, or small-sized) (fig. 4), CV-20 (Type 2, or medium-sized) (fig. 5), and CV-43 (Type 3, or large-sized) (fig. 6). In the excavation of CV-43, we also excavated a number of Type 1 units that were found in the immediate vicinity. All three of our major excavations yielded substantial amounts of pottery and artifacts, as well as most of our chronological information. We did not attempt excavation of any of the very large-sized, or Type 4, units, lacking the funds and the time for such an enterprise; however, Sanders, during his operations, excavated the largest of the Type 4 units in the Las Sepulturas zone (fig. 7).

RESEARCH OBJECTIVES

On the most general level, the research objective of the Harvard Copan Project was to describe and understand the nature of settlement patterning and the settlement system in the environs of Copan. Both survey and excavation were directed to this end. What were the functions of the many structures that now appear as surface mounds on the landscape? How were they constructed? What were their relationships to each other in the little plaza units in which they were arranged? What were the relationships between plaza units? Were there spatially distinct clusterings of units in the valley, and what was the significance of these? And, finally, what was the relationship of all of this outlying settlement to that large agglomeration of monumental buildings that we know as the Copan Main Center?

As we began, we asked the very simple question, Were these settlement units the remains of dwelling places or house platforms? We are still forced to say, as have others working within probable domestic Maya remains, that we have no direct proof of such activities as cooking, storage, sleeping, or living; nevertheless, we continue to assume that the majority of these structures served such purposes. We also explored some structures within plaza units that appeared to have had special functions, and our results here were more substantive. We identified some buildings that were almost certainly related to ritual activities and probably community governance.

More specifically, as our work progressed, we asked the question, Did our simple site unit typology reflect the relative status and wealth of the inhabitants? This was a fairly easy hypothesis to test, and our excavations, particularly the more extensive and intensive ones, gave us an affirmative answer. The bigger and more elaborate units did show more evidence of elite status.

More difficult questions and objectives addressed family size and organization. What could the settlements tell us of kin organization?

These were and remain the broad goals of our Copan settlement study. They will be dealt with more directly in Leventhal's forthcoming monograph; however, the immediate purposes of this ceramic and artifact monograph articulate with these broader issues. These purposes are threefold. The first is systematic ceramic and artifact description—by word, drawing, and photograph. Such description, along with quantitative and contextual information, constitutes our basic data set. It facilitates detailed comparisons to materials from other Maya excavation programs and future reanalysis and interpretation of the Copan material. The second purpose is to fix our data, especially our ceramic data, within the unified type-variety system that has been developed for the Maya area over the past several years (Sabloff and Smith 1969, 1972; Sabloff 1975). In this way we can strengthen the ceramic chronology for the Copan region and discuss Copan interrelationships with other Maya sites and regions more effectively. In attempting to do this we not only have worked with the available literature, but have benefited from consultation with colleagues who have worked in the other recent Copan projects and with those who have been involved with ceramics at Quirigua in Guatemala. A third objective or purpose of this study is to explore how far we may go in determining the uses or functions of ceramics and artifacts within the Copan contexts and within the larger context of Maya society. Clearly, settlement arrangement, site architectural information, and burial and cache information have to be examined in concert with ceramics and artifacts.

FIELD AND LABORATORY PROCEDURES

In the field, all excavated soil and refuse from test pits and more extensive architectural-clearing proveniences was sifted through a 1-inch-square mesh screen. All potsherds, other artifacts, and all possible artifacts from these proveniences were then saved and placed in provenience-labeled field bags. These field bags were then removed to a laboratory at our headquarters in Copan, where they were cataloged and their contents were washed, cleaned, or otherwise cared for. All such materials were then numbered with their appropriate catalog number. In addition to regular provenience lot materials, any ceramic vessel, artifact, or other object that, because of its nature or its context, was an item of special interest was assigned a "Special Find" number in the field, with the exact particulars of its context, and given a separate catalog number in the laboratory. Study and classification of ceramics and other artifacts were begun in the Copan laboratory; however, the bulk of such materials was shipped, on loan, from Honduras to the Peabody Museum for further study. Such collections were then returned to Honduras after the completion of classification and description in mid-1983.

In the Peabody Museum laboratory, ceramics were examined provenience by provenience and classified according to the type-variety system. We worked directly with the sherd materials, segregating them on the bases of their various properties of paste, temper, form, and surface treatments and, by so doing, forming tentative or working types and varieties. We also worked comparatively, relying on ceramic type descriptions in the published literature for Copan (Longyear 1952) and for other Maya sites, both lowland and highland. During the period of classification we were helped by Sharer and his colleagues, of the University of Pennsylvania, who had been similarly studying their pottery collections from Quirigua, the major Maya site nearest

to Copan in the southeastern Maya region. We were also kept informed of the ceramic classificatory work being carried on by Rene Viel, at Copan, during the 1978–79 operations directed by Baudez. All of this necessitated constant revisions and reclassifications before we were ready for our final tabulations of types and varieties by provenience. Eventually, we tabulated a total of 247,591 sherds from all of our excavations. These counts, by types, varieties, and proveniences, were then fed into a computer in order to better manage the data and also to check further on the validity of the types. Type and variety descriptions were prepared from large collections of sherds that we had set aside during our sortings and that, in our opinion, best represented the types and varieties under consideration.

We sent substantial samples of various types to Ronald Bishop, formerly of the Brookhaven National Laboratories and now of the Smithsonian Institution, for compositional analysis. Bishop and Marilyn Beaudry's compositional identifications have allowed us to develop a picture of the indigenous pottery production and distribution of types within the Copan Valley and the southeastern Maya region (Bishop et al. 1986). They have addressed and preliminarily answered such questions as the places of origin and manufacture of the well-known polychrome type Copador.

Artifacts other than ceramics were classified by inspection, description, and a comparative examination of the literature from other lowland and highland Maya sites, as well as sites lying to the east of Copan, in Honduras.

This monograph, then, is a presentation of these ceramic and other artifactual classifications, together with our observations and comments upon their site contexts and their more general chronological and distributional contexts in southern Mesoamerica and the Mesoamerican borderlands to the east and south.

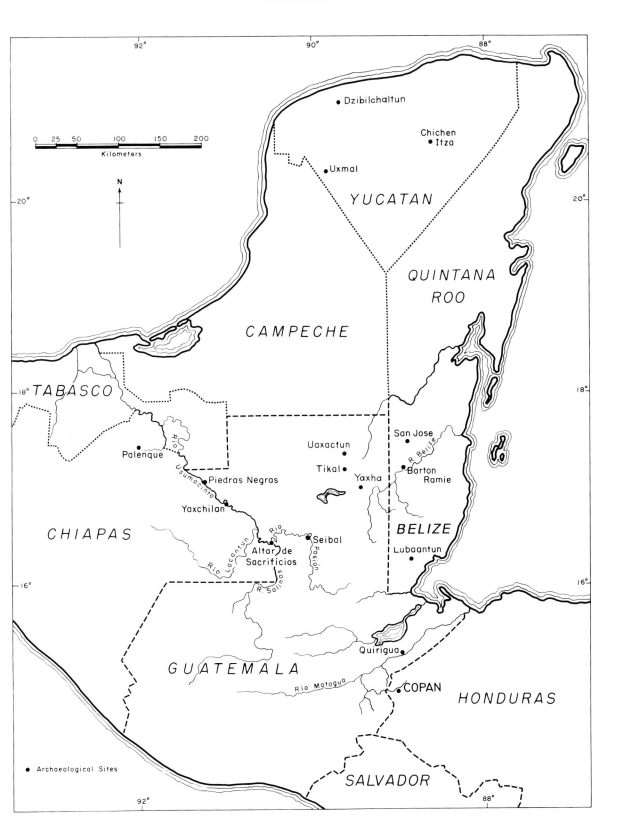

Figure 1.   Map of Maya area with location of Copan

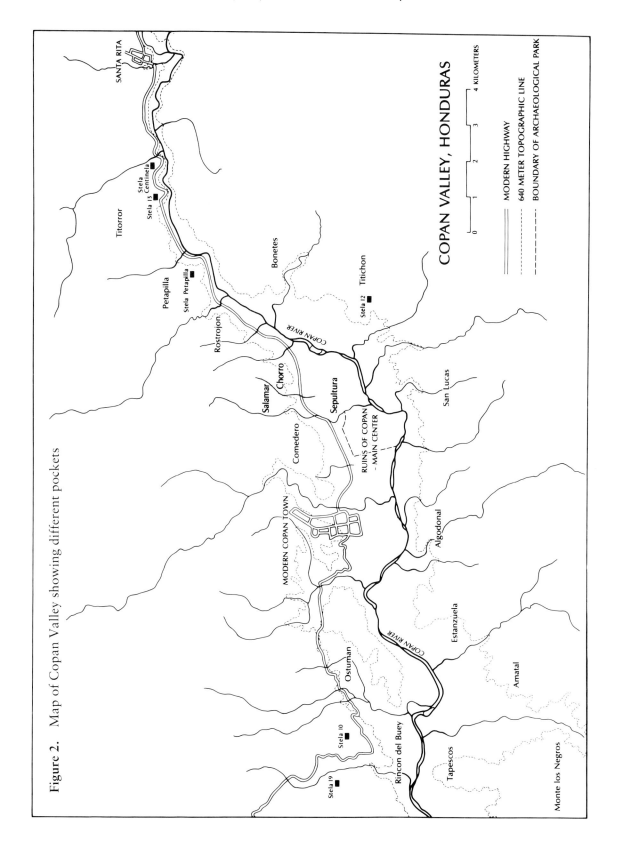

Figure 2.   Map of Copan Valley showing different pockets

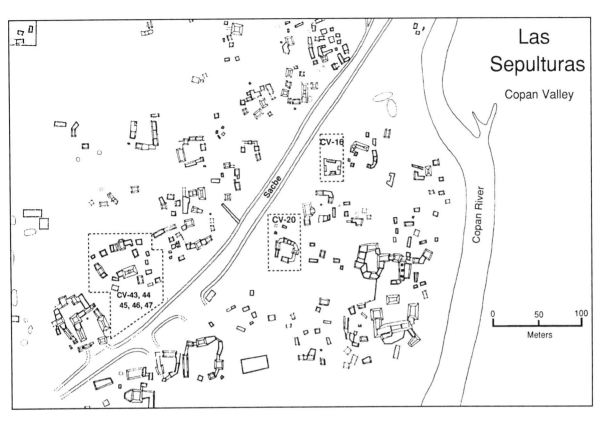

Figure 3. Location of CV-16, CV-20, CV-43–47 within Las Sepulturas section of Copan Valley

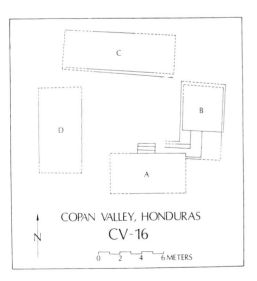

Figure 4. Detailed map of CV-16

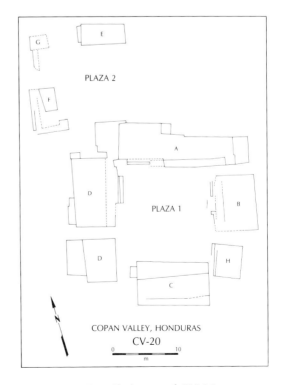

Figure 5. Detailed map of CV-20

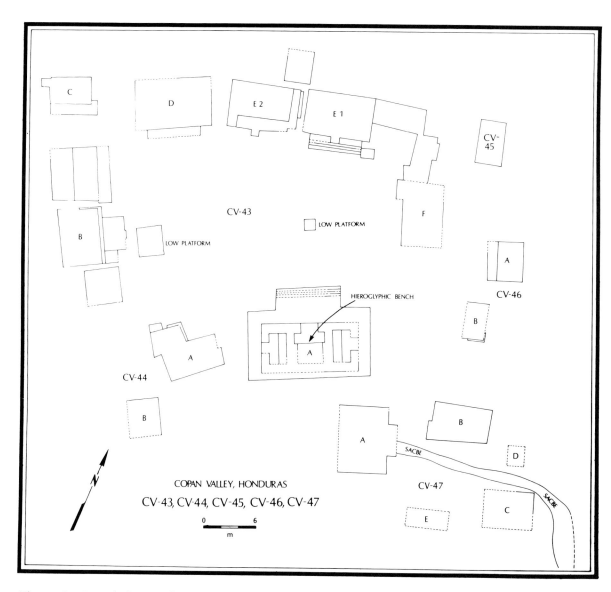

Figure 6.   Detailed map of CV-43–47

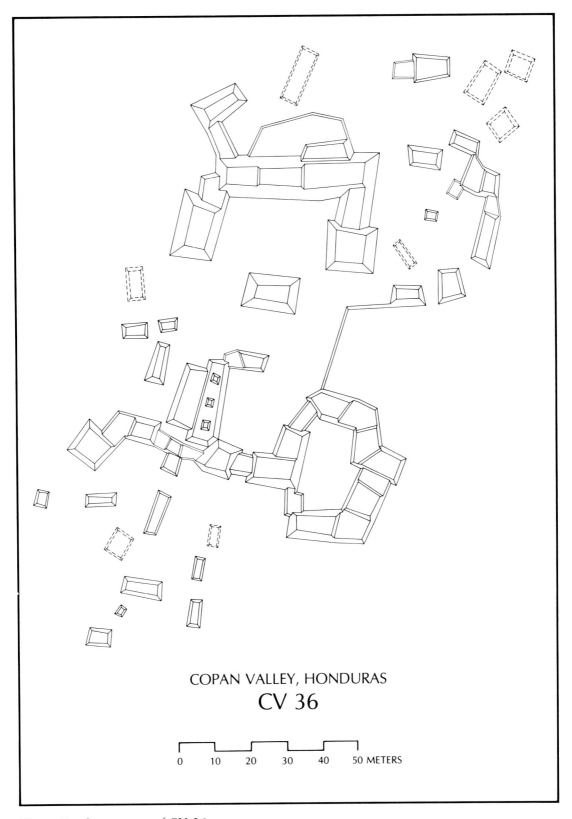

COPAN VALLEY, HONDURAS
CV 36

0   10   20   30   40   50 METERS

Figure 7. Survey map of CV-36

2 Ceramics

There is a long ceramic sequence at Copan that begins in the Maya Early to Middle Preclassic periods and continues up into the Early Postclassic. While the Harvard Copan Project excavations of 1976–77 were concerned largely with the Classic period span of that sequence, it might be well to summarize, briefly, the full pottery chronology of the site and the immediate Copan Valley as it is known at the beginning of the 1990s, following not only our work but that of the Honduran government excavation programs that succeeded ours.

The principal archaeologists involved in these ceramic studies were R. Viel (1983, as well as personal communications 1978–84; see also Viel and Cheek 1983) and D. Webster (1988), and it is from them that we offer the following chronological outline.

The initial Copan phase is designated as the Rayo (see chronological chart in Webster 1988). It is placed at the end of the Early Preclassic period and bracketed by the estimated dates of 1100 to 900 B.C. Evidence for it comes from deep tests in the alluvial flats of the Las Sepulturas zone of the Copan residential settlement. This is a location only a little more than a half-kilometer to the east of the Copan Main Center. This zone is where the Harvard Copan Project excavated its principal residential units, CV-43, CV-20, and CV-16; however, the deep tests referred to were made by our successors in the Copan excavations.

Rayo is succeeded by the Gordon and Uir phases of the Middle Preclassic. Gordon, as it has been defined by Webster, may be a funerary ceramic complex that is a subphase, or facet, of the Uir phase. It is estimated to have lasted from 900 to 600 B.C., and it is marked by ceramic types that are consistent with Early to Middle Preclassic funerary ceramics found elsewhere in southern Mesoamerica as burial furniture at this time, types featuring dark surfaces decorated with incised-bordered red bands. The Uir phase spans the full Middle Preclassic, from 900 to 400 B.C., thus subsuming the Gordon phase.

Chabij is the Copan Late Preclassic ceramic phase, and it is dated from 400 B.C. to A.D. 100.

Chabij is succeeded by Bijac, dated from A.D. 100 to 400, spanning what some would consider the Protoclassic and the early part of the Early Classic period.

The Acbi phase follows the Bijac, and Viel (1983) and Webster (1988) equate Acbi with a Middle Classic period, which they extend from A.D. 400 to 700. We have modified this somewhat, so that the Acbi phase, as used in this report, dates only from A.D. 400 to 600. We call the interval from A.D. 600 to 700, or the last part of the Viel-Webster Acbi phase, the Cueva phase. This was our working term for this early part of the Late Classic period at Copan while we were carrying out our excavations and were engaged in our preliminary ceramic classifications, and we have retained it.

With Viel and Webster, we use the name "Coner" for the Late Classic phase, which dates from A.D. 700 to 900.

Webster, in his chart, places an Ejar phase at A.D. 900 to 1000; however, recent obsidian hydration studies on numerous samples from the Copan Valley give strong indication that there was a substantial occupation of many of the valley residential zones well past even this date, extending, perhaps, up to A.D. 1100/1200, so the terminal date on Ejar is still unsettled.

This sequence, as listed, is thus:

Rayo	1100–900 B.C.
Gordon	900–600 B.C.
Uir	900–400 B.C.
Chabij	400 B.C.–A.D. 100
Bijac	A.D. 100–400
Acbi	A.D. 400–600
Cueva	A.D. 600–700
Coner	A.D. 700–900
Ejar	A.D. 900–1000/1200

In our own excavations we found very little Preclassic or Preclassic/Protoclassic pottery. The early sherds we found were recovered in the constructional fill of later (Classic period) structures. Quite probably, judging from the presence of such debris, there were once Preclassic period structures in these same general residential locations; however, if so, they had long been destroyed.

PRECLASSIC/PROTOCLASSIC PHASES

The Uir Phase

From our collections we identified only 14 sherds as pertaining to this phase. Mostly rims, some of these served as chronological markers for the Middle Preclassic period (fig. 8a–d). These were from deep dishes or bowls with slightly outslanting or outcurving sides. Typically, rims were thickened, usually with a bulge or thickening on the exterior edge, and these rim thickenings were often underscored with an incised line. Other sherds showed a secondary thickening or bulge below the rim edge, and in these cases the two bulges were separated by a shallow channel or chamfering. Wider relationships of these Uir ceramics are of a rather general southern Mesoamerican nature.

The Chabij Phase

The Chabij phase is better represented in our sherd collections than the preceding Uir phase. It is also more distinctive in its general affiliations. We describe three pottery types under the phase: Pacheco Zoned Bichrome, Okla Brown, and Bozo Incised. Together these totaled less than 100 sherds. To these we could also add the types Povmec Red-on-orange, Moscova Red, and Izalco Usulutan, which have their beginnings in Chabij but continue into the Bijac and Acbi phases and are described under those phase headings. Pacheco, Okla, and Bozo are particularly characteristic of central and eastern Honduras, eastern El Salvador, and what is known as the Uapala ceramic sphere of this region. To this was added an influx of the strong western Salvadoran and Guatemalan highland Usulutan (resist) painting tradition as represented in the inception of Povmec Red-on-orange and Izalco Usulutan.

Pacheco Zoned Bichrome Type

Variety Name: Pacheco
Established as a Type and/or Variety: By this description and description by Viel (1983).
Frequency: A total of 33 sherds. This is a very minor type in our collections, which include very few primary deposits of Preclassic materials. It is, however, a fairly common type in the Late Preclassic Chabij phase.
Ceramic Group: Pacheco
Ceramic Complex: Chabij
Illustrations: Figures 9a–d, 10. See also Longyear (1952: figs. 32a–e, 33).

Description:

Principal Identifying Modes.

1. Notched or pinched appliqued ridges on vessel exteriors (fig. 9a–d);
2. red-painted zones bordered or set off by the appliqued ridges;
3. subglobular bowl and subglobular collared jar forms (fig. 10).

Paste, Temper, and Firing. Paste ranges in color from reddish brown to dark brownish gray. It is a fairly compact uniform paste, although somewhat friable. Unslipped surfaces are often pebble-polished and quite hard.

Surface Finish and Decoration. The disposition of the appliqued ridges described above forms both rectilinear and curvilinear patterns. Often these form triangular zones filled with red paint. Others are arranged in vertical rows of closely spaced ridges. The one whole specimen (Cat. No. 1-1016) has an anthropomorphic design modeled in ridges. The ridges themselves vary in width from 1 to 4 mm and are 3 mm or less in height. The notches on the ridges are very closely spaced, varying from wide finger-punched notches to small slash punctations. Most of the surface is unslipped, except for deep red-slipped zones. However, most of the vessel surface is heavily pebble-polished.

Form. The restricted bowl and olla form is evident in our few rim sherds. One is simple, direct, and unmodified, but others are fragments of short vertical to outflared collars. One rim sherd has a small string handle on an outflared jar neck. The direct rim sherd has a horizontally placed finger-sized loop handle.

Whole, Restorable, or Partially Restorable Vessels: We recovered one whole vessel (Cat. No. 1-1016) in a cache deep below CV-43 (Operation 49(A), Level 7-A, Special Find 39). The vessel is in a typical Pacheco Bichrome subglobular deep bowl or jar with a short (1.5 cm) outflared collar. Total vessel height is 8.1 cm with an orifice diameter of 9.8 cm and a maximum diameter at midpoint of 14 cm. On one of the vessel walls there is a pair of hollow effigy heads with appliqued eyes, nose, and head ornamentation and punctated mouth. A pinched appliqued ridge encircles the vessel below the collar.

Classificatory Comments: This type represents a specific local identification of the generic Ulua bichrome ceramics of western Honduras. Our ability to classify Pacheco Zoned Bichrome is clearly based upon the identification of the appliqued ridges on a sherd. The appliqued ridge is the primary identifying trait, and some sherds of this type, without the ridge, may easily have been classified as another type.

At the same time, the number of primary Preclassic contexts found in our excavations was very few, and this is reflected in the small number of Pacheco sherds.

Intrasite Locations, Contexts, and Associations: The location of sherds and the single cache vessel is consistent with a placement of this type in the Late Preclassic or Early Classic period. No statistical evaluation was appropriate or necessary with our tiny collection, but visual inspection of lot counts of proveniences with Pacheco sherds confirms this placement and a contemporaneity of the type with Izalco Usulutan.

John M. Longyear (1952:23, 90, figs. 32a–3, 33) reports similar sherds in his Coarse Ware category and attributes them to the Archaic period (i.e., Late Preclassic) by context and association with Usulutan ceramics.

Intersite Locations, Contexts, and Associations: Together with Izalco Usulutan and Okla Brown, Pacheco Zoned Bichrome completes the major types of Copan's Late Preclassic Chabij complex. The Pacheco Type and the general structure of this complex at Copan tie the valley directly into the general Ulua Bichrome assemblage configuration found in the Late Preclassic throughout western and central Honduras as well as eastern El Salvador. John B. Glass's Ulua Zoned Bichrome Type (1966:163–165) appears to be Pacheco Zoned Bichrome. It has also been reported from Playa de los Muertos (Strong, Kidder, and Paul 1938:62–75; Strong 1948: fig. 15), Santa Rita where the Ulua Bichrome complex was first recognized (Strong, Kidder, and Paul 1938; Strong 1948), and other sites in western Honduras and the Comayagua region (Glass 1966:163–165). Very similar, if not identical, zoned bichrome jars with appliqued decoration have been reported (always in association with Usulutan) at Colonia CARE in the Sula Valley (Sheehy n.d.:9–11), in the Naco Valley (Henderson et al. 1979), in the Eden I phase at Los Naranjos on Lake Yojoa (Baudez and Becquelin 1973), at Lo de Vaca in the Comayagua (Baudez 1966:305–312), and Yarumela (Canby 1951).

It is obvious that Pacheco Zoned Bichrome and similar appliqued and/or incised zoned red-painted types are characteristic of much of western and central Honduras, generally corresponding to the original concept of the Ulua Bichrome assemblage.

The pattern of Pacheco Zoned Bichrome's correlates can be extended to eastern El Salvador by including the very similar appliqued, incised, and zoned red-painted San Esteban and Placitas Red jars and bowls of Quelepa (Andrews 1976: 48–56). A very similar assemblage of zoned red types found with Usulutan types has recently been reported at Gualjoquito in the Middle Ulua area (Schortman, Urban, and Ashmore 1983: 29–30). This broad distribution for Pacheco Zoned Bichrome and a series of closely related zoned bichrome types, always in association with plain and incised unslipped types and Izalco Usulutan, confirms the existence of an Uapala ceramic sphere of closely related ceramic complexes across most of central and western Honduras and eastern El Salvador (see below).

Functional Interpretation: The Pacheco Zoned Bichrome forms indicate the vessel's possible use in serving. However, the number of sherds is too small to provide secure contextual information on function.

Cultural Significance: As detailed above under "Intersite Locations, Contexts and Associations," Pacheco Zoned Bichrome is a critical type in its significance for the cultural affiliations of the Late Preclassic of the Copan Valley. Its presence at Copan ties the site into the pattern identified above for other Ulua Bichrome sites (i.e., ceramic assemblages composed of zoned-red bichrome ceramics, Izalco Usulutan, and plain, incised, and appliqued unslipped ceramics).

This pattern ties Copan into the Late Preclassic Uapala ceramic sphere first proposed by E. Wyllys Andrews V (1976:180–181) and more recently described by Arthur Demarest (1986) and Demarest and Sharer (1986). This pattern of closely associated ceramic assemblages covers much of Honduras and eastern El Salvador. Andrews (1976:180–181; Andrews 1977) has proposed that this ceramic sphere corresponds to the distribution of the Lenca linguistic and ethnic group. Regardless of the validity of the Andrews Lenca hypotheses, the existence of this ceramic pattern cannot be denied.

Note that Usulutan ceramics have also been found at all of the sites of the proposed Uapala ceramic sphere. Izalco Usulutan and other Usulutan types are also characteristic of the adjacent highland areas of western El Salvador and southern Guatemala, where a distinct closely related series of complexes has been included within the sequential Providencia and Miraflores ceramic spheres (Demarest 1985: chap. 6; Demarest and Sharer 1985). However, Copan and the related Uapala sphere sites are distinguished by the presence of Pacheco Zoned Bichrome and its correlates, and the absence (except as rare trade sherds) of the characteristic red, orange, and black Providencia and Miraflores sphere monochromes. This overlap, yet distinction, between the shared artifactual patterns of western El Salvador and western and central Honduras continues from the Late Preclassic through the Postclassic. Copan's complexes alternate between the complexes of these separate regions and the combination of these contrasting regional patterns in the Late Classic. However in the Late Preclassic, Copan is squarely in the eastern (i.e., Honduran) sphere of related ceramic assemblages.

Okla Brown Type

Variety Name: Okla.
Established as a Type and/or Variety: By Viel at Copan.
Frequency: This is a very minor type. A total of 13 sherds were identified from these collections.
Ceramic Group: Unknown.
Ceramic Complex: Chabij.
Illustrations: None.
General Description: With the small number of sherds recovered of this type, only the briefest and most general of descriptions is possible. Okla Brown is a brown-black-colored type. The surface is unslipped but smoothed and in some places slightly polished, possibly pebble-polished. The paste also has this brown-black color. The few rim sherds recovered show a globular body with an incurving shoulder and everted rim. There is no evidence of any type of surface decoration.
Form. The forms for Okla Brown include jars with incurving shoulders and everted rims. Strap handles are also found around the necks of these vessels.

General Comments: As mentioned above, Okla Brown is only a very minor part of our ceramic collection. However, Viel has identified this type as being one of the most important during this Chabij phase. In discussions, Viel has argued that upwards of 30 to 40 percent of the Preclassic sherds from his collections are Okla Brown.

Perhaps this type represents the beginning of an important ceramic technical tradition at Copan, the pebble-polishing of large storage vessels. This tradition clearly continues into the later periods with Antonio Buff and Arroyo Red.

Bozo Incised Type

Variety Name: Bozo.
Established as a Type and/or Variety: By this description.
Frequency: This is a minor type. Only 38 sherds were recovered from our excavations.
Ceramic Group: Unknown.
Ceramic Complex: Chabij.
Illustrations: Figure 11a–h.
Description:
Principal Identifying Modes.
1. Thick white or cream slip;
2. deep, wide, incised line designs on the exterior of the vessel. This incising approaches gouging or carving.

Surface Finish and Decoration. As listed above, one of the primary attributes is the thick white or cream slip on both the exterior and interior of the vessel.

Surface incisions appear to have been made after air-drying and average 0.03 cm in width and 0.02 to 0.03 cm in depth. These incisions appear to have been rather slovenly executed. Occasional excised or punctated areas are seen at the ends of the incised lines.

The incised designs on the surface of the vessel remain unclear from the small fragmentary sherd sample available. They appear to consist of bold and somewhat complex curvilinear elements. A whole vessel, recovered during the Premier Fase del Proyecto Arqueologico Copan (PAC-1), seems to show what might be a human hand in profile, although there are only four digits and not five.

On all of the rim sherds of our collection, there is an interior and exterior red-painted band on the lip of the vessel.

Form. The primary forms include open bowls or dishes. There is one basal sherd within our collection, indicating the existence of flat-bottomed dishes.
Whole, Restorable, or Partially Restorable Vessels: None recovered.
General Comments: This is a very distinctive type, although very few sherds were recovered from our excavations. The white slip is unusual for Copan, which seems to have developed a ceramic tradition based more upon red, orange, and buff slips.

Incised vessels with red rims are common throughout this southeast region, and red-on-white miscellaneous types have also been described (Andrews 1976); however, the distinctive combination of a very thick white slip, a red band around the exterior and interior of the rim, and an incised geometric design is uncommon.

The Bijac Phase

The phase, as it has been defined for Copan, straddles the Protoclassic (A.D. 100–250) and the earlier part of the Early Classic period, or until an estimated date of A.D. 400. During this time, Copan appears to have been—at least from the standpoint of ceramics—still within the Uapala (Honduran–eastern Salvadoran) and Maya highland (western Salvadoran–Guatemalan) traditions. The two types described under the Bijac heading, Povmec Red-on-orange and Moscova Red, so relate. A single mammiform vessel support in our Povmec collection is a Protoclassic chronological marker; however, we encountered no basal-flanged bowls or anything that would denote the Maya lowland Early Classic Tzakol tradition. Such elements had not yet begun to appear at Copan.

Povmec Red-on-orange Type

Variety Name: Povmec.
Established as a Type and/or Variety: By Viel at Copan.
Frequency: Only 15 sherds. A very minor Prospero group type.
Ceramic Group: Prospero.
Ceramic Complex: Bijac and possibly Acbi.
Illustrations: Figure 12a–e.

Description:

Principal Identifying Mode. Complex red designs painted over an orange and buff Usulutan-technique background.

Paste, Temper, and Firing. See Adan Red-on-buff (Acbi phase).

Surface Finish and Decoration. The original well-smoothed surface was buff-slipped so that the orange color, achieved by a resist or Usulutan technique, overlies the buff surface. The positive red-painted designs were then applied to the exterior vessel surfaces. The most frequent decoration is a band or row of rectangular panels formed by broad and narrow lines and filled with crosshatched lines. A variation on this is a panel filler of short wiggly lines and dots.

Form. Our sample of sherds is probably too small to be representative; however, large heavy-walled jars are indicated, as are bowl forms. These last seem to have been both simple subglobular and collared olla shapes. There is one sherd of a small mammiform support with an interior painted decoration (fig. 12a)—the only interior decoration in our small sample collection for the type. Presumably this was from an open bowl form.

Whole, Restorable, or Partially Restorable Vessels: None recovered.

Classificatory Comments: The inclusion of this type in the Prospero group recognizes the traditional linkage between orange resist-applied or Usulutan-type decoration and the positive red on orange, buff, or cream painting that characterizes the other types of the group. In Povmec, the positive red-painted (not a specular hematitic red) designs are painted over the orange-on-buff Usulutan streaking or stripes of the vessel surfaces.

Intrasite Locations, Contexts, and Associations: The sherd sample is too small for any meaningful statement.

Intersite Locations, Contexts, and Associations: See comments under this heading for Adan Red-on-buff. See also references to Usulutan technique painting with red overpainting at various Maya highland and lowland sites. This subject, as well as the matter of origins of Usulutan painted pottery, has been treated in detail by Demarest and Sharer (1982).

Functional Interpretation: Another intermediate ware on the scale from fine to coarse and utilitarian.

Cultural Significance: Povmec Red-on-orange is an example of the continuance of the Usulutan technique into the Terminal Preclassic (or Protoclassic) and Early Classic times. While there seems to be a time trend for the disappearance of the technique and its replacement by only positively painted red-on-buff, red-on-orange, and red-on-cream types, as seen in the Prospero group, there was also a continued parallel manufacture of Usulutan-painted vessels, at least here at Copan.

Moscova Red Type

Variety Name: Moscova.

Established as a Type and/or Variety: By Viel at Copan.

Frequency: In total, 46 sherds of Moscova Red were recovered from our excavations.

Ceramic Group: Undefined.

Ceramic Complex: Bijac.

Illustrations: None.

Description:

Principal Identifying Modes.

1. Vertical wall composite silhouette bowls;
2. red polished surface.

General Description. The red surface finish is distinctive in that it is smoothed and sometimes polished, producing a distinctive red-brown color.

Moscova Red is known from Preclassic cache vessels. These cache vessels are vertical walled, composite silhouette bowls with rounded basal angles and slightly rounded bases. Lids are associated with these vessels.

Intersite Locations, Contexts, and Associations: Vessels similar to this type have been identified from the Protoclassic Balam phase at Zacualpa by Robert Wauchope (1948). This coincides with the chronological placement of Moscova Red at Copan.

Functional Interpretation: This type is a fairly restricted one in that all the sherds and vessels that have been recovered (including the material from the PAC-1) are of the same basic form. It appears that they were used as the Preclassic cache vessel at Copan. The Burdalu Red Type of the Early Classic period continues this cache vessel tradition.

EARLY CLASSIC PHASE

The Acbi Phase

During what we define as the Acbi phase (A.D. 400–600), Copan ceramics maintained their strong participation in the highland-derived Usulutan tradition, as represented by the type Izalco Usulutan. At the same time, they retained their roots in the old local Uapala sphere or tradition, as seen in such a type as Cementerio Incised. Also, influences from the Maya lowlands began to make themselves felt and grew more pronounced during the Classic period. At Copan, however, there was an ongoing process of interaction between Maya highland and lowland traditions within the context of the older, local Uapala tradition. Copan pottery makers drew upon all of these antecedents, and certainly by the succeeding Late Classic period they had created a definite Copan ceramic sphere of their own.

Izalco Usulutan Type

Variety Names: Provisional A, B, C, and Unspecified.
Established as a Type and/or Variety: By R. J. Sharer at Chalchuapa, El Salvador (1978:3: 39–41).
Frequency: 1,227 sherds in our collection or 0.5 percent of all of our sherds. Of these, 180 or 14.7 percent of the Izalco collection were of the provisional Izalco A Variety, 296 or 24 percent were of the proposed B Variety, and only 16 sherds were of the proposed C Variety. Most of our Izalco sherds, 735 or 60 percent, we have left unspecified as to variety. Clearly, Izalco Usulutan is a minor type in our collections, but it is quite common in the few proveniences that date to the very Late Preclassic or initial Early Classic periods.
Ceramic Group: Izalco.
Ceramic Complexes: Chabij, Bijac, and Acbi.
Illustrations:

Izalco A: Figure 13a–i.
Izalco B: Figures 14a–l, 15.
Izalco C: Figure 16a–b.

See also Longyear (1952: figs. 44–52, 102a–c, 105h, h', 11d, 117b, b').
Description:
Principal Identifying Modes.
1. Usulutan decoration in salmon-pink to buff designs on a slightly darker pale pink to orange background;
2. hard, durable surface finish with a shiny, highly polished appearance in well-preserved specimens.

Variety Distinctions. Based on excavations in deep midden deposits, Viel (personal communication 1983) has proposed a chronological subdivision of Izalco Usulutan into three varieties—Chabij, Bijac, and Acbi phase varieties. Our own sample and contexts for Izalco Usulutan are insufficient to confirm or negate this hypothesis. However, following Viel's criteria, we have been able to classify about 40 percent of our Izalco Usulutan finds into the three varieties, the remaining 60 percent being left in the Unclassified Variety.

The distinctions are as follows:

1. Variety A (fig. 13a–i) (Chabij complex, Late Preclassic period); characteristic modes are everted grooved or incised rims on both open bowls and jars; tabs, ears, or projections on open bowls; medial flanges; spouts on jars; small string handles; and chamfering on bowls.
2. Variety B (figs. 14a–l, 15) (Bijac/early Acbi phase, Initial Classic period); characteristic modes are large mammiform tetrapod supports, basal flanges of 1 to 2 cm, sometimes scalloped, sharply outflared rims joining vessel walls at 45-degree angle (i.e., cuspidor-shaped rims).
3. Variety C (fig. 16a–b) (Acbi phase, Early to Middle Classic periods); characteristic modes are reduced basal flanges and smaller mammiforms with many perforations.

The validity of this distinction was explored via statistical study of contexts with Izalco Usulutan, comparing the co-occurrences of the three varieties. A Spearman Correlation for nonparametric data was computed for 706 excavation proveniences. Analysis of this correlation shows that these three Izalco varieties do not correlate with one another within the excavation units. This suggests that there are valid distinctions, quite possibly chronological, among these three varieties of the Izalco Type. Still, if 60 percent of our Izalco sherd sample could not be readily classified by the Viel system, his varietal divisions should be viewed with caution until more classifications and analyses of Copan materials are carried out. Obviously, given the long persistence of the type in the Copan region, it would be of great advantage in Preclassic to Early Classic (Chabij-Bijac-Acbi) dating if successful Izalco varietal-chronological distinctions were discovered.

Paste, Temper, and Firing. A generally hard, fine paste, with inclusions of fine (0.5–0.05 mm) subangular particles of sand or, occasionally, mica. Paste is pale pink to buff in color (5YR 7/4, 6/4, 5/4, 4/4; 2.5YR 7/4, 6/4, 5/4), although darker cores, often black, are common. Paste surfaces are usually very hard.

Surface Finish and Decoration. The surface finish is the unique identifying characteristic of this type. Well-preserved specimens have a lustrous, glossy finish and are usually quite hard. The Usulutan decoration appears as lighter lines, buff or pale pink (often the same as the paste color; see above) against a background of darker color, pale pink to a more common light orange. The exact nature of the surface is a subject of debate. As originally defined by Sharer (1978: 3:39–40), the surface on which these designs are executed is believed to be the unslipped or "self-slipped" paste with distinctive Usulutan designs created by differential firing (i.e., differential degrees of surface oxidation). However, others have suggested that a very thin, well-fused slip of pink-orange color lies on the paste surface, providing the darker background for the designs executed on the surface, or showing through the surface in the lighter paste color.

The question of whether the surface is unslipped, "self-slipped" in a colloidal suspension of the same clay as the paste, or subtly slipped in a very thin slightly darker color draws us into the unresolved twenty-year controversy over how the resist-like Usulutan decorated surfaces were manufactured. We refer the reader to

Demarest and Sharer (1982) for background on this Usulutan controversy and to Edwin M. Shook and Alfred V. Kidder (1952:100), Sharer (1978:3:134–135), Ronald K. Wetherington (1978b: 101–102), and most recently Mary R. Hopkins (1986) for hypotheses about manufacture and discussions of experiments to confirm or negate these hypotheses. From the perspective of macroscopic classification, all analysts agree that Izalco Usulutan has a distinctive and characteristic surface finish and style of Usulutan decoration, distinguishing it from other less well made Usulutan and resist ceramics of upper Central America. The latter include types characterized by a heavy cream or orange slip.

Regardless of how the Usulutan designs were executed against Izalco's pink to orange surfaces, they can be characterized as to pattern and placement. The actual designs are generally curvilinear lines in wiggles, swirls, loops, or volutes. However, straight lines are also common. Often the lines are executed in parallel sets, as if somehow applied with a multiple-brush technique. Large, irregular blotches or blobs of lighter color are also common Usulutan designs. Sometimes Izalco surfaces have a cloudy, irregular orange to pink-orange surface, but without any sharp distinct designs. Decoration is on the interiors and exteriors of bowls, but only on the exteriors of jars.

Form. In Late Preclassic contexts Izalco Usulutan is found in a wide variety of forms of many sizes. These forms include vertical-wall bowls, flaring-wall bowls with flat or convex bases, flanged flaring-wall bowls with sublabial or medial flanges, flaring-wall bowls with composite silhouettes and scalloped shoulders or scalloped basal flanges. All of these bowl forms can be found with rims that are simple direct, direct-grooved, everted, wide-everted, wide-everted-and-grooved, wide-everted-and-modeled bolstered, or slightly thickened. These open bowl forms vary in orifice diameter from 25 to 40 cm and in height from 13 to 20 cm.

Other forms are restricted or convex-wall bowls, deep hemispherical bowls, deep neckless jars, or olla forms with vertical or outflaring necks and direct, everted, or wide everted rims. Olla forms usually have restricted orifices of 6 to 12 cm and heights estimated as ranging from 12 to 40 cm. Elaborate animal effigy forms are also common here as well as throughout the highlands and southern periphery. These include fish, turtle, and frog effigy bowls, the lattermost having elaborate rim heads or faces molded in very wide everted rims or sublabial flanges.

Later (Protoclassic and Early Classic) forms of Izalco Usulutan have basal flanges and/or large mammiforms. According to Viel (personal communication 1983), the size and shape of mammiform and attributes of flanges are specific to time periods and can be used to define chronologically distinct provisional varieties (see discussion of "Variety Distinctions," above).

Whole, Restorable, or Partially Restorable Vessels: Our own excavations encountered a few primary Preclassic or Initial Classic proveniences and many large sherds, but no whole vessels were recovered. One large sherd is an archetypal Protoclassic (Izalco B Variety) mammiform support (fig. 15). This sherd was recovered from Operation 49(A), CV-43. It measures over 7.5 cm wide and 6 cm high, with a conical nipple/nubbin foot 2 cm wide at its base. The fragment also has part of a scalloped, wide basal flange.

Classificatory Comments: Classificatory problems include the exact definition of the characteristic surface of the type (see "Paste, Temper, and Firing" above) and the uncertainty of the provisional variety distinctions (also discussed above). Izalco Usulutan sherd counts are probably also inflated slightly in our counts by the occasional inclusion of Usulutan-decorated body sherds of the later Chilanga Red-painted Usulutan Type. However, generally, paste, surface, and form differences allow the distinction of these later types of the Usulutan tradition.

Intrasite Locations, Contexts, and Associations: The small number of Izalco sherds makes it difficult to identify specific locations and contexts within the excavations. There is clearly no specific association between the differential distribution of Izalco and any specific structure of CV-20, CV-16, or CV-43. Of the CV-20 collection of sherds, Izalco makes up .2 percent of the total, at CV-43 4 percent, and at CV-16 2 percent.

It should be noted that in clearing and trenching operations conducted within the sacbe at two points along its extent, Izalco sherds were found in slightly higher frequency than in other excavations. We suggest that the fill used in the sacbe construction may have come from buildings

erected during this Late Preclassic to Early Classic period.

Intersite Locations, Contexts, and Associations: Izalco Usulutan is ubiquitous in the Late Preclassic and Protoclassic of southeastern Mesoamerica. It originated in the long Usulutan tradition of western El Salvador (Demarest and Sharer 1982; Demarest 1986). Between the beginning of the Late Preclassic and the Protoclassic and Initial Classic periods (ca. 400 B.C.–A.D. 300), the distinctive Izalco Usulutan Type or very similar local versions spread in popularity across all of El Salvador, the highlands of Guatemala, most of Honduras, and even Guatemala's Lower Motagua Valley. Occasional sherds of this type also appear in the Maya lowlands, in some cases due to long-distance trade (e.g., Demarest 1986; Bishop 1984). The development, spread, and distribution of this type have been described and discussed in detail elsewhere (Demarest and Sharer 1982; Andrews 1976:65–66, 142–144, 179–181; Demarest 1986; Demarest and Sharer 1986). Published Late Preclassic occurrences, cited in these sources, of Izalco Usulutan or very similar hard-surfaced, unslipped or single-slipped, fine-pasted finds include Bilbao, Monte Alto, Kaminaljuyu, and the Salama Valley in the Guatemala highlands; Chalchuapa, Santa Leticia, Atiquisaya, Jayaque, and the Zapotitan Basin in western El Salvador; the Cerron Grande Basin and Quelepa in central and western El Salvador; the middle Ulua, Sula, and Comayagua regions of western Honduras; the Naco and Copan valleys of far western Honduras; and the Lower Motagua Valley at numerous sites, including a few deep deposits at Quirigua. Thus, by the end of the Preclassic period, Izalco Usulutan is a shared element indicating the communication of ideas about style, form, and specialized manufacturing and decorative techniques across all of the southern periphery of Mesoamerica.

As discussed above under the Pacheco Zoned Bichrome Type, there are indications of two large ceramic co-traditions in these Usulutan-dominated Late Preclassic sites of the southern Mesoamerican periphery. One is the series of sites in western El Salvador and highland Guatemala, including Santa Leticia, Kaminaljuyu, Monte Alto, Chalchuapa, and Bilbao. These sites all participate in the sequential Providencia (500–100 B.C.) and Miraflores

(100 B.C.–A.D. 250) ceramic spheres, characterized by large frequencies of Izalco Usulutan and by other fine monochrome types in black, red, orange, and, less frequently, cream (see Demarest and Sharer 1986 for more detailed discussion of these ceramic spheres). These sites also have local, coarse-ware jars in red on buff. This pattern contrasts with the simpler assemblages of western and central Honduras and eastern El Salvador, where Late Preclassic ceramic assemblages are characterized by far fewer types. These simpler Uapala sphere assemblages have a very large frequency of Izalco Usulutan (from 20 to 70 percent) accompanied usually by unslipped plain and incised ceramics and Pacheco Zoned Bichrome or similar local zoned red bichrome ceramics. Copan, Quelepa, and numerous excavated sites in Honduras participate in this Uapala Sphere. Andrews (1976:65–66, 142–144, 179–181) defined this sphere pattern, which has been further detailed by Demarest, Sharer, and others (e.g., Demarest and Sharer 1986; Demarest 1986).

The distinction between these two regional sets of spheres apparently has great cultural significance. Andrews (1976, 1977) has proposed a linguistic and ethnic Lenca affiliation for the Uapala sphere, while Sharer (1974, 1978) has proposed highland Maya affiliations for the Guatemala and western Salvadoran Providencia and Miraflores spheres. Of particular significance to us here is that two ceramic spheres of the southern periphery overlap at Copan during most of the Classic period. Earlier, however, in the Late Preclassic Chabij complex, Copan was clearly in the more eastern Uapala sphere.

Functional Interpretation: Izalco Usulutan is so common in the Late Preclassic and Initial Classic, so widely distributed, and so varied in vessel forms that it must have included vessels of many different functions—domestic, ritual, and probably even storage.

Cultural Significance: As discussed above under "Intersite Locations, Contexts, and Associations," the common presence of Izalco Usulutan (together with Pacheco Zoned Bichrome and the plain Okla Type) indicates that from the Late Preclassic Chabij complex, if not earlier, the Copan Valley's ceramic ties and artifactual affiliations are with El Salvador and Honduras, rather than to the Maya lowlands to the north.

This southern and eastern pattern in Copan's household artifacts and ceramics persists throughout the rest of the history of the site, despite the spectacular Classic Maya presence manifested in Copan's monumental architecture, sculpture, elite burials, and a very few elements of the artifactual assemblage (e.g., glyphs on Don Gordon Modeled-carved, moldmade figurines).

This dual pattern is the central motif of Copan's archaeology: ties of elite public culture to the Maya north, but affiliations in most other aspects of ceramics, artifacts, and household culture with the southern periphery to the south and east. The exact meaning of this dual pattern is the primary question regarding the site's development and its role as the southern frontier outpost of Classic lowland Maya civilization.

A second series of questions regards Copan's clear and distinctly different patterns of shared ceramic and artifact types with western El Salvador, on the one hand, and Honduras, on the other. In the Chabij phase of the Late Preclassic, Copan's ceramic affiliation is clearly (and nearly entirely) with the east (i.e., with Honduras). As we have noted, the dominance of Okla plain, Izalco Usulutan, and Pacheco Zoned Bichrome places the Copan Valley squarely in the Uapala ceramic sphere, which includes sites such as Quelepa in eastern El Salvador and Los Naranjos in the Lake Yojoa region of Honduras. This Late Preclassic ceramic sphere, with its three major groups of types, contrasts with the more varied and complex Miraflores ceramic sphere pattern of the highlands of western El Salvador and southeast Guatemala. This latter western pattern tends to be associated with the more developed and complex "epi-Olmec" chiefdoms of that region (e.g., at Chalchuapa, Kaminaljuyu, Santa Leticia, and Monte Alto).

Cementerio Incised Type

Variety Name: Zigoto.
Established as a Type and/or Variety: By Viel at Copan.
Frequency: Rare in the predominantly Late Classic Harvard Copan Project lots. See frequency comments for Cementerio Incised: Cementerio Variety and Mapache Grooved.

Ceramic Group: Cementerio.
Ceramic Complexes: Bijac/Acbi.
Illustrations: Figures 17a–g, 18, 19.
Description:

Principal Identifying Modes.
1. Appliqued ridges marked with pinches on indentations;
2. medium-line incision in geometric patterns;
3. rough to slightly smoothed unslipped surfaces.

Paste, Temper, and Firing. See Cementerio Variety description.

Surface Finish and Decoration. Incised ornamentation occurs in small triangular zones filled with parallel lines, and in larger areas with more widely spaced parallel lines. Punctations are sometimes associated with incisions usually in rows but also in fields. Width between incised lines varies from 3 to 9 mm. Appliqued ridges appear to have encircled vessels near the collar or near the maximum midpoint of jar diameter. These ridges average about 7 mm in width and 3 to 5 mm in height. Indentations or pinches are located directly on top of the ridge and may be very closely spaced (2 or 3 mm) or more widely placed (1 cm). It is possible that the applique ornamentation in some instances was a zoomorphic representation (a possible eye of a human, bird, or animal). As to distribution of decoration on the vessel, some sherds suggest that the upper vessel wall above the maximum diameter and the appliqued ridge were given over to incision and punctation, whereas the lower portion was left plain.

Form. The present collection is inadequate to give a good idea of vessel form range of the type, but all sherds we have indicate a collared jar or olla form. These would appear to have been somewhat smaller than the related types of the Cementerio group.

Four sherds give evidence of vertically placed loop handles located on or just below the collar area of the jars. These handles are 2.5 to 5 cm in length, rise to 2 to 2.5 cm in height, with the handle element itself being between 1 and 1.5 cm in thickness. The aperture of the handle is in two instances large enough for the insertion of a forefinger and in one instance too small for this.

No rim or basal sherds are present in this collection.

Whole, Restorable, or Partially Restorable Vessels: Two partial vessels (Cat. Nos. 1-306 and 1-672) in globular jar form were recovered.

Cat. No. 1-672 (fig. 18) has an estimated original height of 20 cm and a maximum diameter at midpoint of 21.5 cm. Remains of the collar bear coarse incised lines as does the upper half of the jar, with alternating patches of parallel vertical lines and fields of slash punctations. At the midpoint of the vessel wall is an appliqued fillet or strip that has been pinched to form a notched effect. This last feature is diagnostic of the Zigoto Variety.

Cat. No. 1-306 (fig. 19) is a large collared olla of Cementerio Incised coarse-ware with a height of 33 cm, collar height of 7 cm, and collar orifice diameter of 14 cm. The collar is slightly outflared. The vessel surface from rim to below the neck is covered with crude crosshatched incised lines. From the shoulder down the vessel is plain.

Classificatory Comments: This is an earlier, slightly more elaborate version of Cementerio Incised and contrasts with the later Cementerio Variety. Sherds of the Zigoto Variety are very hard to distinguish from those of the Cementerio Variety. Therefore, Zigoto cannot be fully defined on the basis of the Harvard Copan Project.

Intrasite Locations, Contexts, and Associations: Only a small number of sherds of this Cementerio Incised: Zigoto Variety were recovered in these excavations. No specific distributional pattern can be identified.

According to studies and excavations by Viel (personal communication 1983), the Zigoto Variety dates earlier than the Cementerio Variety of Cementerio Incised, going back to the very beginning of the Classic period. Our statistical counts do not include separate evaluation of Cementerio Incised's varieties, so we are unable to evaluate this interpretation. See discussions for Cementerio Incised (Cueva phase) for further comments.

Intersite Locations, Contexts, and Associations: See Cementerio Incised description (Cueva phase).

Functional Interpretation: Same as for Cementerio Incised: Cementerio Variety.

Cultural Significance: This is an earlier version of Cementerio distinguished by Viel (personal communication) on the basis of a larger Preclassic and Early Classic sample. It seems possible that there is a developmental connection between this type and other appliqued ridge types of the Late Preclassic in the periphery (e.g., Pacheco Bichrome).

See section on "Cultural Significance" for Cementerio Incised: Cementerio Variety (Cueva phase) for further discussion.

Hijole Unslipped Type

Variety Name: Hijole.
Established as a Type and/or Variety: By Viel at Copan.
Frequency: There are only 81 sherds that we have classified within this Hijole Type.
Ceramic Group: Unknown.
Ceramic Complexes: Bijac/Acbi.
Illustrations: Figure 20a–k.
Description:
Principal Identifying Modes.
1. Thick, coarsely tempered, rough surfaced ware of brownish tint;
2. globular collared jars with outflared rims;
3. subglobular bowls with thickened or folded rims;
4. large shallow open bowls or plates.

Surface Finish and Decoration. The surface of these vessels has a general brownish tint (5YR 5/4); however, there is no slip on the surface. Some of the surfaces of the sherds are very rough, whereas others show evidence of smoothing and even some polishing. Occasionally, one finds red banding on both the interior and exterior of the rims or lips of the vessels.
Form. Note also the presence of large, heavy strap handles, which apparently were placed vertically on the body of the vessel.
Whole, Restorable, or Partially Restorable Vessels: None recovered.

Prospero Red-on-buff Type

Variety Name: Unspecified.
Established as a Type and/or Variety: By Viel at Copan.
Frequency: 148 sherds or 35 percent of the Prospero group. The entire Prospero group is less than 0.1 percent of Copan's total collection.

Ceramic Group: Prospero.
Ceramic Complexes: Bijac/Acbi.
Illustrations: Figure 21a–j.
Description:
Principal Identifying Mode. Slovenly executed red linear designs on buff to buff-orange background.
Paste, Temper, and Firing. See Adan Red-on-buff.
Surface Finish and Decoration. Both curvilinear and rectilinear elements in positive red-on-buff painting. The red is the same as that of Adan Red-on-buff. These red elements are almost always blurred so that it is difficult to distinguish formal designs; however, cross-hatching is one recognizable design. The decorative scheme is clearly related to Adan Red-on-buff; the main difference is the extremely slovenly execution of the Prospero painting in contrast to the more carefully formed Adan designs. Decoration seems to be principally on vessel exteriors; however, there are a few sherds of open bowl forms that have interior designs.
Form. The principal form is either a jar or an olla, but lacking information on vessel heights it is impossible to say what the numerical proportions between these two may have been. Some sherds come from large, thick-walled vessels that had a pronounced medial (or approximately medial) angle. Other sherds indicate thinner-walled vessels, either jars or ollas. As implied by the "jar" and "olla" designations, orifices of the vessels were restricted, and the few rim sherds found indicate rims with short flared or outslanted collars. Some pieces show vertical loop handles, and these had been placed to arch over the medial angle of the vessel. There is one sherd in our collection that has a small circular nubbin attached to the vessel wall. The nubbin is 3 cm in diameter and 1.5 cm high and has a deep indentation or pit in its center. There are a few sherds of open bowl forms.
Whole, Restorable, or Partially Restorable Vessels: None recovered.
Classificatory Comments: One of the Prospero group, with Bijac/Acbi phase beginnings. Like Adan Red-on-buff, it is probably related to an Usulutan tradition; however, and again like Adan, it is executed entirely in positive red-on-buff painting with no evidence of Usulutan resist on vessel surfaces.

Intrasite Locations, Contexts, and Associations: Again, the small number of sherds makes it impossible to attempt to identify any specific pattern of distribution within the excavations.

Intersite Locations, Contexts, and Associations: See commentary under this section for Adan Red-on-buff.

Functional Interpretation: For domestic functions. Along with other Prospero group types, Prospero Red-on-buff has an intermediate position on a scale of fineness, somewhere between coarse unslipped plain and striated vessels and the more finely made and decorated polychrome types.

Cultural Significance: Another recognizable type in the ample tradition of red painting in a buff, orange, or cream ground that is so well represented at Copan, beginning with the Usulutan tradition wares in the Late Preclassic and continuing in both the Early and Middle Classic in both Usulutan techniques and positive painting techniques.

Chitam Red-on-cream Type

Variety Name: Chitam.
Established as a Type and/or Variety: By Viel at Copan.
Frequency: Only 20 sherds. A very rare Prospero group type in our collections.
Ceramic Group: Prospero.
Ceramic Complexes: Bijac/Acbi interface.
Illustrations: Figure 22a–b.
Description:
Principal Identifying Modes.
1. Specular hematitic red broad-line and sloppily executed geometric designs on cream slip;
2. coarser paste with heavier tempering particles than other Prospero group types.

Paste, Temper, and Firing. Similar to other types of Prospero group but with larger sand or grit temper particles.

Surface Finish and Decoration. The red lines of the decoration are broad (1–1.5 cm in width) and frequently blurred or smeared. The red color is a dark red (10R 3-6). All design arrangements are rectilinear-rectangles, triangles, and so on. The sloppy execution of the decoration is closer to the mode of Prospero Red-on-buff than to Adan

Red-on-buff. Buff surfaces are probably self-slipped for the most part. There is smoothing but little or no polishing of surfaces.

Form. Sherds indicate two forms: (1) a collared jar with short outflared collar and (2) an open bowl with a very slightly incurved rim and a slight medial angle on the body.

Whole, Restorable, or Partially Restorable Vessels: None recovered.

Classificatory Comments: Another type within the Prospero group. This type is set aside from Adan Red-on-buff and Prospero Red-on-buff by somewhat different colors in surface treatment and by a coarser paste.

Intrasite Locations, Contexts, and Associations: No data.

Intersite Locations, Contexts, and Associations: See comparative comments under Adan Red-on-buff.

Functional Interpretation: Similar to Adan Red-on-buff and Prospero Red-on-buff.

Cultural Significance: See Adan Red-on-buff and Prospero Red-on-buff. The use of a specular hematite red paint for the surface decoration, in contrast to the lighter reds used in other Prospero group types, is of some interest. In general, in southern Mesoamerica, specular red paint has Early and Middle Formative or Preclassic uses and may disappear afterward. Here at Copan, however, Chitam Red-on-cream provides a continuity in this kind of paint through Late Preclassic and into Early Classic times. Then, of course, specular hematite paint has an unusual vogue in the Late Classic Copador Polychrome Type at Copan.

Adan Red-on-buff Type

Variety Name: Adan.
Established as a Type and/or Variety: By this description.
Frequency: 207 sherds or nearly half of our Prospero group sherds. However, the entire Prospero group is only 0.1 percent of our collection.
Ceramic Group: Prospero.
Ceramic Complex: Acbi.
Illustrations: Figure 23a–g.
Description:
Principal Identifying Modes.

1. Broad parallel lines with attached solid geometric zones in red on a buff or orange-buff ground color;
2. large jars with short, slightly outflared collars.

Paste, Temper, and Firing. Sand tempered, fairly compact paste. In general, slightly coarser than the paste texture of the Tipon group types. Surfaces tend to be buff-fired.

Surface Finish and Decoration. The most frequent designs are close-spaced red parallel lines, running both horizontally and vertically on the vessel. A common arrangement is for the horizontal lines to be placed near the top or the collar of the jar and for the vertical lines to descend from these down over the shoulder and sides of the jar. The individual red lines are fairly constant in width (3–5 mm) and have intervening spaces of about the same width. The line arrangements are sometimes combined with attached dot or flag-like elements. There are also some indications of nested chevrons and triangles and some cross-hatching. Another design element variation is that of a wavy line placed between two straight lines. The execution of the decoration is bold rather than tight and neat; and there is a range from well laid out patterns to much more slovenly executed ones. Among the latter there are instances of blurring of the lines. The red pigment has a range of 2.5 YR 5-8 to 5-6. The underlying buff surface is, in some instances, a definite slip; but, in most instances, it appears to be self-slipped or the smoothed surface of the vessel. The buff surfaces range from 5 YR 6-4 to 5 YR 6-6. With the common jar form, the exteriors are the well-smoothed to polished surfaces; however, some jars show slipping and smoothing-polishing on collar interiors. Usually the orifice of the jar has an interior red band that overlaps onto the top of the lip.

Form. The large collared jar form has a wide orifice, estimated from sherds at 17 to 23 cm in diameter. It is unlikely that the maximum diameters of the jars (probably at body midpoint) were much greater than the orifice diameters. There is no reliable information on vessel height. Several loop handles are in our collections for the type. These are 3 x 2 to 2 x 1.5 cm in thickness, and the loops are large enough to permit the insertion of two or three fingers. The handles were placed parallel to the vertical axis of the vessel, and they were attached to points just below the rim and at the top of the shoulder. All handles were red-painted.

Whole, Restorable, or Partially Restorable Vessels: None recovered.

Classificatory Comments: One of a series of Prospero group types. These types have their beginnings in Late Preclassic (Bijac) times at Copan, and, although entirely positively painted, they apparently relate to the red-on-buff, red-on-orange, or red-on-cream treatments seen in some types that combine Usulutan resist techniques with positive painting.

Intrasite Locations, Contexts, and Associations: Longyear (1952:28–30, 96–97) refers to red-on-orange ware occurring in both the latter part of the Early Classic and in the Full or Late Classic periods; but none of this material that he describes has the collared jar form so typical of Adan Red-on-buff.

Intersite Locations, Contexts, and Associations: Adan Red-on-buff and other red-on-buff, red-on-orange, or red-on-cream types of the Prospero group probably derive from an Usulutan tradition that has its origins in the Salvadoran-Guatemalan highland regions (Demarest and Sharer 1982). This tradition impinged on the Maya lowlands, influencing pottery developments there. For instance, the type Guacamallo Red-on-orange, which is found at Altar de Sacrificios (Adams 1971:29) and at Barton Ramie (Gifford 1976:137–140), has a similar color scheme to some of the Prospero group types although still retaining some evidences of resist painting in addition to the red overpainting. Guacamallo is a Protoclassic period type. San Ignacio Red-on-brown from Barton Ramie (Gifford 1976:156) should also be mentioned. It occurs in jar forms, like Adan, and dates to the Early Classic. What appear to be possible resist-painted stripes occur on some specimens.

Sharer (1978:47) describes red-painted Usulutan-decorated in the Maya highlands pottery as part of his Chilanga group.

In Honduras, at Los Naranjos, Claude Baudez and Pierre Becquelin (1973:170–193) list two types, Muerdalo Orange and Bolo Orange, which have Usulutan painting. Closer to Adan Red-on-buff and to Prospero Red-on-buff, however, are their types Urupa Red-on-buff (Baudez and Becquelin 1973:235–237, fig. 94g) and Meambar Red-on-buff (ibid.:238–240, fig. 94a–e), which are somewhat later (dating to the very end of the late Preclassic and into the Early Classic) than Muerdalo and Bolo. Urupa and Meambar are both entirely positive painted, as are Adan and Prospero, and they both include jar forms (in some cases with handles). Thus, a survey of the literature would find the closest parallels to the Prospero group types in Honduras.

Functional Interpretation: Probably food-holding or food-serving vessels. Adan does not run to truly fine luxury wares, but neither is it a coarse utility ware.

Cultural Significance: Adan Red-on-buff and other types of the Prospero group represent a developmental continuity out of the ancient highland Usulutan tradition. One of the processes of this tradition was the increasing emphasis on red overpainting and the dropping out of resist painting. All but one of the Prospero group types (the exception being Povmec Red-on-orange) are entirely positive painted. This development seems to have taken place primarily in the vicinity of Copan or in western Honduras, as evidenced by the information from Los Naranjos. At least there seem to be more of the red-on-buff decorated Early Classic types in these regions than in the Maya highlands or, certainly, than in the Maya lowlands proper.

Ricardo Composite Type

Variety Name: Ricardo.

Established as a Type and/or Variety: By this description.

Frequency: 36 sherds. Only 8.5 percent of our small Prospero group ceramic collection.

Ceramic Group: Prospero.

Ceramic Complex: Acbi.

Illustrations: Figure 24a–d.

Description:

Principal Identifying Modes.
1. Crosshatched incised collar or neck area;
2. red-on-buff painting on body of jar;
3. collared jars or olla forms.

Paste, Temper, and Firing. Similar to most other Prospero group types of relatively fine-grained paste and temper.

Surface Finish and Decoration. Incision on neck or collar exteriors varies from deep to shallow. Design is usually that of crossed diagonal lines with individual diamonds of cross-hatching varying from about 1 to 4 cm in length or width. Some few sherds indicate that incised decoration is simple parallel diagonal line arrangements rather than cross-hatching. Exterior vessel surface of jars below crosshatched incision is well smoothed to polished and varies from definite buff-orange slip to a buff self-slip. Red-painting decoration includes bold crosshatched arrangements, parallel horizontal lines encircling the vessel, or large solid red bands or areas below incised neck zone. The red color ranges from 10 R 4/6 to 10 R 5/8.

Form. Only collared jars or ollas are represented. The collars are quite short (3–5 cm in height). Vessel orifices appear large in proportion to maximum widths of vessels. Two orifice examples were 20 cm in diameter. We had no good measurements of maximum vessel diameters or heights. On two sherds there were small vertically placed strap handles on the vessel collars.

Whole, Restorable, or Partially Restorable Vessels: None recovered.

Classificatory Comments: The incised decoration on this composite type is similar to that of the type Cementerio Incised: Cementerio Variety, both in the slash-like quality of the incised lines themselves and in the crosshatch or diamond arrangement. Paste, temper, and especially surface finish and the use of a red-on-buff or red-on-orange decorative scheme, in addition to the incision, are like those types of the Prospero group with which Ricardo Composite is lumped.

Intrasite Locations, Contexts, and Associations: No data.

Intersite Locations, Contexts, and Associations: A search of Peten and Maya lowland literature reveals nothing that seems close to or comparable with Ricardo Composite. As with other Prospero group types, relations point in the direction of the highlands and, even more so, eastward into Honduras. Sharer's (1978:49–50, figs. 21g, 1–3 and 1–4) Chapia Grooved-punctated and Pilapa Red-painted types from Chalchuapa in El Salvador have slight resemblances to Ricardo Composite; Baudez and Becquelin's (1973:218–219, figs. 89, o–w, 90,1) Tiligua Incised from Los Naranjos, in Honduras, is closer. Tiligua forms are collared jars; the incision is slash-like; and there is red paint in zones marked by incision or otherwise disposed on the vessel body. From

their description, the paste and temper of Tiligua sounds somewhat coarser than that of Ricardo Composite or most of our Prospero group types.
Functional Interpretation: See comments on other Prospero group types.
Cultural Significance: One of the positive painted red-on-buff or red-on-orange types deriving from the Usulutan tradition.

Burdalu Red Type

Variety Name: Burdalu.
Established as a Type and/or Variety: By Viel at Copan.
Frequency: A total of two sherds have been identified within this collection.
Ceramic Group: Unknown.
Ceramic Complex: Acbi.
Illustrations: None.
General Description: Viel (1983) has identified this type as the cache jars for the Acbi period. He states that they are a continuation of the Moscova Red cache vessels from the Bijac time period. These cache vessels are open bowls with straight or slightly outslanting sides and everted rims.

The surface of these vessels is slipped and polished with a red slip that is typical of the Copan cache vessels.

Melano Carved Type

Variety Name: Melano.
Established as a Type and/or Variety: By this description.
Frequency: A total of 95 sherds were placed within the Melano group, which includes three types: Melano Carved, Melachrino Brown, and Con Permiso Red-on-brown.
Ceramic Group: Melano.
Ceramic Complex: Acbi.
Illustrations: Figures 25a–o, 26, 27.
Description:
Principal Identifying Modes.
1. A combination of fine and broad incision-carving on highly polished brown to black exterior surfaces;
2. cylindrical jars;
3. jar lids.
Paste, Temper, and Firing. No data.

Surface Finish and Decoration. The incision-carving on the surface of the vessels was done after air-drying so that the individual lines sometimes present a scratched appearance. There are instances of substantial portions of the vessel surface having been excised or cut out, particularly at points of the intersection of lines in the decoration. This sometimes results in medallion-like areas left at the level of the vessel surface. These elements are sometimes decorated with very fine line incision.

Decoration appears to have been placed in bands at some 0.1 to 3 cm below the vessel rim. There are some sherds that indicate that such decorated zones probably extended some distance down the vessel wall, possibly to near the base. There are also panel-like arrangements.

The design motifs themselves consist of glyphic or pseudo-glyphic elements along with running geometric arrangements combining both rectilinear and curvilinear elements. In addition to hieroglyphic and geometric design units, there are central human figure designs as evidenced by Cat. No. 1-319 (fig. 27; see below for a detailed description of this particular piece).

Small fields of fine-line or crosshatched incisions are part of the designs. Two sherds in the collection show small, appliqued button-like features that were probably incorporated into the design. There is also one example of red pigment rubbed into the design after firing. In addition, Cat. No. 1-319 shows a similar use of pigment in the design.

The use of white and colored thin plaster coatings was noted on several sherds and the one restored vessel, Cat. No. 1-319.

Finally, there is evidence that the lids of this vessel type also had incised-carved decorations.
Form. The cylinder or near-cylinder jar is the most common form. The restored vessel of this type (Cat. No. 1-319) is 15.2 cm high and has an orifice diameter of 14.3 cm and a basal diameter of 13.1 cm. This specimen has a very low ring base (2–3 mm) that is 10.8 cm in diameter.

Rim sherds from the collection indicate that the orifice diameter of this specimen is within the general size range, although there are a few pieces that indicate a slightly larger diameter.

In addition to the cylinder jar form, there is at least one sherd that appears to be a fragment of a squat open bowl or barrel-shaped vessel.

Lids are also found with the vessels of this type. As mentioned above, they also have carved and incised designs similar to those found on the vessel bodies. The lids have a slight overhanging lip or edge.

Feet found with these sherds are solid or hollow slab-shaped. They are sometimes decorated with deep slashes.

Appliqued hollow button-like features with a horizontal slash were added to the side walls of the vessel just above the bottom break.

Whole, Restorable, or Partially Restorable Vessels: Two Melano Carved: Melano vessels were recovered in our excavations.

1. Cat. No. 1-319, Operation 19(C), Special Find 59, CV-20, Level 6. This vessel was found in Level 6 of a deep trench through Structure A, CV-20. It was the burial furniture associated with Burial 16, CV-20.

This vessel is a carved cylinder jar with a carved and incised decoration on one side. Vessel dimensions are as follows:

Height: 15.2 cm
Orifice diameter: 14.3 cm
Basal diameter: 13.1 cm
Ring base diameter: 10.8 cm

The outline of this vessel is slightly constricted toward the midpoint—bulging below this and flaring toward the rim. Wall thickness is 5 to 6 mm. The ring base is extremely low, only 2 to 3 mm in height. The walls of this vessel break in sharply to the base about 2 cm from the bottom of the jar.

The exterior of the vessel has a high polish. This polish extends at least halfway down the interior wall with the lower interior sections and the bottom only smoothed.

About 1 cm below the lip of the vessel is a glyph band, 2 cm in width. This band has been defined by deep carved incision, executed when the clay was dry but before it was fired. Such deep carving separates and partially defines some glyphs. Some of the glyphs are also defined by fine-line and dot incision or possibly engraving. These glyphic forms appear to be pseudo-glyphs. For example, one that appears to be an ahau is repeated several times. Red pigment (cinnabar?) has been liberally rubbed along the glyph band.

The plain, lower part of the vessel has been covered with a very thin layer of stucco or plaster and then painted green. Much of the stucco has eroded away, but enough remains to confirm this description.

One side of the vessel presents a carved panel with a finely incised and engraved figure. The rectangular panel is 12 cm high and 11 cm wide. The figure depicted appears to be a male, with his body facing forward and the head in profile. He wears a large belt and long hip pads or sashes. These paraphernalia indicate that this may be a representation of a ball player. His spread-leg stance, the position of one hand up and the other down, and the flair of his hip pads or sashes suggest motion, again emphasizing the possibility that this is a ball player. This individual also wears a feathered headdress, a necklace, and a central sash that hangs down between his legs.

The carved-out area of this panel and the incisions and engraved lines that define the figure are all heavily impregnated with red pigment.

2. Cat. No. 1-329, Operation 26(A), Special Find 4, Salvage Excavation in group south of Main Copan group (L11-93, El Bosque Map), Level 2.

This vessel was found as part of a cache within a crypt beneath structure L11-93. Associated with this vessel were several artifacts:

a. a small jade pendant or perforated plaquita (1-326)
b. a Babilonia Polychrome tripod vessel (1-327)
c. a small, eroded polychrome bowl found within 1-327 (1-328)

This Melano Carved: Melano vessel is a cylinder vessel and has the following dimensions:

Height: 15.9 cm
Diameter at base: 9 cm

Portions of the rim had been destroyed, and no further dimensions could be taken.

The upper portion of the vessel is smoothed and polished. Below this plain band is a 2-cm-wide glyph band located 1.8 cm below the rim. It is defined at the top and bottom by a set of broad-line incised lines. The band itself is filled with what appears to be a series of pseudo-glyphs formed with broad-line incision.

Below this glyph band is another plain band, 1.8 cm in width. In turn, below this band is a field of diagonally placed, closely spaced flutings, each 1 cm apart. The top of this field of flutings is marked by a roughly dotted incised line. These flutings end at another dotted incised line 1.8 cm from the base. This final 1.8-cm band is plain, similar to the upper portion of the vessel.

As with Cat. No. 1-319 described above, the glyph band appears to have been impregnated with a red pigment.

Classificatory Comments: This appears to be the beginning of a polished black or brown ware tradition at Copan. The persistence of this tradition through later time periods does create some problems in distinguishing Melano Carved from other later polished black sherds. Melano Carved sherds are, of course, identified by carved or incised designs; consequently, many plain vessel body sherds from Melano vessels must have been grouped within the undecorated Melachrino Brown type.

Intrasite Locations, Contexts, and Associations: There are too few sherds to make a proper assessment of the distribution of this type; however, one should note that the two whole or partially whole vessels were found within specific ritual contexts: a burial and a cache within a crypt.

Intersite Locations, Contexts, and Associations: Although fairly rare within our collections from Copan, this polished black-brown ware is common throughout the southeast Maya area and the Guatemala highlands. It is also found within the southern Maya lowlands proper. Within the southeast area, there are definite similarities between the Melano group materials at Copan and the Chiquihuat group at Chalchuapa in El Salvador (Sharer 1978). One of the major differences between our collection and that from Chalchuapa is the presence of the cylinder jar form. Bowl forms are characteristic of Chalchuapa, but Viel (1983) also has identified bowl forms in the type from the PAC-1 collections. In the Guatemalan highlands, the Melano connections are with the Esperanza phase at Kaminaljuyu where Melano-like features include polished black-brown ware, slab vessel supports, cylinder jars with lids, and painted stucco over-decoration (see Kidder, Jennings, and Shook 1946; Wetherington 1978b). In the Maya lowlands proper, see the carved and stuccoed vessels from Uaxactun (R. E. Smith 1955).

Cultural Significance: Melano-like pottery, especially with its stuccoed decoration, suggests a new course of influence coming into Copan ceramics, a course related, perhaps ultimately, to Teotihuacan and moving, via Kaminaljuyu and the Guatemalan highlands, into the southeast Maya region. It is also related, as witnessed by the glyph-like carved panels on the vessels and the iconography of the designs, to the southern Maya lowlands proper, which were also caught up in the Teotihuacan-Kaminaljuyu influences of this time. All of this is in contrast to the earlier relationships of Copan-produced pottery, which seem to have been essentially within the El Salvador–Honduran orbit of influences.

Functional Interpretation: The rather elaborate nature of the Melano Carved vessels and the proveniences of the two whole specimens that we found suggest a ritual function.

Melachrino Brown Type

Variety Name: Melachrino.
Established as a Type and/or Variety: By this description in consultation with Viel (1983).
Frequency: See Melano Carved.
Ceramic Group: Melano.
Ceramic Complex: Acbi.
Illustrations: Figure 28a–j.
Description:
Principal Identifying Modes.
1. Polished brown to black slip;
2. slab-footed cylinder jars with lids;
3. open bowl forms with ring bases.
Paste, Temper, and Firing. No data.
Surface Finish and Decoration. The surfaces of these vessels are well smoothed to hard polished on both the exterior and the interior. The surface coloring tends to be black-brown with some mottling and fire clouding.
Form. There are two primary forms:

1. One of the forms is a cylinder jar with slab-footed, hollow tripod supports. These cylinders also have lids that are conical in form and

are, in some cases, quite thick and heavy. The lids show smoothing on both the interior and exterior, although the exterior surfaces tend to be generally more polished.

2. The other form for Melachrino Brown is a bowl form with straight to outslanting walls. Some of these bowls were probably subhemispherical in outline and had small ring bases. There is one sherd in the collection that shows a basal flange.

Sample cylindrical dimensions:

Rim diameter: 15 cm
Basal diameter: 13 cm
Lid diameter (outer) 16 cm

Slab foot:

Height: 8.5 cm
Width: 3 cm

Whole, Restorable, or Partially Restorable Vessels: None recovered.
Classificatory Comments: See Melano Carved.
Intrasite Locations, Contexts, and Associations: See Melano Carved.
Intersite Locations, Contexts, and Associations: See Melano Carved.
Cultural Significance: See Melano Carved.
Functional Interpretation: See Melano Carved.

Con Permiso Red-on-brown Type

Variety Name: Con Permiso.

Established as a Type and/or Variety: By this description in consultation with Viel (1983).
Frequency: See Melano Carved.
Ceramic Group: Melano.
Ceramic Complex: Acbi.
Illustrations: Figure 29a–i.
Description:
Principal Identifying Modes:
1. Red banding on polished brown surface. This red banding is usually located on the exterior of the vessel rim;
2. open bowl forms with a ring base.
Paste, Temper, and Firing. No data.
Surface Finish and Decoration. The surface finish of this type is similar to that described above for Melachrino Brown. These vessels have a smoothed to polished interior and exterior with red banded designs. This red banding is most frequently found on the vessel exteriors. The width of the band extends about 1 cm below the lip. Sometimes the banding extends over the lip of the vessel into the interior of the bowl. In addition to this rim banding, there are some indications that such bands were also painted lower down on the vessel exteriors.
Form. The primary form of this type is the open bowl, similar to that described above for Melachrino Brown. These open bowls are medium to small in size with straight or outsloping walls. Orifice diameters range from 22 to 30 cm.
Whole, Restorable, or Partially Restorable Vessels: None recovered.

LATE CLASSIC PHASES

The Cueva Phase

Our ceramic collections are the largest for the two Late Classic period phases at Copan, the Cueva and the Coner, and because of this our type descriptions for these phases are more detailed. The two phases were separated in the field through both ceramic and architectural stratigraphy, and this chronological separation has stood up well in our typological comparisons with other sites and regions. It should be noted that the Cueva phase (A.D. 600–700) corresponds to what Viel (1983; see also Bishop et al. 1986 for further discussion of Copan's ceramic chronology) calls late Acbi, and there is substantial continuity and overlap from Acbi to Cueva.

Usulutan resist or negative painting is prominent in both phases. The prime Usulutan type of the Cueva phase is Chilanga Red-painted Usulutan in its several varieties. The ground or slip color on all of these varieties is a light orange-over-cream Usulutan resist, overpainted with positive red designs. There are, of course, old local Honduran continuities reflected in the Arroyo Red and Antonio Buff large monochrome-slipped and pebble-polished jars; but, at the same time, many of the finer household wares of the phase resemble Maya lowland types. Most specifically, this can be seen in the use of carved glyphic, glyph-like, or Classic Maya iconographic motifs as vessel decoration. Also, the well-smoothed or polished types of the Tipon and Capulin ceramic groups would seem to point in the direction of the Maya lowlands; however, the lines of influence here are complicated by the fact that Classic pottery from the Maya highlands includes wares very simple in surface treatment and composition to those of the Tipon-Capulin groups.

Chilanga Red-painted Usulutan Type

Variety Names: Chilanga, Osicala, and Unspecified.
Established as Types and/or Varieties: By Sharer at Chalchuapa (1978:3:47).
Frequency: 5,617 sherds or 2 percent of our total collection. By variety the breakdown is as follows:

Osicala Variety: 3,185 sherds or 56.7 percent of the Chilanga group;
Chilanga Variety: 790 sherds or 14 percent of the Chilanga group;
Unspecified Variety: 1,587 sherds or 28.3 percent of the Chilanga group; and
Arturo Incised Variety: 55 sherds or 0.9 percent of the Chilanga group.

Clearly, Chilanga Red-painted Usulutan: Osicala Variety is the dominant type and variety of the Chilanga group ceramics. As discussed below, most of the Unspecified Variety and many of the Chilanga Variety sherds would have been classified as Chilanga Red-painted Usulutan: Osicala Variety if more complete specimens, showing side wall painting, had been available. It is probable that over 80 to 90 percent of the Chilanga Red-painted Usulutan ceramic vessels were of the Osicala Variety.
Ceramic Group: Chilanga.
Ceramic Complexes: Acbi and Cueva.
Illustrations:
Chilanga Variety: Figure 30.

Osicala Variety: Figures 31–39.
Description:
Principal Identifying Modes.
1. Red slip painting over light orange and cream Usulutan resist decoration;
2. a generally fine white paste.
Variety Distinctions. Following Sharer's original type description (1978:3:47), the Chilanga Variety is characterized by red slip painting only as a simple rim band and usually an exterior band near the base of vessel walls or near the tip of ring bases. The area of the wall between these bands is left without red slip painting, leaving exposed the Chilanga group's characteristic Usulutan resist designs. The Osicala Variety is characterized by the addition of more complex red-painted designs on vessel walls, usually on the exterior between the red rim and base bands and also sometimes on vessel interiors. Osicala Variety red-painted motifs include simple lines, squiggles, blobs, curvilinear designs, simple geometric designs, and stylized profiles of birds, monkeys, or other animals. The Unspecified Variety was a typological construct we used to classify sherds that could not be placed definitively in either the Chilanga or Osicala Variety (see "Classificatory Comments" below).
Paste, Temper, and Firing. A fine-to-medium textured paste with few inclusions. Paste is uniform in color, a light cream or buff to pink (7.5 YR 7/4, 8/4, 8/2, to 10 YR 8/2). Occasionally dark cores (black or gray) are found, but most specimens are fully oxidized. Paste texture is slightly porous.

Although paste is macroscopically consistent in appearance throughout the Copan Valley and in other regions, neutron activation analyses (see appendix B; Bishop et al. 1986) show that a variety of different clay sources were used to produce Chilanga Red-painted Usulutan. Copan's Chilanga appears to be locally manufactured.
Surface Finish and Decoration. Surfaces are smoothed and often polished to high-gloss finish. Surfaces were probably self-slipped in a thin layer of slip made from the same clay as the cream/buff paste; but a "wet smoothing" could have created the same effect.

As with earlier Usulutans (see Izalco Usulutan Type descriptions), this underlying cream, buff, or pale pink surface was somehow covered with a darker pink to orange (2.5 YR 5/6, 5/8, 6/6, 6/8) surface layer through which areas left in the original lighter paste color show through as resist designs. The negative-effect motifs include parallel multiple-brush wavy-line designs, straight multiple lines, or indistinct blobs of lighter surface color. As with Izalco Usulutan, the method used for creating this resist or resist-like appearance has been, and remains, an issue for discussion and continuing research (Demarest and Sharer 1982; Sharer 1978:3:134–135; Hopkins 1986).

Over the polished cream/orange Usulutan-decorated surfaces, red painting was applied as rim and base bands and, in the Osicala Variety, as more complex exterior and interior wall designs (see "Variety Distinctions" above). Red paint is a deep, rich red (7.5YR 5/8, 4/8).

Form. There are three principal vessel forms. The most common form is the simple hemispherical bowl, usually with an annular base. Four whole vessels of this form were discovered by the Harvard Copan Project, three of the Osicala Variety and one of the Chilanga Variety. Bowl shape is from subhemispherical to hemispherical. Dimensions of the bowl form range widely: in height from 5.8 to 12 cm and in orifice diameter from 5 to 29 cm. Bases range from a low ring to a pedestal ring base and vary from 0.2 to 3 cm in height. All whole examples and most rim sherds have simple direct rims. This bowl form usually has a wide red-painted rim band on both the interior and exterior of vessels and often another red circling band at the bottom of the vessel wall or tip of the ring base. Three of the four whole vessels are of the Osicala Variety, with simple red-painted designs on their exterior walls. The one Chilanga Variety whole bowl has a high annular base and only a simple rim band painted in red. All whole vessels and most sherds in this form have elaborate multiple wavy-line (three to five lines) Usulutan designs on both interiors and exteriors with designs in cream to pale pink paste color surrounded by the orange surface color. Occasionally, less elaborate designs of wide lines or even blobs are found in the Usulutan-decorated surfaces beneath the red-painted rim bands and wall motifs.

A second common form is the small jar or deep low-necked bowl. Our project recovered three restorable vessels of this shape. This form is delicate with thin walls (less than 0.6 cm) and direct but slightly outturned rims. This form has a small, subglobular body gently curving inward to a slight restriction and then outward to form a short collar. Some of these forms take a squat pear shape. Heights range from 11.5 to 16 cm, orifice diameters from 13 to 14 cm, and maximum diameter at the midpoint of the vessel from 15 to 19 cm. Bases are simple, small, and flat. This form still has a wide red rim band, sometimes covering all of the low collar. But sometimes the side wall designs are extremely complex, including elaborate curvilinear or geometric patterns, which may be combined with animal profiles. Simpler designs, red lines, blobs, or circles are also used to decorate some olla forms. In this form the Usulutan surfaces beneath the red painting are more often characterized by blobs of lighter resist, rather than lines. This olla form is largely, if not exclusively, of the Osicala Variety because of its red-painted designs on side walls. It may also be a slightly later form (largely Cueva, rather than Acbi).

A third common form is the simple plate, open plate, or dish, with wide outturned or everted rims and open outsloped walls. This form is found with a variety of bases including flat, simple bases, ring or annular pedestal bases, and occasionally large hollow tripod feet. Some examples have a basal flange. This flanged form may be slightly earlier (i.e., more common to the Acbi than to the later Cueva phase). Dimensions on the five whole vessels of this form range in height from 4 to 5 cm with diameters of the dish mouths ranging from 17 to 28 cm. Wide-everted rims on vessels and sherds are often as large as from 4 to 5 cm in width. Our five whole examples of this form have wide simple red painting in wide lines and circles. The wide-everted rims are often painted entirely red. Red designs are simpler and sloppy. On the whole vessels the Usulutan surface had only cloudy and mottled appearance, rather than distinct designs. Walls are thick in this form, often about 1 cm.

Whole, Restorable, or Partially Restorable Vessels: Twelve whole or restorable vessels were recovered in the form categories mentioned above. One is of the Chilanga Variety and the remaining dozen are of the Osicala Variety.

The one Chilanga Variety bowl (Cat. No. 1-225) (fig. 30) has a low pedestal base (2.2 cm in height, 10.4 cm in diameter) on a hemispherical bowl of 10 cm in height and 22 cm in orifice diameter. The rim is simple and direct. A single wide red band (1.4 cm in width) is found on both the interior and exterior of the bowl rim. The Usulutan designs on the bowl are well defined, in sets of three parallel lines flowing across the interior and exterior of the vessel.

Of the Osicala vessels, three are simple hemispherical or slightly subhemispherical bowls. One (Cat. No. 1-223) (fig. 31) has a pedestal base 2.6 cm in height and 10.8 in diameter with the bowl body 10 cm high and 14.1 cm in its orifice diameter. There is a slight angle on the lower bowl wall. Interior decoration is a wide interior rim band with pendant hook elements painted over a multiple wavy line Usulutan background. Exteriors are decorated in the wall panel defined by encircling wide rim and base red-painted bands. Between these are wide red vertical lines.

A second Osicala Variety pedestal-based bowl (Cat. No. 1-238) (fig. 32) has an orifice diameter of about 20 cm. Over a blotchy Usulutan-design decorated cream and orange background, red-painted designs are a wide red rim band, a wide red basal band, and large solid red rectangles (3 x 4 cm) between these bands.

Another Chilanga Red-painted Usulutan: Osicala Variety specimen (Cat. No. 1-226) (fig. 33) is a simple bowl form with a height of 5.8 cm and orifice diameter of 4.9 cm. Red painting consists of a single wide rim band, below which are two other wide encircling red bands. A vague, mottled Usulutan surface with no clear designs lies below the red painting.

Three of the Chilanga whole vessels recovered by our project were small olla or deep bowl forms. One (Cat. No. 1-228) (fig. 34) is a beautiful, elaborately painted deep bowl with a height of 14 cm and an orifice diameter of 13.5 cm. The bowl has a composite-silhouette wall that curves slightly inward and then outward to form a low collar. Maximum diameter at midpoint was 18.6 cm. The collar or recurved upper wall (3 cm in height) was painted entirely red. Three wide red bands encircle the lower wall near the base of the vessel. The zone between these red bands is painted in narrower line designs of multiple inset triangles and single line squiggles. The background is a sharply contrasting orange surface with cream or buff Usulutan blob motifs.

Another deep bowl form (Cat. No. 1-1017) (fig. 35) has an incurving wall with no real collar, but a rim band, over 2 cm in width, which gives

the effect of a collar. The vessel has a height of 11.7 cm, orifice diameter of 14 cm, and a midpoint diameter of 15.3 cm. There are four modeled ridges on the lower vessel wall below the shoulder, and these extend down to the base. Between the wide red, collar-like, rim band and a wide red band on the lower vessel wall were complex designs including hook elements, squid-like forms, and bird profiles. The largely obscured, underlying Usulutan surface has no clear design elements.

A third Usulutan deep bowl or olla form (Cat. No. 1-361) (fig. 36) has a height of 16 cm, orifice diameter of 14 cm, and maximum diameter of 19.3 cm. This vessel has a simpler global form with a short (4.4 cm) red-painted incurving collar. Designs in red paint are a single wide irregular band around the vessel midpoint with large solid red circles, 5 cm in diameter, above the midpoint of the vessel wall. The Usulutan background below this red paint has its lighter designs in blobs and irregular lines. This vessel has simpler and more carelessly executed designs than the ones described above.

Five vessels of Chilanga Red-painted Usulutan are open bowl or plate forms with outflaring walls. Two of these (Cat. Nos. 1-1203 and 1-1204) (for 1-1203 see fig. 37) are virtually identical, with heights of 4.7 cm and 5 cm, orifice diameters of 28.3 and 27.7 cm, and interior orifices (within wide-everted rims) of 23 cm. Both vessels have a simple flat base, outflaring walls, and nearly horizontal wide-everted rims (over 5 cm wide). These rims are painted red, and there is also a wide red band on the exterior vessel walls near the base. The rest of the vessel is covered with orange Usulutan surfaces with ill-defined designs. On each vessel, the interior surface bottom has a single, very large (diameter 8 cm) solid red ball at its center.

Another simple flat-bottomed bowl with outflaring walls (Cat. No. 1-382) has a height of 3.9 cm and an orifice diameter of 17 cm. The only red-painted decorations were encircling red bands, one at the rim and several others below.

Another whole specimen (Cat. No. 1-1210) (fig. 38) is an outflaring-wall bowl with a wide-everted rim and large, crude tripod supports. This vessel has an orifice diameter of 28 cm, 6 cm of which is the wide-everted rim. The plate body is 11.8 cm in height, and there are large hollow tripod supports of 7.5 cm in height and 4.5 cm in diameter. The everted rim is painted red, and red painting, in the form of thin, curving lines, composes a vague polygon in the interior of the vessel bottom. The Usulutan orange surfaces of this vessel are without discernable designs.

One restored plate or open bowl (Cat. No. 1-207) (fig. 39) has large (4.5 cm in diameter) tripod supports and a clear basal ridge. The bottom is convex and the body height (without the tripods) is 8 cm, with an orifice diameter of 29 cm. Vessel walls are thick (1 cm). The entire vessel is covered with splotchy Usulutan designs. There is an exterior red rim band, and the basal ridge is red. There is a wide red rim band on the interior. Below this are two encircling red bands between which are red chevrons. Below this, in turn, are two more encircling red bands, and at the center of the bottom interior is a large red circular spot. The basal ridge suggests an Early Classic period, or Acbi phase, date.

Classificatory Comments: Sharer's original definition of the Chilanga group placed it primarily in the Vec ceramic complex at Chalchuapa, dated from A.D. 100 to 200. However, the Early Classic is in general poorly represented at Chalchuapa, presumably because of the site's decline and partial abandonment after the eruption and ash fall from Volcan Ilopango at about A.D. 250 (Sharer 1974, 1978; Sheets 1979). Our Chilanga sample is more reliable in context and sample size than Chalchuapa's relatively small and sporadically distributed initial Classic Vec phase. The Copan sample indicates a far longer period of popularity for Chilanga group ceramics. They are common at Copan in the Early Classic Acbi complex, but are especially common in the Middle Classic to early Late Classic Cueva complex.

The distinction between the Chilanga Variety and the Osicala Variety is difficult to maintain in actual sherd sorting. The primary distinguishing factor, red painting on side walls in addition to red rim and base bands, is highly sensitive to sherd size; only larger sherds with a portion of side wall can be securely judged on this criterion. Our Chilanga Red-painted Usulutan: Unspecified Variety was created to account for this problem in sorting. It is a residual category of sherds that are small or are fragmented in such a way that side wall painting cannot be judged. The large number of sherds in this Unspecified Variety,

over 28 percent of the total in the Chilanga group, suggests that the Chilanga vs. Osicala Variety distinction is not a very satisfactory one. (See also "Intrasite Locations, Contexts, and Associations" below.)

Note also that Gualpopa Polychrome is characterized by Chilanga-like surfaces and red-painted designs with the addition of some black-painted designs and less frequent use of distinct Usulutan designs on the cloudy orange surfaces. It is probable that a large number of Gualpopa sherds fragmented to exclude black-painted wall designs and have been tabulated as Chilanga Red-painted Usulutan.

Intrasite Locations, Contexts, and Associations: The intrasite and stratigraphic associations of this type indicate a temporal placement in the Acbi and Cueva phases with a particular prevalence in the latter phase. The excavations at CV-20 and CV-43 revealed architecture, burials, and caches pertaining to the Cueva phase.

Intrasite correlations between ceramic types confirm placement of this type in the Acbi and Cueva complexes. The Spearman Rank-Order Correlation chart indicates that the correlations, while tending to be somewhat weak statistically, reveal a correlation among all three varieties of Chilanga material—Chilanga, Osicala, and Unspecified. There is also a correlation of association between this type and the Antonio group ceramics. This confirms our use of these two primary ceramic groups to define the Cueva phase.

Intersite Locations, Contexts, and Associations: As discussed above ("Classificatory Comments"), Chilanga Red-painted Usulutan is common at the site of Chalchuapa, in El Salvador, where it was first defined as a type (Sharer 1978:3:47). Originally, Sharer placed it in the Early Classic Vec phase, but it appears to have had a much longer and later period of popularity at Copan and also in western El Salvador. It is common at other sites in El Salvador (Longyear 1944, 1966) where it is generally reported as simply red-painted Usulutan. At Quelepa, in eastern El Salvador, the Shila phase (A.D. 200–600) Chaparrastique Red-on-orange group and Hato Nuevo Red-on-orange-on-white group are closely related to Chilanga Red-painted Usulutan, sharing many vessel forms, red painting over Usulutan decoration, some design elements, and red banding and other vessel wall designs.

Generally, red painting in rim bands and vessel wall designs on Usulutan surfaced bowls is common throughout the southeast highlands of Mesoamerica and the southern periphery. At Kaminaljuyu it is present in the Early Classic in small quantities (Wetherington 1978b:107–109; Longyear 1944:65). At Bilbao in the Protoclassic, Lee A. Parsons reports red-rim-painted Usulutan (Parsons 1969:86), and in the Early Classic the closely related Colmenera Red-on-orange type red paint is also found on exterior walls of bowls (ibid.:100–101). Turning to western Honduras we find that Chilanga Red-painted Usulutan, or very similar red-on-Usulutan ceramics, are reported as a common type in the Naco Valley and on the Sula plain (Henderson et al. 1979; Patricia Urban, personal communication 1984). In the Middle Ulua area at the site of Gualjoquito, Chilanga Red-painted Usulutan appears as a very minor type in Early Classic contexts (Schortman, Urban, and Ashmore 1983). Note that compositional analyses indicate local pastes and manufacture for each of these Chilanga occurrences, implying that shared stylistic concepts, not trade, were primarily responsible for the Chilanga group's distribution.

It is significant that Chilanga Red-painted Usulutan occurs only sparsely at Quirigua in the Classic period, and that only occasional Usulutan sherds are found in the Late Preclassic and Protoclassic periods at that site. Elsewhere in the Motagua Valley, Chilanga Red-painted Usulutan appears only occasionally and then as a minor type (Edward Schortman, personal communication 1983).

Functional Interpretation: Vessel forms and general sherd distribution are both consistent with functions as serving vessels in household contexts; however, the common placement of Chilanga vessels in caches and burials indicates some ritual associations for the type.

Cultural Significance: This type is highly significant as an indicator of the strong cultural affiliation between western El Salvador and the Copan Valley. The Chilanga group's importance in the Acbi and Cueva phases at Copan underscores the general southern peripheral (rather than lowland Maya) nature of Copan's "household" culture.

At Copan, as throughout El Salvador and western Honduras, red painting on Usulutan was the starting point for the evolution of the polychrome tradition. This tradition begins with red rimming on an Usulutan or cloudy orange background, is followed by the red wall designs of the Osicala Variety of Chilanga, and becomes elaborated in the Late Classic with the addition of black, and then specular red (purplish) paint to produce a variety of local polychromes (including Gualpopa, Copador, Arambala, and others). Some of these polychromes are painted on an Usulutan background, others on a cloudy orange or cream base; however, it is clear that all of these southern periphery polychromes are derived stylistically from the red-painted Usulutans of the Early Classic, most notably the Chilanga group.

Arturo Incised Type

Variety Name: Arturo Incised.

Established as a Type and/or Variety: By this description and description by Viel (1983).

Frequency: 55 sherds. A very minor variant of the Chilanga group, constituting less than 1 percent of the sherds of that group.

Ceramic Group: Chilanga.

Ceramic Complexes: Acbi and Cueva.

Illustrations: Figure 40a–g. See also Longyear 1952: figures 59f,h, 111c.

Description:

Principal Identifying Modes.

1. Red-painted Usulutan decorated surfaces as characteristic of the Chilanga group;
2. red bands and zones outlined with fine-line post-firing incision;
3. painted and incised designs on bowl wall exteriors.

Paste, Temper, and Firing. Same as Chilanga Red-painted Usulutan.

Surface Finish and Decoration. Surfaces are basically the same in finish, red paint, Usulutan design and slip colors, and Usulutan decoration as Chilanga Red-painted Usulutan. Red designs include bands just below the rim exterior and areas of red paint in vague shapes on vessel walls. An encircling interior red rim band is noted on both open bowls and on constricted mouths of deeper bowls.

The incised lines that zone or ornament the red areas are rather imperfectly drawn. They vary from a fine scratching that approaches engraving to somewhat larger smoother lines of clearer incision. The incised decorative motifs are single circles or ovals, concentric circles, curved or straight pairs of parallel lines, triangles, and other rectilinear elements. Open bowl forms have both linear and blob-like Usulutan designs especially visible on bowl interiors and also sometimes on exteriors.

Small, button-like appliqued nodes, bosses, and ridges are found on some sherds. In a few cases it is apparent that incised designs, painting, and appliques combine to depict human or animal faces. In these cases the entire bowl may have been intended as a highly stylized effigy.

Form. Vessels all appear to be relatively small, thin-walled, and delicate. The two main forms are open bowls and small jars (or deep bowls) with slightly constricted orifices but without distinct necks or collars. The open bowl form includes simple, hemispherical forms and dishes with outsloped sides and vestigial basal flanges.

Orifice diameters on the deep bowls or neckless jars are 10 to 16 cm. Open bowl orifice diameters are usually about 20 to 22 cm. Vessel wall thickness on all forms is about 5 mm or slightly less.

Whole, Restorable, or Partially Restorable Vessels: None recovered.

Classificatory Comments: No classificatory problems. This type is a minor incised variant of Chilanga Red-painted Usulutan.

Intrasite Locations, Contexts, and Associations: This type is too infrequent to warrant statistical evaluation of distributional patterns. Review of contexts indicates a distribution parallel to that of Chilanga Red-painted Usulutan, placing this type in the late Acbi and the Cueva complexes.

Intersite Locations, Contexts, and Associations: Intersite associations for the Chilanga group have been given above for Chilanga Red-painted Usulutan. Note that this specific incised type, Arturo Incised, has also been reported at Gualjoquito, where one incised Chilanga vessel was found (Schortman, Urban, and Ashmore 1983:31). Arturo Incised is not reported at Chalchuapa, where the Chilanga group is relatively common (Sharer 1978:3).

Functional Interpretation: Probable function was serving bowls.

Cultural Significance: Arturo Incised is a rare incised variant of Chilanga Red-painted Usulutan. (See Chilanga for further discussion.)

Cara Gorda Composite Type

Variety Name: Cara Gorda.
Established as a Type and/or Variety: By this description.
Frequency: A rare variant of the Chilanga group.
Ceramic Group: Chilanga.
Ceramic Complex: Cueva.
Illustrations: Figure 41a–e.
Description:
Principal Identifying Modes.
1. Deep, coarse incision and red-zoning forming exterior surface decorations;
2. Chilanga group surfaces and paste;
3. small jars or deep bowls with incurved or insloped walls.

Paste, Temper, and Firing. Same as for Chilanga Red-painted Usulutan.

Surface Finish and Decoration. Chilanga group surface, but with Usulutan designs either absent or unclear. Smooth, polished, orange to cream-orange slip with dark red painting in rim bands and surrounding incised zones on vessel walls. Incised designs are rectilinear or complex, but examples are too fragmentary to fully characterize. Incisions were executed after air-drying, and the lines are 1 to 2 mm in width and about 1 mm deep. One large sherd has an incised circular design, possibly an ahau-glyph face form, just below the rim. The vessel wall outside of the glyph-like design is painted red.

Form. Small thin-walled restricted or incurved-wall deep bowls. Two sherds show straight or slightly outcurved walls.

Whole, Restorable, or Partially Restorable Vessels: No whole vessels and few large sherds were recovered.

Classificatory Comments: This is a variant within the Chilanga group ceramics, and it is possible that many sherds from vessels of the type were classified into other types of this group.

Intrasite Locations, Contexts, and Associations: See Chilanga Red-painted Usulutan.

Intersite Locations, Contexts, and Associations: See Chilanga Red-painted Usulutan. However, deep-incised Chilanga variants are not reported elsewhere within this southeast zone.

Functional Interpretation: See Chilanga Red-painted Usulutan.

Cultural Significance: Another minor variant of this western Salvadoran Usulutan-based tradition. See comments on Chilanga Red-painted Usulutan.

Capulin Cream Type

Variety Name: Uogistus.

Established as a Type and/or Variety: Capulin Cream: Capulin Variety was established by Sharer and colleagues at Quirigua. The Uogistus Variety pertains to the Copan collections.

Frequency: Only 40 sherds total. A minor white-slipped Tipon group variant in our collections. Composes about 38 percent of our total Capulin subgroup sherd collection.

Ceramic Group: Capulin subgroup of Tipon group.

Ceramic Complexes: Acbi and Cueva.

Illustrations: Figure 42a–h.

Description:

Principal Identifying Modes.

1. A heavy cream slip showing smoothed to polished surfaces;
2. flat-bottomed bowls or cylindrical jars.

Paste, Temper, and Firing. Paste cores are variegated in color and variously layered, including grays, reds, and browns. The paste texture is uniform, consistent, and slightly porous. Temper is fine sand, and density of temper within paste may be quite variable. Surface hardness is usually in excess of 2.0 on Moh's scale and generally falls within a 3.5-to-5.5 range.

Surface Finish and Decoration. The slip appears to be on vessel exteriors only. Bases, however, are sometimes unslipped. Color is 10 YR 8/2, white.

Form. Flat-bottomed bowls or cylinder jars seem the most common. Sherds also indicate bowls with either slightly incurved or slightly outsloped sides. One sherd is a ring base fragment from a bowl, with the ring base about 2 cm high.

Whole, Restorable, or Partially Restorable Vessels: None recovered.

Classificatory Comments: One of a Capulin subgroup of cream-slipped types found at Copan.

Has generic relationship to smoothly slipped or slipped and polished Tipon group types as well as to similar cream and brown wares found elsewhere in the Maya lowlands.

Intrasite Locations, Contexts, and Associations: Longyear (1952:98) describes a White Ware from Copan that resembles Capulin Cream in slip color and thickness of slip. He refers to cylindrical vessels with tripod legs. Longyear's White Ware also includes both negative or resist painting and incised decoration, suggesting the related Capulin subgroup types, Sombra Resist and Champona Incised.

As mentioned above, there are only a very small number of Capulin Cream sherds from these excavations and therefore there are no data as to differential distribution of the material. The small number of sherds also makes any attempt at correlating this type with other types almost impossible.

Intersite Locations, Contexts, and Associations: As noted, there are general resemblances to lowland Maya white, cream, and brown wares, especially to those of the Early Classic horizon. The presence of Capulin Cream: Capulin Variety at Quirigua (Sharer, personal communication) has also been noted. At Barton Ramie, James C. Gifford (1976:167–168) refers to a type, Pucte Brown, which is Early Classic in time and which possesses cylindrical vessel forms; and Richard E. W. Adams (1971:22) also refers to this type from Seibal. Gifford (1976:272–273) describes a Yaha Creek Cream that occurs in cylindrical vase forms; however, this is essentially a Late, rather than Early, Classic type. Pertinent to our comparisons are ceramics from the highlands, in El Salvador, where the Huiscoyol Ceramic group of the Vec complex (A.D. 400–650) (Sharer 1978: 46–47) shows similarities to the Capulin subgroup and the Tipon group types of Copan and Quirigua. Also, Sharer's (ibid.) Chilanga ceramic group, which includes resist-decorated material, has similar forms to Capulin Cream and the related Sombra Resist at Copan.

Functional Interpretation: This appears to be a fine ware type, probably associated with eating and drinking rather than cooking or storage. Although we have no examples in our collection or from our excavations, Capulin Cream appears to be the sort of pottery that might occur as burial furniture.

Cultural Significance: A type that is in a lowland Maya tradition of polished cream, white, or brown wares. This tradition is associated with the cylindrical vessel form, and, more distantly, there is a probable relationship with Teotihuacan influence into the Maya lowlands and the Maya highlands. At Copan and Quirigua it is possible that Capulin subgroup and Tipon group types result from Salvadoran-Guatemalan highland contacts.

Champona Incised Type

Variety Name: Capsicum.
Established as a Type and/or Variety: By Sharer and associates at Quirigua. The Capsicum Variety pertains to Copan.
Frequency: 12 sherds. A rare type of the minor Capulin subgroup of the Tipon group.
Ceramic Group: Capulin subgroup of Tipon group.
Ceramic Complexes: Acbi and Cueva.
Illustrations: Figure 43a–g.
Description:
Principal Identifying Modes.
1. Heavy cream to white slip, smoothed to polished. Same as Capulin Cream and Sombra Resist;
2. deep incisions, and sometimes carved-out areas, forming geometric patterns and sometimes glyph-like figures.
Paste, Temper, and Firing. See Capulin Cream and Sombra Resist. Compact paste, fine sand temper.
Surface Finish and Decoration. The white slip is always found on vessel exteriors and sometimes on interiors as well. The incised decoration is frequently arranged in parallel lines below the rim on vessel exteriors. Often such parallel lines border intermediate wavy lines or rows of slash punctations. More complex designs include panels of rectangular form that contain glyph-like elements or scrolls, hooks, and volutes. A few sherds in our collection have carved-out zones or backgrounds that tend to be combined with finer-line incised decorations.
Form. Sherds indicate medium-sized and medium-deep bowls with slightly outslanted sides and rims. Some of these bowls appear to have had

pronounced basal angles. We have no sure evidence for bases, but these were probably rounded with small flattened central portions. Vessels were thin-walled (under 5 mm) and delicate.
Whole, Restorable, or Partially Restorable Vessels: None recovered.
Classificatory Comments: The incised division of the Capulin subgroup.
Intrasite Locations, Contexts, and Associations: See comments under this section for Capulin Cream and Sombra Resist. Longyear (1952:98, fig. 67d–g) describes and illustrates the type from his Copan excavations. The specimens he shows have the more complex and glyphic designs referred to above.
Intersite Locations, Contexts, and Associations: Within the Maya lowlands proper, Early Classic incised and gouged-incised types, often featuring complex or glyphic designs in addition to simpler geometric ones, are frequently met with, although they are usually black-slipped rather than cream-slipped. An example would be the type, Lucha Incised, found in two varieties at Barton Ramie (Gifford 1976:164–166) and at Seibal (Sabloff 1975:110–112, figs. 212, 213f). Another Early Classic incised black ware type is Urita Gouged-incised (Adams 1971:52; Sabloff 1975:112), occurring at both Altar de Sacrificios and Seibal. There seems to be some chronological continuity of this polished, well-slipped, incised ware tradition on into Late Classic, as seen in a Pasion phase Unnamed Cream Gouge-incised type at Altar de Sacrificios (Adams 1971: fig. 57a). There are no good parallels from Los Naranjos in Honduras (Baudez and Becquelin 1973) or, apparently, from the Guatemalan highlands. In the Salvadoran highlands, Sharer (1978: 48–49) describes a type, Chingo Plano-relief, which, in its glyph-like designs, shows some similarities to Champona; however, Chingo Plano-relief is black-brown in surface color and is a Late Classic rather than an Early Classic type.
Functional Interpretation: A fine ware for household use.
Cultural Significance: Included in Capulin Cream group, although the type was not found by us in cylinder jar forms, which are characteristic of both Capulin Cream and Sombra Resist. It is, however, apparently contemporaneous with the

other Capulin types, falling in the latter part of the Early Classic period and in the earlier part of the succeeding Late Classic.

Sombra Resist Type

Variety Name: Styx.
Established as a Type and/or Variety: Sombra Resist: Sovedeso Variety was established by Sharer and colleagues at Quirigua. The Styx Variety pertains to the Copan collections.
Frequency: 54 sherds or 51 percent of the Capulin subgroup sherds (106 total) found by our excavators.
Ceramic Group: Capulin subgroup of Tipon group.
Ceramic Complexes: Acbi and Cueva.
Illustrations: Figures 44a–f, 45.
Description:
Principal Identifying Modes.
1. Heavy cream slip with smoothed to polished surfaces;
2. very faint, blurred, blackish decoration (designs uncertain or unclear) resulting from resist technique;
3. flat-bottomed cylinder jars or bowls with lids;
4. medium-deep bowl with outslanted sides, basal flange, and hollow tripod supports.
Paste, Temper, and Firing. Essentially the same as Capulin Cream—consistent, compact, fine sand tempered.
Surface Finish and Decoration. A cream slip— 10 YR 8/3 very pale brown—applied to exteriors and, less frequently, to interiors. Interior slips sometimes white (10 YR 8/2). Interiors also have a buff self-slipping and, sometimes, a polished surface that resembles that of Tipon Polished Brown. Resist decoration is on exteriors and has a blurred or blotchy gray-black aspect. Design patterns may have been both curvilinear and rectilinear, but nothing more can be said about them because the sherds are extremely eroded or faded. In addition, red banding of the lip area is fairly common. Application of red may be on both exterior and interior, or only on one or the other. Red banding is sometimes applied to the flange on basal-flanged bowls.
Form. Cylinder jars with basal diameters of about 14 cm. These jars had lids (at least in some instances) of a subconical or scutate shape. Of

the two lid specimens available, one has a direct edge, the other a slight downturned flange. There are also flat-bottomed bowls with straight or only slightly outslanting sides. The orifice diameters of these are estimated at 12 to 17 cm. Presumably, heights of vessels were less than diameters. The third vessel form is well represented by a single restored specimen (Cat. No. 1-1024). This is a medium-deep bowl with outslanted or outcurved sides, a basal flange, and evidences of hollow tripod supports. (These supports, or the remnants of the supports, are not visible in either the photograph or the drawing of the vessel in figure 45.) The rim diameter of the restored vessel is 35 cm; the height, without the tripod supports, is 10 cm.
Whole, Restorable, or Partially Restorable Vessels: The bowl (Cat. No. 1-1024) (fig. 45) just referred to is the only restorable specimen in our collections. It has the blotched, eroded resist-technique decorations on the walls of the exterior. There is an encircling red band on the interior edge of the rim that extends over onto the top of the vessel lip.
Classificatory Comments: A Capulin subgroup type for which we have taken Quirigua data (Sharer personal communication) as our lead in establishing a Copan variety.
Intrasite Locations, Contexts, and Associations: As noted in our discussion of Capulin Cream, Longyear (1952:98) lists and describes resist- or negative-painted decoration and illustrates three specimens (ibid.: fig. 67a–c). The vessel he shows as his figure 67, a, a′, a″ is a cylinder jar with tripod slab feet in the Teotihuacan tradition.

The partial vessel (Cat. No. 1-1024) described above was found within Level 8 of a deep trench through Structure A, CV-45 or 9M-139. This provenience (Cat. No. 1-1024) typifies the Cueva phase. A total of 306 sherds were found within this level. Of these sherds, 178 or 58 percent have been typed within the Antonio group. Another 38 sherds or 12 percent are part of the Chilanga group. The majority of the remaining sherds were too eroded to be classified.
Intersite Locations, Contexts, and Associations: Sombra Resist appears to be linked to other Early Classic period cylinder jar vessels found at a number of places in the Maya lowlands. These are always relatively rare and, where fine-grained dating can be obtained, appear to fall into the lat-

ter part of the Early Classic. Such would correspond to the Acbi/Cueva or late Acbi dating
assigned to the type at Copan. Robert E. Smith
and Gifford (1966:171, 158) refer to a late Tzakol Uaxactun type, Japon Resist, which closely
resembles Sombra Resist (see illustrations of
cylinder jars in Smith [1955:vol. 2: figs. 1k, 5f–g,
8e]). Excellent examples of Japon Resist are also
described and shown by Raymond E. Merwin
and George C. Vaillant (1932:69, pl. 28a,c) from
Holmul where they appear to date to the end of
the Holmul III phase or the latter part of the Early Classic. Adams (1971:58) has noted Japon
Resist at Altar de Sacrificios. On the other hand,
Sabloff (1975) does not report it from Seibal;
however, that author (ibid.:233) specifically
notes that Teotihuacanoid traits, including cylinder jars, are rare or absent in the collections from
that site. At Barton Ramie, Gifford (1976:162)
does not specifically list Japon Resist, but the
only possible Classic resist-decorated sherds he
does describe are in an Early Classic context.
Although cylinder jars of various polished wares
are a common feature of the Kaminaljuyu Early
Classic, none of these is reported as showing
resist decoration (Kidder, Jennings, and Shook
1946:159–170). In the Salvadoran highlands we
have already referred to Chilanga group resist-
decorated cylinders that fall on this general Early
Classic to Late Classic time horizon (Sharer
1978:46–47).

Functional Interpretation: Most of these vessels
were probably elite goods. Like Capulin Cream,
Sombra Resist vessels were fine wares. They
could have served as household drinking or eating vessels. They were used, as were the Japon
Resist examples from Holmul, as funerary offerings.

Cultural Significance: There seems to be an adhesion between the cylinder jar—frequently the
cylinder jar with Teotihuacanoid lid—and resist
decoration. This adhesion or association characterizes the Early Classic, and probably the latter
part of the Early Classic, in the Maya lowlands.
Curiously, the Kaminaljuyu cylinder jars, from
the Guatemalan highlands, do not show this
association; none seems to have been decorated
with resist painting. This makes it seem less likely
that Kaminaljuyu could have been the source of
the Sombra or Japon Resist cylinder jars that are
found in the Maya lowlands. Perhaps the Sal-

vadoran highlands and the Chilanga ceramic
group context was the focus of this cylinder
jar–resist painting association. In any event,
resist-painted cylinder jars are, while rare in
numbers at any site, a frequently occurring item
in the Maya lowlands in the Early Classic.

Mapache Grooved Type

Variety Name: Mapache.
Established as a Type and/or Variety: By Viel at
Copan.
Frequency: See Cementerio group counts given
below. Specific counts are not given, since the
Cementerio group sherds were tabulated only by
group. In the overwhelmingly Late Classic counts
of the Harvard Copan Project, the later Cemente-
rio Incised Type of this group predominates,
while Mapache Grooved is less frequent and
Zigoto Incised is quite rare. Note, however, that
it is very difficult to distinguish body sherds of
Cementerio Incised from Mapache sherds;
Mapache Grooved may be somewhat more frequent in our lots. All things considered, group
level counts were deemed more appropriate for
this group.
Ceramic Group: Cementerio.
Ceramic Complexes: Acbi and Cueva.
Illustrations: Figures 46a–g, 47, 48.
Description:
Principal Identifying Modes.
1. Broad, rough, shallow grooving in parallel
   line formations;
2. large, collared jar forms;
3. rough to slightly smoothed unslipped ware.
Paste, Temper, and Firing. See Cementerio
Incised description above.
Surface Finish and Decoration. The grooves are
imperfectly spaced but average about 5 to 7 mm
apart. Individual grooves are fairly uniform in
width, ranging from 3 to 5 mm. The groove presents a rough-bottomed scraped appearance, and
the lines of the design are somewhat irregular and
uneven. Grooves on vessel collars are arranged
either vertically or on a slight diagonal. There are
also horizontal encircling grooves around the
base of the collar. Decoration on some vessel
bodies may incorporate panels of zigzag incision,
very shallowly impressed. There are also some
instances of rows of deep-dot punctations paral-

leling vertical grooving on vessel bodies. Additional elements on vessel bodies are diagonal arrangements of parallel grooved lines. Decoration on the vessel probably extended down to the maximum mid-diameter of the jar and possibly below this.

Form. The only form is a large water jar with a collar and outflared or outturned rim. The orifice diameter on one such partially restored specimen is 24.5 cm, with the maximum body diameter of about 40 cm, height about 40 cm, and the height of the collar 10.5 cm.

Mapache vessel bases were left plain, and for this reason they have not been classified with the type. However, it is probable that they were small, round, and indented, much as some identified with other Copan water jar types.

There is no evidence of handles.

Whole Vessels: There are two whole vessels (Cat. No. 1-450 and 1-307). Both are large jars with collars, outflared rims, and large mouths. The form of the best restored specimen (Cat. No. 1-307) is described above (see "Form"). It also has a slightly everted small rounded lip that has traces of a red slip. It is decorated in a characteristic Mapache pattern with deep, broad (2–5 mm) incised lines running from the lip to the base of the collar. These vertical coarse incisions are parallel and about 0.5 to 1 cm apart. Several parallel lines also run horizontally, encircling the vessel just below the neck. Below this, the upper half of the jar body was decorated with haphazard incised slashes, zigzags, triangles, and punctations.

The other specimen (Cat. No. 1-450) is a partial vessel with a simple collar. It is decorated from the lip to the base of the neck with fine crosshatch incised lines.

Classificatory Comments: Considerable overlap with Cementerio Incised and Zigoto Incised. See "Classificatory Comments" for Cementerio Incised below and comments on frequencies below for both Cementerio and Mapache.

Intrasite Locations, Contexts, and Associations: According to Viel (personal communication 1983), and with reference to the chronology of this type at Quirigua (Sharer personal communication 1983), Mapache Grooved begins earlier than Cementerio Incised: Cementerio Variety, starting in the Early Classic Acbi component.

See Cementerio Incised: Cementerio Variety for further discussion.

Intersite Locations, Contexts, and Associations: See Cementerio Incised intersite comparisons given above.

An interesting connection for Mapache Grooved is the type's near identity to the Cementerio group types at Quirigua. There the grooved and incised jars are decorated like Mapache Grooved with vertical or diagonal grooving and incision on collars rather than with the more complex variety of incised and punctate designs that characterize Cementerio and Zigoto Incised. Thus, this type is one of the very few that show ceramic similarities between Copan and Quirigua.

Functional Interpretation: Same as discussed for Cementerio Incised: Cementerio Variety.

Cultural Significance: In addition to the comments given in the Cementerio Incised description, note again that Mapache Grooved shows a specific similarity to Quirigua incised jars. Also, as at Quirigua, this type tends to be somewhat earlier than Cementerio Incised.

Cementerio Incised Type

Variety Name: Cementerio.

Established as a Type and/or Variety: By this description.

Frequency: Counts made by group only. A total of 3,923 sherds or 1.42 percent of Harvard Copan Project sherds are of the Cementerio group. The vast majority of these are of the Cementerio Incised type. The other two types of the Cementerio group, Mapache and Zigoto varieties, are earlier and as a result tend to be rare in the Harvard Copan Project lots, which are predominantly Late Classic in date. The infrequency of these variants in our collections, as well as their general similarity (in small sherds) to each other, made counts on the type level impractical.

Note also that since only incised sherds of Cementerio could be distinguished from Lysandro Unslipped, these counts do not accurately reflect the considerably higher relative frequency that one can project for the manufacture of whole vessels of the Cementerio Incised Type. That is, only incised portions of the vessel (about one-third of its surface) would, as sherds, be classified into the type.

Ceramic Group: Cementerio.
Ceramic Complexes: Acbi and Cueva.
Illustrations: Figure 49a–d.
Description:
Principal Identifying Modes.
1. Crudely incised line patterns on vessel collar or immediately below rim;
2. slashed or deep-dot punctations;
3. large collar jar forms.

Paste, Temper, and Firing. Paste is variable in color running from buff to gray. Paste consists of fine clay particles uniformly tempered with variable sized subangular particles of mixed colored sand in temper density of less than 25 percent. Paste is slightly porous and clay matrix is somewhat variable in its homogeneity. Hardness ranges from 3.5 to 5.5 on Moh's scale.

Surface Finish and Decoration. Vessel exteriors and interiors are smoothed but not polished, and interiors are more markedly smoothed than exteriors. Incised line arrangements are usually diagonal to the vertical axis of the vessel extending from rim down onto the collar and sometimes onto vessel shoulders. Incised lines are arranged in nested sets of diagonal lines, sometimes parallel vertical lines, and sometimes crosshatched lines. All are rather roughly and haphazardly executed. Space between lines varies greatly but averages about 1 cm. Punctations are used as filler between incised lines, usually slash punctations 0.5 to 1 cm long or rough dot punctations 3 to 4 cm in diameter. Occasional curvilinear but simple incised designs are seen as lines bordered by fine, ticked punctations.

Form. The single dominant form is a globular or subglobular jar with a low outflared collar.

There is considerable variation in the diameter of the orifice of these vessels, ranging from 14 to 30 cm. Collar height ranges from 3 to 6 cm. Maximum diameter of jars was probably at about midpoint on the body. In the one restored vessel, height was 42 cm, although a considerable range in height is estimated. Height is often about the same as diameter, and orifices are usually about one-third of the vessel's maximum diameter. The incised and punctated decoration was applied to collars and upper shoulders of vessels. Rims vary from horizontal eversion to an angle of about 45 degrees. They are occasionally painted red, as in most other Late Classic utilitarian types at Copan.

Bases were probably mostly classified as Lysandro Unslipped, as were lower portions of vessels lacking incision.

Loop handles are characteristic of the type, placed at the juncture of shoulder and collar with the upper part of the handle just below the rim. The handles are 1.5 to 2 cm in thickness and 5 to 8 cm in length, forming a loop aperture for one or two fingers. The number of handles per vessel is unknown.

Whole, Restorable, or Partially Restorable Vessels: There is one partial vessel (Cat. No. 1-305). It is a globular jar with an outflaring collar. Size estimates are as follows: total height, 40 cm; orifice diameter, 25 cm; and midpoint diameter, 30 cm. It has splashes of orange-red daub on the collar and body and characteristic slash-incision in crosshatched lines accompanied by long slash punctations.

Classificatory Comments: This type is defined by its coarse incisions. Body portions without these incisions would be sherds of Lysandro Unslipped, and undoubtedly have been classified and counted as Lysandro. Thus, sherd frequency counts represent only a portion of the sherds originally from Cementerio Incised vessels.

Intrasite Locations, Contexts, and Associations: Cementerio group ceramics were found predominantly in the Cueva proveniences in our test excavations and architectural excavations; however, Cementerio group types start during the Acbi phase and continue into Cueva.

Statistically, we have not been able to identify any significant differential distribution of any Cementerio group type in our excavations.

Intersite Locations, Contexts, and Associations: Coarse-incised unslipped utilitarian jars are not uncommon in the southern periphery of Mesoamerica; however, Cementerio is unusual in the variety of its line, slash, and punctate decoration and the varied combination of techniques and designs on each vessel. Generally, similar coarse-incised unslipped types are recorded at a number of sites in the periphery. Obrajuela Plain and Broad Incised of the Lepa Complex (Late Classic) at Quelepa (Andrews 1976:96–104, fig. 23) are somewhat similar, as are Candungo and Tiligua Incised Types of the Eden II complex (Early to Middle Classic) at Los Naranjos (Baudez and

Becquelin 1973:213–219, fig. 89). As with Masica Incised, the closest correlates for this type are found in central Honduras. In addition to the Tiligua and Candungo Incised at Los Naranjos, Stone (1957: figs. 39, 67) illustrates similar coarse-incised sherds from the Comayagua Valley and from the Sulaco region.

The Cececapa Incised with Red Type of the site of Gualjoquito, Honduras, appears to be related to Cementerio, as the two share forms, coarse-incised hatching, simple designs, and red neck and rim painting (Schortman, Urban, and Ashmore 1983:29, 31). But at Gualjoquito and other middle Ullua drainage sites, Cececapa Incised goes back to the Late Preclassic period. Schortman, Urban, and Ashmore (1983:31) believe that the Early Classic version of this type may be transitional between a Cementerio-like Cececapa and the finer Masica Incised type of the Late Classic. Such a continuous tradition would be expected for central-western Honduras, the area of greatest frequency and probable origin of these incised types. Note, however, that at Copan there is neither typological nor chronological continuity between Cementerio and Masica Incised. The two types are distinctive in style, with Cementerio being very crudely incised and Masica Incised quite finely done.

In addition to its connections to central Honduras, Cementerio is also one of the few types showing some degree of affinity with Quirigua. Thus it is broadly similar to the Quirigua Guayabal and Chilmecate varieties.

Functional Interpretation: The type's form and its distribution are consistent with an interpretation of its use as a water jar. The surface incisions would facilitate cooling as do striations on the later Casaca Striated water jar type of the Late Classic Coner complex. Its common presence in household refuse and fill is consistent with this interpretation.

Cultural Significance: Because Cementerio group types are difficult to separate in classification, and because they display considerable continuity and overlap through time, they do not serve as good phase diagnostics. Thus, Zigoto and Mapache begin in Acbi times, although Mapache peaks in popularity in the Cueva phase; and while Cementerio Incised is most common in the Cueva phase, it continues on into Late Classic Coner.

As indicated above, intersite comparisons show that Cementerio weakly reinforces the pattern more sharply defined by Masica Incised and Babilonia Polychrome. That is, it shows ceramic connections to central and western Honduras, as well as the broadly peripheral (i.e., not Classic lowland Maya) nature of the Copan ceramics. The extant archaeological literature does not often include the description of homely utilitarian vessels and sherds such as those of the Cementerio group. Consequently, there is less intersite information.

It is interesting to note the strong negative statistical correlation between Cementerio Incised and its functionally equivalent Late Classic water jar type, Casaca Striated. It appears that in the latter part of the Late Classic period, Casaca Striated rapidly became the major Copan water vessel, completely replacing Cementerio Incised. As discussed below (see Casaca Striated, "Cultural Significance"), Casaca Striated follows the Maya lowland Tzakol and Tepeu trait of striated water jars. In contrast, Cementerio Incised is a rather typical water jar type for the southern periphery. It seems likely that the Late Classic replacement of Cementerio Incised by Casaca Striated reflects the increasingly strong ties of the Copan Valley to the Maya lowland sites to the north.

Arroyo Red Type

Variety Name: Arroyo.
Established as a Type and/or Variety: By this description.
Frequency: This description is based upon 3,277 sherds. This collection represents 1.2 percent of the total sherd collection recovered within the Copan Valley.
Ceramic Group: Antonio.
Ceramic Complex: Cueva.
Illustrations: Figure 50a–n.
Description:
Principal Identifying Modes. There are two surface identifying characteristics of this type:

1. The exterior surface of the vessel shows clear pebble-polishing as was evident with Antonio Buff;
2. the exterior surface is covered with a red slip;

3. the primary forms are deep bowls with incurving sides, deep bowls with vertical or slightly
outsloping walls, and small collared jars.

Paste, Temper, and Firing. The color of the surface finish varies slightly from a red self-slip, 10R
5/8 and 2.5 YR 4/8, to a light red, 2.5 YR 6/8.
Surface hardness ranges on the exterior from 2.5
to 3.5 on Moh's scale and on the interior is less
than or equal to 2.0. The paste consists of predominantly silty particles. Its density ranges from
dense/compact to slightly porous with a uniform
homogeneity.

The temper material is evenly distributed
between sand and sand-pumice, and the temper size
ranges from fine to very coarse. Finally, the size of
the temper is predominantly subangular, with some
particles being fully rounded.

Surface Finish and Decoration. Although the
surface of these vessels has been pebble-polished,
a thin red slip has also been applied to the exteri-
or of the vessels. Occasionally, this red slip is also
evident on the interior, depending on the vessel
form. This application of a slip contrasts with
Antonio Buff, which has no slip.

As indicated in the detailed description above,
there is a considerable range in the surface color
from red to orange. Fire clouding is also evident.

Form. The basic forms of this type are very similar to the forms evident within the Antonio Buff
type. They include bowls with incurved rims,
bowls with vertical walls or slightly outsloping
walls, deep bowls with marked everted rims, and
small collared jars.

Bowl rims are generally markedly thickened.
As with the Antonio Type, the thickening is more
characteristic of incurved walled bowls than other forms. Bowls with incurved rims have orifice
diameters ranging from 30–35 cm to as little as
20 cm.

One definite basal sherd was identified. It has a
small circular indentation and probably came
from a small collared jar.

Numerous loop handles were also identified
with the type. Some were placed vertically on the
collared jars. Whether they occur on other forms
is unclear.

There are two straight dipper-like handles,
both fragmentary, and a third fragment of a handle with a crudely modeled quadruped adorno.

**Whole, Restorable, or Partially Restorable Ves-
sel:** One partial Arroyo Red vessel was identified.
Only the basal portion of the vessel remains. This
vessel is identified as Cat. No. 1-253, and the
context is described in detail below.

Classificatory Comments: As with Antonio Buff,
this type is defined by a pebble-polished exterior;
however, the surface color, in this case, is red.
Basal portions of vessels are difficult to classify,
but one was identified (see below).

Intrasite Locations, Contexts, and Associations:
One large basal fragment (Cat. No. 1-253, Operation 20(A), CV-20, Special Find 49) of Arroyo
Red was recovered from a dedicatory cache in the
fill of Structure D, CV-20. This basal fragment,
as mentioned above, had a convex indentation on
the base and was probably part of a collared jar.
It was found in association with the following
artifacts:

1. one large round mano
2. one small round mano
3. one barkbeater
4. one diorite polishing stone
5. three large fragments of other collared vessels:

    a. Sopi Incised (Cat. No. 1-305, Operation
    20(A), CV-20, Special Find 46);
    b. Cementerio Incised (Cat. No. 1-306, Oper-
    ation 20(A), CV-20, Special Find 47);
    c. Mapache Grooved (Cat. No. 1-307, Oper-
    ation 20(A), CV-20, Special Find 48)

The artifacts appear to be associated with domestic activities, as does the structure in which the
cache was found.

Intersite Locations, Contexts, and Associations:
See intersite section for Antonio Buff. Arroyo
Red resembles Moncagua Plain from Quelepa, El
Salvador (Andrews 1976).

Functional Interpretation: See functional section
under Antonio Buff. Also see section above on
intrasite contexts.

Cultural Significance: See section under Antonio
Buff.

Sopi Incised Type

Variety Name: Sopi.
Established as a Type and/or Variety: By this
description in consultation with Viel.

Frequency: See the counts and frequency data for Arroyo Red. As will be clear in the description below, the only difference between this type and Arroyo Red is the incising along the collar. Sherds, therefore, would not be an accurate reflection of frequency of vessels of this type.

Ceramic Group: Antonio.

Ceramic Complex: Cueva.

Illustrations: Figures 51a–h, 52, 53.

Description:

Principal Identifying Modes.

1. Fine-line incision in a crosshatch and other geometric patterns on the vessel collar exteriors;
2. pebble-polished surface resulting in a buff/orange/red surface color;
3. large collared jar forms.

Paste, Temper, and Firing. See Antonio Buff and Arroyo Red for details.

Surface Finish and Decoration. The most common surface color is light red, 2.5 YR 6/6, but there is a great variation in the surface color from vessel to vessel and in fact on a single vessel. The surface of the exterior is largely self-slipped. The only evidence of an added slip is a red pigment seen on some of the vessel rims or lips. Occasionally, this pigment extends slightly down the interior walls of the vessel.

The defining surface incision is found around the collar of the vessel. The most common design is a band of crosshatched incision just below the lip. This results in rather irregular diamond forms averaging about 1.5 cm in length and 0.7 cm in width. These incised lines, which were made prior to firing, are fine and sharp. Other designs include parallel diagonal lines, parallel vertical lines, and combinations of parallel lines and long slash punctations.

Form. The most common form is a large collared jar. One partially restorable vessel (Cat. No. 1-256) (fig. 52) has the following measurements:

Rim diameter: 18 cm
Base diameter: 9.5 cm
Maximum diameter at midpoint: 33 cm
Height: 26.5 cm
Height of collar: 6 cm

Generally, the collars of these jars are short, as in the vessel described above. Rims are always outflared or outturned, at a horizontal or near-horizontal angle.

The few identified bases were fairly small, round, and indented.

Small loop handles were placed vertically on these vessels from near the rim lip to the top of the shoulder. It is uncertain how many handles would have been placed on a single vessel—two or four? The loops vary in length from 3 to 4.5 cm and in height from 1.5 to 2.5 cm. Handle thickness ranges from 0.9 to 1.1 cm. The loop aperture is large enough for the insertion of a single finger. The apparent delicacy of these handles makes it unlikely that they would have been used to lift the vessels, especially if they were filled with a liquid.

Whole, Restorable, or Partially Restorable Vessels: Two partial vessels have been recovered. One of these vessels is Cat. No. 1-256 and is described in detail above.

The second vessel is Cat. No. 1-305, Operation 20(A), Special Find 46, CV-20, Level 5. It was part of a cache found within Structure D of CV-20. It is a partially restored large olla (fig. 53). The dimensions are as follows:

Height: approximately 17 cm
Maximum diameter at midpoint on the body of the vessel: 30 cm
Orifice diameter: estimated at 25 cm

This vessel is unslipped. Along the interior rim and in patches on the exterior shoulder is evidence of an unevenly applied red wash or thin red paint. The exterior incised decoration of this vessel, on the collar area, is an encircling band, about 3 m in width, consisting of very coarse, slash-incised cross-hatching. The bottom of the band is marked by a simple, crudely incised, encircling line.

Classificatory Comments: Due to the similarity in color and surface pebble-polishing between this type, Antonio Buff, and Arroyo Red, it is probable that most of the body sherds of vessels of this type were classified within these other types.

Intrasite Locations, Contexts, and Associations: Sopi Incised is a clear temporal marker for the Cueva complex, associated in refuse with Arroyo Red and Antonio Buff. It is associated with Arroyo Red in a cache found within Structure D, CV-20.

Intersite Locations, Contexts, and Associations: As with Antonio Buff and Arroyo Red, the closest affiliate for Sopi appears to be the Moncagua Plain Incised from Quelepa; however, this Salvadoran type does not appear to be as clearly pebble-polished as is Sopi.

Functional Interpretation: See functional interpretation for the collared jars of Arroyo Red and Antonio Buff.

Cultural Significance: See description for Antonio Buff and Arroyo Red.

Antonio Buff Type

Variety Name: Antonio.

Established as a Type and/or Variety: By this description. This type is based upon 12,566 sherds, including one partially restorable vessel. This represents 4.5 percent of the total sherd collection recovered by the Harvard Copan Project.

Ceramic Group: Antonio.

Ceramic Complexes: Cueva and possibly Middle and Early Acbi.

Illustrations: Figure 54a–i.

Description:

Principal Identifying Modes.

1. Pebble-polished surface with slight striations, particularly on the exterior and upper portions of the vessel. Pebble-polishing is less pronounced on the interior;
2. a buff to mottled gray-buff to gray color or self-slip;
3. a variety of forms, primarily including deep open bowls, shallow bowls, and comales.

Paste, Temper, and Firing. The color of the paste of this Antonio Type ranges considerably from a buff to a gray. On the Munsel chart, some of these ranges include

1. a light reddish brown—5 YR 6/4
2. a pinkish brown—7.5 YR 7/4
3. dark grayish brown—10 YR 4/2

The hardness of the interior of the vessel is generally less than or equal to 2.0 on Moh's scale. The exterior is slightly harder, ranging from 2.5 to 3.5.

The texture of the clay particles within the paste is predominantly silty. The paste is homogeneous with a uniform distribution of clay inclusions.

The temper used in Antonio seems to be both sand and sand-pumice. The size of the temper is divided between fine and coarse. The shape of the temper ranges from subangular to subangular and fully rounded.

Surface Finish and Decoration. The pebble-polished, slightly roughened exterior and interior surfaces of this type vary greatly in color. The range is evident in the previous section. It is unclear if an actual slip or wash has been added to the surface of these vessels. The surface color of the vessel is almost identical to the paste color. The smooth treatment of both the interior and exterior surfaces approximates a slip in appearance, especially in contrast to a completely unslipped type such as Lysandro or Casaca. The compromise term "self-slip" was selected to identify the surface treatment, implying that the clay of the vessel has been substantially smoothed and semi-polished on the surfaces. This polishing has been done with what appears to be the rather small surface of a pebble or artifact. Such surface treatment has left polishing striations that range in width from approximately 2 to 3 cm. These polishing marks are tightly packed together, creating a smoothed and uniform surface. This pebble-polishing is most evident on the neck, shoulder, and central portions of the vessel. The areas immediately around the rims and basal portions of the vessels are usually left rough, probably because it was more difficult to polish these areas.

The variation in exterior vessel surface color—from buff to blotchy, gray-black patches and streaks—appears to be the result of imperfect and differential firing during manufacture. Often such blotches occur only on the shoulders of vessels and not on their bases, seemingly ruling out domestic cooking functions as the cause of the blotches.

Form. There are three principal forms within this Antonio Buff Type:

1. Deep open bowls: The walls of these deep open bowls range in their orientation from vertical to slightly insloping to slightly outsloping. There is a thickening of the wall near the rim on all of these open bowls. The thickness of the vessel wall at the rim ranges from 0.8 to 1.5 cm. The vessel wall thins out lower on the vessel to a minimum of 0.4 cm. Diameters of these vessels range from 30 to 40 cm. Vessels with incurving rims tend to be smaller in rim diameter than those with vertical or outsloping walls. Vessel height or depth is presently undetermined but appears to be less than the orifice diameter.

2. Very shallow plates/bowls and handled comales: Although there are two distinct forms being grouped within this category, the exact relationship between them is uncertain. Probably, there is a gradation from a shallow bowl to a flat comal. Loop handles are affixed horizontally to the edges of the comales. One partially intact comal specimen includes a handle with the following dimensions: length—10 cm; thickness—1.5 cm; handle to plate-edge aperture—6 cm x 2 cm. The diameter of the shallow open bowl ranges from 38 to 42 cm. The comal fragments were not complete enough to get a good diameter measurement. Wall thickness near the rim of the vessel ranges from 0.9 to 1.4 cm; lower on the vessel it is between 0.8 and 1 cm.

3. Collared jar: This third common vessel form of the type is a smallish (25-cm average diameter) collared jar. The collars are short and vary from slightly outflared to markedly outturned. Vessel walls average from 0.4 to 0.6 cm. Some specimens showed little vertical loop handles, extending from the rim to the base of the collar.

In addition to the handles described above for the comales and small collared jars, there are other loop handles that were affixed to either deep bowls or the jars. These handles average about 2 cm in diameter and are at least 10 cm in length. From the few specimens available, these handles would probably have been placed horizontally on the vessel.

There are several other handles in our collection that have a pebble-polished Antonio-like surface. These include a single fragment of a dipper-like handle. This fragment measures about 3 cm in diameter and may have been attached to a shallow bowl. Three others appear to have projecting handles. Two of these were formed by doubling and squeezing together a projecting loop of clay. These are probably similar to the handles from the ladle forms described in our Sepultura type and also described by Longyear (1952).

Whole, Restorable, or Partially Restorable Vessels: Only one Antonio Buff vessel (Cat. No. 1-361) was recovered. It came from debris after the salvage excavation in Structure L11-93 was destroyed. There is therefore no stratigraphic context for this vessel. The vessel is a simple circular comal with a diameter of 19.5 cm and a thickness of 0.9 cm.

Classificatory Comments: The type is very clearly defined by the marked pebble-polishing and self-slip on the surface of the vessels; however, as pebble-polishing decreases toward the lower portions of the vessels, sherds from these lower portions might often have been classified as Lysandro Unslipped. Another classificatory problem is that Antonio Buff and Arroyo Red tend to blend, in surface color, one into another; however, both appear to be contemporaneous and related types that define the Cueva phase and complex.

Intrasite Locations, Contexts, and Associations: Antonio Buff, as was Arroyo Red, was found as frequent fill material in Cueva phase constructions underlying those of the later Coner phase.

Intersite Locations, Contexts, and Associations: Pebble-polishing as a pottery surface treatment—an identifying mode of Antonio Buff—is found elsewhere in the southeast periphery of the Maya area. At Chalchuapa, in El Salvador, Sharer (1978) notes such surface treatment, although there it is always combined with various types of surface decoration. The only pebble-polished type without surface decoration that we have come across is Moncagua Plain, from Quelepa in eastern El Salvador (Andrews 1976), which resembles both Antonio Buff and Arroyo Red. Moncagua also has vessel forms similar to those of Antonio Buff.

Functional Interpretation: Domestic cooking and serving functions seem most likely. The comal form relates to the modern-day comal, or pottery griddle, found widely in Mesoamerica, which is used for cooking tortillas and other foods. We cannot, however, support this interpretation by the presence of cooking or burning marks on the comales we found. Perhaps our sherd sample was too small for this determination.

Cultural Significance: Along with Arroyo Red, this is one of the marker types of the Cueva phase. Wider relationships are indicated in the southeast peripheral area.

Switch Molina Striated Type

Variety Name: Sandoval.

Established as a Type and/or Variety: Switch Molina Striated: Switch Molina Variety was established at Quirigua by Sharer and associates (personal communication 1980). The Sandoval Variety is presented here for the first time, based upon two whole vessels and a collection of 1,200 sherds. This is less than 2 percent of the Switch Molina (Striated Jars) collection.

Ceramic Group: Switch Molina.
Ceramic Complex: Cueva.
Illustrations: Figures 55a–o, 56, 57.
Description:
Principal Identifying Modes.
1. Close-spaced, medium-to-fine striations, relatively lightly impressed, on vessel exteriors;
2. subglobular or tecomate-like bowls with unmodified rims;
3. deep open bowls with slightly outcurving walls and short, outflaring rims.

Paste, Temper, and Firing. Very similar to Casaca Striated: Casaca Variety.

Surface Finish and Decoration. Interiors are smoothed. The exteriors are covered with striations that are 1 to 2 mm in width and about the same distance apart. These average as somewhat more lightly impressed than the striations of Casaca Striated: Casaca Variety. Striations are found virtually covering the vessels except for the base. They begin at the lip and are frequently arranged diagonally, running from left to right; sometimes they are placed horizontally on the vessel; and sometimes there are combinations of diagonal and horizontal placements. A complete subglobular olla (Cat. No. 1-580) shows a combination of diagonal and horizontal striation arrangements; another complete vessel, a small collared olla or jar (Cat. No. 1-745), is covered with horizontally placed striations.

Red pigment, like that described for Casaca Striated, is usually present on vessel lips, on rim exteriors, and sometimes as body splotches.

Some vessels show exterior fire-blackening.

Form. The subglobular bowl or tecomate-like vessel is probably the most common form. These apparently range from 15 to 30 cm in maximum diameter, with orifice diameters of about 7 to 13 cm. The rims for this form are direct and unmodified, lips rounded. Deep open bowls occur, and sherds for this form indicate orifice diameters as much as 30 cm. Depth of these bowls can only be guessed at, but it was probably less than the orifice diameter. Some of the open bowls had vertical walls; others show a slight constriction a short distance below the orifice,

with a slightly outflared upper portion. Otherwise, rims are unmodified and rims rounded or flattened. There are also some collared ollas or jars. These are smaller than the large collared jars of the Casaca Striated type.

Appendages include plain, horizontally placed loop handles on subglobular bowls and little button-like appliqued nodes also attached to this same vessel form.

Whole, Restorable, or Partially Restorable Vessels: Two of these were recovered. One, a subglobular bowl (Cat. No. 1-580, CV-43, Op. No. 33(Z), Special Find 16) (fig. 56), has a maximum diameter of 17 cm, is 10 cm high, and has an orifice with a diameter of 8 cm. It also has two horizontally placed loop handles. No complete open bowl forms were found, but one small collared jar (Cat. No. 1-745, CV-43, Op. No. 33(FF), Level 4-B) (fig. 57) is 8.8 cm high and 8.8 cm in maximum body diameter. The rim reflares above a short collar, and the orifice is 6.8 cm in diameter. The jar has a small, flat, round base.

Classificatory Comments: With small body sherds it is difficult to separate Switch Molina Striated: Sandoval Variety from Casaca Striated: Casaca Variety; however, close inspection of a number of sherds from each of the two types does indicate a finer and more lightly impressed striated line for Switch Molina. In our sorting, this difference was picked up after we noticed that striated sherds from deeper stratigraphic levels, in places where some depth of refuse did obtain, often showed subglobular bowl rims. The consistent association of the finer striations with such rims led us to establish the type and variety for our Copan collections. Subsequent study of the collections, particularly in the light of excavation and stratigraphic information, enabled us to expand the type description to include small collared jars and deep open bowl forms as well.

Intrasite Locations, Contexts, and Associations: Found in residential refuse and building fills. Two large concentrations of sherds were found, respectively, in CV-20, Structure A, Op. No. 19(C), Level 4 (Cat. No. 1-220) and in CV-43, Structure E, Op. No. 102(A), Level 3 (Cat. No. 1-953). These and other deposits of Switch Molina sherds were found in relatively deep excavation levels, and the associations seem to be mainly with the Acbi phase of the site's history. At the same time, it is probable that Switch Molina and Casaca have chronologically overlapping frequencies of occurrence in the Acbi through Cueva to Coner sequence, with Casaca Striated gradually replacing Switch Molina Striated.

Intersite Locations, Contexts, and Associations: Our Sandoval Variety of Switch Molina Striated is, of course, related to the Switch Molina Variety of the type from the site of Quirigua (Sharer and associates, personal communication). Other similar types are found elsewhere in the Maya lowlands, as at Seibal (Sabloff 1975:101–102) and Altar de Sacrificios (Adams 1971:19–20), where the Early Classic striated type is known as Triunfo Striated. Triunfo has the lightly impressed striations characteristic of Switch Molina. In these Peten sites the Late Classic parallel to Casaca Striated is Encanto Striated. The Triunfo vessel forms, however, are mostly collared jars with outflared rims and do not include the subglobular bowl so characteristic of Switch Molina Striated: Sandoval Variety. At Altar de Sacrificios, Adams has designated two varieties of Triunfo, and one of these, the Ak Variety, has little button-like appliqued nodes on vessel exteriors, similar to such appendages noted for Sandoval.

Moving outside of the Maya lowlands, we find no close similarities to Switch Molina Striated or to any of the striated types found at Copan or in the Peten sites. As noted in searching for comparisons to Casaca Striated, the Honduran Los Naranjos type, Jaitique Grossier (Baudez and Becquelin 1973:123–130) and the Salvadoran type described from Chalchuapa, Casa Sucia Striated (Sharer 1978:28), are not very similar to Sandoval.

Functional Interpretation: Presumably, a utility ware. Water and food storage and, perhaps, cooking—as in the case of Casaca Striated—are all suggested.

Cultural Significance: Switch Molina Striated: Sandoval Variety is an indicator of the long chronological persistence of the striated surface finishing technique for apparent storage and water vessels in the Maya lowlands. This Sandoval Variety has been dated to the Early Classic and, perhaps, the earlier part of the Late Classic period at Copan. As such, it finds parallels in other lowland Maya sites, where similar striated surface vessels were produced at this time and where they form a part of a continuum of striated wares, one beginning in the Preclassic period and

persisting through the Late Classic period. At Copan, where there appears to have been a mixture of Classic lowland Maya ceramic traits and traits pertaining to a local regional tradition, it is of interest to note that these striated wares link to, and probably derive from, the lowland Classic Maya sphere rather than to the peripheral zones of Honduras to the east of the Guatemalan–Salvadoran highlands to the south.

Chalja Red-painted Type

Variety Name: Copan.
Established as a Type and/or Variety: By this description in consultation with Sharer and Viel.
Frequency: Although this type is part of the Tipon group, it is similarly classified as part of the Chalja subgroup, which consists of at least four separate types. The total number of sherds within this subgroup is 77. This represents 0.02 percent of the total sherd collection under study.
Ceramic Group: Tipon.
Ceramic Subgroup: Chalja.
Ceramic Complexes: Cueva and Acbi.
Illustrations: Figures 58a–c, 59, 60, 61.
Description:
Principal Identifying Modes.
1. Hematite dark red paint on polished brown surfaces;
2. simple band and ball designs for this hematite pigment;
3. open bowl and cylinder jar forms.
Paste, Temper, and Firing. See technical description for Tipon: Moni Variety.
Surface Finish and Decoration. The primary surface decoration consists of red banding on the exterior rims and walls of the bowls or cylinders. On the exterior of the vessel, the red band begins from 0.5 to 4 cm below the rim itself. Some specimens show evidence of interior rim banding, usually confined to a relatively narrow strip at the uppermost section of the interior. There are also some occasional solid red ball painted elements. They measure 4 to 6 cm in diameter. In one case (see vessel Cat. No. 1-137, below) they have been placed on the exterior wall of an open bowl and on the interior base of the same specimen.
Form. One of the most complete specimens (Cat. No. 1-137, Operation 6(N), CV-20) (fig. 59) is a

shallow open bowl or dish with a marked basal angle, flat bottom, small hollow tripod supports, outsloped rim, and flat everted lip. Diameter at the orifice is 26 cm. The diameter at the basal angle is slightly less than this. Total vessel height is 7.5 cm. The tripod supports are 2 cm high and 3.3 cm in diameter. Additional open bowl forms include a casuela form with a slight medial angle and a slightly outflared rim. The base on this form is rounded, although it probably rested on a flattened circle.

Whole, Restorable, or Partially Restorable Vessels: Three complete vessels were recovered. One, Cat. No. 1-137, is described above. Two other complete specimens were recovered in the excavations. These are both small cylinders with a single red hematite band around the exterior rim of the vessel. The following are the measurements:

Cat. No. 1-807 (fig. 60), Operation 63(A), CV-135, Special Find 2: height 5.5 cm, orifice diameter 4.25 cm.

Cat. No. 1-1183 (fig. 61), Operation 83(A), CV-16, Special Find 3: height 8.25 cm, orifice diameter 6 cm.

Classificatory Comments: Only a small number of sherds were identified of this Chalja Red-painted Type. One of its identifying features, hematite red paint, may have caused confusion with other hematite red-painted vessels, such as Caterpillar Polychrome or Copador Polychrome.

Intrasite Locations, Contexts, and Associations: Due to the small number of sherds recovered, little can be said about the distribution of this type throughout our excavations; however, two of the whole or partial vessels were found in direct association with burials. Cat. No. 1-1183 was found with Burial 4, CV-16. Cat. No. 1-807 was found within a test excavation and was associated with a small stone burial crypt. Chalja Red-painted seems, therefore, to have had some ritual association.

Intersite Locations, Contexts, and Associations: According to Sharer (personal communication), a type of Chalja Red-painted was found at Quirigua during the late Maudsley phase and the Hewett phase at that site. This chronological placement correlates exactly with that at Copan. Although this Chalja Red-painted is part of the

Tipon group and this group is probably associated with the Chiquihuat group at Chalchuapa, there is no evidence of a type similar to Chalja Red-painted at Chalchuapa.

Cultural Significance: First, this type shows one of the few connections between Copan and Quirigua. Second, we see the early use of specular hematite red paint for a surface decoration. This surface decoration becomes much more important during the following Coner phase.

Molanphy Modeled-carved Type

Variety Name: Molanphy.
Established as a Type and/or Variety: By this description.
Frequency: This description is based upon 43 sherds.
Ceramic Group: Chalja (Tipon).
Ceramic Complex: Cueva.
Illustrations: Figure 62a–j.
Description:
Principal Identifying Modes.
1. Modeled-carved glyphic and other complex designs;
2. fine dentate stamped zones and combinations of these zones with the modeled-carved designs described above;
3. orange slip with specular hematite red banding in combination in the modeled-carved designs and the dentate stamped zones.

Surface Finish and Decoration. Both the exterior and interior of these vessels are slipped orange (5YR 6/8 reddish yellow). Red bands are located on both the interior and exterior of the rim (red:7.5 R 4/6). Similar red bands are located above the basal angle of straight-sided jars or bowl forms. On the interior of some of the vessels, there is evidence of streaky brown to black bands below the red rim.

The exterior red bands are separated from the zones of dentate stamping by incised lines. The dentate stamping includes small linear rows of dentate pits. These rows vary from 1 to 1.5 cm in length. Individual pits are 1 to 2 mm in diameter. It would appear that such rows were made with the dentate edge of a stick or similar carved instrument. The number of dentates in the rows is usually either four or eight. The rows are placed vertically on the vessel or at a slight diagonal axis. Other variations to this basic pattern include larger bar-like dentations, 0.5 to 1 cm in length and 1 to 2 mm in width. These longer dentations are sometimes arranged horizontally on the vessel, and it seems likely that they were made as individual impressions with the end of a stick or similar instrument.

Modeled-carving ranges from flat surfaces that are slightly incised or carved and punctated to more deeply carved cameo-like surfaces. Some sherds show fluting on surfaces that have also been red-painted. When the dentations are associated with the incising or modeled-carving, the number and form of the dentations change slightly. Unfortunately, not enough material of this type was recovered to enable us to describe in detail the modeled-carved designs.

Form. The primary form of this type is a medium-deep bowl with a basal angle and a flattened bottom. The rims of these bowls are direct and unthickened.

Whole, Restorable, or Partially Restorable Vessels: None recovered.

Intrasite Locations, Contexts, and Associations: No information.

Intersite Locations, Contexts, and Associations: No information.

Chalja Incised Type

Variety Name: Peck.
Established as a Type and/or Variety: By this description in consultation with Sharer.
Frequency: This description is based upon 62 sherds.
Ceramic Group: Tipon.
Ceramic Complex: Cueva.
Illustrations: Figure 63a–g.
Description:
Principal Identifying Modes.
1. Thick white slip (similar to Capulin);
2. incised and carved decoration in complex designs including glyphic designs;
3. the application of a dark red slip over the primary white slip.

Paste, Temper, and Firing. See technical description of Tipon: Moni.
Surface Finish and Decoration. The thick white slip is combined with the incised and carved decoration and the red-slipped designs on the exterior surfaces only; however, the white slip is some-

times found on the interior surfaces. The incised and carved designs are of medium depth with small cut-out areas at line intersections. Designs include rectilinear panels, scroll and volute elements, and hieroglyphs.

Form. The primary vessel form of this type is an open, medium-deep bowl that may have had a basal angle. Orifice diameter is about 14 cm. Another form might be a cylinder jar with an outflaring rim, although the evidence for this form is uncertain.

Whole, Restorable, or Partially Restorable Vessels: None recovered.

Intrasite Locations, Contexts, and Associations: No information.

Intersite Locations, Contexts, and Associations: This type has connections with Quirigua, according to Sharer (personal communication). It is interesting to note that while Copan seems to develop numerous types based upon a red slip, Quirigua goes in a different direction with an emphasis upon white slipping.

Cultural Significance: See above.

Gualpopa Polychrome Type

Variety Name: Copan.
Established as a Type and/or Variety: By Sharer (1978) from Chalchuapa, El Salvador. The Copan Variety is defined by this description.
Frequency: A total of 1,317 sherds from our excavations or 0.5 percent of the total collection under study.
Ceramic Group: Gualpopa.
Ceramic Complex: Cueva.
Illustrations: Figures 64a–j, 65.
Description:
Principal Identifying Modes.
1. Cream-colored, fine, untempered paste;
2. red (not specular hematite) and black designs on an orange-cream background;
3. open hemispherical bowl forms.

Paste, Temper, and Firing. See Sharer (1978:51).
Surface Finish and Decoration. Design motifs include animals, geometric designs, and what appear to be simple glyphs. Design motifs are outlined in red and black over a thin slip of orange-cream color. The interior vessels of Gualpopa tend to be plain, with only the orange-cream slip with the design motifs most common on the exterior.

Sharer has defined a set of four varieties based upon exterior decoration. His first variety, the Gualpopa Variety, is defined as having elaborately painted motifs, including glyphic elements and naturalistic birds, on both the interior and exterior of the vessel. There is no evidence from the material recovered from our excavations or those of the Carnegie Institution (Longyear 1952) that this variety is found at Copan. Sharer's second variety, the Geometric Variety, is defined as having simple geometric motifs confined to the exterior of the vessel. Sharer's third variety, the Mono Variety, is defined by silhouette monkeys on the exterior of the vessel. This is one of the most common varieties found within our Copan excavations. Sharer's fourth variety is the Glyphic Variety, where glyph-like design elements are outlined in either red or black.

Form. The hemispherical bowl is the most common. Marilyn Beaudry (1983) states that 61 percent of all Gualpopa artifacts found within the southeastern region are open hemispherical bowls. Other forms include vertical-walled bowls and composite-walled bowls; however, these are rare in the Copan material.

Whole, Restorable, or Partially Restorable Vessels: One Gualpopa bowl (Cat. No. 1-130) was recovered from a test excavation in CV-17, Operation 10(A), Special Find 3.

This is a small, partially eroded Gualpopa bowl (fig. 65). The vessel is 7.3 cm high with an orifice diameter of 15.2 cm. The walls converge ever so slightly toward the rim. The exterior has a light orange slip. There is a solid dark red band just below the lip, on both the vessel exterior and interior. Below this red band, on the vessel exterior, two black bands, 2.7 cm apart, encircle the bowl. Between these black bands are a number of small design elements—perhaps monkey silhouettes, perhaps glyphs, or both. These smaller elements are badly eroded. These design elements may have been painted alternately in red and black. A solid red encircling band goes around the vessel base below the above design arrangement.

Classificatory Comments: A problem with this type was differentiating eroded Gualpopa Polychrome from other fine-paste eroded polychromes, such as Chilanga and Copador.

Intrasite Locations, Contexts, and Associations: Gualpopa sherds were found consistently in Cueva phase contexts.

Intersite Locations, Contexts, and Associations: Gualpopa Polychrome is a defining type for the southeastern Maya region on the time level of the Cueva phase. This follows, chronologically, the Acbi phase (with its Chilanga Polychrome) and precedes the Coner phase (with its Copador Polychrome); however, Gualpopa has its inception as early as Acbi and continues into Coner.

There are some element continuities (orange background color, fine paste) from Chilanga Polychrome into Gualpopa, and Gualpopa also shows links (red and black designs, use of glyph-like design elements) to later Copador Polychrome.

Functional Interpretation: Beaudry (1983), in her study of the fine-paste types of the southeastern region as a whole, notes that Gualpopa Polychrome designs and design execution are on a lower level of competence than those found on Copador Polychrome. She also states that there was little standardization of Gualpopa design; Copador had more evidence of motif standardization. Beaudry then hypothesizes that Gualpopa, because of its restricted distribution, was an important, locally produced, household ceramic type. Copador, according to Beaudry, had a ritual function. We are skeptical of the functional differences assigned to these two polychrome types by Beaudry. The great abundance of Copador Polychrome in household contexts in the later Coner phase certainly suggests its daily usage as a serving ware, although this does not preclude Copador's use in ritual contexts. Our opinion is that the two polychromes functioned much the same—in effect, largely as household nice ware. We see the difference between the two as largely chronological, with the aesthetically superior Copador gradually replacing the more crudely painted Gualpopa over time.

Cultural Significance: Gualpopa Polychrome is a major defining ceramic type of the southeast Maya region during this earlier part of the Late Classic period.

The Coner Phase

During the Coner phase, Copan enjoyed its greatest growth in population and public architecture as well as its political and artistic climax and sculptural magnificence.

The dating of the Coner phase is set at A.D. 700 to 900. The date for the inception of the phase is set by the first appearance of the distinctive pottery type Copador Polychrome and the correlation of this highly distinctive pottery with Copan Initial Series hieroglyphic dates (Leventhal 1986; Willey 1988). The terminal date of A.D. 900 is an arbitrary one selected at a point in time a few decades after the last Copan Initial Series monument (Morley 1920). It was once assumed that the site and the valley were abandoned at about that time, an abandonment that appeared to coincide with the period of the Classic Maya collapse throughout the southern lowlands; however, recent obsidian hydration dates taken from samples obtained from numerous residential sites in the Copan Valley strongly suggest that Copan, at least in its outlying environs, continued to be occupied at least until A.D. 1000, or perhaps even as late as A.D. 1100/1200 (Sanders and Webster, personal communication 1989). Whether or not a full Coner ceramic complex, including Copador Polychrome, continued into these later centuries has not yet been determined.

Copador Polychrome, with its synthesis of lowland Maya design elements, including hieroglyphs or pseudo-glyphs, with other designs and vessel forms reminiscent of antecedent Uapala and Maya highland traditions, appears to have originated at Copan, or at least in the Copan Valley. It is found in great abundance here. It occurs only to a limited extent in the Maya highlands, and it is virtually nonexistent elsewhere in the Maya lowlands.

The remainder of the ceramic types of the Coner phase show an interesting division in their heritages. Tipon Orange-brown and Don Gordon Modeled-carved continue in the fine ware traditions of the Maya lowlands. But interestingly, the very common water jars of Casaca Striated also have parallels in the Maya lowland Peten sites. So the selections in pottery styles from this source and direction were not all limited to elite wares. The types Masica Incised, Reina Incised, and Raul Red all seem to have been derived from old local Honduran prototypes. Caterpillar Polychrome looks like a local Honduran debasement of Classic Maya polychrome ideas; Babilonia Polychrome, also Classic Maya–derived, is a handsome ware from northwestern Honduras, in the Ulua Valley (often better known as Ulua

Polychrome). Sepultura Unslipped refers to incensarios that point back toward the Maya lowlands. In the Coner phase, the one regional tradition that seems to have dropped out of the Copan ceramic interaction center is the Maya highlands. By this time, the powerful Usulutan custom of painting was largely dead.

Ardilla Gouged-incised Type

Variety Names: Ardilla and Crapo.
Established as a Type and/or Variety: By this description in consultation with Viel (personal communication 1980).
Frequency: A total of 212 sherds were recovered, a very small percentage of the collection under study.
Ceramic Group: Tipon.
Ceramic Complexes: Cueva and principally Coner.
Illustrations: Figures 66, 67a–dd.
Description:
Principal Identifying Modes.
1. Polished brown surfaces, usually both exterior and interior;
2. deep, broad-line gouged-incision-and-excision;
3. deep to medium-deep, flat-bottomed open bowl or dish.

Variety Distinctions: The distinction between the Ardilla and Crapo varieties focuses upon the design elements. The Crapo Variety features design elements such as stylized frogs or deities located within panels.
Paste, Temper, and Firing. See the "Paste, Temper, and Firing" section for Tipon Orange-brown.
Surface Finish and Decoration. The surface finish of this Ardilla Gouged-incised Type consists of smoothed and polished surfaces that generally have a dark brown color, although the color range extends from black-brown to buff on most sherds/vessels. Fire mottling is evident on many of the sherds.

The surface decoration—consisting of incising, excising, and some punctations—is found usually on the exterior wall of the bowls or dishes. This decoration may extend from just below the rim down to the basal angle. Incised decoration is also found on vessel supports. It appears that the incision and excision of the vessel walls was done after air-drying of the vessel surface, resulting in a slightly ragged or fractured quality of the incised or engraved lines. Excised portions very clearly display this rough or fractional appearance.

The design elements are generally interlaced rectilinear designs, although there are examples of intertwined curvilinear elements. Other designs include rectilinear panels composed of concentric, inverted U-shaped elements combined with areas filled with multiple lines. There are also very complex designs that may combine all the elements described above. Such designs include curvilinear and rectilinear zones and dot punctations. Some of these seem to form flower or petal-like designs. Some sherds show only parallel line incisions or simple line incisions below the rim. These may have been combined with the more complex designs, described above, on the entire vessel.

The one slab-footed support that bears an incised decoration apparently represents a stylized face (Tlaloc?).

The execution of the design elements varies from careful and skillful to rather sloppy and haphazard, with the majority of the recovered specimens falling within the latter category.

One partial vessel of this type shows evidence of specular hematite red paint on rectangular panels. These panels are defined by gouged incised lines on the exterior sides of a flaring-walled flat-bottomed bowl.

One specimen of the Crapo Variety shows a highly stylized frog that is outlined in both deep-gouged and fine-line incisions. It is located within a rectilinear panel on the exterior wall of a polished-brown cylinder jar.

Form. There appears to be only one primary form represented within this type: a deep to shallow bowl with slightly outslanted side walls. Subdivisions of this basic form include bowls with simple or direct rims and bowls with thickened and markedly everted rims. The orifice diameter of an everted rim, flat-based bowl is approximately 39 cm. The orifice diameter of a direct rim, flat-based bowl is 20 cm. Vessel bases were flat or approximately so. Some probably did not have supports; others have slab feet or hollow rounded feet. The slab feet include both solid and hollow forms. They vary in height from just

under 2 cm to just over 4 cm. The length-to-width dimensions range from 4 x 2 cm to 7 x 2.5 cm. The one rounded, bulbous support is 4.5 cm high and 6.5 cm in diameter, tapering to a base with a 3.5-cm diameter.

Whole, Restorable, or Partially Restorable Vessels: A partially restorable vessel (Cat. No. 1-137; CV-20, Operation (N), Level 1) was recovered in the clearing operations associated with Structure A, CV-20. It is flat-bottomed with outslanting walls. It probably had three hollow rounded feet. A zone circling the central part of the exterior wall of the vessel is the focus of the decoration. This is executed in vertical and horizontal deep-gouged incised lines. At intervals within this zone are curved-line elements that are vaguely reminiscent of the Preclassic flame-eyebrow designs found widely in Mesoamerica.

Orifice diameter of the vessel is 26 cm; height, 7 cm.

Classificatory Comments: The only sherds that were placed within this Ardilla Type are those that clearly show evidence of gouge-incising, excising, or perhaps punctations. It is clear that many sherds from other sections of Ardilla vessels were probably classified as simply Tipon Orange-brown.

Intrasite Locations, Contexts, and Associations: Longyear illustrates an Ardilla: Crapo vessel in figure 110f. It is similar to one of the specimens recovered in our excavations, for it shows the outline of a frog on the side of a cylinder vase. This was found within Tomb 1-41, which was located within the western or Ostuman section of the Copan Valley. Longyear correctly dates this tomb within the Full Classic, confirming our placement of the type within late Cueva to early Coner time span.

Intersite Locations, Contexts, and Associations: There are no highly specific matches between Ardilla Gouged-incised and other types within the southeast Maya region, the western Salvadoran–Guatemalan highlands region, or the region of the Maya lowlands proper, yet there are general resemblances to dark brownish or blackish wares that have been decorated with incision and carving in all of these regions. Some of these are somewhat earlier than Ardilla; others are contemporary. We will refer to some of these below under our description of the Coner phase type, Don Gordon Modeled-carved.

Reina Incised Type

Variety Names: Bolo and Reina.
Established as a Type and/or Variety: By this description.
Frequency: 562 sherds, or 0.2 percent of total sherds at the site. Frequency of whole vessels was certainly higher than this, however, as red-slipped body sherds would be classified as Raul Red: Unspecified Variety. This is a minor (but not rare) type of the Cueva and Coner complexes, especially the latter. This type shows some relationships to the more popular Masica Incised Type: Cruz Variety.
Ceramic Group: Marina.
Ceramic Complexes: Cueva and Coner.
Illustrations: Figure 68a–q.
Description:
Principal Identifying Modes.
1. Fine-line, imperfectly drawn, close-spaced, rectilinear designs;
2. red painting on rims, handles, and shoulders in bands or sloppily painted rectilinear designs;
3. medium to small collared jars;
4. strap or loop handles from collars to shoulders.

Variety Distinctions. Bolo Variety has a paste and slip identical to Masica Incised: Cruz Variety. The Reina Variety has a darker pinkish-brown paste and a darker, almost maroon slip on the collars.
Paste, Temper, and Firing. Bolo Variety, as noted, has paste characteristics identical for Masica Incised: Cruz Variety. Reina Variety has a homogeneous light reddish-brown paste (5 YR 6/3, 6/4) with colored sand temper containing occasional pumice and sherd particles. This paste is dense to slightly porous and has a silty clay texture with soft interiors (under 2.0 on Moh's scale) and harder exteriors (2.0 to 3.5).
Surface Finish and Decoration. Surface decoration of both varieties can be broadly characterized as a sloppy version of Masica Incised's combination of zoned incision and red slip. The Bolo Variety has exactly the same red-orange slip as Masica Incised; the Reina Variety (in addition to its distinctive paste) has slip-painting in a slightly darker red to red-brown color (2.5 YR 4/6, 5/6, 4/8, 5/8, 6/8, 3/4).

Reina incisions are usually in fine-line patterns of rectangles, serried or intersecting triangles, or other geometric arrangements defined by sets of two, three, or four parallel lines. Above and below the central band of decoration, which runs around the neck or collar of the vessel, are raised or pendant triangles often filled with hatching. In addition to fine-line incision there are some designs carried out with deeper, wider slashed lines.

Painting commences on the lip (occasionally slopping over into the vessel interior) and extends down to the area of the incised band on the neck or collar. Width of this upper painted band varies from 1 cm to 5 or 6 cm. Handles are generally also painted. The lower portion of the incised decoration marks the starting point for a lower painted zone. This lower zone covers the middle portion of vessel and, in some cases, extends to the base. The most common painted design below the incised zone is composed of an alternating field of horizontal bands and squiggly (or wavy) horizontal lines. Painted decoration on the vessel rim, when this occurs, consists of nested triangular arrangements of broad lines or triangles. All painting is in broad, bold, sloppily executed lines. The paint is cracked into a characteristic mosaic pattern, particularly on hard fired specimens with a dark brown colored paint.
Form. The only form is a collared jar. The collars are relatively high, averaging 7 to 8 cm, and approach the vertical with only a slightly outflared upper rim and lip. In general, these jars tend to be smaller than collared jar forms of the Cruz Variety of Masica or of Raul Red, Casaca Striated, and other Copan utility types.

Orifices range from 12 cm up to 20 cm in diameter and narrow slightly at the neck. Vessel wall thickness ranges from 1 cm at the rim to 0.5 cm on the vessel wall. Bases are indented. Handles are vertical straps or loops averaging 7 cm in length and from 1.2 to 2 cm in width. There are four handles to a vessel. Handles extend from just below the rim to the upper shoulder.
Whole, Restorable, or Partially Restorable Vessels: One partial vessel was recovered. It had an estimated height of about 25 to 30 cm with a maximum diameter of 19 to 20 cm restricting to 11 cm at the base of the neck with a 14-cm slightly outflared rim.

A whole Reina Incised vessel is shown by Longyear (1952: fig. 1091).
Classificatory Comments: Reina Incised can generally be regarded as a sloppily executed variant

of Masica Incised having a somewhat distinct four-handled jar form and a slightly different repertoire of incised designs. The Reina Variety paste variant also has a darker pinkish-brown paste and red-brown slip as compared to the buff paste and more orange slip of Masica Incised and the Bolo Variety of Reina Incised.

Intrasite Locations, Contexts, and Associations: This type is clearly found within primarily Coner proveniences, but beyond this, we have not been able to identify any differential distribution for the type. We had anticipated a correlation with Masica Incised, but the correlation chart does not indicate a particularly strong tie.

Intersite Locations, Contexts, and Associations: See comparisons (below) for Masica Incised. Note that Reina Incised's characteristic jar form with its four vertical handles is a common form in many types in central Honduras.

Cultural Significance: Like the dominant Masica Incised Type, Reina Incised underscores the Copan Valley's ceramic ties to the east (see discussion above for Cruz Variety). There is some stratigraphic evidence that Reina may begin earlier than the Cruz Type (i.e., during the preceding Cueva phase); however, the two types may be largely contemporary. Frequency of Reina at no point approached that of Masica Incised. We see no particular cultural or chronological significance in the distinction between the Bolo and Reina paste variants. They may represent only the individual potter's choice of clay.

Functional Interpretation: Form and context of this type, as with Masica Incised, are consistent with an interpretation of its use as a domestic ware, possibly a serving vessel for liquids. High correlations did not exist, however, with artifacts or other pottery types frequently associated with kitchen debris.

Tipon Orange-brown Type

Variety Name: Moni.
Established as a Type and/or Variety: By this description. Other types and varieties of Tipon are currently being described by Sharer and associates at Quirigua. Longyear (1952:30) described vessels of this type, but without isolating and defining it as a distinct taxon.
Frequency: This description is based on the full collection of Tipon Orange-brown: Moni Variety pottery found at Copan, 6,557 sherds or 2.37 percent of the total recovered by the Harvard Copan Project.
Ceramic Group: Tipon.
Ceramic Complexes: Cueva and Coner.
Illustrations: Figures 69a–b, 70a–b, 71, 72, 73a–k.
Description:
Principal Identifying Modes.
1. Smooth to polished self-slipped surfaces on both exteriors and interiors but with polishing most common on exteriors;
2. surface varies widely in color, but light orange-brown to chocolate brown is the general range of well-preserved surfaces;
3. fairly uniform wall thickness 0.4 to 0.7 cm, but usually about 0.5 cm or less;
4. diagnostic forms are cylindrical jars and open to hemispherical bowls;
5. small nubbin or podal supports are common.

Paste, Temper, and Firing. Paste surfaces range in color from reddish yellow or pink (5 YR, 7/6-7/8) to brownish yellow (10 YR, 7/3-7/6), gray brown (10 YR, 6/2), or dark gray (7.5 YR, 3/0). Cores are often dark, sometimes gray-black. The paste is slightly porous with fine clay particles. The paste is uniform with an even distribution of homogeneous fine clay particles and fine to very coarse subangular sand inclusions. Temper density is less than 25 percent. Surface hardness on interior surfaces is generally about 2.0 on Moh's scale and from 3.5 to 5.5 on Moh's scale on exterior surfaces. Compositional analyses by Bishop and Beaudry (see appendix C) have indicated two distinct compositional groups and two presumed sources for Tipon group pastes.

Surface Finish and Decoration. Surfaces are smooth, self-slipped, often polished on exteriors, and when eroded they have a velvety feel. Surface color is from light orange-brown or pink to dark brown.

Form. The most characteristic forms are cylinder jars and low bowls.

Cylinder jars have vertical to slightly outflaring walls. Rims are direct and lips rounded. Occasionally, cylinder walls slant inward gently to a very slightly restricted orifice. Cylinder dimensions range in height from 13 to 18 cm, with orifice diameters from 8 to 18 cm and basal diameters from 8 to 16 cm.

The bowls are medium deep to shallow with flat bottoms, slightly outsloped to outflared sides, and direct rims with rounded or pointed lips. Bowl heights are from 6 to 9 cm, orifice diameters from 16.5 to 20.5 cm, and basal diameters from 11.5 to 16.5 cm. One variant of the bowl form is a composite silhouette bowl with a basal angle and a rounded base resting on either a ring or an indented bottom. A typical example of this form would have an orifice diameter of about 17 cm. Another bowl variant is a smaller hemispherical bowl (orifice diameter less than 16 cm) with very thin walls (less than 0.5 cm).

One rare but interesting variant in form is a miniature cylinder form with a height of less than 8 cm and a diameter of less than 6 cm.

Supports occur on both cylinders and bowls. There are small solid podal supports. They vary in diameter from 1.5 to 5 cm and in height from 0.5 to 1.5 cm. Some are cylindrical in shape; others taper slightly. (The tapered ones may be somewhat earlier.) The supports occur as both tripods and tetrapods.

Other appendages are rare, although a few sherds have punched nodes, raised ridges, effigy modeling, or other appliqued elements. Also, there are a few small, open, trough-like spouts.

Whole, Restorable, or Partially Restorable Vessels: There were 17 whole, restorable, or partial vessels recovered by our project in a variety of contexts, from caches and burials to domestic middens. Twelve of these are cylinder forms. All are simple but elegant, with a hint of an hourglass profile narrowing just a bit toward the midpoint of the vessel. All are well smoothed with a typical range of Tipon colors: buff or cream to light cocoa brown. All examples have thin walls, ranging from 3 mm to about 8 mm. These simple cylinder forms and their dimensions are as follows:

Cat. No. 1-510, Special Find 12, CV-43: small restored cylinder jar, height 11 cm, orifice diameter 8.2 cm, and basal diameter 6.9 cm.

Cat. No. 1-214, Special Find 24, CV-20: height 13.3 cm, orifice diameter 10.5 cm, basal diameter 8.8 cm.

Cat. No. 1-1044, Special Find 48, CV-43: height 13.3 cm, orifice diameter 10.1 cm, basal diameter 8.2 cm.

Cat. No. 1-1209, Special Find 102, CV-43: height 12 cm, orifice diameter 10.8 cm, basal diameter 9 cm.

Cat. No. 1-1205, Special Find 98, CV-43: height 12.3 cm, orifice diameter 10.6 cm, medial diameter 9 cm, basal diameter 8.7 cm.

Cat. No. 1-20, Special Find 4, CV-20: height 18 cm, orifice diameter 13.5 cm, basal diameter 10.9 cm.

Cat. No. 1-355, surface find: partial vessel, height estimated at 20 to 22 cm, orifice diameter 14 cm, basal diameter 14 cm.

Cat. No. 1-720, Special Find 5, CV-115: partial vessel, bottom diameter 15 cm, upper half missing. This specimen has three nubbin feet.

Cat. No. 1-745, CV-43: partial vessel, bottom diameter 16 cm, no upper half recovered, especially thin walls 2.5 to 3 mm thick.

Cat. No. 1-722, CV-115 (fig. 72): whole vessel with pedestal base, an unusually fine specimen. Height 20.5 cm, orifice diameter 15 cm, basal diameter 12.8 cm, giving the vessel an hourglass shape. The pedestal base is 2.2 cm high, 13 cm at base, constricted to 11 cm where it joins the cylinder jar body.

Cat. No. 1-1199, Special Find 92, CV-43: a partially destroyed cylinder vessel.

Cat. No. 1-1200, Special Find 93, CV-43: a partially destroyed cylinder vessel.

Four Tipon Orange-brown vessels are simple, flat-based bowls with flaring walls. All are well smoothed or polished with typical buff or light brown Tipon surfaces. The vessels of this form are:

Cat. No. 1-1201, Special Find 94, CV-43: height 7.5 cm, orifice diameter 18.6 cm, basal diameter 13.8 cm.

Cat. No. 1-1202, Special Find 95, CV-43: height 7.2 cm, orifice diameter 19.4 cm, basal diameter 14.3 cm.

Cat. No. 1-1206, Special Find 99, CV-43: height 7.2 cm, orifice diameter 18.9 cm, basal diameter 14 cm.

Cat. No. 1-1208, Special Find 101, CV-43: height 7.8 cm, orifice diameter 19 cm, basal diameter 14 cm.

One whole vessel (Cat. No. 1-361) (fig. 71) has an unusual tray form with a spout. It has a height of 4 cm, orifice diameter of 15.7 cm, basal diameter of 12 cm, and open spout of 2.5 cm. It has outsloped walls, notched lips, and a simple flat bottom. The spout is small, open, and trough-shaped.

Classificatory Comments: The frequency of sherd counts of this type is undoubtedly greatly inflated by inclusion of plain body sherds broken from vessels of the Don Gordon Modeled-carved, Tasu fluted, and Claudio Incised Types. In all of these types the diagnostic decorative mode covers less than half of the vessel. This taxonomic overlap partly explains the potentially significant associational correlations between Tipon Orange-brown, Don Gordon Modeled-carved, and Tasu fluted.

Note that Bishop and Beaudry's compositional analyses have isolated two distinct pastes as defined by chemical groups. The taxonomic correlates of this compositional distinction could not be isolated by macroscopic reexamination.

Intrasite Locations, Contexts, and Associations: As will be discussed in detail in chapter 4, Tipon cannot be closely connected with any specific proveniences. Nevertheless, most of the whole or restorable Tipon vessels were found in burial or cache contexts. As examples, the vessel Cat. No. 1-20 was found beneath the plaza floor at CV-20 in association with a primary burial, Burial 1; a secondary burial, Burial 3; and several artifacts. Also, the tomb discovered within Structure B of CV-43 (Burial 24) contained eight Tipon Orange-brown: Moni vessels in association. Four of these were cylinder vases and the other four were simple, flat-based bowls with flaring walls. One of each form was located within a small niche in each wall of the tomb.

Thus, Tipon Orange-brown Type served as elite burial furniture. It should be noted that several of these burial contexts with Tipon are correlated with the Cueva phase. Although Tipon was an important type during the Coner phase at Copan, it also functioned as an elite burial item in the earlier phase.

Intersite Locations, Contexts, and Associations: In the Middle to Late Classic period, black ware cylinders and bowls in plain, incised, fluted, and modeled-carved variants are common throughout the Maya lowlands, highland Guatemala, and western El Salvador. At Copan itself there is a tradition extending back into the Early Classic of decorated and plain black wares in groups like the Melano and Ardilla (see discussions of these types). This plain, carved, and incised black-brown ware tradition at Copan probably relates to the Teotihuacanoid black and black-brown cylinders and bowls of Kaminaljuyu (Kidder, Jen-

nings, and Shook (1946: figs. 171, 172). For evidence of this connection, see the vessels of our Acbi phase Melano group.

However, the Tipon group at Copan shows numerous characteristics that distinguish it from the earlier black groups at the site. It has a soft, self-slipped velvety-textured surface in pale pink to dark chocolate brown, whereas the earlier black bowls and cylinders at Copan have a shiny, hard, dark black surface. The decoration of these earlier black wares tends to be incision, and sometimes post-fired incision, rather than the modeled-carving as seen in the Tipon group ceramics type, Don Gordon Modeled-carved (see below). Indeed, the surface and paste characteristics, and to a certain extent even the decorative modes, of the Tipon group are closer to the indigenous western Salvadoran and highland Guatemalan black-brown tradition than to either the Teotihuacanoid black wares of Kaminaljuyu or the highly polished, deep black Balanza group of the Tepeu ceramic sphere in the Maya lowlands proper.

Turning then to western El Salvador, we find that Tipon Orange-brown (as well as the incised, fluted, and modeled-carved types of the Tipon group) fits squarely into this long tradition of soft-surfaced, polished, black-brown ceramics often characterized by elaborate surface decoration. It begins with the Jinuapa group in the Middle Preclassic at Chalchuapa (Sharer 1978:3:23–24) and continues with the Late Preclassic Pinos black-brown types at Santa Leticia (Demarest 1986), Chalchuapa (Sharer 1978:3:36–38), Atiquisaya (Haberland 1958), and Kaminaljuyu (Wetherington 1978b:55–68). Note that at Kaminaljuyu the groups and types of the entire black-brown tradition are identical to those at the other sites, but a different terminology was applied. See Demarest and Sharer (1986) for a clarification of the unity of these types. Bilbao has a parallel and entirely similar tradition of black-brown groups and types (Parsons 1969:1: chap. 3). These black-brown groups of the highlands and Pacific coastal plain show remarkable similarity in color, texture, and even range of surface treatments to the later Tipon group types at Copan. This highland tradition sees its Middle to Late Classic culmination in the Teotihuacanoid blacks of Kaminaljuyu, the Barranquilla ceramic group at Bilbao (with plain, incised, and modeled-carved types; Parsons 1969:1:124–128), and the Chiquihuat ceramic group at Chalchuapa (Sharer 1978: 3:47–49).

It is the lattermost, the Late Classic Chiquihuat group, that is most similar to Copan's Tipon group in all characteristics. This similarity is not surprising in view of the fact that most other fine wares (Chilanga, Gualpopa, Copador) are shared by Chalchuapa and Copan. In addition to a similarity in surface color, texture, and paste characteristics, Chalchuapa's Chiquihuat and Copan's Tipon groups share most forms, including the predominance of deep vertical-walled bowls or cylinders, and shallow bowls, including composite-silhouette forms. Decorative variants are also parallel, with types in both groups defined by plano-relief modeled-carving, fine incision, and fluting. Even the zones for surface treatments are parallel with modeled-carving in bands above the shoulders of composite-silhouette bowls and below the rim of deep vertical-walled bowls or cylinders.

While the similarities underscore the fact that the Tipon and Chalchuapa's Chiquihuat groups are both Late Classic manifestations of the Salvadoran black-brown tradition, the differences between these two groups are equally significant because they point to the Maya lowlands to the north. Both Tipon and Chiquihuat share geometric, curvilinear, and pseudo-glyph motifs in their modeled-carved types (Chingo Plano-relief at Chalchuapa, Don Gordon Modeled-carved at Copan); however, as detailed in the type description below, Don Gordon has far more elaborate designs and many more true Maya hieroglyphs than the Chiquihuat tradition. Furthermore, Don Gordon vessel forms are more elaborate—including gadrooned bottoms, combinations of gadrooning and fluting, and taller cylinder forms—than the Chiquihuat group. The Tipon group also has a softer, smoother surface texture, a finer paste, and generally better execution of design elements.

The finer, more elaborate design elements in the Tipon group's Don Gordon Modeled-carved type show striking similarities to specific motifs and treatments in the Balanza Black and related ceramics of the Maya lowland Tepeu ceramic sphere. These shared forms, motifs, and designs are described below under the Don Gordon type description (see "Intersite Locations, Contexts, and Associations" section).

The Tipon ceramic group also has close connections to the site of Quirigua, Copan's Motagua Valley neighbor. Tipon types at both sites share similar characteristics in color, texture, paste, and form; and both sites have high frequencies of the plain Tipon Orange-brown type defined here. Neutron-activation analyses (see appendix B) indicated that Tipon was locally made at each site. Nevertheless, decorative modes of the Tipon group at each site are completely distinct, not only in detail but in general emphasis and frequency. At Copan, surface manipulation, especially modeled-carving, incision, and fluting, is extremely common, whereas at Quirigua it is rare. The Quirigua Tipon ceramics are more frequently decorated with painting in red, white, and pink in broad bands, zones, circles, and other simple, bold patterns.

The ceramic assemblages of western and central Honduras are notably lacking in any black-brown Late Classic type even remotely similar or parallel to Tipon. Urban and Schortman observe (personal communication 1984) that such pottery is not present, even as an import, at any excavated or surveyed site in the middle Ulua Valley.

Cultural Significance: Overall, the Tipon group is a kind of microcosm of Copan's complex and eclectic ties. The group is essentially a late variant of the southern highland black-brown tradition, as seen in Chalchuapa's Chiquihuat group. In addition to the Tipon group's southern affiliations, it shows strong ties to the Maya north. The sharing of the Tipon group by Copan and Quirigua reflects the close interaction of those two sites. Their very distinct approaches to decorating Tipon group types may have resulted from a conscious effort on the part of their inhabitants to underscore their ethnic or political identities.

Functional Interpretation: Tipon Orange-brown and the other Tipon types are common in caches, burials, and elite contexts. They are also all highly correlated statistically with the Late Classic polychromes. It is, therefore, likely that the Tipon group in general was a higher status, perhaps an elite status, type. Still, Tipon is neither rare nor sharply restricted in its distribution. Sherds of all Tipon types, especially the plain Tipon Orange-brown, are common in domestic middens and fill contexts. Thus, Tipon pottery must have been popular as a general fine ware for serving food and drink in Copan households.

Don Gordon Modeled-carved Type

Variety Name: Don Gordon.
Established as a Type and/or Variety: By this description.
Frequency: A count of 898 sherds or 0.32 percent of our total sherds. This type constitutes 10.6 percent of the total Tipon group in our collection.
Ceramic Group: Tipon.
Ceramic Complex: Coner.
Illustrations: Figures 74, 75, 76, 77a–m.
Description:
Principal Identifying Modes.
1. Deeply modeled-carved decoration (prefiring);
2. polished brown surfaces (Tipon);
3. designs of Maya hieroglyphs, pseudo-glyphs, human, animal, deity, or demonic representations.

Paste, Temper, and Firing. See descriptions of other Tipon group types and also Capulin subgroup types. In general, Don Gordon paste, temper, and surfacing tend to be a little more homogeneous and finer-grained than that of other Tipon types; however, they are very similar.
Surface Finish and Decoration. Well-smoothed or polished surfaces range from a dark brown to a light buff, and jar and bowl exterior and interior surfaces are so treated. In some instances it seems clear that a definite slip was added before firing; in others the surface was probably only self-slipped. Surfaces always show a buff-fired color. In cross section this can be seen overlying a gray-black paste core.

The modeled-carved decoration, which ranges from 1 to 3 mm in depth, is always confined to exterior surfaces. There is always an undecorated rim or lip band, from 0.6 to 3.7 cm wide, encircling the vessels. The frequent hieroglyphic modeled-carved ornamentation consists of relatively few glyphs in clauses or sequences. There are two basic patterns or dispositions of the hieroglyphs: (1) a band of glyphs carved just below the rim of the vessel (the most common); (2) raised panels of glyphs within larger panels in which human figures and/or mythological figures are the central motifs.

The hieroglyphic inscriptions on these vessels are generally arranged in series of from five to eight glyphs which appear to represent a local variant of Michael D. Coe's (1973) "primary standard sequence." Occasional exceptions to this sequence are fragments of Calendar Round dates and ruler's titles, indicating some historical content to these exceptional pieces. It is likely that the glyphs appearing on or in the raised panels are exclusively of historical content. The scenes on vessels—Maya dignitaries, animals, birds, and possibly deities—are usually accompanied by glyphic texts of some kind or another. Some Don Gordon Modeled-carved vessels, however, have no such life scenes and are ornamented instead with bands of relatively simple rectilinear decoration, such as concentric cartouche forms, rectangles, nested triangles, and cross-hatching. Although we cannot be certain from our present sample, it seems likely that these vessels had no hieroglyphic decoration. This geometric decoration, without life scenes, seems to be most commonly associated with medium-deep open bowls rather than the cylinder jars. There are also some Don Gordon specimens that combine modeled-carved decoration with fluting, gadrooning, and chamfering (see below for descriptions of such specimens).
Form. Principal form is a cylindrical or near-cylindrical jar. These have flat bases and straight or very slightly outslanted or outflared sides. Orifice diameters are about 14 cm and heights are in excess of this (sherd sample does not allow accurate height estimates). Vessel walls are about 5 mm thick except toward rim or base where they are a little thicker. A second form, the medium-deep bowl, has a slightly outflared rim and a basal angle. Diameters of bowls are 15 to 19 cm with heights or depths slightly less than one-half of the diameters. Some few specimens of this form have small horizontally everted rims. A third form is a small hemispherical bowl. These tend to be thinner-walled and in general more delicate than the other two forms. A fourth, and rare, form is a little rectangular, necked flask shape (see description below).
Whole, Restorable, or Partially Restorable Vessels: We have five of these. Cat. No. 1-137 (fig. 76) is a fragmentary bowl with a basal angle and an outflared rim. It is buff-colored ware, slightly eroded. There is a decorative band of carved

pseudo-glyphs about 1 cm below the lip edge. The base of the bowl has, or had, several wide, deep, smooth-bottomed flutes radiating out from the center up to the basal angle. It came from Operation 6(N), CV-20, Level 1.

Cat. No. 1-206 (fig. 75) is about two-fifths of another open bowl. Estimated orifice is 17 cm and height is 7 cm. There is a low, sharp basal angle and a small, almost flat, circular base. Walls and rim are outslanting. The ware has well-smoothed buff-to-brown fired surfaces. There is a plain band, 1.1 cm wide, below the lip, and a 3.8-cm design band is below this. There were probably six to eight large, boldly carved glyphs in this band, one of which appears to have been the Copan emblem glyph. It came from Operation 21(A), CV-20, Level 2.

Cat. No. 1-668 (fig. 74) is another basal angle bowl with outslanting sides. Orifice diameter is 19.7 cm, height 6.7 cm, diameter at basal angle 16 cm, and there is a small, circular, flat, slightly inset base that measures 6.9 cm in diameter. The surfaces are a fine polished brown. The encircling decorated panel is 1.7 cm below the lip and is 3 cm wide. The design consists of a series of glyph-like elements. Below the basal angle the bowl is divided into eight equal portions by deep, broad flutes or grooves. The basal exterior shows some black fire-clouding. This vessel came from Operation 54(A), CV-94, Level 8, Burial 1, Special Find 1.

Cat. No. 1-719 is a thin-walled cylinder jar. It probably had a nicely polished brown surface, although it has been badly eroded showing buff-fired surfaces. It measures 19.4 (height) x 15.9 (orifice diameter) x 14.2 (basal diameter) cm. As measurements indicate, the walls slope outward very slightly. Decoration is confined to a 2.5-cm band 2 cm below the lip. It consists of a row of glyphs or glyph-like elements. The jar came from Operation 55(A), CV-115, Special Find 4. Within the jar were found the bones of a bird, possibly a hummingbird.

Cat. No. 1-1214 is a complete little rectangular flask of fine-quality light-buff ware. It has been classified as a Miniature Vessel (fig. 162). This is the original firing color, and there are indications that the vessel was entirely coated with a very light buff slip before firing. The flask measures 9.1 cm in height. At the top it is 5.7 x 5.4 cm, and at the bottom the measurements are 3.8 x 3.5 cm.

The flask has a short neck ending in a small orifice (diameter 2.9 cm) that has a slightly thickened and flattened lip. Each of the two wider sides of the flask bears a panel of six very carefully executed hieroglyphs. The arrangement is in two vertical rows of three glyphs each. The glyphs on the two sides of the flask are identical. The glyph panels are bordered by a band about 5 mm in width. At the sides and the bottom of the panels this border has been left plain, but at the top it has been divided by short incisions or ticking. The two narrower sides of the flask have been left plain. The base of the flask is slightly inset. After firing, it appears that the flask was rubbed with a red powdered pigment (probably cinnabar), and some of this pigment still adheres, in patches, to the vessel surfaces. Cat. No. 1-1214 was found in Operation 100(B), CV-43, Feature 13, Special Find 107.

Classificatory Comments: Because of its distinctive surface treatment and decoration, Don Gordon Modeled-carved was readily and easily set aside as a type. As is common with decorated types, sherd count frequencies are probably much lower than original vessel frequencies, since undecorated body and base sherds would be classified as the plain Tipon Orange-brown type.

Intrasite Locations, Contexts, and Associations: Don Gordon Modeled-carved is well represented at Copan. Longyear (1952:98, figs. 68, 69) described it under the name "Carved Brown Ware" and illustrated it in both cylinder jar and bowl forms. As with other Tipon Orange-brown types, it is an elite ware found in what appear to be mainly ritual contexts such as caches and burials.

Statistically, this type correlates with the other Tipon group ceramics. However, this is not a stronger correlation than we find with other types within this ceramic collection.

Intersite Locations, Contexts, and Associations: As discussed above for Tipon Orange-brown (see "Intersite Locations, Contexts, and Associations" and "Cultural Significance"), the Tipon group ceramics are part of a generically related southern highland/western Salvadoran tradition of smoothed, polished, and decorated black-brown ceramics, paralleling Chalchuapa's Chiquihuat group, Bilbao's Barranquilla group, and the Miraflores and Verbena black-brown wares at Kaminaljuyu (Sharer 1978:3:42–49; Parsons

1969:2:124–128; Wetherington 1978b). It is notable that all of these black-brown groups of the highlands have modeled-carved or coarse-incised variants with complex designs. In the Chingo Plano-relief type of Chalchuapa's Chiquihuat group (Sharer 1978:3:48–49), the modeled-carved designs even include anthropomorphic, zoomorphic, and complex geometric patterns, similar to those of Don Gordon. The Chingo designs, however, also include pseudo-glyphs.

With the exception of carved Early Classic period vases from Kaminaljuyu (Kidder, Jennings, and Shook 1946:183–185, 159–171, fig. 177), which reflect strong lowland influence, the carved and coarse-incised highland black-brown wares do not approach Don Gordon in either complexity of design or quality of execution. Rather, in the arranging, execution, and design elements themselves, Copan's Don Gordon Modeled-carved is more similar to the modeled-carved pottery of the Late Classic Tepeu sphere types of the Maya lowlands. This Classic Maya iconographic corpus and style appears to have been imposed upon or blended with the southern highland black-brown tradition at both Copan and Quirigua.

R. E. Smith (1955: fig. 42a, 16, 18–21b, 2,3) illustrates a number of incised or gouged-incised sherds from Uaxactun that bear some general resemblances to Don Gordon Modeled-carved. These sherds, which were later classified in a formal typology (Smith and Gifford 1966), include those of the Canoa Incised, Carmelita Incised, Geronimo Incised, and Calabaso Gouged-incised Types, with the Calabaso type being closest to Don Gordon. All date to Tepeu 2 or Late Classic times. This would be chronologically consistent with a Don Gordon Modeled-carved dating at Copan. A slightly later (Tepeu 3) modeled-carved type from Uaxactun, which shows some Don Gordon similarities, is Sahcaba Modeled-carved (R. E. Smith 1955: fig. 44m; see Smith and Gifford 1966 for type identifications). To continue in this Tepeu 3 time bracket (A.D. 800–900), we cannot overlook the fine Orange ware type, Pabellon Modeled-carved (R. E. Smith 1955: fig. 86b–h, j–l, n, p; Sabloff 1975:195–198, figs. 384–385), which also has some very clear technological resemblances to Don Gordon Modeled-carved although iconography of the designs differs as do some of the vessel shapes. For further

references to Maya lowland Tepeu, or Late Classic, incised, gouged-incised, or modeled-carved types see Gifford (1976:254, fig. 159e), Adams (1971:49–51, figs. 67, 68), R. E. Smith (1955: fig. 86i, m, o), and Smith and Gifford (1966).

Before leaving the Maya lowlands in this survey of comparative material, we should note that a carved surface decorative technique does antedate the Late Classic period here. Thus, Adams, from Altar de Sacrificios, shows a type, Urita Gouged-incised (Adams 1971:52, fig. 31c) which incorporates pseudo-glyphs in its carved decorations, and another, San Roman Plano-relief (ibid.: fig. 33), which has a quite elaborate Classic Maya–style carving on the wall of a lidded cylinder tripod jar. Both Urita Gouged-incised and San Roman Plano-relief are Early Classic, rather than Late Classic, and thus suggest local prototypes for the modeled-carved technical and decorative tradition in the Maya lowlands. San Roman and Urita are polished black types, but another Altar de Sacrificios Early Classic type, Contrabandista Gouged-incised (ibid.:52, fig. 36a), is a polished brown ware.

Outside of the Maya lowlands, polished modeled-carved wares, similar to Don Gordon Modeled-carved, do not appear on a Late Classic time level with any frequency. Baudez and Becquelin (1973) report nothing of this sort from Los Naranjos; Sharer (1978) has nothing comparable from Chalchuapa in El Salvador; and the only similar occurrences from the Guatemalan highlands are the previously referred to carved Early Classic period vases at Kaminaljuyu.

The statistical correlations of Don Gordon's distribution pattern with those of other types appear to have more chronological than status-related significance. Indeed, Claudio Incised and Tasu fluted of the Tipon group appear to be somewhat more elite in the nature of their contextual associations.

Cultural Significance: Intricate vessel surface carving—usually on the polished surfaces of black or dark brown vases—has Maya area beginnings, in both the highlands and lowlands, as early as the Early Classic period. Such carved designs were recognizably Maya in style, incorporating mythic and possible historical human or humanoid subjects, animals, and glyphic or glyph-like elements. Quite frequently, such carving or gouged-incising was done on cylinder tripod vases. Some of the pieces have a Teotihuacanoid cast. Whether these appear earlier in the Maya highlands or lowlands is still uncertain; however, it was in the lowlands that this form of ceramic decoration enjoyed the greatest vogue, especially subsequently in Middle Classic and Late Classic times. Just where this evolution of modeled-carved pottery, from Early to Late Classic, took place remains to be determined, although it seems likely that there was more than one center of such development. Obviously, Copan was one such center.

Generally consistent with other Copan findings is the fact that the making of Don Gordon Modeled-carved pottery is not found to the east, in Honduras. It is clearly a ceramic in the elite Maya tradition with all of its iconographic relationships lying back to the west, either in the Classic Maya lowlands or in the Maya highlands.

Claudio Incised Type

Variety Name: Claudio.
Established as a Type and/or Variety: By this description.
Frequency: A total of 401 sherds of Claudio Incised were recovered, or less than 0.15 percent of the total number of sherds recovered by the Harvard Copan Project. Claudio Incised accounts for about 5 percent of the sherds of the Tipon ceramic group.
Ceramic Group: Tipon.
Ceramic Complex: Coner.
Illustrations: Figures 78, 79a–dd.
Description:
Principal Identifying Modes.
1. Fine-line incised decoration in a variety of complex design motifs including stylized life-forms, combined with curvilinear, rectilinear, or geometric motifs;
2. smooth Tipon group characteristic buff to brown polished surfaces. This Tipon type tends to be more buff-colored.
Paste, Temper, and Firing. See Tipon Orange-brown descriptions.

Note that paste color tends to be predominantly pale pink to buff (5 YR 7/6-7/8) in this Tipon group type.
Surface Finish and Decoration. Surfaces are smoothed or self-slipped as with other Tipon group types. Occasional red painting or slipping is found on vessels. This includes red bands encircling the exterior of bowls just below the lip and a few sherds, apparently from cylinders, that indicate a pale to medium red.

The characteristic fine-line incisions have an engraved appearance, apparently resulting from their execution on an air-dried surface prior to firing. This execution is sometimes rather scratchy and imperfect, with designs incised unevenly and the lines themselves unsteady or broken.

The designs themselves are quite complex, including life-forms, pseudo-glyphs, and geometric motifs. The animal or mythical forms are difficult to identify. A partially restored vessel shows one of these as a quadruped, the eye formed by concentric circles and a center dot and the body outlined by a continuous line and then filled with short slashes or elongated punctations. Sherds in the collection include this form and other animals. Some are birds or fish with feathers or scales indicated by wavy lines. Glyph-like figures and numbers sometimes form rim bands. These "glyph" rim bands tend to be incised more deeply than other Claudio designs, approaching the appearance of the modeled-carved rim bands on Don Gordon Modeled-carved.
Form. There are three principal forms:

1. vertical-walled bowls or cylinder jars,
2. subhemispherical bowls, and
3. flaring-walled open bowls with a basal angle.

Vessel walls on all forms are fairly uniform, about 5 mm in thickness. Occasionally there is a slight thickening at the rim.

Dimensions on the three principal forms are difficult to estimate, but a subhemispherical bowl, represented by the one restorable vessel, had a diameter of 24 cm, a height of 9 cm, and a small, circular, and slightly indented base of about 8 cm diameter. The cylindrical jars or deep vertical-walled bowls are represented only by sherds, but they appear to have had large diameters, approximately 20 cm, and to have been generally of large size. Flaring-walled bowls are represented only by small sherd fragments. Bases on the subhemispherical bowls were round and indented. Cylinders or vertical-walled bowls had solid, nubbin, tripod feet.

Whole, Restorable, or Partially Restorable Vessels: Cat. No. 1-530 (fig. 78) is the subhemispherical bowl with the measurements given above. It had the characteristic fine-line incision, in this case illustrating a strange quadruped form.

Classificatory Comments: There is the usual probable reduction in sherd counts (as compared to original vessel frequency) due to the tabulation of plain body sherds and bases of Claudio Incised with the type Tipon Orange-brown. Also, as noted above, some glyphic rim bands are very similar to those in Don Gordon Modeled-carved.

This type is very close to the Tipon group type Tarro Incised: Tarro Variety, as defined at Quirigua by Sharer (provisional classification notes, 1983); however, the Copan type shows more consistency in style of incision and a different range of naturalistic representations. Nonetheless, it is possible that Tarro Incised of Quirigua and the Claudio Incised of Copan eventually may be redefined as varieties of a single type.

Intrasite Locations, Contexts, and Associations: See discussion above for Tipon Orange-brown: Moni Variety.

Intersite Locations, Contexts, and Associations: The closest intersite association of this type is with the aforementioned Tarro Incised type of Quirigua (see "Classificatory Comments" above).

Claudio parallels other Tipon group types in indicating a general western Salvadoran cultural affiliation for the site's black-brown ware ceramics. Zompopa Incised and Titihuapa Red-painted-incised (red rimmed) of Chalchuapa's black-brown Chiquihuat ceramic group are broadly parallel to Copan's Claudio-incised and Quirigua's Tarro Incised; however, Zompopa and Titihuapa lack the complex naturalistic designs and pseudo-glyphs, showing instead only geometric motifs. Similarly, the complex incised examples of Bilbao's Late Classic Barranquilla ceramic group are of a generally similar southern highland black-brown tradition, but surface finish is inferior to that of the Tipon incised types and the incised motifs, while occasionally complex, do not include the glyph panels or animal forms of Claudio Incised or Tarro Incised.

Cultural Significance: This type, like the Tipon group in general, indicates some interaction and communication between Copan and its rival center to the north, Quirigua. The significance of the type as an indicator of contact with other areas is less clear. While a weak generic similarity to fine-incised black-brown wares of the Late Classic highlands has been noted, resemblances in specific design elements to ceramics of the Maya lowland sites may be of greater interest.

Functional Interpretation: Probably a high quality serving vessel, an interpretation consistent with functions of the other decorated types of the Tipon group.

Tasu Fluted Type

Variety Name: Blandina.
Established as a Type and/or Variety: By this description.
Frequency: This description is based on 612 sherds or 0.22 percent of the total number of sherds recovered from Copan. Tasu fluted constitutes 7.7 percent of the total sherds of the Tipon group.
Ceramic Group: Tipon.
Ceramic Complex: Coner.
Illustrations: Figure 80a–v.
Description:
Principal Identifying Modes.
1. Tipon Orange-brown polished brown surfaces and paste characteristics (see Tipon Orange-brown definition above);
2. deep, round-bottom, smoothed vertical flutings, gadrooning, and/or horizontal chamfering on vessel exteriors.

Paste, Temper, and Firing. See paste description for Tipon Orange-brown.

Surface Finish and Decoration. Both interior and exterior surfaces are well smoothed with polishing on exteriors. Color ranges from buff to brownish black with most specimens a medium to light brown color (see Tipon Orange-brown surface description).

Decoration is by grooving or fluting, often combined with low-relief ridges, on vessel exteriors. Grooves or flutes may be arranged vertically ("fluting") or horizontally ("chamfering"), or in gadrooned formations, the lattermost sometimes creating a phytoform appearance. The flutes vary in width from 1 cm to 2 mm with an average of about 5 mm or from a very broad line preslip incising to very wide grooves or channels. Ridged areas between the grooves also vary in width ranging from 3 to 4 mm.

Design elements include vertical grooving running entirely around the vessel or groups of two or three parallel vertical grooves separated by large plain zones. Chamfering may sometimes be found in combination with fluting in arrangements where three or four chamfer grooves encircle the vessel forming a border, above which are flutes. Gadroons tend to divide the vessel walls of bowls into lozenge-like segments, giving the vessel a phytoform appearance. While there are some instances where fluting, chamfering, or gadrooning extends virtually to the lip of the vessels, there is usually a plain exterior band, from 1 to 5 mm in width, just below the lip. No grooving is found on the small bases of Tasu vessels.

Form. There are three principal vessel forms:

1. The most common is an open hemispherical bowl with direct, outslanting-to-vertical rims and orifice diameters of 16 to 20 cm. Bases on this form are small, circular, and indented, measuring about 6 cm in diameter.
2. A second popular form is the cylindrical jar or deep vertical-walled bowl. The walls on these deep bowls may be slightly outsloped or curving to effect a barrel-like shape. Limited material and the paucity of complete specimens make measurements unreliable, but orifice diameters are about 14 cm and heights range from deep bowls to true cylinder jars. Bases were circular and flat, although some may have small nubbin tripod supports.
3. The third vessel form is a medium to shallow open bowl with outsloped sides and a slightly outflared rim. These bowls often have a basal angle below which the sides slope down to a small, circular flat or indented base. Orifice diameters on some of these bowls measure up to 40 cm.

Whole, Restorable, or Partially Restorable Vessels: No whole Tasu fluted vessels were recovered by the Harvard Copan Project, although some vessels that may be Tasu fluted are illustrated in Longyear's study of Copan ceramics (1952: figs. 104c, 106f).

Classificatory Comments: Tasu fluted is the fluted, gadrooned, or chamfered type of the Tipon group. Consequently, the sherd frequency counts are probably reduced substantially, since plain bottoms or walls of Tasu fluted vessels would be included in the plain Tipon Orange-brown types.

The only other classificatory problem with this type involves occasional composite forms that may have been rare funerary ceramics. A few examples of Don Gordon Modeled-carved were found to have fluting or gadrooning below their rim band of modeled carved glyphs. These have been classified as Don Gordon Modeled-carved. One whole vessel of this fluted and modeled-carved composite is shown by Longyear (1952: fig. 108j). Other, perhaps even more unusual, composite ceramics were Tasu fluted cylinders or deep bowls with rim bands of Copador Polychrome painted glyphs. We found only a few sherds of this very rare variant, but one such sherd may be represented by Longyear (1952: fig. 74a). He does not describe the paste of this sherd, but it may have been similar to that of Copador.

Intrasite Locations, Contexts, and Associations: See discussion above for Tipon Orange-brown: Moni Variety.

Intersite Locations, Contexts, and Associations: Tasu fluted also appears at Quirigua (Sharer, provisional classification notes 1983), where it is a very minor type of Quirigua's Tipon group ceramics.

The only other similar ceramics are the fluted types in the parallel polished black-brown ceramic groups of western El Salvador and highland Guatemala. Most notably, these include the fluted vessels of Chalchuapa's Chiquihuat Black-brown: Chiquihuat Variety (Sharer 1978:3:47–48) and the fluted and gadrooned examples of Bilbao's Barranquilla ceramic groups. Note that these and other black-brown types of western El Salvador and highland Guatemala are less finely executed and less consistent in both decoration and finish than Tasu.

Cultural Significance: Like other types of the Late Classic Tipon ceramic group, Tasu fluted reflects Copan's close interaction with Quirigua and its more general cultural affiliations with western El Salvador and the southern highlands of Guatemala.

See extensive discussion of "Intersite Locations, Contexts, and Associations" and "Cultural Significance" for Tipon Orange-brown: Moni Variety.

Functional Interpretation: The form, intrasite contexts, and statistical associations of this type are all indicative of functions as a serving vessel in elite households and as an elite funerary ceramic.

Copador Polychrome Type

Variety Name: Glyphic Varieties A–E.
Established as a Type and/or Variety: Copador was first described by Boggs (1945) and then detailed by Longyear (1952). It was first established as a type by Sharer (1978).
Frequency: A total of 5,110 Copador sherds were recovered in our excavations. This represents 2 percent of the total sherd collection.
Ceramic Group: Copador.
Ceramic Complex: Coner.
Illustrations: Figures 81, 82, 83, 84, 85, 86, 87, 88, 89, 90, 91, 92, 93, 94, 95, 96, 97.
Description:
Introduction. Copador pottery, found throughout the southeast Maya region (although in very small numbers at Quirigua), is one of the most distinctive pottery types from Copan. It is recognizable in very small sherds or even if the sherd is slightly eroded.

Numerous works and reports have focused upon this type. The three most detailed studies to date, Longyear's *Copan Ceramics* (1952), Sharer's *The Prehistory of Chalchuapa, El Salvador, Vol. 3, Pottery and Conclusions* (1978), and Beaudry's *Production and Distribution of Painted Late Classic Maya Ceramics in the Southeastern Periphery* (1983), will therefore be used as the basis of the following description, modified and supplemented by recourse to our own collection. Drawings, photographs and detailed descriptions of our whole or partially restorable Copador vessels will highlight the details of the Copador ceramic type.
Principal Identifying Modes.
1. Specular hematite red, orange, and black painted designs on a cream slip (fig. 81);
2. distinctive glyphic and figure elements on the vessels;
3. a soft, fine, tan/cream colored paste.
Paste, Temper, and Firing. The paste utilized in the production of Copador pottery at Copan is very distinctive. It is a very fine cream to buff colored paste. The temper is minimal and includes only extremely small pieces of fired clay that are similar in color and composition to the paste.

The uniform coloring of all sherds and vessels argues for standardization in production, in terms of both clay preparation and firing (Beaudry 1983).
Surface Finish and Decoration. Longyear (1952) and Sharer (1978) have both described Copador surface decoration. Longyear defined the individual elements of the designs, and Sharer created a set of varieties that grouped these design elements and often the forms.

Let us begin with a statement of Longyear's design elements.

Glyphic Element A: This seems to be a two-part glyphic element. The primary part appears to be defined by a cartouche with an internal spiral or U-shaped element. The second part, either a prefix or an affix, seems to represent the number two, showing two dots located within a half cartouche.

Glyphic Element B: This is again a two-part glyphic element. The main part appears to be a head in profile with a clearly defined mouth, eye, and nose. Longyear has identified this head form as being possibly associated with several defined hieroglyphs: the head variant of tun; a generalized statement of "deity"; and a stylized serpent head. We would like now to include another possibility—the profile of a bat or zotz. The heavily defined eye, the blunt, almost upturned nose, and the partially opened mouth of the head might be a stylized bat as represented in the Copan emblem glyph. The second part of this glyphic element is the same two-dot prefix or affix found within glyphic element A.

Glyphic Element C: Longyear defines two varieties:

C1: "It consists of a grotesque head, usually with a scroll issuing from the mouth. The back of the head is generally encircled by a conventionalized hand and arm." (Longyear 1952:60)

C2: This second variety is again a face with a scroll emanating from the mouth. This form seems to be always associated with the bar-and-dot numerals for 7 or 8. Longyear identifies the C1 form as being a conventionalized glyph referring to either "Lord" or "Lord of the North." His identification of the C2 form is more hesitant, although he does mention that this may be a local variant of the generalized "Lord" glyph.

In addition to these glyphic elements, Longyear also defines two other major components in the Copador designs. These are human figures and birds.

Longyear defines three primary positions for the human figures represented on Copador vessels:

1. Reclining figures are drawn in profile with extended arms and legs, bent at the elbows and knees. A diagnostic costume consists of a "headband or cap, a string of beads around the neck, wristlets, anklets, and belt around the waist" (Longyear 1952:62). Reclining figures with what appear to be similar costumes are found on the Hieroglyphic Stairway in the Copan Main Center.
2. Seated figures are shown cross-legged and in profile, either leaning forward or sitting straight up. The costumes are very similar to those of the reclining figures. In front of the figure, and perhaps being reached for by the figure, is an object described by Longyear as a "flower-like double scroll"; however, this again appears to be similar to the prefix or affix described above for glyphic elements A and/or B.
3. Longyear provides two possible interpretations of standing figures. First, if the figures are all presented with the same pose, he argues that they may be part of a procession; however, if the poses vary from figure to figure, a dance may be represented.

Longyear defines three forms associated with birds on Copador vessels. Naturalistic birds are described as "grotesque in the extreme, with long, curving bills and necks, and huge eyes." Semi-conventionalized birds appear to show fairly standardized birds, standing with fruit-bearing branches in their mouths. Conventionalized birds are described as a more stylized and simplified form of the semi-conventionalized birds.

Numerous other glyphic and figural elements are mentioned by both Longyear and Sharer, but these are not common and need not be included in a primary description of the decorative elements on Copador vessels.

Sharer, in his analysis of the Chalchuapa ceramics (1978), reviews Longyear's glyphic and design elements and discusses them as varieties of the Copador Polychrome type, showing how these various designs are combined on vessels.

Glyphic Variety A: Sharer defines this variety as having a single band of glyphic elements on both the interior and exterior of the vessel walls. These elements might include Longyear's glyphic elements A and B, either separately or combined, or glyphic element C. Design motifs on the bottom portion of these same vessels do not fit any of the design motifs defined by Longyear and seem to be more geometric in form—stripes, spirals, and so on. This Glyphic Variety A is said by Sharer to be rare at Copan, and the analysis of the material recovered from our excavations supports this claim.

Glyphic Variety B: A single band of glyphic elements (either Longyear's A or B) is found on the exterior of the vessels. In addition, the lower exterior zone includes reclining human figure elements. On the interior of the vessel, a single band of glyphic elements (A, B, or C) is commonly found, while the interior base of the vessel is covered with a circle-and-dot geometric design.

Glyphic Variety C: This variety is defined by small seated human figures or a serpent figure located within the upper zone of the exterior of the vessel. The interior of the vessel either has undefined glyphic elements (tentatively assigned by Sharer to Longyear's Glyphic Element A) associated with the bar and dot number 8 or semi-conventionalized birds. Interior bottoms again have the circle-and-dot motif. According to Sharer, this variety is absent from Copan, and, again, our findings support this statement.

Glyphic Variety D: The upper zone of these vessels may include one or several bands of glyphic elements or sometimes glyphic elements in panels. According to Sharer, these glyphic elements may occasionally be outlined in black rather than the common red with orange fill. The lower zone of the vessel usually includes seated human figures, occasionally also located within panels. The interiors of these vessels are plain.

Glyphic Variety E: On the exterior of these vessels, Sharer notes a single band of glyphic elements. The lower section has seated monkeys with their hands and arms extended. On the interior of the vessels, this type is defined by semi-conventionalized birds or monkeys within the upper zone and by the circle-and-dot motif within the bottom zone. Sharer states that this variety is absent from Copan.

Figure Variety A: The exterior of the vessels of this figure variety show predominantly geometric forms, including vertical twists, linked scrolls, and so on. The interior walls have large, naturalistic birds. The bottom of the interior is usually decorated with the circle-and-dot motif.

Figure Variety B: The exterior of these vessels has seated human figures, while the interior has semi-conventionalized birds. The interior bottom sections of these vessels are most commonly decorated with the circle-dot motif or the knotted-rope motif.

As our detailed description of the numerous whole or partially restorable vessels found during our excavations within the settlement zones of Copan will reveal, the descriptive classificatory structure as outlined above stands up well.

Form. Numerous vessel forms of Copador ceramics recorded by us include the following:

1. Bowls. The most common form of Copador found at Copan is the bowl form, which may be subdivided into simple hemispherical bowls with decoration on both the interior and exterior; composite-walled bowls with slightly outcurving rims and basal breaks about two-thirds of the way down the vessel; a variant of this composite-walled bowl with faceted flanges or scallops along the basal break; and a slightly less common bowl form that is a simple hemisphere with slightly incurving walls, slightly restricted orifice, and exterior decoration.
2. Cylindrical Vessels. This is not a common form at Copan. The walls of these are either straight, slightly outflaring, or slightly outcurving. The base is flat. As with the restricted-orifice bowls described above, the distinctive Copador design is found only on the exterior of the vessel.
3. Effigy Forms. Another form, less common than the bowl, is the effigy vessel, which often takes the form of a small jar with vertical neck and outflaring rim. The body of the jar is molded into the form of an animal. Most often, the animal represented seems to be a frog or, sometimes, a turtle. The modeling includes a face, legs, and occasionally other portions of the animal body.

Whole, Restorable, or Partially Restorable Vessels: A detailed description of each of the Copador vessels found in our excavations is not necessary with the photographs and drawings along with the detailed description of the type above.

1. Cat. No.1-299 (fig. 82), Operation 21(A), CV-20, Special Find 58
2. Cat. No. 1-212 (fig. 83), Operation 20(A), CV-20, Special Find 27
3. Cat. No.1-211 (fig. 84), Operation 21(A), CV-20, Special Find 26
4. Cat. No. 1-322 (fig. 85), Operation 24(A), CV-20, Special Find 65
5. Cat. No. 1-19 (fig. 86), Operation 2(C), CV-20, Special Find 4
6. Cat. No. 1-315 (fig. 87), Operation 21(A), CV-20, Special Find 63
7. Cat. No. 1-251 (fig. 88), Operation 19(C), CV-20, Special Find 50
8. Cat. No. 1-383, Operation 27(B), Santa Rita I, Special Find 2
9. Cat. No. 1-206 (fig. 89), Operation 21(A), CV-20, Level 2
10. Cat. No. 1-352, Operation 26(A), Structure L11-93, Level 1
11. Cat. No. 1-473 (fig. 90), Operation 33(E), CV-43, Special Find 1
12. Cat. No. 1-1147 (fig. 91), Operation 102(A), CV-43, Special Find 87
13. Cat. No. 1-1148 (fig. 92), Operation 102(A), CV-43, Special Find 86
14. Cat. No. 1-1140 (fig. 93), Operation 102(A), CV-43, Special Find 82
15. Cat. No. 1-1141 (fig. 94), Operation 102(A), CV-43, Special Find 69
16. Cat. No. 1-1184 (fig. 95), Operation 83(A), CV-16, Special Find 2
17. Cat. No. 1-902 (fig. 96), Operation 49(A), CV-43, Level 4
18. Cat. No. 1-1139 (fig. 97), Operation 102(A), CV-43, Special Find 80

Classificatory Comments: The distinctive and hard surface finish with specular hematite red paint and distinctive design motifs made Copador Polychrome an easily identifiable pottery type. The only potential confusion was with completely eroded sherds in which the fine paste criterion could cause confusion with other types such as Chilanga.

Intrasite Locations, Contexts, and Associations: As with most of the other fine-ware types of the Coner phase, Copador is found commonly within ritual contexts, such as burials or caches; but at the same time, it frequently occurred within household trash.

An examination of the Spearman Correlation chart shows that Copador groups strongest with distinctive Coner types, including Sepultura Unslipped, Casaca Striated, Lorenzo Red, Raul Red, and Caterpillar Polychrome. It also correlates with Gualpopa Polychrome, from the Cueva phase, which may indicate a similar function for these two polychrome types.

Intersite Locations, Contexts, and Associations: As stated above, Copador is one of the most distinctive pottery types found within the southeastern zone of the Maya lowlands. It was identified early in the work of this region, and its name derives from Kidder's combination of the two locations where the type was most commonly found: Copan and El Salvador.

Copador has been found in western and central El Salvador (Boggs 1945) and within this region, particularly at the series of sites at Tazumal, which includes Chalchuapa (Sharer 1978). In addition, Copador has been found in eastern Guatemala at Asuncion Mita (Stromsvik 1950) and San Agustin Acasaguastlan (Smith and Kidder 1943). On the other hand, Copador is virtually nonexistent in the Late Classic Hewett phase at Quirigua—or, indeed, in any context at that site. This lack of Copador Polychrome at Quirigua may be due to the break in Copan–Quirigua relations that occurred in A.D. 737, or just prior to the origins of the type (Leventhal 1986). Although by no means abundant, Copador is slightly more common at other sites of the Lower Motagua Valley than it is at Quirigua. As an example, it is known from Playitas (Schortman and Urban, personal communication). It also occurs as a minor type along the Pacific Coast (Shook 1965).

Copador Polychrome is known from only scattered locations in the Maya lowlands proper. Several pieces are reported from Piedras Negras (Butler 1935; W. R. Coe 1959), and other sherds of the type may have been found at Pusilha.

These Pusilha specimens are of some interest in that the compositional studies of Bishop and Beaudry (Beaudry 1983) suggest that they are not trade pieces from the southeast Maya region but may have been manufactured somewhere in the lowlands as relatively rare imitations of Copador.

Cultural Significance: Copador Polychrome fits tightly into the Coner phase at Copan. Just how late the type may extend into the Terminal Classic to Postclassic occupation of Copan is uncertain. Recent obsidian hydration studies by Sanders and Webster (personal communication) have indicated that there was a considerable occupation of the residential zone of Copan which lasted well after A.D. 900, perhaps as late as A.D. 1100/1200. While we do not question this late occupation of Copan, we think it unlikely that Copador Polychrome continued to be made—at least in quantity and in full definition of that type—much after about A.D. 950. Dating on the Copador type from elsewhere, as at Chalchuapa, would seem to place it in the Late Classic period; however, admittedly, as Copador is used as a time marker for the latter part of the Late Classic, there can be a circularity to this reasoning.

A question of major interest about Copador Polychrome has been the location of its origins and primary production center or centers. As noted, Kidder, in fashioning the name "Copador," implied a probable Copan–Salvadoran derivation. Longyear (1952:64) wanted to be more specific, and he argued, on the basis of abundance, that Copan was the most likely production center. For him, Salvadoran occurrences were the result either of importation from Copan or (as in the case of the false Copador type, Arambala Polychrome) of local imitations. Recent ceramic compositional studies of Copador Polychrome (see Beaudry 1983; Bishop et al. 1986; and especially appendix B of this volume) have established three geographic-compositional groupings: western Honduras, which pertains to Copan and immediately surrounding sites; western El Salvador (Chalchuapa–Tazumal, Zapotitan); and the Motagua Valley. Unfortunately, these studies have been unable, so far, to pinpoint any clay sources within these three zones. To return, again, to Longyear's arguments, and to the principle of abundance, Copan and its immediate environs seem the most likely place for the origin and primary production of Copador Polychrome.

Copador Polychrome Type

Variety Name: Geometric.
Established as a Type and/or Variety: By this description.
Frequency: Unknown.
Ceramic Group: Copador.
Ceramic Complex: Coner.
Illustrations: Figure 98a–i.
Description:
Principal Identifying Modes.
1. Red (specular hematite red) or red-and-black designs on an orange slip;
2. geometric and essentially rectilinear design motifs;
3. cylinder jars.
Surface Finish and Decoration. Design motifs of these vessels appears to be glyphic or glyph-like. These are generally arranged in rectangular block-like arrangements. Vessels all appear to have had a red exterior rim band. Below this band are rows and/or panels of decoration on the upper portion of the vessel. Hieroglyphic identifications are difficult to determine, and in most cases we are probably dealing with pseudo-glyphs or glyph-like elements similar to those found on the Copador Variety vessels.
Form. The only form evident is the cylinder jar with outflared rims.
Whole, Restorable, or Partially Restorable Vessels: None recovered.
Classificatory Comments: See Copador Polychrome for details.
Intrasite Locations, Contexts, and Associations: See discussion under Copador Polychrome: Glyphic Varieties.
Intersite Locations, Contexts, and Associations: See Copador Polychrome: Glyphic Varieties.
Cultural Significance: See Copador Polychrome: Glyphic Varieties.

Doric Composite Type

Variety Name: Doric.
Established as a Type and/or Variety: By this description, although similar vessels have been illustrated by Longyear (1952).

Frequency: Unknown.
Ceramic Group: Copador.
Ceramic Complex: Coner.
Illustrations: Figure 99a–h.
Description:
Principal Identifying Modes.
1. Combined use of incised and modeled-carved surfaces with specular red banding and zones;
2. cylinder jar forms.
Surface Finish and Decoration. Glyph-like bands encircle the upper portions of the cylinder jars of this type. There are also indications of vertical bands or panels with glyph forms on the exterior surface of the jars. The glyphs are left unpainted. The bands or panels of glyphs are bordered with red slipped zones. One specimen shows evidence of deeply defined vertical fluting on the vessel walls.

Some jars show only an interior red rim band. Another vessel, however, has a series of alternating red and brownish-black interior bands extending down the interior vessel wall. The interior red bands of this specimen do not appear to be the dark hematite red typical of this and Copador vessels, but instead are more of an orange-brown-rust color.

The modeled designs are glyphic or glyph-like.
Form: The only form evident of this type is the cylinder jar, slightly outflared at the top.
Whole, Restorable, or Partially Restorable Vessels: None recovered.

Caterpillar Polychrome Type

Variety Name: Caterpillar.
Established as a Type and/or Variety: By this description in consultation with Viel (personal communication 1980).
Frequency: A total of 814 Caterpillar Polychrome sherds were recovered from these excavations. This represents 0.3 percent of the total collection.
Ceramic Group: Caterpillar.
Ceramic Complex: Coner.
Illustrations: Figures 100, 101.
Description:
Principal Identifying Modes.
1. Bold red and black designs on an orange background;

2. large open bowls or flaring-sided plates with hollow tripod supports;
3. consistently thick-walled vessels averaging about 1 cm in thickness.

Surface Finish and Decoration. The primary background slip of these vessels is orange, which was applied to the interiors of the plates and usually the upper portions of the exterior. Decoration in red (sometimes specular hematite) and black is most common on the interior, although it occurs occasionally on the exterior.

The interior designs usually have an encircling red band at or slightly below the lip. In the latter instances, the area below the red band is ornamented with black, lobate forms that alternate with black vertical or diagonal tickings. The main portion of the design, however, is on the outsloping interior wall of the vessel and consists variously of stylized jaguar faces (?) and glyph-like elements. This main portion of the design has a basal banding that marks the edge of the design. The interior flat bottom of the bowl or plate may or may not have additional design elements. Exterior decoration on vessel walls seems to have been entirely in red. These exterior designs are more boldly and slovenly executed than the interior designs. In addition to these designs, there are exterior red rim bands and bands at the basal angle.

Form. The open dish or plate has a markedly outflared rim. Frequently, this is outturned at a point about 3 cm below the lip. An exterior basal angle is well defined and sometimes marked by a low ridge or flange. Orifice diameter of these vessels ranges from 30 to 50 cm.

Tripod supports for the plates are hollow with rounded or slightly flattened points. Average size is 6 cm in height and 4 cm in diameter. The supports are most frequently left unpainted, although in a few instances they bear red pigment on their exterior sides.

There are some indications that some of these plates may have had loop handles arranged horizontally or parallel to the rim. However, we found no handle fragments attached to large body sherds.

Whole, Restorable or Partially Restorable Vessels: There are two partially restorable Caterpillar vessels.

1. Cat. No. 1-229 (fig. 100), CV-20, Op. 21(A), Level 2, Special Find 37. This complete speci-men has a total height of 10.4 cm, an orifice diameter of 33.8 cm, and a diameter at the basal angle or basal flange of 22.1 cm. The tripods on this vessel are about 5 cm high. Each hollow tripod has two holes in its side and one at the bottom.

2. Cat. No. 1-1207 (fig. 101), CV-43, Op. 100(B), Special Find 100. This is a fragmentary tripod plate with a positive red and black design on an orange background. The estimated original height of the vessel is 10 cm, and its orifice diameter is 28 cm. The plate is very shallow and open with interior vessel walls rounding gradually into an everted lip. The tripod supports were hollow and probably elongated. The interior decoration of the plate is black-and-red-on-orange. There is an encircling broad black line at the juncture of the plate floor and wall. A short distance above this is an encircling red band. Above this is a panel decoration composed of a black continuous voluted line. The upper edge of this panel is formed by another encircling broad red line. Around the lip of the plate are a series of broad, black scallops. The exterior may have been orange slipped but now is only a buff or gray. There is an encircling red band just below and under the lip edge. There is another red band located just above the angle of the exterior wall and base.

Classificatory Comments: Caterpillar Polychrome presented some problems in the classification, especially with some of the smaller sherds which may have been grouped in other types, such as Copador Polychrome.

Intrasite Locations, Contexts, and Associations: Both of our restorable vessels came from grave contexts and, as in the case of our other polychrome types, were of ritual use. We found relatively few sherds, but enough within trash contexts to indicate a possible household use.

Intersite Locations, Contexts, and Associations: The strongest ties are with western and west-central Honduras. Thus, similar pottery was found by William D. Strong, A. V. Kidder, and J. Drexel Paul, Jr. (1938), in the Ulua-Yojoa region of Honduras, as well as by Baudez and Becquelin (1973) (see their Chichipate Polychrome) at Naranjo in the same general region. The use of specular hematite paint is in keeping with our southeastern Maya region; however, neither Caterpillar nor an equivalent is reported from

Chalchuapa in El Salvador. The type's common vessel form, the tripod plate with the slight basal angle, is, of course, a common one in the Maya lowlands proper, being known among other places at Uaxactun (R. E. Smith 1955), Altar de Sacrificios (Adams 1971), and Seibal (Sabloff 1975).

Babilonia Polychrome Type

Variety Name: Uncertain if Copan occurrences (at least as examined by us) constitute a separate variety from that described from Los Naranjos.
Established as a Type and/or Variety: Formally, and under this name, by Baudez and Becquelin (1973) at Los Naranjos in Honduras. Previously, however, there was some recognition given the type under the name "Ulua Mayoid" (Strong, Kidder, and Paul 1938; Strong 1948).
Frequency: A total of 559 sherds or 0.20 percent of total collection.
Ceramic Groups: Babilonia or Ulua Yojoa.
Ceramic Complex: Coner.
Illustrations: Figures 102, 103, 104a–l.
Description:
Principal Identifying Modes.
1. A polychrome color scheme, with red and black on orange;
2. Maya-like glyph form or pseudo-glyph form and life-form designs;
3. a cylindrical jar form, often with short slab-tripod supports;
4. a slightly thickened rim that is slightly incurved and pointed at the lip.
Paste, Temper, and Firing. This has been discussed in great detail by Baudez and Becquelin (1973:256–257) in their description of Babilonia Polychrome from Los Naranjos. Essentially, the Copan collection of the type falls within the scope of their description. The paste of the type is very compact and fairly homogeneous, although, as Baudez and Becquelin indicate, white quartz particles and other darker, vitreous appearing material is evident in paste cores. Their estimate that tempering material is, usually, less than 60 percent of total paste core approximates what we have found. Generally, the surfaces of vessels, both interior and exterior, have been oxidized to a buff, red-buff, red, or brownish color. Frequently, sherds show a more or less uniform oxidization throughout, although some have cores

that are lighter than surfaces and others have cores that have been reduced to a gray color.
Surface Finish and Decoration. (See Baudez and Becquelin 1973:257, 261–278). Surfaces are slipped on both exteriors and interiors. This slip varies from buff or yellowish to orange. Surfaces are well smoothed to brilliantly polished. The most distinctive designs, as noted under the "Principal Identifying Modes" heading, are Maya glyph forms, pseudo-glyph forms, and life (human, animal, demon, deity) forms. However, it should be noted that many vessels bear geometric elements (rectangles, panels, cruciforms, scrolls, and so on), and although these are often or usually combined with glyph forms or life-forms, there are instances where they probably were the only decorative designs on the vessels. At least this is indicated by the data from Los Naranjos (Baudez and Becquelin 1973: fig. 102), and some of our sherds suggest this for our Copan collection. This leads us to the problem of the related type, Ulua Bold Geometric. We originally—following Strong, Kidder, and Paul (1938: pl. 7)—separated out certain of our sherds under this heading, in contrast to the bulk of our Babilonia Polychrome material, which we had defined (following Strong, Kidder and Paul, ibid.: pl. 8) as being characterized by glyph-like or life-form decorations; however, the Baudez and Becquelin definition of Babilonia Polychrome subsumes both Ulua Bold Geometric and Ulua Mayoid because these had been defined previously by Strong, Kidder, and Paul, and we have followed this latter definition here. For a detailed review of all of the decorative elements of Babilonia Polychrome the reader should consult Baudez and Becquelin (ibid.:261–278). Although we cannot be sure, because of the very fragmentary and eroded nature of much of our material, that our Copan collection duplicates all of the decorative variation that those authors describe and illustrate for Los Naranjos, it seems probable that a very great proportion of it is represented in our collections. This would include a few pieces of Babilonia Polychrome which incorporate incised, carved, or low-relief modeled modes.
Form. Baudez and Becquelin (1973:257–261) list a great number of forms for Babilonia Polychrome: open bowls, open bowls with tripod supports, cylinder jars, cylinder jars with very low slab-like tripod supports, globular bowls, and globular bowls or jars with collars, including

some with handles. This lattermost form, incidentally, seems particularly characteristic of the Bold Geometric decorated examples of the type (Baudez and Becquelin 1973: fig. 102a,b; Strong, Kidder, and Paul 1938: pl. 7a–d). Our Copan collection of Babilonia Polychrome seems heavily weighted, as to vessel form, to the cylinder jar with low slab-like feet.

Whole, Restorable, or Partially Restorable Vessels: There are two of these in our collections.

Cat. No. 1-327 (fig. 102) is a cylinder jar with red, dark orange, and black decoration on an orange slip. The jar measures 14.3 cm in height, with an orifice diameter of 16.6 cm and a basal diameter of 15.6 cm. The rim shows the characteristic Babilonia thickening and incurve or inward bevel. It has round, small, but hollow tripod feet (1.2 cm high and 4.5 cm in diameter). Each foot has an air hole or vent in the center of its base. The interior vessel walls were orange-slipped; the base probably was not, although its fired color is a similar color. All painted decoration is on the exterior of the jar. The painting style is distinctly Maya-like. Three seated dignitaries are depicted in black outlining but with red, dark orange, and black costuming or accoutrements. Each personage is elaborately dressed, with an elaborate feather headdress attached to a turban. Each is belted, displays a sash, and holds a fan. Between the figures, in two of the intervening spaces, is the figure of a moan bird. The individual, in each case, faces toward the bird, but the bird faces away from him, toward the back of the next individual. The third intervening space, with no bird, is very small; the fan of one dignitary almost touches the downward hanging headdress of the next. All three dignitaries face to the right. The drawing, execution, and spacing of the three human figures and the two birds, despite the elegance of the theme, are sloppily done. Above the heads of the dignitaries is a row of glyphs or pseudo-glyphs, done in red, dark orange, and black. Above the glyphs is an encircling narrow black band from which rises a series of stepped, scroll-end elements. These elements extend up to the lip-edge of the vessel. The bottom of the jar is also bordered with a black band that extends down under the vessel base and also covers the sides of the three supports. The vessel base was orange-slipped. Cat. No. 1-327 came from the Copan Main Ruin, Operation 26(A), Level 2, Special Find 2.

Cat. No. 1-342 (fig. 103) is another cylinder jar, also painted in a Maya-like style. The slip is orange, and the decoration has been carried out in red, black, dark orange, and cream. The orange slip covers both interior and exterior walls; but the exterior base, which is unslipped, is orange-fired. All painted decoration is on the exterior. The jar is 17.8 cm high, with an orifice diameter of 19 cm and a basal diameter of 17.6 cm. The tripod legs are slab-shaped and measure 1.6 cm high x 7.2 x 2.5 cm. The design consists of a repeated pattern of three standing men. Their bodies are in front view, but heads are in profile and turned to the right. The quality of the drawing is rather poor. The individuals are also shown as similarly garbed, with feather headdresses, necklaces, and belts. The belts appear to hold side-pads in place along the individual's body and suggest ball players. There is a narrow border, both above and below the central design, of a small, repeated, geometric element in black on orange. Each of the individuals of the main design stands between vertical stave-like elements. The arms and hands of the men are outstretched; however, they can be seen to be in front of, rather than holding, the stave-like elements. Between the men are upright pillar-like elements with bent or drooping tips ending in ornamented flares. The human figures are in cream with red and black features and ornamentation. The background to the figures is black; however, this negative design effect has all been achieved by positive painting. The vessel orifice is tipped with a broad black band that extends down the interior walls below the lip. Below this, on the interior, is a separate, narrower black band. Cat. No. 1-342 came from the Copan Main Ruin, Operation 26(A), Level 5, Special Find 11.

Classificatory Comments: In the course of this description one of our classificatory problems has already been commented upon. This includes our decision to include bold geometric sherds with those of more typically Maya-like glyph and life form designs, a procedure in which we follow Baudez and Becquelin. We suggest, however, that future researchers might attempt to separate these two, possibly somewhat distinct, decorative systems. It seems likely—or at least it might be a useful working hypothesis—that the bold geometric increment in the type or style has Honduran roots and that the type, as it eventually emerges in the Late Classic period, represents a fusion of resident traditions with a Classic Maya lowland Polychrome tradition. There are probably other subdivisions of this ceramic, as well as numerous modal patterns, worthy of future exploration.

Note that current descriptions of this polychrome group use variously the terms Babilonia, Ulua Polychrome, and Ulua-Yojoa Polychrome for the same ceramic. We hope terminological standardization will also be possible in the future.

Intrasite Locations, Contexts, and Associations: Babilonia Polychrome is well known at Copan. Longyear (1952:75, 101, figs. 104g, 105a, 109h, 110c, 117c) describes and dates it to the Late Classic period there and shows numerous illustrations of it, but the type is certainly not local to that region.

Babilonia Polychrome's statistical correlations with other types in their distributional patterns reflect chronology and, to a lesser degree, status. Positive but weak correlations are found only with other Coner phase types: Lorenzo Red, Copador Polychrome, Casaca Striated, Tipon Orange-brown, Don Gordon Modeled-carved. Note, however, that of the positive correlations, those with Copador, Tipon, and Don Gordon probably also reflect the similar contexts and status reinforcing functions of these types.

Intersite Locations, Contexts, and Associations: Baudez and Becquelin (1973:278–282) plot out the distribution of Babilonia Polychrome. The type seems at home in the Ulua–Yojoa–Comayagua region of Honduras. It is also common in central and southern Honduras, and Viel (1978) sees the Copan presence of the type related to these regions. It would appear to be an element of foreign ware or trade in parts of El Salvador, and Baudez and Becquelin so interpret its presence at Copan, where, indeed, it seems to be a minority type in contrast to the contemporaneous ceramics. In both earlier published reports (Stone 1957; Baudez and Becquelin 1973; Strong, Kidder, and Paul 1938; Glass 1966; and others) and current excavations (Wallace 1977; Henderson et al. 1979; Schortman, Urban, and Ashmore 1983; Hirth, Schortman, and Urban, personal communication 1983) in western and central-western Honduras, the evidence and the consensus of interpretation are that this type is a Maya-influenced Late Classic fine ceramic, but

one that is entirely indigenous to the Ulua–Yojoa–Comayagua region.

Functional Interpretation: Babilonia Polychrome is clearly a fine or luxury ware, perhaps reserved for funerary and ritual purposes although it may have had some household uses as well. Its presence at Copan suggests that it was a luxury import there; however, it seems to have been relatively common, since it is found in outlying residences, such as those investigated by us, as well as within the precincts and tombs of the Copan Main Center. Statistical evaluations of distribution patterns do not conclusively demonstrate this functional interpretation, but they are consistent with it (see "Intrasite Locations, Contexts, and Associations" above).

Cultural Significance: From the data available now it seems reasonably certain that Babilonia Polychrome was a development of the Ulua–Yojoa–Comayagua region, a zone peripheral to the area of Classic Maya lowland civilization lying directly to the west. The type embodies many elements in color scheme, decorative motifs, and vessel forms from ceramics of the Maya Classic period. These elements, however, have been reworked in this peripheral setting and the final product undoubtedly represents a fusion of these ideas—however they were transmitted—with local Honduran traditions. The Classic Maya inspirations for Babilonia are mainly those deriving from Tepeu or Late Classic times, especially such decorative features as the glyph, life forms, and cylinder jar forms.

The principal cultural significance of this type at Copan is to reflect strong ties in trade or elite interaction with western and central Honduras. These ties in an elite ceramic type reinforce the pattern seen in domestic wares like Masica Incised and Cementerio Incised. Thus, they reflect the strength of the site's ties to Honduras, while indicating a certain complexity in the probable mechanisms of interaction involved.

Masica Incised Type

Variety Name: Cruz.
Established as a Type and/or Variety: By Baudez and Becquelin (1973:296–299), although description was not framed in type-variety terminology.
Frequency: 3,312 sherds—1.2 percent of total sherds found at Copan. A major ceramic of the

Coner phase, Masica Incised vessels were more common than these sherd counts indicate since many Raul Red sherds probably were originally part of Masica Incised vessels, which are red-slipped and unincised below the shoulder. See "Classificatory Comments" below for a clarification of this problem.

Ceramic Group: Marina.
Ceramic Complex: Coner.
Illustrations: Figures 105a–q, 106a–d, 107a–d, 108a–r.
Description:
Principal Identifying Modes.
1. Fine-line incised and fine punctation in complex rectilinear-curvilinear designs, often composed of parallel incised lines;
2. restriction of incised design to collar and shoulder of narrow-mouthed jars;
3. red-orange slip applied below design on vessel and sometimes on upper portion of rim;
4. collared jar form with vertical loop handles.

Paste, Temper, and Firing. Gray-black cores with buff surfaces on both interior and exterior. Color is consistently above 10 YR 7/4. Paste texture ranges from densely compact to finely porous. Paste consists of fine clay particles with fine to very coarse inclusions of sand and quartz, probably mostly added as temper. Particles are uniformly distributed with a density ranging from less than 25 percent to 50 percent. Particles are subangular in shape. Surface hardness ranges from 2.0 to 5.5 on Moh's scale, although exterior surfaces tend to be at the higher end of this scale. Bishop and Beaudry's neutron activation analyses have indicated that this is a typical local valley paste (see appendix B).

Surface Finish and Decoration. Unslipped surfaces are smooth on the exterior. Interior surfaces have a light texturing, perhaps the result of smoothing with a soft instrument (smoothing with leaves or a piece of cloth produces such a pattern).

Exterior surfaces are often slipped in bright orange-red (2.5 YR 6/8). Slipped surfaces are bright in color, but are usually matte, rather than shiny, and often have a powdery feel and texture. The red pigment is of the carmen shade typical of the Marina group and of all of the red-slipped (e.g., Raul, Lorenzo) and red-daubed (Casaca Striated, Cementerio Incised) types of the Copan Valley. Zones of incised designs on the collar and shoulder of vessels were smoothed but left unslipped. Bases and the bottom portions of the jar walls were usually left unslipped.

On most vessels there is a zone filled with incised designs extending from the neck or collar down to the mid-shoulder of the jar. Occasionally, incised designs are placed elsewhere on the exterior. The incised designs were finely executed, apparently while the clay surfaces were still wet and soft. These designs included fine-line (less than 1 mm) incisions and dot or slash punctations. Sometimes hollow reed punctations also appear. Design motifs are rectilinear and curvilinear patterns formed by sets of three or four closely spaced parallel incised lines. The most common designs defined by these parallel lines include triangles, rectangles, and continuous curvilinear or zigzag bands. The designs and zones formed by multiple-line incision are often filled with small dot and slash punctations. Occasionally modeled or appliqued decoration is found on vessel surfaces or handles in the form of ridges, nubbins, and anthropomorphic or zoomorphic faces.

Form. The single characteristic common form is a collared jar with a globular or subglobular body, a restricted orifice, and an outflared neck or collar. A few sherds of an apparently collarless variant were found at Copan and are also reported in Masica Incised: Cruz Variety vessels from Los Naranjos (Baudez and Becquelin 1973: 297, fig. 115) and central Honduras (Stone 1957: fig. 53). One aberrant wide cylindrical form (46 cm diameter) was also found at Copan.

Orifice diameter on the jar necks ranges from 9 to 19 cm, depending largely on vessel size. Average orifice diameter is about 14 cm. Vessel heights are difficult to estimate, but heights of 30 to 40 cm may have been common. Wall thickness ranges from 0.8 to 1.5 cm near the rim, but walls are much thinner on the jar bodies (0.4–1.2 cm). Most body sherds are characteristically thin, with an average thickness of about 0.5 cm.

Bases were probably small and indented. However, it appears that most bases lacked red slip or incision and so were classified with Lysandro Unslipped material.

Most vessels had vertical loop handles attached to the shoulder or collar of the vessel just below the rim or slightly lower. Handles are predominantly unpainted, although some are slipped or daubed with the red-orange slip. Handles are usually plain and smoothed, but decoration variants include incision, nodes, and one appliqued zoomorph. Some handles consist of double, joined strips, with some examples in which the two are twisted into a braid. Handles are 5 to 10 cm in length and 1 to 2.5 cm in width. Vessels had two or four handles each, although some were handleless.

Whole, Restorable, or Partially Restorable Vessels: None recovered.

Classificatory Comments: The frequency of Masica Incised: Cruz Variety whole vessels at Copan was probably much higher than sherd counts indicate, since only sherds actually bearing incision (i.e., incised neck and upper shoulder fragments) were classified as Masica. Incision probably covered only about one-fourth of vessel surfaces. Red-slipped Masica sherds lacking incision cannot be distinguished from Raul Red sherds because the types share both the same paste and slip. Unslipped bases have probably been classified as Lysandro Unslipped, since paste is the same for these types. Frequency comparisons show that only a total of four Masica sherds were found in contexts that did not contain any Raul Red sherds. This correlation confirms our observation that Masica vessels were covered by red-orange slip over much of their surface. Therefore, it is safe to assume that many sherds classified as Raul Red are fragments of the lower two-thirds of Masica Incised vessels. So the frequency of Masica Incised vessels at Copan was probably considerably higher than the sherd counts indicated.

Nonetheless, the definition of separate Masica Incised and Raul Red types is justified, since some unincised, entirely red-slipped Raul Red vessels have been found recently at Copan (Viel, personal communication). Furthermore, statistical review of all ceramic lots shows that 215 contexts and a total of 2,273 Raul Red sherds were found with no associated Masica Incised sherds. Also note that the correlation matrix for all types indicates only a very weak correlation between Masica Incised (Cruz Variety) and Raul Red (Raul Variety). These statistics confirm that a proportion of the Raul Red sherds were originally part of unincised red-slipped vessels. Thus, the definition of separate types and separate counts is justified.

Note that Longyear (1952:91, fig. 31f,g,k) described and illustrated Masica Incised sherds, although he erroneously placed them in the Postclassic period.

Intrasite Locations, Contexts, and Associations: Masica Incised: Cruz Variety is found in residential refuse and building fills.

There is no consistent pattern of correlations that could be interpreted as social or functional in nature. Types of funerary function and of elite status (e.g., Don Gordon Modeled-carved) as well as household jars (Casaca Striated) are both highly correlative with the Cruz Variety because of its sharply defined Late chronological associations.

Intersite Locations, Contexts, and Associations: Masica Incised and related types appear to be widely distributed throughout the southern periphery of Mesoamerica, but Masica is particularly common in central Honduras. The type was first described by Baudez and Becquelin at Los Naranjos (1973:296–299), and description and photographs indicate near identity to the Masica material at Copan. Masica or closely related ceramics also appear sporadically in the descriptions of material from other sites in Honduras. In her regional survey Doris Stone (1957: figs. 45c, 53c, 59a:c) illustrates Masica sherds from Las Vegas and Lo de Vaca in the Comayagua and from a site in the Siguatepeque region—all in the highlands of central Honduras. Motifs and treatment appear to be the same as at Copan. Strong, Kidder, and Paul (1938:42, 49) describe Masica Incised ceramics from the Ulua Valley in western Honduras at the sites of Las Flores Bolas and Santa Rita. In his synthesis of Honduran material, Glass (1966:173) describes Comayagua vessels that are probably within the Masica Incised type. Recent excavations by Wendy Ashmore, Edward Schortman, and Patricia Urban in central-western Honduras have found large quantities of Masica Incised at several Late Classic sites in the Middle Ulua drainage. Its frequency there is high (over 10–15 percent of Late Classic materials), and Masica Incised appears to be one of the common diagnostic types of the Late Classic of western and central Honduras (Urban and Schortman, personal communications 1984). Most of these ceramics are identical to Masica Incised: Cruz Variety; a minor portion have simpler designs and daubing more similar to Copan's

Reina Incised or to the Tipante Variety of Masica Incised found at Quirigua.

Turning to Quirigua and the Motagua Valley of southeastern Guatemala, we find several varieties of Masica Incised at Quirigua, none of them similar in design elements to the Cruz Variety at Copan. Quirigua's Tipante Variety has a coarser incision with more simple parallel-line incised designs. On the other hand the Matesano Variety of Quirigua's Masica Incised has very fine (almost faint) incision in patterns somewhat distinct from Copan's Cruz Variety. It is also distinguishable by its more brown paste and darker red, rather than red-orange, slip. Nonetheless, Quirigua obviously also shares the broader Masica modes with Copan and sites throughout western and central Honduras.

It is significant that Masica Incised is not a common type at any excavated site in El Salvador and is also absent from highland Guatemalan assemblages. At Chalchuapa three Late Classic sherds described by Sharer (1978:3:73) are probably of one of the Masica types. In the Late Classic Lepa phase at Quelepa some sherds of the Chapeltique Orange-red Incised type show designs and treatment similar to Masica Incised (Andrews 1976: figs. 147d,e, 148p). Otherwise the distribution of Masica Incised in its several varieties appears to be limited to Honduras and the adjacent Lower Motagua Valley of Guatemala.

Functional Interpretations: Intersite associations, evidence from other sites, and the type's dominant handled jar form are all consistent with a utilitarian household function, possibly as a serving vessel for liquids. The incised decoration across the vessel shoulders might have aided cooling of liquid contents.

Cultural Significance: Masica Incised was a major type of the Coner phase and one of the most important indications of Copan's close ties to the east and south. Together with Chilanga, Babilonia, Gualpopa, and Copador, it indicates that the Copan assemblage was essentially a southern periphery assemblage rather than a lowland Classic Maya complex. Unlike Babilonia, Copador, or Chilanga, Masica Incised is a nonpolychrome, utilitarian type, and its presence here indicates that Copan's ties to the south and east go well beyond elite trade and interaction. One might speculate that Masica Incised along with other shared traits implies a more general

cultural affiliation of Copan's population with those of other western and central Honduran sites lacking those hallmarks of Maya elite culture that are found in the Copan and Motagua Valleys. Note that Copan's Masica Incised (in all varieties) is definitely locally made, since Bishop and Beaudry's neutron activation analyses have demonstrated typical local profiles of trace elements for Masica's pastes (see appendix B).

Masica Incised is absent from assemblages in El Salvador, even from those Late Classic complexes that share the Copador, Gualpopa, and Chilanga polychromes with the Copan Valley (e.g., Chalchuapa, the Zapotitan Basin, Cerron Grande Basin). Thus, while Copador and Gualpopa are shared by Coner phase Copan and Late Classic Salvadoran sites, Masica Incised, Reina Incised, and Babilonia Polychrome are shared by Copan and central Honduras. These two sets of ties show the intensity, breadth, and complexity of Copan's interaction across the entire southern periphery of the Maya area. This contrasts with the relative scarce indications of shared *ceramic* features between Copan and lowland Classic Maya sites to the north.

Note also that Masica Incised may have a developmental antecedent in the Cececapa Incised with Red Type of Gualjoquito and other sites in the middle Ulua Valley (Schortman, Urban, and Ashmore 1983:29, 32). This possible developmental tradition for Masica is further evidence of the strong Honduran affiliation of the type and another indication of Copan's ties to central and central-western Honduras.

Raul Red Type

Variety Names: Raul and Unspecified.
Established as a Type and/or Variety: By this description.
Frequency: 29,837 sherds—10.8 percent of the total number of sherds recovered by the Harvard Copan Project. Sixty-four percent of these Raul Red sherds are of the Raul Variety, and the remaining 36 percent are of Unspecified Variety. These frequencies are inflated because many sherds of the Raul Variety and some of the Unspecified were probably from various types of incised vessels. The Unspecified category is also inflated by the inclusion of much badly eroded and only tentatively classified red-slipped sherds.

Ceramic Group: Marina.
Ceramic Complex: Coner.
Illustrations:

Raul Red: Raul: figure 109a–y.
Raul Red: Unspecified: figure 110a–h.

Description:
Principal Identifying Modes.
1. Tomato red slip on vessel exteriors. Slip has soft matte quality and erodes easily;
2. collared jar with constricted to slightly constricted orifices and short outflared necks, often with outturned rims.

Variety Distinctions. The Raul Variety sherds tend to be thinner-walled and come from slightly smaller vessels. This variety is better defined and less variable than the Unspecified. It probably includes most of the red-slipped body sherds from Masica Incised vessels, as well as sherds from all-red incised vessels (see "Classificatory Comments" in the Masica Incised section). The Unspecified Variety includes a range of Raul-like material, probably including the heavier and more eroded sherds of Raul Red; some sherds from slightly different red-slipped vessels; and possibly a genuine heavier-walled and coarser variant of the Raul Red type. Again, Unspecified Variety (about 36 percent of the Raul Red type) also may include body sherds from unincised portions of Masica and Reina Incised vessels.

Paste, Temper, and Firing. Paste is approximately the same as for Masica Incised (see above), although the Unspecified Variety of Raul Red also includes a wider variation in pastes. Raul Red pastes are slightly porous, with silty to fine clay particles (the latter more common) and very fine to medium fine sand temper in subangular to fully rounded uniformly distributed particles (25 percent to 50 percent density range). Temper is occasionally much coarser in some Unspecified Variety examples (larger than 1.5 mm). Paste color is buff 10 YR 6/3, and its hardness is 2.0 to 5.5 (Moh's scale) on sherd interiors and 3.5 to 5.5 on outer surfaces.

Surface Finish and Decoration. Orange-red (2.5 YR 6/8) covers the exterior surface of sherds. Occasional unslipped areas have a buff surface with lightly textured smoothing. Slip is matte and easily erodes. Interiors and the lower portions of vessels were probably left unslipped. All of these characteristics are shared with Masica Incised. It appears that the unincised red-slipped vessels

represented by a portion of the Raul Red sherds may have had the area from above the shoulder to just below or onto the vessel neck left unslipped. This unslipped zone was smoothed but not polished. In Masica Incised vessels this unslipped zone was filled with fine-line incisions and punctations. Red-slipped body sherds below this zone and upper neck sherds above it would have been classified as Raul Red. Clearly, however, some vessels did not bear incised designs, the unslipped zone being left empty. It is the presence of these vessels that requires the distinction between the Raul Red and Masica Incised Types.

Interior surfaces on Raul Red sherds (as with Masica Incised) show a textured, smeared smoothing effect.

The Unspecified Variety also includes sherds with a coarser and sometimes darker red slip, often badly eroded.

Form. The diagnostic Raul Red form is the same as that for Masica Incised, a collared globular jar with a restricted orifice, slightly outflaring neck, and loop handles. Some vessels (largely in the Unspecified Variety) have a shorter, more markedly everted collar; and a few large open bowl fragments with interior as well as exterior red slipping were also found (again, placed in the Unspecified Variety). A few sherds were from restricted bowls, and some sherds even imply zoomorphic or anthropomorphic bowl forms.

Rim profiles vary from outflaring to horizontally everted with the latter being more common. Everted rims are substantially thicker than the vessel walls, with an average rim thickness of 1.5 cm and wall thickness of 0.4 to 0.5 cm in the Raul Variety; Unspecified Variety tends to have thicker body walls (0.7–1 cm). Orifice diameters are 12 to 22 cm in the Raul Variety but are often larger (30 to 43 cm) in some of the Unspecified Variety examples. Rims usually flare outward an additional 1 to 1.75 cm. Vessels were large with maximum diameter much wider than the orifice diameter.

Bases were small and circular, 7 to 8 cm in diameter, and were indented.

Handles are all loop forms and appear to have been placed both horizontally and vertically on the vessels. They vary in length from 10 (most commonly) to 3 cm. Most handles are unornamented although frequently red-slipped. Unslipped handles include examples with vertical bifurcation, protuberances, and some crude modeling and applique in the form of notched ridges or, rarely, small, crudely modeled animals. Such applique and modeled elements also appear on some Raul Red body sherds.

Whole, Restorable, or Partially Restorable Vessels: There is only one restorable vessel of this type, although it has not been restored, because of the highly destroyed nature of the remains. The context of this vessel is: Operation 6(I), Level 1, CV-20, Special Find 15.

This is a large collared jar with a short collar. It has an everted rim with a thickened lip. Two loop handles were found which were placed horizontally on the shoulder of the vessel. No dimensions of the vessel could be determined.

Viel (personal communication 1981) reports that two whole Raul Red jars have recently been found in the Copan Valley.

Classificatory Comments: The overlapping typology of Masica Incised and Raul Red has been mentioned above; and one should keep in mind that Raul Red frequencies are, thereby, exaggerated. Raul Unspecified remains a poorly defined variety that should be considered provisional.

Intrasite Locations, Contexts, and Associations: Both varieties are found in quantity in household refuse around the sides and backs of house platforms. Such occurrences are similar to those of other domestic types. The best associational occurrences of the two varieties are with Masica Incised and Tipon Orange-brown, both strong Coner phase types.

Intersite Locations, Contexts, and Associations: The strongest ties seem to be with the Tepeu sphere (Late Classic) red-slipped wares of the Maya lowlands (R. E. Smith 1955; Adams 1971; Sabloff 1975), although it should be noted that Raul Red is not usually as well made and finished as these Peten types. Raul Red and its Copan Coner phase companion type, Casaca Striated, do not have good counterparts in the southeastern Maya region, including western Honduras, the Ulua-Yojoa regions, and all of El Salvador (Sharer 1978; Andrews 1976; Schortman and Urban, personal communication 1976).

Casaca Striated Type

Variety Name: Casaca.
Established as a Type and/or Variety: By this description in consultation with Sharer and col-

leagues who describe similar material in the Switch Molina ceramic group at Quirigua. The present description is based on 63,922 sherds, including rim, body, and appendage pieces and partially restorable vessels. This is 23.1 percent of the total sherd collection from Copan under consideration in this monograph.
Ceramic Group: Switch Molina.
Ceramic Complex: Coner.
Illustrations: Figure 111a–m.
Description:
Principal Identifying Modes.
1. Striated vessel exteriors;
2. red-daubed lips;
3. large jars with short, everted collars;
4. large loop handles placed horizontally on vessels.

Paste, Temper, and Firing. Gray-black paste cores with buff to light gray surfaces (usually both exterior and interior but sometimes only exterior) resulting from firing. Color range of these surfaces is 7.5 YR to 10 YR. Paste texture ranges from dense and compact to slightly porous. Silty clay particles, sand, and pumice are in the paste. Some of this material may be natural inclusions in clay used, but the pumice and most of the sand were probably intentionally added as temper. Size of the particles varies from fine to coarse, and shape varies from subangular to rounded. Temper density within paste is estimated at 25 to 75 percent. Surface hardness is usually about 2.0 on Moh's scale, although some specimens are harder.

Surface Finish and Decoration. Interiors are scraped, sandy, but generally smoothed. Exteriors are unslipped and bear the diagnostic striations. These striations are usually 2 to 3 mm wide, about 1 mm deep, and separated from each other by about 1 mm. They always occur in groups of parallel markings, suggesting that they were made with a toothed or comb-like instrument on the wet clay. They begin just below the rim and extend down the neck and onto the body of the vessel. Their orientation is most often diagonal, descending from left to right on the vessel body. At about midpoint on the vessel body this rather uniform diagonally disposed orientation of the striations is replaced by a more random disposition of the striated lines. Vessel bases seem to have been left plain.

A red pigment of a carmen shade, comparable to that of the painted surfaces of the Coner complex type, Raul Red (2.5 YR 6/8 average), is nearly always applied to the vessel lips. Sometimes this pigment extends for a short distance down the insides of the vessel walls. It is also frequently applied to the vessel exteriors, just below the rims, in a daubed or carelessly splashed fashion.

Vessel surfaces, both interior and exterior, but particularly the latter, often have fire-blackened spots.

Form. The most common form—indeed, the only certain form—is a large jar with a relatively low or short collar and an everted or outflared rim. Such jars may be as much as 45 cm in height, although about 30 cm is the more usual size. Maximum diameters of these jars are slightly less than height. Necks or collars are from 2 to 4 mm in height; orifices are relatively large. The rim flare or eversion varies from the horizontal to about a 45-degree angle.

Vessel walls are often quite thin but average at about 5 mm. Necks and bases are generally thicker, being, in some cases, as much as 1.5 cm.

Bases are round, relatively small (about 8 cm in diameter), and indented. Only very rarely are there signs of striation marks on these bases. Because of this, many Casaca Striated base sherds were probably classified by us as Lysandro Unslipped.

Loop handles are the only appendages. They range from 7 to 14 cm in length and from 1 to 3 cm in handle diameter, and are placed horizontally on the jar shoulders. They were so arched in their attachment to the vessel walls that it is easy to insert one or more fingers through the loops, and it seems certain that they were quite functional carrying handles. The handles were attached to the vessel walls when the clay of both was wet. Handle ends were simply pressed against the vessel, and little tool impressions usually can be seen where the adhesion was reinforced in this manner. Handles are never striated, and for this reason many have probably been classified as Lysandro Unslipped.

Whole, Restorable, or Partially Restorable Vessels: In spite of the abundance of Casaca Striated in our sherd collections, whole, restorable, or partially restorable vessels were rare or virtually absent.

One partially restorable specimen (Cat. No. 1-108) was recovered from CV-20, Op. 6(K), Level 1. The complete rim and collar were put together, and many of the remaining body sherds were fitted to each other. One sherd has a large loop handle. Rim diameter measures 19.4 cm, and maximum body diameter is estimated at about 25 cm with vessel height probably a little greater than this. Rim lip is red painted, and there are red smears on the body exterior. The body sherds are thin-walled, averaging about 4 mm.

Classificatory Comments: We have already alluded to the problems of classifying Casaca Striated plain bases and handles as Lysandro Unslipped. Ware and paste qualities of the two types are very similar or identical. What this may mean is that perhaps another 5 percent of the total sherds in our Copan collections may also have been Casaca Striated, with this figure subtracted from the Lysandro percentage total.

There seem to be other classificatory problems when we attempt to coordinate our classification with Longyear's. That author (Longyear 1952: 89–90) describes "Coarse Ware, Storage Jars," a category that probably includes some Casaca. Longyear also refers to striated surface finish as "raking," and at one place he states that "raking appears toward the end of the Early Classic period and is very common in Full Classic (Late Classic) times." It should be noted, however, that several of the sherds illustrated in Longyear's figures 30 and 31, which he designates as raked, would not have been classified by us as striated but as Mapache group ceramic types, such as Cementerio Incised or Mapache Incised. Longyear's figures 30u and 31a probably are, however, true striated types.

Intrasite Locations, Contexts, and Associations: As indicated previously, Casaca Striated: Casaca Variety is a numerically important type in our Copan collections. It is found abundantly in household refuse contexts, implying domestic, everyday usage. It is also a frequent type in constructional fill proveniences. Site stratigraphy and associations indicate a Coner phase temporal context or a Late Classic date. This observation would accord with that just cited from Longyear. It is our opinion that Casaca Striated: Casaca Variety was preceded in Copan chronology by a related type, Switch Molina Striated: Sandoval Variety. Presumably, this latter named type would be the "raked" ware that Longyear states appears toward the end of the Early Classic period.

Intersite Locations, Contexts, and Associations:
Striated surface vessels are common in the Maya
lowlands, and they have a long chronological
range, extending from the Preclassic period
through the Classic periods. Several striated types
were first formally named by Smith and Gifford
(1966) in their supplement to Smith's (1955)
Uaxactun pottery study. The one of these that is
closest typologically to Casaca Striated, as well
as being contemporaneous with it, is the Late
Classic Encanto Striated type; earlier types are
the Preclassic Sapote Striated and the Early Classic Triunfo Striated. Encanto Striated has the
deep, wide, closely, and carefully spaced striation
marks characteristic of Casaca. Its jar forms are
similar to Casaca, with flared or everted collars.
Encanto has been well described and illustrated
by Adams (1971:19–20) from Altar de Sacrificios
and by Jeremy A. Sabloff (1975:155–158) from
Seibal. There are some differences between the
two types: Encanto does not have the handles
characteristic of Casaca; and the latter does not
have the little appliqued pellet and band features
of Encanto. Nevertheless, the similarities are evident, and some kind of an affiliation is indicated.
Another Late Classic striated type is Tu-tu Camp
Striated, which has been described and illustrated
by Gifford (1976:273–276) from Barton Ramie
in Belize.

When we turn away from the Maya lowlands
proper, however, and look to the south or to the
east, there are few close parallels to Casaca Striated or to the typically Maya lowland striated
wares. To begin with, striated pottery seems not
to be represented in the Guatemalan highlands,
judging at least from the long Preclassic to Classic sequence at Kaminaljuyu (see Kidder, Jennings, and Shook 1946:205–213; Wetherington
1978a:3–51; Lischka 1978:233–246; Rice 1978:
414–420). It is reported from Chalchuapa, in
western Salvador; however, there are no close
similarities with Casaca. Sharer (1978:43, 59,
64) refers to three types with this kind of surface
treatment: Ozatlan Striated (Protoclassic-Early
Classic), Zacamil Striated-Applique (Late Classic), and Joateca Striated (Late Postclassic-
Historic). All, however, are radically different
from Casaca Striated or the Maya lowland striated types.

In the east, around Lake Yojoa and the Ulua
drainage, the Casaca similarities or parallels are
weak. Strong, Kidder, and Paul (1938), Stone

(1957), Nedenia C. Kennedy (1977, 1981), and
Kennedy, Messenger, and John Yonk (1982)
report no striated wares. James Sheehy (personal communication), however, mentioned
striated pottery being found associated with
Masica Incised, also a Copan Coner phase
type, at the site of Choloma. The more detailed
site monograph and pottery descriptions from
Los Naranjos (Baudez and Becquelin 1973) also
include some references to surface treatments
that are striated, raked, or brushed; but these,
as in the types Jaitique Grossier (ibid.:123–130),
Mongora Brun (ibid.:164–169), and Custeca
Simple (ibid.:304–307), appear to pertain to
occasional sherds within a context of what
are otherwise plain or unslipped types. Such
specimens may have been casually or acciden-
tally scraped, brushed, or raked; certainly, they
do not present the aspect of the systematically scored or striated Casaca or Encanto
type.

Functional Interpretation: Abundance of Casaca
Striated in domestic rubbish contexts and its
absence from graves or special cache contexts
strongly suggests utilitarian functions for the
type. Size and shape further suggest that Casaca
Striated jars were used as water jars or food storage jars. The appearance of burned areas on the
bases and sides of vessels might imply they were
sometimes used for cooking. The vessel orifices are proportionately large enough, in relation to vessel size and shape, to have per-
mitted such use. The striated surfacing has
been explained in at least two ways by archaeologists. The roughening would possibly prevent slipping from the hands when the jar
was filled and heavy, although, of course, the
large loop handles appear to have been the
main devices for handling and carrying. It is
also possible that the striated surface roughening of vessels aided in water cooling by, in
effect, presenting more surface for drying and
evaporation.

Cultural Significance: To sum up, Casaca Striated
and its related types at Copan find their closest
parallels and similarities in the Maya lowlands
or, at least, the southern Maya lowlands. The
nature of the spread or diffusion of this type must
remain largely speculative. In a very general way,
brushed, scraped, or striated surface roughening
of large vessel utility wares is a very widely distributed trait in Mesoamerica, other parts of the

Americas, and even the world; hence, historical relationships among such appearances cannot be postulated on formal similarity alone. It is a surface treatment technique that could have evolved independently on many occasions in response to simple functional needs or advantages. Nevertheless, in the Maya context it seems likely that the striation idea did diffuse, as a mode, throughout the Maya lowlands, and Copan was very likely one locus in such a diffusion network. One line of reasoning that supports this interpretation is that there is a similarity in the general trend of development of these striated wares as these are found from one lowland region to another and from site to site. Thus, at Barton Ramie, Uaxactun, Altar de Sacrificios, Seibal, and elsewhere, wherever we have chronological data on large sherd collections, we find that striated types of the Preclassic and Early Classic periods have fainter and more haphazardly arranged striations, while the Late Classic types (such as Encanto Striated and Tu-tu Camp Striated) have bolder, more definitely impressed and oriented striation marks. This trend is observed at Copan, where the earlier (Early Classic) Switch Molina Striated: Sandoval Variety is more faintly and irregularly striated than the later Casaca Type.

That Casaca Striated and the other Copan striated types are more closely related to the Maya lowlands proper than they are to the highlands to the south or the Ulua-Yojoa country to the east is of special interest. Striated pottery would certainly appear to have been a part of ordinary or commoner culture at Copan, and much of Copan commoner culture has links to the south and east. Casaca Striated, however, like elements of hierarchical culture at Copan—sculpture, hieroglyphics, calendrics, and minority polychrome wares—appears to link to the lowland centers of the Peten.

Casaca Striated Type

Variety Name: Crud.
Established as a Type and/or Variety: By this description, which is based on only 85 sherds. A minor striated ware variant.
Ceramic Group: Switch Molina.
Ceramic Complex: Coner.
Illustrations: Figure 112a–g.
Description:

Principal Identifying Modes.
1. Striated vessel exteriors with wide-spaced, faint, and rather wide lined striations;
2. small, thin walled, collared globular ollas or jars with short everted rims.

Paste, Temper, and Firing. Same as Casaca Variety.

Surface Finish and Decoration. Interiors are smoothed. Exteriors are unslipped and tend to be bumpy and more uneven than the Casaca Variety. The striations on the exteriors are wide-spaced (5 mm apart), relatively wide (1–2 mm), and quite shallow. The orientation of the striations is generally parallel to the vertical axis of the vessel. This is especially the case near the top of the vessel; lower down on the vessel body the orientation is more haphazard.

A red pigment like that seen on the Casaca Variety specimens is frequently seen as splotches on interiors and exteriors.

Form. Collared jars and ollas are the only form (or forms) recorded. We have only one partially restorable vessel of the type. This piece is probably near the small end of the size range. It measures 9 cm in height and 12 cm in diameter. Heights on larger vessels probably are as much as 20 cm. Collars, which are 1.5 to 3.5 cm in height, vary from nearly vertical to moderately outflared. None is completely everted.

Vessel walls range from 3 to 10 mm in thickness, with area of mid-body and bases being the thinnest.

Small loop handles were placed both vertically and horizontally just below the collar. These handles are 4 to 5 cm long and 1.5 cm in diameter.

Whole, Restorable, or Partially Restorable Vessels: None recovered.

Classificatory Comments: The correlation between the rather faint, wide-lined, and wide-spaced striations and the small jars suggests that the specimens so classified as Crud Variety were purposeful creations aiming at certain modal combinations rather than simply occasional poorly or carelessly striated vessels or portions of vessels.

Intrasite Locations, Contexts, and Associations: In general, contexts are those of household refuse. There was a substantial concentration of Crud Variety sherds in CV-43, Op. 49(A), a deep trench made into Structure E-2. Several of these were pieces of the same vessels, but not all of them were. Other specimens were found scattered through various proveniences, usually in association with Casaca Variety sherds.

Intersite Locations, Contexts, and Associations: This minor variety of striated pottery at Copan is not easily traced through the literature. In general, faintness of striation lines and haphazardness of application tend to be early modes within the striated wares of the Maya lowlands, preceding the Late Classic; however, our data indicate Casaca Striated: Crud Variety is essentially contemporaneous with Casaca Variety.

Functional Interpretations: Following the suggestions made for Casaca Striated: Casaca Variety, the vessels of Crud Variety may have been small water jars.

Cultural Significance: Appears to be a minor variety of striated pottery, dating to the Late Classic period, at Copan. Its distribution at other sites in the Maya lowlands and in surrounding regions is not known and is difficult to determine because classification procedures for such types and varieties of utility wares have not been precise enough.

Lorenzo Red Type

Variety Name: Lorenzo.
Established as a Type and/or Variety: By this description.
Frequency: 15,292 sherds or 5.3 percent of our total collection.
Ceramic Group: Lorenzo.
Ceramic Complex: Coner.
Illustrations: Figures 113, 114a–h, 115a–f.
Description:
Principal Identifying Modes.
1. Roughened, scraped, or wiped exterior surfaces in which markings frequently appear as semi-obliterated striations;
2. red-slipped interiors in which slip has a thin, streaky appearance;
3. large, hemispherical cauldron-like open bowls.

Paste, Temper, and Firing. Paste color tends to conform to two modes: (1) gray-black cores with buff surfaces in which the fired surface (as on the exterior of the bowls) varies from 5 YR 3/6 to 10 YR 2/7; and (2) a reddish-brown color throughout that is closer to the 5 YR end of the scale. The

first color mode is usually associated with a sandy temper, whereas the second color mode has less sand. Specimens pertaining to the second mode may be somewhat earlier in their chronological range, dating back to the Cueva phase; however, this chronological distinction is not always a clear one, because there is considerable grading in paste color and tempering material. The texture of the paste, in general, is fine to slightly porous. Sand is the only observed temper, and it ranges from fine to coarse, with subangular particles. The temper density range is 25 to 50 percent. Surface hardness ranges from 2.0 to as much as 5.5 on Moh's scale, with the exterior surfaces harder.

Surface Finish and Decoration. The scraped, wiped, roughened, and slightly striated surfaces show temper extrusions and drag marks from these extrusions. These exterior surfaces vary in color from buff to red, following the observations on paste coloring. They also show frequent evidences of burning. Interior surfaces are completely slipped, including the lips of the vessels. Slip color varies from 2.5 YR 5/8 to 10 R 4/8. Prior to this slipping the interiors of the bowls were carefully smoothed.

Form. Four form variants were recorded.

Variant 1 is a deep, cauldron-bowl with a thickened direct rim and a rounded lip. About 45 percent of the rim sherds pertain to this variant, including three restorable or partially restorable vessels (Cat. Nos. 1-1211, 1-227, and 1-108) (fig. 113). The diameter at the rim of this variant is about 58 cm, and depth on two specimens where it could be accurately estimated was 28 and 19 cm, respectively. Body wall thickness ranges from 0.5 to 1 cm and rim thickness from 1 to 1.5 cm.

Variant 2 is similar but has a thickened and outturned or outflared rim. This outturning or outflaring varies from a horizontal to only a slightly diagonal upturning. Lips tend to be more flattened than with Variant 1. About 45 percent of the rim sherds pertain to this variant, including one partially restorable vessel (Cat. No. 1-271). Orifice diameter of these bowls is slightly less than Variant 1, ranging from 25 to 45 cm. Height is always less than diameter and varies considerably. Vessel wall thickness is same as Variant 1, but rims tend to be thicker (1.5–2 cm).

Variant 3 is a subglobular or tecomate-like bowl. About 8 percent of the sherds pertain to this form. The form range is from a notably restricted orifice to a very slightly constricted one. The interior red slip completely covers the interior, however, even with bowls that have the markedly restricted orifices. Vessel maximum diameters—usually at a point slightly below the orifice—range from 25 to 40 cm. Vessel height was less and varies proportionately, probably from about 20 to 30 cm. Wall thickness is slightly less than with Variants 1 and 2, ranging from 3 to 6 mm; rims range from 8 to 9 mm in thickness.

About 2 percent of the specimens belong to Variant 4. This is a comal or plate. It is not perfectly flat but has a slightly rounded bottom and a slightly upward curve or slant to the sides. Vessel diameters are estimated at 55 to 60 cm. These comales or plates have loop handles or lugs on the rim. There seem to have been two to a plate. They turn up slightly from the rims.

Bases on all of the bowl forms are rounded to very slightly flat-rounded. While handles were probably present on all comal forms, only a single handle was found associated with the bowl forms. This was a vertical handle placed 3.5 cm below the rim edge of a Variant 1 bowl. The handle was 6.5 cm long and 1.5 cm in diameter.

Whole, Restorable, or Partially Restorable Vessels: There were four partially restorable vessels of Lorenzo Red, pertaining, as indicated above, to form Variants 1 and 2. One of these (Cat. No. 1-227) was found with Burial 9, CV-20 (Op. No. 21(A), Level 2, Special Find 35). Another (Cat. No. 1-1211) was found associated with Feature 13 in CV-43 (Op. No. 100(B), Special Find 104).

These are described in detail above with the form descriptions.

Classificatory Comments: In the early stages of our classification some sherds of Lorenzo Red were classified with the type Casaca Striated; however, the consistency of the interior red-slip mode on these was soon detected in time to switch classification to the Lorenzo Type. In general, the identifying modes of Lorenzo defined the type fairly tightly, although one small classificatory problem did emerge. This was a confusion between a few Lorenzo rim sherds of form Variants 2 and 4 with rim edges bearing interior red pigment from the type Sepultura Unslipped.

Intrasite Locations, Contexts, and Associations: Lorenzo Red has an interesting distributional pattern. First, several vessels have been found within a burial context. This includes Cat. No. 1-1211, which was found within the tomb of Burial 24, CV-43. It was placed rim down within a corner of the tomb. Another was found in association with Burial 9, CV-20. This was another complex burial within Structure B of CV-20.

At the same time, large quantities of this type of ceramics were found in household refuse, indicating some sort of domestic function.

Longyear does not describe the type in his Copan report, or at least not to any great extent. The closest thing would be a mention under his "Coarse Ware Category" where he refers to Shallow Bowls (Longyear 1952:91, fig. 37), noting that some examples had buff-to-dark-brown exteriors, scraped and smoke-blackened, and interiors covered with an orange wash or slip. This would be closest to the Variant 4 form described above.

Intersite Locations, Contexts, and Associations: Gifford (1976:230–231) describes a type, Garbutt Creek Red, from Barton Ramie, in central Belize, that has some similarities to Lorenzo Red. The Garbutt Creek forms are open bowls or bowls with very slightly incurved rims. The interiors are red-slipped, and the exteriors are sometimes, but not always, unslipped and scraped. Garbutt Creek bowls, however, tend to be somewhat shallower than the Lorenzo examples, and the Belize type is also different in being calcite-tempered. Garbutt Creek Red is a Spanish Lookout phase type at Barton Ramie, dating to what would be Tepeu 2-3 or Late Classic, or contemporaneous to the Copan Coner phase. A further search of the Peten-Belize literature disclosed no other ceramics that resemble Lorenzo Red. Nor did a search through the Ulua-Yojoa, Chalchuapa, or Kaminaljuyu literature turn up anything.

Functional Interpretation: The abundance of the type at Copan, at least in our investigations, implies utility functions. The shallow bowls could have been used for cooking as well as serving.

Cultural Significance: Linkages of Lorenzo Red to other sites or regions appear to be few. It may be a local Copan region (type?) although the Garbutt Creek Red type from Belize suggests ties in this direction. At Copan, from the evidence at hand, it would certainly appear to be a Late Classic, Coner phase time-marker.

Sepultura Unslipped Type

Variety Name: Unspecified.
Established as a Type and/or Variety: By this description; however, Longyear (1952:92) does identify both incensarios and cache jars that are the same as this Sepultura Type.
Frequency: The present description is based upon 9,192 sherds and 19 partially restorable vessels. This is 3.3 percent of the total sherd collection from Copan under consideration in this monograph.
Ceramic Group: Sepultura.
Ceramic Complex: Coner.
Illustrations: Figures 116, 117, 118, 119, 120, 121, 122, 123, 124, 125, 126, 127, 128, 129, 130a–b, 131a–c, 132a–b, 133a–g, 134a–d, 135a–e.
Description:
Principal Identifying Modes. Sepultura vessels are made from a heavily tempered, coarse paste ware. The surfaces are rough or irregular. The ware is generally fired to a brick red color, although there is some variation in this coloring due to fire clouding and possibly post-firing secondary burning.

There are three very distinctive vessel forms subsumed under this type. Although 19 partial or whole vessels were recovered from the excavation program, much of our information comes from sherds. Therefore, we are uncertain as to how diagnostic form features of this type are associated with one another. The three most common basic forms are these:

1. large, cylindrical incensario form jars;
2. smaller cylindrical barrel-shaped forms—often with lids—which also appear to be incensarios;
3. pedestal-based shallow bowls or plates with interior prongs.

There are also three other forms, minor in frequency:

4. small jars with markedly outflared rims—buckets;
5. box forms;
6. ladle forms.

Paste, Temper, and Firing. The hardness of the surface of Sepultura vessels was found to be rather variable, ranging from 3.5 to 5.5. The paste color ranges from a primary red to black, gray, and buff, specifically 2.5 YR 5/4 to 2.5 YR 6/4. The texture of the clay particles is fine. The paste is of medium compactness. The temper for Sepultura is sand. The size of the temper is variable, and the shape of the temper ranges from subangular to fully rounded. The temper density is 25 to 50 percent.
Surface Finish and Decoration. As indicated above, surfaces of Sepultura vessels generally range from rough or bumpy to partially smoothed. The interiors of all the vessels tend to be somewhat smoother than the exteriors.

In some instances, red daubing (10 R 5/8) is evident on the surface of all the vessel forms except for the large cylindrical jars.

Form 1 large jars are ornamented with vertical flanges, solid pointed nodal projections or spikes, and a variety of low-relief modeling. Such features may or may not occur together on a single vessel. In addition to these appliqued features, broad horizontal incisions or grooves are frequently combined with the flanges and/or spikes.

Form 2 smaller jars often have small appliqued adornos affixed to the vessel wall. These adornos are tentatively identified as cacao pods. They may be either solid or hollow. They are generally about 6 cm long, 3 to 4 cm wide, and 2 cm high; however, there are some that are considerably smaller, being only half this size or less. The individual pods are fluted or grooved vertically down the middle, suggesting this cacao identification. All of the specimens observed are single pods with one exception. This exception shows two small pods attached to a common stem. In addition to these cacao pods, these smaller jars also have spikes or nodes for ornamentation. There are a few sherds with slightly more elaborate ornamentation, including button-like nodes, flutings, and hollow reed punctations. Most of these more elaborate decorations were probably part of the lid. There is one large sherd of a high-relief modeled face.

For Form 3, the pronged, shallow bowls or plates, we have only one instance of ornamentation or decoration. This is a single prong that shows three vertical ridges separated by a series of diagonal grooves or incisions. Peter Mathews (personal communication) suggests this may depict a stingray spine.

The only decoration on the Form 4 small jars is the common use of red daub paint over the entire exterior surface of the vessel.

Only one Form 5 Sepultura box was recovered in our excavations. The body of the box was without decoration other than being covered with red paint; however, the lid had two elaborately modeled projecting serpent or reptilian heads at opposite ends. These heads are painted with a white and/or blue pigment.

Only one ladle (Form 6) was recovered from the excavations. The red daub is evident over part of the hollow handle of this vessel. The only decoration is a slight upturning at the end of the handle, creating a slight upward projection. Several other vessels of this form were found during the earlier excavation programs at Copan, and generally, these show an elaboration of the end of the handle sometimes resulting in an elaborate incised or modeled serpent face.

Form. Eight complete specimens of the Form 1 large cylindrical jars were recovered from the excavations of CV-20. Their height varies from 30 to 46 cm with the majority of the vessels nearer the larger size. Orifice diameters range from 25 to 30 cm. This diameter includes a horizontally flared or everted rim, which is a characteristic feature of this form. The jars tend to bulge out slightly, starting at a point just below the rim so that at the vessel midpoint, the diameter is greater than that just below the rim; however, this midpoint diameter is not equal to the maximum orifice diameter. The bases have a slightly smaller diameter than the vessel midpoint. Two good examples with complete data are presented below.

Vessel 1-75:
Height: 46 cm
Rim diameter: 28.5 cm
Diameter below rim: 24 cm
Diameter at midpoint: 26 cm
Diameter at base: 24 cm

Vessel 1-97:

Height: 41.5 cm
Rim diameter: 24.5 cm
Diameter below rim: 23 cm
Diameter at midpoint: 24 cm
Diameter at base: 21 cm

The bases of the vessels of this form are extremely rough and thin, being not more than 1 cm in thickness. The thickness of the vessel walls ranges from 6 mm to 8 mm. The thickness of the rim is 1.5 cm.

Several of the vessels have vertical flanges. These range from 18 to 20 cm in length. They are a little over 1 cm thick, and extend out from the vessel 2.5 to 3 cm. Many of the Form 1 vessels are also decorated with nodes or spikes that appear to be solid. The diameter of these spikes at the base ranges from 3 to 4 cm, and they are 1.5 to 2.5 cm in height. These spikes terminate in a blunt, rounded point.

The flanges occur in pairs on the sides of vessels and tend to be located on roughly opposite sides of the jar. Although, they are usually situated more toward the front or decorated side. This decoration, including the applique, modeling, and spikes, is located within the field between the flanges. This front side of the vessel, as defined by the flanges and/or other decoration, consists of about one-third of the vessel circumference; the remaining surface may be left plain. Spikes or nodes are generally placed in vertical rows. Sometimes, these spikes are located in a single vertical row down the middle of the vessel between the flanges; at other times, they are in multiple rows on the sides or back of the jars.

Two complete specimens of the smaller jar, Form 2, offer good details about this form. They measure in height, respectively, 21.9 cm (Cat. No. 1-356) and 13.8 cm (Cat. No. 1-213). The orifice diameters are 27.7 (Cat. No. 1-356) and 19 cm (Cat. No. 1-213), and the basal diameters are 21 cm (Cat. No. 1-356) and 13 cm (Cat. No. 1-213). Both these vessels have a bucket form with a markedly everted rim. The fairly large sherd collection representing this form generally conforms to the descriptions of the two vessels above.

Modeled ornamentation for Form 2, as mentioned above, is most commonly in the form of the cacao pod adornos. On one of the whole specimens (Cat. No. 1-213), there are four of these pods, one on each of the four sides of the vessel, just below the rim. The other complete specimen (Cat. No. 1-356) is decorated with spikes. These are arranged in three fields, each field extending from lip to base. The individual fields comprise three vertical rows of spikes with five spikes in each row. The spikes measure 2.5 cm in diameter at the base, and they are 2 to 2.5 cm in height.

Both of the complete Form 2 specimens have lids, and it appears from the sherd collection that this is a common accompanying feature of this vessel form type. These lids most commonly have a subconical or scutate form. Frequently, they have close-spaced, deep scorings running parallel to the rim of the lid. Quite possibly, these scorings were to steady the lid as it rested on the edge of the vessel orifice. Some lids have cacao pod adornos on the sloping sides of the lids and, in one case (Cat. No. 1-213), there is a loop handle on top of the lid.

There are other lid forms, including those that appear to be flatter or only slightly rounded on top. This form often has slight projections (often three in number) resulting in an approximate rounded triangular shape. The top of one such lid has been stippled with closed space and small circular or hollow reed punctations. Other variations in lid form include plain dome shapes and conical shapes with upward-pointing leaf-like projections. These last may be effigy plant representations, perhaps symbolic of a cacao tree, which would be a continuation of the same symbolism seen in the pod representations. (See Longyear 1952: fig. 114a.) It might even be possible to extend the cacao tree interpretation further and argue, as Julie Benyo does (1978), that the spikes on these vessels represent the spikes on the limbs and trunk of the cacao tree.

All of the lids probably had openings or holes in them. In the truncated conical form, the holes appear to have been punched through the sloping sides. For the flat or slightly rounded form, they were placed on the vertical sides or edges; and for those with the elaborate conical projections or superimposed effigy adornos, the holes were probably in the projecting adornos, as well as in the top and sides of the lid.

The third major form of the Sepultura type is the pronged pedestal bowl. Lacking whole specimens, we are uncertain of the number of prongs attached to each vessel; three seems the most likely, although possibly there were four. The bases of these bowls measure 4 to 5 cm in height and 10 to 20 cm in diameter. All flare outward slightly from the point of their attachment to the bowl to their bases. The bowls themselves are shallow (7–8 cm deep) with widely sloping sides. Interiors are smoothed and almost invariably smudged or clouded black or gray. Exteriors, including the underside of the bowl and the outer and inner sides of the pedestal, are left extremely rough. They show no evidence of blackening or fire-clouding.

The prongs—which are one of the diagnostics of this form—are placed on the interiors of the bowls, usually less than 1 cm below the lip. They vary in size, with lengths ranging from 7 to 11 cm, basal diameters from 4 to 7.5 cm, and pointed-end diameters from 1 to 3 cm. All of the prongs are hollow, and their openings on the undersides of the bowls may vary, according to the prong sizes, from 2 to 6 cm. There is also a small opening at the pointed end of each prong. In many instances, we found a thin red wash on the surfaces of the prongs, and this wash extended to the edges of the rims of the bowls to which the prongs were attached; however, there is no evidence that the red wash covered the entire bowl interior, nor did it occur on vessel exteriors. The exteriors of the prongs almost always showed evidence of fire-clouding. Some prongs show such clouding all around the surface; in others, the two lateral sides show such discoloration, but the side toward the bowl rim and the opposite side do not. In no case did we see fire-clouding on the interiors of the hollow prongs.

Form 4, the small or bucket-shape, ranges from 6.5 to 8 cm in height, from 10.5 to 11.5 cm in orifice diameter, from 8.5 to 9 cm in body diameter, and from 7 to 7.5 cm in basal diameter. Four were recovered from our excavations. These were plain except for thin red pigment on some.

Form 5 is the box shape. We found one. It is roughly square and has a loosely fitted detachable lid. As mentioned in our descriptions of decoration, two reptilian or serpent heads adorn the lid.

Form 6 is a ladle, of which we found one example. Its basin portion measures 19.5 cm at the orifice, narrowing to 8.5 cm at the base. The interior of this dipper or basin is smoothed and shows smudging. The handle is a hollow tube projecting horizontally from the basin and opening into the upper wall of the basin. Length of the handle is 15 cm. Its end is open and upturned. Its surface has been partially smoothed and daubed with a red wash.

Whole, Restorable, and Partially Restorable Vessels: We recovered 19 whole, restorable, or partially restorable vessels of the type, and several of these have already been described by us under decoration and form categories; however, we also offer the following complete inventory list.

1. Cat. No. 1-75 (fig. 116), CV-20, Operation 4(K), Special Find 11. A large cylindrical vessel of the Form 1 shape. On one side of the vessel are low-relief modeled ridges (see drawing for details of design). The upper portion of both, extending about 12 cm down from the rim, is smudged or burned. Vessel dimensions: height, 46 cm; rim diameter, 28.5 cm; diameter just below rim, 24 cm; midpoint diameter, 26 cm; basal diameter, 24.3 cm.

2. Cat. No. 1-92 (fig. 117), CV-20, Operation 6(I), Special Find 13. This is another cylinder vessel of Form Type 1, with an outflared rim. Burning or smudging is evident on its upper portions, extending 18 cm below the rim on the exterior and 25 cm on the interior. The interior base shows no evidence of smudging. About three-quarters of the surface of the vessel is decorated. There are two fields of small spikes (2 cm in length and 2 cm in width) located on approximately opposite sides of the vessel. These fields each consist of five vertical rows of spikes, starting just below the rim and extending down almost to the base. The rows are about 5 cm apart. On one side, there are 59 spikes—four rows with 12 spikes and one row with only 11; on the opposite, there are 58 spikes—three rows of 11, one row of 12, and one row of 13. One area between the two fields of spikes has been left plain; on the other side, there is a low-relief "key-hole" figure. Vessel dimensions: height, 41.2 cm; rim diameter, 26 cm; diameter below rim, 20.5 cm; diameter at midpoint of vessel, 22.5 cm; diameter at base, 20 cm.

3. Cat. No. 1-97 (fig. 118), CV-20, Operation 6(I), Special Find 14. This is another Form 1 cylinder vessel with an outflared rim. Burning or smudging is seen only on the upper portions of the vessel, extending down about 10 to 15 cm on the exterior and 15 to 20 cm on the interior. About one-third of the exterior surface is decorated, the decorated area being démarcated by two long vertical flanges. The flanges are 28 cm long and extend out from the vessel wall about 2.5 cm. The decorated area is further framed by two low horizontal ridges that connect the flanges at the top and bottom. The decoration consists of six spike-like nubs or nodes placed vertically and equidistant from each other between the two flanges. Each node is about 3.5 cm in diameter and extends out 2.5 to 3 cm from the vessel wall. The nodes are separated by five horizontal incised lines, imperfectly drawn. Vessel dimensions: height, 41.5 cm; rim diameter, 24.5 cm; diameter below rim, 23 cm; diameter at midpoint of vessel, 24 cm; diameter at base, 21 cm.

4. Cat. No. 1-109 (fig. 119), CV-20, Operation 6(J), Special Find 16. Another partially restored vessel of Form 1 with a straight rim and an outwardly beveled lip. Smudging and burning is seen on both the upper half of the exterior and interior walls. There is also some blackening or burning on the interior base of the vessel. The decoration consists of eight vertical rows of nubbin spikes, each spike being about 2.5 to 3 cm in diameter, rounded on the end, and 1.5 cm high. The rows of spikes are from 10 to 20 cm apart. The five spikes in each row are spaced vertically at intervals of 5 to 7 cm. Vessel dimensions: height, 34.5 cm; rim diameter, approximately 31 cm; diameter below rim, 25 cm; diameter at midpoint of vessel, 25 cm; diameter at base, 22 cm.

5. Cat. No. 1-117 (fig. 120), CV-20, Operation 6(J), Special Find 19. Another vessel of Form 1 with the upper third of the exterior wall of the vessel, including the rim, fire-smudged and blackened. On the interior, the upper half of the wall shows evidence of smudging. The decoration is very similar to Vessel 1-97, being defined by two pronounced vertical flanges. It consists of six horizontal incised lines over which a column of six spikes had been placed. The spikes are 3 cm in diameter

and 5 cm in height, each tapering to a point and each being scored with one of the six incised lines. On each side of the column of spikes are thin appliqued strips, forming a serpentine design that extends the length of the column of spikes. Vessel dimensions: height, 33.8 cm; rim diameter, 24.7 cm; diameter at midpoint of vessel, 22.7 cm; diameter at base, 22.5 cm.

6. Cat. No. 1-120 (fig. 121), CV-20, Operation 6(K), Special Find 18. Another cylinder vessel with outflared rim of Form 1. There is evidence of burning or smudging on the upper sections of both interior and exterior walls. This blackened area covers the top 10 cm of the vessel. The decoration is framed by two vertical flanges, with low raised ridges connecting these flanges at the top and bottom. Three incised lines, equidistantly spaced, run horizontally across the vessel, extending from one flange to the other. Four spikes are located in a vertical column equidistant between the two flanges. Each spike is about 3.5 cm in diameter, 4.5 cm in height, and pointed. Vessel dimensions: height, 42 cm; rim diameter, 28 cm; diameter below rim, 24 cm; diameter at base, 23 cm.

7. Cat. No. 1-131 (fig. 122), CV-20, Operation 6(M), Special Find 20. A large cylinder with outflared rim of Form 1. It is similar in form and decoration to the two previously described vessels. Again, smudging occurs on only the upper few centimeters of the interior wall of the vessel. The decoration covers about one-third of the surface and is framed by two vertically placed flanges that are connected at both the top and bottom by low appliqued ridges. A vertical column of six spikes is located equidistant between the flanges. Each spike is 5 cm in diameter and 3 cm in height, and they are separated from each other by five evenly drawn, deep, broad, horizontal incised lines that extend across the decorated area of the vessel and onto the edges of the flanges. Vessel dimensions: height, 40.5 cm; rim diameter, 28 cm; diameter below rim, 23.5 cm; diameter at base, 24 cm.

8. Cat. No. 1-140 (fig. 123), CV-20, Operation 6(M), Special Find 23. A large Form 1 vessel very similar to those described above. There is smudging or burning on the upper 7 to 9 cm of both surfaces of the vessel. The decorated area has the two defining vertical flanges, with the basal ends of the flanges connected by a low appliqued ridge. A vertical column of spikes is located equidistant between the flanges. The spikes are 5 cm in diameter, 2.5 cm high, and slightly pointed. Estimated vessel dimensions: height, 30 cm; rim diameter, 26 cm; base diameter, 23.5 cm.

9. Cat. No. 1-213 (fig. 124), CV-20, Operation 19(C), Special Find 25. Unlike all the vessels described above, Cat. No. 1-213 is a smaller jar with a lid and fits into Form 2. This vessel was found as part of a cache within the fill of Structure A, CV-20. Similar to the other Sepultura vessels, it also has smudging near the rim and on the exterior upper vessel wall. The basic shape is bucket-like, with an everted rim. There are four small lugs, probably representations of cacao pods, equidistantly spaced on the vessel walls just below the everted rim. These lugs measure 4 cm in length, 2.5 cm in width, and 3 cm in height. Vessel dimensions: height, 13.8 cm; orifice diameter, including flange at rim, 19 cm; diameter at base, 13 cm.

This vessel also has a lid. It is scutate in form and has a loop handle and three cacao pod lugs, identical to those on the vessel wall, placed equidistantly around its sides. There are also three holes, each about 2 cm in diameter, which were punched out from the inside before firing. The loop handle arches over the top, spanning from one side to the other. This handle is 2.4 cm in diameter, and the loop is wide enough for all four fingers of the hand to be inserted through it. The lid has some fire-clouding spots on both the interior and exterior, although this appears to be clouding from the original firing and not from use as an incensario. Lid dimensions: height, 10 cm including the handle; diameter at base, 21.2 cm; diameter at top, 11 cm.

10. Cat. No. 1-249, CV-20, Operation 19(C), Special Find 51. This partial vessel is a large fragment of a Form 1 large cylinder. It shows no decoration.

11. Cat. No. 1-303 (fig. 125), CV-20, Operation 19(F), Special Find 66. This is the one ladle, Form 6, recovered from the excavations. It has been described in detail above.

12. Cat. No. 1-356 (fig. 126), Site #1975-216, Operation 3, Special Find 1. This vessel was found during the renovation of a street within the modern village of Copan. It was found below what appears to have been a pre-Columbian paved area. It is a bucket-shaped jar (Form 4) with an outflared rim and lip and a high scutate lid. Decoration consists of three fields of nubbin spikes. Each field extends from the lip to the base, is about 10.5 cm in width, and has three vertical columns of spikes with five spikes in each column. The spikes are about 2 to 2.5 cm in height and about 2.5 cm in width at the base. Vessel dimensions: height, 21.9 cm; rim diameter, 27.7 cm; diameter at base, 21 cm. The lid also has a spike decoration, with three fields of nine spikes each on the lid sides and at least one spike on the top. The lid top had also been perforated with several holes, each 2.5 cm in diameter. The original number of these holes could not be determined because of breakage. The height of the lid was approximately 8 cm.

13. Cat. No. 1-626 (fig. 127), CV-43, Operation 37(N). This is a partial barrel-shaped vessel (Form 2). Only the body and base are intact. The walls are outflaring and had two appliqued lugs probably of the cacao pod shape. Diameter at the base was approximately 10 cm.

14. Cat. No. 1-671 (fig. 128), CV-43, Operation 33(FF), Special Find 20. A small bucket-shaped vessel that formed one side of a lip-to-lip cache (with Special Find 21, which was completely eroded) found under the plaza of CV-43. It is a very rough and coarsely made vessel with no surface decoration. It has been fired to a salmon-red color with no evidence of a slip or wash. Vessel dimensions: height, 9 cm; rim diameter, 13.5 cm; diameter at base, 7 cm.

15. Cat. No. 1-751, Operation 37(O), CV-43, Level 1. This is a small section of what appears to be the upper portion of a Sepultura Unslipped lid. There appears to be a leaf-like design at the very top, and there are holes cut out on the side of the lid—as if to allow smoke or incense to escape.

16. Cat. No. 1-809, Operation 33(GG), CV-43, Special Find 28. This is a small basal portion of a Sepultura Unslipped large cylindrical vessel. No prongs or spikes are in evidence. Only part of a ring-base is visible with this fragment.

17. Cat. No. 1-970 (fig. 129), Operation 104(A), CV-43, Level 2. This is a square cache vessel with lid that was recovered from the fill of Structure A, CV-43. The square cache box is 17.25 cm per side. Each side appears to have been made individually and then joined, roughly, at the edges. The lid of this box is rather elaborate. It also measures about 17.25 cm square and has an elaborately modeled serpent head at each end. The modeled heads show fine details of the eyes, mouth, and fangs. They are unslipped but have evidence of blue paint (unfired) on the surface. The rest of the lid and the surface of the box reveal a fine polished red finish on the exterior, although the interior surfaces of both were left unpolished.

18. Cat. No. 1-1079 (fig. 130a), Operation 102(A), CV-43, Special Find 56. This is a very small, simple cup-like vessel (probably a small cache vessel) with a markedly outflared rim. The paste and surface decoration fit the Sepultura Unslipped type. There is some evidence of smudging around the sides of the vessel. Vessel dimensions: height, 6.6 cm; orifice diameter, 11.2 cm; body diameter, 8.8 cm; basal diameter, 7.5 cm.

19. Cat. No. 1-1080 (fig. 130b), Operation 102(A), CV-43, Special Find 57. This is the companion cache vessel to that described above, Cat. No.1-1079. Vessel dimensions: height, 7.5 cm; orifice diameter, 10.9 cm; body diameter, 8.5 cm; basal diameter, 7 cm.

Classificatory Comments: Sepultura is a distinctive type, based upon its ware qualities, thickness of vessel walls, surface decorations, and overall appearance.

Intrasite Locations, Contexts, and Associations: The Sepultura Type was found throughout the excavation proveniences within the studied Copan groups.

All eight whole specimens of the large, cylindrical, incensario form (Form 1) were recovered at CV-20. Seven of them were found in direct association with Structure A, CV-20: 1-92, 1-97, 1-109, 1-117, 1-120, 1-131, and 1-140. Six were along the back wall, embedded into the ground surface below the activity or ground level of occupation. Careful excavation revealed that a small area of dirt around the rim of the vessel had been burned and hardened. This burning is reflected in the darkening of the upper wall portions of the embedded vessels, as referred to in the above descriptions.

One specimen of Form 2, the smaller barrel-shaped form, was found in situ as part of a cache of diorite rubbing and polishing stones and a miniature table. This cache was located below the floor of the main room of Structure A, CV-20. The other whole vessel of this form was also found beneath an apparent house floor, although it was recovered as part of a salvage operation within the village of modern Copan. The form, with its lids, seems likely to have been associated with household rituals, perhaps serving as an incense burner.

The pronged, pedestalled bowls (Form 3) were not found in situ within any of our excavations. Little information is therefore available as to the distribution of this form.

Form 4, the small jars or buckets, appear to be small cache vessels that form the fairly common lip-to-lip caches within the Maya area. Several of these vessels were found under the floor of the plaza of CV-43 in front of Structure A.

The cache box, Form 5, was found broken within the fill of Structure A, CV-43. It may have been broken as part of a dedicatory ceremony during the construction of this building, since most of the pieces were in close proximity to one another.

Finally, the one ladle (Form 6) recovered in the excavations (1-303) was recovered on the floor of one of the rooms on the surface of Structure A, CV-20. It was not associated with any other artifacts or materials.

Sepultura Unslipped correlates strongly with Copador Polychrome, Don Gordon Modeled-carved, Tipon Orange-brown, Masica Incised, Raul Red, Casaca Striated, and Lorenzo Red. There is a weak correlation with other Coner types, however, including Babilonia Polychrome,

Caterpillar Polychrome, Claudio Incised, Tasu fluted, and Reina Incised. There are also correlations with two Cueva types: Gualpopa Polychrome and Cementerio Incised.

Intersite Locations, Contexts, and Associations: Incense burners or incensarios, to which our type, Sepultura Unslipped, largely pertains, are common Maya ceramic forms, in both the lowlands and the highlands.

Our Form 1, the tall cylinder with appliqued spike and flange decorations, has some general but no specific similarities to large incensarios found in the Maya lowlands proper. The latter are much more complex in decoration and design than the ones we found at Copan. For instance, they often incorporate human elements (see, for examples, specimens from Palenque, as shown by Barbara Rands and Robert L. Rands [1959]).

It is with our Form 2, the smaller, barrel-shaped modifications of the cylinder shape, that we find more similarities in other sites. Some, as we have seen, have spiked decorations and associated lids. This Form 2 is found at Quirigua, where Benyo (1978) describes such Late Classic jars with spike and cacao pod features, as well as accompanying lids. Elsewhere within the Southeast Region, there are such Late Classic incensarios with spikes and flanges at Los Naranjos in Honduras (Baudez and Becquelin 1973). At Quelepa, in eastern El Salvador, Andrews (1976) defined a Late Classic censer that he named Lolotique Spiked. To the west, the type seems to be missing from the Late Classic complex at Chalchuapa (Sharer 1978), but it is present further west at Kaminaljuyu (Wetherington 1978b) in Middle and Late Classic contexts—or slightly earlier than the Copan occurrences. In the Peten lowlands, the Form 2 incensario has an approximate match with the vessels of the type Miseria Applique at Seibal (Sabloff 1975), occurring there toward the end of the Late Classic (Bayal phase of Tepeu 3 time level).

The pedestal-bowl shape with the interior prongs, our Form 3, recalls the three-pronged incense burners that Stephan F. de Borhegyi (1950, 1951a, 1951b, 1951c) has described from the Maya highlands and elsewhere within the southeast Maya region. The ones he describes date to the Late Preclassic and the Early Classic periods. His are cylindrical with three prongs on the top of the vessel. A large bowl or plate was probably placed on the prongs to create the final working incense burner. Our Copan Form 3 incense burners do not duplicate those described by Borhegyi. Ours are pedestal bowls rather than cylinders and have the prongs on the interiors of the bowls; still, we think the Copan form was also used with a plate or bowl placed on top of the prongs. Our Copan Form 3 has a close match with a pedestalled and pronged bowl from Uaxactun, one that R. E. Smith (1955) refers to as a "bowl with inner-inverted feet." At Uaxactun, this specimen dates to the Early Classic period. The type is reported from Quirigua (Benyo 1978), where it occurs contemporaneously with the Late Classic Form 2 in the Quirigua Cacaguat ceramic group.

The Copan pottery cache box, our one representative of Form 5, seems rare within the Maya area in general; however, one was found at Quirigua in the early excavations at that site by Edgar L. Hewett.

Form 4, the ladle, occurs in the Maya highlands and lowlands and also in the southeast region. Sabloff (1975) describes such a form within the Miseria Applique type of the Late Classic Bayal phase at Seibal in the Peten; Dora de Gonzalez and Wetherington (1978) define a similar ladle from Kaminaljuyu, in the Guatemalan highlands, where the form dates anywhere from the Middle Classic into the Postclassic periods. They are also present at Los Naranjos, in Honduras, during the Late Classic (Baudez and Becquelin 1973) and also from Quirigua (Benyo 1978).

Cultural Significance: The widespread distribution of the incensario form—vessels of a generally rough-surfaced ware but with flanges, spikes, prongs, and other forms of modeled decoration—seems to characterize the entire Maya area, lowlands and highlands as well as that territory we refer to as the southeast Maya region (which includes parts of the Maya lowlands and highlands as well as substantial portions of western Honduras). There are indications that some incensario forms date back as early as the Late Preclassic and Early Classic in the Guatemalan highlands and at least as early as the Early Classic in the Peten lowlands. For Copan, however, the earliest occurrences appear to be in the Late Classic period.

Functional Interpretation: It is obvious that not all of our six vessel forms of the Sepultura Unslipped ceramic type served as incensarios or incense burners. Almost certainly, Forms 2 (the barrel-shaped cylinder with the lid), 3 (the pedestal-based shallow bowl with the interior prongs), and 6 (the ladle) did so serve. Form 1 (the tall cylinder with an incensario-like shape) is also likely to have been used for some special burning functions. On the other hand, Form 5 (the cache box), gives no indication of having been so employed, and all the contextual evidence we have for Form 4 (the small, bucket-shaped vessel) suggests that it, too, was used as a cache receptacle.

RESIDUAL TYPES

In pottery classification, residual types are usually plain, unslipped wares that, indeed, may constitute valid types; however, it is frequently the case that numerous plain and unslipped vessel portions of various related slipped or decorated types are classified as sherds into the plain, unslipped type. There is one such plain, unslipped pottery type in our Copan collection and our classification of this collection: Lysandro Unslipped. It probably has some validity as a type. That is, we are convinced that there were complete vessels that, if we had been fortunate enough to have found whole, we would have classified as Lysandro Unslipped. But it is also a residual category, for we are equally certain that plain and unslipped body sherds (especially basal sherds) and plain and unslipped handles from such types as Masica Incised, Casaca Striated, Raul Red, and others have also been classified as Lysandro Unslipped. This situation is not uncommon in large-scale classification of potsherds.

Lysandro Unslipped Type

Variety Name: Unspecified.

Established as a Type and/or Variety: By this description. This is a very tentative definition (see "Classificatory Comments").

Frequency: 53,880 sherds or 19.5 percent of the entire collection of sherds recovered by our project. This total is probably *greatly* inflated by inclusion of eroded sherds, unslipped bottoms, handles, and body sherds from various decorated types into this plain unslipped ware type.

Ceramic Group: Lysandro (See "Classificatory Comments").

Ceramic Complex: Primarily Coner, although some material so classified may be earlier.

Illustrations: None.

Description:

Principal Identifying Modes.

1. An unslipped coarse surface without decoration;
2. large jars with short collars or necks.

Paste, Temper, and Firing. These criteria are much like those of the type Casaca Striated. Paste cores are usually fired to a dark gray, and one or both surfaces to a buff or gray-buff. Sand and pumice are the tempering materials. There is considerable variation in density or compactness of paste. Surface hardness ranges from 2 to 3.5 or, occasionally, higher.

Surface Finish and Decoration. Surfaces, both interior and exterior, have been smoothed by scraping or smooth-wiping; however, they remain coarse and sandy to the touch, with temper particles frequently extruding through onto the surface.

Form. Large storage jars with short necks or collars are the most common. Smaller jars and deep cauldron-like bowls are also represented. Large loop handles are present. These are of a size, and a size range, comparable to that for the type Casaca Striated. Most of these were probably oriented horizontally on the vessel. Vessel bases are round-flat and round-indented. Little indented or impressed button-like nodes appear on some vessels. These were placed high on the vessel shoulders.

Whole, Restorable, or Partially Restorable Vessels: None recovered.

Classificatory Comments: A disproportionately large number of basal and handle sherds were classified into Lysandro Unslipped, and, conversely, relatively few rim sherds were so tabulated. This makes it virtually certain that plain and unslipped bases, handles, and other sherds from slipped, decorated, or otherwise surface-treated types (such as Casaca Striated) were classified as Lysandro Unslipped. At the same time, as we have stated in the residual introductory section above, we are reasonably sure that Lysandro Unslipped is a valid type and was represented by some complete vessels.

Intrasite Locations, Contexts, and Associations: Material that has been classified as Lysandro Unslipped was common in most of the proveniences within our excavations. The strongest associational correlations of this type are with Coner phase types such as Babilonia Polychrome, Caterpillar Polychrome, Copador Polychrome, Tasu fluted, Don Gordon Modeled-carved, Tipon Orange-brown, Masica Incised, Raul Red, Lorenzo Red, and Sepultura Unslipped.

It appears, from his descriptions, that Longyear found sherds of Lysandro Unslipped at Copan (Longyear 1952:89–92). Certainly, his general designation of Coarse Ware includes large collared jars that fit our projected image of the type; however, Longyear does not specify that such vessels had completely plain, unslipped surfaces.

Intersite Locations, Contexts, and Associations: Unslipped plain wares are found throughout the Maya lowlands in Late Classic contexts, a situation that increases the possibility that Lysandro Unslipped, from Copan, is, indeed, a true or valid type. Cambio Unslipped is such a type, found at Uaxactun (Smith and Gifford 1966), at Altar de Sacrificios (Adams 1971:18), and at Seibal (Sabloff 1975:153–155). At Barton Ramie, Gifford (1976:276–287) describes three plain unslipped types: Alexanders, Cayo, and Humes Bank. Some of the vessels of these types have little punched appliqued nodes on jar or bowl shoulders, generally similar to such node features seen on sherds we have classified as Lysandro Unslipped from Copan.

Functional Interpretation: Utility water or storage vessels.

Cultural Significance: While close historical relationships are not necessarily implied by similarities seen in unslipped plain, striated, or coarse red-slipped wares found throughout the Maya lowlands, as well as at Copan, we suggest a basic common tradition.

COMPARATIVE PERSPECTIVES ON CERAMICS: A SUMMARY

In our excavations in the several structures of the Las Sepulturas residential zone of Copan, we encountered a very few sherds that we identified as belonging to the Preclassic Uir phase (900–400 B.C.). As the structures we were exploring dated to the Classic period Acbi, Cueva, and Coner phases—or from a time span of about A.D. 400 to 1000—we have assumed that the sherds typologically identified as pertaining to the Uir phase were from earlier refuse that had been used in the fill of the later constructions. The Uir phase, along with the Early Preclassic Rayo (1100–900 B.C.) and Gordon (900–600 B.C.) phases, is documented from the research of other archaeologists who have been working at Copan (see Webster 1988). It is our understanding that, in general, the ceramics of all of these early phases bear resemblances to similarly dated early complexes found elsewhere in southern Mesoamerica (e.g., Chiapas, the southern Gulf lowlands of Mexico, and the Ulua Valley of Honduras); however, we have little direct knowledge of this material, which was scantily represented in our diggings.

In chronological order, the next ceramic phase at Copan is the Chabij (400 B.C.–A.D. 100), which corresponds to the Late Preclassic period. The Pacheco Zoned Bichrome type of the phase would seem to continue this kind of decoration from the preceding Middle Preclassic phases, and, along with monochrome incised types, to relate to the ceramics of western and central Honduras and eastern El Salvador and to what is known as the Uapala ceramic sphere.

Later, in the Bijac phase (A.D. 100–400), Copan Uapala sphere ceramics show strong western El Salvadoran and Guatemalan highland influences, especially in the inception of an Usulutan painting tradition, beginning with the type Povmec Red-on-orange, and continuing with the very distinctive type Izalco Usulutan. Izalco became a dominant painted ware in the succeeding Acbi phase (A.D. 400–600) of the latter part of the Early Classic period. The Usulutan, or resist-painted, decoration was then amazingly persistent at Copan, lasting well into the Cueva phase (A.D. 600–700), or into the beginnings of the Late Classic period.

During the Acbi and Cueva phases, there was a balanced interaction among the three ceramic traditions at Copan: (1) the old Honduran–eastern Salvadoran Uapala patterns; (2) the Usulutan-dominated strains from the western El Salvador and the Guatemalan highlands; and (3) the Maya lowlands. The types Cementerio Incised, Mapache Grooved, Arroyo Red, and Antonio Buff are representative of the first of these traditions. By and large, these are monochromes or more simply decorated vessels, generally vessels of large-to-medium size and of an apparent utilitarian purpose. The Maya highlands of the second tradition are represented by the strong Usulutan continuity, by Izalco Usulutan, Chilanga Red-painted Usulutan, and related positive painted types such as Prospero Red-on-buff, Chitam Red-on-cream, Adan Red-on-buff, and Gualpopa Red-painted. It is to be noted, of course, that the Honduran–eastern Salvadoran Uapala sphere was also influenced early on—back as early as the Late Preclassic—by this western Salvadoran–Guatemalan Maya highland Usulutan tradition so the lines of relationships, and influences and counter-influences are complex as we try to trace them out. The Maya lowlands of the third tradition are represented rather weakly by such types as Melano Carved in the Acbi phase; but by Cueva times this line of influence had grown much stronger with Molanphy Modeled-carved and the Tipon-Capulin finely finished wares.

In the Coner phase the old Honduran–Salvadoran tradition still continues in such types as Reina Incised, Masica Incised, and Raul Red—in general, utility-type wares. Lowland Maya influence is seen in a number of ways. Don Gordon Modeled-carved continues the idea of modeled-carved glyphic or glyph-like decoration of fine ware vessel surfaces. But Casaca Striated, a type largely devoted to coarse-finished large water jars, seems to be either Peten-derived or with very close parallels in the Maya lowlands proper. Sepultura Unslipped is made up, to a large extent, of rough-finished and modeled incensarios, and these vessels at Copan rather closely resemble lowland Maya counterparts. Classic Maya polychromy is seen reflected in three ways at Copan:

(1) in crude imitations, such as Caterpillar Polychrome; (2) in the form of Ulua Valley Babilonia Polychrome (or Ulua Polychrome), which is a distinctive northwest Honduran reflection of Maya polychrome traditions; and (3) most important of all (at least in terms of volume of the product), in the handsome Copador Polychrome, almost certainly a type originating at Copan (or in the Copan Valley). Its prototypes are surely Classic Maya polychromes, with glyphs or pseudoglyphs, human or grotesque figures, and monkeys, and, we think, such an Usulutan tradition type as the immediately antecedent Gualpopa Polychrome. Gualpopa does not have an actual Usulutan or resist-painted ground color, but it is orange-slipped and painted with positive red and black designs, including some life-form figures. It died out in popularity at Copan just as Copador increased in vogue, and there can be little doubt but that Gualpopa is the immediate antecedent of Copador. In a sense, it represents the last contribution of the Maya highland tradition to Copan ceramics, which by Coner times are now more strongly influenced by the Maya lowlands, although, to a great extent, Copan pottery now might be thought of as sui generis.

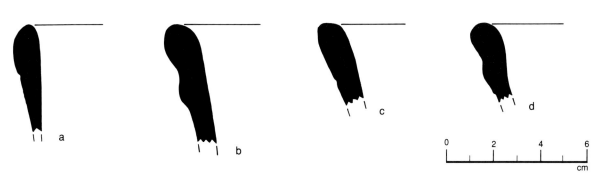

Figure 8a–d. Uir phase profiles (Scale for drawings throughout the book is 1:1, unless otherwise noted.)

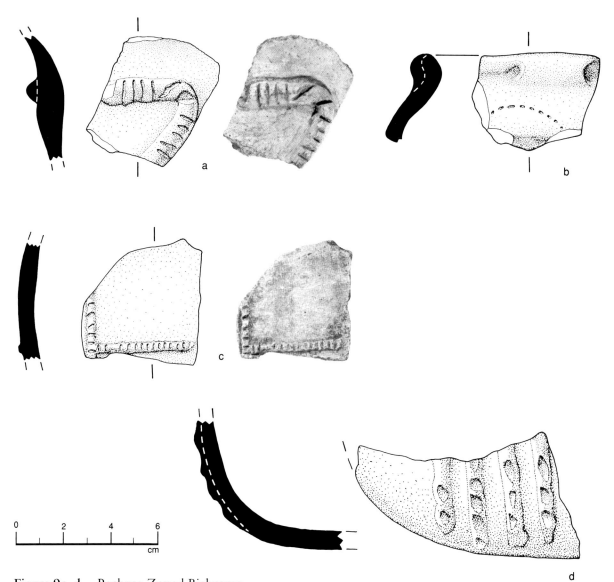

Figure 9a–d. Pacheco Zoned Bichrome

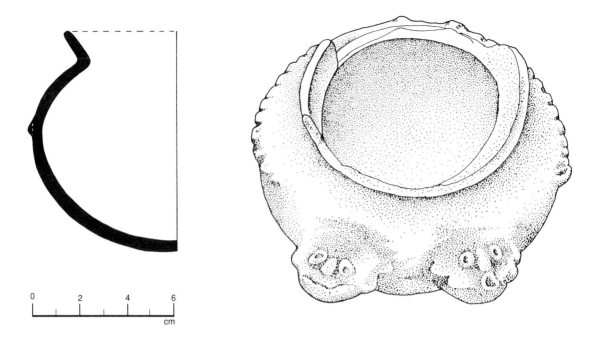

Figure 10. Pacheco Zoned Bichrome 1-1016

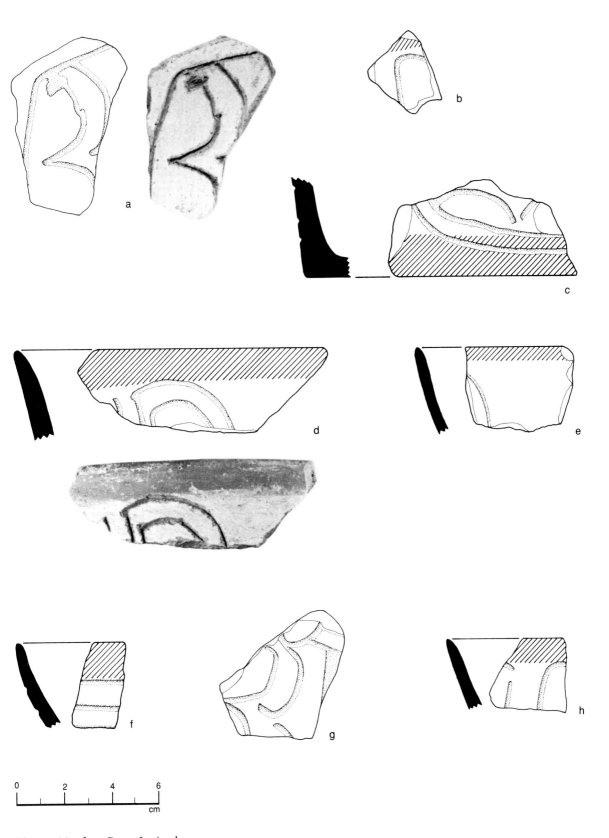

Figure 11a–h. Bozo Incised

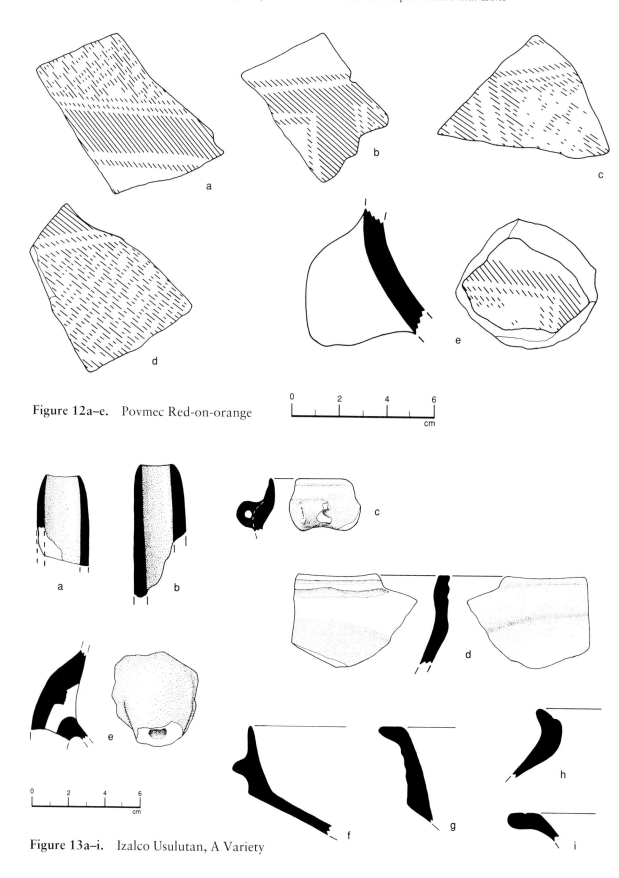

Figure 12a–e.   Povmec Red-on-orange

Figure 13a–i.   Izalco Usulutan, A Variety

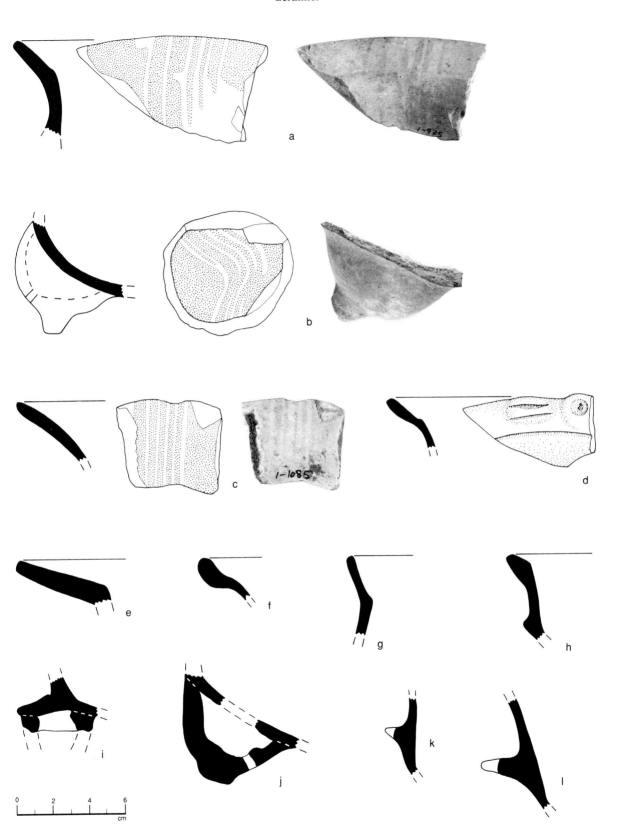

Figure 14a–l. Izalco Usulutan, B Variety

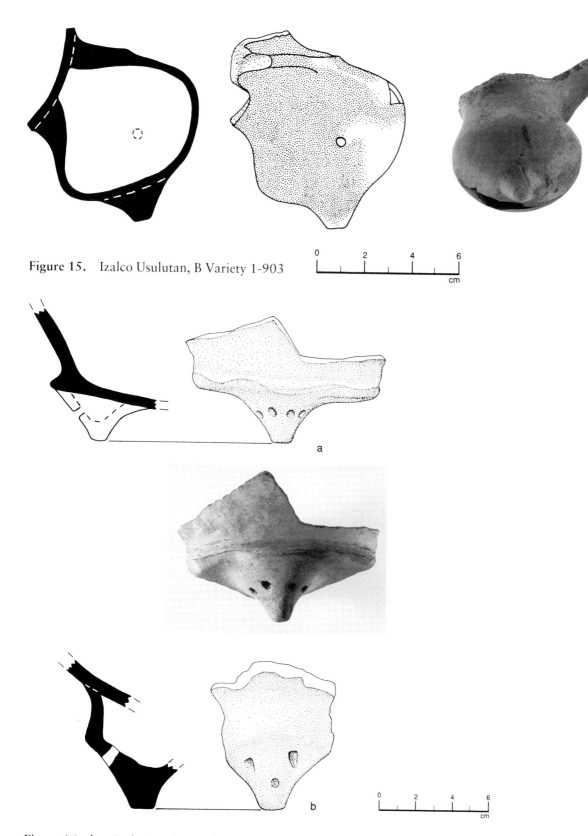

Figure 15.   Izalco Usulutan, B Variety 1-903

Figure 16a–b.   Izalco Usulutan, C Variety

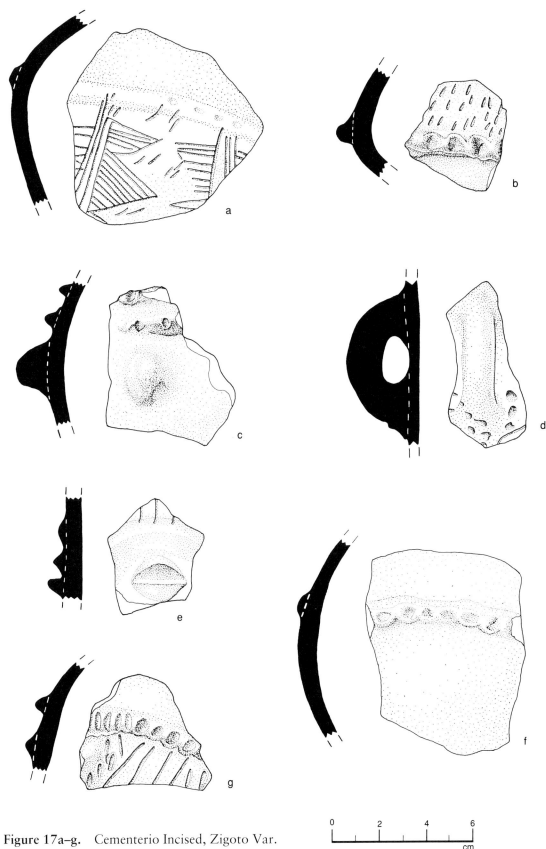

Figure 17a–g. Cementerio Incised, Zigoto Var.

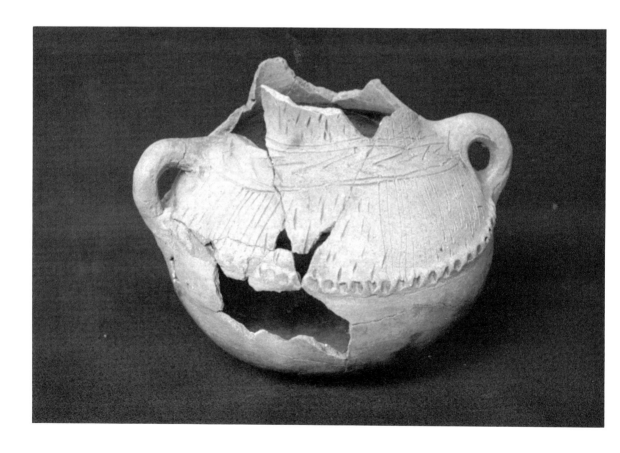

Figure 18.   Cementerio Incised, Zigoto Var. 1-672

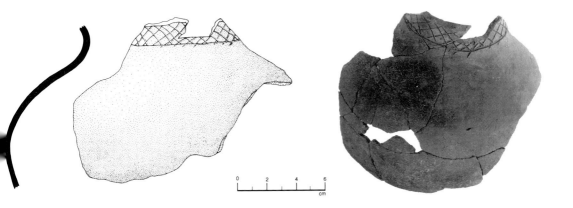

Figure 19. Cementerio Incised, Zigoto Var. 1-306

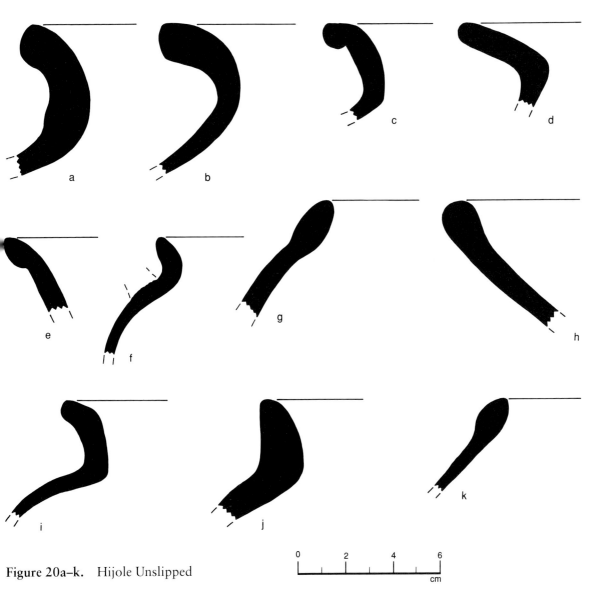

Figure 20a–k. Hijole Unslipped

Figure 21a–j.   Prospero Red-on-buff

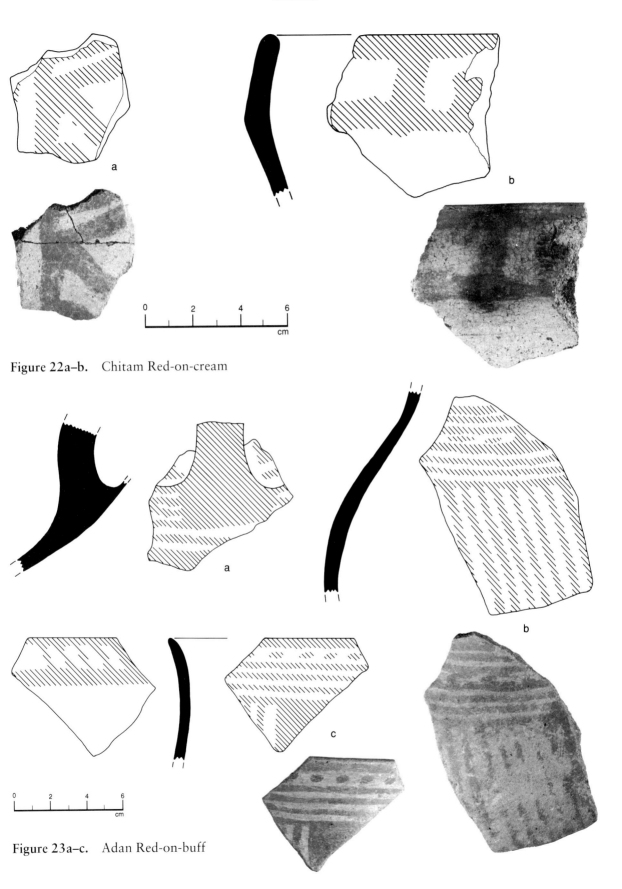

Figure 22a–b. Chitam Red-on-cream

Figure 23a–c. Adan Red-on-buff

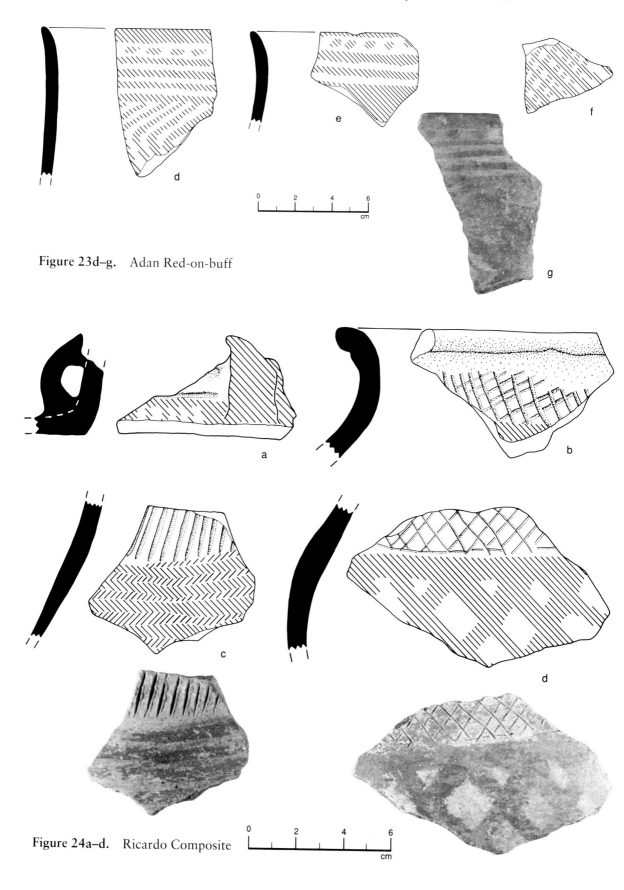

Figure 23d–g.   Adan Red-on-buff

Figure 24a–d.   Ricardo Composite

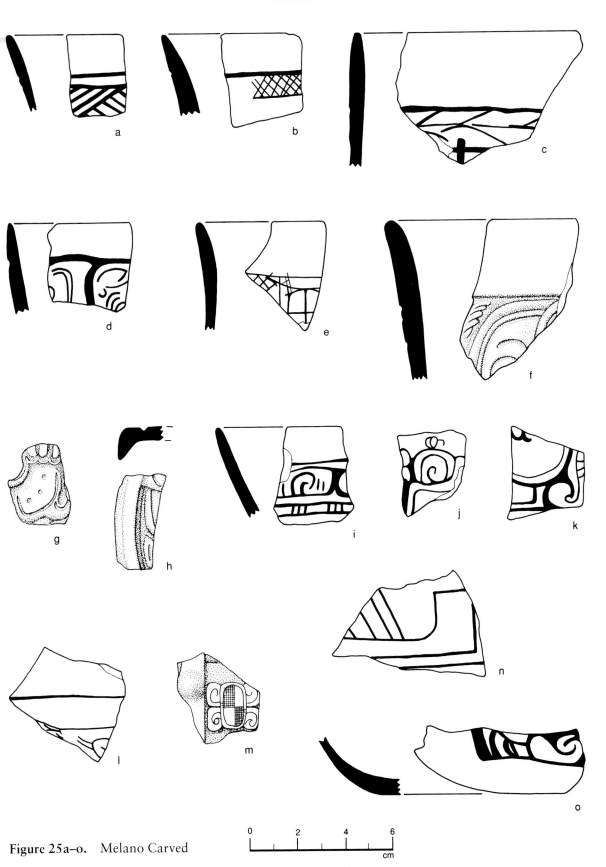

Figure 25a–o. Melano Carved

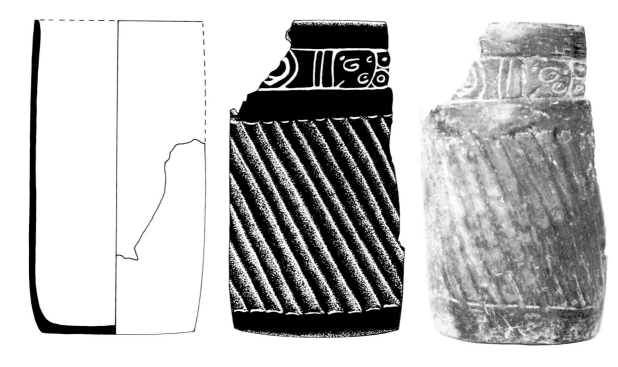

0   2   4   6
                cm

Figure 26.   Melano Carved 1-329

Figure 27.   Melano Carved 1-319

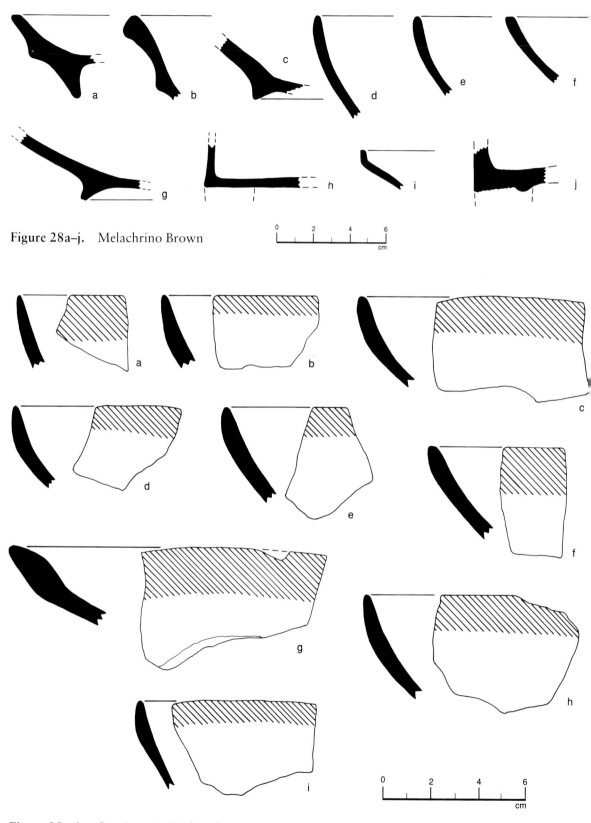

Figure 28a–j.   Melachrino Brown

Figure 29a–i.   Con Permiso Red-on-brown

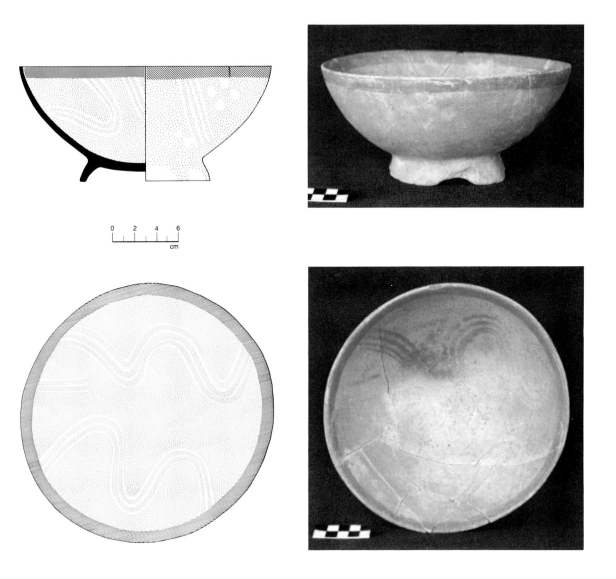

0   2   4   6
cm

Figure 30.   Chilanga Red-painted Usulutan, Chil. 1-225

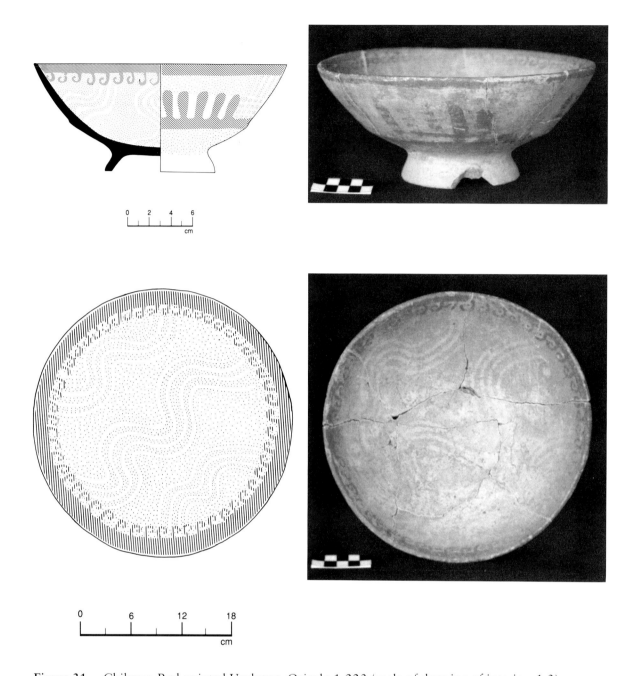

Figure 31.   Chilanga Red-painted Usulutan, Osicala 1-223 (scale of drawing of interior: 1:3)

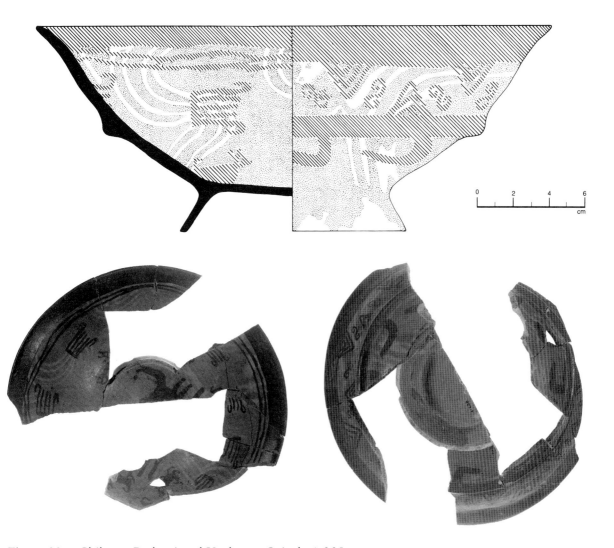

Figure 32.   Chilanga Red-painted Usulutan, Osicala 1-238

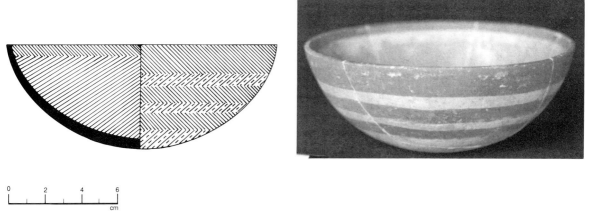

Figure 33.   Chilanga Red-painted Usulutan, Osicala 1-226

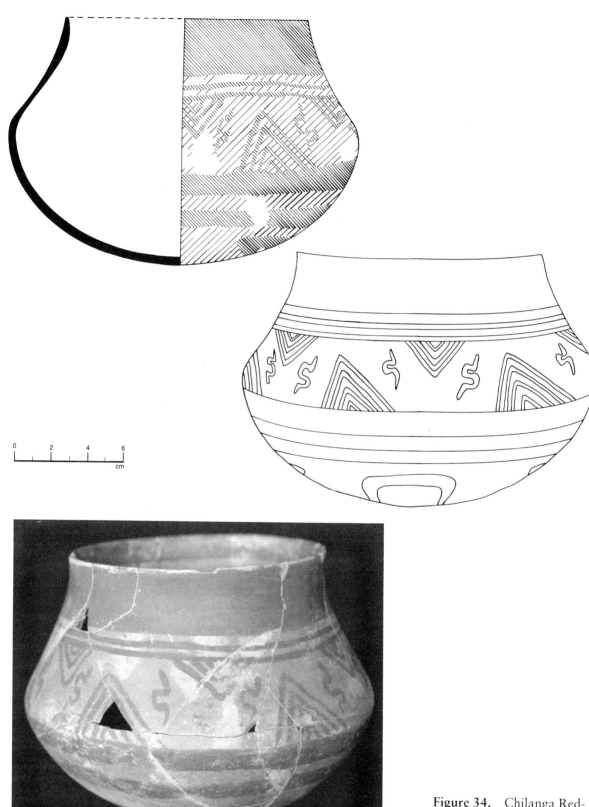

0   2   4   6
cm

Figure 34. Chilanga Red-painted Usulutan, Osicala 1-228

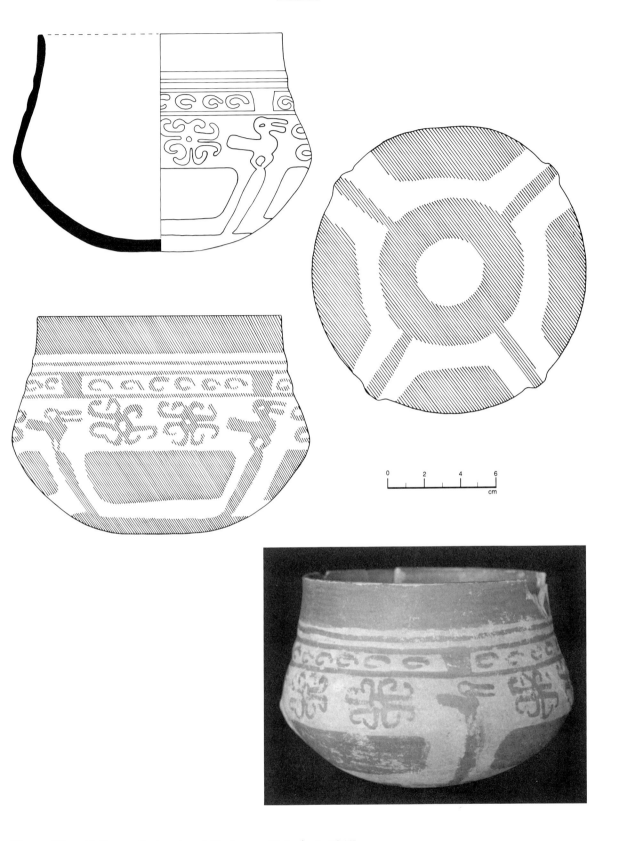

Figure 35.   Chilanga Red-painted Usulutan, Osicala 1-1017

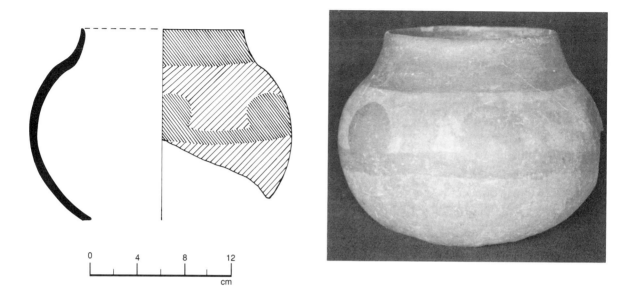

Figure 36.   Chilanga Red-painted Usulutan, Osicala 1-361 (scale of drawing: 1:2)

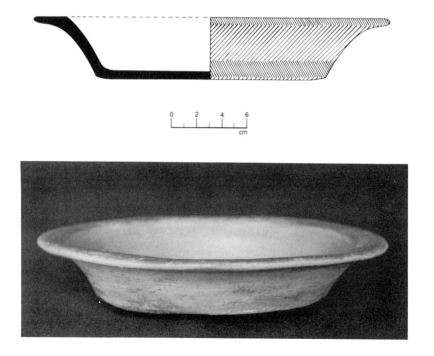

Figure 37.   Chilanga Red-painted Usulutan, Osicala 1-1203, side view and profile drawing

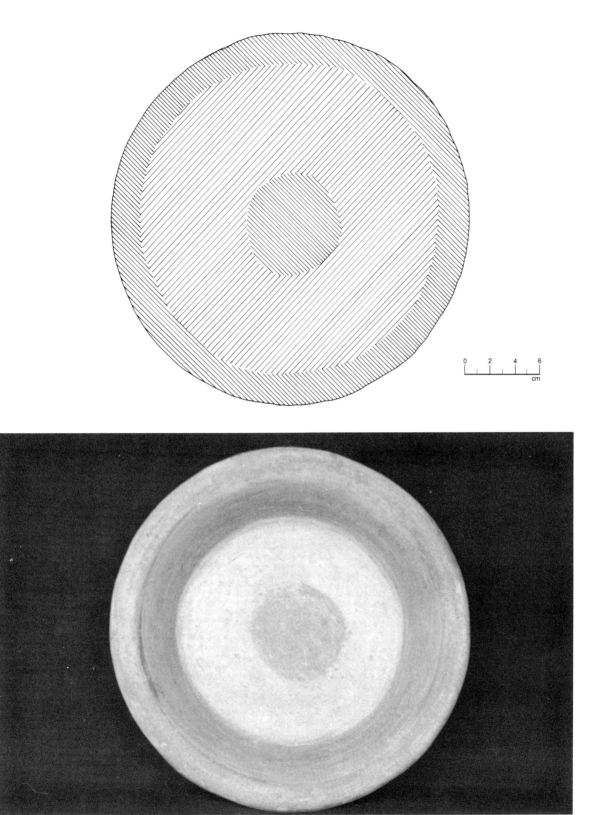

Figure 37 continued.   Chilanga Red-painted Usulutan, Osicala 1-1203, interior

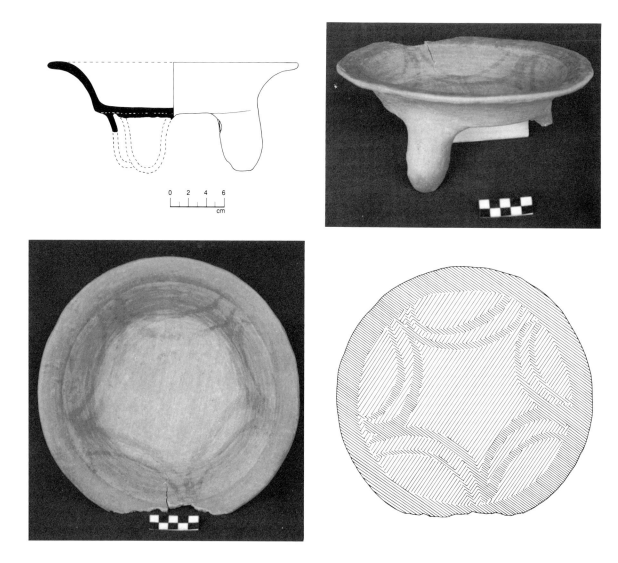

Figure 38.   Chilanga Red-painted Usulutan, Osicala 1-1210

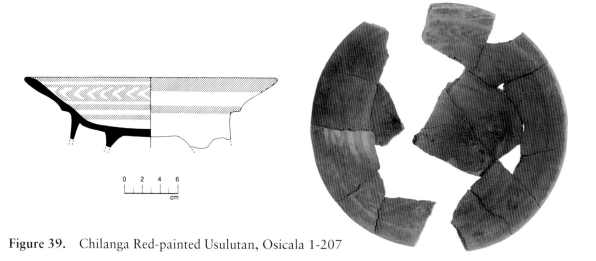

Figure 39.   Chilanga Red-painted Usulutan, Osicala 1-207

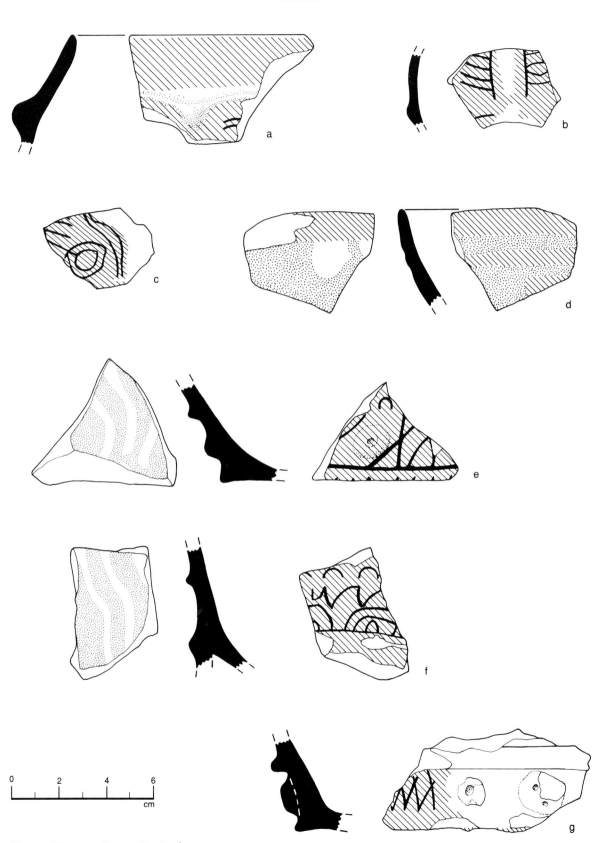

Figure 40a–g. Arturo Incised

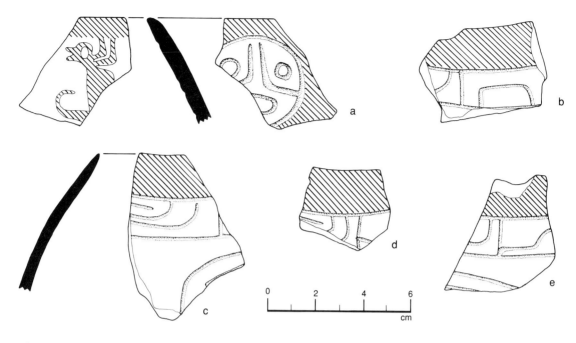

Figure 41a–e.   Cara Gorda Composite

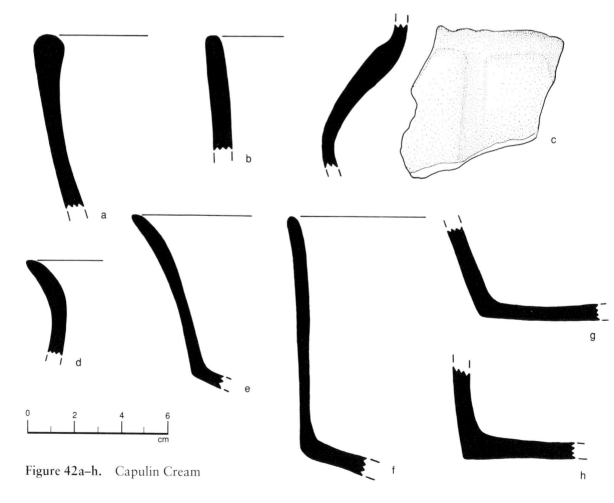

Figure 42a–h.   Capulin Cream

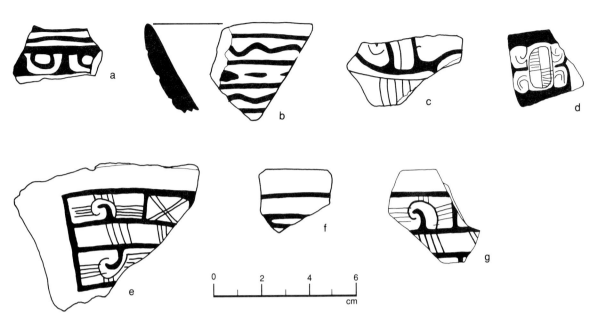

Figure 43a–g.   Champona Incised

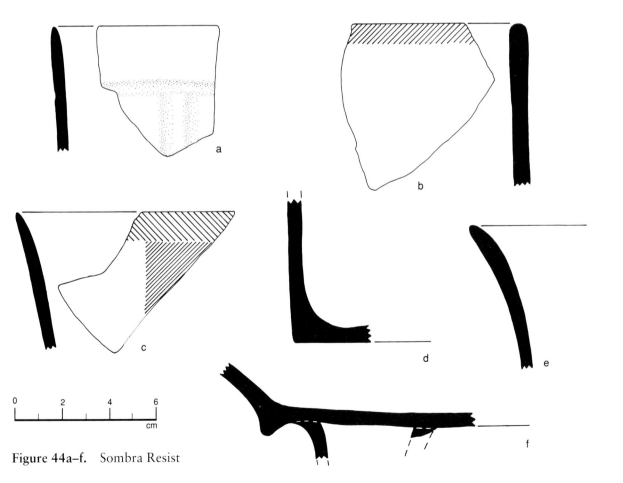

Figure 44a–f.   Sombra Resist

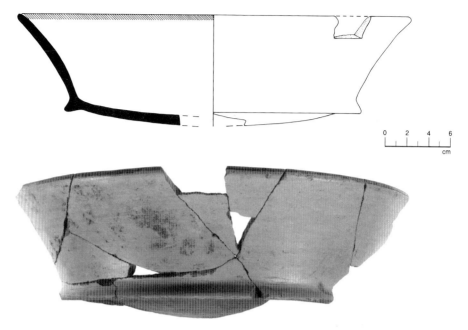

Figure 45.   Sombra Resist 1-1024

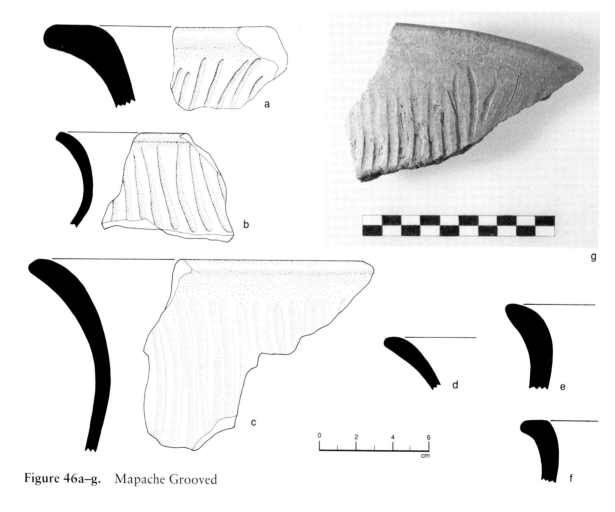

Figure 46a–g.   Mapache Grooved

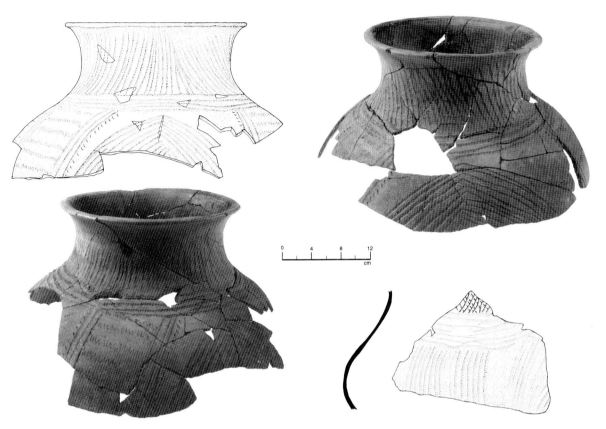

Figure 47. Mapache Grooved 1-307 (scale of drawing: 1:2)

Figure 48. Mapache Grooved 1-450 (scale: 1:2)

Figure 49a–d. Cementerio Incised

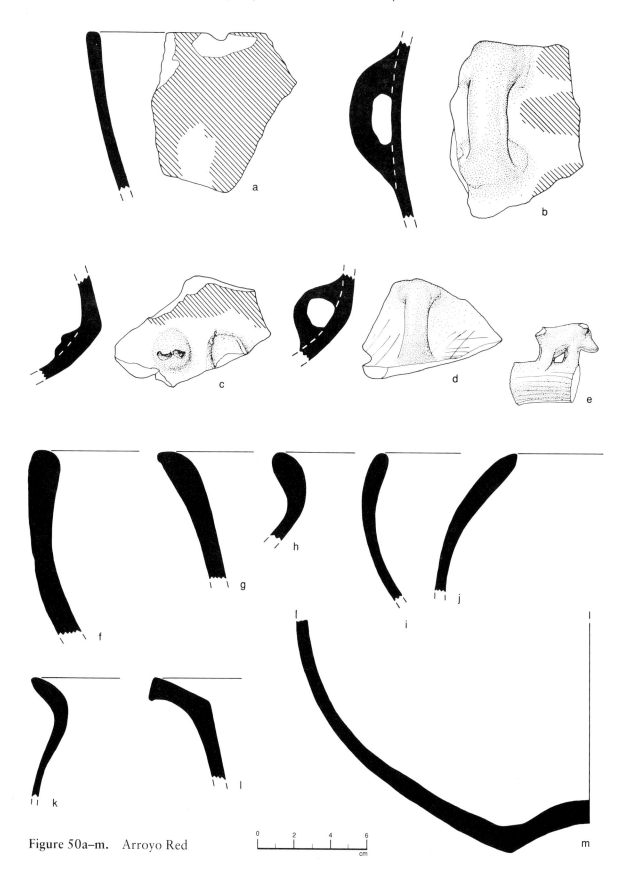

Figure 50a–m.   Arroyo Red

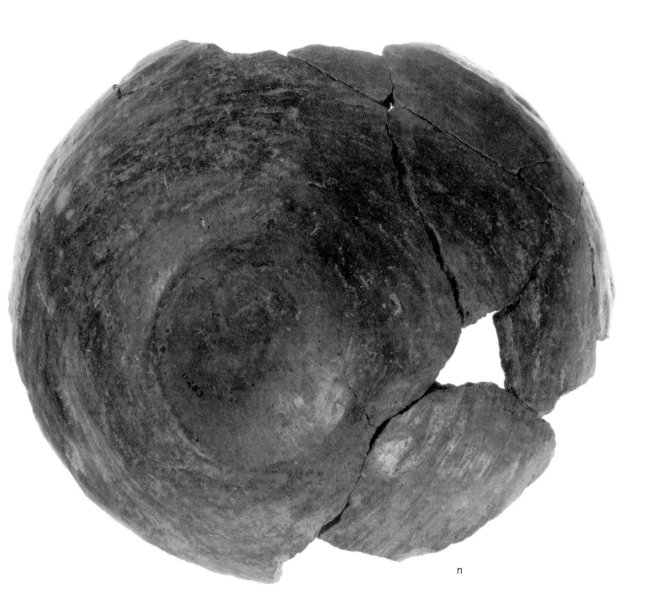

Figure 50n. Arroyo Red, photo of base

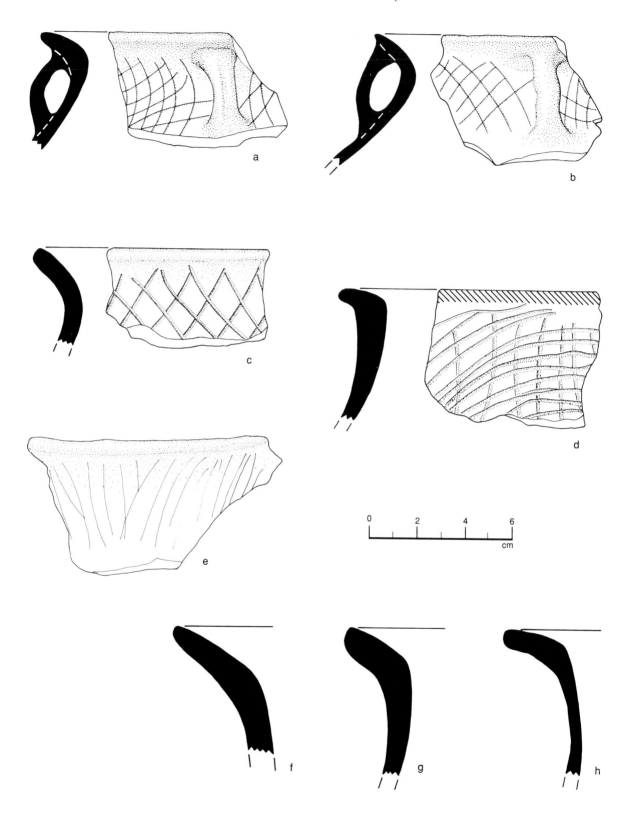

Figure 51a–h.   Sopi Incised

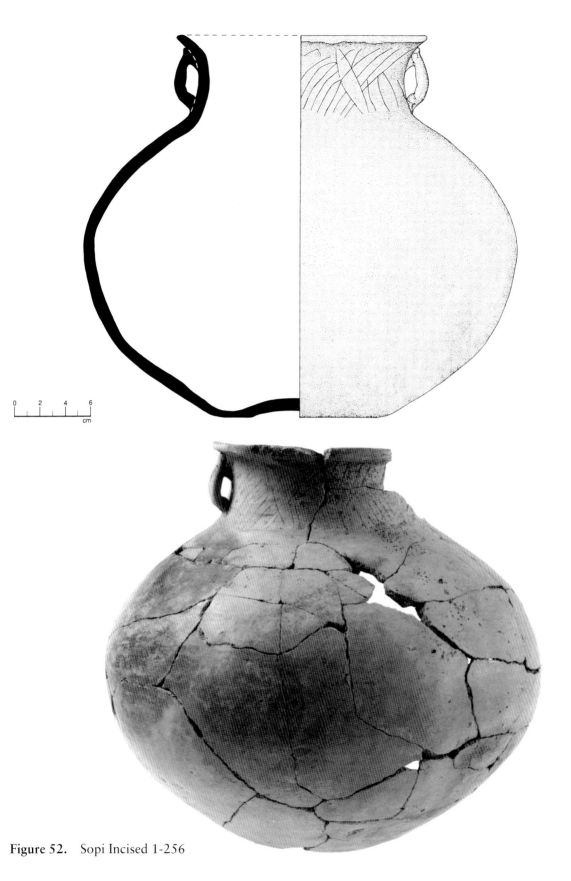

Figure 52. Sopi Incised 1-256

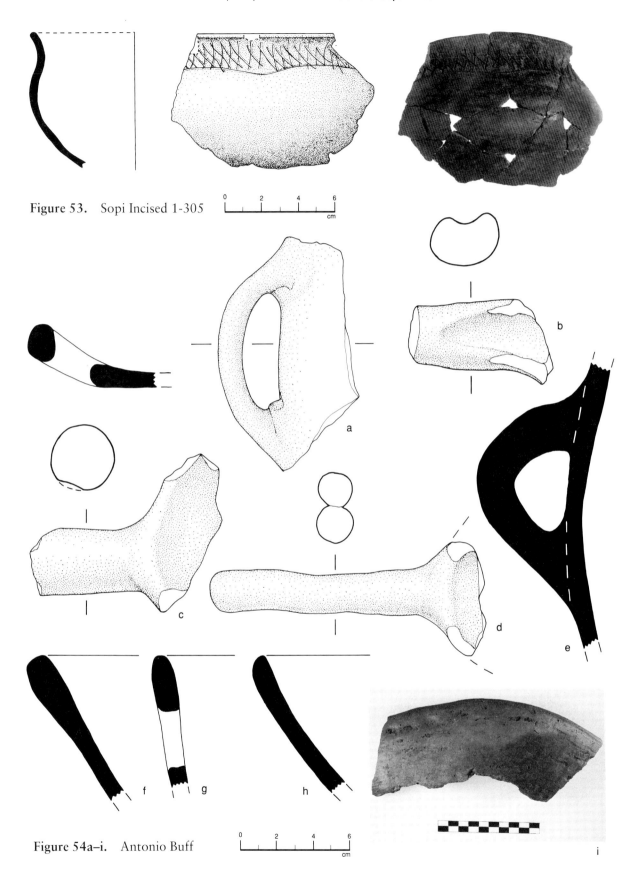

Figure 53. Sopi Incised 1-305

Figure 54a–i. Antonio Buff

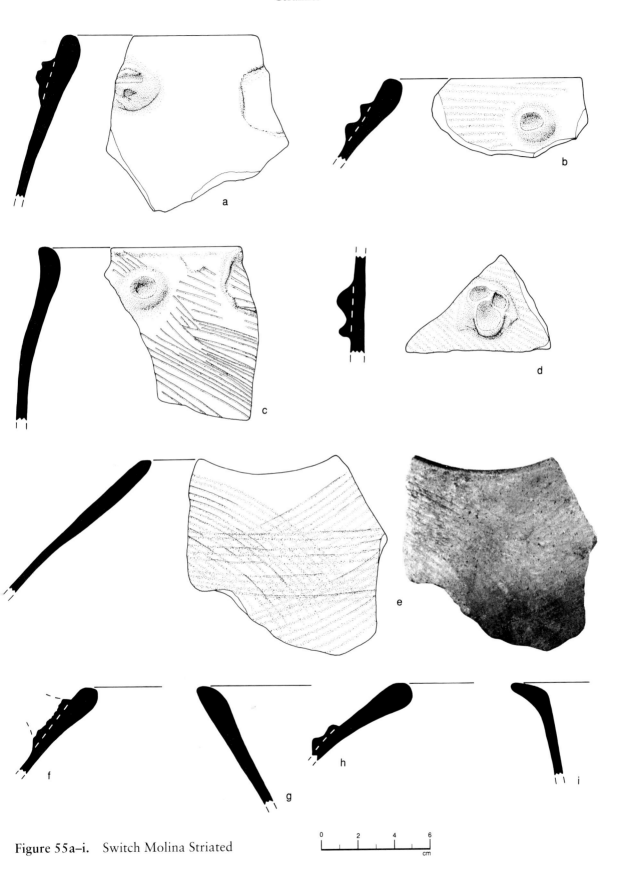

Figure 55a–i. Switch Molina Striated

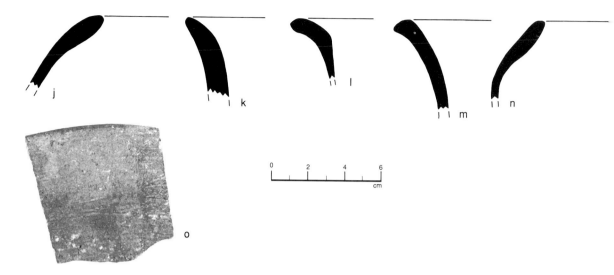

Figure 55j–o.   Switch Molina Striated

Figure 56.   Switch Molina Striated 1-580

Figure 57.   Switch Molina Striated 1-745

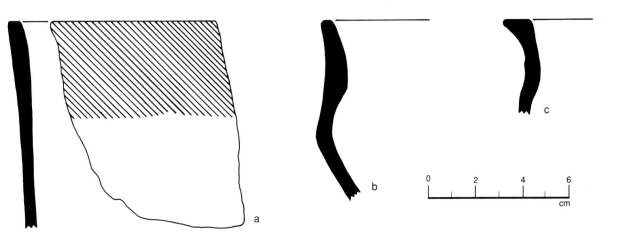

Figure 58a–c.   Chalja Red-painted, profiles and surface decoration

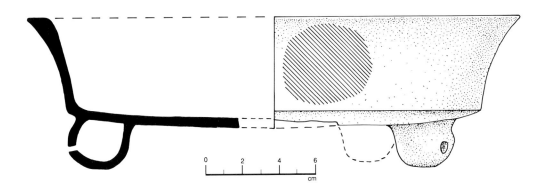

Figure 59.   Chalja Red-painted 1-137

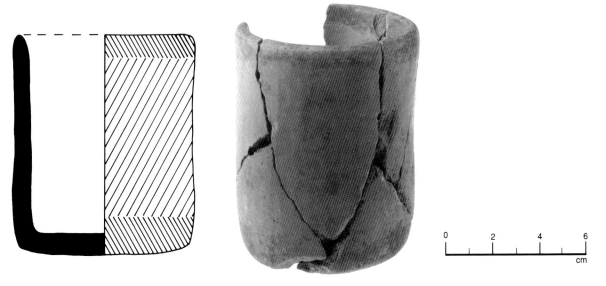

Figure 60.   Chalja Red-painted 1-807

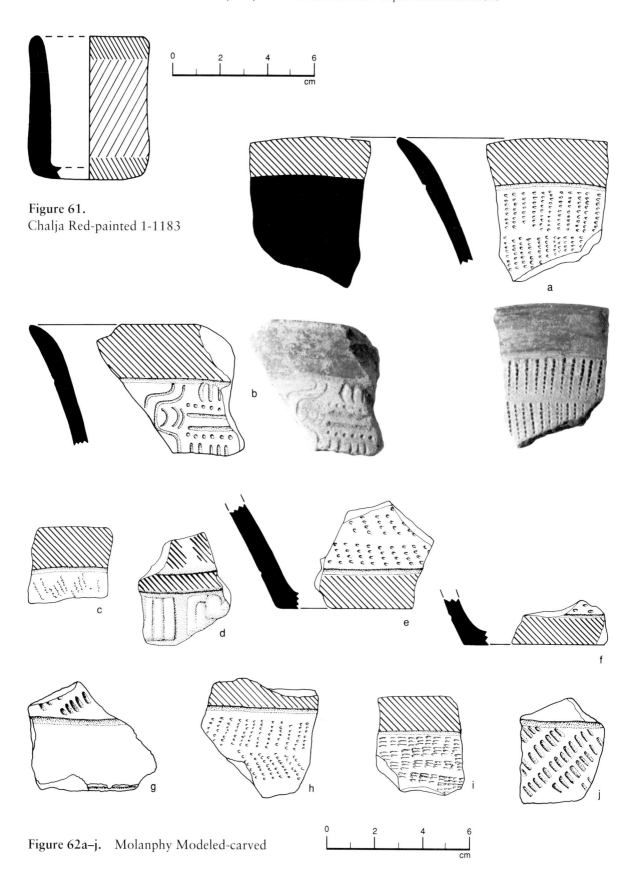

Figure 61.
Chalja Red-painted 1-1183

Figure 62a–j.   Molanphy Modeled-carved

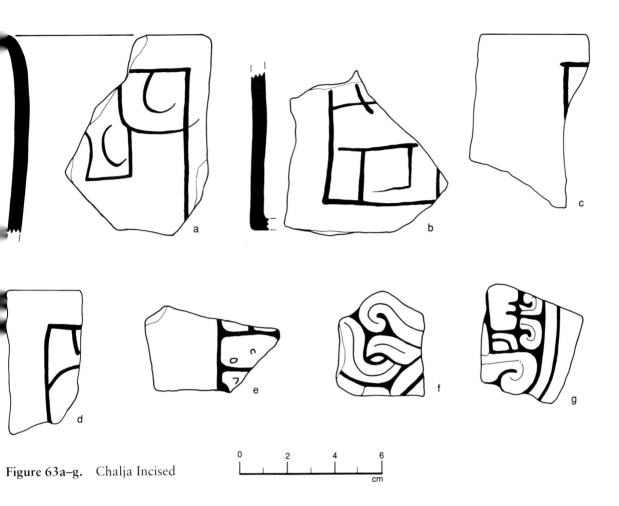

Figure 63a–g. Chalja Incised

Figure 64a–j. Gualpopa Polychrome

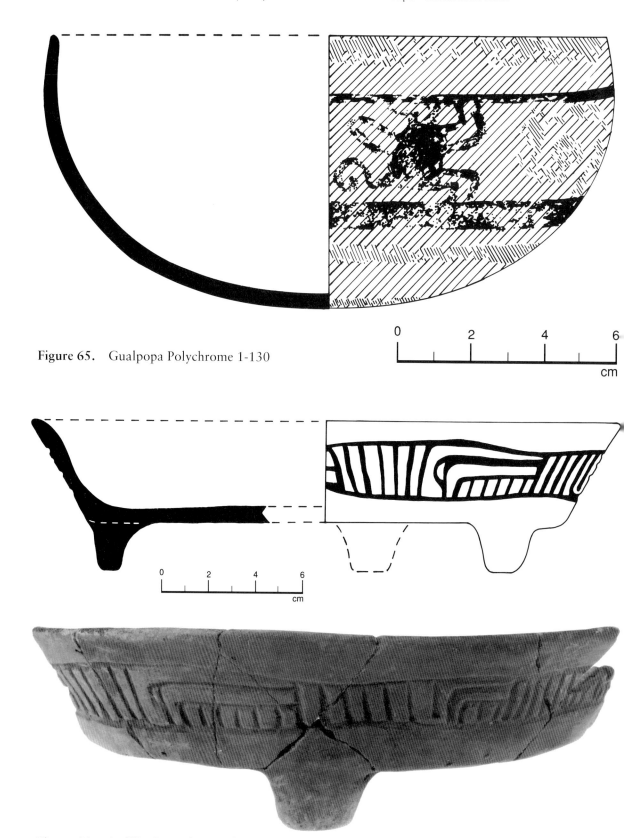

Figure 65.   Gualpopa Polychrome 1-130

Figure 66.   Ardilla Gouged-incised 1-137

Figure 67a–s. Ardilla Gouged-incised

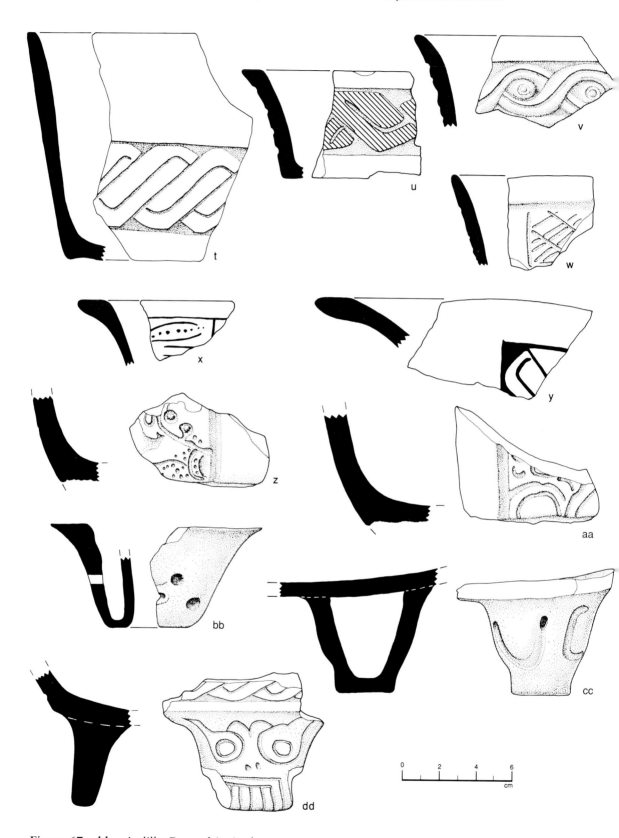

Figure 67t–dd.   Ardilla Gouged-incised

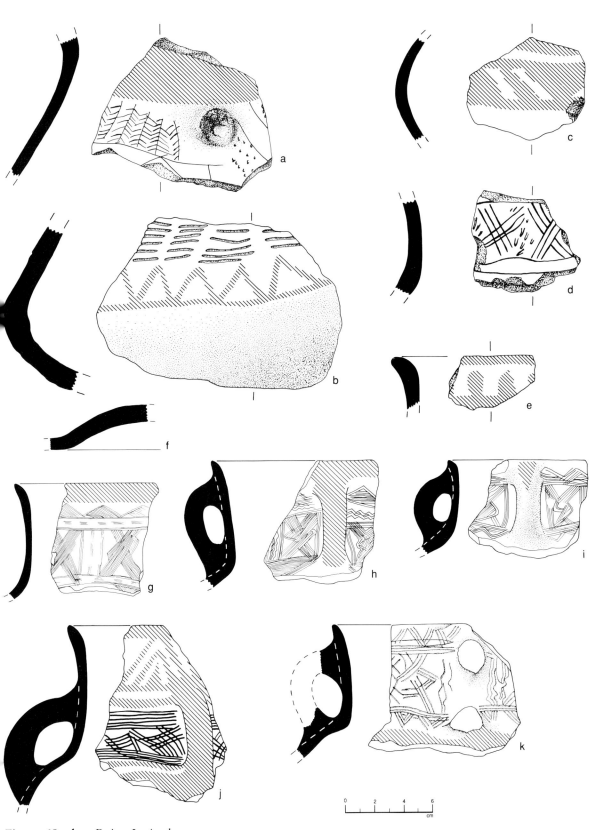

Figure 68a–k. Reina Incised

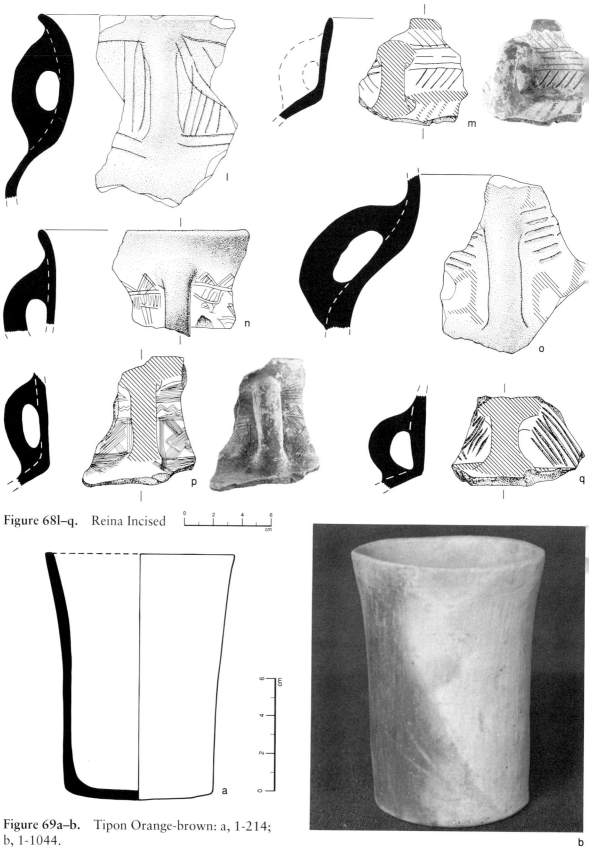

Figure 68l–q.   Reina Incised

Figure 69a–b.   Tipon Orange-brown: a, 1-214; b, 1-1044.

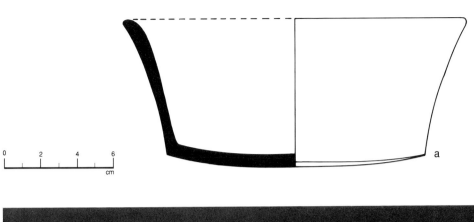

Figure 70a–b.   Tipon Orange-brown: a, 1-1208; b, 1-1202.

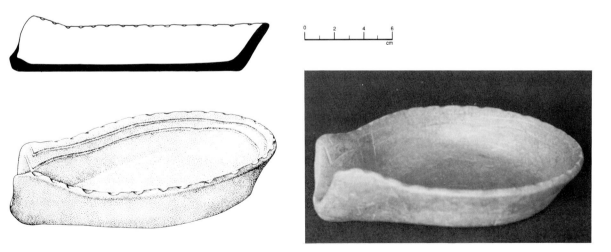

Figure 71.   Tipon Orange-brown 1-361

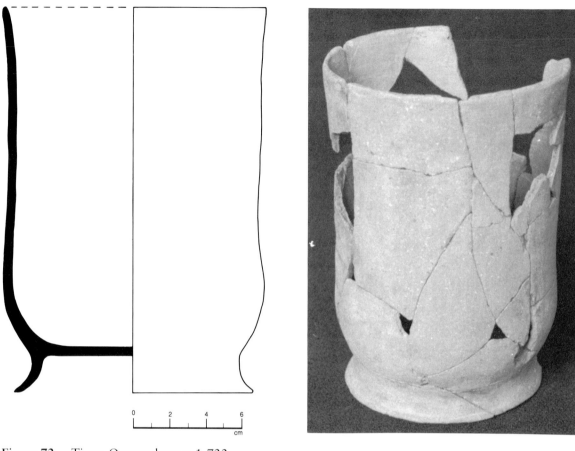

Figure 72.   Tipon Orange-brown 1-722

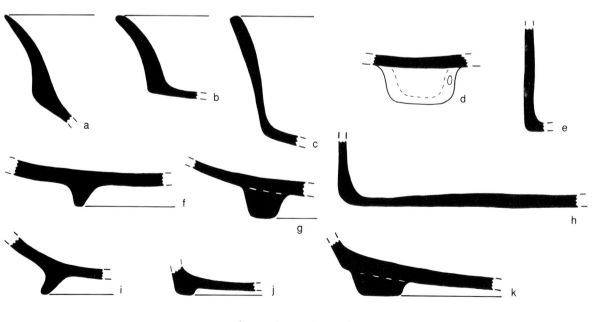

Figure 73a–k.   Tipon Orange-brown

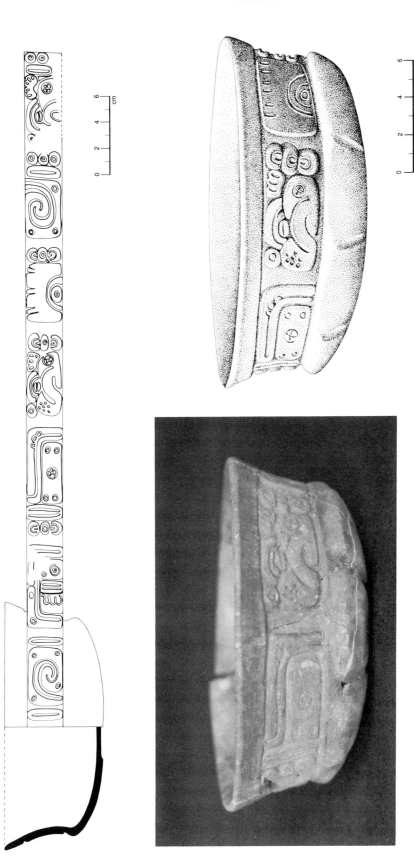

Figure 74. Don Gordon Modeled-carved 1-668

Figure 75.   Don Gordon Modeled-carved 1-206

Figure 76.   Don Gordon Modeled-carved 1-137

Figure 77a–m. Don Gordon Modeled-carved

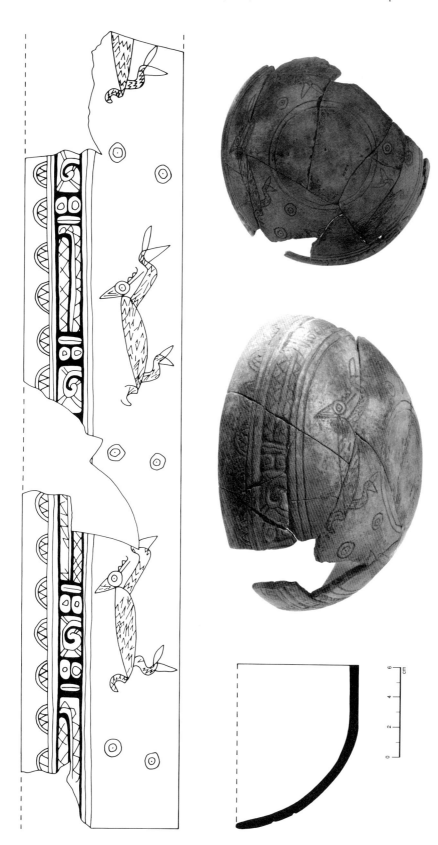

Figure 78. Claudio Incised 1-530

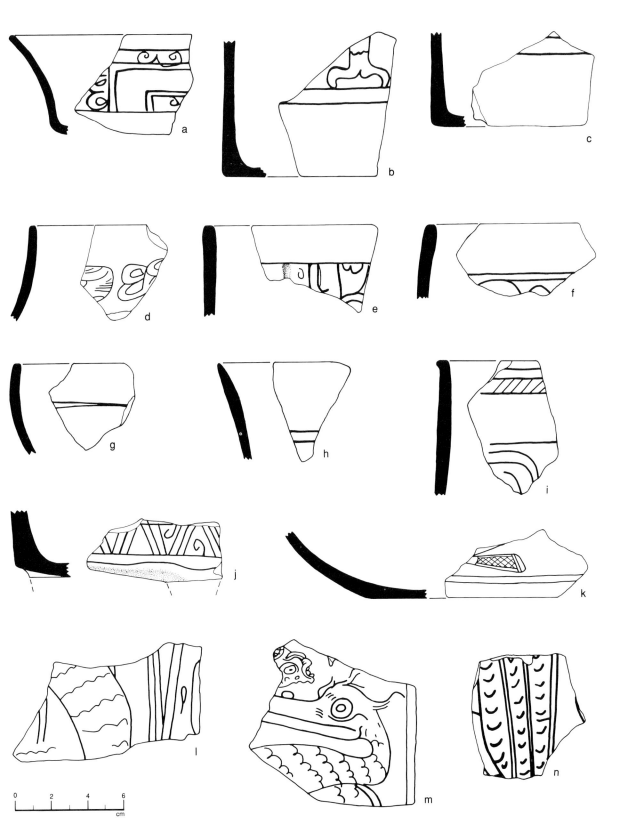

Figure 79a–n. Claudio Incised

Figure 79o–dd.   Claudio Incised

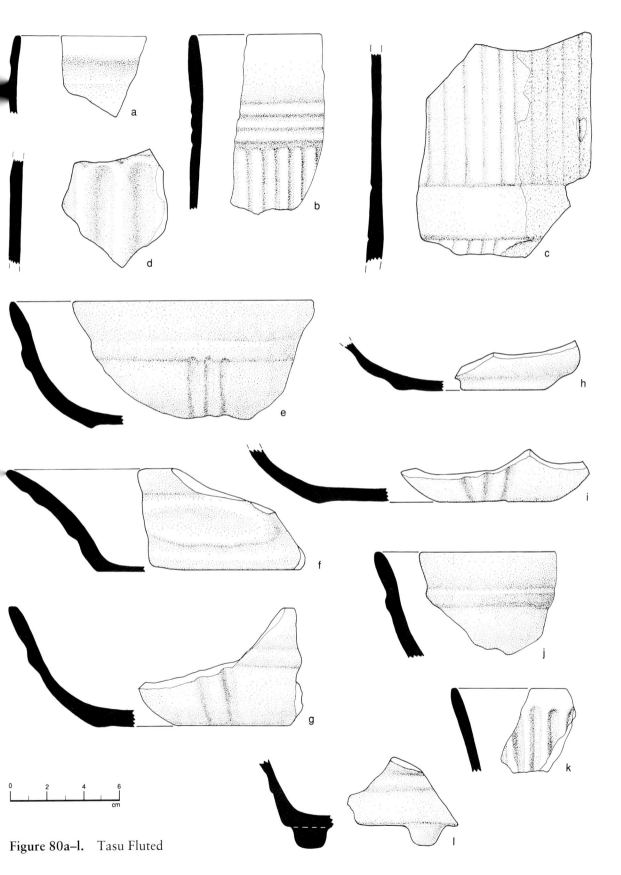

Figure 80a–l. Tasu Fluted

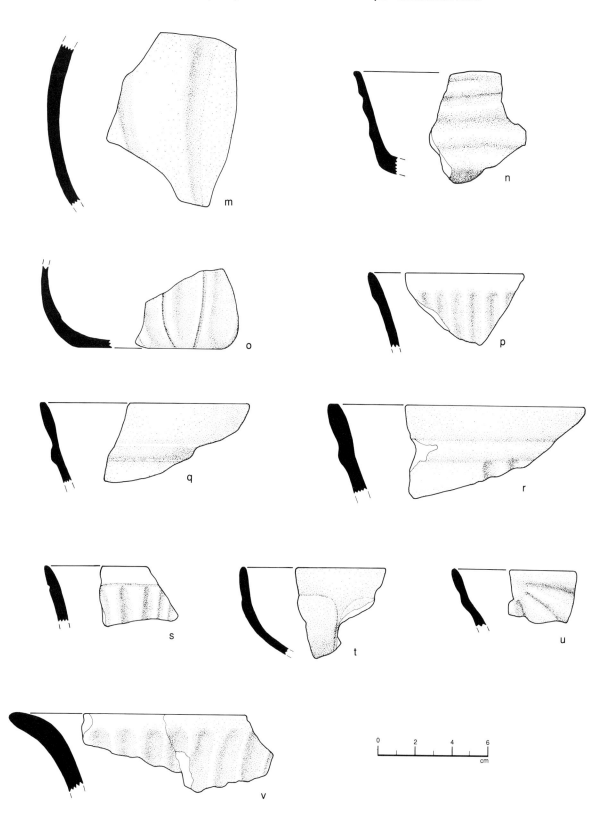

Figure 80m–v.   Tasu Fluted

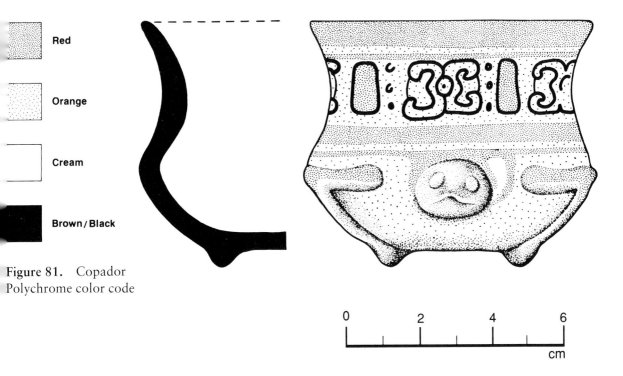

Red

Orange

Cream

Brown/Black

Figure 81. Copador
Polychrome color code

Figure 82. Copador Polychrome, Glyphic Vars. 1-299

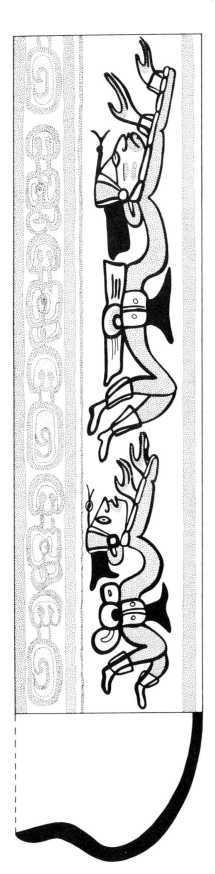

Figure 83.   Copador Polychrome, Glyphic Vars. 1-212

Figure 84.   Copador Polychrome, Glyphic Vars. 1-211.

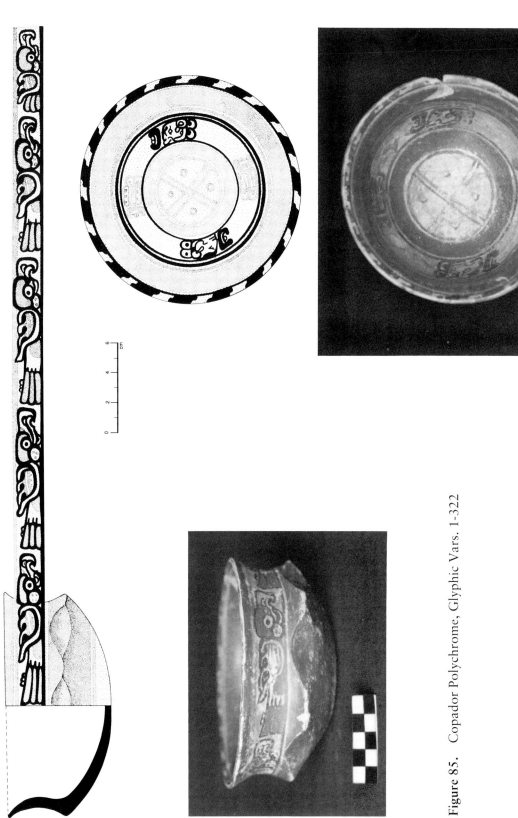

Figure 85.   Copador Polychrome, Glyphic Vars. 1-322

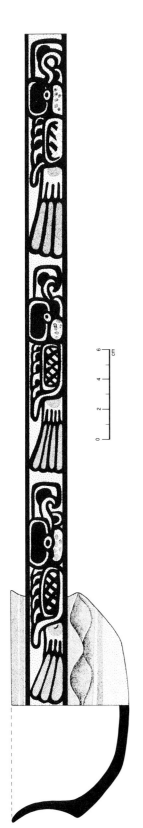

Figure 86. Copador Polychrome, Glyphic Vars. 1-19

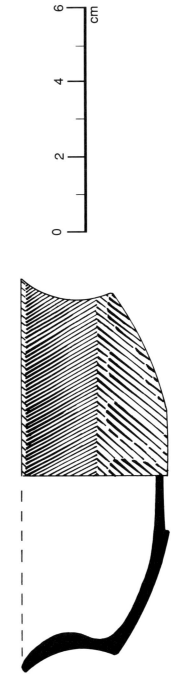

Figure 87. Copador Polychrome, Glyphic Vars. 1-315

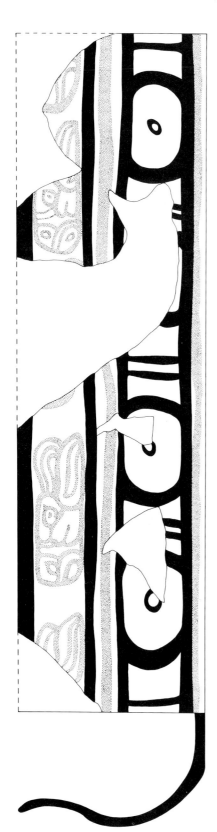

Figure 88. Copador Polychrome, Glyphic Vars. 1-251

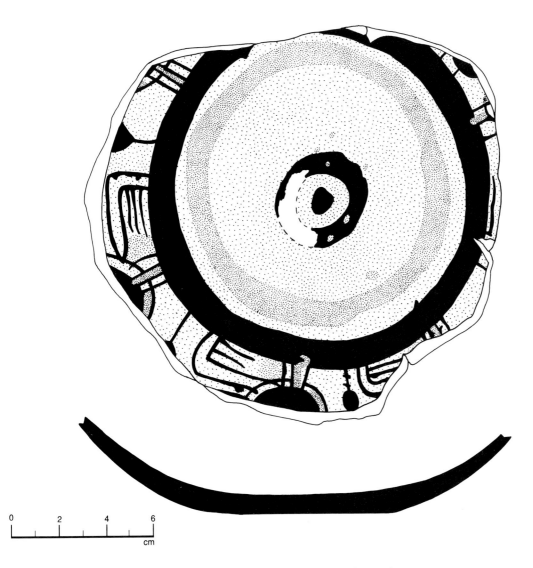

Figure 89.   Copador Polychrome, Glyphic Vars. 1-206, profile and interior

Figure 90.   Copador Polychrome, Glyphic Vars. 1-473

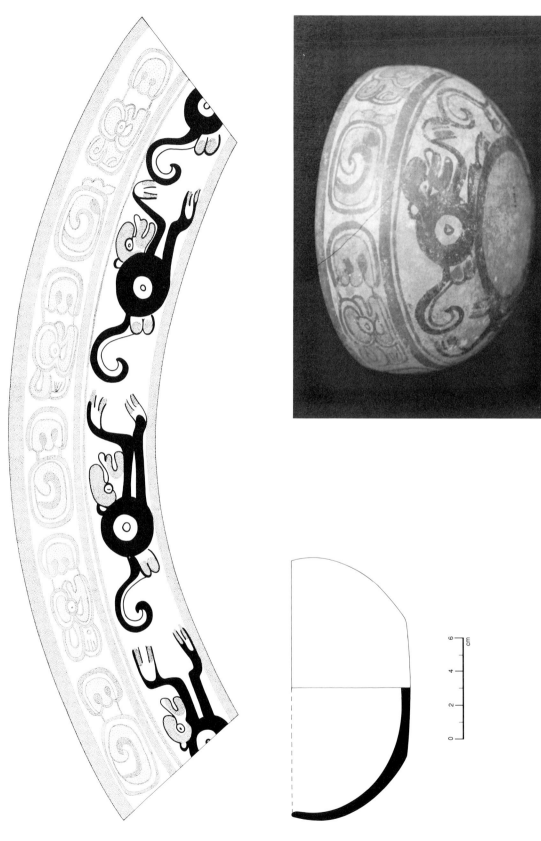

Figure 91.   Copador Polychrome, Glyphic Vars. 1-1147

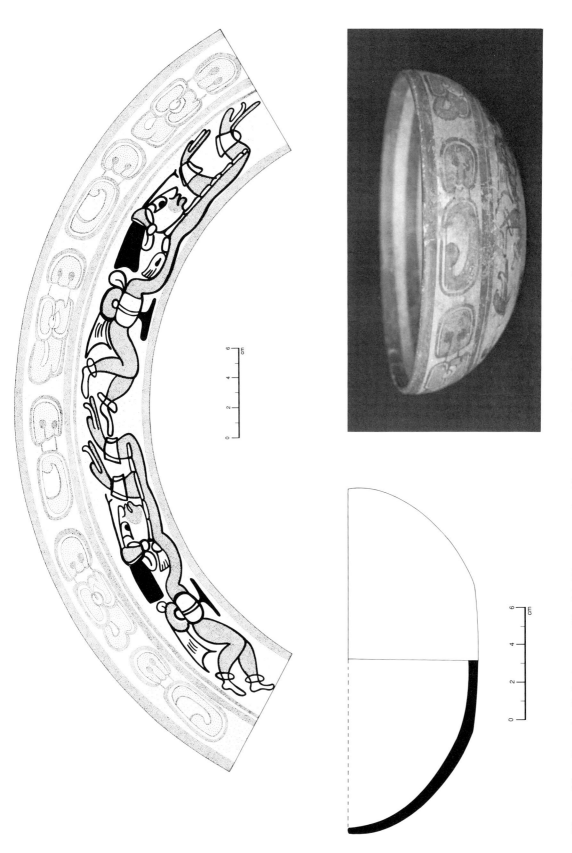

Figure 92. Copador Polychrome, Glyphic Vars. 1-1148, side view, profile, and drawing of surface decoration

Figure 92 continued.   Copador Polychrome, Glyphic Vars. 1-1148, interior view and drawing of interior decoration

Figure 93. Copador Polychrome, Glyphic Vars. 1-1140

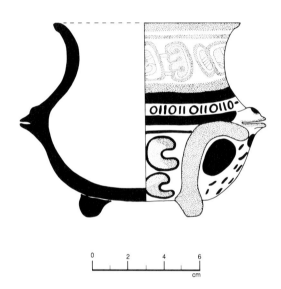

Figure 94.   Copador Polychrome, Glyphic Vars. 1-1141

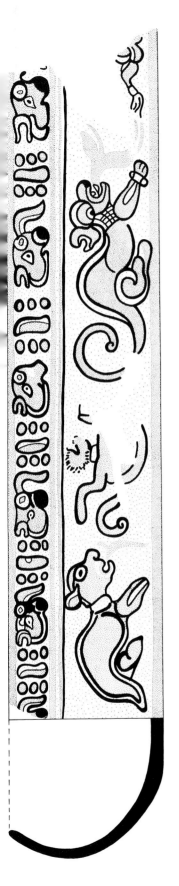

Figure 95. Copador Polychrome, Glyphic Vars. 1-1184

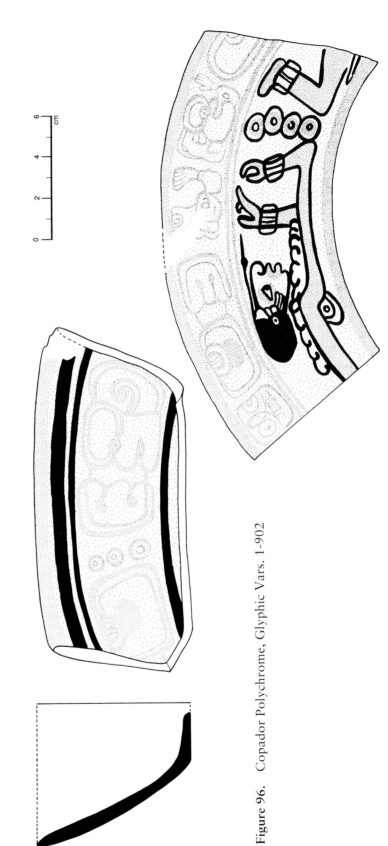

Figure 96. Copador Polychrome, Glyphic Vars. 1-902

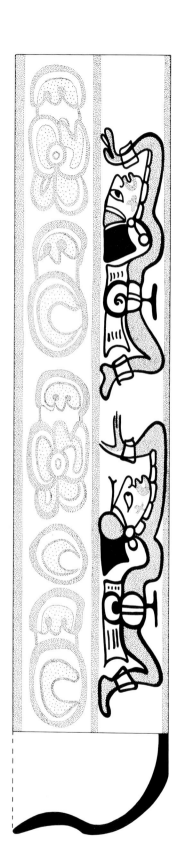

Figure 97.   Copador Polychrome, Glyphic Vars. 1-1139

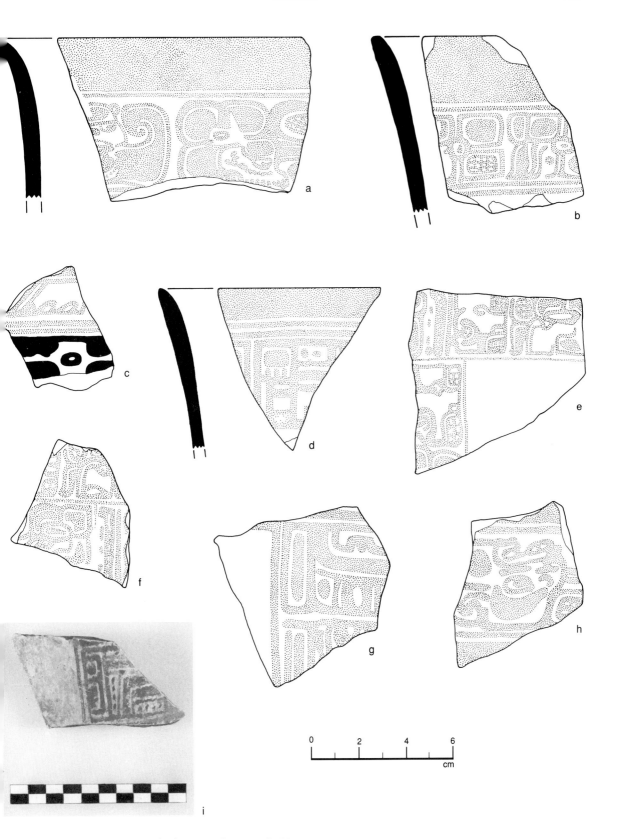

Figure 98a–i. Copador Polychrome, Geometric Var.

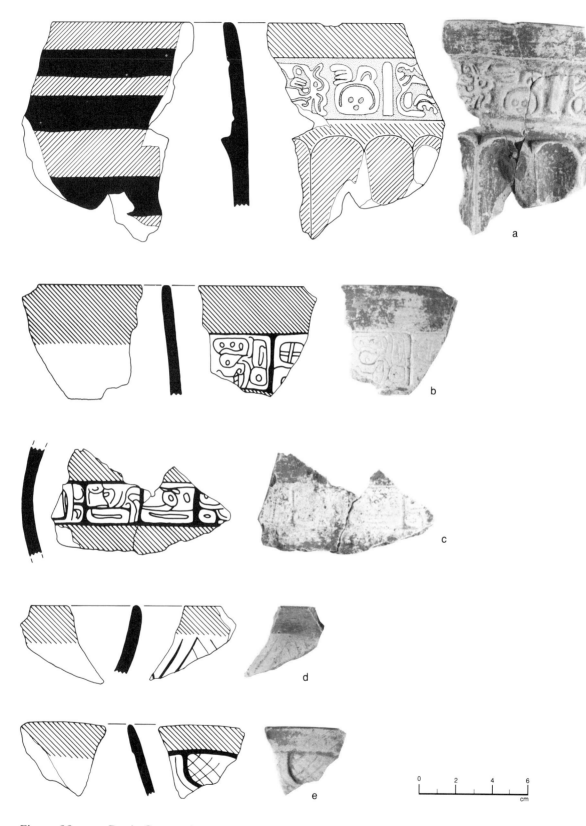

Figure 99a–e.   Doric Composite

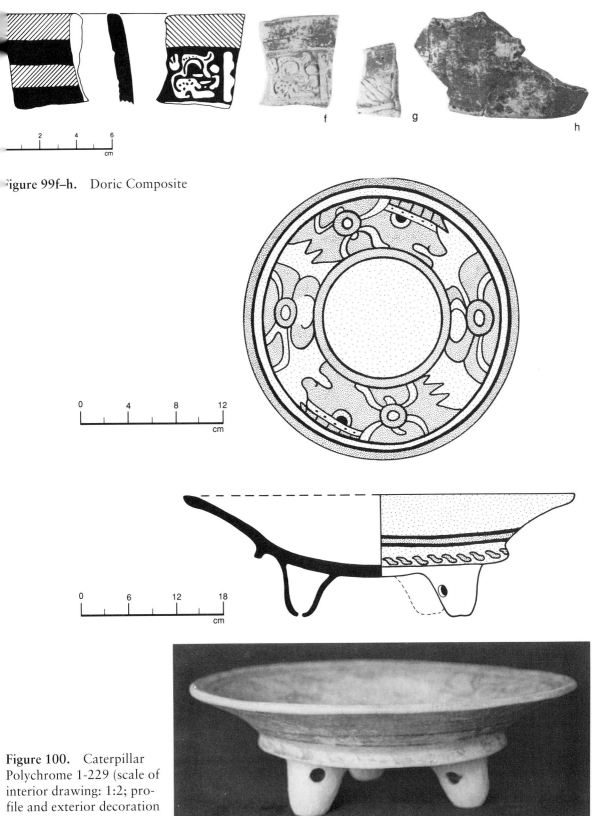

Figure 99f–h.   Doric Composite

Figure 100.   Caterpillar Polychrome 1-229 (scale of interior drawing: 1:2; profile and exterior decoration drawing: 1:3)

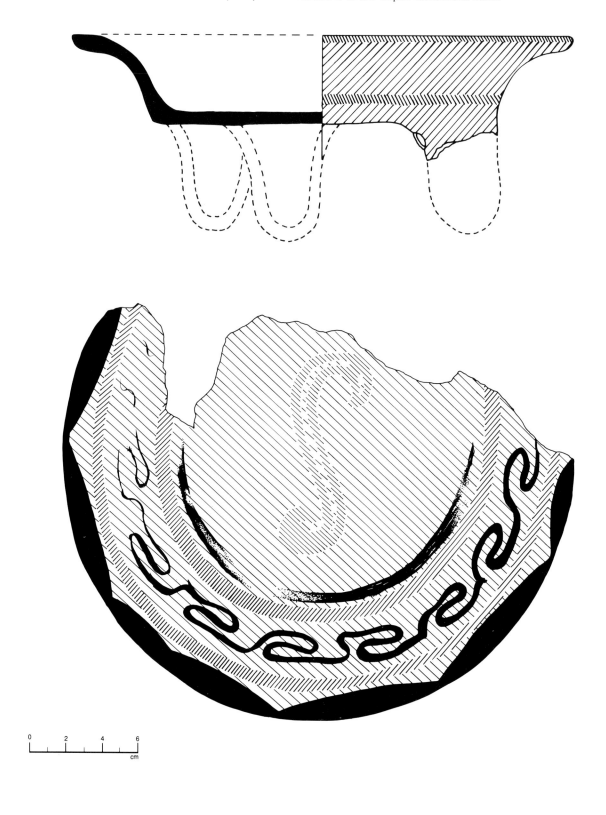

Figure 101.   Caterpillar Polychrome 1-1207

Figure 102.   Babilonia Polychrome 1-327

Figure 103.   Babilonia Polychrome 1-342

Figure 104a–l.   Babilonia Polychrome

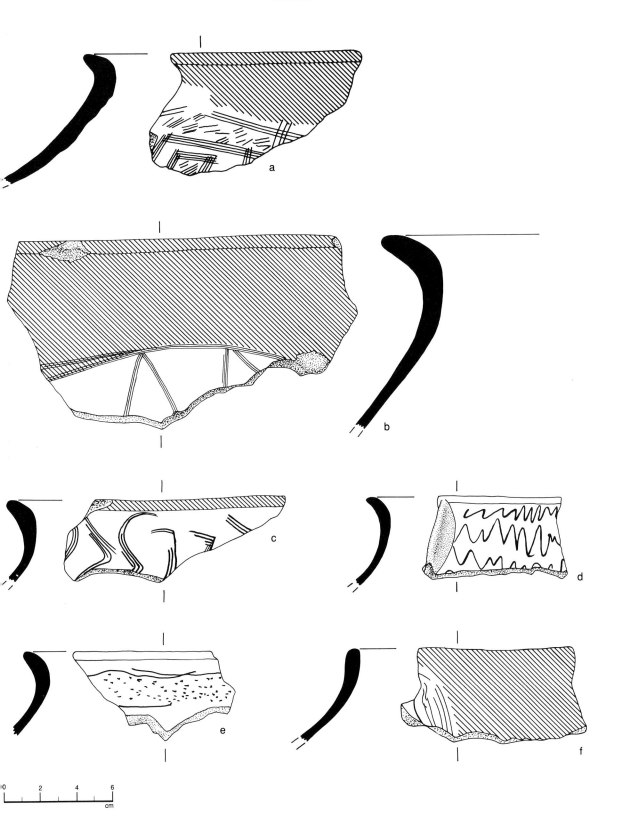

Figure 105a–f. Masica Incised, rim profiles and surface decoration

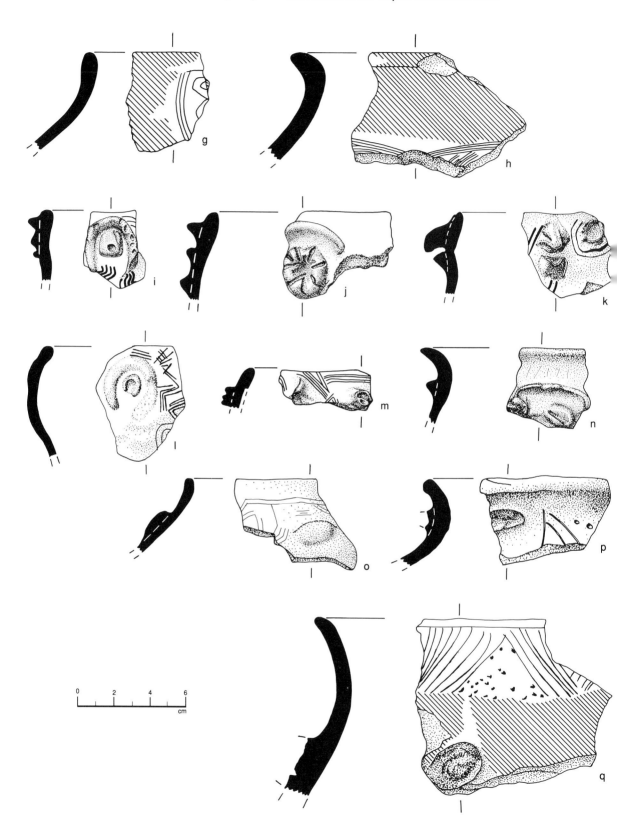

Figure 105g–q. Masica Incised, rim profiles and surface decoration

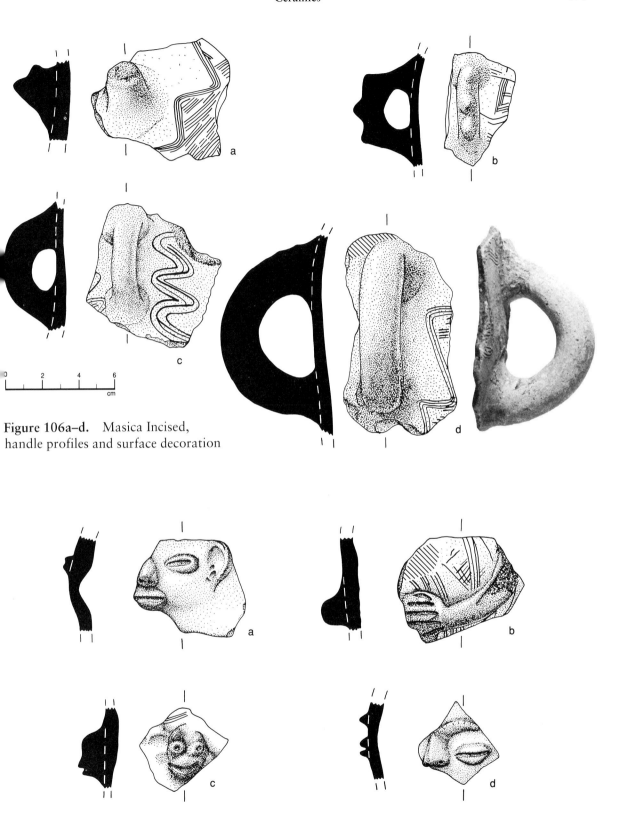

Figure 106a–d. Masica Incised, handle profiles and surface decoration

Figure 107a–d. Masica Incised, miscellaneous modeling

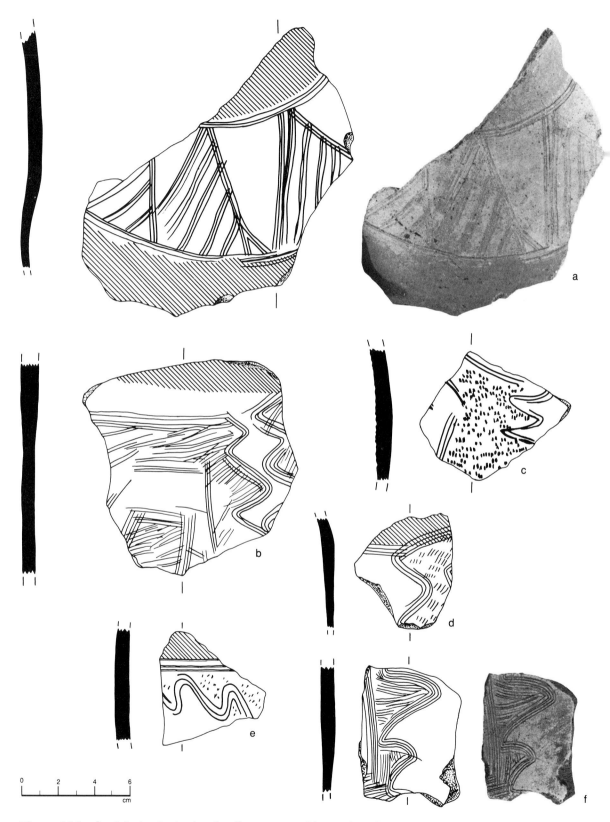

Figure 108a–f.   Masica Incised, miscellaneous profiles and surface decoration

Figure 108g–p. Masica Incised, miscellaneous profiles and surface decoration

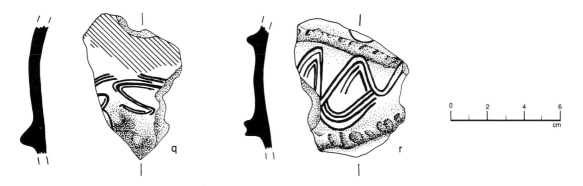

Figure 108q–r.   Masica Incised, miscellaneous profiles and surface decoration

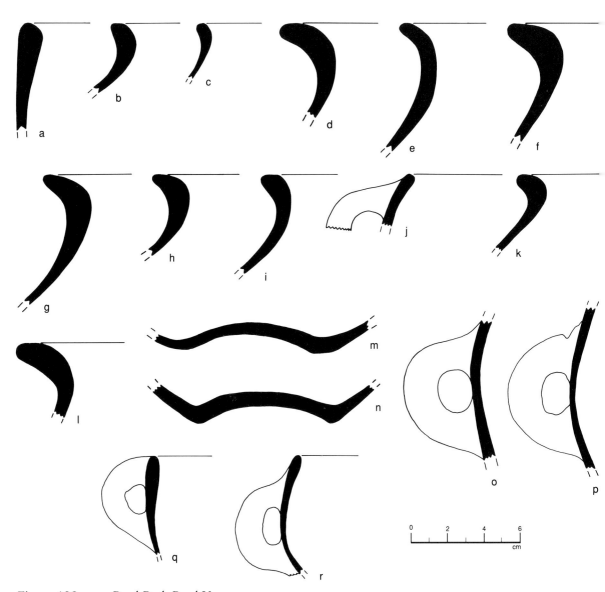

Figure 109a–r.   Raul Red, Raul Var.

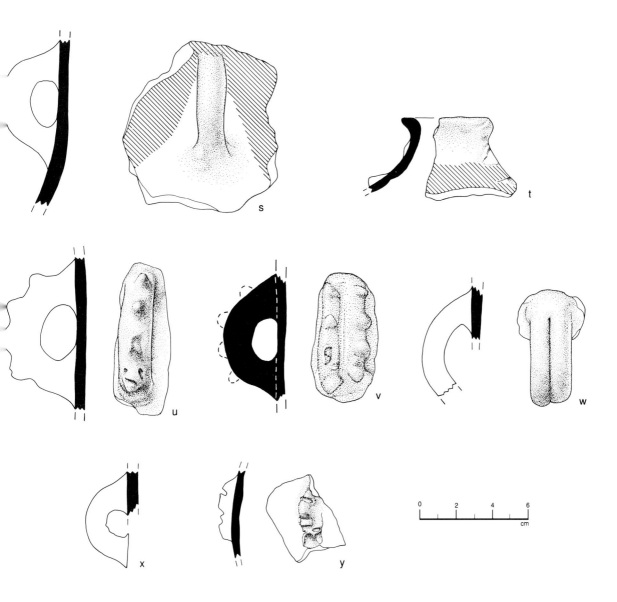

Figure 109s–y. Raul Red, Raul Var.

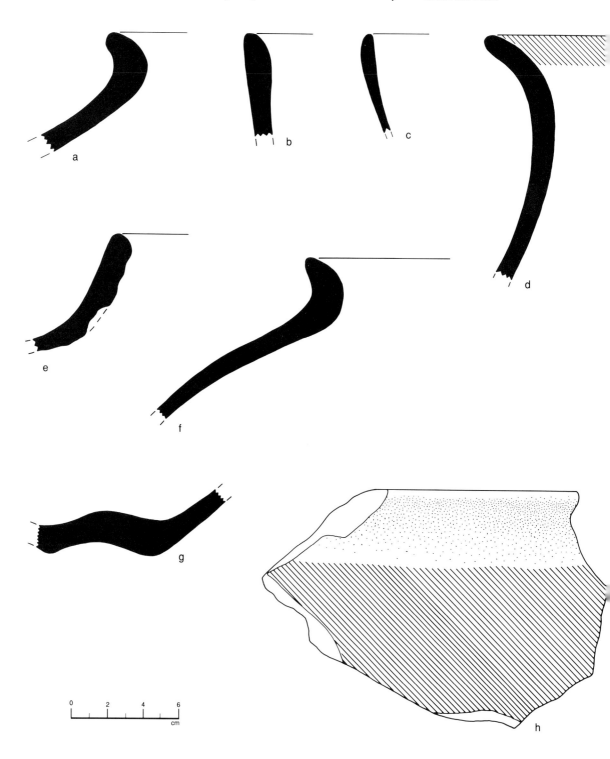

Figure 110a–h.   Raul Red, Unspecified Var.

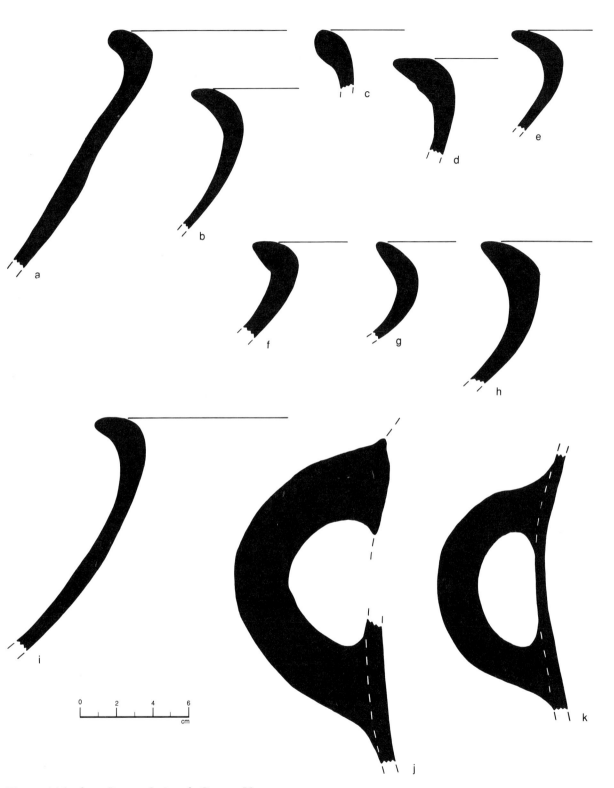

Figure 111a–k. Casaca Striated, Casaca Var.

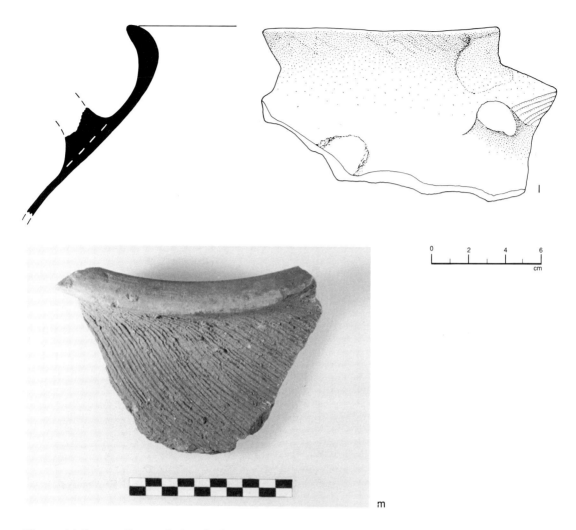

Figure 111l–m.   Casaca Striated, Casaca Var.

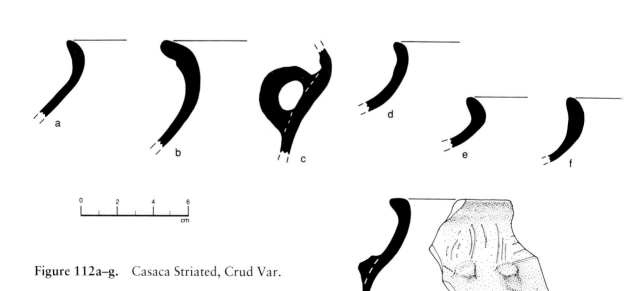

Figure 112a–g.   Casaca Striated, Crud Var.

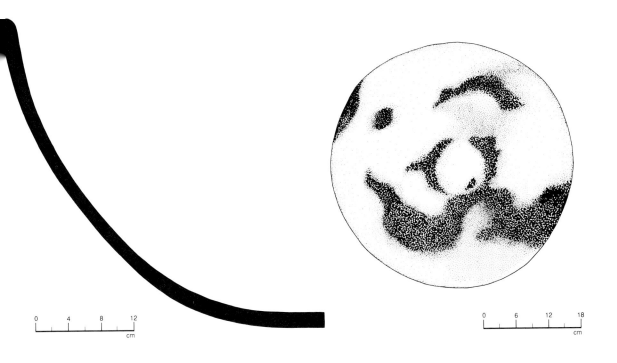

Figure 113. Lorenzo Red 1-1211 (scale of profile drawing: 1:2; surface decoration drawing: 1:3)

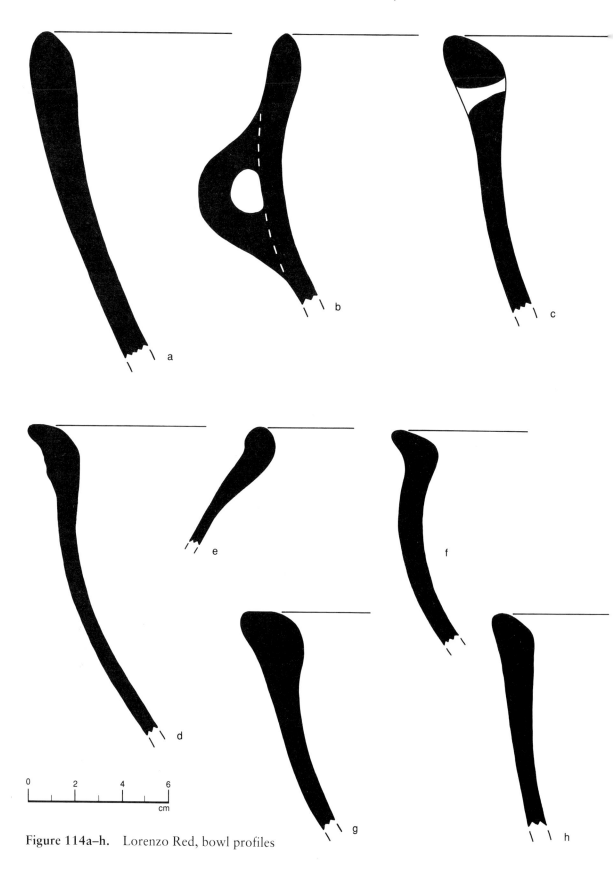

Figure 114a–h.   Lorenzo Red, bowl profiles

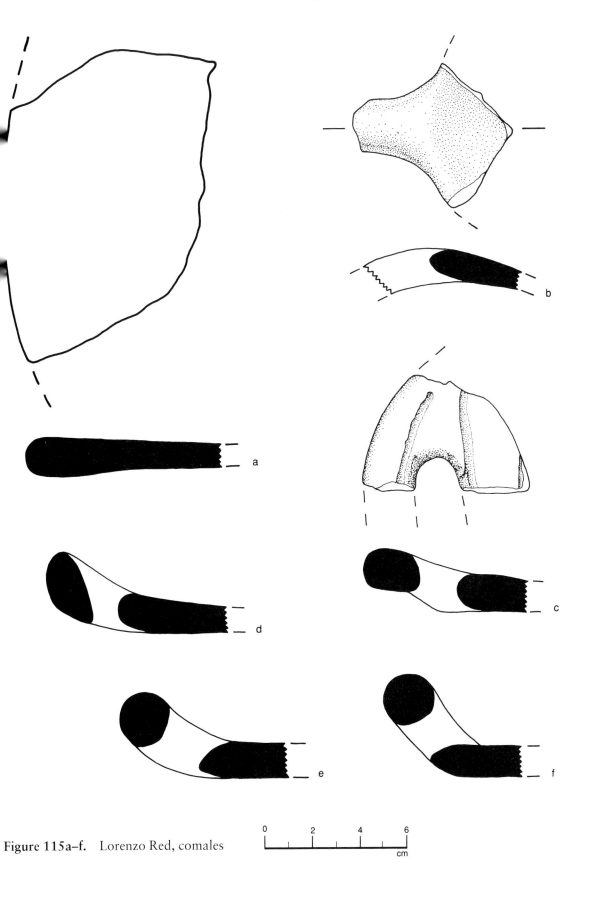

Figure 115a–f. Lorenzo Red, comales

Figure 116.   Sepultura Unslipped 1-75 (scale of drawing: 1:2)

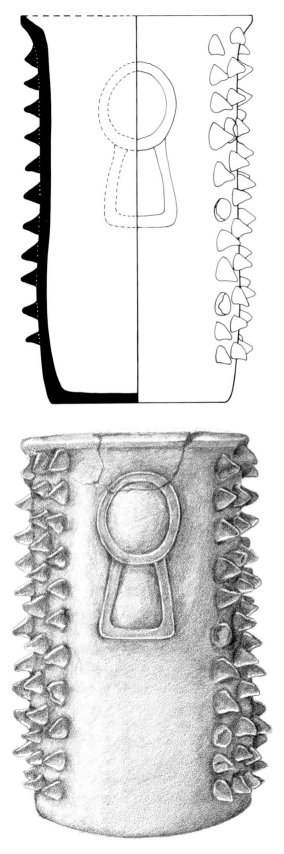

Figure 117. Sepultura Unslipped 1-92
(scale of drawings: 1:2)

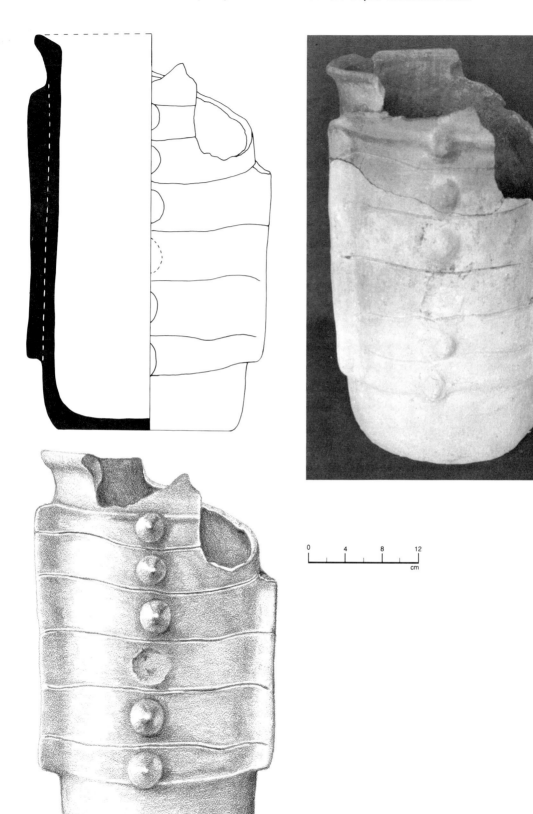

Figure 118.   Sepultura Unslipped 1-97
(scale of drawings: 1:2)

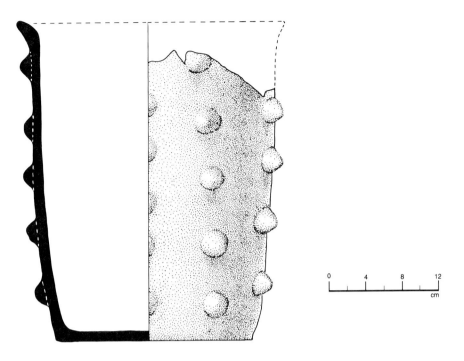

Figure 119. Sepultura Unslipped 1-109 (scale of drawing: 1:2)

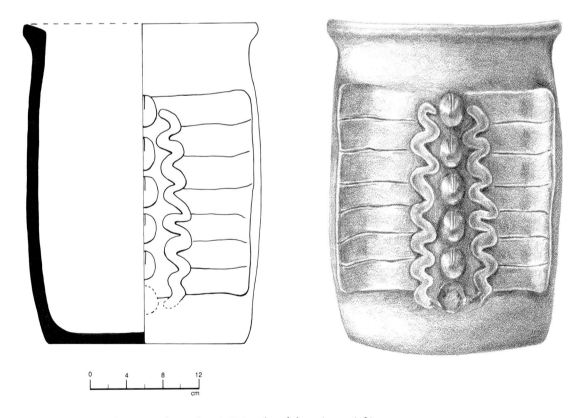

Figure 120. Sepultura Unslipped 1-117 (scale of drawings: 1:2)

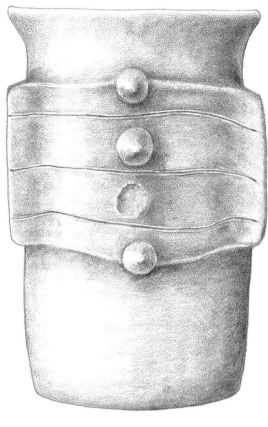

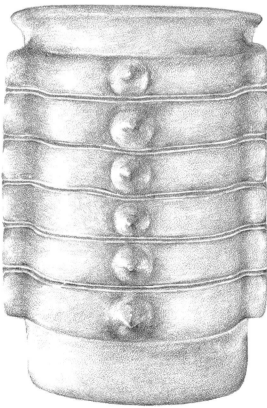

Figure 121 (left). Sepultura Unslipped 1-120 (scale of drawing: 1:2)

Figure 122 (below, left and right). Sepultura Unslipped 1-131 (scale of drawing: 1:2)

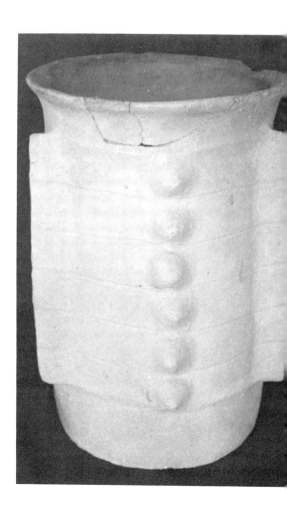

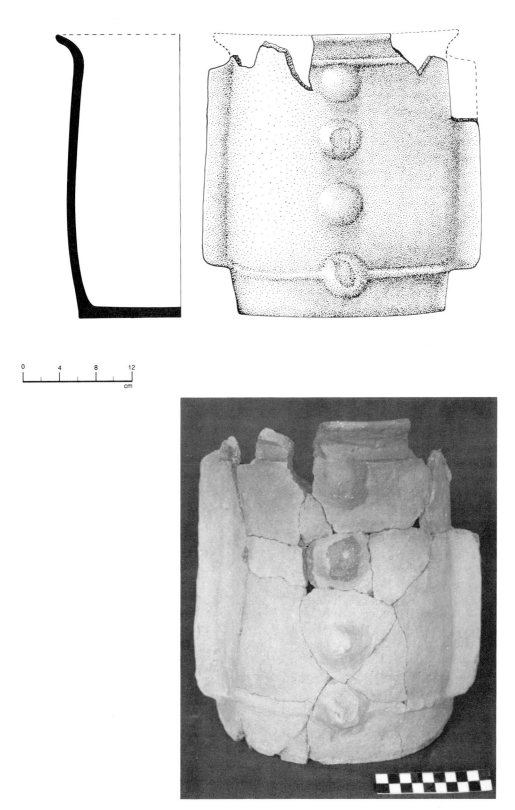

Figure 123. Sepultura Unslipped 1-140 (scale of drawing: 1:2)

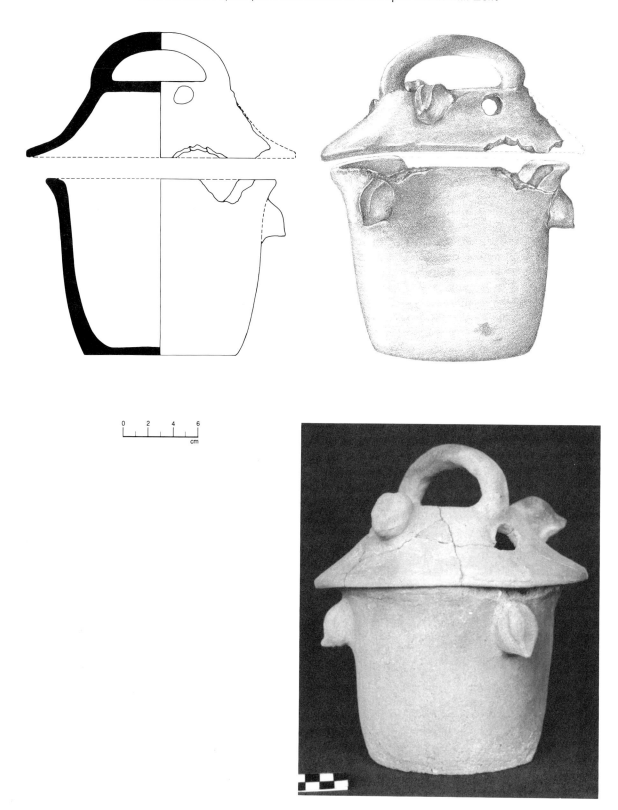

Figure 124.   Sepultura Unslipped 1-213

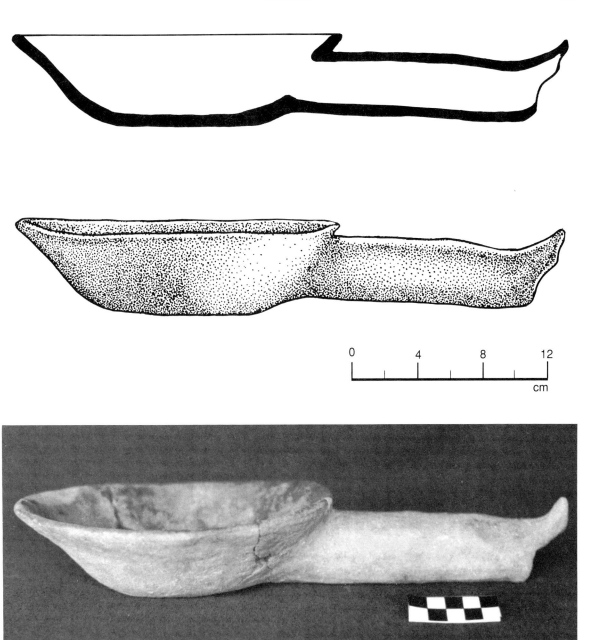

Figure 125. Sepultura Unslipped 1-303 (scale of drawings: 1:2)

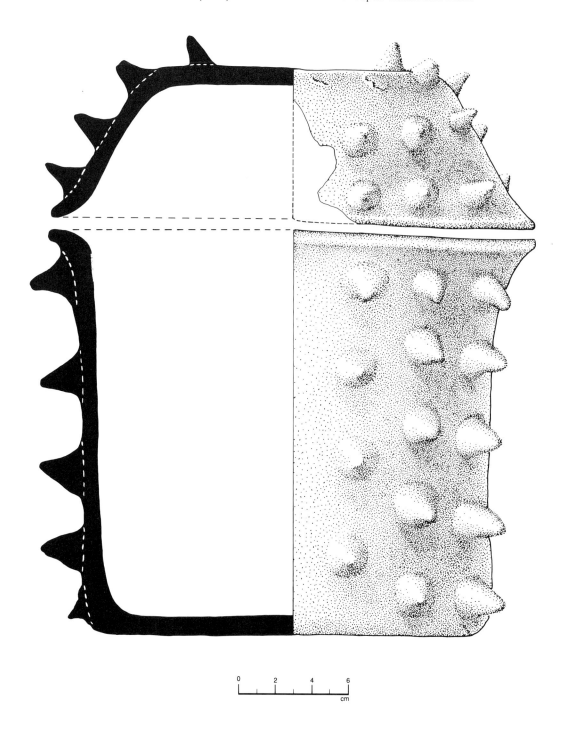

Figure 126. Sepultura Unslipped 1-356

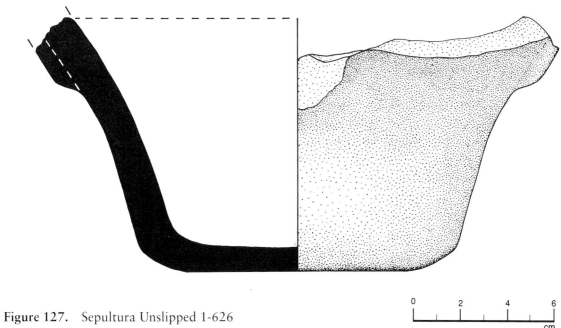

Figure 127. Sepultura Unslipped 1-626

Figure 128. Sepultura Unslipped 1-671

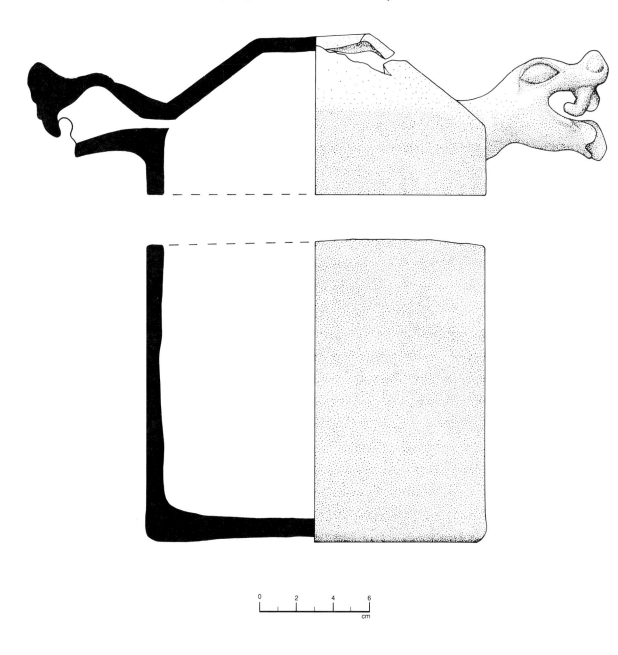

Figure 129. Sepultura Unslipped 1-970, square cache box and lid, profile

Figure 129 continued. Sepultura Unslipped 1-970, square cache box and lid, side views

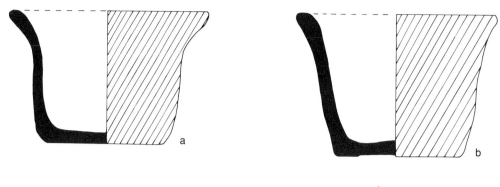

Figure 130a–b.   Sepultura Unslipped: a, 1-1079; b, 1-1080.

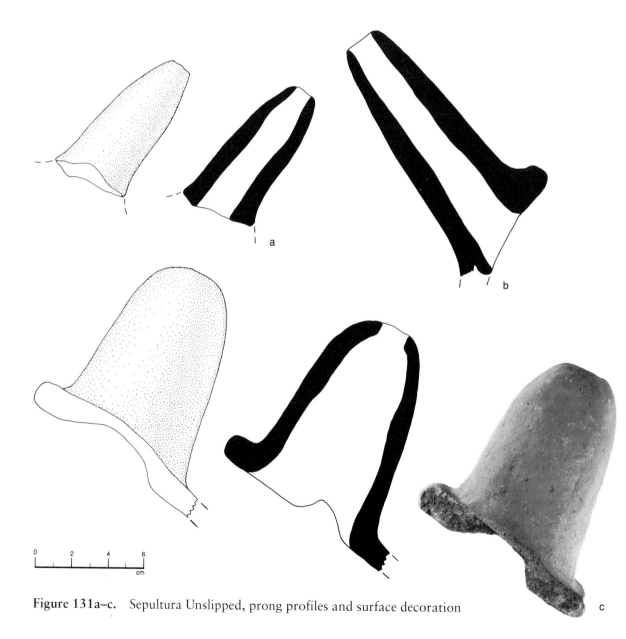

Figure 131a–c.   Sepultura Unslipped, prong profiles and surface decoration

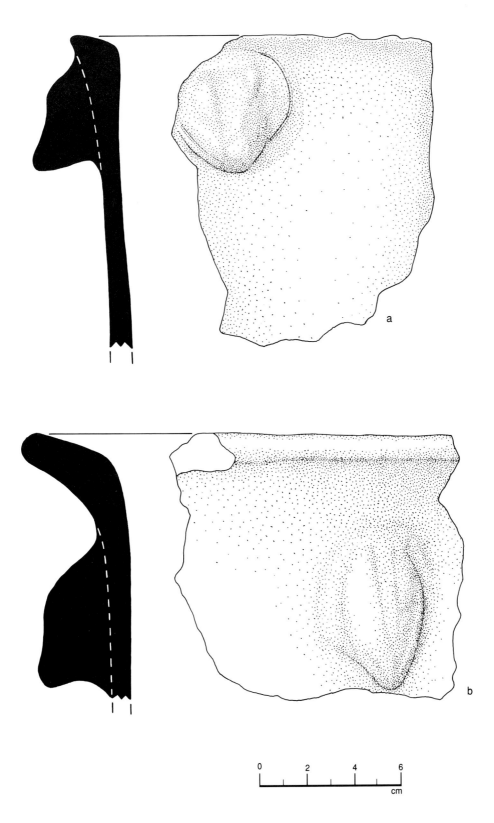

Figure 132a–b.   Sepultura Unslipped, rim profiles and surface decoration

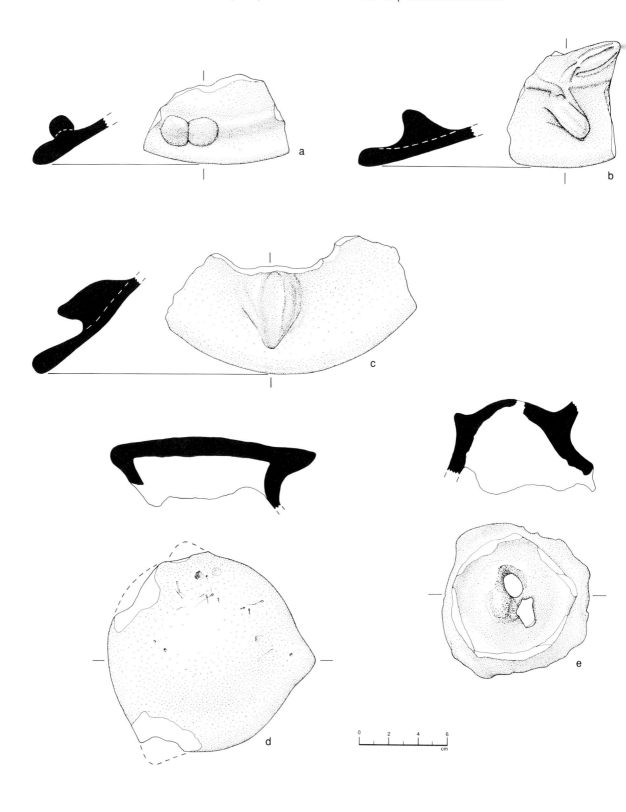

Figure 133a–e.   Sepultura Unslipped, lid profiles and surface decoration

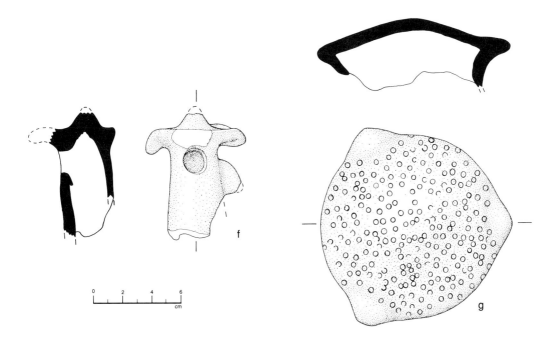

Figure 133f–g. Sepultura Unslipped, lid profiles and surface decoration

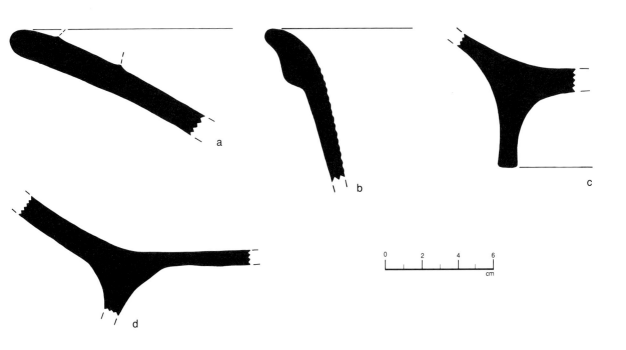

Figure 134a–d. Sepultura Unslipped, bowl profiles

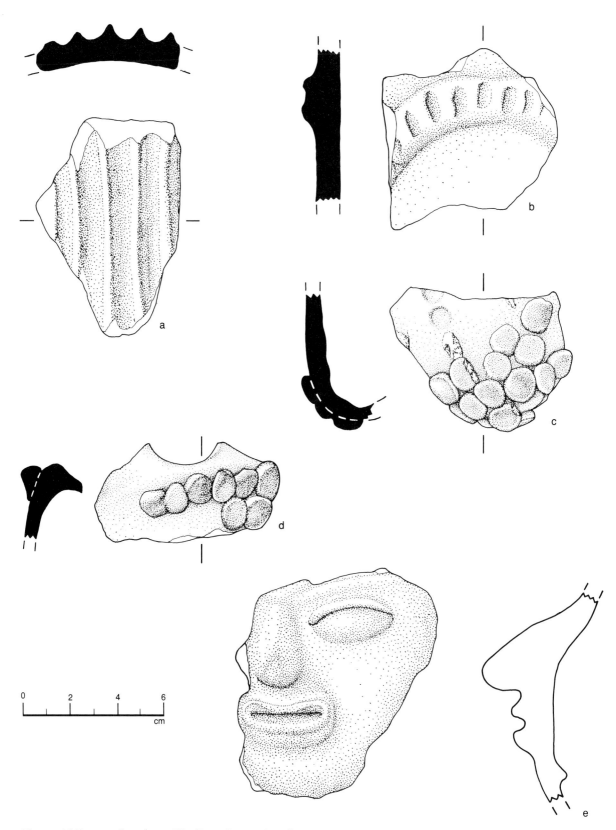

Figure 135a–e.   Sepultura Unslipped, exterior decoration

3 Other Artifacts

General, Comparative, and Summary Comments

Figurines in our Copan collections were of two basic categories: the handmade forms, generally attributed to Preclassic times, and the usually moldmade figurines or figurine-whistles so characteristic of the lowland Maya Late Classic period.

We found only five figurine fragments that could be identified typologically—if somewhat uncertainly—with the Preclassic period at Copan. Two of these were head fragments similar in face and eye treatment to one illustrated by J. M. Longyear (1952: fig. 86e) and classified by him as Archaic or Preclassic, although indicated as coming from an Early Classic provenience. In a general way, these two head fragments resemble those from Preclassic contexts elsewhere in the Maya area, both lowlands (Willey 1972, 1978) and highlands (Dahlin 1978). There is also a resemblance to the Preclassic figurines from the Ulua–Yojoa region of Honduras to the east (Strong, Kidder, and Paul 1938: pl. 15c ; Baudez and Becquelin 1973: fig. 150). Generally, such handmade figurine types date to the Middle Preclassic period, although some have been found in lowland Maya Late Preclassic contexts (Willey 1972: fig. 5a–b). The remaining three handmade figurine pieces in our collection have been classified by us as large, solid figurine body fragments. Because of their amorphous nature they are difficult to compare. Inasmuch as our excavations were largely in Classic period structures and deposits, it is not surprising that we found so few Preclassic figurine specimens; however, Longyear (1952:104), whose tests penetrated into

Preclassic levels in various excavations, comments on the scarcity of such figurine material at the site.

In contrast to our Preclassic, handmade figurine finds, we encountered many Late Classic, usually moldmade, figurine and figurine-whistle specimens, although over half our total of 149 was in small fragments. From the more complete specimens we could identify the standard lowland Maya moldmade varieties such as the Maya Men: Elaborately Attired, Maya Warrior, and Grotesque forms, together with the usual run of animals and birds (Willey 1972:14–78; Willey 1978:12–36). Of special interest were several pieces of a variety classified previously (Willey 1972:45–50) as the Semi-solid, Simply Dressed Type. At Altar de Sacrificios this type or variety appeared to be older than the other moldmade forms and dated, we thought, to the very end of the Early Classic and the beginning of the Late Classic. Such a dating would harmonize well with the Middle Classic date we put upon several of the structures and deposits that were excavated at Copan.

In general, our Copan Middle Classic and Late Classic moldmade figurines are clearly in the Peten lowland Maya tradition. They would be at home in sites such as Altar de Sacrificios, Seibal, Uaxactun, and Tikal. By way of interesting contrast, this is not the case for Maya highland (Kidder, Jennings, and Shook 1946; Dahlin 1978) or Honduran (Strong, Kidder, and Paul 1938: fig. 7; Baudez and Becquelin 1973: fig. 152a–d) regions, where moldmade figurines are either lacking or rendered in a quite different style.

Preclassic–Early Classic (?) Figurines (?) (2)

There are two of these. Both are fairly large heads, about 7 cm in height. Cat. No. 1-737 (fig. 136a) is heavy and has a relatively narrow hollow chamber. This was not a whistle chamber, and it was not connected with a body chamber (if such existed). The head appears to have been broken away from a body; however, the break is not rough but has been ground smooth. Only about two-thirds of the head remains; the right

side of the face and upper portion of the head have been lost through breakage. The facial features are well modeled—a slightly open mouth, nose (now eroded), and eye. The eye is a long oval depression with a central deep-dot punctation. The face has a white slip, which extends around to the back where there is evidence of a flat-rectangular hairdo or headdress. The upper part of the head is rather pointed or peaked. It has white paint at the back but not the front. A vent hole (for firing) is in one side of the head, just above the ear. Perhaps there was a paired hole in the other side of the head that has been lost in breakage.

Cat. No. 1-777 (fig. 136b) is solid. The features are nicely modeled—chin, mouth, nose, and elongated, depressed ovals for eyes. A visored headdress is indicated above the forehead, and a conical cap or hat crown rises above this. The head has been broken away from a presumed body at the neck. The back of the piece is smoothed, well flattened, but slightly imperfect in surface smoothness. The ware is coarse, red-buff fired, and there is no evidence of a slip as on the first head.

Cat. Nos.	Op. No. and Provenience
1-737	39(I) CV-44, Lev. 1
1-777	64(A) CV-160, Lev. 4

Large Solid Figurine Body Fragments (3)

Cat. No. 1-127 is an elbow or knee joint from a figure. The limb is about 3 x 2 cm in diameter and its overall length is about 5 cm, much too large for a limb of a smaller moldmade figurine. It is unslipped but of medium-fine buff ware.

Cat. No. 1-261 is rather amorphous. It may be a leg fragment. It is 2.6 x 2.5 cm and solid. It bears a red-orange slip on its unbroken surfaces.

Cat. No. 1-1091 appears to be the buttocks, lower back, and a portion of a leg of a large figurine. The individual was in a seated position and was probably wearing a short skirt. It measures 5.7 cm long, 4.3 cm high, and 3.7 cm wide. Its general aspect is that of a fragment of a fairly large, handmade Preclassic figurine. It is unslipped and of a medium-fine buff paste.

Cat. Nos.	Op. No. and Provenience
1-127	4(O) CV-20, Lev. 1
1-261	21(A) CV-20, Lev. 4
1-1091	105(A) CV-44, Lev. 3

Late Classic Figurines and Figurine-whistles (149)

Animals or Birds (17)

Cat. No. 1-534 (fig. 137a) is the only complete specimen. It represents a very crudely modeled frog, clearly handmodeled and not moldmade. The frog is extended, with all four legs out-stretched, on the top of the whistle. The animal faces the whistle mouthpiece. This latter consists of two apertures. One of these extends through so that air blown in would pass over the whistle chamber hole on the bottom of the piece; the other is partially broken and may never have penetrated all the way through to allow a passage for air. The two whistle chambers, each of which has a single large round vent at the bottom, are bulbous or spheroid. The ceramic of the piece is coarse and unslipped and fired to a gray-black. Its closest counterpart in the ceramic inventory of our Copan sites is the Lysandro Unslipped Type. The facial features of the frog are indicated with incisions. The specimen measures about 6 x 5 cm in diameter and 4 cm in height.

Cat. No. 1-522 (fig. 137b) is a peccary, a solid head broken away from a hollow body. It may have been moldmade, although this is uncertain. The eyes, snout, mouth, and tusks are indicated with realism. The paste is buff in color, rough, and unslipped. The head is 4 cm long and 3 cm across.

Cat. No. 1-950 (fig. 137c) is a little, solid handmade jaguar (?) head about 2.3 cm in diameter. Eyes, nose, mouth, and a cranial furrow are rather simply depicted. The underside of the head has been ground and smoothed after breakage. It might have been attached to a hollow-bodied figure.

Cat. No. 1-540 (fig. 137d) is probably the head of a pisote. It is solid and was probably broken from a hollow body, although we cannot be sure of this. We are uncertain if it is handmade or moldmade. The paste is the coarse ware noted in the specimens above. The eyes of the animal are indicated by punched incised circles, there are incised lines indicating furrows or wrinkles on top of the head, and the mouth is indicated by incision. Height 4 cm, diameter 2.7 cm.

Cat. No. 1-115 (fig. 137e) is a hollow monkey head, clearly a part of a whistle. There are two vent holes in the piece. The facial features of the monkey are moldmade, and the animal is shown wearing ear ornaments and, possibly, a neck ornament. The paste is coarse, but the piece may have been slipped and is now much eroded. Height 4 cm, width 3 cm.

Cat. No. 1-517 is a tiny monkey (?) head, probably moldmade, very badly eroded, that was probably part of a hollow body. Eyes, nose, and mouth can be made out; the conformation of face and snout suggests a monkey. Measurements are 2.4 x 2 cm.

Cat. Nos. 1-556 and 1-615 are little hollow-headed fragments of felines or jaguars. Both are moldmade and nicely designed, showing eyes, teeth, snout, and, on one specimen, ears. Both are made of a pottery paste that approaches Fine Orange (Near Fine Orange) (see Willey 1972:28). These fragments are, respectively, 3 x 2.5 cm and 2 x 2 cm.

Cat. Nos. 1-98 and 1-615 (second specimen), probably moldmade, are fragments of hollow animal bodies, otherwise unidentified. For Cat. No. 1-98 this animal identification is based on the shape of the front legs of the beast; human figures are not so depicted. The specimen is of a buff-fired ware that has been red-slipped but with the surface much eroded. The fragment is about 5 x 5.5 cm. For Cat. No. 1-615 the animal identification is based on the presence of two short front legs and a tail behind. It measures 3.5 x 3.5 cm. This specimen is of a similar ware to the other and was also red-slipped. There seems little doubt that these are figurine-whistle fragments.

Cat. Nos. 1-31, 1-545, and 1-704 are all little stylized bird heads, probably moldmade, that were probably broken from hollow bodies; this last, however, cannot be demonstrated. All are made of a Near Fine Orange paste. All show a similar beaked bird in stylized profile, with an eye on each side done with an appliqued punched pellet. The fragments vary in length from 2.5 to 5 cm.

Cat. No. 1-1177 (fig. 137f) is a strange little object. It is a fragment of the rear half of a quadruped. One hind leg remains; the other has been lost. A tail is indicated as turning up over the animal's back. An anus (vulva?) is indicated by a punctation just below the tail. The body is more or less flat. The piece is obviously handmade, of buff ware that may have been redslipped. Length 3.6 cm, width 3 cm, and thickness 1.2 cm.

Cat. Nos. 1-21 and 1-128 are very small moldmade fragments of either animals or birds.

Cat. Nos.	Op. No. and Provenience
1-21	2(I) CV-20, Lev. 1
1-31	4(C) CV-20, Lev. 1
1-98	6(J) CV-20, Lev 1
1-115	7(G) CV-20, Lev. 1
1-128	10(A) CV-17, Lev. 4
1-517	33(BB) CV-43, Lev. 4
1-522	33(CC) CV-43, Lev. 1
1-534	34(H) CV-43, Lev. 1
1-540	36(G) CV-43, Lev. 1
1-545	33(CC) CV-43, Lev. 2
1-556	37(C) CV-43, Lev. 1
1-615 (2 spec.)	35(O) CV-43, Lev. 1
1-704	43(E) CV-43, Lev. 1
1-922	50(A) CV-45, Lev. 3
1-950	39 (S) CV-44, Lev. 1
1-1177	83(A) CV-16, Lev. 2

Maya Men: Elaborately Attired (9)

This type follows the categorization of figurines as used at Seibal (Willey 1978:19–23), where this general term was used to subsume various elaborately attired types as these had been described from Altar de Sacrificios (Willey 1972:27–40). All of these figurines are moldmade; all came from hollow-bodied forms; and it is likely that they were whistles. Because they will be described individually here, further varietal classification is unnecessary.

Cat. No. 1-196 (fig. 138a) is a head with an elaborate, turban-like headdress. The individual wears ear ornaments and a heavy necklace. The paste is Near Fine Orange. Total height is 4 cm.

Cat. No. 1-615 is a portion of a hollow head. The nature of the high, fan-like headdress suggests a man. Paste is dark brown. Total height is 5 cm.

Cat. No. 1-617 is a badly eroded solid head that was probably attached to a hollow body. The headdress, although largely broken away, was of an elaborate fan or turban type. Paste is reddish, coarse. Height is 4.3 cm.

Cat. No. 1-643 is a fragment showing one ear ornament and a portion of a high headdress. The head was hollow. The paste is reddish, coarse. Height is 4.7 cm.

Cat. No. 1-770 is a headcrest fragment, a high, comb-like feature. It is solid, but the fracture on the bottom of the fragment shows that the head of the individual was hollow. The paste is reddish, coarse. The fragment is 3 cm high and 5.3 cm wide.

Cat. No. 1-777 is an eroded, red-paste specimen of a solid head. The headdress was fan-like or turban-like and similar to Cat. No. 1-617. From the breakage in the neck area it is clear that the head was once attached to a hollow body. Height is 4.3 cm.

No cat. number—8 (fig. 138b) is a flat, solid head, probably broken from a hollow body. The headdress is a tall one, appearing as plumes rising from a headband. Paste is buff-colored. Height is 4.8 cm.

Cat. Nos. 1-285 and 1-622 are body fragments from hollow, moldmade bodies. Both indicate wide, heavy belts, very probably ball-game belts, worn by the individuals depicted. Such gear was worn only by males, usually elaborately attired ones. Cat. No. 1-285 (fig. 138c) is of black paste (possibly black-slipped?) and is 7.5 cm tall. No. 1-622 is about 4 x 4 cm in diameter and is of Near Fine Orange paste.

Cat. Nos.	Op. No. and Provenience
1-196	19(A) CV-20, Lev. 2
1-285	24(A) CV-20, Lev. 6
1-615	35(O) CV-43, Lev. 1
1-617	33(FF) CV-43, Lev. 2
1-622	38(G) CV-43, Lev. 1
1-643	39(D) CV-43, Lev. 1
1-770	47(D) CV-47, Lev. 1
1-777	64(A) CV-160, Lev. 4
No cat. number—8	

Maya Warriors (1)

This type has been defined from Seibal (Willey 1978:23).

Cat. No. 1-1025 (fig. 139) is a fragment of a hollow moldmade figurine of red-buff paste which depicts a circular shield, in incisions and appliqued modeling. A tassel depends from the center of the shield. The shield was undoubtedly held in the hand of a warrior figure. The fragment is 4.3 x 2.6 cm.

Cat. No. 1-1025 came from Op. No. 49(A) CV-43, Level 7-C.

Maya Women (1)

Only one fragment can be identified as a woman, Cat. No. 1-31 (fig. 140). This shows the front body section of a hollow, moldmade figurine. Dress, necklace, crossed hands, and exposed breasts (above the dress) are all depicted. Paste is a coarse buff. Height is 5.1 cm.

Cat. No. 1-31 came from Op. No. 4(C) CV-20, Level 1.

Monsters (1)

Following an earlier classification (Willey 1972:50), this designation is applied to a half-human, half-bird figurine (Cat. No. 1-922). It is a hollow, moldmade figurine-whistle, or the upper portion of one. The head is that of a broad-beaked bird with a crest above the head done in rather stylized fashion with what may be indications of a ruff (or wings?) at the sides of the head. As the drawings (fig. 141) show, both the head and body chambers are hollow. The latter has been broken away at the bottom. It measures 5.8 x 5 x 4 cm. The face of the bird—beak, nostrils, and eyes—is depicted quite forcefully. The body below this appears to be the breast of a woman.

Cat. No. 1-922 came from Op. 50(A) CV-45, Level 3.

Semi-solid, Simply Dressed Type (4)

This type was noted and described from Altar de Sacrificios (Willey 1972:45–49), and there are a few specimens in our Copan collections that probably fit the type. The most definite of these is Cat. No. 1-861 (fig. 142a), a human male torso. It has been broken off at the waist. The head, which may have been moldmade, is missing. A fragment of one freestanding arm remains. The figurine is hollow, but the body cavity is small and tubular, a characteristic of the type. The figure appears to be wearing a simple, shirt-like garment. There is no visible ornamentation, although a small patch at the center of the chest suggests that a small ornament (such as that seen in the figurine shown in Willey 1972: fig. 37a) has been broken off. This rather severe, simple garb is another characteristic of the type from which the name is derived. There is no indication that this figurine was ever used as a whistle. Measurements: height, 6 cm; width, 5 cm; and thickness, 2.6 cm.

Cat. No. 1-1060 (fig. 142b) is similar to the above. It shows the shoulders and upper torso of a human male. There is no evidence that this piece was hollow; however, the break occurs high enough up on the body to have destroyed all evidence of this. There is just a suggestion on the shoulders of a plain, shirt-like garment. Remains of a simple necklace are depicted at the base of the throat. Measurements: height, 2.6 cm; width, 5.5 cm; and thickness, 2 cm.

Where human head portions were found, they were clearly moldmade; however, the simply dressed bodies appear to have been handmade. Other characteristics of the type are freestanding limbs and, probably but not certainly, appliqued ornamental features. Cat. No. 1-846 is a human arm of an appropriate size for such a figurine. It has been broken away from a body. There is a glove or gauntlet on the hand and a bracelet around the wrist. Another possible specimen is Cat. No. 1-747, a freestanding plumelike decorative element that might have been broken from a headdress.

Cat. Nos.	Op. No. and Provenience
1-747	39(J) CV-44, Lev. 1
1-846	47(H) CV-47, Lev. 1
1-861	71(A) CV-204, Lev. 4
1-1060	79(A) CV-16, Lev. 3

Semi-solid, Simply Dressed Type: Crude (4)

Again, following descriptions from Altar de Sacrificios (Willey 1972:49–50), these specimens appear to pertain to this type. The suggestive characteristics of the type are heavy appliqued belts and ornaments, modeled rather crudely.

Three specimens (Cat. Nos. 1-206, 1-690, and 1-952) are portions of lower human bodies, two standing and one seated. All were probably hollow figurines. The remaining piece (Cat. No. 1-1024) is a human head with a crudely modeled turban. The head is solid but the missing body was probably hollow. The facial features were clearly moldmade. There is no clear evidence here that any of these were whistles, but, by analogy with specimens elsewhere (Willey 1972: fig. 39), they may have been. The height of the head fragment is 4 cm. The heights of the other two pieces are between 3 and 4 cm.

Cat. Nos.	Op. No. and Provenience
1-206	21(A) CV-20, Lev. 2
1-690	34(P) CV-43, Lev. 1
1-952	50(A) CV-45, Lev. 6-A
1-1024	50(A) CV-45, Lev. 8

Human Figurine Fragments (24)

These are fragments of hollow-bodied, moldmade figurines or figurine-whistles. The fragments are not large enough or distinctive enough to identify for certain as to sex; however, it is probable that most came from male figurines of the type, Maya Men: Elaborately Attired. One or two limb fragments may be of the Semi-solid, Simply Dressed Type.

Cat. Nos.	Op. No. and Provenience
1-14	2(B) CV-20, Lev. 3
1-33	5(B) CV-20, Lev. 1
1-77	6(H) CV-20, Lev.1
1-156	15(A) CV-20, Lev. 1
1-186	15(B) CV-20, Lev. 1
1-196	19(A) CV-20, Lev. 2
1-200	20(A) CV-20, Lev. 2
1-231	21(A) CV-20, Lev. 2, Special Find 39
1-503	36(A) CV-43, Lev. 1
1-519	36(B) CV-43, Lev. 1
1-550	38(A) CV-43, Lev. 1
1-561	35(I) CV-43, Lev. 1
1-565	36(K) CV-43, Lev. 1
1-615	35(O) CV-43, Lev.1
1-626 (2 spec.)	37(N) CV-43, Lev. 1
1-629	43(C) CV-43, Lev. 1
1-633	37(M) CV-43, Lev. 1
1-680	53(A) CV-91, Lev. 8
1-747	39(J) CV-44, Lev. 1

1-782	45(F) CV-45, Lev. 1
1-859	49(A) CV-43, Lev. 2
1-890	68(A) CV-68, Lev. 2
1-1057	49(A) CV-43, Lev. 8-C

Human or Animal Figurine Fragments (83)

This still larger residual category is for all of those figurine fragments, mostly of a hollow-bodied, moldmade kind, that cannot be identified as animal or human but are probably all from some life-form or another. Probabilities favor most of these as being from human figures.

Cat. Nos.	Op. No. and Provenience
1-28	5(A) CV-20, Lev. 1
1-69	5(L) CV-20, Lev 1
1-70	4(J) CV-20
1-72 (2 spec.)	8(B) CV-20, Lev. 2
1-76	5(M) CV-20, Lev. 1
1-77	6(H) CV-20, Lev. 1
1-79	5(O) CV-20, Lev. 1
1-88 (2 spec.)	7(F) CV-20, Lev. 1
1-125	7(H) CV-20, Lev. 1
1-126	6(M) CV-20, Lev. 1
1-146 (2 spec.)	12(B) CV-20, Lev. 1
1-184	16(D) Sacbe, Lev. 4
1-197	19(B) CV-20, Lev. 2
1-219	20(A) CV-20, Lev. 4
1-220 (2 spec.)	19(C) CV-20, Lev. 4
1-238	19(C) CV-20, Lev. 5
1-247	21(A) CV-20, Lev. 3, associated with Burial 11
1-477 (3 spec.)	33(E) CV-43, Lev. 4
1-503	36(A) CV-43, Lev. 1
1-517 (2 spec.)	33(BB) CV-43, Lev. 4
1-522 (4 spec.)	33(CC) CV-43, Lev. 1
1-524 (2 spec.)	35(E) CV-45, Lev. 1
1-525	34(E) CV-43, Lev. 1
1-526 (2 spec.)	33(Z) CV-43, Lev. 4
1-532	34(G) CV-43, Lev. 1
1-555 (2 spec.)	33(EE) CV-43, Lev. 2
1-556	37(C) CV-43, Lev. 1
1-565	36(K) CV-43, Lev. 1
1-569 (2 spec.)	34(K) CV-43, Lev. 1
1-573	36(L) CV-43, Lev. 1
1-589 (2 spec.)	41(A) CV-47, Lev. 1
1-602	35(M) CV-43, Lev. 1
1-609 (2 spec.)	54(A) CV-94, Lev. 2
1-614	52(A) CV-88, Lev. 2
1-615 (2 spec.)	35(O) CV-43, Lev. 1
1-617 (5 spec.)	33(FF) CV-43, Lev. 2
1-618	36(N) CV-43, Lev. 1
1-620	37(I) CV-43, Lev. 1

1-627	40(D) CV-45, Lev. 1
1-641	35(P) CV-43, Lev. 1
1-662	54(A) CV-94, Lev. 5
1-687	35(Q) CV-43, Lev. 1
1-688	33(FF) CV-43, Lev. 3
1-711 (2 spec.)	44(G) CV-46, Lev. 1
1-733	35(S) CV-43, Lev. 1
1-761 (2 spec.)	42(I) CV-43, Lev. 1
1-842	39(M) CV-44, Lev. 1
1-850	65(B) CV-177, Lev. 3
1-857	100(A) CV-43, Lev. 1
1-950 (2 spec.)	39(S) CV-44, Lev. 1
1-952	50(A) CV-45, Lev. 6-A
1-1021	49(A) CV-43, Lev. 6-C
1-1037	77(B) CV-16, Lev. 1

No Number (6 spec.)

Large Human Figurines (5)

There are five human head fragments that are from moldmade hollow figurines of a much larger size than those of the usual figurine or figurine-whistle categories.

Cat. No. 1-30 is a facial fragment of a hollow, moldmade head. Height from mouth to top of eyes, which is all that remains, is 2.5 cm.

Cat. No. 1-115 (fig. 143a) is a partial hollow head, showing one side of a hairdo or headdress and a circular ear ornament. The height of the face is estimated as about 3 to 4 cm. The ware is Near Fine Orange.

Cat. No. 1-632 (fig. 143b) is the nose of a large human face broken from a hollow-headed figurine. The nose, which has a bar-like ornament showing on each side of the septum, is 2.4 cm in height, suggesting that the entire face must have been about 5 to 6 cm high. The paste is Near Fine Orange.

Cat. No. 1-895 (fig. 143c) shows the upper portion of the face and a part of a headdress of a hollow-headed figurine. Total head height was probably 5 to 6 cm. The moldmade face is well done, with eyes, eyelids, ears, nose, and septum nose-ornament all portrayed. There is a head-band with a central ornament on the brow. The ware is fairly fine quality and fired a clouded buff-black with no definite evidence of pigment or slip.

Cat. No. 1-1085 (fig. 143d) is a facial fragment of an eroded hollow-headed figurine. Mouth, nose, and eyes are all moldmade and well styled. Original total facial height was probably 5 to 6 cm.

Cat. Nos.	Op. No. and Provenience
1-30	4(B) CV-20, Lev. 1
1-115	7(G) CV-20, Lev. 1
1-632	42(B) CV-43, Lev. 1
1-895	68(A) CV-68, Lev. 4
1-1085	102(A) CV-43, Lev. 5

MISCELLANEOUS POTTERY OBJECTS

Unperforated Potsherd Disks	47	Conical	4
Perforated Potsherd Disks (Spindle Whorls)	30	Rectangular	2
Other Worked Potsherds	3	Multi-chambered	8
Spindle Whorls (Specially Manufactured)	4	Miscellaneous Forms	3
Potsherd Pendants	3	Miniature Vessels	33
Beads	3	Briquette Materials	150
Ear Ornaments	18		
Ceramic Ornaments or Ritual Objects	11		
Seals or Stamps	5		
Collanders	36		
Candeleros	271		
Cylindrical	167		
Bottle-shaped	87		

General, Comparative, and Summary Comments

We have a substantial number of potsherd disks, both unperforated and perforated, in our Copan collections. Longyear (1952:103–104) also noted these in his excavations. They are, of course, common in the Maya lowlands (see Willey et al. 1965:402–407; Willey 1972:78–82; Willey 1978:40–44, and also for other Peten lowland citations). Sherd disks are mentioned from Los Naranjos, in Honduras, (Baudez and Becquelin 1973:400), and a fragment of a perforated disk is illustrated from that site (ibid.: fig. 149l). These appear to be from Late Classic contexts. Both perforated and unperforated disks are common in the Chalchuapa collections from El Salvador (Sheets 1978:66–68).

Our specially manufactured or molded spindle whorls include both the hemispherical and the flat disk varieties. Longyear (1952: fig. 82j–l) illustrates moldmade whorls from Copan. They are found throughout the Maya lowlands and pertain to the Late Classic horizon (see Willey et al. 1965:402; Willey 1972:86; Willey 1978:40, 46–47). They do not appear in the Los Naranjos account (Baudez and Becquelin 1973), but W. D. Strong, A. V. Kidder, and J. D. Paul (1938: pl. 4i–j) illustrate moldmade whorls from the Naco region of Honduras. They seem abundant at Chalchuapa (Sheets 1978:62–63), but Kidder (Kidder, Jennings, and Shook 1946:215–216) speaks of the rarity of spindle whorls at Kaminaljuyu, a circumstance that would appear to pertain to both Preclassic and Classic periods at that site.

Among our miscellaneous worked potsherds are three classified as pendants. One of these is the rather distinctive notched-end pendant or weight that is known widely in southern Mesoamerica, occurring in Maya lowland Preclassic and Classic contexts (Willey 1978:44–46; Willey 1972:82) and especially in Postclassic deposits (Willey et al. 1965:408; see also Proskouriakoff 1962:402; Sanders 1960; Bullard 1973). C. Baudez and P. Becquelin (1973: 399–400, fig. 143a–d) illustrate the form from Honduras, and M. D. Coe (1961:101, 105) notes it for the Pacific Coast of Guatemala. The Honduran Los Naranjos examples are Late Classic; those from Pacific Guatemala are Preclassic. While the notched-end pendant (or net or line weight) does seem to be particularly characteristic of the Postclassic period in the Maya lowlands, it obviously has an earlier history here as well as elsewhere.

All of our definitely identified pottery ear ornaments from Copan were of the napkin-ring type,

or probably so. A few of our fragmentary specimens could have been pieces broken from an ear spool type that is annular and hollow but is closed at one end. This closed-end form was found by Longyear (1952:102–103: fig. 82d–f) a Copan, where he also found the napkin-ring type (ibid.: fig. 82 a–c). The napkin-ring form is common in the Maya lowlands. G. Willey (1972: 89–93, fig. 74a–g) found it at Altar de Sacrificios where it occurs from Late Preclassic through Late Classic contexts. There is a Preclassic specimen reported from Uaxactun (Ricketson and Ricketson 1937: pl. 69), and the type occurs in the Late Classic at Piedras Negras (W. R. Coe 1959:70) Baudez and Becquelin (1973:398, figs. 148g–j 149f) found Preclassic specimens at Los Naranjos in Honduras; Smith and Kidder (1943: fig. 34c) show a napkin-ring from the Motagua Valley; and they are present at Kaminaljuyu (Kidder, Jennings, and Shook 1946:215). At this latter site they date as Preclassic.

We found both flat and cylindrical seals or stamps at Copan. Longyear (1952:103, fig. 83) did as well. Ours are mainly from Classic period contexts; his are from both Preclassic and Classic, with a flat stamp dating as Late Preclassic and cylindrical seals from Late Preclassic and Early Classic. Both forms are found in the Maya lowlands. At Barton Ramie, a cylindrical specimen (Willey et al. 1965:410, fig. 258l) came from Middle Preclassic levels. At Altar de Sacrificios, two cylindrical seals can be dated as Middle Preclassic and Protoclassic, respectively (Willey 1972:94, figs. 77, 78), while a flat stamp from that site is placed as Protoclassic (ibid.:93–94, fig. 75). From Seibal, there was a cylindrical seal in Middle Preclassic levels (Willey 1978:50, fig. 56) and a flat stamp that probably dates as Terminal Classic (ibid.:49–50, fig. 55). In the Guatemalan highlands, at Kaminaljuyu, both a flat stamp (Kidder, Jennings, and Shook 1946: 215, fig. 166g) and a roller or cylindrical stamp (ibid.:214–215, figs. 92b, 187n,o) were recovered, all uncertainly dated. Payson D. Sheets (1978:65–66) reports both forms from Chalchuapa. Baudez and Becquelin (1973:399, fig. 148k–n) found both flat and cylindrical stamps at Los Naranjos, where a flat one was dated as Late Classic and two cylindrical ones as Late Preclassic. Strong, Kidder, and Paul (1938: pl. 9l, fig. 57) also found flat stamps in Honduras, with Late Preclassic and Late Classic dates. As a general statement we can say that both cylindrical and flat seals or stamps made of pottery are found in the Maya lowlands and in bordering territories to the south and east. They seem never to be very numerous, and both forms occur from at least Middle Preclassic through Late Classic times.

Of all of the types subsumed under the heading of miscellaneous pottery objects, candeleros are by far the most common in our Copan collections. They also appear to be, if not unique to that site, at least unusually characteristic of it. Longyear (1952:101–102) discusses them at some length. He notes that they first appear in the site sequence in the early part of the Early Classic period and reach their peak of frequency in the latter part of that period. Thereafter, in the Late Classic, they gradually die out. Our excavation data do not directly confirm this chronological disappearance of candeleros during the Late Classic period. Longyear found little in the Mesoamerican literature that was truly similar to the Copan candeleros. He found that something similar occurred at Teotihuacan; indeed, the general form, a small pottery object suggesting a socketed candle holder, was first so named from Teotihuacan data. The Copan candeleros, however, are not a good match for the ones from Teotihuacan. The latter are usually multi-chambered; those from Copan are almost all single-chambered objects.

In turning to the Maya highlands and lowlands, Longyear found a few candeleros described in the literature. One is described and illustrated from Kaminaljuyu (Kidder, Jennings, and Shook 1946:216, fig. 93). It is a double-chambered form with nearly squared sides and base—quite unlike those from Copan. The authors of the Kaminaljuyu report cite similar squared candeleros for elsewhere in the Guatemalan highlands and for the Pacific Coast of Guatemala, implying, however, that such objects are never found in large numbers. Longyear (ibid.) also made reference to an occasional candelero from Maya lowland sites, noting specifically Yaxchilan and Piedras Negras. Again, these seem to be the multi-chambered forms. W. R. Coe (1959:72, fig. 60f-g) described and illustrated those from Piedras Negras. They are little, shallow double-cups, quite unlike the

Copan candeleros. Interestingly, the closest similarities to the Copan candeleros all lie to the north or the east, in Honduras. There are some from Los Naranjos (Baudez and Becquelin 1973:342–343, fig. 133r–t). These are single-chambered cylinders, some with incised decoration, and much like, or identical to, the Copan specimens. Strong, Kidder, and Paul (1938: fig. 7j) also show such a candelero from the Ulua Valley; and Baudez and Becquelin (1973) refer to others from this general region as shown by D. Stone (1941: fig. 94e) and George B. Gordon (1898: fig. 34, pl. 12, fig. 1d). More recently, candeleros have been found at Gualjoquito and at Naco. We have information on six from the former site. Most of these seem to have been of the cylindrical variety, and one had four chambers. One of the single-chambered form was decorated with punctations on its outer surface (W. Ashmore, personal communication 1986). Four specimens from Naco include two with multiple chambers (J. S. Henderson, personal communication 1986). It should be emphasized, however, that these candeleros from Honduran regions to the east and north of Copan are rare, or at least scant in number. So far, Copan is the only place where the type is found in large numbers. Perhaps like Copador Polychrome, the candelero is primarily a Copan type, diffusing from there, in a limited way, to other parts of Honduras.

Unperforated Potsherd Disks (47)

This classification follows others (see, for example, Willey 1978:40–41). All are worked potsherds with edges trimmed or ground to circular or disk shapes, with varying degrees of workmanship in shaping and in approximating a perfect circular form (fig. 144a–e). Fifteen of the specimens belong to the large variety (more than 6.5 cm in diameter); the others are of the small variety. There are only two complete large variety specimens; 17 of the small ones are complete.

It is, of course, possible, and even probable, that the small specimens were blanks, meant to be finished into perforated spindle whorls. This is also possible for some of the large variety. For instance, Cat. No. 1-779 is only 7.5 to 8 cm in diameter. Other large variety disks, however, seem too big for this. Thus, Cat. Nos. 1-845 and

1-95, although incomplete and presenting less than half a disk, were probably in excess of 12 cm in diameter; and their purpose must have been for something other than that of a spindle whorl.

In general, coarse-ware pottery types—Casaca Striated and Lysandro Unslipped—predominate in the disks, especially the large variety ones; but other types are also represented, such as Cruz Incised, Lorenzo Red, Raul Red, and even a few sherds of the Tipon and Chilanga groups.

Cat. Nos.	Op. No. and Provenience
1-1	1(A) CV-20, Surface, Large Plaza
1-21 (2 spec.)	2(I) CV-20, Lev. 1
1-43	4(D) CV-20, Lev. 1
1-61	6(F) CV-20, Lev. 1
1-77	6(H) CV-20, Lev. 1
1-82	7(E) CV-20, Lev. 1
1-85	5(P) CV-20, Lev. 1
1-88	7(F) CV-20, Lev. 1
1-126	6(M) CV-20, Lev. 1
1-142	12(A) CV-20, Lev. 1
1-150	13(A) CV-20, Lev. 1
1-206	21(A) CV-20, Lev. 2
1-207	19(C) CV-20, Lev. 3
1-217	22(A) CV-48, Lev. 1
1-245	22(B) CV-48, Lev. 3
1-452	30(A) CV-45, Surface
1-508	33(E) CV-43, Lev. 8
1-522	33(CC) CV-43, Lev. 1
1-529	34(D) CV-43, Lev. 1
1-542	33(CC) CV-43, Lev. 4
1-543	35(F) CV-43, Lev. 1
1-560	35(J) CV-43, Lev. 1
1-590	37(E) CV-43, Lev. 1
1-605	51(A) CV-84, Lev. 3
1-617 (2 spec.)	35(FF) CV-43, Lev. 2
1-619	34(M) CV-43, Lev. 1
1-626	37(N) CV-43, Lev. 1
1-635	44(B) CV-46, Lev. 1
1-689	44(C) CV-46, Lev. 1
1-745	33(FF) CV-43, Lev. 4-B
1-760	48(B) CV-47, Lev. 1
1-779	42(H) CV-43, Lev. 1
1-815 (2 spec.)	39(L) CV-44, Lev. 1
1-842	39(M) CV-44, Lev. 1
1-845	35(T) CV-43, Lev. 1
1-872	65(B) CV-177, Lev. 4
1-905	103(A) CV-46, Lev. 2
1-919	39(P) CV-43, Lev. 1
1-950 (2 spec.)	39(S) CV-43, Lev. 1
1-953	102(A) CV-43, Lev. 2

1-972	49(A) CV-43, Lev. 5-C
1-1023	50(A) CV-45, Lev. 7
No Number	

Perforated Potsherd Disks (Spindle Whorls) (30)

These are centrally drilled or perforated potsherds of the sort usually identified as spindle whorls (fig. 145a–g). In our Copan collections the size range is from about 3–3.5 cm in diameter to about 6.9 cm in diameter. Thus, except for one specimen (Cat. No. 1-733), all of the Copan sherd whorls fall into the small variety as has been defined for Seibal (Willey 1978:41–42). Most of the Copan whorls in this collection fall in the 4 to 6 cm range. Six are complete; the rest are fragments.

A little less than half of these whorls have carefully trimmed and ground edges and are nearly perfect circles; the others are moderately to notably ragged around the edges, giving the appearance of being unfinished or being carelessly made. Drilling on all of the whorls is biconical. The actual perforation diameters range from 4 to 9 mm; in all cases, however, the beginnings of the hole, on either side of the sherd, are somewhat larger than this. Three specimens show unfinished perforations.

There seems to have been little or no flat surface grinding or smoothing of the sherds; that is, they remain as they were except for the edge trimming and shaping and the perforation. They can be readily identified as to pottery types—Casaca Striated, Lorenzo Red, Raul Red, and Lysandro Unslipped all being represented.

Cat. Nos.	Op. No. and Provenience
1-28 (2 spec.)	5(A) CV-20, Lev. 1
1-31	4(C) CV-20, Lev. 1
1-33	5(B) CV-20, Lev. 1
1-53	7(A) CV-20, Lev. 1
1-77	6(H) CV-20, Lev. 1
1-82	7(E) CV-20, Lev. 1
1-88 (2 spec.)	7(F) CV-20, Lev. 1
1-93	6(I) CV-20, Lev. 1
1-98 (3 spec.)	6(J) CV-20, Lev. 1
1-128	10(A) CV-17, Lev. 4
1-537	34(I) CV-43, Lev. 1
1-573 (2 spec.)	36(L) CV-43, Lev. 1

-609	54(A) CV-94, Lev. 2
-617 (2 spec.)	33(FF) CV-43, Lev. 2
-621	35(N) CV-43, Lev. 1
-707	38(H) CV-43, Lev. 1
-733	35(S) CV-43, Lev. 1
-842	39(M) CV-44, Lev. 1
-859	49(A) CV-43, Lev. 2
-892	45(O) CV-46, Lev. 1
-910	39(Q) CV-44, Lev. 1
-942	72(A) CV-205, Lev. 7
-973	39(T) CV-44, Lev. 1
-1035	104(A) CV-43, Lev. 1

Other Worked Potsherds (3)

There are three worked sherds, other than disks or perforated disks, that are comparable to some of the worked sherd forms seen elsewhere in the Maya area (see Willey, 1978:44–46).

Cat. No. 1-574 is a rectangular piece, measuring about 3.8 cm in diameter. The four edges have all been carefully ground. It is a sherd of polychrome pottery, probably Copador Polychrome.

Cat. No. 1-617 is a fragment of a worked sherd, probably originally of ovoid form. The fragment measures 6.4 x 2.4 cm. It is of eroded polychrome, probably Copador.

Cat. No. 1-745 is a thick, coarse, red-slipped (on the exterior) sherd, best classified as Raul Red. It has been trimmed, although the edges are not well ground, to an oval, 9.3 x 5.8 cm.

Cat. Nos.	Op. No. and Provenience
1-574	35(L) CV-43, Lev. 1
1-617	33(FF) CV-43, Lev. 2
1-745	33(FF) CV-43, Lev. 4-B

Spindle Whorls (Specially Manufactured) (4)

These are pottery whorls made especially as whorls, not reworked from sherds.

Cat. No. 1-98 (fig. 146a) is less than half of a semispherical whorl. Diameter of the original was 3 cm, and height or thickness was just a little over 1 cm. The base is smooth, plain, and polished. Around the base is a plain band about 3 mm wide, set off from the design above it by an incised line. This design on the whorl was also executed in incision. The perforation is about 6 mm in diameter.

Cat. No. 1-566 (fig. 146b) is a plain semispherical whorl of eroded buff ware that may have been slipped. Diameter is 2.4 cm, and height or thickness is 1.2 cm. The hole or perforation is 6 mm in diameter.

Cat. No. 1-602 (fig. 146c) is half of a hemispherical whorl, 2.8 cm in diameter x 1.6 cm in thickness. The perforation of the whorl is 6 mm in diameter. On the bottom there is a light, incised line design of a circle divided by four attached semicircles. The top of the whorl shows a nested series of triangles between two encircling lines. The whorl is made of a nicely smoothed gray-buff ware that was slipped with red.

Cat. No. 1-1086 (fig. 146d) is a circular whorl that has been ground around the edges to approximate a truncated cone. Both the bottom and the top are smooth and plain. Diameter is 2.3 cm and thickness is 0.7 cm. The perforation is 4 to 5 mm in diameter. The ware is fine and dark brown.

Cat. Nos.	Op. No. and Provenience
1-98	6(J) CV-20, Lev. 1
1-566	39(A) CV-43, Lev. 1
1-602	35(M) CV-43, Lev. 1
1-1086	104(A) CV-43, Lev. 6

Potsherd Pendants (3)

These are sherds reworked as pendants.

Cat. No. 1-237 is a Raul Red sherd, 5.5 cm long and 4.2 cm wide at the top. The overall shape is an elongated oval with one flattened and eared end. It could have been suspended as a pendant by attaching a cord around the ears.

Cat. No. 1-268 is a notched-end pendant. It is elongated, 3.2 cm in length and less than this in width. One of the ends has been notched to form a little suspension nubbin. It was made from a sherd of Raul Red.

Cat. No. 1-954 (fig. 147) is an almost complete circular sherd pendant. It is 3.7 cm in diameter. The edges have been very carefully ground. There is a hole near the rim, 6 mm in diameter, which has been biconically drilled. The sherd belongs to the Chilanga ceramic group.

Cat. Nos.	Op. No. and Provenience
1-237	22(B) CV-48, Lev. 1
1-268	19(C) CV-20, Lev. 8
1-954	50(A) CV-45, Lev. 5

Beads (3)

These are all specially manufactured as pottery beads; they are not reworked sherds or other pottery fragments.

Two are subspherical in form. The larger of these, Cat. No. 1-361, is 2.7 cm in diameter and 1.9 cm in height. This size suggests that it may have been a spindle whorl rather than a bead; however, the form is subspherical rather than semispherical, the latter being the more common form for a specially manufactured whorl. The perforation is 5 to 6 mm in diameter. The object is made of a smoothed brown-black ware. The smaller subspherical bead is Cat. No. 1-1249. It measures 1.3 x 0.9 cm and is made of a buff ware.

The third bead (Cat. No. 1-771) is tubular in form. One end has been broken off, but the length of the remainder, 5.9 cm, is probably close to the original full length. Diameter is 1.5 cm, and the longitudinal hole that pierces the cylinder or tube is 5 mm in diameter. The intact end is rounded. The paste is a rough gray-black, and the bead has not been polished.

Cat. Nos.	Op. No. and Provenience
1-361	26(A) Main Center, Struct. L11-93, Lev. 10
1-771	34(S) CV-43, Lev. 1
1-1249	100(B) CV-43, Special Find 141, associated with Feature 13

Ear Ornaments (18)

Fifteen of these are of the well known, delicate, napkin-ring earspool type. A few were recovered complete; others are fragments. There is also a definite ear ornament of a tubular-pin type which is complete. The remaining two specimens clas-

sified under this heading are possible, but no definite, earplugs. Both of these are little effigies.

Of the napkin-ring type, Cat. No. 1-110 (fig. 148a) is a complete, elegant ring, with an outer diameter of 4 cm. It has a quadrate or rosette form marked by four indentations in the outer or flared side. The impressed or incised design, which consists of little V-shaped and key-shaped figures, is on this flared side. The other side is slightly flared but plain.

Cat. No. 1-224 (fig. 148b) is another napkin ring specimen. It measures 2.2 cm at the larger flared end and is 1.7 cm high. Walls of the ring are 1 to 2 mm in thickness. The ware is fine brown, but not polished. The larger flared end has been crimped or notched at four equidistant points to effect a kind of rosette configuration. At the smaller flared end there are four little ridges on the interior of the ring that correspond in position to the crimps or indentations at the larger flared end. A design, rectilinear in nature and not expertly incised, runs around the exterior of the ring.

Cat. No. 1-310 refers to what was probably a matched pair of napkin-ring ornaments. One is complete, with a larger diameter of 3.7 cm, a smaller diameter of 3.3 cm, and a height of 1.3 cm. The larger or outer flared end has four equidistant crimps or notches in the rim, and there is incised ticking visible between these crimps. The ware is a fine polished brown or buff, and the walls are delicately thin. The mate to the complete one is a half-fragment.

Cat. Nos. 1-312 and 1-313 (figs. 148d and 148c respectively) are another pair (although cataloged separately). They are of plain polished brown ware. Identical in size, they measure 2.3 cm at the outer diameter, 1.7 cm at the smaller diameter, and 1.6 cm high. The walls are 1 mm thick. Both are complete.

Cat. Nos. 1-14, 1-31, 1-93, 1-238, 1-259, 1-316, 1-975, 1-1023, and 1-1053 are all napkin-ring fragments. Cat. No. 1-316 was a fine polished black specimen with a running design of scrolls around its exterior (fig. 148e). These had been rubbed with red cinnabar. Cat. No. 1-259 is another polished black specimen. This one has an incised design on the interior. Cat. Nos. 1-238 and 1-1023 both have exterior band incised designs of rectilinear key-like and nested triangular elements, respectively. Both of these are of a fine polished buff ware, and the ornaments have been red-slipped on the exterior. Cat. No. 1-31 is a polished buff piece that has designs on the interior of the ring but not the exterior, as in the case of Cat. No. 1-259. Cat. Nos. 1-975 and 1-1053 are of buff ware and red-slipped, and have incised designs on both the exterior and interior of the spool. Cat. No. 1-93 is a plain, buff-ware, red-slipped fragment. Cat. No. 1-14 is also a red-slipped buff-ware piece that was decorated with an appliqued node or nodes.

Cat. No. 1-314 is the tubular pin-shaped ornament (fig. 148f). It is made of well-smoothed brown ware. Length is 1.8 cm, diameter at large or outer end is 1 cm, and diameter at small straight end is 0.7 cm.

The two earplug type ornaments—if such they are—are Cat. Nos. 1-496 and 1-1085. The first is a hollow, moldmade human head (the back now broken away) attached to a small, solid tapered stem. Without the stem it would have been classified as another moldmade human figurine. Overall length is 3.9 cm. Assuming this is an ear ornament, the stem element would have been inserted in the lobe of the ear. Cat. No. 1-1085 is a little handmade animal or bird head (fig. 148g), rather crudely executed, attached to a solid, rounded stem or base. The latter would have been inserted in the ear lobe if this piece had been worn as an ear ornament. Height is 2.9 cm.

Cat. Nos.	Op. No. and Provenience
1-14	2(C) CV-20, Lev. 3
1-31	4(C) CV-20, Lev. 1
1-93	6(I) CV-20, Lev. 1
1-110	10(A) CV-17, Lev. 2, Special Find 1, associated with Burial 1
1-224	21(A) CV-20, Lev. 2, Special Find 32
1-238	20(A) CV-20, Lev. 5
1-259	20(A) CV-20, Lev. 6
1-310 (2 spec.)	24(A) CV-20, Lev. 8, associated with Burial 21
1-312	20(A) CV-20, Lev. 5, Special Find 56
1-313	20(A) CV-20, Lev. 5, Special Find 57
1-314	24(A) CV-20, Lev. 4, Special Find 64, associated with Burial 19
1-316	20(A) CV-20, Lev. 6, Special Find 67
1-496	34(B) CV-43, Lev. 1
1-975	100(B) CV-43, Lev. 3
1-1023	50(A) CV-45, Lev. 7
1-1053	102(A) CV-43, Lev. 4
1-1085	102(A) CV-43, Lev. 5

Ceramic Ornaments or Ritual Objects (11)

This rather general category includes a number of specially manufactured pottery items that appear to be fragments of objects that served either as ornaments or as some kind of ritual objects.

The two pieces under Cat. No. 1-82 appear to be ornamental fragments. One of them looks like half of a ring or circle. If so, the circle was about 6 cm on its outer diameter. The piece itself is thin (6 mm thick) and flat (1.7 cm wide). On opposite sides at the same place are two little, round, punched appliqued buttons. This could be a circular pendant. On the other hand, it may be a decorative element from a vessel, perhaps an effigy or incensario form.

The other piece is rectangulate and flat or slightly concave. It measures 3.2 cm long and varies in width from 2.7 to 2 cm. It has been broken off at the smaller end. Thickness is 6 mm. It could be a part of a pendant or an element from an elaborate vessel. Both pieces are of Near Fine Orange paste.

Cat. No. 1-108 is a nicely finished piece of brown ware that could be an end of a pendant (with the suspension end broken away). The three remaining edges are very nicely rounded by modeling before firing; it is clearly not a worked sherd. It is 5 cm long and 3 cm wide at the bottom end. The two long sides curve outward so that the width of the object at the end, which is now lost, was greater than 3 cm. The piece is very smooth on both sides and 5 mm thick.

Cat. Nos. 1-283 and 1-617 are similar to 1-108. That is, they are nicely made flat, rectanguloid pieces with clearly modeled rather than ground edges. Cat. No. 1-283 is of a sandy buff ware. It measures 3.6 x 3.5 (the complete width) x 7 mm. It was longer than this originally, and a suspension piece may have been broken off. Cat. No. 1-617 is a similar sherd, the base or end of a flat, rectanguloid, smooth-surfaced object. It measures 3.2 x 3 x 0.7 cm.

Cat. No. 1-238 (fig. 149a) appears to be the corner of an ovate or ovate-rectangular plaque of pottery. There is a deeply carved (before firing) design on one surface, suggestive of an arching frame with a feather border. The other side is smooth, and the finished edge had obviously been cut and smoothed before firing. The ware is very coarse tempered and gritty. The paste is buff. The fragment measures 7.5 x 6.5 x 1 cm. It could have been made as a separate object, possibly a very large pendant, or a ritual plaque of some sort. On the other hand, it might have been part of a very elaborate vessel. The ware suggests the quality of the Sepultura Unslipped pottery type.

Cat. No. 1-361 is a complete pottery disk that has been manufactured as such. It is 18.7 cm in diameter and 1.1 cm thick. It is well smoothed on both surfaces; and the edges, which are slightly rounded, were obviously modeled before firing. One side is almost perfectly flat; the other is very slightly concave. Perhaps the designation of "ornament" or "ritual object" is unsuited to this specimen. It may have been only a lid for a cylinder jar; but this remains as a speculation. The ware is buff-fired but not polished. It may have had a buff slip.

Cat. No. 1-524 (fig. 149b,c) consists of two fragments that almost certainly came from the same specimen, apparently a small, carved pottery disk. From the arc of the curve of the outer edges of these two pieces, the original diameter is estimated as about 8 cm. Thickness is 5 mm. The edges are clearly modeled. The slightly convex side is the carved one and bears a decoration of a modeled-carved nature. This consists of very close spaced elements—glyphs and geometric panels. The opposite side is smooth and flat or perhaps very slightly concave. One possibility is that this may have been a mirror-back, once set with something like pyrite plaques, but there is absolutely no evidence of this. If perforated at some point near the rim, it could have been a pendant-like ornament. Or it may have been backed with wood or some other material (now lost) as an ornament of an undisclosed nature. The ware is a fine white-fired clay.

One specimen under Cat. No. 1-815 is the most sherd-like of any in the group. It is about 4.5 cm across and 1 cm thick. On what looks like an outer surface there is a deep incision-

punctation design. On the other side a circular raised element may have been broken off and the edges of this break then ground smooth. The complete form remains a mystery.

The other Cat. No. 1-815 (fig. 149d) specimen is made of fine-quality brown paste and is well formed, smoothed, and highly polished. Only a fragment now, it could have been a pendant or possibly a handle of some sort. Present length is 5.7 cm, but one end has been broken off. It is composed of four banded elements, not unlike a molding or pediment in architecture. These elements would have been in a vertical position if this had been a pendant, for the hole (1 cm in diameter) that runs through the object is at right angles to the bands. Somehow this disposition of the piece seems unlikely; it is aesthetically more satisfying to see the bands as horizontal. The object is 1.9 cm thick, but its width or other dimension cannot be determined because of breakage. If the specimen had been a handle—perhaps of a feather fan?—it would have been held with the bands horizontal and the perforation upright.

Cat. Nos.	Op. No. and Provenience
1-82 (2 spec.)	7(E) CV-20, Lev. 1
1-108	6(K) CV-20, Lev. 1
1-238	20(A) CV-20, Lev. 5
1-283	20(A) CV-20, Lev. 12
1-361	26(A) Main Center, Struct. L11-93, Lev. 10
1-524 (2 spec.)	35(E) CV-43, Lev. 1
1-617	33(FF) CV-43, Lev. 2
1-815 (2 spec.)	39(L) CV-44, Lev. 1

Seals or Stamps (5)

Three of these are flat stamps or seals; the other two are cylindrical.

Cat. No. 1-418 is a small, oblong flat seal. Both ends of the stamp face have been partially broken away. There is a plain, solid, conical handle on the middle of the back of the stamp. Present size of the seal or stamp face is 3.4 x 1.8 cm. The original length was probably about this; the two ends of the seal face have been broken diagonally, leaving what appear to be original corners on each end. The body of the seal is about 6 mm thick. The conical handle is 1.7 cm in length. The design of the seal or stamp is done in deep incisions and is a combination of rectilinear and curvilinear elements (fig. 150a).

Cat. No. 1-561 is a complete seal (fig. 150b). It is oblong, 5.2 x 2.7 cm, and 1.2 cm thick. In the center of the plain back there is a small nubbin handle. The stamp design on the front is a series of little incised rectangles, each with three (or, in one case, two) punctations within it. These little rectangles are bordered by a double incised line, above and below.

Cat. No. 1-686 (fig. 150c) is a fragment (about one-quarter) of a flat circular stamp or seal. The object was probably about 7 cm in diameter. It is quite flat and only about 0.7 mm thick. The main design, of which only a portion remains, was a stylized, curvilinear one, perhaps an animal. The incisions or carving of the stamp are as much as 2 mm deep. There is a border band, which ran around the circular stamp, which is 6 mm wide and decorated with a serried row of little trianguloid elements. A handle appears to have been broken from the center of the back.

Cat. No. 1-595 (fig. 150d) is an approximate two-thirds of a cylinder seal. It is made of a medium-coarse gray-buff ware. The diameter of the roller is 2.4 cm. The intact end is flat and smooth. The decoration on the roller is done with deep, wide incised lines. The design is carefully executed. Two encircling parallel lines form a border at the intact end, and it is a reasonable assumption that two such lines were at the other end of the roller, which is now broken away. The design on the main body of the roller consists of a running volute, or a series of nested triangles separated by a running volute. There are six such triangles, three depending from each border. One set of triangles is plain; the other set has a central punctated dot in each. Present length of the roller is 3 cm, but its length when complete was probably about 4 cm. The perforation hole through the cylinder is 4 mm in diameter.

Cat. No. 1-1024 (fig. 150e) is about one-half of a cylinder seal. The ware is a coarse gray-black. Both ends of the roller have been broken, although the one that is more nearly intact may have lost only a slight portion of its surface, which was left rather rough in manufacture. The incisions of the design are very deep and broad. There is a single encircling bordering line around the near-intact end, and perhaps there was such a border at the other end. The framed design probably was divided into two rectangular panels, but

beyond this little more can be said, owing to the fragmentary nature of the seal. Diameter is 2.8 cm. The fragment is 3.7 cm long, but the original was probably about 4.5 cm. The perforation hole is large, 1.3 cm in diameter, and well smoothed throughout the length of the roller.

Cat. Nos.	Op. No. and Provenience
1-413	27(J) Santa Rita 1, Lev. 1
1-561	35(I) CV-43, Lev. 1
1-595	54(A) CV-94, Lev. 1
1-686	39(G) CV-44, Lev. 1
1-1024	50(A) CV-45, Lev. 8

Collanders (36)

These are sherds of vessels with perforated bottoms (fig. 151a), which were used, presumably, as collanders or strainers. They appear to pertain to several pottery types, generally relatively coarse-ware types. The largest portion of them has been assigned to the residual type, Lysandro Unslipped; and the only two rim sherds in the collection belong to this type. There are a few sherds classified as Raul Red; three sherds pertain to the type Lorenzo Red; two are Antonio Buff; and one is Arroyo Red.

From the rim sherds (fig. 151b,c), and from other sherds in the collection, a medium-deep open bowl with slightly outslanting sides, a simple unmodified rim, and a flattish bottom seem to be the characteristic vessel form. Vessel wall or bottom thickness varies from 0.4 to 1.2 cm.

The collander holes vary in size, in the care with which they have been punched through the unfired vessel, and in the side from which they were punched. Hole diameters range from 5 to 9 mm, with about 6 mm as the most common size. Some collander holes have been punched very cleanly, with the surfaces afterward wiped or smoothed, so that it is difficult to tell from which side of the vessel the perforation was made. Others show clay piled up around the edges, indicating pretty definitely the side from which the puncture was made and the side from which the punch extruded. Approximately half of these were punched from the interior and half from the exterior. In a few cases, especially with the larger holes, there are some indications that the perforations were made by drilling after the vessels were fired. Holes are spaced about 2 to 2.5 cm apart.

Cat. Nos.	Op. No. and Provenience
Lysandro Unslipped	
1-69	5(L) CV-20, Lev. 1
1-70	4(J) CV-20
1-115	7(G) CV-20, Lev. 1
1-136	4(R) CV-20, Lev. 1
1-139	10(A) CV-17, Lev. 6
1-153	13(B) CV-20, Lev. 1
1-202	20(A) CV-20, Lev. 3
1-144	11(A) CV-13, Lev. 2
1-469	33(F) CV-43, Lev. 3
1-542	33(CC) CV-43, Lev. 4
1-564 (2 spec.)	36(J) CV-43, Lev. 1
1-587	39(C) CV-43, Lev. 1
1-613	53(A) CV-91, Lev. 2
1-614	52(A) CV-88, Lev. 2
1-639	39(E) CV-43, Lev. 1
1-651	42(D) CV-43, Lev. 1
1-686	39(G) CV-44, Lev. 1
1-761	42(I) CV-43, Lev. 1
1-763	39(K) CV-44, Lev. 1
1-829 (2 spec.)	66(A) CV-190, Lev. 9
1-903	49(A) CV-43, Lev. 5-A
1-1059	74(H) CV-16, Lev. 1
1-1099	77(D) CV-16, Lev. 1
Raul Red	
1-137	6(N) CV-20, Lev. 1
1-575	38(C) CV-43, Lev. 1
1-596	38(E) CV-43, Lev. 1
1-663	53(A) CV-91, Lev. 4
1-742	42(F) CV-43, Lev.1
Lorenzo Red	
1-623	37(K) CV-43, Lev. 1
1-1024	50(A) CV-45, Lev. 8
1-1027	100(B) CV-43, Lev. 4
Antonio Buff	
1-260	19(C) CV-20, Lev. 6
1-859	49(A) CV-43, Lev. 2
Arroyo Red)	
1-1027	100(B) CV-43, Lev. 4

Candeleros (270)

This is the term that has been applied to little pottery containers that may have had a ritual function. They are small, with an average height of 6 cm or less and a diameter of about 3 cm. Longyear (1952:101–102), who found a good many such objects in his diggings at Copan, has written:

> Candeleros presumably were made by building up a rude lump of clay over an armature of wood or reed which, when removed or burnt out, left the central cavity with its opening or openings. Decoration, if any, was then applied, and the vessel was fired. Usually, no effort was made to smooth or even up the outer contour.

Although he refers to this possible burning of a stick or a reed in the course of the making of a candelero, Longyear states, farther along:

> The Copan candeleros give no hint of their function; only a very few have any traces of carbonization on the interior, and the great majority appear to be absolutely clean and unused. It is, indeed, hard to see how anything could have been burnt in these vessels, as only a few have perforations or vent holes, in their sides. Still, their great abundance at Copan, especially near concentrations of burials, suggests that they enjoyed some kind of ceremonial usage.

In our collection, the majority of the candeleros examined did show interior burning or carbonization. Whether this resulted from the burning of a stick or reed around which they had been formed, from the burning of copal or some other substance within them, or from still some other procedure must remain speculative. Except for this, we would concur with Longyear's description and discussion of the Copan candeleros. Certainly, most of the candeleros in our collection were rather crudely made and appear to have been fashioned hastily. This applies both to their shaping and to their incised, punctated, or modeled decoration; however, as Longyear also observed, we noted exceptions that had been more carefully formed, smoothed, and ornamented.

We have divided our collection into a number of varieties, which are discussed below. In general, these correspond to Longyear's form varieties, except that we have grouped his bottle and globe forms together under our Bottle-shaped.

Cylindrical (167)

This is one of the more common varieties. These are cylindrical or very slightly barrel-shaped (fig. 152a–b). Bottoms are always round and quite flat; sides are straight or slightly outcurving; and the rims or lips are usually pointed or straight, although there are some exceptions to this where the lip curves inward, making a slightly constricted orifice. They are 4 to 6 cm in height, are about 3 cm in diameter, and have an orifice about 1.5 cm in diameter. The chambers are sometimes straight-walled and sometimes pointed toward the bottom. The bottoms of the cylindrical candeleros are relatively thick, so the chamber tends to be relatively shallow in relation to the height of the object. The great majority of the cylindrical candeleros are made of a relatively fine grained paste and fired to a buff color, at least on the outer surface. Some of the more nicely smoothed ones may have been slipped, either a buff or red, but this is uncertain.

A number of surface treatment or decorative subvarieties are included under the cylindrical classification. These are plain, incised, incised-and-punctated, modeled, perforated, and red-painted.

We counted 63 plain specimens, including a few complete or near-complete specimens (fig. 153a–g). This number is probably proportionately high for the actual number of original complete plain cylindrical candeleros, for many small fragments that bore no surface decorative treatment (for instance, base pieces) were totaled with this subvariety. In general, the plain subvariety candeleros tend to be a little more crudely formed, with less attention to surface smoothing than the decorated specimens. Some plain fragments are among the largest of the candeleros and range from about 6.5 to 7 cm in height and 3.3 to 3.7 cm in diameter.

We counted 63 incised-and-punctated specimens (fig. 154a–e). Several were complete or nearly so. Incised line designs were carried out both with quite deep, slash-like incisions and with very fine incisions. Punctations were of both the dot and slash forms. There is one example of hollow-reed punctation. Punctations were sometimes contained within incised boundaries and sometimes in separate rows or otherwise disposed independently of incised decoration.

Design elements, as these can be determined, are simple, geometric, and usually rectilinear.

The incised subvariety numbers 26 specimens. Some of these, observed only as fragments, may have been parts of candeleros that had the combined incision-punctation treatment. Some candeleros bore only incised lines bordering the rim, just above the base, or in both places. Others had two or three lines in a multiple-band arrangement. Some had close-spaced vertically arranged lines running from top to bottom of the candelero. On others, lines were placed diagonal to the vertical axis of the specimen. Both broad-deep and fine-shallow incised lines were employed.

The modeled subvariety numbered 12 specimens (fig. 155a–c). These include little appliqued human features, monkeys modeled in low-relief, and other eroded, unidentifiable relief features.

Two specimens are distinguished by holes or perforations, punched through from the outside of the candelero before firing, and compose the perforated subvariety.

A single small fragment of a candelero of cylindrical form had red paint applied to the exterior.

Cat. Nos.	Op. No. and Provenience
1-14 (3 spec.)	2(C) CV-20, Lev. 3
1-17	2(B) CV-20, Lev. 3
1-22 (7 spec.)	2(B) CV-20, Lev. 4
1-27 (2 spec.)	2(C) CV-20, Lev. 4
1-47	5(E) CV-20, Lev. 1
1-61	6(F) CV-20, Lev. 1
1-82 (2 spec.)	7(E) CV-20, Lev. 1
1-90	9(A) CV-18, Lev. 2
1-95	9(A) CV-18, Lev. 3
1-97	6(I) CV-20, Lev. 1, Special Find 14
1-98	6(J) CV-20, Lev. 1
1-105	10(A) CV-17, Lev. 2
1-108	6(K) CV-20, Lev. 1
1-159	14(A) CV-22, Lev. 3
1-165 (2 spec.)	14(A) CV-22, Lev. 4
1-190	17(A) CV-56, Lev. 1
1-205	17(A) CV-56, Lev. 4
1-254	21(A) CV-20, Lev. 3
1-277	23(A) CV-43, Lev. 4
1-424	27(K) Santa Rita I, Lev. 1
1-467 (3 spec.)	33(F) CV-43, Lev. 4
1-474 (2 spec.)	33(E) CV-43, Lev. 5
1-477 (3 spec.)	33(E) CV-43, Lev. 4
1-479	33(F) CV-43, Lev. 4, Special Find 2
1-481	33(F) CV-43, Lev. 4, Special Find 3

Cat. Nos.	Op. No. and Provenience
1-482	33(F) CV-43, Lev. 4, Special Find 6
1-483	33(F) CV-43, Lev. 4, Special Find 4
1-487 (2 spec.)	33(E) CV-43, Lev. 6
1-526	33(Z) CV-43, Lev. 4
1-528	36(D) CV-43, Lev. 1
1-531	33(Z) CV-43, Lev. 5
1-533 (2 spec.)	36(E) CV-43, Lev. 1
1-535 (2 spec.)	35(H) CV-43, Lev. 1
1-539	33(DD) CV-43, Lev. 1
1-542 (2 spec.)	33(CC) CV-43, Lev. 4
1-543	35(F) CV-43, Lev. 1
1-549	36(I) CV-43, Lev. 1
1-555	33(EE) CV-43, Lev. 2
1-556	37(C) CV-43, Lev. 1
1-569	34(K) CV-43, Lev. 1
1-577 (3 spec.)	38(B) CV-43, Lev. 1
1-579	38(C) CV-43, Lev. 1
1-606 (2 spec.)	37(H) CV-43, Lev. 1
1-609	54(A) CV-94, Lev. 2
1-615	35(O) CV-43, Lev. 1
1-617	33(FF) CV-43, Lev. 2
1-619	34(M) CV-43, Lev. 1
1-620	37(I) CV-43, Lev. 1
1-633	37(M) CV-43, Lev. 1
1-639	39(E) CV-43, Lev. 1
1-642 (2 spec.)	42(C) CV-43, Lev. 1
1-650	54(A) CV-94, Lev. 8
1-655 (2 spec.)	54(A) CV-94, Lev. 7-A
1-657 (2 spec.)	54(A) CV-94, Lev. 7-B
1-661 (2 spec.)	54(A) CV-94, Lev. 6
1-692	43(D) CV-43, Lev. 1
1-707	38(H) CV-43, Lev. 1
1-734	46(A) CV-44, Lev. 1
1-763	39(K) CV-444, Lev. 1
1-769	48(C) CV-47, Lev. 1
1-779	42(H) CV-43, Lev. 1
1-786	46(C) CV-44, Lev. 1
1-811	33(GG) CV-43, Special Find 27, associated with Feature 2
1-825	42(J) CV-43, Lev. 1
1-829	66(A) CV-190, Lev. 9
1-836	66(A) CV-190, Lev. 6
1-843	39(N) CV-44, Lev. 1
1-856	33(HH) CV-43, Lev. 1
1-859	49(A) CV-43, Lev. 2
1-899	71(A) CV-204, Lev. 2
1-903 (2 spec.)	49(A) CV-43, Lev. 5-A
1-905	103(A) CV-46, Lev. 2
1-918 (2 spec.)	49(A) CV-43, Lev. 3
1-920	103(A) CV-46, Lev. 1
1-923	100(B) CV-43, Lev. 1
1-925	65(A) CV-177, Lev. 4
1-950	39(S) CV-44, Lev. 1
1-951	49(A) CV-43, Lev. 6-B

Cat. Nos.	Op. No. and Provenience
1-953 (6 spec.)	102(A) CV-43, Lev. 3
1-954 (2 spec.)	50(A) CV-45, Lev. 5
1-971 (2 spec.)	49(A) CV-43, Lev. 7-A, associated with Feature 9
1-972	49(A) CV-43, Lev. 5-C
1-974	100(B) CV-43, Lev. 2
1-975 (4 spec.)	100(B) CV-43, Lev. 3
1-988	49(A) CV-43, Lev. 6-A
1-1002	49(A) CV-43, Lev. 6-A, Special Find 38
1-1003	49(A) CV-43, Lev. 7-A, Special Find 41
1-1006	49(A) CV-43, Lev. 7-A, Special Find 40
1-1009	49(A) CV-43, Lev. 7-A, Special Find 42
1-1010	49(A) CV-43, Lev. 7-A, Special Find 43
1-1012	49(A) CV-43, Lev. 6-A, Special Find 33
1-1013	49(A) CV-43, Lev. 6-A, Special Find 37
1-1020	100(B) CV-43, Lev. 3
1-1026	79(A) CV-16, Lev. 2
1-1027	100(B) CV-43, Lev. 4
1-1045	49(A) CV-43, Lev. 6-C, Special Find 47
1-1053 (2 spec.)	102(A) CV-43, Lev. 4
1-1058 (5 spec.)	100(B) CV-43, Lev. 5-A
1-1063	33(JJ) CV-43, Lev. 2
1-1067	102(A) CV-43, Lev. 4, Special Find 62
1-1070	102(A) CV-43, Lev. 4, Special Find 61
1-1075	49(A) CV-43, Lev. 9-A
1-1077	102(A) CV-43, Lev. 4, Special Find 59
1-1078	102(A) CV-43, Lev. 4, Special Find 58
1-1085 (8 spec.)	102(A) CV-43, Lev. 5
1-1086	104(A) CV-43, Lev. 6
1-1093	105(A) CV-44, Lev. 4
1-1094	106(A) CV-47, Lev. 3
1-1097	80(C) CV-16, Lev. 1
1-1103	83(A) CV-16, Lev. 1
1-1106	105(A) CV-44, Lev. 5
1-1119	102(A) CV-43, Lev. 5, Special Find 78
1-1121	102(A) CV-43, Lev. 5, Special Find 83
1-1137	102(A) CV-43, Lev. 5, Special Find 67
1-1138	102(A) CV-43, Lev. 5, Special Find 81
1-1190	102(A) CV-43, Lev. 6, Special Find 85

Bottle-shaped (87)

This is the second most numerous of the varieties of the candelero type. It has a generally globular or spheroid body with a collar or neck. Sometimes the collar or neck is minimal, a slightly straightened ridge above the body; at other times it is more pronounced and sometimes even slightly outflared. Otherwise—in size, buff paste color, general slovenliness of execution and decoration, and modes of decoration—the bottle-shaped variety is very similar to the cylindrical variety.

A total of 36 specimens have the incised-and-punctated decoration (fig. 156a–f) seen in the cylindrical variety. There are 20 with only incised decoration (fig. 157a–c). The plain category numbers 21. There is a single perforated specimen. Nine are modeled (fig. 158a–b), and among these are some that deviate the most from a strictly bottle shape; however, all have a roughly spheroid body and a constricted neck.

In size, there is a tendency for the bottle-shaped variety specimens to be a little shorter—averaging about 4 cm—than the cylindrical ones; and diameter is often more or less equivalent to height.

Cat. Nos.	Op. No. and Provenience
1-43	4(D) CV-20, Lev. 1
1-93	6(I) CV-20, Lev. 1
1-108	6(K) CV-20, Lev. 1
1-125	7(H) CV-20, Lev. 1
1-138	4(Q) CV-20, Lev. 1
1-162	14(A) CV-22, Lev. 3, Special Find 2
1-164	14(A) CV-22, Lev. 3, Special Find 4
1-169	14(A) CV-22, Lev. 4, Special Find 5
1-173	14(A) CV-22, Lev. 5, Special Find 6
1-191	17(A) CV-56, Lev. 1, Special Find 1
1-204	16(D) Sacbe, Lev. 8
1-260	19(C) CV-20, Lev. 6
1-270	20(A) CV-20, Lev. 8
1-360	26(A) Main Center, Struct. L11-93, Lev. 9
1-361	26(A) Main Center, Struct. L11-93, Lev. 10
1-451	28(A) CV-43, Surface
1-467	33(F) CV-43, Lev. 4
1-472	33(E) CV-43, Lev. 3
1-474	33(E) CV-43, Lev. 5
1-493	33(E) CV-43, Lev. 7
1-511	33(BB) CV-43, Lev. 4, Special Find 10
1-512	33(BB) CV-43, Lev. 4, Special Find 9
1-517 (2 spec.)	33(BB) CV-43, Lev. 4
1-525	34(E) CV-43, Lev. 1
1-528	36(D) CV-43, Lev. 1
1-536 (2 spec.)	35(G) CV-43, Lev. 1
1-544	36(F) CV-43, Lev. 1
1-548	33(Z) CV-43, Lev. 5, Special Find 13
1-552	33(DD) CV-43, Lev. 2
1-553	33(CC) CV-43, Lev. 4, Special Find 14
1-564	36(J) CV-43, Lev. 1
1-572	36(M) CV-43, Lev. 1
1-591	52(A) CV-88, Lev. 1
1-598	53(A) CV-91, Lev. 3
1-608	33(FF) CV-43, Lev. 1
1-636	34(N) CV-43, Lev. 1
1-652	42(A) CV-43, Lev. 1
1-661	54(A) CV-94, Lev. 6
1-693	42(E) CV-43, Lev. 1
1-745	33(FF) CV-43, Lev. 4-B
1-754	59(A) CV-125, Lev. 4
1-810	33(FF) CV-43, Lev. 4-B, Special Find 29
1-879	33(II) CV-43, Lev. 2
1-891	33(II) CV-43, Lev. 3
1-895 (5 spec.)	68(A) CV-68, Lev. 4
1-902	49(A) CV-43, Lev. 4
1-921	101(B) CV-47, Lev. 1
1-951	49(A) CV-43, Lev. 6-B
1-953	102(A) CV-43, Lev. 3
1-970	104(A) CV-43, Lev. 2
1-975	100(B) CV-43, Lev. 3
1-988	49(A) CV-43, Lev. 6-A
1-1004	49(A) CV-43, Lev. 6-A, Special Find 35
1-1008	50(A) CV-45, Lev. 6-A, Special Find 44
1-1012	49(A) CV-43, Lev. 6-A, Special Find 33
1-1014	49(A) CV-43, Lev. 6-A, Special Find 34
1-1024	50(A) CV-45, Lev. 8
1-1027 (2 spec.)	100(B) CV-43, Lev. 4
1-1053	102(A) CV-43, Lev. 3
1-1057 (3 spec.)	49(A) CV-43, Lev. 8-C
1-1058 (4 spec.)	100(B) CV-43, Lev. 5-A
1-1066	102(A) CV-43, Lev. 4, Special Find 60
1-1068	102(A) CV-43, Lev. 4, Special Find 64
1-1069	102(A) CV-43, Lev. 4, Special Find 63
1-1082	50(A) CV-45, Lev. 10
1-1085 (6 spec.)	102(A) CV-43, Lev. 5

Cat. Nos.	Op. No. and Provenience
1-1123	102(A) CV-43, Lev. 5, Special Find 66
1-1124	102(A) CV-43, Lev. 5, Special Find 65
1-1135	102(A) CV-43, Lev. 5, Special Find 68
1-1156	100(B) CV-43, Lev. 9-B

Conical (4)

Two of these are complete and definitely conical (fig. 159). They are just under 4 cm long and have a top diameter of 2.3 cm. Modeling is rather crude and the surfaces bumpy. Two fragmentary specimens are round-pointed bases with walls that appear to slope outward.

Cat. Nos.	Op. No. and Provenience
1-52	6(C) CV-20, Lev. 1
1-57	6(E) CV-20, Lev. 1
1-617	33(FF) CV-43, Lev. 2
No Number	

Rectangular (2)

Cat. No. 1-949 (fig. 160) is a complete specimen measuring 5.8 cm high and 2.9 cm in diameter. The walls are quite straight. It is decorated with an incised line running the height of the candelero on each corner. Between these incised lines are fields of dot punctations. At the top, surrounding the orifice, there is a punctated appliqued button at each corner. The orifice is somewhat restricted and measures 1.2 cm in diameter.

Cat. No. 1-477 is a fragment of the top of a rectangular candelero. The orifice is surrounded by a little collar that is inset from the walls of the object. There are indications of fine-line and dot punctation on the exterior.

Cat. Nos.	Op. No. and Provenience
1-477	33(E) CV-43, Lev. 4
1-949	49(A) CV-43, Lev. 6-A, Special Find 32

Multi-chambered (8)

These are candeleros with more than a single vessel cavity or chamber. Most of the chambers show interior burning as in the single-chambered varieties.

Cat. No. 1-638 (fig. 161a) is a fragment of an object that had four chambers arranged in quadrate form. These chambers were straight-walled, 2.7 cm in depth, and slightly conoidal or pointed-bottomed in form. They measured about 1.6 cm in diameter. The whole object was probably about 3 cm high and a little over 4 cm square. The sides were slightly indented between the chambers, and the bottom is similarly quadrated. Exterior decoration was in rows of long, deep punctations. The ware is coarse, is black-brown in color, and has no slip or finish.

Cat. No. 1-923 is a fragment of another four-chambered candelero. There is little left except the central core; however, this is sufficient to tell that there were four chambers, now largely broken away. Height is 3.1 cm; and the whole piece was about 4 cm square. The chambers were arranged in quadrate form. The ware is fine-grained, the piece well smoothed, the color a red-buff.

Cat. No. 1-537 (fig. 161b) is almost complete and is a three-chambered candelero. It is 4 cm high, 4 cm in diameter, and triangular in shape arrangement. Individual chambers are 1.3 cm in diameter and about 1.5 cm deep, being conoidal in form. Two fairly large perforations (4 mm in diameter) have been punched through each of the chambers, from the outside, a little below the top. The object rests on three pointed feet, each foot being an extension or conoidal prolongation of its respective chamber. The ware is a fairly fine grained, smoothed but not polished buff. There is no decoration.

Cat. No. 1-617 is a fragment of a specimen that was much like the foregoing. The three chambers were arranged in a triangular fashion. Height is 4 cm, and diameter about 4 cm. The pointed extensions or prolongations of the chambers formed three legs or supports. There is no decoration.

Cat. No. 1-1020 (fig. 161c) is a vaguely trianguloid candelero with three tubular orifices or spouts rising straight up from the body. Two spouts remain; a third is missing. Because this third of the candelero is missing, it is possible to see that the three spouts or orifices all entered into a common body chamber. The base is quite flat. Total height is 4 cm, and the diameter was almost this much. The sides of the body of the piece are decorated with fields of fine slash-punctation. On the lower portions of the spouts there are little punched appliqued pellets. Ware is fine and of red-buff color.

Cat. No. 1-1005 (fig. 161d) is a double-chambered candelero. One orifice or spout has a monkey effigy modeled on it; the other spout is broken but may have had a similar form. The two spouts or orifices descended into a common little chamber. The height is 5 cm, the diameters 4.3 and 3.8 cm.

Cat. Nos. 1-696 and 1-1150 are foot fragments that appear to be of the size and shape to have been broken from a four-chambered or three-chambered candelero.

Cat. Nos.	Op. No. and Provenience
1-537	34(I) CV-43, Lev. 1
1-617	33(FF) CV-43, Lev. 2
1-638	37(G) CV-43, Lev. 1
1-696	57(A) CV-122, Lev. 4
1-923	100(B) CV-43, Lev. 1
1-1005	49(A) CV-43, Lev. 6-A, Special Find 36
1-1020	100(B) CV-43, Lev. 3
1-1150	104(A) CV-43, Lev. 7

Miscellaneous Forms (3)

Cat. No. 1-194 is a single-chambered candelero with two nubbin feet or supports. Total height is 3.8 cm. The chamber rises straight up in cylindrical fashion and has an external diameter of 2.3 cm. The interior orifice is 1.3 to 1.5 cm. The chamber is a little over 2 cm deep and pointed at the bottom. The two legs diverge in Y-fashion and are solid. Most of one has been broken off. The ware is coarse and red-brown.

Cat. No. 1-760 (fig. 158c) is a complete olla-like specimen that, perhaps, could have been classified with the bottle-shaped variety; however, it has an unusual appearance. The flattened-globular, olla-like body has an extended flange that stands out 1 cm or more from the cylindrical collar. It has been decorated with appliqued

ornamentation of a now uncertain nature. The piece measures 5.2 cm in maximum diameter (at the body flange); total height is 2.6 cm; the height of the collar is 1.2 cm; the external diameter of the collar is 2.7 cm; and the orifice diameter is 1.7 cm. The base is quite rounded. The ware is black-fired, coarse, and gritty.

Cat. No. 1-1027 is a very crudely made, bumpy surfaced candelero. It is roughly cylindrical in form, although perhaps an effigy of some sort (poorly executed) was intended. Height is 3.9 cm and maximum diameter is 2.9 cm. The chamber is only a little over 1 cm in diameter. Ware is fine-grained and red-brown in color.

Cat. Nos.	Op. No. and Provenience
1-194	17(A) CV-56, Lev. 3
1-760	48(B) CV-47, Lev. 1
1-1027	100(B) CV-43, Lev. 4

Miniature Vessels (33)

This term and classification applies to all of those pottery vessels that are of a very small size and also of a shape and quality to suggest that their uses may have been specialized ones. They are described and listed here under two main group headings—those of fine quality and those of coarse quality.

The one complete fine-quality specimen, Cat. No. 1-1214, is a very handsome modeled-carved flask of a thin, white-fired ware (fig. 162). The ware is comparable to the Capulin subgroup of the Tipon ceramic group in our pottery classification for the Copan Valley. The type is designated as Don Gordon Modeled-carved. The height of the flask is 9.1 cm. It is of a rectangular form, measuring 5.7 x 3.8 cm in width and thickness. These latter measurements are maximum ones; the flask tapers slightly toward the base, where it measures 5.4 x 3.5 cm. The base is, of course, rectangular and is inset to a depth of about 2 mm, resulting in a very small raised ridge running around the basal edges. The orifice is a little straight spout or neck, 1.7 cm high and with a diameter of 2.9 cm. The lip is nicely flattened and thickened. The upper portion of the flask, below the neck, slopes down gently on its four sides. These sides are carefully squared. The top of the body of the flask is marked with a raised ridge, 5 mm wide, which is decorated with ticking marks. Below this, the narrow sides of the flask have been left plain, but the two wide sides display very carefully executed modeled-carved hieroglyphs. These glyphs are arranged in slightly inset panels. The panels consist of two vertical rows of three glyphs each on both sides of the vessel. The two panels and their glyph texts are identical. The object is obviously a quality piece, very likely a ritual item. It was found in a tomb, and red pigment (cinnabar) was found inside of it.

The remaining fine-quality specimens are all small sherds. In regular ceramic classification they would all pertain to Tipon group types. The majority are fired to a white-buff color, suggesting the Capulin subgroup. Some of these bear modeled-carved decoration similar to that of the flask, Cat. No. 1-1214; and it is likely that the flask form is represented among them. Several are short spouts with an everted, thickened lip, virtually identical to Cat. No. 1-1214. Others may gave been little globular bottles; several small (1.2–2.5 cm in diameter) ring bases are in the collection. In one case vertical flutings rise from this ring base. A few other sherds, also with modeled-carved decoration, are fired a black-brown, and these are similar to vessels of the regular Tipon group pottery type, Don Gordon Modeled-carved. These sherds also appear to have been from flask or small bottle forms.

There are two complete coarse-quality miniature vessels. Cat. No. 1-950 (fig. 163a) is a little rectangular vessel with a cylindrical neck. Made of a coarse brown ware, it is similar to the candeleros, although it is somewhat larger: measuring 8.2 cm in height, it is 4.2 and 3.1 cm, respectively, in width and thickness. Cat. No. 1-1118 (fig. 163b) is a small, thick-walled, coarse little olla. Made of an unpolished gray-brown ware, it measures 6.9 cm in height and 6.1 cm in diameter.

The remaining coarse-quality specimens are sherds. Cat. No. 1-61 is a small flat, circular vessel base of thick-walled coarse gray-brown pottery, comparable to the type Lysandro Unslipped. Cat. Nos. 1-98 and 1-132 are small basal sherds of what might be a Tipon group kind of pottery, although the modeling and smoothing on these pieces is very rough. Cat. No. 1-832 is a small,

deeply indented circular vessel base of a Capulin subgroup ware. Cat. No. 1-207 is a rim sherd of a little crudely modeled bowl that would have measured about 4.5 cm in diameter and somewhat less than that in depth. The ware is coarse, suggesting Sepultura or Lysandro Unslipped.

Cat. Nos.	Op. No. and Provenience
Fine Quality	
1-74	5(K) CV-20, Lev. 1
1-83	4(K) CV-20, Lev. 1
1-88	7(F) CV-20, Lev. 1
1-115	7(G) CV-20, Lev. 1
1-132	10(A) CV-17, Lev. 5
1-238	20(A) CV-20, Lev. 5
1-524 (2 spec.)	35(E) CV-43, Lev. 1
1-572	36(M) CV-43, Lev. 1
1-578	39(B) CV-43, Lev. 1
1-608	33(FF) CV-43, Lev. 1
1-617	33(FF) CV-43, Lev. 2
1-618	36(N) CV-43, Lev. 1
1-625	37(L) CV-43, Lev. 1
1-711	44(G) CV-46, Lev. 1
1-747 (2 spec.)	39(J) CV-44, Lev. 1
1-763	39(K) CV-44, Lev. 1
1-843	39(N) CV-44, Lev. 1
1-848 (2 spec.)	45(P) CV-46, Lev. 1
1-919	39(P) CV-44, Lev. 1
1-950	39(S) CV-44, Lev. 1
1-1053	102(A) CV-43, Lev. 4
1-1214	100(B) CV-43, Special Find 107, associated with Feature 13
No Number	
Coarse Quality	
1-61	6(F) CV-20, Lev. 1
1-98	6(J) CV-20, Lev. 1
1-132	10(A) CV-17, Lev. 5
1-207	19(C) CV-20, Lev. 3
1-832	66(A) CV-190, Lev. 5
1-950	39(S) CV-44, Lev. 1
1-1118	102(A) CV-43, Lev. 6, Special Find 84

Briquette Material (150)

Burned clay wall plaster, or briquette material, was found in and around the various building platforms. Chunks ranging from 11 x 10 x 8 cm down to about 3 cm in diameter were recovered, and no doubt still smaller lumps were scattered through refuse but were not saved. The surfaces of these fragments were fired a brick-red; interiors were gray-black. The clay often had admixtures of grit and fine fibers. Usually, one side of a briquette was roughly smoothed, a smeared sort of smoothing, often showing particles of grit or fibers extruding through onto the surface. The opposite side bore heavy fiber or wattel impressions, frequently about 5 mm in width. Presumably, these are impressions made from some sort of a reed or heavy grass wall covering over which the clay had been packed and smoothed. Occasional larger pole impressions were noted, but no matting or woven impressions were observed. It is assumed that these briquette materials all result from subsequent burning of structures. During use or occupancy the building walls were simply coated with a sundried clay.

GROUND STONE

Metates *(In collaboration with Julia A. Hendon)*

A total of 509 metates were recovered during our excavations at Copan. However, this study and analysis was conducted on 108 of these metates, as listed and examined below.

Type 1	43
Type 2	24
Type 3	26
Type 4	13
Special	2

Manos *(In collaboration with Julia A. Hendon)*

A total of 468 manos were recovered during our excavations at Copan. However, this study and analysis was conducted on 144 of these metates, as listed and examined below.

Small Round	13
Large Round	14
Square	3
Triangular	5
Pentagonal	8
Overhang	5
Plano-convex	26
Thin Ovate-rectangular	3
Thick Ovate-rectangular	67

Mortars or Grinding Slabs		48
Type 1	40	
Type 2	8	

Barkbeaters	10

Rubbing and Pounding Stone		44
Rubbing Stones	34	
Pounders	10	

Spherical or Egg-shaped Stones	18
Polishing Stones and Polished Pebbles	61
Pestle	1

Anvil Stones	9
Drill Braces	3
Weight or Anchor	1

Celts		22
Large Variety	1	
Medium Variety	7	
Small Variety	2	
Very Small Variety	12	

Alabaster Vessel	1
Ring Stones	5
Rectangular Perforated Stones	18
Mirrors	7 or 8
Ear Ornaments (Jadeite)	7
Pendants (Jadeite)	8
Adornos (Jadeite)	8

Beads (Jadeite)		77
Flat-rectanguloid Variety	4	
Irregular Variety	2	
Barrel-shaped Variety	1	
Disk Variety	4	
Large Tubular Variety	7	
Small Tubular Variety	26	
Subspherical Variety	33	

Miscellaneous Pebbles (Jadeite)	15
Raw Jadeite	7
Ornaments (Not Jadeite)	12
Stone Figurine	1
Stone Yoke (?)	1
Celt-like Objects or Ritual Maces	5
Star-shaped Stone	1
Stone Disks	4
Incised Stones	3

General, Comparative, and Summary Comments

with assistance from Julia A. Hendon

Our Copan ground stone artifacts include a variety of items, all made by grinding, pecking, and, sometimes, polishing. The only types found in any great number were metates, manos, mortars, and various rubbing and polishing stones. Other less frequent types include barkbeaters, celts, ring stones, mirrors, ear ornaments, adornos, and beads. Most of the ornaments are made of jadeite.

The Copan Type 1 metate is the most numerous in our collections. This type has a flat rectangular grinding surface and base. Longyear (1952:105) reported that the majority of metates found at Copan during his excavations there were "simple, legless troughs of volcanic stone, shaped by pecking. The grinding depression is shallow and bases are gently convex to almost flat." This description fits our definition of Type 1 very closely. The Type 1 metate is not a common lowland Maya type; and it has not been reported from such sites as Altar de Sacrificios (Willey 1972), Seibal (Willey 1978), Piedras Negras (W. R. Coe 1959), Barton Ramie (Willey et al. 1965), and Mayapan (Proskouriakoff 1962). At both Uaxactun (Kidder 1947: fig. 15c–d) and Palenque (Ruz L. 1958: pl.36; Schele and Mathews 1979:870) a few of the more traditional Peten basin-shaped metates (see Willey 1972, 1978) tend toward the flat-bottomed Type 1 shape and suggest that the two forms overlap with each other; and this may also be true of some metate specimens recovered from Cerros, in northern Belize (Garber 1981:45–46); nevertheless, the Copan Type 1 metate is essentially distinct from the Peten basin-shaped or turtle-backed type. Nor is the Copan Type 1 metate reported from the Maya highlands (Kidder, Jennings, and Shook 1946; Sheets 1978). The Type 1 form does appear, however, to the east, in Honduras, where it occurs unequivocally at Los Naranjos (Baudez and Becquelin 1973:379–380, figs. 134–136, 140, 141). Doris Z. Stone (1957:16, 123) also reports, but does not illustrate, legless metates from Comayagua Plain sites, such as Las Vegas, and from the Upper Ulua Valley, where they are associated with Ulua Mayoid pottery, and are presumably of Late Classic age.

Our Copan Type 2 metate is, in effect, the Type 1 form with small nubbin feet or legs, probably always three in number. The type is distinct from our Type 3 in that the Type 2 metates are heavy, thick, and not very carefully shaped. For the most part, the Copan Type 2 metate is absent from the Maya lowlands, the legged forms found there being closer to our Type 3. The closest lowland resemblances to Type 2 that we found are to some of those illustrated by Stromsvik (1931: 148–151, figs. 6–9, pls. 4–5) from Chichen Itza; however, it should be emphasized that the resemblance, while close, is not perfect. Again, as with Type 1, the closest and most numerous resemblances to our Type 2 metate are to the east, in Honduras, as at Los Naranjos (Baudez and Becquelin 1973:380–381, figs. 135, 140), sites in the Choluteca and Yeguare valleys (Stone 1957:91, 96), and at locations at various sites around Lake Yojoa (Strong, Kidder, and Paul 1938:80, 92, 111). Thus, looking at well over half of the 108 metates in our Copan collections, the main ties are toward the east and outside of the Maya area proper.

The Type 3 Copan metate is also a legged form, but the legs are longer and thinner than in Type 2, and the body of the metate is thinner and more delicately shaped than those of either Type 1 or Type 2. It is probable that most of our Type 3 specimens had three legs; however, well-made four-legged metates have been found at Copan. Longyear (1952:105, fig. 89c) describes one that had an animal head carved on one end. Such effigy metates, with three or four legs, are generally common to areas to the south and east of Copan, as in the Motagua Valley of Guatemala (Smith and Kidder 1943:167), in northeastern Honduras (Stone 1957:123), in the Diquis Delta region of Costa Rica (Lothrop 1963:40), and in Panama (Lothrop 1937:95–96, fig. 62a). As a further generalization, the whole tradition of legged metates is very definitely one that is at home in lower Central America, as opposed to

Mesoamerica, and that the numerically high presence of legged forms at Copan probably relates to the proximity of this site to lower Central America. At the same time, it should be noted that well-made legged metates do occur at many lowland Maya sites; however, in these contexts such metates are not very numerous and would appear to be special purpose implements rather than ordinary domestic grinding basins. Thus, the Copan Type 3 metate resembles the thin-flat, legged type at Seibal (Willey 1978:62-64, figs. 65, 66) and at Altar de Sacrificios (Willey 1972:111, fig. 95); and Kidder (1947:33, fig. 76) reports metate leg fragments from Uaxactun that appear to be consistent with the Type 3 form. There is also a legged metate fragment from Chichen Itza (Stromsvik 1935: pl. 2a, b) that is close to the Type 3 mode. Sheets (1978:31–32, fig. 3) shows legged metates from Chalchuapa, in the Salvador highlands, that are similar to the Copan Type 3 in fine workmanship, and these also occur at Kaminaljuyu, in the Guatemalan highlands (Kidder, Jennings, and Shook 1946:140–141). From this it would appear that the fine-quality legged metate idea did spread, to a limited extent, into both Maya lowlands and highlands, presumably from lower Central American contacts.

The Copan Type 4 metate is the turtle-back form typical of the Peten. It occurs in high frequency at such lowland sites as Seibal (Willey 1978:57–62), Uaxactun (Kidder 1947:33), Piedras Negras (W. R. Coe 1959:34), Altar de Sacrificios (Willey 1972:106–110), Barton Ramie (Willey et al. 1965:453-456), San Jose (Thompson 1939:172–173), and Cerros (Garber 1981: 41–45). It also occurs in the Maya highlands and is the common type at Chalchuapa (Sheets 1978:30–31) and Kaminaljuyu (Kidder, Jennings, and Shook 1946:140–141). Elsewhere in Central America the turtle-back form is rare or absent (see Baudez and Becquelin 1973:380; Smith and Kidder 1943:167). Legless walled metates have been reported from some Honduran sites, such as Sensenti (Stone 1957:177), and from some Nicaraguan ones (Healy 1980:174); but these usually have flat bases. At Quelepa, in El Salvador, Andrews (1976:161–162) reports "turtle-backed or basin-shaped metates." While these have recessed grinding surfaces and sidewalls, the bases appear flat in cross section.

Our Copan special metates, the reused building blocks, have counterparts at Chichen Itza, where they seem to have been quite common (Stromsvik 1931: figs. 2–4, pls. 2, 3).

The principal difference between Copan and the Peten sites as far as mano stones are concerned is the scarcity of the square variety at Copan. In the Peten sites, as at Barton Ramie, Altar de Sacrificios, Seibal, and elsewhere, the square variety is common, especially in Late Classic time levels. Out of a total 144 manos in our Copan collections, only three were classified as square, and Longyear reported none from Copan. Comparisons of the occurrences of the various mano varieties for Maya lowland and highland sites are provided in table 1. In preparing this table, which refers to presences and absences only, identification of varieties, in most cases, is based upon illustrations and description since the same terminology was not used. For Altar de Sacrificios, Seibal, and Cerros, however, the same classification system was employed. Further comparative discussions of lowland Maya manos may be found in Willey (1972:123–124; Willey 1978: 54–55; Willey et al. 1965:462–465), Kidder (1947: 33–35), and W. R. Coe (1959:34–35).

At Copan, the most popular mano form—at least on the basis of our collection sample—was the thick ovate-rectangular variety. In contrast, the square variety is most common throughout much of the Maya lowlands. This contrast is the result of a variation in the manner of grinding rather than from different materials being ground. Presumably, maize grains were the primary materials for mano-metate use at Copan as well as at other Maya sites. In other words, where an Altar de Sacrificios or Seibal resident would have turned the mano so as to have used all four sides more or less equally, a Copaneco would have used only two faces of the implement.

Lower Central American sites and mano varieties are given in table 2. There is less information on manos from this area than for the Maya area; however, as at Copan, the most frequent forms are the ovate-rectangular and the plano-convex. The implications, thus, are that Copan was more closely allied to a lower Central American sphere, in manos as well as metates, than to a Maya lowland or highland sphere.

TABLE 1

Distributions of mano types in Maya lowland and highland sites

Site				TYPE					
	Lge Rd	Sml Rd	Sqr	Tri	Pent	Over	Thc OR	Thn OR	P-C
Piedras Negras								x	(x)
Uaxactun	x	x	x	x			x	x	x
Mayapan	(x)		x	x			x	(x)	x
San Jose	x	x	x				x		x
Chichen Itza	x	x		(x)			x	x	x
Calakmul			x				x	x	
Altar de Sac.	x	x	x	x	x	x	x	x	x
Seibal	x	x	x	x	x	x	x	x	x
Barton Ramie	x	x	x	x		x	x	x	x
Cerros	x	x		x	x	x	x	x	x
Copan*	(x)						x		x
Motagua Valley	x	x					x	x	x
Kaminaljuyu							x	x	x
Chalchuapa			x			x	x	x	x
Palenque	x						x		x

Note: Parentheses indicate probable presence.
*From Longyear (1952:105)

REFERENCE TABLE

Coe 1959:34–35	Ricketson and Ricketson, 1937:194	Thompson 1939:173–174
Garber 1981:30–41	Ruz Lhuiller 1958: pl. 36	Wauchope 1934: pl. 5
Kidder 1947:33–35	Sheets 1978:27–30	Willey 1972:116–124
Kidder et al. 1946:140–141	Smith and Kidder 1943:167	Willey 1978:65–76
Longyear 1952:105	Stromsvik 1931:148, 156–157	Willey et al. 1965:457–465
Proskouriakoff 1962:339–341, 347–348	Stromsvik 1935:12	

The question of which mano forms were used with which metate forms is an interesting one. Archaeological associations in the ground form one kind of evidence, but such direct associations were rare in our data. Sizes and shapes of the two kinds of implements may provide other clues as to their conjoined uses. In the discussion of the metates, the lack of side walls or side-to-side concavities on the grinding surface for Types 1–3 was attributed to the use of a mano of equal or greater length than the metate width. Overhang manos would be eminently suited for this, especially with the Type 3 metates, but very few of them were found at Copan. Comparing the mean or actual lengths of the manos given in table 1 with the mean and actual widths of the four metate types shows that the correspondence is close enough to support this interpretation. The metate widths are as follows:

Type 1: x width = 27.65 cm; minW = 16 cm; maxW = 36.6 cm

Type 2: x width = 24.36 cm; minW = 21 cm; maxW = 28 cm

Type 3: only two widths remaining: 17.7 cm and 21.2 cm

Type 4: x width = 27 cm; minW = 23 cm; maxW = 35 cm

We cannot associate specific mano varieties with each of the metates on the basis of these measurements because the range of variation is so great and the sample size for width (metates) and

TABLE 2

Distribution of mano types in lower Central America

Site/Area	Lge Rd	Sml Rd	Sqr	Tri	Pent	Over	Thc OR	Thn OR	P-C
Los Naranjos	(x)	(x)					x	x	x
Rivas Region	x	x	x	x		x	x	x	
Diquis Delta	x	x					x	x	x
Tempisque Valley							(x)	(x)	(x)
Cocle	x	x							x
Chiriqui Gulf				x			x	x	x
Monagrillo							x	x	x
Quelepa		x						x	x

Note: Parentheses indicate probable presence.

REFERENCE TABLE

Andrews 1976:162–163	Linares de Sapir 1968:61–62
Baudez 1967:180–181	Lothrop 1937:96–97
Baudez and Becquelin 1973:381–382	Lothrop 1963: pl. 24
Healy 1980:278–280	Willey and McGimsey 1954:73

length (manos) is so small. The two available lengths for the large round mano variety, for example, are 37 cm and 16 cm. Based on numbers of specimens alone, most of the Copan metates would have been used with a thick ovate-rectangular or plano-convex mano.

Ground stone artifacts classified as mortars tend to be so amorphous that comparisons are difficult. Also, it seems likely that such objects are frequently ignored or underreported. Artifacts reminiscent of the Copan Type 1 mortar, in that they are generally roughly shaped stones used for grinding, have been reported from Seibal (Willey 1978:76–78), Altar de Sacrificios (Willey 1972:124–125), Barton Ramie (Willey et al. 1965:488–489), Uaxactun (Ricketson and Ricketson 1937:193), and Kaminaljuyu, in the highlands (Kidder, Jennings, and Shook 1946:141). The somewhat unusual Type 1 mortar specimen from Copan, Cat. No. 1-615, is duplicated by one from Los Naranjos, Honduras, and both are very similar to specimens from Calakmul (Baudez and Becquelin 1973:382, figs. 136d, 142j; Stromsvik 1935:123, fig. 2, pl. 2). The only reference we found to something like the Type 2 Copan mortar was from Piedras Negras, where W. R. Coe (1959:36) describes a "specialized

grindstone" that is rectangular, well made, and with a rim around all four edges. A shallow trough also follows all four sides between the rim and the grinding surface.

We found both hafted tabular and monolithic club-like barkbeaters at Copan. The first type, rectanguloid or ovoid in outline, is widely distributed in the Maya lowlands, as has been summarized (Willey et al. 1965:471; Willey 1972: 125–127; Willey 1978:55–56). It occurs as well in the Guatemalan highlands at Kaminaljuyu (Kidder, Jennings, and Shook 1946:142–143), in El Salvador at Chalchuapa (Sheets 1978:40), and at Los Llanitos (Longyear 1944:40). It is also found in Honduras, to the east of Copan, Los Naranjos (Baudez and Becquelin 1973:383–384), in the Bay Islands (Strong 1935: pl. 16), and around Lake Yojoa (Strong, Kidder, and Paul 1938:94). Determination of the chronological inception of barkbeater use in the Maya lowlands has been difficult (see Willey 1978:55–56). Formerly thought to be essentially Classic, or at the earliest, Protoclassic, it has been found more recently in Preclassic levels (see Willey 1978:80). The specimens that we found at Copan, however, are probably all of Classic date. While most barkbeaters are of the tabular type, made for hafting to a wooden handle, some are monolithic forms, generally club-like or cylindrical in shape. We found two, or possibly three, of these at Copan. They have been reported from Barton Ramie (Willey et al. 1965:471, fig. 282b) and from the Bay Islands (Strong 1935: pl. 16).

Rubbing and pounding stones, polishing stones, polished pebbles, and odd-shaped, apparently nonutilitarian stones were all recovered from our excavations at Copan. These are, in a general way, similar to such objects found in Maya sites throughout the lowlands, as well as in the highland country and in lower Central America. Their general amorphousness makes specific comparisons to other sites and regions rather unprofitable for culture historical purposes.

Polished stone celts of fine-grained hard stones are a common lowland Maya type. A number of these, mostly of the medium, small, and very small varieties, were found at Copan. These are similar to those described and compared in previous lowland Maya site reports, including those for Barton Ramie (Willey et al. 1965:472–476), Altar de Sacrificios (Willey 1972:130–133), Seibal (Willey 1978:86–89), Uaxactun (Kidder 1947: 38, fig. 78k–q), and many others. Polished stone celts occur at Kaminaljuyu but do not seem to be common there (Kidder, Jennings, and Shook 1946:142). They are present to the east of Copan, at Los Naranjos (Baudez and Becquelin 1973:383, figs. 137, 143). The dating range for polished hard stone celts runs from at least the Middle Preclassic through the Classic and into the Postclassic. Those from Copan are probably all of Classic date. In particular, it is our impression that the very small variety celts tend to be Late Classic at Copan and elsewhere.

We recovered a few ring stones at Copan; Longyear (1952:106, fig. 89d) also found one. It is an artifact—possibly a digging-stick weight—that is more common in the Maya highlands (Kidder, Jennings, and Shook 1946:141–142, fig. 59a; Sheets 1978:37–38; see Willey 1972: 136–137 for a more general discussion) than in the lowlands; however, ring stones do occur at Altar de Sacrificios (Willey 1972:134–137) and Seibal (Willey 1978:90–93). They do not seem to be reported from regions to the east in Honduras. Their chronological position, at least in lowland contexts, is Late Classic, which conforms to our Copan findings.

Slate or mudstone mirror backs, which were once faced with pyrite plaques, are in our Copan collections. These mirrors occur in both lowland and highland Maya sites (see Willey 1972: 142–143 for a discussion of these occurrences). They are also reported to the east, in Honduras, at Los Naranjos (Baudez and Becquelin 1973: 390, fig. 143).

Disk-shaped, central-nubbin, jadeite ear ornaments are a known type in the Maya lowlands (Willey 1972:149–150, fig. 132c–d), and we found several of these at Copan. They differ from the larger earplug flares that Longyear (1952:108, fig. 91) described from the site. Jadeite pendants from our Copan collection are all of modest size, jade quality, and workmanship. Some are plain, some carved. A few jadeite adornos or adorno fragments and quite a few beads were recovered. None of these is exceptional. Beads include several forms: flat rectanguloid, irregular, barrel-shaped, disk, large and small tubulars, and subsphericals. A few jadeite pebbles and some raw, or broken, jadeite lumps make up the collection of this material. The raw material, of a whitish jade, may be residue from jade carving or manufacturing of objects.

Among the miscellaneous ground stone items in our Copan collections are a few fragments of what we have identified as celt-like objects or ritual maces. These were all carved from a gray or black schist-like stone. They resemble, but do not duplicate, some similar objects that were found at Barton Ramie (Willey et al. 1965:479–482, figs. 299a–c, 300). The objects in question could be monolithic axes. Those from Barton Ramie, in some instances, have a wrench-like form. Others have been noted at a few Maya lowland sites, all from Belize (ibid.:482).

Of all of the other ground stone items from our Copan excavations, only the little monolithic stone tables seem worthy of special comment. These are all quite small objects, and, perhaps when complete, were no more than 15 cm in length or width. Their purpose appears to have been of a ritual nature. One may have served as a mortar. There are resemblances to the rather unusual little red sandstone tables from Altar de Sacrificios (Willey 1972:251–254), although those from Altar de Sacrificios were generally larger. Some of those from Altar de Sacrificios showed signs of burning on their tops, as did one specimen from Copan. None of the altar tables had been used as a mortar.

Metates (509, with 108 used for study)

with assistance from Julia A. Hendon

A total of 509 metates or metate fragments were recovered from our excavations, and 108 of these were used for this study. These were made from either tuff or basalt. Both finer and coarser grained brecchia tuffs were used, and the basalt varies from vesicular to nonvesicular.

These metates were divided into four major types, plus a "Special" category. All are described below.

Type 1 (43)

This type is represented by the greatest number of our studied specimens, a total of 43. It appears to be the most common form of metate that was used in the Copan Valley. Metates of Type 1 have a rectangular grinding surface and base. The corners of the grinding surface are well defined, ranging from rounded to square. Edges are straight, although the side edges (long dimension) are not always parallel since the corner angle may be obtuse rather than right (fig. 164a). Walls rising above the grinding surface occur infrequently and usually result from use.

In cross section, these metates vary from trapezoidal (fig. 164b) to semicircular (see fig. 164a). The trapezoidal ones have a flat base and well-defined, straight sides that slope inward from the grinding surface. The junction between sides and base is rounded but obvious (fig. 164c). The other shape, hemispherical, has curving sides that merge imperceptibly into the base (fig. 164d). In these cases, the base is often slightly concave on both axes, presenting a flattened turtle-back aspect (see discussion of Type 4). A great deal of variation exists in cross-sectional shapes, especially in the amount of curvature displayed by the sides. None of the Type 1 metates has the rounded base of the Type 4 category; neither are they perfectly planar.

Wear is visible on many of the artifacts. In some cases, the surface slopes down gently from one or both end edges (short dimension), forming a wedge-shaped cross section. Differences in smoothness and the unevenness of the incline indicate that such a slope results from wear rather than deliberate construction. Cat. No. 1-124 (fig. 165) goes from a height of 6 cm at its highest point at the surviving end to a height of 1.1 cm at the opposite broken edge. The change in height is gradual. The surface of the metate has a few large holes, which may have been deliberate attempts to prolong the life of the metate by renewing the roughness of the grinding surface. The unusually low height of the metate also suggests heavy and long use. Another metate, Cat. No. 1-899 (see discussion below for further details), measures 9.5 cm at its highest point on the wedge-shaped end and 3 cm in the center. A similar wear pattern occurs on Cat. No. 1-486, which, over a distance of 11 cm, goes from 4.8 cm to 3 cm in height. The same difference in smoothness occurs. The flattened area at the edge of the grinding surface is as rough as the base and sides, contrasting with the feel of the sloping surface. The variation in maximum and minimum heights and in their ratios also suggests that the unevenness results from use of the metate.

Differential wear along the side edges is much less obvious. One example of wall formation is visible in figure 165, Cat. No. 1-899, which was also worn at the surviving end (see above). As figure 165 shows, this specimen is a fragment with only one side and corner intact. The wall is found on the longer surviving edge. About 9 cm in from the broken edge, the wall begins to rise, attaining a maximum height of 11.5 cm. Although the junction between wall and surface is not perpendicular, the curve is steep and abrupt enough to contrast, in cross section, with the gently sloping, wedge-shaped form of the ends of Cat. No. 1-124 and Cat. No. 1-899 itself. The wall is 5 cm thick/wide. In the center of the flat surface, the height is 3 cm. This type of wall is found on three other fragments—Cat. Nos. 1-1023, 1-693, and 1-923. None of these fragments has as high or as thick a wall as 1-899, but the contrast between higher and lower sections of the surface is distinct enough to represent less heavily used cases of the same type of wear.

The grinding surface itself in most of the metates examined remains flat in cross section across the short dimension. Any concavity at all is on the order of 1 to 2 cm. The grinding surface is often noticeably smoother than the sides or base. Some have very large holes in their surfaces, even given the vesicular character of much of the stone used, which may represent an attempt to increase the tooth of the surface. A few metates are actually polished in places, usually near the edges. The location of the polish suggests it was caused by contact with the mano rather than from the material, presumably maize, being ground (Sheets 1978:30). The bases on some are also smooth, perhaps from movement during grinding.

Manufacture was through pecking. It is difficult to separate pecking holes from vesicles or from holes resulting from mineral inclusions dislodged during use or manufacture; however, on some metates pecking marks are definite. Although not as well made as Type 3, all Type 1 metates examined had been shaped, with an effort obviously made to produce flat bases and grinding surfaces, symmetrical sides, straight edges, and squared corners.

From the general lack of side wall or concavities, it seems likely that a mano equal to or wider than the width of the metate was used. A longer mano would have required holds similar to those of a rolling pin. If, however, the mano were pushed rather than rolled, a mano of a length equal to the metate's width would have been adequate. In the first instance, a mano with a circular cross section would have worked best; in the second, a square or rectangular-shaped one might have been more effective. The sloping at the metate ends indicates that grinding did not continue all the way to the end edge of the metate. Since all the specimens examined with this wear pattern are fragments, it is not clear if the metate ends were symmetrical. Because this slope results from wear, however, rather than deliberate design, one would not expect both ends to wear down equally. Cat. No. 1-899 and the other ones with distinct side walls were probably used with a mano shorter than the metates' width and with flat ends.

Two complete Type 1 metates will be described. The first one, Cat. No. 1-98, is rectangular with rounded corners. The grinding surface is flat and horizontal. The base, slightly convex, curves smoothly into the sides, giving it a roughly hemispherical cross section (fig. 165c). Pecked from a vesicular basalt, the base is rough. The grinding surface has been worn smooth, but it has only a shallow concavity (1 cm). The metate measures 44 cm long x 30.5 cm wide x 6.2 cm high at the center, the most concave point, and 7.5 cm high at the highest point.

The second whole one, Cat. No. 1-1023 (fig. 165d), resembles Cat. No. 1-98 very closely. The top is roughly rectangular in outline with rounded corners. In cross section, the grinding surface dips 1 to 2 cm, appearing almost horizontal. From the cross section one can also see the metate to be trapezoidal in shape with a flat base and roughly straight sides. The dimensions are 55 cm long x 31 cm wide x 7 cm high.

Some generalizations about dimensions are possible from the two complete metates discussed above and others. There are nine metates, in addition to Cat. Nos. 1-98 and 1-1023, that preserve both corners of one end, allowing width measurements. The widths range from 16 cm to 36.6 cm with the majority (seven) falling between 20 and 30 cm. The mean of these 11 specimens is 27.65 cm with a standard deviation of 5.75 cm. For the same 11, the mean and standard deviation of the height are 5.94 cm and 1.43 cm. In measuring height, the maximum measurement was used whenever large discrepancies existed for one specimen because of differential wear. Several of the metates are worn more near the center than at the ends; in these cases the end measurement was used. In those cases, however, where the grinding surface is virtually flat and without walls, center measurements were used. The other 26 metate specimens that could be measured or for which field notes or drawings were available are too fragmentary for length or width measurements. Heights, however, were taken, and the mean height of these metates plus the 11 above (N=37) is 5.94 + 1.33 cm.

The only two definite length measurements are from Cat. No. 1-98 (44 cm) and 1-1023 (55 cm). The lengths of Cat. Nos. 1-1, 1-137, and 1-195 were estimated at 30, 44, and 36 cm, respectively, by Willey (field notes). Also, Cat. Nos. 1-115 and 1-124 have retained 27 cm of their original length, putting them within the range of the complete ones. In summary, although Cat. No. 1-1 appears unusual with 30 cm estimated length x 16 cm width x 9 cm height, being somewhat shorter, narrower, and taller than the others, a clear separation into small and large categories fails to emerge. Obviously, one must be cautious with so fragmentary and small a sample of measurements, but from the data available, Type 1 metates are fairly homogeneous in size, being on the order of 50 cm long x 28 cm wide x 5 cm high average dimensions, as well as in shape.

Cat. Nos.	Op. No. and Provenience
1-1 (2 spec.)	1(A) CV-20, Surface, Large Plaza
1-31	4(C) CV-20, Lev. 1
1-98	6(J) CV-20, Lev. 1
1-108	6(K) CV-20, Lev. 1
1-115	7(G) CV-20, Lev. 1
1-124	4(P) CV-20, Lev. 1
1-137	6(N) CV-20, Lev. 1
1-195	16(D) Sacbe, Lev. 6
1-455 (2 spec.)	29(A) CV-44, Surface
1-486	33(G) CV-43, Lev. 1
1-522	33(CC) CV-43, Lev. 1
1-524	35(E) CV-43, Lev. 1
1-527	35(C) CV-43, Lev. 1
1-568	37(D) CV-43, Lev. 1
1-587	39(C) CV-43, Lev. 1
1-589	41(A) CV-47, Lev. 1
1-597	40(A) CV-45, Lev. 1
1-602	35(M) CV-43, Lev. 1
1-610	40(C) CV-45, Lev. 1
1-617	33(FF) CV-43, Lev. 2
1-621	35(N) CV-43, Lev. 1
1-628	43(A) CV-43, Lev. 1
1-631	39(F) CV-43, Lev. 1
1-639	39(E) CV-43, Lev. 1
1-651	42(D) CV-43, Lev. 1
1-693	42(E) CV-43, Lev. 1
1-707	38(H) CV-43, Lev. 1
1-734	46(A) CV-44, Lev. 1
1-759	48(D) CV-47, Lev. 1
1-761	42(I) CV-43, Lev. 1
1-815	39(L) CV-44, Lev. 1
1-846	47(H) CV-47, Lev. 1
1-887	67(B) CV-106, Lev. 1
1-899	71(A) CV-204, Lev. 2
1-904	102(A) CV-43, Lev. 1
1-921	101(B) CV-47, Lev. 1
1-923	100(B) CV-43, Lev. 1
1-1023 (2 spec.)	50(A) CV-45, Lev. 7
1-1091	105(A) CV-44, Lev. 3
No Number	

Type 2 (24)

Type 2 metates are Type 1 metates with legs. The shapes and dimensions of the metates, excluding the legs, are squarely within the Type 1 range of variation. Small nubbin feet, usually three in number, have been placed on the base, however. Because feet are the only distinguishing criterion for Type 2, fragments of footed metates not containing a foot would have been placed in Type 1. This makes Type 1, at least in part, a residual category and the total number of Type 2 artifacts a minimum number. Since there are, however, clear cases of both footed and unfooted metates, it does not seem proper to combine the two types.

One complete specimen, Cat. No. 1-706, shows that the feet are arranged in a tripod (fig. 166a). The similarity to the complete Type 1 metates, Cat. Nos. 1-98 and 1-1023, is obvious. The overall form is rectangular with rounded corners, straight sides, and a somewhat curved base. The end with the central foot is narrower than the other end. The metate is concave in the center, where it is about 2 cm deep. The metate itself is of a fairly uniform thickness—4.6 cm in the center, 5 cm at the ends. The legs are set in from the sides of the metate and are roughly ovoid in cross section. The dimensions are 38.6 cm long x 18–21 cm wide x 7.4 cm high. The metate height is 5 cm maximum. The legs are 2 cm high with a cross-sectional measurement of 4 x 5 cm.

Other fragments bear out this tripod arrangement. In cross section, the feet appear roughly rectangular with rounded corners. Occasionally, they are more ovoid. At times the foot's outside edge lies flush with the metate edge. The bottom is generally flat and the sides parallel, although none of the feet (or the metates) show evidence of particularly careful workmanship. The center feet, in many cases, are longer and more rectangular than the corner ones. Of the six end fragments with central feet intact (Cat. Nos. 1-1, 1-77, 1-137, 1-761, 1-1021, and 1-1084), all have feet between 6 and 9 cm in length (long dimension, usually parallel to the metate edge) and five of them have a foot width of 3 to 4 cm. The sixth one, Cat. No. 1-1084 (fig. 166b), has a square foot 7 x 7 cm. The three end fragments with one or both corner feet measure 5 cm in diameter (Cat. No. 1-145) (fig. 166c), 3.5 x 4 cm (Cat. No. 1-867) (fig. 166d), and 3 cm diameter (Cat. No. 1-83) (fig. 166e). Since none of the center foot fragments joins with the corner feet fragments, one cannot insist too strongly on this distinction in size. The complete one, Cat. No. 1-706 described above, does not have a larger central foot. It may be, therefore, that for individual metates feet are uniform in size but that variation exists between metates. It is interesting, however, that for the admittedly small sample of measurements available, all five central feet are longer than all three sets of corner feet.

As mentioned above, metate dimensions are comparable with those of Type 1. The sole length measurement, 38.6 cm, comes from Cat. No. 1-706. It falls below the two complete lengths for Type 1 of 44 cm and 55 cm but seems within an acceptable range of variation. There are seven fragments allowing width measurements. The widths range between 21 and 26 cm with a mean of 24.36 cm + 2.28 cm, very close to the Type 1 mean of 27.65 + 5.75 cm. The metate heights are also like Type 1, ranging between 3.5 and 5.8 cm. Their mean is 4.74 + 0.69 cm (N=10) compared to 5.94 + 1.33 cm for the Type 1 specimens. Type 2 metates are, on the average, somewhat smaller than Type 1 but the ranges of variation of the two overlap. The feet measure 4.5 cm or less, with the majority (six out of nine) 1 to 2.6 cm. The mean leg height is 1.69 + 1.16 cm. Putting leg and metate height together, one finds that the height measurements are virtually the same for Types 1 and 2.

Wear patterns are also similar to Type 1. The grinding surfaces have only small concavities or are flat when viewed in cross section across the short dimension. No side walls appear. Several of those examined, however, slope down slightly from the ends. The complete one, Cat. No. 1-706, as well as two fragments, show this pattern. The lack of side walls coupled with the generally even wear on the surface suggests the use of manos equal to or longer than the metate width. Either round or rectangular ones would work. Overhang manos could also be used with Type 2 metates.

As the figures given earlier show, no increase in overall metate height is gained by adding the legs. Also, the legs are so short in many cases that they do not completely lift the base off the ground. Given the fact that many of the Type 1 bases are somewhat convex and that they are often worn smooth, it is possible that feet were added to decrease movement of the metate, to make it steadier and more stationary. It might also be

that the Type 1 metates were meant to be left in some more or less permanent location where they could be wedged against unwanted movement, whereas the legged ones were designed to be used in more than one location without external stabilization. Type 2 metates are heavy and large enough to preclude considering them as portable over long distances but within a domestic house plaza group they could have been moved without undue exertion.

Cat. Nos.	Op. No. and Provenience
1-1	1(A) CV-20, Surface, Large Plaza
1-77	6(H) CV-20, Lev. 1
1-83	4(K) CV-20, Lev. 1
1-137	6(N) CV-20, Lev. 1
1-145	4(S) CV-20, Lev. 1
1-451 (2 spec.)	28(A) CV-43, Surface
1-549	36(I) CV-43, Lev. 1
1-579	38(C) CV-43, Lev. 1
1-626	37(N) CV-43, Lev. 1
1-633	37(M) CV-43, Lev. 1
1-695	55(A) CV-115, Lev. 3
1-706	42(F) CV-43, Lev. 1
1-707	38(H) CV-43, Lev. 1
1-761	42(I) CV-43, Lev. 1
1-767	45(J) CV-46, Lev. 1
1-779	42(H) CV-43, Lev. 1
1-867	101(A) CV-47, Lev. 1
1-918	49(A) CV-43, Lev. 3
1-962	81(A) Sacbe, Lev. 5
1-1021	49(A) CV-43, Lev. 6-C
1-1054	104(A) CV-43, Lev. 4
1-1084	106(A) CV-47, Lev. 1
1-1102	82(A) CV-16, Lev. 3-A

Type 3 (26)

Type 3 metates have legs, but otherwise they are quite different from the Type 2 variety. The legs are longer and thinner, and the body of the metate is also thinner and more carefully shaped. Because of this relative delicacy and thinness, it is unlikely that legless pieces of Type 2 metates would have been placed in the Type 3 group.

No complete specimens are extant. Fragments with either center or corner-located legs were recovered, suggesting, although not conclusively, that these metates, like Type 2, were three-legged. It is impossible to tell if the legs were all of equal height. The following discussion, therefore, will concentrate mostly on the legs themselves.

Of the six specimens with center legs (Cat. Nos. 1-202, 1-574, 1-853, 1-862, 1-864, and 1-970), measurements and illustrations are available only for Cat. No. 1-202 (fig. 167a). This metate has two rounded corners and roughly parallel sides. The grinding surface is slightly concave in lateral cross section. One side wall merges smoothly with the base; the other is vertical. Dimensions are 11.7 cm (remaining length) x 17.7 cm wide x 3 cm high. The leg is conical with an ovoid cross section, tapering smoothly to a narrow flat tip. Unlike many of the examples discussed below, the leg on Cat. No. 1-202 is set back from the edge of the metate. The metate seems to flare out from the leg. The height of the leg proper is between 4.3 and 3.2 cm, making it somewhat shorter than the other Type 3 specimens that we measured. The leg diameter is 5 cm at the base, directly underneath the metate, and 2 cm at the tip. The metate probably originally had two corner feet on the opposite end.

The following specimens are all corner fragments with one leg remaining. Cat. No. 1-206 (fig. 167b) has a leg whose outer side is flush with the end of the metate. The sides directly joining the metate edge at its corner are quite straight, but the opposite side, underneath the grinding surface, is curved. The leg tip itself is not flat but may be broken. From the leg tip to the top of the metate is 9.9 cm. The metate itself is 4 cm thick. The leg is 7 cm wide at the base and 1 cm wide at its tip.

The leg on Cat. No. 1-686 is squared on the two outside faces and rounded underneath the metate. It blends smoothly into the metate edges and tapers down to a flat, roughly circular tip. The metate itself has a rounded corner and a flat, smooth, and almost polished grinding surface that is 3 cm thick. The leg has a maximum height of 9.5 cm with a minimum of 6 cm.

Cat. No. 1-465 has a leg that is truly four-sided. It slants in markedly from its junction with the metate edge. The two tallest sides, one flush with the end, the other with the side, measure 11.2 cm and 9 cm in height. The two remaining sides, directly underneath the metate, are 6.9 cm each. All sides are flat and straight, if not parallel. The metate proper is 2 to 4 cm high.

A fourth fragment, Cat. No. 1-615, also shows the angled leg rising into the metate edge (fig. 167c). By angling the outside faces, the leg is positioned underneath the metate. The face below the metate is straight. The overall leg shape is rectangular with less tapering than seen on other examples, including Cat. No. 1-465. The leg dimensions are 4.7 cm high, 6.5 cm thick at the base, and 3.3 cm thick at the tip. The metate slopes down very slightly from the end. It may have been concave from end to end when whole, but it is almost flat from side to side. The grinding surface is very smooth. Only one horizontal measurement, the width, is complete. The dimensions of the metate are 17.4 cm length remaining x 21.2 cm maximum width x 3–3.7 cm height at broken edge. The metate has rounded corners with straight and parallel sides.

Further examples of leg-metate junction are found on Cat. Nos. 1-68 (fig. 167d), 1-571, 1-621, and 1-1086. All of these fragments show the leg placed at the edge of the metate. For Cat. No. 1-68, the height from metate surface to tip is 14.5 cm, while it is about 10 cm from metate underside to leg tip. The leg is widest at its base where it joins the metate—8 cm.

Cat. No. 1-146 is a leg broken off from a metate. It displays clearly the rectangularity of many of the Type 3 legs. The sides are straight and parallel, lacking the tapering found on others. It measures 2.7 cm on the cross-sectional short axis and 6.9 cm on the cross-sectional long axis. The maximum remaining height is 5. 8 cm. It is possible that the small lip at the broken end represents a remnant of the metate itself. Cat. Nos. 1-862 and 1-414 mirror Cat. No. 1-146 in having rectangular cross sections and straight sides. Both, however, taper in at their tips. Cat. No. 1-414 is unusually large, measuring between 13 and 15 cm from tip to broken area (where the base would be). Cat. No. 1-862 is made out of a brecchia rather than the usual vesicular basalt. All three legs, as are all the other specimens described above, are carefully crafted with smooth, flat, even surfaces and careful joins.

There are eight specimens, in all, whose maximum and minimum leg heights can be accurately measured. The minimum height ranges between 3.2 and 10 cm, with a mean of 5.73 cm and a standard deviation of 1.91 cm. The measurements of maximum height go from 4.3 to

14.5 cm. The mean is 9.61 cm + 2.68 cm. The ratios of maximum to minimum height fall between 2.2 and 1.34 cm. The leg on Cat. No. 1-202 appears unusually short in comparison to the other seven specimens. It has the lowest minimum height, 3.2 cm, although several of the others cluster around 4 and 5 cm. The maximum height, 4.3 cm, is more of a greater disparity since all the other ones are 8 cm high or more. This difference stems from the fact that only Cat. No. 1-202 is a leg discontinuous with the metate end. The metates have a mean height of 3.81 + 0.83 cm. The only two complete widths are 17.7 cm for Cat. No. 1-202 and 21.2 cm for Cat. No. 1-615. Both the average minimum and maximum leg heights are greater than the Type 2 leg heights. Their mean height is 2.09 cm + 1.11 cm. Individual minimum measurements do overlap with a few Type 2 specimens. The Type 3 metate proper also has a smaller mean height (3.81 cm) than either Type 1 (5.94 cm) or Type 2 (4.83 cm).

Wear on the Type 3 metates is mainly from end to end, although definite conclusions are difficult to draw from fragmentary specimens. The grinding surface slopes down slightly from the end on several fragments, but the specimens are not sufficiently intact to tell whether the metates were concave or tilted with legs of uneven height. No walls have formed on the side or end edges. The smoothness and incipient polishing of some of the grinding surfaces suggest that these were heavily used metates (Cat. Nos. 1-615, 1-571, 1-686, and 1-465). They could have been used with circular, rectangular, or overhang metates.

Cat. Nos.	Op. No. and Provenience
1-68	7(B) CV-20, Lev. 1
1-137	6(N) CV-20, Lev. 1
1-146	12(B) CV-20, Lev. 1
1-202	20(A) CV-20, Lev. 3
1-206	21(A) CV-20, Lev. 2
1-414	27(H) Santa Rita 1, Lev. 1
1-465	33(F) CV-43, Lev. 1
1-571	37(F) CV-43, Lev. 1
1-574	35(L) CV-43, Lev. 1
1-615	35(O) CV-43, Lev. 1
1-621	35(N) CV-43, Lev. 1
1-667	54(A) CV-98, Lev. 8, Burial 7
1-683	54(A) CV-94, Lev. 10
1-686	39(G) CV-44, Lev. 1
1-747	39(J) CV-44, Lev. 1
1-748	45(B) CV-46, Lev. 1
1-853	39(O) CV-44, Lev. 1
1-862 (2 spec.)	47(G) CV-47, Lev. 1
1-864	73(A) CV-185, Lev. 1
1-874	68(A) CV-68, Lev. 5
1-970	104(A) CV-43, Lev. 2
1-991	81(D) Sacbe, Lev. 1
1-1054	104(A) CV-43, Lev. 4
1-1086	1054(A) CV-43, Lev. 6
1-1091	105(A) CV-44, Lev. 3

Type 4 (13)

Type 4 is the turtle-back variety common to the Peten. Only 13 specimens, mostly fragmentary, were recovered at Copan. In appearance, they have concave bases that curve smoothly up to the surface on both axes. The cross section differs from most Type 1 metates in having no distinction between sides and base. There are cases of Type 1 metates, however, that approach a turtle-back cross section but whose flat grinding surface still differentiates them from Type 4. The top of the Type 4 metate is concave from side to side. The depth of the depression varies, probably reflecting degree of use. A difference exists also between those with smooth, evenly curved concavities and those with straighter side walls abutting a flatter, depressed grinding surface. This latter form is what is referred to as basin- or trough-shaped. The height and thickness of the walls vary.

Strictly speaking, the terms "turtle-backed" and "trough-shaped" do not necessarily describe the same form, since one refers to the base and the other to the top of the metate. Examples can be found in the literature of turtle-backed metates with flat grinding surfaces and flat-based ones with deeply sunk basins. Since the practice, in many artifact descriptions, seems to be to combine these two terms (and forms) into one class, we have assigned both metates with concave grinding surfaces and walled basins to Type 4. In essence, it is with the metate top where the contrast with Type 1 is greatest—Type 1 metates are flat, Type 4 metates are either curved or walled.

The one complete specimen, Cat. No. 1-1, is made of gray brecchia. It measures 33 cm long x 23 cm wide x 9 cm high at the center. The grinding surface has only a slight dip. Poorly shaped, it is of crude workmanship.

One fragment, Cat. No. 1-841, has a side wall. The overall shape of the metate and the extent of the walls remain unknown, but enough is left to show that a definite trough had been formed by use. The wall rises steeply above the 3-cm-high grinding surface. The thickness of the wall varies between 4.5 and 5.5 cm (fig. 168b, left).

Cat. No. 1-631 has raised sides and an open end (fig. 168b, right). Made of brecchia, it has a curved cross section resulting from a concave top and a convex base. The thickness of the metate itself, from base to surface, is fairly uniform from sides to center. One side measures 6 cm high, the other 4 cm, and the center 5 cm. The curvature of the base and top give it the appearance of having side walls. The width is 23 cm; the maximum length remaining is 18 cm. The surface is rectangular with rounded corners.

Cat. No. 1-278 is also extremely curved in cross section with a concave top surface and convex base (fig. 168a). Its shape is rectangular with one surviving corner. The stone used is brecchia. The fragment measures 26.4 cm long x 17 cm wide x 7 cm high in the center and 4 cm high at the sides. The concavity of the grinding surface is 2.4 cm deep. The width has been estimated at 30 cm.

The remaining nine specimens (Cat. Nos. 1-454, 1-589, 1-685, 1-688, 1-859, 1-902, 1-984, 1-1022, and 1-1054) are fragments. In the field notes, six are identified as vesicular basalt (Cat. Nos. 1-454, 1-589, 1-688, 1-859, 1-902, and 1-1022) and one (Cat. No. 1-685) as brecchia. The other two (Cat. Nos. 1-984 and 1-1054) are made of a fine-grained, nonvesicular rock of unknown type. Taking all 13 specimens together, one has three (Cat. No. 1-841 being the third) fine-grained nonvesicular metates, four made of brecchia, and six of vesicular basalt.

Cat. Nos.	Op. No. and Provenience
1-1	1(A) CV-20, Surface, Large Plaza
1-278	24(A) CV-20, Lev. 4
1-454	32(A) CV-47, Surface
1-589	41(A) CV-47, Lev. 1
1-631	39(F) CV-43, Lev. 1
1-685	33(FF) CV-43, Lev. 2, Special Find 24
1-688	33(FF) CV-43, Lev. 3
1-841	41(C) CV-47, Lev. 1
1-859	49(A) CV-43, Lev. 2
1-902	49(A) CV-43, Lev. 4
1-984	41(I) CV-47, Lev. 1
1-1022	50(A) CV-45, Lev. 6-B
1-1054	104(A) CV-43, Lev. 4

Special (2)

There are two specimens that do not fit easily into any of the four previous types. They do not resemble one another, but have been placed together in this miscellaneous category.

Cat. No. 1-185 is made from an architectural building block. The stone is andesite tuff, a common building material at Copan. The overall shape is rectangular, measuring 25 cm long x 18 cm wide x 8 cm high. One large side has a trough-like, round-bottomed groove worn in it that is 10 cm wide and 3 cm deep. Reused building blocks are known at other sites. At Chichen Itza, for example, they are the common type (Stromsvik 1931:146–148, figs. 2–4, pls. 2, 3; Stromsvik 1935:123, 127, pls. 1, 2).

The other, Cat. No. 1-107, is a very small piece of an unusual legged metate. The metate has a foot or base running the complete length of the preserved edge. This support, 2.2 cm high, is recessed under the metate, creating a descending ridge below the upper part of the metate (fig. 169). The metate proper is 2 cm thick. The grinding surface is flat with straight edges. It is well made, but too little remains to suggest the original full shape.

Cat. Nos.	Op. No. and Provenience
1-107	4(N) CV-20, Lev. 1
1-185	18(A) CV-20, Lev. 1

Manos (468, with 144 used for study)

with assistance from Julia A. Hendon

A total of 468 manos were recovered in our excavations, and 144 of these were utilized for this study and analysis. The manos from Copan have been divided into nine varieties based primarily on cross-sectional outline. These varieties are overhang, triangular, square, pentagonal, small round, large round, plano-convex, thin ovate-rectangular, and thick ovate-rectangular. The greatest number of specimens are of the thick ovate-rectangular and the plano-convex types. Relatively few of the manos recovered are whole, and many show secondary use as pounders or anvils.

Stone materials for manos are the same as for metates, essentially tuffs and basalt.

In general, it appears likely that the various forms result from wear rather than intentional shaping. Except for the round types, wear, indicated by smoothness and polishing, is usually heaviest on the flat or flatter faces of the manos. The flatness of the faces varies from specimen to specimen. In addition to being flatter, the more heavily used areas are generally wider than the rougher unused spots. Even the round manos, which lack distinct faces, sometimes show slight differences in smoothing on the various facets of their sides.

As a convention to facilitate description, the flat grinding areas on the square, pentagonal, and triangular varieties will be called faces or sides. For overhang, thin ovate-rectangular, and thick ovate-rectangular varieties, the wider, usually smoother and flatter areas will be referred to as top and bottom, and the remaining opposing faces will be called sides. The flat face of the plano-convex ones will be called the bottom, the remaining curved area the top. Width will refer to the distance from side to side in cross section; height (or thickness), to the distance from top to bottom. The round variety manos have diameter measurements.

As table 3 illustrates, all nine varieties are fairly close to one another in overall size: in length, width, and height (or diameter). Length was probably the most variable dimension, but it is also the least often preserved.

We propose that the original shape of most of the manos at Copan was round. Continued use wears down the surface unevenly, forming flat or less curved faces. Therefore, most round manos found in excavation should be either blanks (i.e., manufactured but relatively unused ones) or implements used with a rolling rather than rubbing motion, which distributed the wear evenly.

Support for this interpretation comes from the excavation of Structure D of CV-20. A cache of two manos (Cat. Nos. 1-241 and 1-243), one barkbeater (Cat. No. 1-242), one polishing stone of black diorite (Cat. No. 1-244), and five incomplete storage jars, surrounded by rubble, was placed in the fill of an earlier building (Structure D–Sub 1). It lay at approximately plaza level, just inside of a retaining wall. All of the stone artifacts appear unused. The two manos are described below, Cat. No. 1-241 under the large round category, and Cat. No. 1-243 under the thick ovate-rectangular. The inclusion of a thick ovate-rectangular mano in the cache may cast some doubt on the idea that all mano types result from round originals. Cat. No. 1-243, however, is quite ovoid in cross section and lacks the differential smoothness associated with use. It is probably, therefore, a slightly less well turned round blank, or, possibly, a round blank modified in preparation for use as a thick ovate-rectangular mano.

The round manos are subdivided into small (diameter less than 8 cm) and large (diameter greater than or equal to 8 cm).

Small Round (13)

One complete specimen was recovered, Cat. No. 1-635. It measures 21 cm long x 5.3 cm in diameter. A cross section of this variety may be seen in the illustration (fig. 170) of Cat. No. 1-786. One end of 1-786 is flattened in what appears to be deliberate shaping rather than grinding. A slight

TABLE 3
Dimensions of mano varieties (cm)

Type	Length	Max. Width	Max. Height
Large Round	37*, 16.4*	9.4	(9.4)
Thin Ovate-Rectangular	24.8*	8.7	4.1
Thick Ovate-Rectangular	21.8	7.8	5.9
Plano-convex	22.6*	7.6	6.1
Square	—	6.7	(6.7)
Small Round	21*	6.4	(6.4)
Overhang	31.3*	6.3	5.9
Triangular	—	—	5.5
Pentagonal	23.5	—	5.5

*Not means, actual measurements, usually because only 1 complete specimen

aper toward both ends is evident in all specimens examined.

The surfaces of those specimens examined are uniform in texture. Three have smooth surfaces and rough ends; the fourth has a rougher exterior. One, which preserves one end, is well made with a symmetrical appearance and gradual taper. It is difficult to ascribe the extreme smoothness of these fragments to wear alone, although it is possible. Both these small round manos and the larger round ones described below are much smoother and more polished than most of the other types.

A tentative subdivision of the small round variety could be "small round rough." These specimens, two in number, do not show any signs of deliberate or use-related smoothing. They are irregularly shaped and rough-surfaced, but despite this they are classified as manos rather than pounders because their ends are unbattered. Both are complete. The first, Cat. No. 1-93, measures 12 cm long and 5 cm in diameter with a slight taper. The second, Cat. No. 1-126, is 18.5 cm long with a diameter of 6 cm.

Cat. Nos.	Op. No. and Provenience
1-93	6(I) CV-20, Lev. 1
1-126	6(M) CV-20, Lev. 1
1-451	28(A) CV-43, Surface
1-545	33(CC) CV-43, Lev. 2
1-635	44(B) CV-46, Lev. 1
1-648	34(O) CV-43, Lev. 1
1-786	46(C) CV-44, Lev. 1
1-844	48(H) CV-47, Lev . 1
1-859	49(A) CV-43, Lev. 2
1-867	101(A) CV-47, Lev. 1
1-984	41(I) CV-47, Lev. 1
1-1054	104(A) CV-43, Lev. 4
No Number	

Large Round (14)

Of the round manos with diameters greater than or equal to 8 cm, two are complete and two more almost so. The two whole ones vary greatly in length, with Cat. No. 1-241 measuring 37 cm and Cat. No. 1-361 (fig. 171) only 16.4 cm. The two almost complete ones measure 16 cm (Cat. No. 1-451) and 18 cm (Cat. No. 1-821) in length. In general, all these manos taper slightly

toward either end. Diameters range from 8 to 11.5 cm.

Condition of the surface varies. Some, such as Cat. Nos. 1-842 and 1-241, the latter from a cache, are smooth and even polished all over their exteriors with no signs of grinding. Others are rough and also appear unused. The remainder, by far the majority, exhibit differential smoothness, suggesting the beginnings of transformation into one of the other types. As examples, one may point to Cat. No. 1-651, which has a circumference of 25.5 cm, 7 cm of which is smooth and almost polished while the rest is rough. On Cat. No. 1-587, 14 cm out of the 30.5-cm circumference have been polished. Continued use of this same 14 cm would presumably flatten it, producing a plano-convex mano.

Cat. Nos.	Op. No. and Provenience
1-1 (2 spec.)	1(A) CV-20, Surface, Large Plaza
1-52	6(C) CV-20, Lev. 1
1-241	20(A) CV-20, Lev. 5, Special Find 42
1-361	26(A) Main Center, Struct. L11-93, Lev. 10
1-451	28(A) CV-43, Surface
1-537	34(I) CV-43, Lev. 1
1-587	39(C) CV-43, Lev. 1
1-651	42(D) CV-43, Lev. 1
1-702	44(E) CV-46, Lev. 1
1-821	45(N) CV-46, Lev. 1
1-842	39(M) CV-44, Lev. 1
1-968	78(D) CV-16, Lev. 1
1-1159	102(A) CV-43, Lev. 7

Square (3)

Square manos are very rare, and only three specimens were recovered. Only one, Cat. No. 1-451, is even possibly complete; it is 11 cm long. Cat. No. 1-651 (fig. 172), however, which is broken, measures 13 cm in length remaining. The heights and widths range from 9.5 cm (Cat. No. 1-615) to 4.5 cm (Cat. No. 1-451), with Cat. No. 1-651 in the middle with 6 cm. The latter is really a parallelogram with one face smoother than the others. Both Cat. Nos. 1-451 and 1-615 are crudely made with little evidence of grinding. The smaller one, Cat. No. 1-451, however, was used as a pounder or, more probably, an anvil. This use is suggested by a deeply pitted area in the approximate center of one side.

Cat. Nos.	Op. No. and Provenience
1-451	28(A) CV-43, Surface
1-615	35(O) CV-43, Lev. 1
1-651	42(D) CV-43, Lev. 1

Triangular (5)

Triangular manos have, as the name implies, three grinding surfaces. The faces are not always perfectly flat nor the corners sharp, but the triangular cross section is clear. No complete examples were found. Heights, however, on the four specimens that could be measured, are remarkably consistent—all four measure 5.5 cm. Cross section varies from clearly triangular, as in Cat. Nos. 1-108, 1-596, and 1-704 (fig. 173a), to three-sided but with more rounded angles or curved faces, as in Cat. Nos. 1-686 (fig. 173b) and 1-863. As a general rule, the flatter the face the smoother the surface, supporting the interpretation of the development of this shape through use.

Cat. Nos.	Op. No. and Provenience
1-108	6(K) CV-20, Lev. 1
1-596	38(E) CV-43, Lev. 1
1-686	39(G) CV-44, Lev. 1
1-704	43(E) CV-43, Lev. 1
1-863	50(A) CV-45, Lev. 2

Pentagonal (8)

Five-sided manos are more common in our collection than either three- or four-sided ones. Like the triangular ones, the shape is not always symmetrical; the length of individual sides may vary considerably. Cat. No. 1-1027, for example, has faces measuring 8, 6, 4.5, 2.5, and 2 cm; Cat. No. 1-52 (fig. 174a) measures 5.4, 5, 4, 2.4, and 2 cm; and the faces on Cat. No. 1-615 are 6, 5, 5, 4.5, and 4 cm (fig. 174b).

There are three complete specimens. The lengths are quite disparate: Cat. No. 1-33 measures 31 cm, Cat. No. 1-361 measures 23.5 cm, and Cat. No. 1-156 measures only 16 cm (fig. 174c). Two partially complete ones, Cat. Nos.

1-52 and 1-1027, measure 17 cm and 19 cm long, respectively. Height averages about 5.5 cm. Wear, or smoothness, is most noticeable on the wider faces. One specimen, Cat. No. 1-589, is pitted on one side near the center, suggesting secondary use as an anvil or hammer stone.

Cat. Nos.	Op. No. and Provenience
1-33	5(B) CV-20, Lev. 1
1-52	6(C) CV-20, Lev. 1
1-156	15(A) CV-20, Lev. 1
1-361	26(A) Main Center, Struct. L11-93, Lev. 10
1-552	33(DD) CV-43, Lev. 2
1-589	41(A) CV-47, Lev. 1
1-615	35(O) CV-43, Lev. 1
1-1027	100(B) CV-43, Lev. 4

Overhang (5)

Overhang manos are so named because of a projection or lip at one or both ends which would fit over the side of a metate. At Copan, all examples have only one overhang, but all except one are broken. The overhanging area is small and short but quite distinct. There are five specimens from the excavations.

The one complete example, Cat. No. 1-98, measures 31.3 cm long with a maximum height of 7 cm, including the overhang (fig. 175a). There is definitely only one overhang process on this mano; the other end is intact but shows no such overhang. A partially complete mano, Cat. No. 1-451, measures 13.5 cm in length remaining, 6.5 cm high, and 5 cm wide (fig. 175b).

Two specimens examined, Cat. Nos. 1-615 and 1-686, are ovate-rectangular in cross section but have the overhang process. On Cat. No. 1-686, the overhang was just starting to develop on one end. Both of the flatter, broader faces, the top and bottom, one of which has the overhang, are still rough. The bottom, the face with the overhang, does not seem to be much smoother than the top, but the presence of the beginning of an overhang suggests that the bottom was receiving greater use.

Cat. Nos.	Op. No. and Provenience
1-98	6(J) CV-20, Lev. 1
1-451	28(A) CV-43, Surface

-615 35(O) CV-43, Lev. 1
-686 39(G) CV-44, Lev. 1
No Number

Plano-convex (26)

Manos of this variety are characterized by one flat grinding surface (the bottom). The rest of the mano is curved so that in cross section it looks like a flattened circle. In some cases, use of parts of the curved surface has led to the beginnings of other flat faces, approaching an ovate-rectangular form. This category is numerically the second largest in our Copan sample.

Two subdivisions were noted in the field analysis, the first being rocks shaped only by grinding and the second being rocks shaped to a circular form and then reduced to plano-convex form by use. The first, presumably, were suitably shaped rocks found in stream beds or other locations which were collected and used for grinding with only minimal modification through pecking. The second kind are more finely shaped on their non-grinding surfaces than the first and are assumed to have been originally large or small round variety manos flattened through use. No obvious differences exist between these subvarieties in size; the widths range between 6.5 and 9.5 cm, the heights from 4.5 to 8 cm, but neither larger nor smaller values cluster consistently with one group. The large majority of the manos are of the second type.

Only one whole mano was found, Cat. No. 1-361 (fig. 176a). Its dimensions are 22.6 cm long x 8.4 cm wide x 6.6–6 cm high. Another one, Cat. No. 1-45, is almost complete, measuring 18.5 cm remaining length x 7.5–8 cm wide x 7 cm high. Both of these specimens are of the first or natural subvariety. For contrast, figure 176b shows Cat. No. 1-841, a good example of the second subvariety.

A somewhat unusual specimen, Cat. No. 1-1020, is shown in figure 176c. Here, the upper curved area is uneven enough to produce a cross section approaching a triangular or pentagonal form. The mano is placed in the plano-convex type, however, because the field notes do not indicate whether or not the upper flat surface is natural or the result of grinding. (This specimen was not examined in the Peabody Museum Laboratory.) Furthermore, triangular manos have

three grinding surfaces, and Cat. No. 1-1020 has, at the most, two.

Cat. Nos.	Op. No. and Provenience
1-136	4(R) CV-20, Lev. 1
1-259	20(A) CV-20, Lev. 6
1-361	26(A) Main Center, Struct. L11-93, Lev. 10
1-451 (3 spec.)	28(A) CV-43, Surface
1-454	32(A) CV-47, Surface
1-490	33(P) CV-43, Lev. 1
1-495	35(A) CV-43, Lev. 1
1-524	35(E) CV-43, Lev. 1
1-530	34(F) CV-43, Lev. 1
1-535	35(H) CV-43, Lev. 1
1-544	36(F) CV-43, Lev. 1
1-550	38(A) CV-43, Lev. 1
1-573	36(L) CV-43, Lev. 1
1-587	39(C) CV-43, Lev. 1
1-590 (2 spec.)	37(E) CV-43, Lev. 1
1-705	39(H) CV-44, Lev. 1
1-759	48(D) CV-47, Lev. 1
1-760 (2 spec.)	48(B) CV-47, Lev. 1
1-841	41(C) CV-47, Lev. 1
1-845	35(T) CV-43, Lev. 1
1-975	100(B) CV-43, Lev. 3
1-1020	100(B) CV-43, Lev. 3

Thin Ovate-rectangular (3)

Thin ovate-rectangular manos have a width greater than or equal to twice their height. They are quite rare in our Copan collections. Cat. No. 1-108 is the only complete specimen. It measures 24.8 cm long x 8.8 cm wide x 4 cm high in the middle—one end is much thinner than the other (fig. 177). The type is more ovoid in cross section than many of the thick ovate-rectangular manos.

Cat. Nos.	Op. No. and Provenience
1-70	4(J) CV-20
1-108	6(K) CV-20, Lev. 1
1-1116	77(F) CV-16, Lev. 1

Thick Ovate-rectangular (67)

The thick ovate-rectangular variety, defined primarily by proportions, may be subdivided into three cross-sectional outlines. The first, Subvariety 1, approaches a plano-convex outline but has a more distinct top and sides and a more curved bottom. Subvariety 2 is more oval than rectangular in cross section, with almost no sides and a quite curved top and bottom. Subvariety 3 is the classic ovate-rectangular form, with four distinct but curved faces. Many of this subvariety and a few of the other subvariety have an area of pitting on anywhere from one to four sides, suggesting use as a hammer stone or anvil. The depth and expanse of the pitting varies, but it is usually placed in the center of the broken piece, suggesting that, once broken, the manos were put to a different use.

There are ten complete specimens. None is of Subvariety 1; Subvariety 2 is represented by Cat. Nos. 1-137, 1-203, 1-495, and 1-651. The degree to which they taper off at the ends varies. Cat. No. 1-203 (fig. 178a) appears essentially untapered, whereas Cat. No. 1-137 (fig. 178b) is definitely smaller at both ends. In contrast to 1-203, which has a smooth surface and trimmed ends, Cat. Nos. 1-495 and 1-651 are irregularly shaped, with rounded ends and an uneven surface. They measure 20 cm long x 8.7 cm wide x 7.7 cm high (1-495) and 18.4 cm long x 7.5 cm wide x 7 cm high (1-651). They are shorter than Cat. No. 1-137 or 1-203 but not really narrower or thinner. Cat. No. 1-137 measures 24.8 cm long x 9.2 cm wide x 6 cm high; Cat. No. 1-203 measures 24.7 cm long x 8.4 cm wide x 5.6 cm high.

The remaining six complete thick ovate-rectangular manos fall into Subvariety 3. Dimensions are as follows:

Cat. No. 1-78 (fig. 178c): 22.6 cm long x 8.4 cm wide x 7 cm high;

Cat. No. 1-98: 28.6 cm long x 8.1 cm wide x 5.8 cm high;

Cat. No. 1-98: 19.9 cm long x 8.1 cm wide x 6.9 cm high;

Cat. No. 1-243 (fig. 178d) (from the cache in Structure D of CV-20): 20.2 cm long x 7.2 cm wide x 6 cm high;

Cat. No. 1-361 (fig. 178e): 21 cm long x 10 cm wide x 8 cm high;

Cat. No. 1-647 (fig. 178f): 17.8 cm long x 8.4 cm wide x 5 cm high.

Tapering is much less evident on these specimens than on the Subvariety 2 specimens.

At least 20 of the Subvariety 3 manos are pitted. Most of them have been pounded on one or

two faces. Great variation in depth and area of the pitting occurs, but, as mentioned earlier, almost all pits are centered on the face. It is easy to see why Subvariety 3 would be chosen most often for this sort of use, since it has two flat faces opposite one another. If one wished to use a broken mano as a support upon which to place some item for pounding, a flat underside would be as necessary for stability as a flat upper side would be for holding the object. Instances of such pitting were noted for one specimen each in the square, pentagonal, and overhang varieties. It remains a question as to what was being pounded; nuts seem a reasonable possibility.

Cat. Nos.	Op. No. and Provenience
1-1	1(A) CV-20, Surface, Large Plaza
1-31	4(C) CV-20, Lev. 1
1-52	6(C) CV-20, Lev. 1
1-68	7(B) CV-20, Lev. 1
1-78	7(D) CV-20, Lev. 1
1-98 (2 spec.)	6(J) CV-20, Lev. 1
1-137	6(N) CV-20, Lev. 1
1-186	15(B) CV-20, Lev. 1
1-203	19(C) CV-20, Lev. 2
1-243	20(A) CV-20, Lev. 5, Special Find 44
1-361	26(A) Main Center, Struct. L11-93, Lev. 10
1-451	28(A) CV-43, Surface
1-472	33(E) CV-43, Lev. 3
1-495	35(A) CV-43, Lev. 1
1-517	33(BB) CV-43, Lev. 4
1-522	33(CC) CV-43, Lev. 1
1-524	35(E) CV-43, Lev. 1
1-528	36(D) CV-43, Lev. 1
1-530	34(F) CV-43, Lev. 1
1-535	35(H) CV-43, Lev. 1
1-538	37(A) CV-43, Lev. 1
1-545	33(CC) CV-43, Lev. 2
1-549 (2 spec.)	36(I) CV-43, Lev. 1
1-550 (2 spec.)	38(A) CV-43, Lev. 1
1-556 (2 spec.)	37(C) CV-43, Lev. 1
1-560	33(J) CV-43, Lev. 1
1-568	37(D) CV-43, Lev. 1
1-573	36(L) CV-43, Lev. 1
1-588	38(D) CV-43, Lev. 1
1-596	38(E) CV-43, Lev. 1
1-602	35(M) CV-43, Lev. 1
1-606	37(H) CV-43, Lev. 1
1-612	51(A) CV-84, Lev. 4
1-615	35(O) CV-43, Lev. 1
1-619	34(M) CV-43, Lev. 1

1-621	35(N) CV-43, Lev. 1
1-623	37(K) CV-43, Lev. 1
1-626	37(N) CV-43, Lev. 1
1-627	40(D) CV-45, Lev. 1
1-647	44(A) CV-46, Lev. 1
1-651	42(D) CV-43, Lev. 1
1-687	35(Q) CV-43, Lev. 1
1-693	42(E) CV-43, Lev. 1
1-707 (2 spec.)	38(H) CV-43, Lev. 1
1-712	34(Q) CV-43, Lev. 1
1-735	45(A) CV-46, Lev. 1
1-736	42(G) CV-43, Lev. 1
1-737	39(I) CV-44, Lev. 1
1-750	41(B) CV-47, Lev. 1
1-763	39(K) CV-44, Lev. 1
1-785	48(A) CV-47, Lev. 1
1-821	45(N) CV-46, Lev. 1
1-831	47(E) CV-47, Lev. 1
1-848	45(P) CV-46, Lev. 1
1-856	33(HH) CV-43, Lev. 1
1-859	49(A) CV-43, Lev. 2
1-861	71(A) CV-204, Lev. 4
1-895	68(A) CV-68, Lev. 4
1-970	104(A) CV-43, Lev. 2
1-1095	74(I) CV-16, Lev. 1
1-1100	77(E) CV-16, Lev. 1
1-1174	83(A) CV-16, Lev. 5

Mortars or Grinding Slabs (48)

The class of mortars contains a heterogeneous collection of ground stone artifacts that may be characterized most succinctly as implements obviously used for grinding but unlike any of the metate types in size and appearance. The class is divided into two types, 1 and 2, distinguished by details of shape and workmanship.

Type 1 (40)

Type 1 mortars are generally roughly shaped square or circular slabs. Most show evidence of grinding; none of pounding. They are generally shaped by pecking and, of course, by use.

Cat. No. 1-77 is a complete oval specimen of fine-grained gray stone. It has a curved and partially smoothed base; the top, nearly flat with a slight concavity, is somewhat smoother. The cross section is like that of Type 1 metates. The dimensions are 17.5 cm long x 15.2 cm wide x 5.5 cm high (fig. 179a).

Cat. No. 1-108, another complete specimen, is small, circular, and made of a vesicular rock. The underside is flat and well shaped. The top has a 0.5-cm-deep concavity, and there is a small lip running around the edge. It measures 11.1 cm in diameter and 3.2 cm high (fig. 179b).

A third whole specimen, Cat. No. 1-124, is oval with a round base and a concave surface. The concavity forms a trough running on a diagonal to the long axis of the mortar. The stone is a vesicular lava. The dimensions are 10 cm long x 7 cm wide x 4.6 cm high. The basin is 1.5 cm deep (fig. 179c).

An exceptionally large example is Cat. No. 1-1. It is flat on both top and bottom. No concavity has developed on the grinding surface. It measures 33 cm long x 20.5 cm wide x 8 cm high.

Although broken, Cat. No. 1-633 (fig. 179d) is also larger than most of the other mortars. It is rectangular in shape, with rounded corners and straight, parallel sides. The base and top are flat. The sides bulge outward and are rough, as is the base. The top surface is smooth with a blue or black stain on it. It measures 20 cm long x 25 cm wide x 9 cm high.

Four more mortars show only slight breakage. Cat. No. 1-451 is more or less square. The base, which is curved, and the sides have been shaped by pecking but are still rough-textured. The top surface is smoother, with only a small concavity less than 1 cm deep. Made from a red-buff vesicular stone, it measures 33 cm long x 22 cm wide x 6–7.5 cm high. Cat. No. 1-454 (fig. 179e) is square with rounded corners. Both base and top are curved. The underside is rough and pecked; the top is smoother. It measures 12 cm long x 11 cm wide x 4 cm high at the center. The concavity is 0.6 cm deep. Cat. No. 1-589 is almost whole and roughly square. The top is smooth and slightly curved. One half of it is darkened by a bluish-black stain, possibly the remnant of some material that was ground. The base is convex and also smooth. Its dimensions are 16 cm long x 11 cm wide x 4.5 cm high. Cat. No. 1-577 has three straight edges, with the fourth convex. The two remaining corners present are well defined and square. The top is flat; the base is also flat except for a raised area near the curved edge, which might be a crudely formed nubbin foot. It measures 16.2 cm long x 13.1 cm wide x 1.9–2.3 cm high.

Cat. No. 1-881 is a circular mortar about three-quarters preserved. Made of a red vesicular rock and manufactured by pecking, it has a rough and very slightly concave top. The base is curved and smoothed, probably during grinding. The sides slant inward and downward to the base. Enough remains to show that the mortar measured 25 cm on one dimension and is 6 cm high. Another fragment of a circular mortar, about half complete, is Cat. No. 1-451. Its diameter is 19 cm with a height of 5 cm. Very crudely shaped, Cat. No. 1-978 is also about 75 percent intact. Both horizontal dimensions are preserved. The overall shape is rectangular. A concavity had begun to develop on the surface in an area of greater smoothness. A bluish-black stain is on this surface. The mortar measures 23.5 cm long x 15 cm wide x 8 cm high. A second Cat. No. 1-978 is smaller and more oval than the first, with a flat base and a sloping top. Its dimensions are 12 cm in length remaining x 15 cm wide x 7 cm high at the edge and 4 cm high at the center.

The rest of the mortars are smaller fragments of varying sizes. All have essentially flat grinding surfaces and flat to slightly convex bases. A few of the more circular ones, such as Cat. No. 1-108 and Cat. No. 1-692, have a small rim running around their edges. Some of the fragments have concave grinding surfaces; others are quite flat on the top even though these show some evidence of grinding.

As noted, blue-black stains occur on some of these mortars, and one shows a green stain. It is possible that these are the remains of pigments that were ground on the mortars.

Further examples of Type 1 mortars are Cat. Nos. 1-68 (fig. 179f), 1-78 (fig. 179g), 1-271(fig. 179h), and 1-693.

One exception to the usually rectangular or round shape of the Type 1 mortars is Cat. No. 1-615 (fig. 179i). This specimen is almost complete, with only one end missing. Its overall shape is ovoid, lacking definite corners. Made of a gray-buff vesicular stone, it has high, fairly thick walls of uneven height which enclose the grinding surface. As such it resembles the Type 4 metates from Copan and basin-shaped metates in general; however, the walls of Cat. No. 1-615 slant inward, suggesting that a rotary grinding action was used rather than the back-and-forth rubbing movement used on the metates. The fragment measures 34 cm remaining length x 35 cm wide, with the concavity measuring 29.6 cm x 20 cm. It is between 15.4 and 10.4 cm high.

Cat. Nos.	Op. No. and Provenience
1-1	1(A) CV-20, Surface, Large Plaza
1-68	7(B) CV-20, Lev. 1
1-77	6(H) CV-20, Lev. 1
1-78	7(D) CV-20, Lev. 1
1-108	6(K) CV-20, Lev. 1
1-124	4(P) CV-20, Lev. 1
1-137	6(N) CV-20, Lev. 1
1-156	15(A) CV-20, Lev. 1
1-202	20(A) CV-20, Lev. 3
1-254	21(A) CV-20, Lev. 3
1-271	19(F) CV-20, Lev. 2
1-451 (4 spec.)	28(A) CV-43, Surface
1-453	31(A) CV-46, Surface
1-454	32(A) CV-47, Surface
1-495	35(A) CV-43, Lev 1
1-524	35(E) CV-43, Lev. 1
1-527	35(C) CV-43, Lev. 1
1-577	38(B) CV-43, Lev. 1
1-589 (2 spec.)	41(A) CV-47, Lev. 1
1-615	35(O) CV-43, Lev. 1
1-621	35(N) CV-43, Lev. 1
1-627	40(D) CV-45, Lev. 1
1-633	37(M) CV-43, Lev. 1
1-692	43(D) CV-43, Lev. 1
1-693	42(E) CV-43, Lev. 1
1-822	33(FF) CV-43, Lev. 5-B
1-860	50(A) CV-45, Lev. 1
1-881	72(A) CV-205, Lev. 2
1-921	101(B) CV-47, Lev. 1
1-928	41(H) CV-47, Lev. 1
1-954	50(A) CV-45, Lev. 5
1-978 (2 spec.)	75(A) CV-16, Surface
1-1053	102(A) CV-43, Lev. 4
1-1154	104(A) CV-43, Lev. 10-B
1-1305	3 CV-177, Surface

Type 2 (8)

Type 2 mortars are smaller and more carefully made than those of Type 1. They are square to rectangular in shape. Their main distinguishing characteristic is the presence of a ledge-like rim on all four sides.

The only complete example, Cat. No. 1-569 is almost square, with a flat base and straight sides. Overall dimensions are 11.5 cm long x 10 cm wide x 3.75 cm high. The inner rectangle formed by the rim measures 7.5 cm long x 6.5 cm wide. The grinding surface itself is 0.5 cm deep (fig. 180a).

Two other partial specimens resemble Cat. No. 1-569. Cat. No. 1-126 has only one intact corner, which, although rounded, forms an approximate 90-degree angle. The sides curve outward. The mortar was 13.5 cm on its complete dimension, and it is 4 cm thick with a grinding area 1 cm deep. The rim is 2 cm wide (fig. 180b). Cat. No. 1-1056 is somewhat larger than Cat. Nos. 1-126 and 1-569 but similar in appearance. Both the inner and outer corners of the rim are squared and the surfaces are flat. One corner has a very faint, shallow line or groove crossing it on the diagonal from inner to outer corner. This may have been the beginning of a groove or channel that, as we shall see below, was more pronounced on some other Type 2 mortar specimens. The outer dimensions of Cat. No. 1-1056 are 15 cm (on the complete side) x 10 cm (on the incomplete side), with the corresponding mortar concavity being 10 cm (complete) by 8.5 cm (incomplete). Total height or thickness is 2.5 cm, while the depth of the concavity or recessed surface is only 0.2 cm. The rim ledge varies from 1.8 to 2 cm in width (fig. 180c).

Two other fragments have a very definite groove cut through the rim ledge. Cat No. 1-107 is one of these. Such a groove could have served to pour out liquid contents resulting from grinding in the mortar concavity. Cat. No. 1-107 was a little thicker (3.3 cm) than the previously described specimen although probably of about the same original length and width (fig. 180d). Cat. No. 1-838 (fig. 180e) is another rim-grooved mortar. The groove, within the concavity, runs parallel to one side of the fragment. There was no rim ledge on the specimen, but perhaps the groove was, nevertheless, used to empty contents within the grinding cavity. This mortar was probably about the same original overall size as Cat. No. 1-107.

The three remaining fragments of mortar Type 2 are all too small for further description (Cat. Nos. 1-206, 1-763, and 1-1020).

Cat. Nos.	Op. No. and Provenience
1-107	4(N) CV-20, Lev. 1
1-126	6(M) CV-20, Lev. 1
1-206	21(A) CV-20, Lev. 2
1-569	34(K) CV-43, Lev. 1
1-763	39(K) CV-44, Lev. 1
1-838	42(K) CV-43, Lev. 1
1-1020	100(B) CV-43, Lev. 3
1-1056	80(B) CV-16, Lev. 1

Barkbeaters (10)

All of the Copan barkbeaters in our collection are made of fine-grained gray to gray-buff volcanic stone. Eight of these are of the flat, tabular form. These all appear to pertain to the rectangular variety of that type (see Willey et al. 1965: 469–471; Willey 1972:125–127; Willey 1978: 79–80); however, with some of the smaller fragments it is difficult to be certain of the varietal distinction between rectangular and oval as it has been made in the above-cited literature. Two, or possibly three, barkbeaters are of the club-like type (Willey et al. 1965:471, fig. 282b).

Of the rectangular variety, five are complete or nearly so. Cat. No. 1-1183 (fig. 181a) is a perfect specimen. It measures 7.1 cm long, 6 cm wide, and 3.6 cm thick. The shape is virtually a perfect rectangle. The encircling hafting groove extends along both long sides, completely across one end, and partially across the other end, with only a small space of about 2.5 cm left ungrooved. The functional or pounding grooves run lengthwise on one side. These are 1 mm to a little more in width and are separated by lines that average about 3 mm in width. Depth of these scorings or grooves is about 2 mm. On first inspection, the opposite side appears plain; however, closer study shows very fine incised, although somewhat imperfectly drawn, lines running parallel to the long axis of the beater. Perhaps these indicate tentative beginnings to score this side of the specimen.

Cat. No. 1-353 (fig. 181b) is also complete. It is a rather imperfect rectangle. Length is 9 cm; width at one end measures 6.7 cm and at the other end 6 cm. Thickness is 4.8 cm. The hafting groove encircles the piece completely. One flat beating surface is scored, parallel to the long axis, with grooves that are about 2 mm wide and separated by bands that average between 2 and 3 mm in width. Depth of grooves is about 2 mm. The opposite side is unscored.

Cat. No. 1-242 (fig. 181c), also of the rectangular variety, is another complete specimen. It measures 10.1 cm long and 5.4 by 4.3 cm in width at its respective ends. Maximum thickness is 3.9 cm. The hafting groove is found along both long sides and one end. One of the large surfaces is flat and scored. These scoring lines are rather uneven in drawing and spacing. They are about 2 mm deep, 2 mm wide, and 3 to 4 mm apart. The opposite large surface is plain, smoothed, and markedly convex.

Cat. No. 1-202 (fig. 181d) is an almost complete rectangular barkbeater with one corner broken off. The hafting groove encircles three-fourths of the piece, the long sides and one end. One large surface has a single scored line running the length of the stone on a median axis. The other side was left plain. It appears that the beater was unfinished. Measurements are 10.1 x 7.5 x 3 cm.

Cat. Nos. 1-192, 1-220 (fig. 181e), and 1-1032 are all definite fragmentary pieces of rectangular variety barkbeaters. All indicate circumferential hafting grooves. Two of them, Cat. Nos. 1-192 and 1-220, were scored on one flat surface but not the other. The remaining piece, Cat. No. 1-1032, is too small a fragment to make such a determination.

Cat. No. 1-765 (fig. 181f) is a possible fragment of an unfinished barkbeater; at least this is the most likely identification for this piece. It is made of a slightly vesicular, gray-brown volcanic stone. It measures 11.5 cm long, 5.5 cm wide, and 4.5 cm thick. There is a groove along one long side, and a groove, or the beginnings of one, on the short side. The other short side is missing because of breakage. One of the large flat surfaces has been smoothed, but there are no barkbeater striations on it. The other flat surface is still unsmoothed. Perhaps the implement was broken during manufacture and discarded.

Perhaps the most notable thing about the rectangular variety barkbeaters from our Copan collection is that all were scored only on one surface. Barkbeaters of this kind found at Barton Ramie (Willey et al. 1965:469), Altar de Sacrificios (Willey 1972:125), and Seibal (Willey 1978: 79–80) were usually scored on both flat surfaces.

We have two club-like barkbeaters in the collection. Cat. No. 1-1 (fig. 181g) is a fragment showing a portion of the beater just above the handle end. Total length of the fragment is 9 cm. The piece is approximately cylindrical in cross section, with the smaller, or handle, end measuring 4.4 cm in diameter and the larger end 5.4 cm in diameter. There are scorings along two opposite sides of the larger end; the other two sides were left plain. These scorings are 1 to 2 mm apart and relatively fine and shallow.

For Cat. No. 1-1103 there is only a probable identification as a club-like barkbeater. It is an assumed handle fragment for the type, 11 cm long and about 6 x 4 cm in diametric measurements. As such, it is ovoid rather than cylindrical in cross section. In what may be the basal portion of the club section of the implement, one surface is flattened and slightly concave; however, only the smallest lower edge of this surface remains on the piece. There are no visible barkbeater-type scorings. The other possibility is that this fragment may have been a part of a celt-like object or mace.

Cat. Nos.	Op. No. and Provenience
1-1	1(A) CV-20, Surface, Large Plaza
1-192	17(A) CV-56, Lev. 2, Area A
1-202	20(A) CV-20, Lev. 3
1-220	19(C) CV-20, Lev. 4
1-242	20(A) CV-20, Lev. 5, Special Find 43
1-353	3 General, northeast section of valley
1-765	45(I) CV-46, Lev. 1
1-1032	50(A) CV-45, Lev. 7
1-1103	83(A) CV-16, Lev. 1
1-1183	83(A) CV-16, Lev. 7, Special Find 3

Rubbing and Pounding Stones (44)

Rubbing Stones (34)

The name "rubbing stones" (fig. 182a–f) has here been applied to ground stone implements of not very standardized form or size that could have been employed as abraders or rubbing implements in the manufacture of other artifacts of stone, bone, or wood. They stand apart from pounders in that they do not have evidence of pounding surfaces; presumably, they were all used in a rubbing or grinding action. They are distinct from polishing stones in that the polishng implements have a very smooth, glossy, polished surface, apparently from use with soft materials, whereas the rubbing stones, however well ground these implements may be, have an abrasive surface. Most are made of welded and unwelded tuffs or felsites.

On the basis of size and shape, we have distinguished three varieties of rubbing stones: small, well shaped, and well dressed; flattish or block-like; and large, coarse, boulder-like.

The small, well-shaped, and well-dressed variety includes four specimens. Two of these are rectanguloid. Cat. No. 1-82 is apparently complete, with well-ground surfaces on all six sides. It measures 6.1 x 2.7 x 2.2 cm. The piece has a grainy, sandy surface. Cat. No. 1-238 is similar, although one end seems to have been broken off. It is 4.8 x 2.4 x 2 cm. It is made of a whitish, slightly coarse-grained volcanic stone, and it has a scratchy surface. Cat. No. 1-574 is a little celt-shaped artifact and is unusual in that it is made of soft limestone. It is 7 x 3 x 2 cm. Given the nature of the material, a celt function seems unlikely, and it was probably used as a rubbing stone. Cat. No. 1-905 is an elongated pebble of a yellowish volcanic stone. It is well smoothed and rounded on all surfaces. Some of this probably resulted from natural causes, but there are signs that it was also shaped by rubbing. Measurements are 5.8 (length) x 1.7 (diameter) cm. It is slightly curved or cucumber-shaped.

The flattish or block-like variety, numbering 18 specimens, shows a considerable size range, although most of our smaller specimens are broken. In general, they are all made of fine- to medium-grained stones with relatively sandy or scratchy surfaces. None is as well shaped as is characteristic of the small variety rubbing stones. All are more or less rectanguloid in shape, most being relatively thin on one diameter. A large, apparently complete, stone (Cat. No. 1-451) measures 14 x 8.5 x 4.2 cm; a smaller one from this same provenience is 8.5 x 4.5 x 2.3 cm. Another large specimen (Cat. No. 1-687) is rectanguloid in cross section at one end but tapers toward the other end. It is 18.5 x 5 x 5 cm. One of the long flat surfaces of this stone has been worn down by grinding. There are also two small incised lines or grooves on this surface. Two small fragments of other stones are trianguloid in cross section and have been rubbed on all faces.

Another elongated piece is plano-convex in form, and two other small ones are flat-rectanguloid bar-like fragments, with evidence of rubbing and shaping on all surfaces. Another is very block-like and measures 10.7 x 8.6 x 5.5 cm.

The large, coarse, boulder-like variety numbers 12 specimens. Most are flattened-ovate in form and show use on two large surfaces. Some of these could be reworked fragments of manos; however, their overall shape tends to be somewhat less regular than that of the Manos. There are indications that some of these stones served more than one purpose. Some show slight pittings on the large flat surfaces that suggest they were employed occasionally as anvils; others have one battered edge, suggesting pounding functions. Most are of coarse-grained, vesicular volcanic stones. One of the Cat. No. 1-651 specimens is representative of the large end of the size scale. It is trapezoidal in outline, somewhat wedge-shaped in cross section, and shows evidence of rubbing, pounding, and anvil uses. It measures 14.8 x 12 x 6.2 cm. There are a few specimens of what might be considered a subvariety. All of these are made of the gray-green andesite used commonly in Copan masonry. As a consequence, they are softer than the other rubbing stones. They are bar-like in form, roundish to rectanguloid in cross section. Cat. No. 1-814 is one of these. It shows rough shaping or rubbing on one end and on the long surfaces; the other end has been broken. It is 9 cm long and 4.8 cm in diameter. It is also slightly dumbbell-shaped or larger at the two ends and narrower and concave toward the center.

Cat. Nos.	Op. No. and Provenience
Small, Well-shaped, and Well-dressed Variety	
1-82	7(E) CV-20, Lev. 1
1-238	20(A) CV-20, Lev. 5
1-574	35(L) CV-43, Lev. 1
1-905	103(A) CV-46, Lev. 2
Flattish and Block-like Variety	
1-78	7(D) CV-20, Lev. 1
1-82	7(E) CV-20, Lev. 1
1-126	6(M) CV-20, Lev. 1
1-202	20(A) CV-20, Lev. 3
1-451 (5 spec.)	28(A) CV-43, Surface
1-490	33(P) CV-43, Lev. 1
1-577	34(I) CV-43, Lev. 1

Cat. Nos.	Op. No. and Provenience
Flattish and Block-like Variety (Continued)	
1-589	41(A) CV-47, Lev. 1
1-619	34(M) CV-43, Lev. 1
1-621	35(N) CV-43, Lev. 1
1-687	35(Q) CV-43, Lev. 1
1-692	43(D) CV-43, Lev. 1
1-974	100(B) CV-43, Lev. 2
1-1058	100(B) CV-43, Lev. 5-A
Large, Coarse, Boulder-like Variety	
1-5	2(B) CV-20, Lev. 1
1-615	35(O) CV-43, Lev. 1
1-617	33(F.F) CV-43, Lev. 2
1-651 (2 spec.)	42(D) CV-43, Lev. 1
1-736	42(G) CV-43, Lev. 1
1-763	39(K) CV-44, Lev. 1
1-814	48(E) CV-47, Lev. 1
1-840	48(G) CV-47, Lev. 1
1-843	39(N) CV-44, Lev. 1
1-961	74(F) CV-16, Lev. 1
1-978	75(A) CV-16, Surface

Pounders (10)

These pounders or hammers are distinct from the pebble choppers or pounders listed under the chipped stone category. These have either been shaped by grinding and pecking or are pebbles or small boulders of volcanic rock that show striking marks from use. They are, for the most part, elongated stones (fig. 183a–c), ranging in length from about 7 to 15 cm and in diameter from about 3.5 to 6 cm. Some of them could have served also as relatively small manos (of the thick ovate-rectangular or plano-convex varieties), but none is really well shaped enough to so qualify definitely. All of these elongated pounders show some pounding marks on one or both ends. Usually, these are rather slight. One specimen is conical (fig. 184a). It is 7.5 cm high and tapers from a diameter of 9 cm at one end to 6 cm at the other. On this specimen the pounding marks are all on the larger end. There is also one heavy spherical nodule that has been used as a pounder (Cat. No. 1-115) (fig. 184b). It is similar to those from Seibal (Willey 1978:84–85, figs. 80c, 86). The Copan specimen had a gray-green cortex, but at one spot where this has been removed, a dense, flinty core is revealed. It measures about 7 cm in diameter.

Cat. Nos.	Op. No. and Provenience
1-115	7(G) CV-20, Lev. 1
1-455	29(A) CV-44, Surface
1-496	34(B) CV-43, Lev. 1
1-527	35(C) CV-43, Lev. 1
1-561	35(I) CV-43, Lev. 1
1-636	34(N) CV-43, Lev. 1
1-692	43(D) CV-43, Lev. 1
1-742	42(F) CV-43, Lev. 1
1-747	39(J) CV-44, Lev. 1
1-821	45(N) CV-46, Lev. 1

Spherical or Egg-shaped Stones (18)

This is a type or category that has been referred to before in Maya lowland artifactual assemblages (Willey 1972:138–139; Willey 1978:93). At Seibal, where we found only one of each, we described them under separate headings. Here there are more specimens, and the spherical and egg-shaped stones grade rather easily into each other. All of the objects are made of rather dense volcanic stones, ranging from andesites to basalt.

All have been carefully pecked and shaped. Surfaces are uniformly smooth. On some there are spots that appear as contusions somewhat larger than would have been necessary in the pecking-shaping process, and some could have been used as hammers or pounders. In dividing the spheres or egg-shaped stones from the stone pounders, form and slightness of contusions were the separating diagnostics. The size range of the spheres is from a diameter of about 5 cm to 11 cm. The egg-shaped stones range from measurements of about 4 x 3 cm to 8 x 6.5 cm. The use or function of the stones is unknown.

Cat. Nos.	Op. No. and Provenience
1-1 (4 spec.)	1(A) CV-20, Surface, Large Plaza
1-115	7(G) CV-20, Lev. 1
1-370	3 Surface, northeast section of valley, Chorro Quad, near 7M-23 Str.
1-561	35(I) CV-43, Lev. 1
1-635	44(B) CV-46, Lev. 1
1-650	54(A) CV-94, Lev. 8
1-712	34(Q) CV-43, Lev. 1
1-782	45(F) CV-46, Lev. 1
1-817	48(F) CV-47, Lev. 1
1-839	33(FF) CV-43, Lev. 6-B

-845   35(T) CV-43, Lev. 1
-846   47(H) CV-47, Lev. 1
-853   39(O) CV-44, Lev. 1
-918   49(A) CV-43, Lev. 3
-1027   77(B) CV-16, Lev. 1

Polishing Stones and Polished Pebbles (61)

Two functional types or categories are recognized under this heading: pebbles actually used as polishing tools and pebbles that show polish. There is often difficulty in distinguishing between the two. For the most part, however, the actual polishing stones, or tools, tend to be larger than the others.

Definite Polishing Stones are made of hard, dark (blacks, grays, gray-greens), fine-grained (diorite) stone. These range in size from lengths of 8 to 16 cm, with widths of 5 to 11 cm, and thicknesses of 2 to 5 cm. These measurement ranges indicate an oblong shape, and this is largely true; however, there are some specimens in which length and width are approximately the same. Generally, the stones, whether oblong or of more or less equivalent diameters, tend to be flattish. The polishing surfaces are flat planes, as a rule. Quite often there is more than one such surface on an artifact.

One of the Cat. No. 1-950 (fig. 185a) specimens is an excellent example of a black diorite polisher. It measures 12.8 x 6 x 5.5 cm. As such, it is proportionately a little thicker than most. The two ends show some pounding marks, either from intentional shaping or, perhaps, use as a pounder as well as a polisher. In cross section it is pentagonal. All five of these surfaces show polishing striations as very fine lines. On three surfaces these fine abrasions run parallel to the long axis of the implement; on one face—a relatively narrow one—they run at right angles to the long axis; on the fifth face they run in various directions. The implement is heavy (775 grams) and well suited to the hand.

Another Cat. No. 1-950 specimen is made from a circular, flat, diorite pebble. It is 10 cm in diameter and 1.7 cm thick. Both flat surfaces are highly polished, especially near the center of the pebble. These show numerous fine-line scratches from use, that tend to run in all directions. The third Cat. No. 1-950 specimen is made from a pebble that was prismatic in cross section. It is 11 x 5.5 x 2.5 cm. Only the larger flat surface was utilized. It is polished to a high gloss and shows fine-line striations parallel to the long axis of the tool. The other two surfaces are well smoothed and, in places, even slightly polished; however, these do not seem to have been the primary polishing surfaces.

Cat. No. 1-69 is a highly polished piece of gray diorite. It is only 7.5 cm in diameter and is of irregular shape. Maximum thickness is about 2.5 cm. One flat surface, the more convex one, is highly polished, and striations indicate it was the principal polishing surface; however, the other surface of the piece, which is rather irregular in form and not ideally adapted to a polishing use, bears a nice gloss, presumably from long handling.

These specimens are representative of perhaps two-thirds to three-fourths of the polishing stones. Of the total number of this variety perhaps a half to a third are fragmentary. A number of other varieties remain to be noted.

Cat. Nos. 1-33, 1-78, 1-156, and 1-687 are all obvious polishing tools of a very small, specialized sort. These are little celt-like forms with varying degrees of polishing wear. They range from 8 to 4.5 cm in length. Two are trapezoidal in outline, one tear-shaped, and one is a fragment (probably of a trapezoidal-shaped implement). Maximum widths are 2.1 to 4 cm and thicknesses from 1.3 to 1.6 cm. The fragmentary piece (Cat. No. 1-156) is made of siltstone, the others of diorite. Cat. Nos. 1-33 and 1-78 show little polish use; Cat. No. 1-156 is well ground on both larger surfaces; and Cat. No. 1-687 shows high-gloss polish, particularly on its larger end. This last piece is not wedge-shaped or celt-shaped in cross section outline but maintains a uniform 1.5 cm thickness for its full length. The broad, blunt, larger end, as noted, seems to have been the utility polishing or buffering end.

Two other small pieces deserve special mention. One of these (Cat. No. 1-71) is of gray-green jadeite. It is a trianguloid pebble, 4.5 x 3.2 x 2.4 cm. The larger surface is perfectly flat and highly polished and was obviously the principal polishing surface; however, the three sides and the other large surface (the top) have a smooth handling gloss. Cat. No.

1-639 is an elongated piece of impure quartz, measuring 6.2 cm long and 2.8 cm in diameter. Most of its surface is rough and unworked. The slightly smaller end shows some slight signs of use as a tool. The larger end, which is round-blunted in form, is highly polished as though from use.

A number of other specimens are of lighter colored rocks than the typical black or gray diorite polishers. Some of these, such as Cat. No. 1-454, of a light gray-green hard stone, are of a comparable size to some of the larger black diorite specimens and have clear striation marks on their flat surfaces.

Two pebbles from Cat. No. 1-137 are small, 5–6 x 3–4 cm, and show gloss only from handling. These are polished pebbles rather than polishing stones. They are, respectively, of a white and light yellow quartzite.

Two tiny pebbles, Cat. Nos. 1-1 and 1-1053, are highly polished pieces of agate, one a variegated red-yellow, the other a gray-green. They are, respectively, only 1.5 and 1.8 cm on their longest diameters. Both show a high gloss. Perhaps they were being prepared for beads or ornaments.

Several polished pebbles were found with burials or as special finds. These are fine-quality stones that give evidence of handling polish or other special treatment. Cat. No. 1-110 is a little spheroid of rose quartz that looks as if it was smoothed and polished through handling. Cat. Nos. 1-345, 1-347, and 1-348 are all yellow-brown, semitranslucent pebbles, smoothed through handling, and rubbed with cinnabar. All are about 1.5 cm in diameter. Other specimens include several from a cache at CV-20 (Cat. No. 1-215) (fig. 185b).

Cat. Nos.	Op. No. and Provenience
1-1 (2 spec.)	1(A) CV-20, Surface, Large Plaza
1-21	2(I) CV-20, Lev. 1
1-26	4(A) CV-20, Lev. 1
1-30	4(B) CV-20, Lev. 1
1-33	5(B) CV-20, Lev. 1
1-36	2(C) CV-20, Special Find 10, associated with Burial 3
1-37	2(C) CV-20, Special Find 8, associated with Burial 3
1-38	2(C) CV-20, Special Find 4, associated with Burial 3 and Feature 3
1-69	5(L) CV-20, Lev. 1
1-71	6(G) CV-20
1-77	6(H) CV-20, Lev. 1
1-78	7(D) CV-20, Lev. 1
1-82 (4 spec.)	7(E) CV-20, Lev. 1
1-107	4(N) CV-20, Lev. 1
1-110	10(A) CV-17, Lev. 2, Special Find 1, associated with Burial 1
1-137 (2 spec.)	6(N) CV-20, Lev. 1
1-156	15(A) CV-20, Lev. 1
1-196	19(A) CV-20, Lev. 2
1-202	20(A) CV-20, Lev. 3
1-206 (2 spec.)	21(A) CV-20, Lev. 2
1-215 (8 spec.)	19(C) CV-20, Lev. 3, Special Find 28
1-222	21(A) CV-20, Lev. 2, Special Find 30
1-244	20(A) CV-20, Lev. 5, Special Find 45
1-278	24(A) CV-20, Lev. 4
1-345	26(A) Main Center, Struct. L11-93, Lev. 5, Special Find 13
1-347	26(A) Main Center, Struct. L11-93, Lev. 5, Special Find 15
1-348	26(A) Main Center, Struct. L11-93, Lev. 5, Special Find 16
1-454	32(A) CV-47, Surface
1-573	36(L) CV-43, Lev. 1
1-618	36(N) CV-43, Lev. 1
1-626 (2 spec.)	37(N) CV-43, Lev. 1
1-631	39(F) CV-43, Lev. 1
1-639 (2 spec.)	39(E) CV-43, Lev. 1
1-648	34(O) CV-43, Lev. 1
1-687	35(Q) CV-43, Lev. 1
1-740	59(A) CV-125, Lev. 2
1-837	64(A) CV-160, Lev. 6
1-845	35(T) CV-43, Lev. 1
1-861	71(A) CV-204, Lev. 4
1-950 (3 spec.)	39(S) CV-44, Lev. 1
1-953	102(A) CV-43, Lev. 3
1-974	100(B) CV-43, Lev. 2
1-1053	104(A) CV-43, Lev. 4
1-1173	80(E) CV-16, Lev. 1

Pestle (1)

Cat. No. 1-763 (fig. 186) is a small stone pestle of vesicular volcanic stone. It is 4.9 cm long and measures 4 cm in diameter at the slightly larger or grinding end. This end is flattened, and there is a slight ridge or extension to it so that it is about 4 mm wider than the shaft of the pestle. The opposite end is more rounded than flattened. The pestle end appears to have been used for rubbing or grinding rather than hard pounding, and this seems consistent with the size of the implement.

Cat. No. 1-763 came from Op. No. 39(K) CV-44, Level 4.

Anvil Stones (9)

These are small boulder-like stones, roundish in contour, and flatter, more rectangulate stones. Their characteristic feature is the presence of pecked or contused pits on their flatter surfaces. We presume that these stones had an anvil, or nether stone, function in some sort of pounding operations.

Cat. No. 1-1 (fig. 187a) is an approximately circular, flattish boulder of a vesicular volcanic stone. Its edges have been purposefully, if somewhat roughly, trimmed. It measures 13.1 x 12 x 5.3 cm. There is a central pit on both flat surfaces. These have been made by pecking and are about 3.5 cm wide and less than 1 cm deep.

Cat. No. 1-271 is very similar to Cat. No. 1-1, although it is oval rather than circular, measuring 12.7 x 8.4 x 2.7 cm. The central pits on both flat surfaces are about 3 cm in diameter and less than 1 cm deep.

There are three specimens within Cat. No. 1-451. The largest and most complete is a circular, apple-shaped stone, 12 x 7.5 cm (fig. 187b). One side of this specimen has been heavily fire-blackened. There is a centrally located pit on both sides, about 3 cm in diameter and less than 1 cm deep. A second specimen with this number is a fragment. The stone is soft and friable, and one face has been broken away. It is oval in outline, measures 12 x 10 cm, and probably had a thickness of about 8 cm. This stone, too, shows some fire-blackening. There is a central pit on the intact surface. There may have been a smaller pit on the surface that has been lost. The third specimen of this number is somewhat smaller, being only 8.5 x 5.5 cm. One surface is slightly flatter than the other. The central pit on this surface is 3 cm in diameter; the pit on the more rounded surface is 2 cm in diameter. Both pits are less than 1 cm deep.

Cat. No. 1-530 is a very heavy boulder of hard volcanic stone. It is a flattened sphere in shape. Its circumference has been shaped slightly by rubbing and pounding; however, it qualifies as an anvil stone by the contused central pits on each of its flatter surfaces. Diameter is about 9 cm and thickness 7.5 cm. The pits are somewhat irregular and are 3 to 3.5 cm in diameter and less than 1 cm deep.

Cat. No. 1-545 (fig. 187c) is an oblong, coarse volcanic stone. It probably has been shaped, and it is somewhat mano-like in form although too short for the usual thick ovate-rectangular variety mano. Length is 12.2 cm, and the other two dimensions are 7 x 6 cm. There are deep, irregular pits near the center of both of the flatter surfaces. These are about 3 cm in diameter and less than 1 cm deep; however, this evidence of pounding or pecking extends around one side of the stone, virtually connecting the two pits.

Cat. No. 1-651 is rectanguloid in outline, and it looks like one end of a thick ovate-rectangular mano. One end is slightly rounded and shaped; the other is broken off. The stone is a vesicular volcanic. It measures 1 x 9.3 x 4.3 cm. At the center of both flattish sides there is a pecked pit. It is deeper and more pronounced on the more rounded side, shallower and less well defined on the flatter side. In both cases it is about 3 cm in diameter and less than 1 cm deep.

Cat. No. 1-1298 is a fragment of an anvil stone. Its diameter is 9.5 cm, and its thickness 5 cm. There is a pecked pit on only one flat surface.

Cat. Nos.	Op. No. and Provenience
1-1	1(A) CV-20, Surface, Large Plaza
1-271	19(F) CV-20, Lev. 2
1-451 (3 spec.)	28(A) CV-43, Surface
1-530	34(F) CV-43, Lev. 1
1-545	33(CC) CV-43, Lev. 2
1-651	42(D) CV-43, Lev. 1
1-1298	84(A) Petapilla Dam

Drill Braces (3)

These are small circular stones, each with a small drilled pit in the center of one flat surface. These pits may have been made by a drill shaft that was held against the stone and, perhaps, against the chest of the user. They were originally classified as anvil stones, but it is obvious that they are quite different in size and pit formation.

Cat. No. 1-688 is a small, round, flat pebble of fine-grained volcanic stone. It probably has some overall shaping, both circumferentially and around the edges. At the center of the slightly more convex flat surface there is a small, cleanly defined drill pit 7 mm in diameter and about 5 mm deep. The stone measures 6.2 x 5.5 x 3 cm.

Cat. No. 1-782 is quite small, measuring only 3.7 x 4 on its diameters and about 2.5 cm thick. One flat side has been ground quite smooth. The opposite larger surface was left much more convex. It has a drill hole, conical in form, that is 1.5 cm in diameter at the surface, about 5 mm at the bottom, and a little over 1 cm deep.

Cat. No. 1-822 is of a light purplish tuffa. It has been shaped somewhat on all surfaces and has a flattened egg-like form. Measurements are 7.7 x 6.7 x 4.8 cm. At the center of one of the two larger flat round surfaces is a drill pit 1 cm in diameter and a little less than 1 cm deep.

Cat. Nos.	Op. No. and Provenience
1-688	33(FF) CV-43, Lev. 3
1-782	45(F) CV-46, Lev. 1
1-822	33(FF) CV-43, Lev. 5-B

Weight or Anchor (1)

Cat. No. 1-196 (fig. 188) is a heavy stone with a suspension groove around one end that appears to have been used for an anchor or suspended weight of some kind. It measures 13 cm long and 6.7 cm in diameter. Originally it was a piece of a thick ovate-rectangular mano. It was broken at both ends, and these ends were subsequently smoothed to a slight degree. There is also a longitudinal break along one side. The suspension groove is immediately below one of the ends. It encircles the stone and is 1.3 cm wide and 2 to 3 mm deep.

Cat. No. 1-196 came from Op. No. 19(A) CV-20, Level 2.

Celts (22)

This is the designation referring to well-smoothed and well-shaped chopping or cutting tools made of hard, fine-grained stone (see, for example, Willey 1978:86–90). They include welded tuffs, felsites, fine-grained basalts, and diorites and range in color from dark gray to black. They were obviously manufactured by grinding and polishing riverine pebbles. Those in our sample show varying degrees of polish. Many in this group are fragments, but these pieces, together with complete or near-complete specimens, indicate that a trapezoidal shape or outline is the most common form for the type.

We presume that the celts were used for chopping or cutting—perhaps wood, perhaps the soft stone of the Copan masonry and sculptures. The general utility bifacially flaked chopper or celt, the generally common form throughout much of the Maya lowlands (see Willey 1978:105–108 for examples), is absent from our artifact sample. Perhaps the ground stone celts of the large and medium varieties were used instead. However, these larger celts are quite rare in our sample. Our most common variety is the very small celt. Such an implement would have been suitable for fine carving in wood or stone, but not for heavy work, nor would it have been suitable for the land-clearing function generally ascribed to the bifacial chipped stone celts or choppers.

In classifying this type of tool from other lowland Maya sites (see Willey 1978:86), a rather arbitrary size-range classification was used: large, over 15 cm in length; medium, 15 to 8 cm; small, 8 to 6 cm; and very small, below 6 cm.

Large Variety (1)

Only one fragment (Cat. No. 1-953) may be a sliver from a large variety celt. It is a nicely smoothed piece from the side wall, near the butt end, of a celt. The sliver is 8.4 cm long, and an estimated total length of the implement is in excess of 15 cm.

Medium Variety (7)

Seven specimens have been classed as medium variety. One of these is complete. Cat. No. 1-1 is a well-polished celt of dark green stone (diorite or serpentine?) which is trapezoidal in outline. It measures 9 x 5 x 3.3 cm. The bitt end is flat. It shows the greatest polish near the cutting end. The remaining medium variety specimens are fragmentary. Cat. No. 1-6 is a midsection of a celt. The fragment is 8 cm long, so the complete specimen was undoubtedly in the medium variety size range. It measures 3 to 4 cm wide and 2 to 3 cm thick. The material is a mottled gray dense stone. It is well shaped but not polished.

Cat. No. 1-33 is a small fragment from near the poll end of a well-polished gray-green celt. It measures 5 cm long, 3.1 cm wide, and 1.4 cm thick.

Cat. No. 1-70 is a bitt end, 4.9 cm wide and 2.9 cm thick. Length of the piece is 6 cm. It is a blackish stone. Surfaces are shaped but pitted, except for the actual cutting edge, which is sharp and polished for 1 to 2 cm back from the edge.

Cat. No. 1-126 is a small corner fragment of the bitt end of a beautifully polished gray-green celt. The piece is about 3 x 3.5 x 2.5 cm. It probably came from a medium variety celt.

Cat. No. 1-574 is a midsection piece of a smoothed but not polished celt. It measures 3.8 cm wide and 3 cm thick. Length of the fragment is 5 cm, which suggests an estimated original full length of more than 8 cm. The material is dark gray stone.

Cat. No. 1-615 is a midsection piece of nicely polished gray stone. Width is 4.5 cm, and thickness is 3.2 cm. The fragment is 4.7 cm long, suggesting an original length of over 8 cm.

Small Variety (2)

Cat. No. 1-197 is a complete small variety celt. Made of hard gray stone, it is 7.2 cm long. The width at the blade end is 3.5 cm and at the poll end is 2.1 cm. Thickness is 2 cm. It is well smoothed and shaped but not polished.

Cat. No. 1-108 is a highly polished bitt end sliver of a size to suggest that the specimen was probably in the small variety range, although it could have been larger.

Very Small Variety (12)

There are 12 very small variety celts in the collection. Seven of these are complete. Cat. No. 1-31 is a black trapezoidal specimen, 3.8 x 3.5 (at bitt) x 2.5 (at poll) x 1 (maximum thickness) cm. The little cutting or bitt end is sharp and highly polished on both surfaces. The remaining surfaces show shaping and some polishing but also rough patches. The poll or butt end is flattened and abraded.

Cat. No. 1-52 (fig. 189a) is a tiny wedge-shaped celt, trapezoidal in outline. It is 4 x 2.8 (width at bitt) x 1.8 (width at poll) x 1.6 (thickness at poll) cm. The blade half of the artifact is well polished on both sides, and the blade is still sharp. The upper half and poll end are ground but not polished. The poll is flat and rounded. The material is gray-black, hard, and fine-grained as in most of the celts.

Cat. No. 1-58 (fig. 189b) is also wedge-shaped in cross section and trapezoidal in outline. It measures 5.6 x 3.9 (at bitt end) x 2 (at poll end) x 1.9 (maximum thickness) cm. The blade half shows polish on both surfaces; the remainder is ground but not polished. The blade is dulled and abraded as though from use. The poll is rounded and abraded.

Cat. No. 1-317 is similar in trapezoidal outline and wedge-shaped cross section to the two above-described specimens. Length is 5.8 cm. It is well polished at blade end and otherwise roughly ground.

Cat. No. 1-451, again, is similar to those described above. Length is 4.3 cm, and thickness 1.3 cm. Its polished surfaces and blade are abraded and broken in places.

Cat. No. 1-844 is a wedge-shaped and trapezoidal specimen. Length is 4.7 cm, and width at bitt end is 3.2 cm. Thickness is 1.5 cm. The bitt half is polished, the remainder is not.

Cat. No. 1-1047 is similar to the above. Length is 5.9 cm, bitt width 3.7 cm, and thickness 1.7 cm. The bitt half is highly polished, and the rest is not.

The remainder are small fragments. Cat. No. 1-461 is unusual in that it is made of light gray stone. The bitt-end portion is handsomely polished on all surfaces. Length (fragmentary) is 4 cm, bitt-end width 3.3 cm, and thickness 1.6 cm. It was probably wedge-shaped in cross section. Cat. Nos. 1-902 and 1-973 are pieces of other wedge-shaped, trapezoidal tools of dark gray or black stone. Cat. Nos. 1-69 and 1-76 are very tiny fragments that probably came from similar implements.

Cat. Nos.	Op. No. and Provenience
Large Variety	
1-953	102(A) CV43, Lev. 3

Cat. Nos.	Op. No. and Provenience
Medium Variety	
1-1	1(A) CV-20, Surface, Large Plaza
1-6	2(D) CV-20, Lev. 1
1-33	5(B) CV-20, Lev. 1
1-70	4(J) CV-20, Lev. 1
1-126	6(M) CV-20, Lev. 1
1-574	35(K) CV-43, Lev. 1
1-615	35(O) CV-43, Lev. 1
Small Variety	
1-108	6(K) CV-20, Lev. 1
1-197	19(B) CV-20, Lev. 2
Very Small Variety	
1-31	4(C) CV-20, Lev. 1
1-52	6(C) CV-20, Lev. 1
1-58	6(D) CV-20, Lev. 1
1-69	5(L) CV-20, Lev. 1
1-76	5(M) CV-20, Lev. 1
1-317	20(A) CV-20, Lev. 6, Special Find 1
1-451	28(A) CV-43, Surface
1-461	33(C) CV-43, Lev. 2
1-844	48(H) CV-47, Lev. 1
1-902	48(A) CV-43, Lev. 4
1-973	39(T) CV-44, Lev. 1
1-1047	100(B) CV-43, Lev. 4, Special Find 55

Alabaster Vessel (1)

This is a small (maximum diameter 4.5 cm) body sherd from an alabaster or onyx vessel (fig. 190). The contour of the sherd suggests a bowl form. Sherd thickness is 5 to 6 mm. Both surfaces have been evenly smoothed. It is whitish in color and semitranslucent. The interior is plain. The exterior bears a finely engraved design of some complexity. What appears to be a portion of a human figure, dressed in some regalia, is depicted. This individual holds in his left hand a staff or spear from the top of which depend tassels or, perhaps, feathers.

Cat. No. 1-270 came from Op. No. 20(A) CV-20, Level 8.

Ring Stones (5)

This artifact has been reported in frequency at both Altar de Sacrificios (Willey 1972:134–137)

and Seibal (Willey 1978:90–93). A few came from our diggings at Copan.

Cat. No. 1-86 (fig. 191a) is a complete ring stone of coarse gray lava. It is moderately well smoothed. Diameter is 13.7 cm, and height is 6.4 cm. The minimal diameter of the hole is 2.5 cm.

Cat. No. 1-108 (fig. 191b) is also complete and is made of a whitish volcanic stone. It, too, is well shaped and smoothed and measures 11 x 5.7 cm, with a 2.5-cm hole diameter.

Cat. No. 1-138 (fig. 191c), also complete, is made of coarse volcanic stone and measures 10.2 x 6.4 cm, with a 2.5-cm hole diameter.

Cat. No. 1-710 (fig. 191d), a virtually complete specimen, is made of a flinty limestone. It measures 13.5 x 5.5, with a 2.3-cm hole.

Cat. No. 1-786, another almost complete ring stone, is made of andesite. It measures 12 cm in diameter, and the hole has a minimal diameter of 3 cm.

Cat. Nos.	Op. No. and Provenience
1-86	7(E) CV-20, Lev. 1, Special Find 12
1-108	6(K) CV-20, Lev. 1
1-138	4(Q) CV-20, Lev. 1
1-710	35(R) CV-43, Lev. 1
1-786	46(C) CV-44, Lev. 1

Rectangular Perforated Stones (18)

These are rather irregularly shaped and smoothed, flat, generally squarish or rectangular stones, each with a more or less central perforation (fig. 192a–d). In workmanship they are always inferior to the ring stones in shaping, smoothing, and drilling. All of the specimens listed below conform to the rectangular designation except three (Cat. Nos. 1-746, 1-953, and one from 1-1020). These three are of irregular rather than either rectangular or circular outline; however, their workmanship and general appearance is consistent with that of what we have designated here as the rectangular perforated stone type.

There is a considerable range in the size of the stones. Their maximum diameters range from 6 cm to as much as 23. This casts some doubt on the validity of the objects as a unified type; however, only one was as much as 23 cm, one was 18 cm, and the remainder measured below 14 cm.

The majority of the specimens cluster between 8 and 12 cm. Thickness of the pieces does not always correlate with diameter. Most specimens fall in a thickness range of 4 to 6 cm. The holes are always biconically drilled, a circumstance that makes it unlikely that these stones are drill braces that have been worn through and discarded. The drilling results in a surface pit considerably larger than the actual diameter of the true perforation. The perforations range from less than 2 cm (rare) to 5 cm (rare), with most being 2 cm or a little over. Almost all of the rectangular perforated stones are made of coarse volcanic material.

They may also have served as digging-stick weights.

Cat. Nos.	Op. No. and Provenience
1-1 (2 spec.)	1(A) CV-20, Surface, Large Plaza
1-12	2(B) CV-20. Lev. 2
1-53	7(A) CV-20, Lev. 1
1-57	6(E) CV-20, Lev. 1
1-124	4(P) CV-20, Lev. 1
1-125	7(H) CV-20, Lev. 1
1-271	19(F) CV-20, Lev. 2
1-451	28(A) CV-43, Surface
1-475	33(J) CV-43, Lev. 1
1-615	35(O) CV-43, Lev. 1
1-746	45(C) CV-46, Lev. 1
1-953	102(A) CV-43, Lev. 3
1-973	39(T) CV-44, Lev. 1
1-978	75(A) CV-16, Surface
1-1020 (3 spec.)	100(B) CV-43, Lev. 3

Mirrors (7 or 8)

Four of these are slate or mudstone fragments of what appear to have been mirror backs; another is a highly polished concave stone; and two (or three?) others are pyrite mirror pieces.

Cat. No. 1-625 and 1-842 (fig. 193a) are mudstone or siltstone pieces, carefully smoothed on both flat surfaces as well as on an outer curving edge. These edges are very carefully ground on a bevel, a characteristic of mirror backs found elsewhere (see Willey et al. 1965:490–491; Willey 1972:141–143; Willey 1978:96). There can be little doubt but that these two specimens are mirror back fragments. Cat. No. 1-973 (fig. 193b) is of tuff and has been smoothed carefully on only one side. It has smoothed and rounded, rather than beveled, edges. Its identification as a mirror back is less certain. The three pieces range from about 2 x 4 to 4 x 6 cm in diameter. All are 5 to 6 mm thick.

Cat. No. 1-1097 is a highly polished (both surfaces) piece of black slate. It is not an edge fragment, so the mirror back identification is not certain. It is approximately 4.5 x 3.5 cm in diameter and 3 to 4 mm thick.

Cat. No. 1-88 (fig. 193c) is not a typical mirror or mirror back. It is a roughly semicircular piece of stone, presumably a fragment of a whole object. The material is a dark, red-brown silicified tuff. What looks like a rounded edge has been fashioned from the rough, convex side of the fragment by, apparently, pressure-flaking. The interior or concave side is very highly polished surface of a mottled reddish-brown. The function of the piece may not have been as a mirror, but the high gloss of the concave surface could certainly have served as a reflector. The fragment measures 7.5 x 3.5 cm by 1.5 cm in thickness. The concavity is about 4 mm deep.

Cat. No. 1-1274 (fig. 193d) refers to two iron pyrite pieces that may or may not have been from the same mirror surface. One piece measures 2.5 x 1.4 x 0.2 cm. It has a highly polished reflecting surface and a presumed underside that has been well smoothed but not polished. It is an edge fragment, and the bevel of the edge is away from the polished surface. There are two tiny drilled pits on the polished surface near the edge, and each of these pits is connected to the edge by a little groove. Near the broken edge of the fragment, away from the finished beveled edge, is a tiny hole that was drilled through the mirror from its outer or polished surface. A second specimen under this number is slightly smaller than the first but otherwise similar. It, too, has two little pits on the outer mirror surface near the beveled edge, and these pits are similarly joined to the edge by little grooves. There is no hole in the piece. If these two pieces come from the same specimen, and it is very likely that they do, the complete original might have been of ovate-rectangular form and about 3 x 2.5 cm in outline size. Other pieces, however, presumably were lost, for our two fragments cannot be fitted together.

Cat. No. 1-252 is a tiny piece of pyrite, trapezoidal in outline and less than 1 cm in diameter. It is only about 1 mm thick. One surface has beveled edges; the other surface is coated with cinnabar pigment. If it is not a small plaque from a mirror reflecting surface, it may have been inset into wood, stone, or bone as some kind of a decorative inlay.

Cat. Nos.	Op. No. and Provenience
1-88	7(F) CV-20, Lev. 1
1-252	22(B) CV-48, Lev. 4, Special Find 50
1-625	37(L) CV-43, Lev. 1
1-842	39(M) CV-44, Lev. 1
1-973	39(T) CV-44, Lev. 1
1-1097	80(C) CV-16, Lev. 1
1-1274 (2 spec.?)	102(A) CV-43, Special Find 166, with Special Find 57

Ear Ornaments (Jadeite) (7)

These are all disk-shaped ear ornaments, described as follows.

Cat. No. 1-1040 (fig. 194a) is a thin disk of good-quality green jadeite. Its circular form is somewhat irregular. It measures 2.7 cm in diameter, and maximum thickness at center is 6 mm. One surface is flat; the opposite surface has a small central nub, 1.3 cm in diameter. This nub has a central depression, and the center of this depression has been drilled through, uniconically, from this side of the object, with a small hole 1 mm in diameter. Both surfaces are highly polished.

Cat. No. 1-1041 (fig. 194b) is a circular disk-like ornament, 2.9 cm in diameter and 6 mm thick, with a saucer-like form. On the concave side of the saucer there is a little flattened central boss, 1.1 cm in diameter. The ornament has been centrally perforated through this boss but from the reverse side of the disk. The drill hole is uniconical and is 2 to 3 mm in diameter on the reverse side of the ornament but only 1 mm in diameter where it pierces through the nubbin on the obverse side.

Cat. Nos. 1-1145 and 1-1146 appear to have been a pair of circular ear ornaments. They are almost exactly alike. Both are of a mottled gray-green jadeite, and both measure 1.5 cm in diame-

ter and 3 mm thick. One side of each, highly polished, is flat; the other side is smoothed but not polished and slightly convex. The central perforation has been made through each ornament from the unpolished side. The holes are uniconically drilled and taper from 5 to 2 mm.

Cat. Nos. 1-1212 and 1-1213 are another pair of ear spools (fig. 195a–b). Both are made from nice-quality green jadeite. They are of the dish or saucer form. The more polished side of each is the concave side with a raised central boss; the reverse side of each is less polished. On both, this reverse side shows evidence of string-sawing, with indications that the sawing had gone in from two sides until only a small ridge separated the cuts. Then the ornaments were broken free from their matrices and the thin broken ridges subsequently ground smooth. The outer diameter of the ornaments are 4.7 cm in both cases, and both are 1.1 cm thick. The central bosses measure 1.7 cm in diameter. Both ornaments are made with a small flange or flare to the rim of the concave side. Perforations have been drilled from the flat or unpolished sides through the boss of the opposite side. These perforations are uniconical and taper from about 3 to 1 mm.

Cat. No. 1-1308 (fig. 195c) is an imperfectly circular ear ornament of nice-quality green jadeite, 2.9 cm in diameter and 6 mm thick. It is saucer-shaped, with a central boss on the concave side. The boss is 1.3 cm in diameter and has a flattened top. This concave side is highly polished; the reverse side is not. The perforation is uniconical, drilled from the reverse side, with the drill hole tapering from 3 to 1 mm.

Cat. Nos.	Op. No. and Provenience
1-1040	102(A) CV-43, Special Find 50, Feature 10
1-1041	102(A) CV-43, Special Find 51, Feature 10
1-1145	102(A) CV-43, Lev. 6, Special Find 89
1-1146	102(A) CV-43, Lev. 6, Special Find 88
1-1212	100(B) CV-43, Special Find 105, Feature 13
1-1213	100(B) CV-43, Special Find 106, Feature 13
1-1308	102(A) CV-43, Special Find 171, Burial 18

Pendants (Jadeite) (8)

These are variously shaped ornaments, all perforated for suspension, presumably to be worn around the neck. The only such objects not included under the pendant category are elongated, more or less tubular forms that have been pierced longitudinally. These grade easily into the bead category and so have been classified as beads.

Cat. No. 1-15 is a trianguloid (in outline), prismatic (in cross section) pendant of fair quality green jadeite. It is not very well polished. Length is 5.3 cm, width (at bottom) 2.4 cm, width (at top) 1.2 cm, and thickness 0.8 cm, There is a small, biconically drilled perforation running through the small end of the pendant from one prism face to another.

Cat. No. 1-147 is a highly polished, plain, flat, rectangular pendant of a dark gray-brown stone, probably jadeite. It measures 4.2 x 3 x 0.8 cm. Perforation holes were started at each edge, presumably with the intention that these would meet and effect a transverse suspension hole; however, the drilling was never finished and the pendant remains unfinished.

Cat. No. 1-230 (fig. 196a) is a small pendant carved in human head form. The material is an impure greenish-white jadeite. Length is 2.4 cm; diameter, 1.5 cm. The carving is disposed around all sides of the form so that the rendering is not realistic. There is what appears to be an enormous ear ornament, as large as the face, on one side of the head. The pendant has been perforated longitudinally, from the top of the head to the base. The drilling is biconical.

Cat. No. 1-335 (fig. 196b) is of medium-quality jadeite. It is a pendant that is trapezoidal in outline and has been carved on one side with a highly stylized human face. Length is 4.8, maximum width 2.2, and thickness 1.2 cm. It has been pierced transversely at just above midpoint and near the small end. Both perforations are biconical.

Cat. No. 1-336 (fig. 196c) is an elongated trapezoidal pendant of light green-gray jadeite of medium quality. Length is 6.7 cm, width 3.3 cm, and thickness 1.3 cm. The back surface is smooth, rounded, plain, and not highly polished. The front or carved surface, which is somewhat more green in color than the reverse, has a high gloss. The edges are smoothed but not polished. The pendant has been perforated through the long axis with a biconically drilled hole, 5 mm in diameter. Another drill hole, on the transverse axis of the pendant, was started at the larger end; but this hole does not penetrate through to the hole of the long axis nor to the other side of the pendant. The design, a sophisticated and complex one, shows a human head facing upward or toward the top of the pendant. This head emerges from the mouth of a stylized serpent. While the design is one fully within the canons of the Maya Classic style, the carving technique displayed is of only moderately good quality.

Cat. No. 1-337 (fig. 196d) is a prismatic shaped pendant, perforated transversely through the small diameter at one end. Length is 4.1 cm, and width, at midpoint, is 1.3 cm. It is a nicely polished piece of gray-green jadeite of good quality. There is a low-relief carved design on one of its prismatic surfaces. The design is curvilinear and abstract.

Cat. No. 1-338 (fig. 196e) is a human head or face pendant of gray-green jadeite. The face side is green, the reverse gray, and both are highly polished. Height of face is 3.2 cm, width 4.3 cm, and thickness about 1 cm. Back side is curved or convex. The front is carved in high relief. The face is depicted in a front view. Ear ornaments are shown as well as an arching-stepped hairdo. The quality of the carving is careful and good. The perforation is through the long axis (width) of the piece. It has been biconically drilled and is 3 to 4 mm in diameter.

Cat. No. 1-351 is a small fragment (2 cm in diameter) of what had been a human face pendant. It is of good-quality dark green jadeite.

Cat. Nos.	Op. No. and Provenience
1-15	2(B) CV-20, Special Find 3
1-147	11(A) CV-13, Lev. 3, Special Find 1
1-230	21(A) CV-20, Lev. 2, Special Find 38
1-335	26(A) Main Center, Struct. L11-93, Lev. 2, Special Find 7
1-336	26(A) Main Center, Struct. L11-93, Lev. 2, Special Find 8
1-337	26(A) Main Center, Struct. L11-93, Lev. 2, Special Find 9
1-338	26(A) Main Center, Struct. L11-93, Lev. 2, Special Find 10

Cat. Nos.	Op. No. and Provenience
1-351	26(A) Main Center, Struct. L11-93, Lev. 5, Special Find 19

Adornos (Jadeite) (8)

This rather ambiguous term has been given to quite small objects or fragments of objects that are obviously of an ornamental nature but cannot clearly be identified as ear ornaments, pendants, or beads. In some instances they may have been sewn to clothing; in others they could have been attached to wooden backings as inlays.

Cat. No. 1-326 is a small, flat, rectangular plaque of green jadeite. It measures 1.9 x 1.2 x 0.2 cm. There are two tiny perforations at the center. Each is 2 mm in diameter; they are 3 mm apart; and they are biconically drilled.

Cat. No. 1-350 is a small polished sliver of very high quality green jadeite. It is more polished on one surface than the other and may have been an inlay piece. It measures 1.6 x 0.5 x 0.2 cm.

Cat. No. 1-582 is an interesting little object. It is of very fine green jadeite. It is flattish and slightly concave-convex. The convex surface is highly polished; the other side and edges are less so. It measures 1 x 0.7 x 0.2 cm. At each of the two smaller ends there are paired holes, drilled uniconically from the concave side.

Cat. No. 1-583 is a fragment of irregular shape. It is 2.5 x 2.5 x 1.3 cm. It is not well polished. The most probable identification is that of an adorno fragment.

Cat. No. 1-717 is a small worked lump of pale green jadeite, measuring 2 x 1.3 x 1 cm. It is squarish in cross section. It may be an unfinished ornament.

Cat. No. 1-721 is a well-polished plaque-like fragment of light green and gray-black jadeite. A rectangular panel design has been engraved on both surfaces. Measurements are 3.2 x 1.5 x 1.2 cm.

Cat. No. 1-948 is a little, flat adorno of greenish jadeite. More or less rectangular, it measures 1.7 x 1 x 0.3 cm. A slightly convex surface is highly polished and has a decoration of fine crosshatched lines. The opposite surface is flat and shows sawing marks but no polish. There is a tiny uniconical perforation, drilled from the convex side, near one edge.

Cat. No. 1-1276 is a fragment showing a high gloss on one side which is a convex surface. The other side is a broken surface. Measurements are 1.5 x 1.5 x 0.4 cm.

Cat. Nos.	Op. No. and Provenience
1-326	26(A) Main Center, Struct. L11-93, Lev. 2, Special Find 1
1-350	26(A) Main Center, Struct. L11-93, Lev. 5, Special Find 18
1-582	33(Z) CV-43, Special Find 17
1-583	33(Z) CV-43, Special Find 18
1-717	55(A) CV-115, Lev. 2, Special Find 2
1-721	55(A) CV-115, Lev. 5
1-948	102(A) CV-43, Lev. 1, associated with Burial 12, Special Find 31
1-1276	102(A) CV-43, Special Find 168, within Special Find 57

Beads (Jadeite) (77)

These beads are made of jadeite of varying quality, ranging from some quite clear greens through more mottled gray-whites and gray-greens. For the most part, they show a high polish. Drill holes of any length or depth are biconical in form and technique; only perforations of relatively thin diameters were done uniconically.

Seven varieties have been designated according to form. These will be described seriatim.

Flat-rectanguloid Variety (4)

They range in size from 1.9 x 1.6 x 0.7 cm to 0.7 x 0.7 x 0.1 cm. The thicker specimens, which are rectanguloid to ovate in cross section, have all been pierced through their long diameters. The single thin, small specimen has been drilled uniconically through its thinnest diameter.

Irregular Variety (2)

These are small, nugget-like, irregularly shaped, but nevertheless highly polished, beads. They are about 1 cm at their largest diameter.

Barrel-shaped Variety (1)

This is a modification of the tubular form. The specimen is 1.4 cm long with a maximum diameter of 1.1 cm. It is drilled longitudinally and biconically.

Disk Variety (4)

These are thin, flat, circular beads. Size ranges from 1.6 x 0.6 to 0.8 x 0.4 cm. All are drilled centrally and, in spite of the thinness of some of them, biconically.

Large Tubular Variety (7)

These are the artifacts classified as beads rather than pendants; however, they are of a size so that they might very well have been worn singly in pendant fashion (fig. 197). They range in length from 3.5 to 9.3 cm; however, there is only one specimen (Cat. No. 1-361) measuring at the larger figure; all of the others fall between 3.5 and 4.7 cm. Maximum diameter varies from 0.9 to 1.5 cm. Some of the beads are of more or less the same diameter for their full length; others taper toward the two ends. All are well polished. The jadeite quality varies from good to fair. All specimens are drilled longitudinally and biconically; however, one specimen (Cat. No. 1-863) has another drill hole, extending in from the side of the bead, which connects up with the longitudinal hole. All are plain except one (Cat. No. 1-1226) (fig. 198), which has a pair of incised or grooved lines encircling the bead near each end.

Small Tubular Variety (26)

These are, as the name implies, smaller beads than the above, both in length and diameter measurements (fig. 199). The largest is 2.7 cm long and 1.2 cm in diameter; the small end of the range is 1.2 cm long and 0.5 cm in diameter. In general, the diameter is about one-half that of the length of the bead. The beads are, of course, drilled longitudinally with small, usually biconical perforations.

Subspherical Variety (33)

As the name implies, these are slightly flattened globes (fig. 200). The largest is 2.8 cm in diameter and 2.3 cm in height; the smaller end of the range is about 8 mm in diameter and 6 mm in height. These proportions hold for the middle size ranges. That is, the diameters are slightly more than the heights or thicknesses of the beads. Most are drilled biconically.

Cat. Nos.	Op. No. and Provenience
Flat-rectanguloid Variety	
1-34	2(C) CV-20, Lev. 5, Special Find 6
1-231	21(A) CV-20, Lev. 2, Special Find 39
1-232	21(A) CV-20, Lev. 2, Special Find 40
1-1053	102(A) CV-43, Lev. 4
Irregular Variety	
1-123	10(A) CV-17, Lev. 3, Special Find 2, associated with Burial 5
1-1251	100(B) CV-43, Feature 13, Special Find 143
Barrel-shaped Variety	
1-584	33(Z) CV-43, Special Find 19
Disk Variety	
1-1125	102(A) CV-43, Lev. 5, Special Find 77
1-1126	102(A) CV-43, Lev. 5, Special Find 70
1-1127	102(A) CV-43, Lev. 5, Special Find 72
1-1133	102(A) CV-43, Lev. 5, Special Find 75
Large Tubular Variety	
1-334	26(A) Main Center, Struct. L11-93, Lev. 2, Special Find 6
1-361	26(A) Main Center, Struct. L11-93, Lev. 10 (destroyed level)
1-590	37(E) CV-43, Lev. 1
1-863	50(A) CV-45, Lev. 2
1-1216	100(B) CV-43, Feature 13, Special Find 108
1-1226	100(B) CV-43, Feature 13, Special Find 118
1-1230	100(B) CV-43, Feature 13, Special Find 122

Cat. Nos.	Op. No. and Provenience
Small Tubular Variety	
1-590	37(E) CV-43, Lev. 1
1-716	55(A) CV-115, Lev. 2, Special Find 1
1-1131	102(A) CV-43, Lev. 5, Special Find 73
1-1217	100(B) CV-43, Feature 13, Special Find 109
1-1218	(These and all subsequent numbers in this particular series pertain to Op. No. 100(B) CV-43, Feature 13.) Special Find 110
1-1220	Special Find 112
1-1221	Special Find 113
1-1224	Special Find 116
1-1228	Special Find 120
1-1229	Special Find 121
1-1231	Special Find 123
1-1232	Special Find 124
1-1236	Special Find 128
1-1238	Special Find 130
1-1239	Special Find 131
1-1241	Special Find 133
1-1242	Special Find 134
1-1243	Special Find 135
1-1244	Special Find 136
1-1250	Special Find 142
1-1252	Special Find 144
1-1259	Special Find 151
1-1260	Special Find 152
1-1262	Special Find 154
1-1265	Special Find 157
1-1270	Special Find 162
Subspherical Variety	
1-480	33(F) CV-43, Lev. 4, Special Find 5
1-539	33(DD) CV-43
1-612	51(A) CV-84, Lev. 4
1-1219	100(B) CV-43, Feature 13, Special Find 111
1-1222	(These and all subsequent numbers in this particular series pertain to Op. No. 100(B) CV-43, Feature 13.) Special Find 114
1-1223	Special Find 115
1-1225	Special Find 117
1-1227	Special Find 119
1-1233	Special Find 125
1-1234	Special Find 126
1-1235	Special Find 127
1-1237	Special Find 129
1-1245	Special Find 137
1-1246	Special Find 138
1-1247	Special Find 139

1-1248	Special Find 140
1-1249	Special Find 141
1-1253	Special Find 145
1-1254	Special Find 146
1-1255	Special Find 147
1-1256	Special Find 148
1-1257	Special Find 149
1-1258	Special Find 150
1-1261	Special Find 153
1-1263	Special Find 155
1-1264	Special Find 156
1-1266	Special Find 158
1-1267	Special Find 159
1-1268	Special Find 160
1-1269	Special Find 161
1-1271	Special Find 163
1-1272	Special Find 164
1-1273	Special Find 165

Miscellaneous Pebbles (Jadeite) (15)

These are small pebbles of jadeite. All were waterworn. One of them (Cat. No. 1-34) shows subsequent polish from handling; the others are unpolished. Diameter size varies from less than 1 cm to about 2.5.

Cat. Nos.	Op. No. and Provenience
1-34	2(C) CV-20, Lev. 5, Special Find 6
1-38 (9 spec.)	2(C) CV-20, Special Find 4, associated with Burial 3 and with Feature 3
1-161	14(A) CV-22, Lev. 3, Special Find 1
1-163 (2 spec.)	14(A) CV-22, Lev. 3, Special Find 3
1-346	26(A) Main Center, Struct. L11-93, Lev. 5, Special Find 14
1-1276	102(A) CV-43, Special Find 168 within Special Find 57

Note: Specimen 1-71, which has been classified and listed under "Polishing Stones and Polished Pebbles," but is of jadeite, could also have been grouped here.

Raw Jadeite (7)

These are mostly broken fragments of poor-quality, white-to-pale-green jadeite. Pieces range in size from about 1 cm in diameter to 3 x 4 cm. It seems likely that they are wastage from jadeite manufacturing.

Cat. Nos.	Op. No. and Provenience
1-21	2(I) CV-20
1-874	68(A) CV-68, Lev. 5
1-882	72(A) CV-205
1-895 (2 spec.)	68(A) CV-68, Lev. 4
1-1053	102(A) CV-43, Lev. 4
1-1278	102(A) CV-43, Special Find 170 within Special Find 57

Ornaments (Not Jadeite) (12)

These are ground and polished stone ornaments made of stones other than jadeite. For the most part they are beads, pendants, and fragments. They are described serially.

Cat. No. 1-33 is a fragment of a curved elongate object, probably a pendant. It is ovoid in cross section. The outer side of the curve is rounded and highly polished; the inner side is less well polished and more pointed or ridge-like. Length is 5.8 cm, width is 1.8 cm, and thickness varies from 0.9 to 1.6 cm. The stone is a mottled black, gray, and white; fine-grained; and porphyritic in appearance.

Cat. No. 1-238 is an edge or lip fragment of what probably was a well-polished pendant of gray-white, marble-like stone. It could be a sherd from a rather large bowl of this material, although the pendant interpretation is more likely. The piece is 3.2 x 2.7 x 1.9 cm, the latter being the thickness of the pendant or vessel wall (?). All nonbroken surfaces are polished. Two conical holes have been drilled on and near the lip. One proceeds downward from the middle of the lip top; the other comes in from the side at a point 1.4 cm below the lip top. The two holes barely meet at their conical tips.

Cat. No. 1-252 is a very small plaque-like ornament, apparently of stone. It may have been an inlay into other material. It is of triangular shape, 1 cm long and less than that in basal width. It shows red paint (cinnabar?) on one side.

Cat. No. 1-318 (fig. 201a) is a fragment of a nicely carved human head pendant. The stone is a mottled gray-black and dark green, probably serpentine rather than jadeite. The facial portion is well polished. It has been broken at both the bottom and the top of the head or face, probably in an unsuccessful attempt at transverse biconical

perforation. Rendering is that of the Maya grotesque figurine style of the Late Classic. It depicts a broad-nosed, heavy-featured man with a downturned, grimacing mouth. Carving is low-relief, showing eyes, nose, ears, ear ornaments, and mouth. Height is 3.3, width 2.8, and thickness 1.9 cm.

Cat. No. 1-480 is a disk-bead or, possibly, a stone spindle-whorl of a white crystalline stone. Diameter is 2.8 and thickness 1.2 cm, with a central, biconically drilled perforation 4 mm in diameter. The piece has been smoothed but is not carefully shaped or polished.

Cat. No. 1-664 is a small edge fragment of a pendant, possibly a vessel, or some other unidentified object. The stone is a fine-grained gray-black material. The lip is pointed. One surface is straight; the other rises up abruptly just before the break. It is about 3 cm in diameter and varies in thickness from 1 cm at the lip to 1.9 at the other end of the fragment.

Cat. No. 1-754 is a subspherical bead that was found in pieces. It is of a highly polished dark gray stone. It has been biconically drilled. Estimated measurements are diameter, 3.3 cm; and height, 2.6 cm.

Cat. No. 1-758 appears to be a blank for a cylindrical, as yet undrilled, bead. It is tiny, 1 cm in length and 6 mm in diameter. The material is a medium-hard red stone.

Cat. No. 1-975 is an end fragment of a highly polished gray-black bead. The fragment is 2.3 cm long. The bead was about 1.7 cm in diameter. It was of a tubular, or slightly squared-tubular, form. An attempt was made to pierce it longitudinally by drilling; however, the conical drill hole penetrated to just 1.5 cm of depth before the bead broke.

Cat. No. 1-1043 is a tiny black-brown cylindrical bead, 3 mm in length and 2 to 3 mm in diameter. It has been perforated by a small central hole.

Cat. No. 1-1053 (fig. 201b) is a siltstone or shale pendant of a brown color, 11.6 cm long and about 1.5 cm in diameter (at the center). Its smoothing or shaping appears to have been largely caused by water wear. However, there is a groove around one pointed end, just 1.5 cm below the tip.

Cat. No. 1-1158 is a fragment of an edge or rim, perhaps of a pendant or vessel. It is a nicely polished piece of grayish marble-like stone. The fragment is very similar to 1-238 (described above); however, there is no drill hole, or other hole, in this specimen. It measures about 4 x 3.5 cm and is 2.5 cm thick. The edge or rim is a rounded point.

Cat. Nos.	Op. No. and Provenience
1-33	5(B) CV-20, Lev. 1
1-238	20(A) CV-20, Lev. 5
1-252	22(B) CV-48, Lev. 4, Special Find 1
1-318	20(A) CV-20, Lev. 6, Special Find 67
1-480	33(F) CV-43, Lev. 4, Special Find 5
1-664	53(A) CV-91, Lev. 4
1-754	59(A) CV-125, Lev. 4
1-758	33(GG) CV-43, Lev. 2
1-975	100(B) CV-43, Lev. 3
1-1043	102(A) CV-43, Feature 10, Special Find 53
1-1053	102(A) CV-43, Lev. 4
1-1158	104(A) CV-43, Lev. 9-B

Stone Figurine (1)

Cat. No. 1-602 (fig. 202) is a small human figurine made of a tan-colored tuff or soft volcanic stone. In size and posture it resembles Classic Maya pottery figurines. The head is missing, the remainder intact. It represents a seated human in what appears to be a cross-legged posture. Arms, body, and legs are depicted in deep-scored carving. Back and base are smoothed. Height, without head, is 4.7 cm; basal width, which is the widest point, is 3.8 cm; and basal thickness is 3.2 cm.

Cat. No. 1-602 came from Op. No. 35(M) CV-43, Level 1.

Stone Yoke (?) (1)

This is a well-polished fragment of a black-gray basaltic rock which may have been a fragment of a stone yoke (fig. 203). If so, it would have been a finished edge segment of the U-shaped curve of the stone. It is 2.5 cm in width. The length of the fragment, which is broken at both ends, is 11.5 cm. The original thickness cannot be estimated because the piece has also been broken longitudinally. The width of the stone is thin by comparison with what we know of stone yokes, so the yoke classification may not be appropriate.

Cat. No. 1-98 came from Op. No. 6(J) CV-20, Level 1.

Celt-like Objects or Ritual Maces (4 or 5)

These are celt-like or monolithic axe-like forms. They are, in a general way, reminiscent of specimens found at Barton Ramie, in the Belize Valley (Willey et al. 1965:476–482, figs. 299a–c, 300), although they do not fully duplicate any of these. Their forms suggest ceremonial usage, perhaps as objects carried as insignia of office. The specimens at hand show no definite signs of utilitarian service.

Cat. Nos. 1-901 (fig. 204a) and 1-922 (fig. 204b) probably are fragments of the same specimen. They come from adjacent levels in an excavation. The stone material is a rather friable schist—gray in color and relatively easily broken. The 1-922 portion (or portions—a large piece and four very small fragments) is the handle portion of the mace, showing the remnants of a flat butt end and a small section of an apparent blade-like projection. Total length of the fragment is 20.5 cm. From the butt end of the handle to the beginning of the blade-like projection is 9.6 cm; the broken edge of the projection extends the rest of the way to the top of the fragment. The shaft or handle is ovoid in cross section. The longer diameter, which is parallel to the blade-like projection, is 4.2 cm; the shorter diameter is 3 cm. The remaining small fragments are no more than slivers of rock.

The Cat. No. 1-901 portion (assuming that it belongs to the same original mace) would have been, presumably, the top end of the artifact, being above the blade-like projection referred to in the foregoing. Length of the fragment is 7.5 cm. It is well trimmed or ground and rectangular in cross section with a flat end. Cross-sectional measurements are 4.5 cm (probably not quite complete) x 2.8 cm.

Cat. No. 1-966 (fig. 204c) is a very carefully shaped and smoothed mace of a fine-grained stone. It measures 21 cm in length, 4.5 cm in width, and 3.5 cm in thickness. Both ends are rounded, but there is no taper to the form. On one of the larger flat surfaces, 1.8 cm from one end and approximately centrally located on the shaft of the object, is a rounded hump or protrusion. This protrusion is 2.7 cm wide and 9.3 cm long, and rises 2.4 cm above the flat surface of the shaft. Thus, the object had a crude monolithic axe or mace appearance.

Cat. No. 1-617 (fig. 204d) is a fragment of what appears to be the top of a mace head. It corresponds to such an artifact as is shown in Willey et al. 1965, figure 295, items a or b. The material is a hard, black schist. The piece has been very carefully ground and polished on both flat surfaces as well as along the top, along the side, and in the rectangular notch. The fragment measures about 8 x 9 cm and is 1.2 cm thick. It is of rectangular form, and the notch is 2.6 cm deep.

Cat. No. 1-206 (fig. 204e) probably is a mace head fragment, although it could have been the handle portion of a club-like barkbeater. It is 14.4 cm long. The smooth cylindrical handle tapers from 3.6 cm down to 3.1 cm at its end. At the top or broken end of the object there is an edge or ridge expanding away from the cylindrical handle. This suggests the base of a mace head. There are no scorings in this vicinity that would indicate a club-like barkbeater.

Cat. Nos.	Op. No. and Provenience
1-206	21(A) CV-20, Lev. 2
1-617	33(FF) CV-43, Lev. 2
1-901	50(A) CV-45, Lev. 4
1-922 (frags.)	50(A) CV-45, Lev. 3
1-966	103(A) CV-46, Lev. 3

Star-shaped Stone (1)

Cat. No. 1-738 (fig. 205) is a roughly carved star-shaped piece of soft volcanic tuff of a buff color. One side is quite flat but not smoothed; the other side is rough and bumpy. The object had six points or nubs. Some of these are more or less pointed; others are flattened or squared off. Portions of two adjoining points have been broken away. The overall diameter is 9.8 cm; the thickness is 2.5 cm.

Cat. No. 1-738 came from Op. No. 44(I) CV-46, Level 1.

Stone Disks (4)

These are four stone disks or discoid pieces. Their purpose is uncertain, and it might be questioned if we are dealing with a single type. Most of them appear too small to have been column drums, and the one that is large enough for this purpose has a shaping that makes it seem unlikely.

Cat. No. 1-35 is a fragment, originally probably of circular or oval shape. It had been shaped on all surfaces. The stone is a coarse and soft volcanic. It is 1.7 cm thick, and the estimated diameter is about 8 cm.

Cat. No. 1-765 (fig. 206a) is almost circular and complete. Its two diameters measure 9 and 9.5 cm. It is, however, thicker proportionately than the previous specimen, measuring 4.5 cm on this dimension. The stone is a light-colored, fine-grained, metamorphic. The disk is nicely shaped on both flat surfaces as well as circumferentially. One flat surface is, indeed, quite flat; the other is slightly convex.

Cat. No. 1-1059 (fig. 206b, right) is slightly more ovoid than the above, measuring 10 and 12 cm, respectively, on its two diameters. Thickness is appreciable, 7 cm. The circumference is nicely smoothed. The two flat surfaces have been shaped by pecking but are not smoothly ground. Again, one of these surfaces is flat; the other is convex. The stone is a coarse-grained volcanic.

Cat. No. 1-754 (fig. 206c) is by far the largest of the disks. It is made of a gray-white, moderately soft, medium-grained volcanic stone. It is very carefully shaped and a virtual perfect circle, 19.3 cm in diameter. Thickness is 4.2 cm. The circumference has been ground smooth, as has one flat surface. This surface is actually slightly convex, and the diameter at this surface is 19.3 cm. The other surface is very slightly concave and less well smoothed, and its diameter is about 1 cm less than the other side.

Cat. Nos.	Op. No. and Provenience
1-35	2(B) CV-20, Lev. 6, Special Find 7
1-754	59(A) CV-125, Lev. 4
1-765	45(I) CV-46, Lev. 1
1-1059	74(H) CV-16, Lev. 1

Incised Stones (3)

These are three small incised stones. Cat. No. 1-540 (fig. 207a) is a ground and smoothed hemispherical concretion or geode. The outer portion is a reddish, hematitic-appearing material, the inner a yellowish-buff, fine-grained hard stone. Within the natural circle of the inner, yellowish stone there are two incised concentric circles. Four incised lines divided the space between the inner and outer incised circles. These are not equidistantly placed in a perfect 90- degree quadration but are all a little off-center. The diameter of the object is 4.8 cm; its thickness is 1.9 cm. The outer incised circle is 2.3 cm, the inner circle 8 mm, in their respective diameters. The depth of the incised lines is about 1 mm.

Cat. No. 1-894 (fig. 207b) is a fragment, rectanguloid in outline, of a reddish volcanic stone on which the one smoothed surface has been inscribed with a concentric rectilinear spiral or maze-like design. Measurements are 5 x 4.5 x 2.5 cm. The smoothed surface is completely covered by the incised or inscribed design. These lines are about 3 mm apart, about 1 mm wide in themselves, and 1 mm or less in depth.

Cat. No. 1-611 is considerably larger than the other two incised stones and lacks the pocket-piece, charm-like quality of the little pieces. It is a rough limestone block, more or less cuboid in form (7.5 cm in approximate dimensions). The block is quite weathered, so it is difficult to say to what degree it had once been smoothed. About 2 cm down from one surface there is a continuous thin incised line running around all four sides of the block. At the opposite side of the block it appears that such a line had been started at more or less midpoint on the piece; however, this line does not even extend to the corners of that side.

Cat. Nos.	Op. No. and Provenience
1-540	36(G) CV-43, Lev. 1
1-611	40(E) CV-45, Lev. 1
1-894	46(G) CV-44, Lev. 1

Stone Tables (5)

These are little monolithic table-like objects. They may have served as ritual tables or pedestals of some sort. Their size and fragility would seem to preclude their use as true seats for humans. In at least one case there is grinding evidence on the seat surface that would suggest that this particular specimen, at least, had been used as a mortar. Another specimen shows burning on the surface.

Cat. No. 1-4 (fig. 208a) is a fragment, approximately three-fourths of the original. It is made of a very coarse volcanic stone and has been crudely shaped. The original form was four-legged; most of one leg has been broken away. The table is 12.8 cm long, 11.7 cm wide, and 7.7 cm high. Legs were made flush with the sides of the table, and they are 2 cm high. There is a deep continuous groove, 8 mm wide and 4 mm deep, running around all four sides of the table. This has been placed at a point 2.5 cm below table surface.

Cat. No. 1-215 (fig. 208b), a table fragment, is the most nicely finished of the lot. One leg and one corner of the table have been lost, and two other legs have been largely broken away. The piece is pinkish in color and made of a medium-fine volcanic stone. It measures 13.7 cm wide; the fragmentary length is 12.8 cm. Total height is 7.4 cm. The thickness of the table is 3.3 cm, the height of the legs 4.1 cm. The top surface has been nicely smoothed, as have the edges and the outside surfaces of the legs. The latter rise flush with the edge of the table. They are rectangular, 4.5 x 3.5 cm, and taper slightly toward their bases. The underside of the table and the insides of the legs have been shaped by pecking but are not smoothed. Cat. No. 1-215 was found as one of nine objects in a cache (Special Find 28), together with some polished black stones.

Cat. No. 1-137 (fig. 208c) is a fragment of one end of a table. Width of the top is 13.2 cm, and its height is 8 cm. Legs were set flush with table top and are approximately (4.8 x 4 cm) square. The body of the table is quite thick so that the height of these legs is only 1.7 cm. The surface of the table is well smoothed, but otherwise the piece is not well finished. The material is a soft volcanic stone.

Cat. No. 1-279 (fig. 208d) is complete and might be described as a "mortar-table." Carved or pecked out of a coarse, soft, volcanic stone, it is 11 x 9 x 3.7 cm. There are four rectangular nubbin legs, each set back about 5 mm from the edge of the rectangular table top. The surface and edges of the table are smoothed, but the surface has also served as a mortar so that an oval area, 6 x 5 cm and less than 5 mm deep, is approximately centered on the top surface. The entire top surface of the table also shows evidence of burning. The legs are a part of a thickened underside of the table; in other words, they do not rise flush to the edge of the table surface. Legs measure 1.5 cm high and 3 x 2.5 cm in diameter.

Cat. No. 1-615 is a fragment of a table, probably of limestone. One-half of the table is present, with two legs. The table top is 19 cm wide, and total height is 7.5 cm. Legs are flush with the edges of the top. They are rectanguloid and taper downward on their interior sides.

Cat. Nos.	Op. No. and Provenience
1-4	3 CV-1, Surface
1-137	6(N) CV-20, Lev. 1
1-215	19(C) CV-20, Lev. 3, Special Find 28
1-279	19(G) CV-20, Lev. 2
1-615	35(O) CV-43, Lev. 1

Concretions, Geodes, and Minerals (18)

These are natural formations or minerals, apparently collected by the inhabitants of the Copan residential units and brought into the sites for unknown purposes. Some, but not all, show human modifications. They may be detailed as follows.

Cat. No. 1-1: small shell-shaped geode of ferruginous material. One end is broken off, exposing a hollow interior.

Cat. No. 1-41: small laminated piece of mica.

Cat. No. 1-47: three small flakes of mica. These appear to have been cut into little rectangular plaques 2.5 cm in diameter. They may have been used as inlays or insets into some other material.

Cat. No. 1-70: fragment of large geode.

Cat. No. 1-74: small circular concave concretion. It appears to have been trimmed around the edges and ground on its convex side.

Cat. No. 1-88: little trianguloid piece of soft white limestone that appears to have been shaped by rubbing.

Cat. No. 1-137: four pieces of thin, laminated soapstone.

Cat. No. 1-156: rectangular piece of petrified wood, 5 x 3.5 x 1.5 cm.

Cat. No. 1-221: three small pieces of graphite.

Cat. No. 1-542: fragment of large geode.

Cat. No. 1-609: two small spherical geodes of ferruginous material.

Cat. No. 1-635: a quartzitic concretion, egg-shaped, measuring 5 x 3.5 cm. It has been smoothed, perhaps by being used as a polisher or by repeated handling.

Cat. No. 1-645: small circular concave section of geode.

Cat. No. 1-650: small flattened-spherical geode.

Cat. No. 1-654: half of a flattened-spherical geode, diameter 6.3 cm.

Cat. No. 1-756: half of a small geode.

Cat. No. 1-860: a hard limey concretion of flattened-spherical form. It measures 5.4 x 3.4 cm. One flat side shows a navel-like natural formation. It is well smoothed on all surfaces, from grinding, handling, or both.

Cat. Nos.	Op. No. and Provenience
1-1	1(A) CV-20, Surface, Large Plaza
1-41	4(F) CV-20, Lev. 1
1-47	5(E) CV-20, Lev. 1
1-70	4(J) CV-20
1-74	5(K) CV-20, Lev. 1
1-88	7(F) CV-20, Lev. 1
1-137	6(N) CV-20, Lev. 1
1-156	15(A) CV-20, Lev. 1
1-221	21(A) CV-20, Lev. 2, Special Find 29
1-542	33(CC) CV-43, Lev. 4
1-609 (2 spec.)	54(A) CV-94, Lev. 2
1-635	44(B) CV-46, Lev. 1
1-645	56(A) CV-116, Lev. 2
1-650	54(A) CV-94, Lev. 8
1-654	53(A) CV-91, Lev. 7
1-756	61(A) CV-139, Lev. 2
1-860	50(A) CV-45, Lev. 1

Miscellaneous Worked Stone Fragments (20)

This is a residual category for fragments of ground stone artifacts or pieces of stone that probably show some evidence of grinding, scoring, or drilling. They may be unfinished artifacts or bits of these. All of the stones are relatively coarse in quality and finish. None would qualify as polished (such fragments would have been classified as ornaments), and none would qualify as pebbles of fine-quality stone or otherwise special cache pebbles, which are also classified separately.

Probably mortar fragments or metate fragments compose a large part of the pieces here classified. These are small edge bits—too small to classify with certainty under either the metate or mortar types. Some pieces may have been broken from manos.

Cat. Nos.	Op. No. and Provenience
1-63	5(J) CV-20, Lev. 1
1-73	7(C) CV-20, Lev. 1
1-82	7(E) CV-20, Lev. 1
1-84	5(Q) CV-20, Lev. 1
1-88	7(F) CV-20, Lev. 1
1-126	6(M) CV-20, Lev. 1
1-137	6(N) CV-20, Lev. 1
1-156	15(A) CV-20, Lev. 1
1-186	15(B) CV-20, Lev. 2
1-469	33(F) CV-43, Lev. 3
1-531	33(Z) CV-43, Lev. 5
1-550	38(A) CV-43, Lev. 1
1-577	38(B) CV-43, Lev. 1
1-579	38(C) CV-43, Lev. 1
1-624	40(F) CV-45, Lev. 1
1-626	37(N) CV-43, Lev. 1
1-692	43(D) CV-43, Lev. 1
1-760	48(B) CV-47, Lev. 1
1-970	104(A) CV-43, Lev. 2
1-1027	100(B) CV-43, Lev. 4

Angle Stones or Architectural Stones (17)

This is the term given to a number of stones that are L-shaped, U-shaped, or T-shaped. All are made from the soft andesite tuff characteristic of Copan Valley architecture. It is probable that all were, in some way or another, architectural elements. In the case of some of them, as will be noted below, this is certain because they were found in situ in masonry contexts.

Eleven are L-shaped (fig. 209) or boot-shaped and probably are masonry vault stones. These usually have one arm somewhat longer than the other. Cat. No. 1-573, has for instance, a 23-cm arm and a 15-cm arm. Width of arms is between 5 and 7 cm, and thickness is about 10 cm. This is the largest specimen; others are slightly smaller. On all of them the interior angle of the L is imperfectly fashioned and tends to be rounded rather than squared. The outer angle is a sharp right angle.

Two are U-shaped (fig. 210). Cat. No. 1-454 has a 14.5-cm base, and the two arms rise 8.5 and 10 cm, respectively. Exterior surfaces are well smoothed or flattened and exterior angles are sharp; interior surfaces are less well shaped and the angles are more rounded. One of the two specimens from Cat. No. 1-854 is the other U-shaped stone.

Four are T-shaped (fig. 211). This includes three specimens from Cat. No. 1-451 and one specimen from Cat. No. 1-838. Two of the 1-451 specimens were found in situ in an inverted T position. The measurements on one are 19.5 cm along base, 9 cm in height of base, and the inverted upright of the T is 5 cm high. One of the long arms of the base served as a tenon. Similar stones found elsewhere in Maya building sites have been referred to as "curtain-tie-holders," and these may have so functioned in the Copan sites.

Cat. Nos.	Op. No. and Provenience
1-451 (5 spec.)	28(A) CV-43, Surface
1-454	32(A) CV-47, Surface
1-573	36(L) CV-43, Lev. 1
1-734	46(A) CV-44, Lev. 1
1-760	48(B) CV-47, Lev. 1
1-765	45(I) CV-46, Lev. 1
1-838	42(K) CV-43, Lev. 1
1-844	48(H) CV-47, Lev. 1
1-853	39(O) CV-44, Lev. 1
1-854 (2 spec.)	47(J) CV-47, Lev. 1
1-1059	74(H) CV-16, Lev. 1
No Number	

MINOR SCULPTURES

General, Comparative, and Summary Comments

Architecturally attached sculptures from our excavations are fully consistent with the Copan tradition of architectural adornment through geometric or life-form decorative carving. The pieces described here are relatively simple ones, compared to some of the sculptures found in the Copan Main Center or, for that matter, even within our own excavations (for instance, the hieroglyphic frieze in CV-43).

The freestanding pieces—a crude stone mask, a plain circular altar, a small frog carving, and a fragment of a human torso—are in no way remarkable or definitive as to style.

Architecturally Attached Sculptures (5)

These are all decorative elements that were definitely attached or very probably attached to masonry structures.

Cat. No. 1-185 (fig. 212) is a rectangular, loaf like stone with a deep longitudinal groove running the full length of one of its larger faces. The stone measures 20 x 8 x 6 cm, and the groove is about 2.5 cm deep, 3 cm wide at the top, and narrows toward the bottom. The material is andesite tuff, characteristic of Copan Valley architecture. It seems likely that the block was used as an architectural feature.

Cat. No. 1-449 (fig. 213a) is a carving on the face of a stone block that was obviously set into masonry, perhaps as an element in a frieze. The block is 8.5 x 8.5 x 10 cm. The carved decoration covers the front or outer face, which measures 8.5 x 8.5 cm. It depicts two pendant tassels. Each tassel consists of three hanging or vertical elements, and each is suspended from a circular, button-like element. The material is andesite tuff.

Cat. No. 1-451, also of andesite tuff, is a rounded rectangular stone that measures 9.5 cm

in diameter and 9.5 cm high. There is carving around three sides; a fourth side has been left plain. The carving consists of vertically arranged, widely spaced grooves that are transected by a horizontal groove or constriction. This horizontal groove or constriction corresponds, as can be seen in the drawing (fig. 213b), to the contour of the stone. Perhaps the piece was an element in a row of small false columns, set with the plain side against a building wall.

Cat. No. 1-619 (fig. 213c) is a crude portrayal of an animal, perhaps a jaguar. The material is a soft limestone. The animal head rises from the rectangular block of a tenon, and there can be no doubt that the carving was attached to a building. Eyes of the animal are rendered by two little depressions and a mouth and teeth (or whiskers?) rendered by fine incised lines. Total height is 13 cm, and total length is 17 cm. The tenon element is about 7 cm square in cross section.

Cat. No. 1-747 (fig. 213d) is an apparent building stone that appears ovaloid in cross section. It is andesite tuff and measures 28 cm long or deep (as it would fit into wall masonry), about 16 cm wide, and 10.5 cm high. On the outer or exposed face is a carved spiral design.

Cat. Nos.	Op. No. and Provenience
1-185	18(A) CV-20, Lev. 1
1-449	3 Site L-91
1-451	28(A) CV-43, Surface
1-619	34(M) CV-43, Lev. 1
1-747	39(J) CV-44, Lev. 1

Freestanding Sculptures (4)

These are generally small, freestanding carvings of stone. There is a possibility of overlap here with the minor sculptures–architecturally attached category; however, it is highly likely that all of the pieces described here were not architectural adornment.

Cat. No. 1-451 (fig. 214a) is a mask-like human head or face. It appears to be completely freestanding or not readily interpreted as having been connected with a building or masonry structure. The material is soft white limestone. It measures 18 cm high, 10 to 11 cm wide in profile (measured in the jaw area), and 7.5 cm wide in front view. The face is most schematic, with drilled-pit eyes 4 cm in diameter, a beak-like nose, and a gash for a mouth. It has been fashioned by pecking and grinding.

Cat. No. 1-645 is a plain disk-shaped altar stone made of the standard andesite tuff of the Copan ruins. It is circular or nearly so, 56 cm in diameter and 13 cm thick. There are no decorations on any surface.

Cat. No. 1-657 (fig. 214b) is a small frog or toad sculpture carved from a hard, pink-white, fairly coarse volcanic stone. Although overall shaping remains crude, the head is well, if boldly, executed. The total piece is 11.5 cm high; basal measurements are about 12 cm (front-to-back) x 8.5 cm (across). The winged-shaped frog face has two deeply incised circles for eyes and an incised inverted-V mouth. The top of the head is fashioned to represent a little poll or knob between the eyes. Arms or forelegs are more roughly fashioned, depicting the animal in a sitting position, presumably on its back legs although these are not clearly depicted.

The back and sides are smoothed and finished. The front part of the base is also more or less smoothed, but the back portion of the base is uneven and broken. It is just possible that there was a tenon section here that has been broken away, but this is uncertain so the carving is classed here with the freestanding minor sculptures.

Cat. No. 1-864 (fig. 214c) is an andesite tuff carving of what appears to be a fragmentary human figure. It is about 14 cm high, 16 cm wide, and of approximately comparable length or depth. If it is correctly interpreted as a human figure, the torso and upper arms remain. The head, apparently, has been broken away. It is possible that this may have been tenoned into masonry; but this is so uncertain that it has been grouped here with the freestanding minor sculptures.

Cat. Nos.	Op. No. and Provenience
1-451	28(A) CV-43, Surface
1-645	56(A) CV-116, Lev. 2
1-657	54(A) CV-94, Lev. 7-B
1-864	73(A) CV-185, Lev. 1

CHIPPED STONE (FLINT)

Projectile Points or Knives	22
Straight Stem, Long Blade	1
Laurel-Leaf Blades	21
Scrapers	20
Drills	5
Bifacial	1
Unifacial	4
Pebble Choppers or Pounders	8
Eccentrics	2
Scrap	1,176

General, Comparative, and Summary Comments

Flint, or chert, artifacts are relatively rare at Copan. One of the noteworthy things about our

collection is that it contains no chipped stone choppers or celts, the general utility form or standard biface. Neither does Longyear (1952) record any such artifact. These implements are found in high frequency in Peten and Belize lowland Maya sites (see Willey 1978:102–103 for a discussion of this tool type and its distributions; also Willey 1972:155–156; Willey et al. 1965: 426–429; Stoltman 1975). They have usually been thought of as land-clearing tools, being hafted axe-fashion. Wilk's (1978:139–140) use-wear studies on standard bifaces recovered from other sites in the Maya lowlands confirm that they were used for cutting wood and scrub growth. Based on our sample of artifacts, it is difficult to see what kind of an implement was used for such a function at Copan. The pebble choppers or pounders, of which we found eight specimens, would not have been well suited to a land-clearing purpose.

A single straight stem, long blade projectile point (dart point) is in our collections. It is very similar to one illustrated by Longyear (1952:110, fig. 93d) and is a form found elsewhere in the Maya lowlands, although not in great numbers (Willey 1978:103). A somewhat more common Peten and Belizean type is the broad tapered stem, long blade form (dart point) (ibid.:103, 109, fig. 120b–c). Longyear (1952, fig. 93c) shows one of these from Copan, although we found none in our excavations.

Laurel-leaf blades were the most common flint or chert point or knife form in our Copan collections. Longyear (1952:110, fig. 93a–b) also reported the type. These are a common lowland Maya form and are discussed as to datings and distributions in the Seibal report (Willey 1978: 103–104, 111–112; with reference to wear patterns on such artifacts, see Wilk 1978:142–143).

Flint scrapers and drills that we recovered from our excavations at Copan were largely unifacial implements of no distinctive specialization so that comparisons with other sites and regions is nonproductive. Pebble choppers or pounders recovered are much like those from Seibal (Willey 1978:116), Altar de Sacrificios (Willey 1972: 179–180), and Barton Ramie (Willey et al. 1965:438).

We found only two flint eccentrics. One of these is a small, multiple-notched form generally common among lowland Maya eccentrics (Willey 1972, figs. 164, 173). The other is a fragment of what was probably a monolithic axe-like form (ibid., fig. 176a, for probable comparable example). Longyear (1952, fig. 93e,f) illustrates much more elaborate eccentric forms from his diggings at Copan.

Although flint, or chert, artifacts were scarce, we found over 1,100 pieces of scrap or debitage in our Copan Valley and related excavations. The debitage was generally distributed through our excavations (see section below on debitage description), suggesting that knapping of the material took place in most households; we found no definite indications of specialized workshops. Daniel R. Potter and Fred Valdez, who analyzed this Copan debitage (see below), tell us that the chert is coarse-grained and of poor quality (with voids, fossil inclusions, and bedding

planes) and that the original nodules were generally too small to allow for the easy manufacture of many standard Maya chert or flint tool types, especially the fairly large general utility or standard biface forms, which, as noted, do not occur within our collections. Despite this, the Copan household occupants worked at making chert artifacts. They went through the standard steps of nodule or core reduction, flake or blade production, and subsequent flaking and thinning. All of this was done in the Copan households, and, in the process, they did produce a few tools and weapons; but in the main, they lacked the proper raw resources for a very successful flint or chert industry.

Projectile Points or Knives (22)

Straight Stem, Long Blade (1)

This specimen (Cat. No. 1-79) is a stem fragment of what appears to be a dart point. Although we cannot be certain, the size of the stem suggests the straight stem, long blade type. Length is 2.1 cm, width 2.9 cm, and thickness 0.8 cm. The shoulders of the point were probably very slight. It is of gray chert, carefully chipped on both faces, and with a flat base.

Cat. No. 1-79 came from Op. 5(O) CV-20, Level 1.

Laurel-leaf Blades (21)

This is a well-known chipped stone type in the Maya lowlands, occurring both in the local flint (cherts, calcedonies, etc.) (see Willey 1978:111–112) and in obsidian. Five complete or near-complete laurel-leaf blades were found in our Copan excavations. The remaining specimens are fragments. Most of the fragments are identified to the type with certainty; however, there are three blade tips (Cat. Nos. 1-61, 1-815, and 1-825) that, because of their small size, are more questionable as to type identification.

All blades are of a generally bi-pointed form. All show fine pressure-flaking on both surfaces and on the edges, and all are relatively thin. Light gray, dark gray, dark brown, tan, and honey-colored flints were used.

Laurel-leaf blades were probably used as spear-points or knives. Quite possibly, there was a size division here, with the larger specimens being spear-points and the smaller being knives. This is conjecture, but one correlation in form characteristics may support it. Our larger specimens have their sharper and more effective piercing end near the wider end of the blade. This suggests a spear-point function with the longer, narrower end of the blade held, perhaps, in a slot in a wooden shaft. Our smaller specimens have their sharper end at the longer, tapered end of the blade. The opposite or butt end of these specimens is often quite blunt and rounded. This form would have been more useful as a hafted knife, made to be held and used in the hand.

One specimen bearing Cat. No. 1-16 (fig. 215a) is made of a dark brown fine-quality flint. It measures 19.9 x 6.2 x 1.1 cm. Length was a bit more—one tip has been broken away. Careful parallel-flaking extends from the edges into the median line of the point on both faces. The slightly thinner, sharper end is near the wider end of the point. This width maximum is about one-third of the way back of the point.

The second Cat. No. 1-16 (fig. 215b) specimen is similar in its flint material and fine workmanship to the first. This one measures 21.9 x 6.4 x 0.9 cm. Again, the sharper end is near the broader end of the blade, with the tapered and longer end considerably blunter.

Cat. No. 1-547 (fig. 215c) is smaller than the two just described, measuring only 11 x 3.1 x 0.7 cm. The broader end in this case is rounded and blunt; the longer, tapered end is the sharper. It is made of a nice-quality semitranslucent gray chert. Flaking is lateral, coming in from both edges of each face. There is also some very fine edge retouch.

Cat. No. 1-1046 is, again, a longer specimen, measuring 15 cm now, but perhaps as much as 3 cm was broken off one end. Maximum width is near the broader, and sharper, end and is 4.5 cm. Thickness is 1 cm. The form suggests the spear function, as was the case with the two Cat. No. 1-16 specimens. The material is a pinkish-gray chert.

Cat. No. 1-969 belongs to the longer subtype or spear-point subtype. Now 14 cm in length, it was probably originally 17 to 18 cm long. The broader end, which has its tip broken off, was undoubtedly the sharper end. Maximum width of the specimen is 3.2 cm; thickness, 0.7 cm. The material is a mottled tan chert of good quality. Chipping on both faces and along the edges is excellent.

Thus, of the complete, or near-complete, laurel-leaf blade specimens, four (Cat. Nos. 1-16 with two specimens, 1-1046, and 1-969) belong to the longer, probable spear-point subtype, while one (Cat. No. 1-547) is of the shorter, probable knife subtype form.

Subtracting the three tip fragments (Cat. Nos. 1-61, 1-815, 1-825), this leaves us with 12 fragmentary specimens. Ten of these, judging from their size and general appearance, are almost certainly pieces of the longer, spear-like subtype. The remaining two (Cat. Nos. 1-98 and 1-550) are of the shorter, knife-like subtype with broad, blunt basal ends and sharp, elongated points. Cat. No. 1-98 is a sharp end-point fragment, now 7.4 cm in length and probably originally 8 to 9 cm long. Maximum width is 3 cm and thickness is 0.7 cm. The edge retouch is excellent, and the point is very sharp. Cat. No. 1-550 is a butt-end fragment. Now 5.8 cm long, it was probably originally 8 to 9 cm. The maximum width, near the basal or butt end, is 3.5 cm, and thickness is 0.8 cm. It, too, shows careful surface flaking and excellent edge retouch on the sides and at the rounded butt end. Both specimens are made of a mottled tan chert.

Cat. Nos.	Op. No. and Provenience
1-1	1(A) CV-20, Surface, Large Plaza
1-16 (2 spec.)	2(E) CV-20, Special Find 1
1-43	4(D) CV-20, Lev. 1
1-61	6(F) CV-20, Lev. 1
1-74	5(K) CV-20, Lev. 1
1-76	5(M) CV-20, Lev. 1
1-98	6(J) CV-20, Lev. 1
1-99	4(M) CV-20, Lev. 1
1-200	20(A) CV-20, Lev. 2
1-547	36(H) CV-43, Lev. 1
1-550	38(A) CV-43, Lev. 1
1-573	36(L) CV-43, Lev. 1
1-626	37(N) CV-43, Lev. 1
1-815	39(L) CV-44, Lev. 1
1-825	42(J) CV-43, Lev. 1
1-900	102(A) CV-43, Lev. 2
1-901 (2 spec.)	50(A) CV-45, Lev. 4

1-969	76(H) CV-16, Lev. 1
1-1046	100(B) CV-43, Lev. 4, Special Find 54

Scrapers (20)

These are all unifacial specimens. None is very carefully or elaborately worked (fig. 216).

Cat. No. 1-1 is circular, 7.1 cm in diameter and 2.8 cm thick; and made of white-and-yellow banded flint. There is evidence of use on a part of the circumference. There is no definite evidence of shaping.

Cat. No. 1-37 is elongated and pointed, 9 x 4.8 x 1.8 cm. It is a large plano-convex flake of high-quality dark brown flint. There are possible use nicks on the edges, but there is no sign of definite shaping as a tool.

Cat. No. 1-47 is a roughly circular, high-backed piece of semitranslucent quartz, diameter 4.5 cm and thickness 2 cm. There is very marked evidence of use nicking on the edges.

Cat. No. 1-82. Three of these are irregular-shaped flakes of red or brownish flint. Approximate diameters range from 3 to 5.5 cm and thicknesses from 1 to 1.8 cm. One specimen has a definitely use-nicked edge; the other two may have such nicking. The fourth specimen under this number is a tan and white elongated flake, 5.2 x 3 x 1 cm. It is a prismatic flake struck from a core of gray-white flint. The lower end of the flake has been broken away. Both long edges show clear use nicking.

Cat. No. 1-91 is a tabular block of red-brown flint, 7 x 3.7 x 1.5 cm. There is use nicking along one long edge.

Cat. No. 1-156 is a red-brown flake of rather coarse flint that has been struck from a core. The lower end is broken away. Measurements are 5.5 x 3.7 x 1.1 cm. Both long edges show large chip marks from apparent use.

Cat. No. 1-240 is the striking platform end of a flake, 3.5 cm in diameter and about 1 cm thick. It is honey-colored stone. There is clear evidence of use around the edges.

Cat. No. 1-260 includes a small yellow-brown banded flake, 4 cm in diameter and 1 cm thick. It has use-nicked edges. The other specimen under this number is an elongated form of dark brown flint, 4.2 x 2.6 x 1.3 cm. It has use-nicked edges.

Cat. No. 1-522 is the one specimen that might be bifacially flaked and shaped, although this is uncertain. The material is quite variegated and impure red-brown flint. The piece is triangular in cross section, about 2.5 cm on a side at the larger end, and from this end it tapers down to a sharp point. Length is 6.9 cm. All three of the long sides may have been shaped by flaking, and all surfaces have a sheen or gloss as though from handling. Slight use-nick marks are seen along at least two of the edges.

Cat. No. 1-550 has two specimens. One is a trianguloid piece of what may be a gray quartzite. It has a high, smooth gloss as though from handling. There is evidence of scraping use along one edge. The piece is about 5 x 4 x 2 cm. The remaining specimen under this number may or may not be an artifact. It is a tiny half-disk of flint, 2.2 cm in diameter and 0.2 cm in thickness. The flat surfaces are clearly cleavage or fracture planes; however, the semicircular edges appear to have been trimmed by chipping. The object may have been an ornament of some sort, the fragment of an inlay, perhaps. On the other hand, it could have been a very small, fine-edged scraper.

Cat. Nos.	Op. No. and Provenience
1-1	1(A) CV-20, Surface, Large Plaza
1-26 (2 spec.)	4(A) CV-20, Lev. 1
1-37	2(C) CV-20, Special Find 8, associated with Burial 3
1-47	5(E) CV-20, Lev. 1
1-76	5(M) CV-20, Lev. 1
1-82 (4 spec.)	7(E) CV-20, Lev. 1
1-91	4(L) CV-20, Lev. 1
1-137 (2 spec.)	6(N) CV-20, Lev. 1
1-156	15(A) CV-20, Lev. 1
1-240	22(B) CV-48, Lev. 2
1-260 (2 spec.)	19(C) CV-20, Lev. 6
1-522	33(CC) CV-43, Lev. 1
1-550 (2 spec.)	38(A) CV-43, Lev. 1

Drills (5)

Bifacial (1)

This is apparently the butt end of a nicely chipped drill of gray flint (fig. 217b). The specimen is 4 x 1.2 cm. It tapers slightly toward the point end, the tip of which has been broken off. This tapering is in width (from 1.2 to 1 cm) and thickness (from 0.8 to 0.3 cm). Edges have been carefully retouched.

Unifacial (4)

All are made of gray or gray-white flint (fig. 217a, c–e). Cat. No. 1-126 is a small trapezoidal sliver, length 3.5 cm, width (at top) 1.1 cm, and thickness 0.3 cm. Cat. No. 1-196 is somewhat larger, 4.7 x 2 x 0.5, and has very nicely retouched edges. It is more pronouncedly triangular in outline than any of the other drills. Cat. No. 1-969 was made from an elongated flake that was triangular in cross section. Length is 5 cm, width 2.3 cm, and thickness 1.5 cm. The pointed end of the drill has been carefully trimmed for about half the length of the piece to form a very effective, sturdy point. Cat. No. 1-1037 is a sliver, 4.8 x 1.1 x 1.1 cm. It is triangular in cross section. It has been dressed to a point at one end but otherwise shows little chipping.

Cat. Nos.	Op. No. and Provenience
Bifacial	
1-686	39(G) CV-44, Lev. 1
Unifacial	
1-126	6(M) CV-20, Lev. 1
1-196	19(A) CV-20, Lev. 2
1-969	76(H) CV-16, Lev. 1
1-1037	77(B) CV-16, Lev. 1

Pebble Choppers or Pounders (8)

These are all of flint (chert) or other very hard stone materials that will fracture conchoidally (fig. 218). All specimens show some shaping through pounding or chopping use. They are comparable to the type pebble choppers, as described, for example, from Seibal (Willey 1978:116); and they should not be confused with the more carefully made bifacial type, chopper pounders (ibid.:108).

Two specimens (both from Cat. No. 1-1) are fairly large, 9.5 x 6.5 and 8.5 x 4 cm, respectively. One of these is of fine-quality dark brown flint, similar to that of some of the laurel-leaf blades from the site. The other is of a banded

brown flint. Both have some cortex remaining on the surfaces. The larger specimen has one longitudinal edge that shows considerable battering. The other has pounding abrasions around its circumference.

Cat. No. 1-61 is a small cuboid piece, measuring a little over 2 cm on a side. The material is honey-colored flint, and there is cortex on one face. The edges show evidence of pounding. The specimen also shows some gloss, as though from long handling or use.

Cat. No. 1-259 is an irregular cuboid piece of red and white flint, 7 x 4.5 x 2.9 cm. There are pounding or use marks along one side.

Cat. No. 1-556 is a piece of hard, black metamorphic stone. It is an angular, block-like fragment, 7.8 x 6 x 3.5 cm. There are pounding marks around three edges.

Cat. No. 1-815 is of dark, banded, red and brown flint. There is a small spot of cortex on one face. It measures 6 x 4 cm. There are pounding contusions on its several ridges or edges.

Cat. No. 1- 855 is a rough, prismatic-shaped flake of black flint. One side still shows cortex, while the broad edge and the other side reveal a fresher fracture. The sharp edge shows some signs of pounding or chipping. It measures 8.3 x 6.6 cm on its larger dimensions, and its maximum thickness is 2.8 cm.

Cat. No. 1-1159 is a slab-like piece of reddish and pink-and-white banded flint, 10.5 x 7 x 3.1 cm. There is cortex on one flat side. The other flat side exposes a very smooth cleavage plane where the rock has been broken. The outline of the form is an oval, and one end of this oval shows pounding marks.

Cat. Nos.	Op. No. and Provenience
1-1 (2 spec.)	1(A) CV-20, Surface, Large Plaza
1-61	6(F) CV-20, Lev. 1
1-259	20(A) CV-20, Lev. 6
1-556	37(C) CV-43, Lev. 1
1-815	39(L) CV-44, Lev. 1
1-855	71(A) CV-204, Lev. 3, Plaza 1– Plaza 2
1-1159	37(C) CV-43, Lev. 1

Eccentrics (2)

There are two of these. One (Cat. No. 1-814) (fig. 219b) is complete, a small, irregular, multiple-notched form of a good quality of black flint. It is bifacially flaked and measures 6 x 4.5 cm.

The other specimen (Cat. No. 1-206) (fig. 219a) is a fragment of a monolithic axe-like or baton-like object. The fragment, of mottled white chert, is 10 x 7.5 x 2.5 cm. The chipping is bifacial but rather rough. The fragment appears to be a midsection of the axe or baton. It is generally ovate in cross section. Along one edge there are two small projections, each extending out about 1.5 cm from the body of the object and each measuring about 2 cm on the other axis.

Cat. Nos.	Op. No. and Provenience
1-206	21(A) CV-20, Lev. 2
1-814	48(E) CV-47, Lev. 1

Scrap (1179)

Chert scrap was more plentiful in our Copan excavations than was anticipated from the relatively few finished artifacts we encountered. Most of it consisted of small flakes and fragments, generally not of good quality. We found 99 pieces in our excavations of CV-16, 571 from CV-20, 391 from CV-43, and only 118 fragments from all of our small test excavations within the Copan Valley and at Santa Rita. While generally the amount of chert scrap found appears to correlate with the volume of digging, this was not uniformly the case. Our CV-43 excavations were much more extensive and cut through a greater volume of fill and detritus than did those in CV-20; however, the amount of chert scrap recovered from CV-20 is substantially greater than that found in CV-43 (571 specimens to 391 specimens). CV-43 is a larger and more complex site unit than CV-20, and, in addition, it has certain features, such as the carved stone hieroglyphic bench in Structure A, that imply elite status. CV-20, on the other hand, appears to have been a residential unit of more modest social status. We may ask the question: Was chert working more common in residential units of lower social status than in elite units? But our sample and our information are too small and too limited to allow us to answer this question with any degree of certainty. In neither CV-43 nor CV-20 was there any notable concentration of chert scrap in association with any plaza area or structure.

Chert Debitage: Detailed Descriptions and Comments

by Daniel R. Potter and Fred Valdez

The following results from the examination of several chert (alternatively called flint or chalcedony) debitage lots from the Harvard Copan Project excavations. Materials in this study originated from excavations at CV-16, CV-20, and CV-43, as well as from various test units and from Santa Rita. Most of the assemblage examined was composed of chert debitage, although other lithic forms were observed as well.

Raw Material

In contrast to northern Belize, much of the Peten, and parts of northern Yucatan, debitage collected by the Harvard excavations at the site of Copan is highly variable in terms of color and quality of raw material. "Quality" here refers to our somewhat subjective impressions of what made certain types of chert better than others for the purpose of making chipped stone tools. These impressions have come from our own attempts to fabricate tool forms from indigenous cherts, and also from our experience at several Maya sites that possess ancient chert workshops (included here would be the sites of Colha [Hester, Shafer, and Eaton 1982] and Rio Azul [Adams 1987], both in the southern lowlands, and Xkichmook [Potter 1987], located in the Puuc region of Yucatan).

Briefly, our perception of chert quality refers to three critical attributes: size of nodule, fineness of grain, and consistency of material throughout the nodule or core. Size of nodule simply refers to the size of available chert cobbles or nodules for ancient tool making tasks. The size in which raw chert naturally occurred clearly delimited the size, and therefore types, of tools that could be made within the Copan area. Fineness of grain refers to the microstructure, or texture, of local cherts. Fine-grained materials are easier to work, produce sharper edges, and generally afford the fabricator more control over the knapping process. Coarser cherts, with a less glassy appearance, tend to be tougher, meaning they are physically more difficult to work and control. One type of chert that is commonly coarse-grained, frequently banded in color, and semitranslucent is chalcedony, a type of material that predominates within the Copan sample.

Consistency of material within a nodule or core is perhaps the most important aspect of material quality of the three listed here. By consistency, we refer to homogeneity of material throughout the piece of chert to be worked. Voids, fossil inclusions, pre-fracture anomalies, and bedding planes are deleterious factors that can hinder or halt a toolmaker's attempt to successfully produce a desired tool form. Such imperfections are often invisible from the exterior surface, or cortex, of a nodule and, depending on their frequency and severity, can render even large pieces of raw material unworkable.

With a few exceptions, the Copan material in our sample is generally poor in quality. As noted, the material consists of chalcedony: it is light-colored, translucent, and usually coarse-grained. The primary colors in this material include a clear to milky white, banded white/tan/pink, and a buff to tan. The debitage in our sample indicates that cobble size did not exceed 15 cm in diameter. Nodules of this size would not permit the fabrication of many of the most common Late Classic lowland tool forms, such as the ubiquitous standard utility biface, large celt forms, or large blades. In addition to this problem of nodule size, we noted that small voids, crystalline inclusions, and bedding or other fracture planes were common within the chert. These imperfections would also have limited tool manufacture in terms of tool forms produced and in scale, or potential intensity, of production.

Where cortex is present, it is uniformly rounded and smoothed in a pattern typical of stream-carried materials. This suggests procurement of chert nodules occurred either near the Copan River or perhaps within fossil stream channels in the area.

Classification Analysis

Table 4 shows our classification of the excavated sample. The debitage comprises either flakes or flake fragments, and block fractured chert. The flake category is subdivided into three flake types; primary, secondary, and tertiary. These types are distinguished primarily by amount of cortex

present on the flake's dorsal surface, and are related to certain stages within a lithic manufacturing trajectory. Primary flakes, with 100 percent of their dorsal surfaces covered by cortex, are typical of cobble-shaping or cobble-testing tasks which initiate the toolmaking trajectory. Secondary flakes, which are defined as having only partial coverage of the dorsal surface by cortex (1 percent to 99 percent), are thought to have been produced during core reduction and the initial stages of biface reduction. Tertiary flakes, with dorsal cortex totally absent, were produced during the latter stages of tool manufacture and are generally smaller and more common than flakes of the former two categories. Within the tertiary flake class is a significant subclass of debitage termed biface thinning flake. Flakes in this class share a distinctive type of striking platform and are produced in the final stages of biface manufacture as well as biface resharpening tasks. The other classes within our analysis include hammer stones, which are the percussors used in lithic reduction tasks, cores, and edge-altered flakes.

Copan Debitage

The inconsistent and generally poor quality of the Copan cherts has contributed to the rather amorphous and obscure nature of the debitage assemblage. In many cases, imperfections have altered the form and patterning within the assemblage, making clear interpretation of manufacturing goals and trajectories difficult. Commonly, the presence of these imperfections within the chert was such that attempts to further modify the material were completely arrested at fairly early stages of lithic reduction. In contrast, fine-grained, uniform-quality chert within our sample was commonly associated with the terminal stages of reduction. If our sample is in fact representative of the site in general, it seems likely that good-quality chert was rare and highly prized by Copan knappers.

What does the debitage in the Harvard Copan samples tell us about tool manufacturing and use at the site? A look at columns G through J in table 4 shows that chert debitage from Copan represents all stages of biface manufacture, from decortication of raw nodules to final biface thin-

TABLE 4
Chipped stone debitage from the Harvard Copan Project

A	B	C	D	E	F	G	H	I	J	K	Total
CV-16	3	2	14	21	41	1	5	11	0	1	99
CV-20	3	0	79	76	101	14	123	171	3	1	571
CV-43	1	0	23	84	179	6	44	48	0	6	391
Santa Rita	0	0	3	15	19	0	7	6	3	0	53
Tests	0	0	13	23	8	3	11	6	1	0	65
Total	7	2	132	219	348	24	190	242	7	8	1,179

KEY FOR COLUMNS:

A Provenience
B Hammer stones
C Cores
D Unmodified pebbles
E Block fracture
F Flake fragments
G Primary flakes
H Secondary flakes
I Tertiary flakes
J Biface thinning flakes
K Edge-altered flakes

ning. Therefore we assume that all of these activities took place within the site. Although we do not have the means to quantify chert densities within any of the tested deposits, our rather low flake counts originating from fairly large test excavations give the impression of a low density chert distribution, at least when compared to sites located in more optimal resource zones (Shafer and Hester 1986; Potter 1987; Valdez and Potter 1982). This low density and generalized nature of the assemblage may suggest a lack of specialization and/or central control of chert tool production at the site. This impression is confirmed by John Mallory (1986:153), who states that chert density at Copan was much lower than that of obsidian, even though chert was locally available, while obsidian was coming from a source 90 km distant (the Ixtepeque source: Mallory 1986:153).

Recycling

The scarceness of quality chert at Copan is also indicated by tool recycling. Recycling can be said to have occurred when an artifact was reused in a new context rather than discarded at the end of its primary functional context. Recycling may or

may not entail purposeful remodeling of an artifact.

As an example, of the seven hammer stones (all of chert) noted within the sample, three were exhausted chert cores and one was a large reused secondary flake. All four specimens exemplify the fact that any sizable chert item was likely to go through multiple forms of usage before final discard in midden or structure fill.

Smaller debitage was also reutilized at Copan, in the form of edge-altered or modified flakes. Eight of these were noted in our sample, with modification consisting of lateral trimming, converging retouch, and possibly burin removals. It is important to note here that our survey of flake utilization was largely macroscopic, with only limited low-power scanning. It is therefore likely that we have not detected all cases of secondary debitage use, and that flake utilization was more frequent than our count indicates.

Summary

This analysis of a part of the Harvard Copan Project's chipped stone assemblage revealed information concerning the nature of local chert resources in the Copan area and how these resources were utilized by the valley's ancient inhabitants. Based upon our sample, we have noted that Copan nodule size, a critical factor in determining potential manufactured tool forms, is probably too small to facilitate production of many typical Late Classic tool types. We have also observed that the local cherts of the Copan area are commonly found with a range of imperfections. These include voids, fossil inclusions, bedding planes, and pre-fractured surfaces. All of these would have greatly hindered chipped stone tool manufacture.

Even with all the above-considered problems associated with local materials, the debitage assemblage from the Harvard excavations indicates that all stages of tool making did occur at the site, from the testing and trimming of nodules to biface thinning. However, we know little about the context and intensity of chert procurement and manufacture in ancient Copan. This is unfortunate, because Copan has recently figured importantly in discussions of Maya economics and craft specialization (Mallory 1986; Shafer and Hester 1986). However, even though we cannot quantify chert densities for any of the tested deposits within the site, our impression is that they were quite low and did not occur in aggregation but were dispersed across the site. For this reason, it seems likely that tool manufacturing was a generalized cottage industry rather than a specialized craft. In this we are simply echoing the arguments recently put forward by Mallory for Copan (Mallory 1986), albeit he was largely concerned with the site's obsidian industry.

However, we differ from Mallory in our approach to the causes for this seeming lack of specialized production at the site. If we understand his approach correctly, Mallory believes that this lack of specialization typifies Maya economy in general, regardless of site size, complexity, or surrounding environment. For example, when confronted with the evidence for specialized chert tool production at the Belizian site of Colha, Mallory stated:

I believe the actual differences in the organization and scale of lithic production at Colha and Copan

may be in the techniques and concepts employed in the analysis, rather than in the data, or, ultimately in the prehistoric economies at the two sites (Mallory 1986:152).

Based upon our evaluation of this small chert assemblage, we feel the economies of the two sites were indeed distinctive. The chert resources available within the Copan area, characterized by small nodule size and ubiquitous flaws, would simply not support the demand placed upon them by an intensive production system. In fact it seems clear that chert resources in the Copan area were unable to support even domestic demands at the site. Other workers have noted that obsidian was much more common than were the local cherts in all deposits at Copan (Mallory 1986), even though its primary source (Ixtepeque) was some 90 km distant. Thus, it appears likely that imported obsidian was needed, at least partially, as a supplemental material for tool manufacture, and that it probably functionally replaced chert tools in a number of tasks.

Viewed from this perspective, the unspecialized nature of Copan chert production simply reflects conditions of resource quality and availability, just as the Colha workshops demonstrate a socioeconomic response to the incredible abundance of high-quality cherts present at that site. We believe it is unproductive to view Maya economics, or any other cultural subsystem, as a monolithic entity in space or time. Because economic systems are dynamic, and responsive to local resource situations, we would be very much surprised to see similar modes of labor organization and lithic production at the two sites. Maya settlement spanned a cross section of environments, and we should not be surprised to see differing cultural responses to these.

Until we have a larger sample from the site, or more is published from existing Copan chert collections, our thinking will remain somewhat speculative regarding the relationship between this important pre-Columbian resource and the Copan economic system. We hope the present study demonstrates the utility of even modest lithic collections in understanding ancient Maya economies.

CHIPPED STONE (OBSIDIAN)

by Fred Valdez

Wastage		1,989
Chunks	190	
Flake Fragments	993	
Flakes	739	
Utilized Flakes	67	
Unifacial Artifacts		3,797
Prismatic Blades	3,626	
Macroblades	132	
Scrapers	22	
Pointed Blades	4	
Ridge Flakes	9	
Triangular Blades	3	
Burin Spall-like Artifact	1	
Bifacial Artifacts		84
Arrow Points (Single Side-Notched)	3	
Dart Points		
(Broad Tapered Stem, Short Blade)	7	
Large Biface Fragments		
(Straight Stem, Long Blade)	26	
Eccentric	1	
Prismatic Cores	38	
Flake Cores	2	
Core Tablets	7	
Battered Pieces		31
Drills		1

The Copan obsidian assemblage far exceeds in quantity and quality the recovered chert material. Presented in this section is the result of a technological study of the obsidian. Included here is a description of the obsidian artifacts, which can facilitate interregional comparative analyses (cf. Willey et al. 1965; Sheets 1972, 1978; Willey 1972, 1978; Hester 1975; Hester, Jack, and Selzer 1978; Clark and Lee 1979; Fowler 1981; Valdez 1986).

Part of this study was to review all diagnostics for use-wear characteristics. The obsidian prismatic blades, unifaces (e.g., scrapers), and all bifaces were checked for types of wear and implications of use. The interpretation of obsidian artifact function remains difficult to finalize, although general use can be inferred. For example, certain types of activities can be postulated to include heavy or hard actions such as chopping. However, to identify the actual cause of the use-wear patterns is often complicated. That is, to claim that damage resulted from a chopping activity on a hard surface may be a safe interpretation, but it is then nearly impossible to state that the damage resulted from chopping wood, bone, or having hit stone while digging.

Another objective of the obsidian study was to understand the occurrence of use-wear categories across time and space. This may be useful in determining activities of certain groups as well as in the general analysis of site function. This goal and the results of the study are presented in detail elsewhere (Leventhal, in prep.).

The practice of incorporating use-wear or edge damage studies in chipped stone analyses has progressed at a steady pace. Due to the increased number of studies concerned with determining tool function(s), an effort to compile the accumulated data for the determination of general use-wear trends in the Maya region may be necessitated.

Analysis: Methodology and Presentation

The first stage of analysis was the sorting of general lithic categories. This was accomplished by following traditional lithic groupings such as flakes, blades, unifaces, and bifaces. The more detailed analysis sorted the general classification into more specific morphological groups including arrow points, dart points, and large biface fragments as examples of more exact biface groups. Additionally, sorting based on macroscopic observations of wear allowed for compilation of certain groups. For example, the prismatic blades were sorted into seven categories of observed modification; and unifaces designated as scrapers were grouped according to retouch area. This system of analysis and formatting followed traditional studies as per the reports noted above.

The second stage of the analysis involved the use of a binocular microscope to check the microwear characteristics. All major tools and selected examples of blade use-wear categories were removed to the Center for Archaeological Research, the University of Texas at San Antonio, in the summer of 1981. At the center, all items for microscopic review were studied to verify use-wear categorization. Maximum magnification used was 80X, which proved useful in clarifying use-wear striations and minute edge alteration as seen in microflaking. This low-power magnification allowed the observation of altered and dulled areas, which added support to the macroscopically established use-wear categories.

The use of high-power magnification was not pursued in this study. The dichotomy in microwear studies has been between those using low-power magnification (relying on differences in edge damage patterns), and analysts using high-power magnification (looking at differences in polish appearance). The two schools of thought have been recently presented and reviewed elsewhere (e.g., Tringham et al. 1974; Hayden 1979, 1986; Keeley 1980: McGuire et al. 1982; Bamforth 1986; Siegel 1986).

The descriptive format for the obsidian collection presents the general artifact category (i.e., wastage, unifacial artifacts, and bifacial artifacts) followed by the artifact type (e.g., flakes, macroblades, etc.). Artifacts from the different excavation areas of the Harvard Copan Project (i.e., CV-16, CV-20, CV-43, Santa Rita, and test pits) are incorporated into the descriptive format, keeping area provenience clear. Where available, descriptive statements and measurements are provided for each artifact type.

The Harvard Copan Project Collection

The collection of chipped obsidian artifacts from the Harvard Copan Project as categorized in this analysis numbers over 5,900 pieces. Prismatic blades and blade fragments compose 63 percent of the collection. Scrap or wastage (flake fragments, chunks, etc.) account for 34 percent of the analyzed lot. More formal artifacts, such as bifaces, scrapers, and the like, represent slightly more than 2 percent of the assemblage. Cores form the balance of the obsidian collection at just over 1 percent of the analyzed artifacts.

Specific artifact numbers are provided for each category and excavation area in the descriptions that follow. Measured dimensions are given for maximum lengths, widths, and thicknesses where applicable. Minimum to maximum dimensions are provided when presenting a range for the given artifact type. Proximal fragments of prismatic blades were checked for platform type and platform preparation. More than 85 percent of those viewed were simple platforms with light striations or pecking on the striking surface. Donald E. Crabtree (1968) and Thomas Hester et al. (1978) discuss in detail the technological procedures concerning platform preparation. About 15 percent of the prismatic blade platforms have pointed platforms, and slightly more than 5 percent are represented by multifaceted or crushed platforms. The pointed platforms of the prismatic blades are often formed from careful overhang removals, whereas the crushed platforms may be related to careless or rapid overhang removals (cf. Sheets 1978:11–14).

Typological, Technological, and Use-Wear Descriptions

Specific artifact types have been placed into one of three major categories: (1) wastage; (2) unifacial artifacts; or (3) bifacial artifacts. Each category includes both unmodified and retouched specimens. The representative sample from each excavation area is provided within category and type. A general review of the microwear patterns observed for the entire collection is provided in a later section. Temporal and spatial distributions of specific wear patterns are covered in another study (Leventhal, in prep.).

Wastage

The wastage category, sometimes referred to as scrap or debitage, comprises material that is generally the result of tool manufacture. Discarded flake fragments and chunks make up the largest part of this grouping. There are 1,989 pieces of obsidian in this category, accounting for 36 percent of the total chipped glass collection. The artifacts in this category were not examined under magnification. Table 5 provides a breakdown of the wastage classification by artifact type and excavation area.

Chunks: Chunks are small blocky fragments of obsidian that lack platforms or bulbs of percussion. Of the entire collection, 190 specimens were classified as chunks, representing 9.7 percent of the debitage. Specific distributions of chunks by excavation area is as follows: CV-16 has 15 chunks, representing 7.89 percent of this category; CV-20 with 96 chunks, accounts for 50.53 percent of this artifact type; CV-43 has 38.42 percent of the chunks with 73 specimens; Santa Rita produced 2 chunks (1.05 percent); and the

test pits resulted in 4 specimens (2.11 percent). Eleven of the chunks from CV-20 were noted to have use-wear along one edge. This wear ranged from simple edge retouch to heavy battering/crushing. No other specimens were observed to have modified edges.

Flake Fragments: These are obsidian fragments, usually thin, with evident percussion rings on the ventral surface. However, all lack platforms and bulbs of percussion. Flake fragments number 993 and represent 49.9 percent of the wastage group. Flake fragments recovered per excavation area follows: CV-16, 106 specimens (10.67 percent of

TABLE 5

Counts and distribution of obsidian debitage

Artifact	CV-16	CV-20	CV-43	Santa Rita	Test Pits	Total
Chunks						
A	7.89%	50.53%	38.42%	1.05%	2.11%	
B	15	96	73	2	4	190
C	8.6%	9.5%	9.9%	20.0%	6.9%	
Flake Fragments						
A	10.67%	57.70%	27.29%	.40%	3.93%	
B	106	573	271	4	39	993
C	60.9%	56.7%	36.7%	40.0%	67.2%	
Flakes						
A	6.36%	41.95%	49.39%	.27%	2.03%	
B	47	310	365	2	15	739
C	27.0%	30.7%	49.5%	20.0%	25.8%	
Utilized Flakes						
A	8.96%	46.27%	41.79%	2.99%	0	
B	6	31	28	2	0	67
C	3.4%	3.1%	3.8%	20.0%	0	
Total:						
Number	174	1,010	737	10	58	1,989
% by site	8.75	50.78	37.05	.50	2.92	

KEY:
A   Percentage of artifact type
B   Number of artifact type
C   Percentage of artifact type at site

flake fragments); CV-20, 573 (57.70 percent); CV-43, 271 (27.29 percent); Santa Rita, 4 (.40 percent); and test pits, 39 (3.93 percent).

Flakes: All artifacts classified as flakes must have observable platforms and bulbs of percussion. The count of flakes is 739, representing nearly 37 percent of artifacts in this classification. Of the 739 flakes, 4 may be categorized as biface thinning flakes and 2 as scraper rejuvenation flakes. Hester et al. (1978) and Shafer (1970) provide the descriptive characteristics of scraper rejuvenation flakes. The distribution of flakes is as follows: CV-16 has 47 flakes, 6.36 percent of the flake category; CV-20 has 310 flakes (41.95 percent); CV-43 contains 365 flakes (49.39 percent); Santa Rita produced only 2 flakes (0.27 percent); and the test pits recovered 15 flakes (2.03 percent).

Utilized Flakes: This artifact type is represented by 67 specimens or 3.4 percent of the wastage category. Each flake in this group displays some form of utilization. Most often the flake has the distal or a lateral edge showing minute flake removals. This modification is believed to be associated with some soft or mild work such as slicing or cutting of feathers, fabric, and so on. Six of the utilized flakes were recovered from CV-16 (representing 8.96 percent of the utilized flake category). CV-20 produced 31 specimens (46.27 percent). CV-43 has 28 utilized flakes (41.79 percent). Santa Rita is represented by two utilized flakes (2.99 percent). No utilized flakes were identified from the test pits.

Comments: Except for the utilized flakes category, no artifact group under wastage exhibits any use-wear markings. The evident use-wear noted for the utilized flakes, as has been stated, derives from soft or light use. There is no apparent edge fracturing or steep modification to the flake edges. All wear is in the form of minute and patterned modification.

Unifacial Artifacts

Unifacial artifacts are those that have either the dorsal or ventral side modified, but not both on the same artifact. Most often this modification

occurs as the result of intentional retouch. At times, however, altered edges may result directly from use. Included in this category are artifacts that may not be altered, but are traditionally classified as unifaces. Prismatic blades, macroblades, scrapers, pointed blades, triangular fragments, a burin-like artifact, and ridge flakes have been grouped under the unifacial artifacts category. These seven groups account for 3,809 artifacts and 97 percent of the total obsidian artifact collection.

Each of the seven categories noted above will be defined. The occurrence of each uniface type will be discussed according to individual plaza excavation and then compared to the entire collection.

Prismatic Blades: Prismatic blades are parallel-edged flakes usually exhibiting one or two dorsal ridges. The blades are at least twice as long as they are wide and removed from specially prepared cores (Oakley 1964; Honea 1965; Crabtree 1968; Hester 1972; Fowler 1981). Prismatic blades in the Copan collection number 3,626 specimens, representing 95 percent of the unifacial artifacts and 93 percent of all obsidian artifacts.

More than 99 percent of the obsidian blades recovered in the Harvard Copan Project are in proximal, medial, and distal fragments. Most (2,176) of the blade segments and complete blades have been sorted into seven use-wear categories (see fig. 220a–f). This categorization was applied to samples from CV-16, CV-20, CV-43, and test pits, and is summarized in tables 6 through 13. These categories were established by Hester (1975) in his study of the obsidian indus-

TABLE 6
CV-16 prismatic blades: range of measurements (cm)*

	Proximal	Medial	Distal
Length	1.64–7.32	1.44–6.97	2.04–6.89
Width	0.92–2.46	0.79–2.21	0.81–2.18
Thickness	0.23–0.61	0.21–0.71	0.19–0.57

*No whole specimens were found at CV-16.

TABLE 7

CV-16 prismatic blades: distribution of fragments per edge-wear category

Edge-Wear Type	Proximal	Medial	Distal	Total
1	12	23	4	39
2	3	16	1	20
3	3	3	1	7
4	1	0	0	1
5	4	6	0	10
6	5	6	0	11
7	1	2	0\	3
Total	29	56	6	91

try of Beleh, Guatemala, and utilized by Valdez (1986) for the obsidian assemblage of Santa Leticia, El Salvador. This study uses the terms "use-wear" and "edge-wear" interchangeably. Definitions of the various edge-wear categories are in order before proceeding. The use-wear types are as follows:

1. *Nicking* or miscellaneous wear. Edge damage in this category may result from use, depositional activities, or recent actions including excavation, transportation, and storage. While edge modification is apparent, the cause of the edge damage remains uncertain. One thousand ninety specimens are in this use-wear group.
2. *Dorsal trimming* is observable modification on the dorsal side of the blade. This type of edge-wear is probably the result of much use and is discussed further below. Five hundred twenty-six blades compose the dorsal trimmed group.
3. *Ventral trimming* or edge modification to the ventral face of the blade was identified on 155 specimens. As with dorsal trimming, this is considered intentional use-wear.
4. *Fracturing* of the blade edge is represented by 84 pieces. This type of wear most likely results from some hard activity including the cutting of bone and the incising of stone.
5. *Notching* or concave trimming is an intentional modification as detailed in the removal

of minute flakes from one or both lateral edges of the blade resulting in a clear notch. There are 243 blades categorized with concave trimming or notching.
6. *Miscellaneous patterned wear* is represented by 57 blades. This category has a segment or two of continuous minute flake removals. The use-wear in this group undoubtedly results from activity such as slicing and cutting. The wear is much more distinct than the nicking category. Most blades in this group display patterned wear on the dorsal side.
7. *No wear* is the final category. Only 21 blades have been placed in this group. These are blades that show no edge modification.

Obsidian blade totals and use-wear counts will now be presented for each site and collection category. All measurements are provided in centimeters and as a range unless otherwise noted. The number of blades used for edge-wear categorization is provided where applicable.

CV-16. A total of 131 obsidian blade fragments were recovered from CV-16. Ninety-one specimens were analyzed into use-wear types. The categories of proximal, medial, and distal fragments are provided in table 6 with their applicable range of measurements. The breakdown of use-wear distribution between the three fragments designations is provided in table 7. In nearly 84 percent of the proximal fragments, the blade platform was of the simple preparation type. More than 87 percent showed platform overhang (or platform lip) removals.

CV-20. Obsidian blades and blade fragments from CV-20 numbered 1,669. Categorized into edge-wear types were 1,236 pieces. Tables 8 and 9 provide the various measurements and distributions of the artifacts. Platform preparations for the CV-20 collection are described as simple, and most platform lips had been altered in preparation for the blade removal.

One medial fragment displayed grinding or pecking of the dorsal ridge area. This appears to have resulted from the need to correct a failure in the attempted removal of the previous blade. Often an error in lithic technology will require a section or ridge of the core to be modified, as with pecking and grinding, to ensure the next

TABLE 8

CV-20 prismatic blades: range of measurements (cm)

	Proximal	Medial	Distal	Whole
Length	1.62–7.42	1.37–7.02	2.02–6.96	4.10–9.63
Width	0.95–1.95	0.72–1.94	0.71–1.75	1.14–1.91
Thickness	0.25–0.60	0.23–0.55	0.23–0.51*	0.20–0.60

*Two specimens are much thicker than the provided range and are listed here separately at 0.69 and 0.77 cm.

TABLE 9

CV-20 prismatic blades: distribution of fragments per edge-wear category

Edge-Wear Type	Proximal	Medial	Distal	Whole	Total
1	159	417	24	1	601
2	76	196	12	1	285
3	23	67	2	0	92
4	15	41	1	0	57
5	46	111	6	1	164
6	5	12	0	0	17
7	2	16	0	2	20
Total	326	860	45	5	1,236

blade removal will follow in proper form. The one medial fragment is the only such specimen noted for CV-20.

CV-43. Harvard Copan Project site 43 produced 1,517 obsidian blades and blade fragments. Of these, 851 have been placed into the seven categories of use-wear. Tables 10 and 11 provide the CV-43 measurements and distributional data.

Observations concerning platform preparation and platform overhang modification follow closely to that noted for CV-20.

Test Pits. The test pits produced 309 obsidian blades and fragments (7 are from the sacbe). Ninety have been placed into use-wear groups. Tables 12 and 13 provide all available measurements. The numbers presented here include seven

TABLE 10

CV- 43 prismatic blades: range of measurements (cm)

	Proximal	Medial	Distal	Whole
Length	1.52–7.78	1.46–6.97	1.89–6.94	3.94–9.71
Width	0.96–1.97	0.69–1.88	0.72–1.78	1.08–1.90
Thickness	0.22–0.64	0.23–0.56	0.20–0.53	0.21–0.62

TABLE 11

CV-43 prismatic blades: distribution of fragments per edge-wear category

Edge-Wear Type	Proximal	Medial	Distal	Whole	Total
1	262	153	35	0	450
2	80	113	23	5	221
3	29	25	2	0	56
4	12	13	0	1	26
5	30	34	5	0	69
6	11	12	5	1	29
7	0	0	0	0	0
Total	424	350	70	7	851

blade fragments from an area designated Santa Rita. The Santa Rita specimens were all medial fragments with Type 1 edge-wear.

Special Finds. This category is for blades from special contexts and most often represents cache items. These are not placed into use-wear groupings because most do not exhibit any use-wear. Table 14 provides all measurements for the blades. Catalog number designations have been kept to show the blades' groups as excavated.

Summary: Prismatic Blades. Prismatic blades recovered in the Harvard Copan Project numbered more than 3,600 specimens. Most (2,176) have been analyzed into edge-wear categories. Ninety-nine percent of the blades show some form of edge damage. More than half (1,090) of

the categorized blades were found to have nicking or Type 1 use-wear. Type 2, dorsal trimming use-wear, numbers over 500 specimens or 24 percent of the categorized blades. Eleven percent were placed in the Type 5 group with notching. More than 7 percent have ventral trimming (Type 3); nearly 4 percent (84 specimens) have Type 4 fracturing; and 2.6 percent (57 blades) show Type 6 miscellaneous patterned wear. Less than 1 percent (21 pieces) show no detectable wear.

It is clear that the obsidian blade at Copan was a major tool. The activities associated with obsidian blade use, given the wear types, seems

TABLE 12

Test pit prismatic blades: range of measurements (cm)*

	Proximal	Medial	Distal
Length	1.59–6.89	1.40–6.88	2.01–6.92
Width	1.17–2.41	0.85–1.80	0.90–1.65
Thickness	0.21–0.59	0.25–0.58	0.27–0.35

*No whole specimens

TABLE 13

Test pit prismatic blades: distribution of fragments per edge-wear category

Edge-Wear Type	Proximal	Medial	Distal	Total
1	19	21	9	49
2	7	9	2	18
3	0	2	0	2
4	0	0	0	0
5	3	5	1	9
6	4	6	2	12
7	?	?	?	?
Total	33	43	14	90

TABLE 14
Special finds: prismatic blade measurements (cm)

Catalog No.	Blade Form	Length	Width	Thickness	Comment*
1-11	proximal	1.73	1.43	0.36	1
1-11	proximal	3.10	1.39	0.31	
1-11	proximal	4.71	1.28	0.34	
1-11	proximal	4.18	1.24	0.30	
1-11	proximal	4.96	1.26	0.33	
1-11	proximal	5.63	1.22	0.38	
1-11	proximal	8.07	1.38	0.36	
1-11	medial	2.88	1.70	0.43	2
1-11	medial	1.50	1.28	0.24	
1-11	medial	1.80	1.26	0.22	
1-11	medial	1.32	0.92	0.21	
1-11	medial	1.60	1.21	0.18	
1-11	distal	1.72	0.89	0.33	
1-11	distal	1.39	0.83	0.23	
1-11	distal	1.61	1.07	0.23	
1-11	distal	2.73	1.29	0.29	
1-11	distal	3.33	1.13	0.30	
1-11	distal	2.82	0.76	0.21	
1-11	distal	6.83	1.26	0.34	
1-11	distal	5.49	1.14	0.26	
1-11	distal	6.10	1.29	0.34	
1-11	distal	7.12	1.24	0.30	
1-11	distal	10.50	1.17	0.30	
1-11	distal	11.66	1.23	0.31	
1-11	complete	9.23	0.82	0.24	
1-11	complete	10.03	1.44	0.31	
1-250	proximal	7.33	1.27	0.33	3
1-250	proximal	3.86	1.11	0.29	
1-250	proximal	4.82	1.15	0.36	
1-250	medial	2.15	1.80	0.30	4
1-250	medial	4.33	1.37	0.33	
1-250	distal	5.86	1.12	0.36	
1-250	complete	10.50	1.16	0.34	
1-250	complete	10.81	1.43	0.36	
1-513	proximal	4.96	1.14	0.32	
1-513	proximal	5.98	1.14	0.24	
1-513	proximal	4.82	1.29	0.27	
1-513	proximal	3.68	1.23	0.36	
1-513	medial	3.06	1.26	0.37	
1-513	medial	3.28	1.11	0.33	
1-513	medial	2.02	1.22	0.25	
1-513	medial	2.00	0.93	0.20	
1-513	distal	5.33	1.27	0.20	
1-513	distal	2.09	0.81	0.16	
1-589	complete	10.17	1.44	0.35	
1-669	proximal	3.64	1.89	0.26	

TABLE 14 (*continued*)

Special finds: prismatic blade measurements (cm)

Catalog No.	Blade Form	Length	Width	Thickness	Comment*
1-669	proximal	3.05	1.15	0.37	
1-669	complete	12.55	1.75	0.31	
1-669	complete	11.43	1.73	0.31	
1-669	complete	13.16	1.61	0.46	
1-669	complete	12.34	1.62	0.44	
1-669	complete	11.14	1.74	0.38	
1-669	complete	10.98	1.74	0.45	
1-669	complete	11.37	1.68	0.42	
1-684	proximal	2.97	1.47	0.36	
1-684	proximal	3.43	1.51	0.33	
1-684	proximal	2.23	1.47	0.35	
1-684	medial	2.67	1.20	0.31	5
1-684	distal	2.97	(1.24)	0.28	6
1-684	complete	8.84	1.45	0.27	
1-684	complete	8.80	1.37	0.29	
1-684	complete	9.28	1.39	0.30	
1-685	proximal	4.99	0.89	0.29	
1-685	medial	1.18	1.27	0.26	
1-685	complete	8.92	1.20	0.34	
1-685	complete	8.74	1.14	0.33	
1-685	complete	7.62	1.24	0.32	
1-685	complete	6.78	1.44	0.18	
1-685	complete	7.89	1.35	0.22	
1-685	complete	6.06	1.33	0.24	
1-805	proximal	4.93	1.29	0.33	
1-805	proximal	8.78	1.51	0.43	
1-805	proximal	3.52	1.70	0.29	
1-805	medial	4.39	1.62	0.36	7
1-805	medial	1.06	1.02	0.24	
1-805	distal	3.55	1.35	0.31	8
1-805	distal	6.10	1.48	0.27	
1-805	splinter	1.94	n/a	0.18	9

*Comments—Special Finds:

1. One of the proximal fragments from Cat. No. 1-11 shows edge-wear attributable to Type 5. The specimen has two small notches along one lateral side. Both notches were formed by the removal of minute flakes.
2. Of the five medial fragments from Cat. No. 1-11, three have minor edge modification relating to Type 1 use-wear. One of the three specimens has end modification in the form of beveling. This beveling has produced, in morphological and technological terms, an artifact that could be described as an end scraper. However, it is of minute size, and function was not determined for the blade fragment.
3. One proximal fragment, from Cat. No. 1-250, has edge modification along a distal, lateral edge. The wear form is attributable to Type 6 and almost forms a notch, thus bringing it close to the Type 5 edge-wear.
4. The medial fragments from Cat. No. 1-250 are both of the Type 1 edge-wear with nicking along one lateral edge.
5. Five other medial fragments were noted for Cat. No. 1-684. However, these were fragmented to the extent that no accurate measurements were possible. All seem to be medial fragments, and each is fractured rather oddly, making edge-wear designation questionable. Therefore, no attempt was made to measure or categorize these specimens.
6. A distal fragment from Cat. No. 1-684 has edge fracturing. This specimen has been assigned to the Type 4 edge-wear. The width measurement provided for this fragment is presented in parentheses, indicating an approximation of the dimension.
7. Two of the medial fragments from Cat. No. 1-805 are too fractured for measurement. These were omitted from the table of measurements for reasons similar to those noted in comment 5.
8. A distal fragment from Cat. No. 1-805 has Type 3 edge-wear. The lateral edge exhibits modification from use, as seen in the removal of minute flakes, for an edge length of 1.3 cm.
9. An obsidian splinter from Cat. No. 1-805 has been placed in the prismatic blade section, and its measurements are provided. It appears to be a sliver from a prismatic blade edge. No use was observed on the piece. It measured 1.94 cm long and 0.18 cm for its thickness. Width was not determined due to its form.

quite varied. These include minor slicing and cutting of soft material (e.g., plants, cloth) to the working of hard substances including bone, shell, and stone.

Included in the use-wear observations were specimens showing bidirectional striations along the lateral edges that may be associated with some sawing motion. The minute flakes along lateral edges that form the nicking and various trimming categories most often are feather terminations rather than edge crushing or step-fracturing. This may result from intentional resharpening or from unidirectional stroking. Fowler (1981) has associated notching with shaft straightening and notes this artifact type as a spokeshave. However, some notched specimens from Copan have notches that are very small and appear intentionally formed to serve in a hafting capacity.

The Copan obsidian blade industry served a wide range of functions. This is supported by the edge-wear types present in the collection. Exact functions are difficult to determine because many may have been used in several different activities to produce similar edge damage. Some of the categories may result from combined activities (e.g., in the edge fracturing group, since we no longer are able to see the damaged or cutting edge, it is difficult to determine whether this artifact served in a soft function before being relegated to the hard activity). Given the number of blades compared to the number of other tools, the obsidian blade seems to have provided much of the required cutting and slicing. The obsidian blade undoubtedly served as the all-purpose tool for the ancient Maya at Copan.

Macroblades: Macroblades are technologically similar to the prismatic blades in general form. Both are generally at least twice as long as they are wide. The major differences are in size (macroblades are usually much larger) and in mode of production. Macroblades are produced by percussion and maintain several attributes including large platforms, clear bulbs of force, and compression rings. Table 15 provides a composite of all analyzed macroblades and available measurements. We made some distinction in this study between medium-sized macroblades and large macroblades, since the grade in the Copan collections shows some distinction between the two as analyzed for CV-20.

CV-16. A total of 16 macroblades were recovered from this group. Four are complete specimens. One of the four is irregular in shape; it is not as parallel-sided as most obsidian blades. Proximal and distal fragments are represented at CV-16 by two pieces of each. Medial fragments number eight. No distinctive wear or edge alteration was noted for the CV-16 sample, aside from minor nicking. This modification may have resulted from natural causes or post-depositional activity.

CV-20. Macroblades excavated at CV-20 totaled 37. Five specimens are complete; 13 are proximal fragments; 14 are medial fragments; and 5 are distal portions. Placed into the large macroblade category were one medial and two distal fragments. The large macroblades were found only within the CV-20 excavations. The maximum measurements for the three fragments are 9.46 x 6.2 x 2.04 (length x width x thickness). The medium-sized macroblades tend to have "pointed" ends that formed naturally as they were removed from the core. The larger-sized specimens are fragments that do not show termination features. Most of the macroblades show some form of edge alteration (i.e., minute chipping). However, the nature of the modification may relate to natural causes as opposed to use-wear alterations. None of the medium-sized specimens shows any special edge modification indicating use. One of the large-sized blades has extensive edge damage both laterally and at the distal surfaces. This edge-wear is primarily in the form of large step fracturing caused by heavy chopping activities. The mass of this blade type may also serve as an indication for possible uses.

CV-43. The macroblades from CV-43 are all of the medium-sized category. Seventy-three specimens of this type have been identified in the collection. Five are whole or complete blades; 13 are proximal fragments; 48 are medial sections; and 7 are identified as distal portions. Unlike the CV-20 macroblades, all of the CV-43 specimens show some form of edge modification. These worked edges display step fractures, minute flake removals, or other alterations indicative of use-wear. On one specimen, both lateral edges were retouched to the tip, producing a beveled scraper-like tool (see fig. 221).

Test Pits. Only three macroblade fragments were recovered from these excavations. Two of the specimens are medial fragments and the other is a distal section. No obvious use-wear was noted for the three artifacts.

Summary: Macroblades. Macroblades and macroblade fragments from all excavations numbered 129. Three, all from CV-20, have been classified as large macroblades, while the rest of the collection is medium macroblades. One of the large specimens showed extensive use-wear most likely associated with chopping activities. The edge damage is in the form of step fracturing caused by sharp, hard blows. The size and mass of the large macroblade section would lend itself to axe-like usage.

All of the CV-43 specimens show some edge modification. The use-wear includes flake removals and step fracturing. The flake removals, more regular than occurs in nicking, may have resulted from general use including slicing and cutting. The wear probably resulted from several activities in the processing of raw materials including, for example, plants, meat, or hides (skins). The step fracturing was caused by more edge-damaging activity such as the cutting or shaping of hard substances like bone or wood. The macroblade edge-wear was caused from combined uses and not from a singular activity.

CV-16 with 16 macroblades (12 percent), CV-40 with 37 (29 percent), and CV-43 with 73 specimens (55 percent) show an increase in macroblade occurrence that may correlate

TABLE 15

Macroblades: range of measurements (cm)

CV/Dimension	Proximal	Medial	Distal	Complete
CV-16				
Length	2.30–4.30	2.33–4.87	5.33–5.71	4.00–5.48
Width	2.90–2.94	2.14–2.98	2.84–2.94	2.02–2.88
Thickness	0.55–0.91	0.61–0.94	0.71–0.76	0.63–0.86
No. of Blades	2	8	2	4
CV-20				
Length	2.26–5.02	2.31–4.91	4.88–5.56	3.87–6.16
Width	2.10–3.94*	2.61–2.90	2.35–2.75	2.23–2.87
Thickness	0.35–1.49	0.50–1.21	0.40–0.72	0.33–0.77
No. of Blades	13	14	5	5
CV-43				
Length	3.47–6.32	1.75–5.16	3.09–6.41	5.05–8.60
Width	2.46–4.00	2.30–3.84	2.54–4.24	2.60–4.38
Thickness	0.69–1.28	0.61–1.23	0.73–1.53	0.55–1.39
No. of Blades	13	48	7	5
Test Pits				
Length	n/a	3.23–4.39	5.39	n/a
Width	n/a	2.34–3.41	2.50	n/a
Thickness	n/a	0.71–0.92	0.84	n/a
No. of Blades	0	2	1	0

*One specimen is irregularly shaped at the distal end. The width dimension for this specimen is 4.15 cm.

with group size. The larger structural groups, perhaps with larger populations, may have required more macroblades for household activities. Interesting and unanswered questions remain. First, why do the macroblade specimens showing use-wear occur only at CV-43? Second, why are the large macroblades found only at the CV-20 group?

Scrapers: The definitions of the scraper tool type and probable function(s) have been discussed elsewhere (Hester 1972, 1978; Hester, Jack, and Heizer 1978; Sheets 1978; Fowler 1981). I have studied the Copan specimens for use-wear attributes and feel confident in their placement.

Twenty-two obsidian artifacts have been identified as scrapers or scraper fragments. Interestingly, all of the scrapers come from CV-20. Fourteen of the scrapers are complete or nearly complete artifacts. Nine of the specimens are identified as end scrapers, four as ovoid scrapers, and one as a circular specimen. The circular scraper is made on a flake, whereas the end and ovate scrapers are all made on macroblades. Figure 222a–c illustrates the three scraper forms. The remaining eight scrapers are too fragmented to determine form, size, or original artifact shape (i.e., flake or macroblade). Table 16 provides the maximum metric measurements for the 14 definable scrapers.

Summary: Scrapers. All identified scrapers were recovered from CV-20. Fourteen of the 22 specimens were typed by scraper form. The circular scraper had been modified and used on all

edges. Some undercutting or nibbling was noted along two lengths of 2.6 cm and 3.2 cm. The ovoid specimens showed beveling along distal and lateral edges. One of the ovoid form scrapers shows beveling along the distal edge as well as the left lateral segment of the dorsal surface. This specimen could be categorized as an end-and-side scraper, but maintains an ovoid form. The end scrapers have beveled edges on the distal portion only. Eleven of the 14 specimens showed ventral scratching extending from the bitt end toward the proximal/platform end. This scratching occurs only on the ventral side and may be associated with planing activity.

Scrapers of the types found at Copan have been identified in other collections both of obsidian tools (cf. Sheets 1978; Fowler 1981) and chert (Willey et al. 1965). The use of the term "scraper," with its functional implications, does seem to be an appropriate designation given the types of use-wear identified with scraping or planing actions. The importance, if any, of producing scrapers on flakes or blades has not been determined. A large collection of scrapers may show a direct relationship between scraper form and original material (i.e., flake or macroblade).

Pointed Blades: Four pointed blades were recovered in the Copan Valley excavations. One specimen is from CV-20; the remaining three come from CV-43. Pointed blades are prismatic blade segments that are intentionally shaped at one end to a point. Figure 223a–b illustrates these speci-

TABLE 16
CV-20 scrapers: maximum measurements (cm)

Type	No.	L	W	TH	BL A	BIT A
End	9	6.30	5.61	2.24	84	81
Ovoid*	4	4.22	3.96	1.20	86	80
Circular	1	4.32	4.82	2.20	86	76

*One of the ovoid scrapers was fragmented; length and blade angle could not be determined for maximum measurement consideration. In addition, one of the ovoid specimens could be best categorized as an end-and-side scraper, but was maintained in the ovoid classification.

mens, and table 17 provides the measured dimensions.

Summary: Pointed Blades. All four pointed blades were made on snapped segments of prismatic blades. Similar artifacts are known from other Maya sites (cf. Sheets 1978; Fowler 1981). The edge modification on these specimens is not characteristic of drills or awls. No distinctive use-wear was observed for the pointed artifacts. The CV-20 specimen, as noted above, had alternate trimming, giving a twist effect to the blade's pointed end.

Ridge Flakes: Ridge flakes are specialized artifacts formed when preparing a core for the removal of blades. The ridge flake serves as a guide to the first blade removal from the core and sets the structure for subsequent blade removals. Ridge flakes are more extensively defined elsewhere (Sanger 1968; Hester, Jack, and Heizer 1978). Nine specimens in the Copan collection have been classified as ridge flakes. Table 18 provides the range of dimensions for this artifact type. Figure 224a–b illustrates several examples.

Summary: Ridge Flakes. Nine ridge flakes have been identified. Five are from CV-20; four are from CV-43. Two of the CV-20 specimens were removed in the preparation of macroblade cores. No evidence of use-wear is associated with these artifacts, and none was expected. The observed modification is limited to a row of small flakes removed along the proximal to distal line, forming the ridge required in subsequent blade removals.

Triangular Blades: Three triangular blade fragments are in the Copan obsidian collection. All three specimens come from CV-20. These are obsidian artifacts that resemble prismatic blades except that the dorsal ridge is relatively high, producing very thick specimens. The cross section is triangular in form, inspiring the descriptive designation of triangular blade. One of the pieces has a lateral edge with some use-wear in the form of battering. The cause of this type of wear is uncertain. No other information was gathered for these specimens.

Burin Spall-like Artifact: One specimen resembling a burin spall was noted in the collection. The artifact is 3.82 cm long, 0.45 cm wide, and 0.34 cm thick. It appears to have been removed from the edge of a core since it does have three small frontal facets. It does not show any use-wear, and its designation of burin spall-like is intended as a descriptive effort and not as a functional implication.

Bifacial Artifacts

Bifaces are those artifacts that have been worked on two or more surfaces. Included in this category are cores that are multifaceted. The specific artifact groups under bifaces are arrow points, dart points, large biface fragments, eccentrics,

TABLE 17

Pointed blades: maximum measurements (cm)

CV	Length	Width	Thickness
20*	3.11	1.82	0.32
43	4.36	1.29	0.32
43	2.83	1.31	0.34
43	2.38	1.38	0.34

*This specimen has edge modification on one dorsal and one ventral edge, creating a twist effect to the pointed blade.

TABLE 18

Ridge flakes: maximum measurements (cm)

CV	Length	Width	Thickness
20	3.88	1.21	0.80
20	3.92	1.23	0.79
20	4.08	1.30	0.80
20*	2.04	3.14	1.76
20*	4.04	3.92	1.35
43	1.62	1.28	0.82
43	3.98	1.23	0.79
43	4.11	1.17	0.77
43	4.18	1.18	0.77

*These ridge flakes are much wider and thicker; probably removed from macroblade cores.

prismatic cores, flake cores, core tablets, battered pieces, and drills.

Each group will be briefly described, and measurements will be provided in textual discussion or table form. Eighty-four artifacts have been sorted into the nine biface groups listed above. Bifacial artifacts account for slightly more than 2 percent of the obsidian collection.

Arrow Points: Three arrow points were identified in the obsidian collection. This figures to 2.5 percent of the bifacial artifacts. The arrow points in this collection are all made on prismatic blades. They are of a size to have functioned as true projectiles. Each is discussed below according to site designation.

CV-43. Two of the three arrow points come from CV-43. One is a notched specimen, and the other is a distally shaped point. The shaping of the points was accomplished through the intentional removal of small flakes. This was achieved through pressure flaking. Table 19 provides measurements of all arrow points in the collection. Figure 225a–b illustrates the arrow points. No special notice was made of use-wear characteristics.

Special Finds. One arrow point was cataloged under special finds. It is a side-notched specimen made from a prismatic blade. See table 14 for dimensions and table 14, note 1 for form.

Summary: Arrow Points. The three arrow points described are similar in technology. Each has been briefly described, and all measurements are provided in table 19. All were made from prismatic blades and probably served in a projectile

capacity. No use-wear differentiation was observed on any of the specimens.

Dart Points: Dart points are heavier and larger than arrow points. For most dart points in the Copan collection it is difficult to determine whether the points were made from blades or flakes. However, given their size, they were most likely made from flakes. A total of seven (5.9 percent) recognizable dart points were recovered in the Copan excavations. Table 20 outlines available measurements, and figure 226a–b illustrates several of the dart points.

CV-20. Two of the seven points came from CV-20. Both are completely bifaced. No use-wear modifications were noted for the CV-20 dart points.

CV-43. Five dart points were excavated at CV-43. As seen in the CV-20 sample, all dart points were completely bifaced. One of the specimens is made of green obsidian. In form it is identical to a specimen from Tres Zapotes illustrated by Hester, Jack, and Heizer (1978: pl. 1). No distinctive use-wear alterations were observed, aside from possible impact fractures on three of the points and edge dulling on two of the specimens.

Summary: Dart Points. Seven dart points from the Copan excavations have been documented. Similar specimens have been identified in other

TABLE 19

Arrow points: maximum measurements (cm)

CV	Length	Width	Thickness
43*	1.67	1.40	0.27
43	2.85	1.35	0.25
Sp. Finds	3.04	1.35	0.38

*This is the unnotched specimen.

TABLE 20

Dart points: maximum measurements (cm)

CV	Length	Width	Thickness
20	5.14	2.78	0.79
20	4.87	2.91	0.88
43	5.02	3.63	0.92
43	4.43	2.15	0.64
43*	(5.32)	4.10	1.11
43	(3.42)	2.74	0.79
43†	(4.80)	2.99	0.78

*Figures in parentheses are estimates for fragmented points.

†This is the green obsidian dart point. The distal tip is missing and length is an approximation.

obsidian collections (cf. Sheets 1978; Fowler 1981). Use-wear comments for the dart points are limited to traditional interpretations including usage as points on the ends of long shafts, or perhaps with short handles and used as knives. In any case, the edge-wear on several dart points is minor dulling of the lateral edges probably resulting from use as a cutting or slicing instrument. Three of the points, all from CV-43, have impact fractures. The three points are approximated in length, and the observed fracturing has been attributed to impact stress.

The green obsidian dart point from CV-43 suggests some form of communication with Teotihuacan. The green obsidian source is located in central Mexico at Pachuca. Identical dart point forms to the CV-43 specimen are known from central Mexico (M. Spence, personal communication 1982). The exact nature of the green obsidian at Copan is not clear, but its presence makes certain the use of long-distance trade.

Large Biface Fragments: Twenty-six large biface fragments are in the obsidian collection, representing 22.2 percent of the bifacial artifacts. In all cases, these biface fragments are larger and heavier than dart points. Some of these are comparable to the chert laurel-leaf blades. No complete examples are in the collection. All large biface fragments come from CV-20 and CV-43 and are most likely made from large macroblades. Table 21 lists all measurements for these artifacts. Figure 227a–b illustrates several of the fragments.

CV-20. Six large biface fragments were recovered from CV-20. Three of the bifaces are medial sections. One has a burin scar along a lateral edge. Two specimens are ovate basal (proximal) fragments without other noticeable modification. The sixth fragment is also a basal section, but appears to have two ears or tangs. One of the tangs had broken and only a small remnant remains. This biface fragment was made on a blade, and only the lateral edges are bifaced. No use-wear aside from fragmentation was discerned.

CV-43. Twenty large biface fragments were excavated at CV-43. Four of the specimens are too fragmentary for measurements and are not included in table 21. These are edge fragments belonging to large bifaces, but are of little diagnostic value. Of the 16 remaining fragments, 3 are proximal; 4 medial; 7 are distal; and 2 are stems. One of the proximal segments is clearly a bifaced blade. As with CV-20, little can be interpreted concerning use-wear; however, several general observations are provided below as a commentary.

Summary: Large Biface Fragments. The large biface fragments recovered in the Copan excavations numbered 26, although 4 of the fragments are too small to provide any comparative value. The fragments comprise proximal, medial, and distal segments. Nearly 77 percent of these large bifaces were recovered from CV-43. Several of the specimens proved to have been produced on large blades. It seems likely that most large bifaces were produced from macroblades.

Use-wear observations are somewhat limited by the fragmentation of the artifacts. However, several comments concerning edge damage seem in order. Edge-wear is limited to two major forms: dulling and fracturing. The dulling may be associated with slicing similar to dart point usage. This type of wear is found on three distal and two medial fragments. The edge fracturing is found on two medial specimens. In one case, a burin-blow was struck to remove the lateral edge. Another form of fracturing is impact fracturing. How this occurs on the large bifaces is uncertain. These may be stress-snaps associated with heavy slicing or cutting activities and not true impact breaks. Little else can be positively stated for the cause of the observed edge-wear.

Eccentric: One obsidian artifact has been categorized as an eccentric. It was cataloged as a special find. This artifact is bifacial and L-shaped. It is not of any known functional shape and no use-wear could be observed. The long arm of the L measured a maximum of 4.76 cm as an outside measurement and 3.16 cm along the inside of the arm. The short arm measured 3.79 cm on the outside measure and 2.08 cm along the arm on the inside. The width of the long arm is 1.66 cm; the short arm, 1.50 cm; and at the central area (or bend), 2.11 cm. Thickness ranges from 0.65 cm at the short arm to 0.77 cm at the long arm to 0.90 cm at the center. The bifacial eccentric is illustrated in figure 228.

TABLE 21
Large biface fragments: maximum measurements (cm)

CV	Segment	Length	Width	Thickness
20	proximal	3.81	3.02	0.79
20	proximal	4.66	3.11	1.08
20	proximal	4.76	3.33	0.64
20	proximal?	5.10	3.83	0.83
20	medial	2.72	3.08	1.14
20	medial	4.44	4.12	0.94
43	proximal	6.92	3.15	1.20
43	proximal	2.22	3.01	0.69
43	proximal	3.21	2.41	1.21
43	medial	3.24	2.41	1.19
43	medial	4.77	3.11	1.20
43	medial	5.48	4.73	1.32
43	medial	5.93	4.86	1.20
43	distal	3.37	1.86	0.73
43	distal	2.06	3.20	0.68
43	distal	2.85	2.64	0.92
43	distal	3.59	2.85	0.70
43	distal	3.92	2.44	0.92
43	distal	6.17	4.07	1.06
43	distal	7.03	3.66	1.31
43	stem	2.28	2.22	0.71
43	stem	2.47	2.24	1.18

Prismatic Cores: Thirty-eight prismatic cores and core fragments were analyzed in this study. Prismatic cores account for more than 32 percent of the bifacial artifacts category. These are cores from which prismatic blades were removed (fig. 229b). The remaining blade scars are the primary guide to defining the core type.

CV-16. One core and two core fragments were recovered from CV-16. The larger specimen has very worn facets. This facet weathering may be from stream rolling or possibly from using the core as a planing instrument where the facet ridges serve as a scraping edge. One end of the core has been splintered from some recent activity. The large core fragment measures 9.5 cm long and 3.51 cm wide at maximum points. The two fragmentary cores are only identifiable as prismatic cores from several blade scars on the arti-

facts. No attempt was made to measure the two segments. Figure 229a illustrates the CV-16 core.

CV-20. Fifteen core fragments have been identified in the CV-20 collection. Most (nine) are too fragmented to provide useful measurements. Two of the fragments were identified as medial sections and two are distal segments. The remaining two core fragments had other interesting detail. First, one is part of a plunging blade (cf. Hester 1975). Five facets are identified on the specimen and the platform is scratched, a technique often used to facilitate the removal of blades by providing a slip-free surface for the pressure tool (Crabtree 1968). The other core fragment is a medial section that has one modified edge. The lateral edge has minute flakes removed as if it had been used in a slicing or perhaps sawing motion. The artifact was not reviewed under magnification for detailed use-wear markings. All core fragments from CV-20 were used beyond the production of blades to make other useful segments of obsidian.

CV-43. Excavations at CV-43 produced 19 cores and core fragments. The only complete core is a bipointed core that is 3.7 cm long and 1.62 cm thick. The small core seems to have had bladelets removed from both poles of the core. The remaining 18 fragments are divided as follows: 6 proximal, 4 medial, and 8 distal. All of the proximal fragments show scratching on the platform surface. This was a modification to aid in blade production. One of the medial fragments has a patina, perhaps because it was exposed for a long period of time; another appears stream rolled or used as described for the CV-16 specimen.

Special Finds. The special finds core is a complete specimen measuring 13.4 cm long and 2.55 cm thick. There are eight facets that run the length of the core. The platform area has been removed with two parallel blows (see fig. 229a). This may have been executed to establish a new platform. This specimen is identical to a core illustrated by Henry S. Washington (1921). Sylvanus G. Morley obtained some Copan obsidian in 1920 and allowed Washington to study the sample. In Washington's (ibid.) description of the collection he noted:

> The cores are from 10 to 13 cm long, and from 2.5 to 3 cm at the greatest thickness. They are roughly spindle-shaped with the greatest width near the middle in some of them, but near one end in others. The ends are not sharply pointed, but broken cleanly across.

It appears that the cores and core fragments in this study are very similar to those collected earlier by Morley.

Flake Cores: Two flake cores are in the obsidian collection, and both are from CV-20. These differ from prismatic cores in that they have regular flakes removed from several directions. The cores measured, in centimeters, respectively: length, 3.35 and 3.15; width, 3 and 3.27; thickness, 1.89 and 2.02. No other observations were made concerning these flake cores.

Core Tablets: Seven core tablets and fragments have been identified in the collection. Core tablets are sections of the core removed to expedite blade removals. The tablets remove a used section of the core so that a new platform area may be available for blade production.

Three of the specimens are from CV-20, but show no special features. The other four core tablets are from CV-43. All of the CV-43 specimens show platform grinding, and two of the four also show pecking. Both grinding and pecking are used to provide a slip-free surface in the removal of blades.

Summary: Cores and Core Tablets. A total of 47 cores, core fragments, and core tablets have been studied in this collection. It is apparent from the cores, fragments, and tablets that much of the prismatic blade production took place at the site locales. The tablets reflect the consumer's attempt at core rejuvenation, while the fragmented sections show usage beyond the intended core function. Several prismatic cores showed ridge dulling that may be associated with planing activities, but that remains speculation at best.

Battered Pieces: Thirty-one artifacts have been categorized as battered pieces. These are artifacts that show flake removals from at least two (usually opposing) edges. I will leave the technical discussions of this artifact type to others (e.g., Sollberger and Patterson 1976; McDonald 1968; Clark 1979; Patterson 1979; Hayden 1979). The intent here is for a descriptive rather than a strictly functional designation.

Twenty-two pieces were analyzed from CV-20. These range in size (cm) as follows: length, 2.11 to 5.61; width, 1.87 to 3.1; thickness, 0.74 to 1.19. CV-43 produced nine battered pieces with the following dimensions: length, 2.2 to 5.3; width, 1.8 to 2.81; thickness, 0.8 to 1.15. In all cases, these are artifacts that do indeed appear to be battered (i.e., they have many flakes, often step-fractured, removed from opposing ends). No use-wear analysis was attempted with specimens aside from the obvious edge damage noted.

Drills: CV-20 produced two artifacts that have been classified as drills. Both are fragments of the drill portion. One fragment is 1.34 cm long and 0.42 cm thick. It does not have apparent wear associated with punching leather or the drilling of other materials. The other specimen is much smaller, and may in fact be best classified as a graver. Its minute size, 0.53 cm long, prevents an accurate assessment of this artifact. Therefore, both fragments are termed "drills" for descriptive purposes. No other effort was expended on defining these two items.

The Copan Obsidian Assemblage and Use-Wear Comments

The Copan obsidian collection contains a wide range of tool forms. Documented are 5,902 specimens. Several observations concerning the assemblage and edge-wear are presented below.

The obsidian assemblage at Copan as represented by CV-16, CV-20, and CV-43, and test pits indicates that most of the raw material was arriving in some prepared state. Very little (less than 1 percent) of the debris has any cortex. Cores and debris account for 38 percent of the collection and are the remnants of tool production. Most of the identifiable flakes are as tertiary flakes in final shaping of tools or cores. The ridge flakes in the collection indicate the need to shape or reshape cores in preparation for blade removals. Small prismatic blades represent 60 percent of the collection. These blades served as all-purpose tools for most household tasks of slicing, cutting, and carving. More formal tools, such as scrapers and bifaces, make up only 2 percent of the assemblage. The Copan collection resembles Chalchuapa (Sheets 1978) in that a whole range of artifact types is present.

There are some distributional differences within the Copan groups. Generally, debitage and blades are distributed in a relationship of number to group size (i.e., the larger the group the greater the number of particular artifacts). However, in several cases, certain artifacts occur only in a particular group. For example, scrapers, drills, and the triangular fragments are all found only at CV-20. This may relate to craft activities within the group, or some other functional need. The distribution of obsidian artifacts is discussed in greater detail elsewhere.

The use-wear comments for the Copan obsidian follow traditional observations. Prismatic blades were placed into six types of edge-wear. The edge modifications were noted to be caused by a range of activities, including soft usage such as plant processing and hard activities of cutting and shaping bone, wood, and possibly the incising of stone. Other edge-wear observations centered on the macroblades with some edge nibbling and step fracturing occurring from use on hard substances.

Scrapers also exhibit some wear with beveled edges and ventral striations related to planing activities. These tools are not limited to the activities listed, but certain functions are ascribed from combined use-wear and morphological characteristics. This is also the case for biface fragments where several activities may be performed with the same tool. An excellent example is the CV-16 core with weathered (used?) blade ridges. Brian Hayden (1986) carries this point further in discussing end scrapers by noting that in cases where wear patterns from secondary, incidental uses of tools obscures use-wear from obviously intended primary tasks, as may be the case with at least some collections of end scrapers, it seems clear that use-wear may not be a reliable guide to the intended and predominant use of these tools. Rather than rely on use-wear in these cases to infer primary tool uses, the specialized morphology and design of these tools should be used as the key to understanding their primary use and to reconstructing the relative importance of various site activities—for example, the extreme importance of hide working.

The various use-wear comments provided throughout the text are intended as a guide to use-wear characteristics and probable edge-wear causes. The artifacts/tools are not, however, limited to those listed. In several cases, the observed wear may be related to several activities. Therefore, the Copan obsidian collection is quite representative of a nearly complete assemblage, from raw material to finished tool to used and discarded tool.

BONE ARTIFACTS

Whistle	1
Effigy	1
Tubes	2
Awls	28
Pins	5
Animal Teeth	4
Antler Tine	1
Turtle Shell Spines (?)	2 lots

General, Comparative, and Summary Comments

We found relatively few bone artifacts, and they consist of rather ordinary or typical items— awls, pins, tubes, and other miscellany. Longyear (1952:111–112) reported similar items. It may be that some of the pieces that we have designated as pins were actually needle shaft fragments, as described and illustrated by Longyear; however, we found no needle-eye fragments. The specimens that Longyear calls pins are much more elaborate than those so designated by us. Longyear states that bone awls were extremely rare in his collections. This is not true for us, since well over half the specimens in our small bone artifact collection are awl fragments. For references to bone artifacts, animal teeth, turtle shells, and antler spines found in other Maya lowland sites, see Willey et al. 1965:491–504; Willey 1972: 229–242; and Willey 1978:168–171.

Whistle (1)

Cat. No. 1-918 (fig. 230) is a bird bone whistle, 6.5 cm long and averaging 0.7 cm in diameter. The two ends have been smoothly and evenly cut; the surfaces are well polished. The natural conformation of the bone has resulted in three facets or surfaces. On one of these, near the center of the whistle, there is a single hole, 4 mm in diameter. On another facet are two smaller holes, about equidistantly spaced and each being about 2 cm in from their respective ends of the whistle.

Cat. No. 1-918 came from Op. No. 49(A) CV-43, Level 3.

Effigy (1)

Cat. No. 1-1129 is a bone carving of a little animal, probably a dog (fig. 231). Length is 2.1, height 1.2, and thickness 0.5 cm. There is a tiny suspension hole drilled through the center of the back of the animal.

Cat. No. 1-1129 came from Op. No. 102(A) CV-43, Level 5, and is designated as Special Find 79 from that site.

Tubes (2)

These are carefully cut and polished sections of bird or animal bone. It is unlikely that they were intended as whistles, as they are too short.

Cat. No. 1-115 was probably made from the leg bone of a deer. It measures 4.3 cm long and about 2 cm in diameter. The ends were neatly cut and polished, and the sides are polished. About 6 mm up from one end there are the marks of the beginnings of another cut. These show only on one facet of the bone and did not cut through the wall of the bone.

Cat. No. 1-207 (fig. 232) is a tube of bird bone, 2.3 x 0.7 cm. The ends were clearly cut, and the surfaces show polish.

Cat. Nos.	Op. No. and Provenience
1-115	7(G) CV-20, Lev. 1
1-207	19(C) CV-20, Lev. 3

Awls (28)

These are implements made from animal bones—probably in most instances from leg bones of deer or brocket—that show smoothing, polishing (from intentional dressing, use, or handling), and, frequently, effective awl or punch points (fig. 233a–k). Ten specimens are, without much question, fragments of awls. These implements probably ranged from about 8 to 12 cm in length. At their butt ends they were about 1.5 to 2.5 cm wide, and from here they usually tapered toward a sharpened point. On three of these specimens the articular end of the bone, ground down to a degree, served as the butt end that would be pressed against the palm of the hand in the use of these implements.

The remaining 18 specimens are all small fragments. Most probably they were pieces of awls, although some, which are of rather large size (in width), might have come from hand-held tools that were used as blunt-ended polishers rather than awls or punches. In three instances (Cat. Nos. 1-88, 1-972, and 1-1027) where more than one specimen is listed it may be that these all came from the same implement.

Cat. Nos.	Op. No. and Provenience
Definite Awls	
1-108	6(K) CV-20, Lev. 1
1-136	4(R) CV-20, Lev. 1
1-202	20(A) CV-20, Lev. 3
1-239	19(C) CV-20, Lev. 5
1-537 (2 spec.— not same awl)	34(I) CV-43, Lev. 1
1-574	35(L) CV-43, Lev. 1
1-918	49(A) CV-43, Lev. 3
1-1025	49(A) CV-43, Lev. 7-C
1-1027 (may be part of same awl listed below)	100(B) CV-43, Lev. 4
Probable Awls or Polishers	
1-41	4(F) CV-20, Lev. 1
1-88 (3 spec.)	7(F) CV-20, Lev. 1
1-114	6(L) CV-20, Feature 6
1-219	20(A) CV-20, Lev. 4
1-254	21(A) CV-20, Lev. 3
1-918	49(A) CV-43, Lev. 3
1-972 (4 spec.)	49(A) CV-43, Lev. 5-C
1-1020	100(B) CV-43, Lev. 3
1-1024	50(A) CV-45, Lev. 8
1-1027 (3 spec.)	100(B) CV-43, Lev. 4
1-1086	104(A) CV-43, Lev. 6
No Number	

Pins (5)

These are fragments of bone pins. They are too small in diameter to have served effectively as awls or punches, and their purpose was probably ornamental. The shafts of four of these are solid bone. The surfaces are very highly polished. Cat. No. 1-535 is 2.2 x 0.5 cm; Cat. No. 1-1057 is 2.8 x 0.3 cm; and one Cat. No. 1-866 specimen is 1 x 0.2 cm. All three of these are midshaft fragments. Another Cat. No. 1-866 fragment is a point. It is 3 x 0.3 cm and nicely pointed. There is a remaining Cat. No. 1-866 fragment that appears to have come from near the head of a pin (as indicated by the expansion of the bone shaft for an articular end). It is hollow, probably from a delicate bird bone. The shaft is nicely polished. It measures 2.9 x 0.4 cm.

Cat. Nos.	Op. No. and Provenience
1-535	35(H) CV-43, Lev. 1
1-866 (3 spec.)	71(A) CV-204, Lev. 5
1-1057	49(A) CV-43, Lev. 8-C

Animal Teeth (4)

These are animal teeth that appear to have been used as artifacts, probably ornaments.

Cat. No. 1-126 is a small canine of a carnivore, probably a dog. It is unperforated but shows polish as though from handling.

Cat. No. 1-134 appears to be another dog canine. It has been perforated biconically through the root.

Cat. No. 1-202 is a deer tooth. A perforation has been started through the root but does not go all the way through.

Cat. No. 1-861 is a fragment of a tooth, probably of a carnivore. It may have been perforated at one end, but this portion has been broken away.

Cat. Nos.	Op. No. and Provenience
1-126	6(M) CV-20, Lev. 1
1-134	6(K) CV-20, Lev. 1, Special Find 21
1-202	20(A) CV-20, Lev. 3
1-861	71(A) CV-204, Lev. 4

Antler Tine (1)

An antler tip, 2.8 cm long, shows definite use striations on point. The specimen is calcined.

Cat. No. 1-951 came from Op. No. 49(A) CV-43, Level 6-B.

Turtle Shell Spines (?) (2 lots)

These are curious little objects of slightly porous bone. They have been cataloged in two lots, 1-861 and 1-866, from adjacent excavation levels in a pit in CV-204. Cat. No. 1-861 contains 20 specimens, including both complete and fragmentary pieces; Cat. No. 1-866 contains, similarly, 44 specimens. A whole specimen is a little plaque-like or platelet object, for which an average, and very uniform, size is 2.3 x 0.5 x 0.1/0.2 cm. One surface is quite flat and smooth. The opposite surface has a thickened end, measuring 0.5 x 0.5 cm, and a thinner part,

0.5 x 1.8 cm. On this thinner part there is a slightly indented, pointed-arch depression, with the point toward the thickened end. The lines of this arch are marked with a row of tiny holes. This surface is apparently natural and not carved by man, and it is probable, although not certain, that all of these little objects are completely natural in form.

They have been identified, tentatively, as pieces from the spiney material separating the turtle shell platelets of a large turtle, *Dermatemys mawii*. This identification was made by Dr. James Knight, Museum of Comparative Zoology, Harvard University.

Cat. Nos.	Op. No. and Provenience
1-861 (1 lot)	71(A) CV-204, Lev. 4
1-866 (1 lot)	71(A) CV-204, Lev. 5

SHELL ARTIFACTS, SHELLS, AND MARINE MATERIALS

Pendants	2
Adornos	3
Tinkler	1
Beads	5
Rectangular or Cut Pieces	9
Spondylus sp. Shells	6
Pachychilus corvinus Shells	84
Pachychilus largillierti Shells	15
Other Shells	9
Crab Claw	1
Stingray Spines	2
Coral Sections	6
Marine Worm Tubes	49

General, Comparative, and Summary Comments

Longyear (1952:110–111) describes various small shell ornaments as well as *Spondylus* sp. shells from Copan. Except for a Tinkler ornament, none of his items seems quite like any of those which we recovered; however, both collections are small. The *Spondylus* shell seems more common at Copan than in the Peten sites. For references to comparable shell artifactual items see Willey et al. 1965:503–511; Willey 1972:220–228; Willey 1978:162–165.

Pendants (2)

These are pendant ornaments other than beads.

Cat. No. 1-349 (fig. 234a) is a roughly diamond-shaped pendant made from a *Spondylus* shell. The perforation is in one corner of the diamond. The vertical or longer measurement of the diamond is about 2 cm. One surface of the pendant has been ground smooth, the other left more or less as it was.

Cat. No. 1-361 (fig. 234b) is made from the valve of a *Spondylus*. It is a nearly circular pendant, 8.5 x 7.9 cm on its outer diameters and 4.8 x 3.3 cm on its interior diameters. The form is that of a slightly ovoid ring. In other words, a large oval section has been carefully cut out of the center of the shell. Edges are all carefully trimmed, and the outer or convex side of the shell has been ground almost smooth. There are two small suspension holes, uniconically drilled, near the edge. These are 4.8 cm apart and 0.8 cm in from the outer edge of the ornament.

Cat. Nos.	Op. No. and Provenience
1-349	26(A) Main Center, Struct. L11-93, Lev. 5, Special Find 17
1-361	26(A) Main Center, Struct. L11-93, Lev. 10

Adornos (3)

These are shell ornaments other than pendants or beads.

Cat. No. 1-333 (fig. 235a) is a rectangular little rosette-like ornament, 2.3 x 2 x 0.3 cm. It was carefully carved on one surface, the edges were evenly trimmed, and the back side was left plain and smoothed. The design consists of a central circle. Four petaloid elements radiate out from this to the corners of the rectangle. These are separated from each other by little wedge-shaped elements at the center of each side. At these points the edges of the piece are very slightly notched. There is a small (1 mm) biconically drilled hole through the center of the central circle. The specimen appears to have been made from a piece of a *Spondylus* shell.

Cat. No. 1-953 may have been an ornament of some sort. It is an ovoid piece of shell, lustrous or nacreous in appearance, and carefully trimmed around the edges. It measures 2.4 x 1.5 x 0.1 cm. Possibly it was an inlay. Shell is not identified.

Cat. No. 1-1275 (fig. 235b) is a fragment of a little shell crescent or ring. It was probably made from a piece of *Spondylus*. Measurements are 2.3 x 1.6 x 0.5 cm. Edges and flat surfaces have been carefully ground.

Cat. Nos.	Op. No. and Provenience
1-333	26(A) Main Center, Struct. L11-93, Lev. 2, Special Find 5
1-953	102(A) CV-43, Lev. 3
1-1275	102(A) CV-43, Special Find 167, within Special Find 57

Tinkler (1)

Tinklers are fairly typical lowland Maya artifacts or ornaments, presumably strung as beads or serried pendants. In the latter case they would rattle or "tinkle" together. Usually they are made from *Oliva* sp. shells. Cat. No. 1-162 appears to be a fragment of an *Oliva spicata* shell.

Cat. No. 1-162 came from Op. No. 14(A), CV-22, Level 3, and was designated Special Find 2.

Beads (5)

Cat. No. 1-82 is a small flat bead made from the wall of an unidentified shell. It is ovate-rectangular in outline, 1.7 x 1.3 cm and about 1 mm thick. There is a central perforation 3 mm in diameter.

Cat. No. 1-1042 is a long bead made from a conch columella. It measures 4.2 x 1.7 cm and has been perforated through the long axis with a small biconical hole. It is rather irregular in shape, is not well smoothed, and appears to have been subjected to burning.

Cat. No. 1-1128 is a small tubular bead of shell (unidentified), 1.4 x 0.5 cm.

Cat. No. 1-1130 and 1-1132 are small disk beads made from *Spondylus* sp. shell. They are, respectively, 1.6 x 0.4 and 1.2 x 0.4. Both have been biconically drilled with perforations 4 mm in diameter.

Cat. Nos.	Op. No. and Provenience
1-82	7(E) CV-20, Lev. 1
1-1042	102(A) CV-43, Feature 10, Special Find 52
1-1128	102(A) CV-43, Lev. 5, Special Find 74
1-1130	102(A) CV-43, Lev. 5, Special Find 76
1-1132	102(A) CV-43, Lev. 5, Special Find 71

Rectangular Cut Pieces (9)

These were found together as Cat. No. 1-1277 (fig. 236a–i). All are small, measuring 2 x 1.5 x 1 cm. Six are of *Spondylus* sp.; the other three are of a nacreous, unidentified shell. Perhaps they vere blanks, trimmed and prepared for being made into beads.

Cat. No. 1-1277 came from Op. No. 102(A) CV-43, and was designated Special Find 169 found within Special Find 57.

Spondylus sp. Shells (6)

Spondylus shells are known to have been valued items in trade among the Maya. The ones listed here give evidence, however slight, of having been worked or treated.

Cat. No. 1-206 consists of three fragments from the valve of a single *Spondylus princeps* shell. This specimen does show some working on the back, where a portion of the ridges has been cut away. In this area there are some crude curvilinear carvings, although only a portion of this design, if such it was, remains.

Cat. No. 1-238 consists of two hinged valves of a *Spondylus princeps*. The shell measures about 8 cm in diameter. Red pigment, probably cinnabar, had been placed within the opened bivalve.

Cat. No. 1-343 also consists of two hinged valves; this, however, was a *Spondylus calcifer*. It is about 7 cm in diameter. Red pigment is found within one of the valves.

Cat. No. 1-718 (fig. 237) consists of two hinged valves of a *Spondylus* (not further identified). A fragment of cloth was found inside the bivalve whose interior also shows traces of red pigment.

Cat. No. 1-1020 is a single valve of a large *Spondylus calcifer*. It measures about 12 cm in diameter. There are two short saw-marks across the back of the shell.

Cat. No. 1-1191 consists of fragments of a *Spondylus* shell (species undetermined) and is part of a cache with a coral section and a stingray spine.

Cat. Nos.	Op. No. and Provenience
1-206	21(A) CV-20, Lev. 2
1-238	20(A) CV-20, Lev. 5
1-343	26(A) Main Center, Struct. L11-93, Lev. 5, Special Find 12
1-718	55(A) CV-115, Lev. 2, Special Find 3

1-1020	100(B) CV-43, Lev. 3
1-1191	104(A) CV-43, Lev. 9-B, Special Find 90

Pachychilus corvinus Shells (84)

According to Lawrence H. Feldman, who did the shell identifications for us, well over half of these shells had been tipped, broken in back, or broken above lip, probably by human agency.

Cat. Nos.	Op. No. and Provenience
1-82 (2 spec.)	7(E) CV-20, Lev. 1
1-125	7(H) CV-20, Lev. 1
1-202 (12 spec.)	20(A) CV-20, Lev. 3
1-206	21(A) CV-20, Lev. 2
1-238 (3 spec.)	20(A) CV-20, Lev. 5
1-259	20(A) CV-20, Lev. 6
1-264 (13 spec.)	20(A) CV-20, Lev. 7
1-564	36(J) CV-43, Lev. 1
1-573	36(L) CV-43, Lev. 1
1-650	54(A) CV-94, Lev. 8
1-655	54(A) CV-94, Lev. 7-A
1-699	55(A) CV-115, Lev. 12
1-828 (2 spec.)	66(A) CV-190, Lev. 8
1-829 (4 spec.)	66(A) CV-190, Lev. 9
1-832	66(A) CV-190, Lev. 5
1-859	49(A) CV-43, Lev. 2
1-861 (23 spec.)	71(A) CV-204, Lev. 4
1-897	71(A) CV-204, Lev. 1
1-899 (3 spec.)	71(A) CV-204, Lev. 2
1-953 (2 spec.)	102(A) CV-43, Lev. 3
1-981 (3 spec.)	81(A) Sacbe, Lev. 3
1-1030	102(A) CV-43, Feature 10
1-1159 (4 spec.)	102(A) CV-43, Lev. 7
No Number	

Pachychilus largillierti Shells (15)

According to Feldman, these shells were not worked or modified.

Cat. Nos.	Op. No. and Provenience
1-78	7(D) CV-20, Lev. 1
1-88	7(F) CV-20, Lev. 1
1-206 (3 spec.)	21(A) CV-20, Lev. 2
1-698	36(O) CV-43, Lev. 1
1-699 (7 spec.)	55(A) CV-115, Lev. 2
No Number (2 spec.)	

Other Shells (9)

A number of other shells were recovered from the various diggings. Most of these were identified by Feldman as detailed below. Several of them are fragments, but there is no clear evidence of human workmanship on any of them.

Cat. Nos.	Op. No. and Provenience
Oliva sp. (marine)	
1-206	21(A) CV-20, Lev. 2
1-828	66(A) CV-190, Lev. 8
Ostrea palmula (marine)	
1-206	21(A) CV-20, Lev. 2
1-343	26(A) Main Center, Struct. L11-93, Lev. 5, Special Find 12
Orthalicus princeps (land)	
1-26	4(A) CV-20, Lev. 1
Petaloconchus erectus (marine)	
1-206	21(A) CV-20, Lev. 2
Nephronais goascoranensis (freshwater, local)	
1-528	36(D) CV-43, Lev. 1
Unidentifiable or Unidentified	
1-62	8(B) CV-20, Lev. 1
1-1027	100(B) CV-43, Lev. 4

Crab Claw (1)

This is not an artifact but, obviously, an exotic in the context in which it was found (fig. 238a). Cat. No. 1-953 came from Op. No. 102(A) CV-43, Level 3.

Stingray Spines (2)

These spines had both been worked by trimming the edges and sharpening (fig. 238b). Both were found in fragments.

Cat. Nos.	Op. No. and Provenience
1-1151	104(A) CV-43, Lev. 8
1-1179	104(A) CV-43, Lev. 9-B, Special Find 91

Coral Sections (6)

These are sections of coral formations. They are about 1.5 to 2 cm in diameter and vary in length from 3 to 6 cm. They show no evidence of working. They are obviously exotics in their contexts here.

Cat. Nos.	Op. No. and Provenience
1-135	7(H) CV-20, Lev. 1, Special Find 22
1-648 (2 spec.)	34(O) CV-43, Lev. 1
1-749 (2 spec.)	34(R) CV-43, Lev. 1
1-1191	104(A) CV-43, Lev. 9-B, Special Find 90

Marine Worm Tubes (49)

These are marine worm tubes, calcareous in appearance. Most are straight and vary from 3 to 6 cm in length; diameters are 0.5 to 1.5 cm. The natural longitudinal hole within the tubes is uniformly 4 mm in diameter.

Cat. Nos.	Op. No. and Provenience
1-135 (27 spec.)	7(H) CV-20, Lev. 1, Special Find 22
1-206 (17 spec.)	21(A) CV-20, Lev. 2
1-494 (3 spec.)	35(B) CV-43, Lev. 1
1-644	57(A) CV-122, Lev. 1
1-699	55(A) CV-115, Lev. 2

COMPARATIVE PERSPECTIVES ON OTHER ARTIFACTS: A SUMMARY

Some comparative comments have been made in the sections on categories and types of other artifacts. It might be useful to touch on the highlights of these here in a summary statement.

To begin with pottery figurines, few Preclassic specimens were identified from our Copan excavations, and these identifications were made primarily upon the basis of comparative chronology rather than by excavation provenience. Some of those we found bear a general resemblance to Middle Preclassic figurines from the Maya highlands and lowlands and southern Mesoamerica in general.

The majority of our Copan figurines belong to the Classic Maya lowland tradition of moldmade figurines and figurine-whistles. They include the usual representations of elaborately costumed men, god-figures, grotesques, and animals. In iconography and style, they would have been completely at home in Classic period Peten sites and in contexts of Tepeu 2 or 3 date. We also had a few Copan specimens of partially moldmade, partially handmade figurines of a style that we believe to be of an earlier date, perhaps Tzakol 3–Tepeu 2. All of our Classic moldmade figurines or figurine-whistles came from household refuse, none with burials or caches; and such, generally, are their contexts in the Maya lowlands proper.

No miscellaneous pottery objects that we encountered—the unperforated potsherd disks, the perforated (spindle whorl) specimens, various ear ornaments, and seals or stamps—can be very profitably compared with other regions; all seem to be of a rather general southern Mesoamerican nature.

The odd little ceramic candeleros, which we found in such numbers at Copan, are neither a typical lowland nor highland Maya artifact; however, they do occur to the east, in Honduras, although not in such large quantity as they do at Copan. The ones we found dated to the Classic period, both Early and Late.

The common ground stone metate at Copan is of a flat, rectangular form, often with small, nubbin feet. In general, the flat, rectangular metate form is typical of lands to the east—Honduras and lower Central America. In contrast, the Maya metate, for both highlands and lowlands, is of a turtle-back or basin-shaped form. We found some of these at Copan, but they were vastly outnumbered by the flat, rectangular type. The typical Copan mano stone is of ovate-rectangular form. This form occurs in lowland Maya sites, although there it often tends to be replaced in the Late Classic by a mano that is square in cross section, a type rare to absent at Copan.

Nothing very meaningful can be said about the relationships of most of our other ground stone artifacts from Copan—mortars, barkbeaters, ring stones, polished stone celts, mirror backs, and jadeite ornaments. They occur in both Maya highlands and lowlands and, occasionally, to the east in Honduras. We recovered one quite distinctive ground stone celt-like mace of a ritual form at Copan, and this links directly to such objects in the Peten and Belize. They resemble objects sometimes held in the hands of personages carved on Classic Maya stelae.

Our chert was generally of poor quality, and while we found a fair amount of scrap and wastage, we recovered only a few artifacts. These included laurel-leaf blades, small projectile points, larger dart points, and an eccentric. All are types common to the Maya lowlands; however, the large chert biface chopper or celt, a tool that is ubiquitous in the Maya lowlands, was absent at Copan.

Obsidian is more common at Copan than chert, most of it identified as coming from the Ixtepeque source in the Maya highlands. It was brought in in the form of partially dressed cores, large flakes, and bifaces, and then worked into small bladelets, scrapers, points or knives, and occasional other artifacts. These last, including one obsidian eccentric, are linked to lowland Maya traditions.

In sum, Copan other artifacts point to contacts and the sharing of traditions with Honduras, the Maya highlands, and the Maya lowlands, with a general increase, perhaps, of contacts with the latter area in the later periods. In all of this, the ties are similar to the Copan ceramic relationships.

A SUMMARY OF INTRASITE DISTRIBUTIONS AND THEIR IMPLICATIONS

This section focuses upon an examination of the distribution of the artifacts from two perspectives. The first is the horizontal or differential distribution between the excavated groups and among the structures of each excavated unit. The second is a vertical or chronological view of the artifacts.

Not every artifact was examined from both the horizontal and chronological perspective. When the category of artifact was not tightly defined but rather a more general category (e.g., ceramic ornaments or ritual objects), this artifact type was not included. Also, if there were too few artifacts within a category, it was not included.

The examination of the possible horizontal clustering was not done statistically, for we have shown (see chapter 4) that there is no clear clustering of artifacts in relation to structures to help identify the function of these structures. Rather, each individual artifact within a type has been located on a plan map of each of the excavated plaza groups. Surface finds are not included on the maps. Possible clusters of artifacts have then been identified, checked, and reported in the following section.

The chronological placement of artifact types has also been examined. Quantities of an artifact type were computed for six basic chronological periods.

Phase 1: Preclassic and Early Classic—consisting of the Copan phases of Uir, Chabij, Bijac, and Acbi.

Phase 2: Early Classic/Late Classic overlap—Acbi/Cueva.

Phase 3: the early part of the Late Classic—Cueva.

Phase 4: general grouping of pre-Coner material—Cueva, Acbi, Chabij, Bijac, and Uir—artifacts not found within Phases 1, 2, and 3.

Phase 5: general Late Classic—Cueva/Coner overlap.

Phase 6: end of the Late Classic—Coner.

In addition to these six chronological phases, a category of unknown chronological placement has also been created.

This chronological classification of proveniences was based upon two primary criteria first, the percentage of classifiable sherds relating to each of these phases within each provenience second, the specific excavation/architectural provenience. In the end, all 812 of our Copan excavation proveniences were classified as follows:

1. Uir, Bijac, Chabij, and Acbi phases	6 proveniences	1%
2. Acbi/Cueva	3 proveniences	0.5%
3. Cueva	19 proveniences	2%
4. Uir, Bijac, Chabij, Acbi and Cueva	27 proveniences	3%
5. Cueva/Coner	62 proveniences	8%
6. Coner	494 proveniences	61%
7. Unknown	78 proveniences	10%
8. Sterile	123 proveniences	15%

It is clear that the large majority of excavation proveniences relate to the final Late Classic phase at Copan—the Coner phase (see tables 22 and 23). Therefore, almost all of the artifact types seem to be related to this late phase.

Each artifact type or grouping is presented in terms of both the horizontal distribution throughout the excavated groups and the chronological information available.

It is important to differentiate between primary and secondary deposits in the analysis of artifact distributions. The fill of a structure is a secondary deposit and does not have the same significance as a primary deposit, for instance, the refuse found along the retaining walls of a platform.

Figurines

There seems to be an even distribution of figurines throughout the excavations of CV-43 and CV-20 (fig. 239a–b). They are found within the deep trenches, test excavations, plaza areas, structures, and refuse that collected around the basal retaining walls of the structures.

We found only a few primary concentrations of figurines. The heaviest concentration, located

TABLE 22

Distribution of artifact types by phase

	Phase 1	Phase 2	Phase 3	Phase 4	Phase 5	Phase 6	Unknown
Figurines	0	0	4	5	13	122	10
	0%	0%	3%	3%	8%	79%	6%
Projectile Points & Chert Artifacts	0	0	1	2	8	43	3
	0%	0%	2%	4%	14%	75%	5%
Polishing Stones	0	0	0	0	1	55	5
	0%	0%	0%	0%	2%	90%	8%
Pounding & Rubbing Stones	0	0	0	1	1	38	4
	0%	0%	0%	2%	2%	86%	9%
Celts	0	0	0	0	2	18	2
	0%	0%	0%	0%	9%	82%	9%
Mortars							
Type 1	0	0	1	1	0	37	1
	0%	0%	3%	3%	0%	92%	3%
Type 2	0	0	0	0	1	6	1
	0%	0%	0%	0%	13%	75%	13%
Manos							
Thick Ovate-Rect.	0	0	3	8	65	231	7
	0%	0%	1%	3%	21%	74%	2%
Thin Ovate-Rect.	0	0	0	0	1	14	1
	0%	0%	0%	0%	6%	88%	6%
Large Round	0	0	1	0	3	38	3
	0%	0%	2%	0%	7%	84%	7%
Small Round	0	0	0	0	2	31	2
	0%	0%	0%	0%	6%	88%	6%
Plano-Convex	0	0	1	2	3	35	3
	0%	0%	2%	5%	7%	80%	7%
Pentagonal	0	0	0	1	1	14	3
	0%	0%	0%	5%	5%	74%	16%
Triangular	0	0	0	0	1	9	0
	0%	0%	0%	0%	10%	90%	0%
Square	0	0	0	0	1	4	0
	0%	0%	0%	0%	20%	80%	0%
Overhang	0	0	0	0	0	7	0
	0%	0%	0%	0%	0%	100%	0%
Metates							
Type 1	1	0	4	14	35	351	16
	0%	0%	0%	3%	8%	83%	4%
Types 2 & 3	0	0	1	2	4	40	2
	0%	0%	2%	4%	8%	82%	4%
Type 4	0	0	0	1	3	9	0
	0%	0%	0%	8%	23%	69%	0%
Obsidian							
Blades	0	0	36	108	217	3,009	256
	0%	0%	1%	3%	6%	83%	7%
Scrap	3	0	20	100	318	1,272	258
	0%	0%	1%	5%	16%	64%	13%
Artifacts	0	0	2	7	14	205	2
	0%	0%	1%	3%	6%	90%	1%

Table 22 *(continued)*

Distribution of artifact types by phase

	Phase 1	Phase 2	Phase 3	Phase 4	Phase 5	Phase 6	Unknown
Cores	0	0	0	0	1	43	3
	0%	0%	0%	0%	3%	91%	6%
Pottery Whorls*	0	0	0	0	2	32	0
	0%	0%	0%	0%	6%	94%	0%
Worked Sherds†	0	1	0	3	3	42	4
	0%	2%	0%	6%	6%	79%	8%
Briquettes	0	0	5	39	4	84	19
	0%	0%	3%	26%	3%	56%	13%
Ring Stones	0	0	0	0	0	5	0
	0%	0%	0%	0%	0%	100%	0%
Perforated Stones	0	0	0	0	4	14	0
	0%	0%	0%	0%	22%	78%	0%
Stone Spheres	0	0	0	0	0	15	1
	0%	0%	0%	0%	0%	96%	6%
Miniature Stone Tables	0	0	0	0	0	3	2
	0%	0%	0%	0%	0%	60%	40%
Barkbeaters	0	0	0	2	1	4	2
	0%	0%	0%	22%	11%	44%	22%

*Includes specially made whorls and perforated disks
†Includes unperforated potsherd disks, other worked potsherds, and potsherd pendants

behind Structure E-1 of CV-43, was a clustering of eight figurines or figurine fragments. Another concentration was located on the eastern side of the low platform located within the western side of the CV-43 plaza.

No clear concentrations of figurines are evident within the CV-20 excavations.

One interesting note is the apparent decrease in figurine numbers within the smaller outlying structures of a residential group. Adjacent to CV-43, we found only two figurines in association with the entire CV-47 unit, only three in CV-46, and only one in a possible primary deposit in association with CV-45. In CV-20, the secondary plaza yielded only four figurines. This distributional difference may indicate that although figurines are common throughout all portions of society, they do indicate some status, with more of them found in larger residential contexts.

Most of the figurines found in our excavations were in Coner proveniences (Phases 5 and 6).

Drills and Scrapers—Chert and Obsidian

One of the most obvious differences in the distribution of drills and scrapers is seen in the presence of numerous of these implements in the CV-20 residential unit and their relative scarcity in the CV-43 unit (fig. 240a–b). Twenty-seven scrapers and drills were found in CV-20, with a concentration of them in the refuse around Structure A, suggesting that the people who lived in this building were performing tasks in which these tools were needed. Only four chert scrapers and one obsidian drill came from all of the CV-43 excavations.

Projectile Points and Chert Artifacts

In contrast to the above, there was a fairly even distribution of projectile points found in the CV-20 and CV-43 excavations (fig. 241a–b). Almost all points found in each were concentratd within the central areas of the CV-20 and CV-43 units, the only exception being a single point in the fill of CV-45 (Level 4), a peripheral group of the CV-43 complex. Perhaps significantly, in CV-20, Structure B, and in CV-43, Structure A, the buildings identified as the religious structures (Leventhal and Baxter 1988; on the bases of their architectural features) of their respective residential units, there were no projectile points.

Most of the chert artifacts that were recovered from our Copan Valley excavations were found within a Coner context (Phases 5 and 6).

Polishing, Pounding, and Rubbing Stones

The distribution of both polishing stones and pounding and rubbing stones (presumably implements of similar function) appears to be fairly uniform throughout the CV-20 and CV-43 plaza groups (fig. 242a–b). The only cluster was in a cache of nine objects found below the floor of Structure A, CV-20. These artifacts included eight polishing stones and a miniature table, possibly associated with an incense burner.

Celts

Almost twice as many celts were found at CV-20 (12) as at CV-43 (7) (fig. 243a–b). Again, we note that Structure A of CV-43 and Structure B of CV-20, presumed ritual structures, have no associated celts.

Mortars

Mortars seem to be distributed rather evenly across the structures of both main groups (fig. 244a–b). Only one main structure from each group, Structure C of CV-20 and Structure F of CV-43, have no mortars associated with them.

The clusterings that are identifiable are in Structure A of CV-20, with five mortars, and Structure E-1 of CV-43, with four mortars. Mortars are found both within the fill of these structures and within the trash bordering the structures.

Typologically, mortars have been divided into two types: 1 and 2. The chronological position of each mortar type is presented separately.

Manos

A large number of manos were found during our excavations, with the ovate-rectangular type the most common.

Many more manos were recovered from CV-43 than from either CV-20 or CV-16 (fig. 245a–c). Perhaps this density of manos in the CV-43 unit could be correlated with a larger number of residents. In both CV-43 and CV-20, the implements were fairly evenly distributed around the various structures of each group. Because we had speculated that the functions of the peripheral structures for these two units— CV-44, CV-45, CV-46, CV-47, all adjacent to CV-43, and Structures E, F, and G, all adjacent to the central plaza and principal buildings of CV-20—might have been food preparation areas, we were particularly alert to the possibility that more manos, as well as metates, might be found associated with these peripheral buildings. We found no such concentrations of manos or metates in these peripheral proveniences; nor were there any concentrations of hearth areas or primary charcoal/ash deposits in them.

The chronological information for each mano type is listed separately. It appears that the predominant phase for all the manos is the late Coner time period (Phase 6).

Metates

As is evident from the maps, metates have a similar distribution to the manos throughout the excavations (fig. 246a–c). There does not appear to be any real focal clustering point for these artifacts in any of the structure groups. Some of the structures have four to six metates associated with them, but others have fewer. The presumed ritual buildings, Structure A of CV-43 and Structure B of CV-20, have fewer metates than other structures of their group. In fact, there is only one metate from a primary deposit in association with Structure B of CV-20, the other being found within the structure fill. And while Structure A of CV-43 has five associated metates, all of these are part of the structure fill. The pattern seems to place these structures outside of a food preparation function.

Also as indicated above with the manos, the outlying structures of both groups CV-43 and CV-20 do not have more metates than the central, larger buildings.

As with most of the other artifacts, most of the metates found were associated with the Coner phase.

Obsidian

The following is an examination of the differences in the obsidian assemblages as seen at CV-20 and CV-43. While both areas share a number of obsidian artifact types, several forms seem to be concentrated at one or the other of the residential groups.

Macroblades: The large macroblade variety is found only at CV-20. It is this form from which scrapers were made; thus, the inhabitants of CV-20 had access to the obsidian required to produce the scraper tool.

Medium-sized macroblades occur in both CV-20 and CV-43; however, there is a significantly higher occurrence of them at CV-43. While CV-20 produced 27 medium macroblades, CV-43 produced 73. This difference is most likely associated with site function and not differential site size. Most of the macroblades do show some edge modification, probably related to their use.

Scrapers: As noted earlier, all scrapers recovered from our Copan excavations were found at CV-20. The use of scrapers could be related to the processing of hides or possibly woodworking. Whatever the case, it seems reasonable to assume that CV-20 was the locus of an activity, or activities, that did not take place at CV-43.

Large Biface Fragments: As with medium-sized macroblades, large biface fragments at CV-43 (16) outnumber those from CV-20 (6). The function of these bifaces and the reason for their differential distribution are unknown.

Eccentric and Green Obsidian: CV-43 produced both the single obsidian eccentric that we found and the only green obsidian dart point. Both items are of special value or significance. These occurrences may be another indicator of the status differentiation between CV-43 and CV-20.

Flake Cores: Two flake cores were discovered both in the excavations of CV-20. This is another clue to obsidian toolmaking in this residential unit.

Battered Pieces: Battered pieces are noted in greater frequency at CV-20 (22) than at CV-43 (9). Again, this tool debris may be related to woodworking or some other activity that was carried on at CV-20.

Drills and Burins: The two drill and burin-like artifacts were excavated from CV-20. None were found at CV-43. Again, this is another datum for work activities at CV-20.

The chronological distribution of the obsidian throughout the excavated sites indicates the heaviest occurrence in the last phase at Copan—the Coner phase. While there is some obsidian in the earlier Cueva/Coner time period, any obsidian earlier than this in our sample is relatively rare.

Other Artifact Types

We noted no unusual concentrations for the following artifact types, and simply list their chronological frequencies in table 23. The exception to this is the pottery candelero. These were found in large numbers in our Copan collections. They seem to be a specialty of the site. We were interested in learning something of their function, and because of this we devote some detailed attention to their site distributions and contexts.

Candeleros

Candeleros were one of the most common artifacts found during our excavations at Copan. As has been detailed in the typological description, they have been found occasionally, but only in small numbers, at other Maya cities. Also what have been termed candeleros have been found at Teotihuacan, although these are rather different in their form from the ones at Copan.

The possible function of candeleros remains unclear, although the name given to these artifacts does imply a function, perhaps, of holding candles or burning incense; however, there is no pecific archaeological evidence for such possible unctions.

In our excavations we discovered many candeleros in situ, especially in association with ourials and caches, where they were placed around, although not immediately within, such eatures.

In the following tabulations, the catalog number for each candelero is preceded by a C, B, or M, indicating a cylindrical, bottle-shaped, or miscellaneous variety. The number in parentheses following the catalog number indicates the number of candeleros found within that provenience. Maps (fig. 247a–b) identify the location of the excavation units.

CV-43
Feature 9
Operation 49(A), trench through Structure E2, CV-43. Numerous candeleros were found associated with Feature 9, which consisted of a small cluster of uncut rocks, originally thought to be a crypt, although no bones were recovered. Under and among the rocks was found a ceramic vessel—Special Find 39. The candeleros were scattered around and in clear association with this cache/crypt. Burial 25, consisting of very small bone/skull fragments, was found in the wall of the trench during profiling. It is possible that there is some association between the candeleros and this burial, although this is uncertain.

C1-903 (2)	Level 5-A
C1-988	Level 6-A
B1-988	Level 6-A
M1-949	Level 6-A Special Find 32
C1-1012	Level 6-A Special Find 33
B1-1014	Level 6-A Special Find 34
B1-1004	Level 6-A Special Find 35
M1-1005	Level 6-A Special Find 36
C1-1013	Level 6-A Special Find 37
C1-1002	Level 6-A Special Find 38
C1-971 (2)	Level 7-A associated with Feature 9
C1-1006	Level 7-A Special Find 40
C1-1003	Level 7-A Special Find 41
C1-1009	Level 7-A Special Find 42
C1-1010	Level 7-A Special Find 43
C1-1075	Level 9-A

Burial 15. Two candeleros were possibly associated with Burial 15 within Level 5-B. The burial is a tightly flexed individual within a small crypt

of uncut stones. While there is no clear association between the candeleros and the burial, little else was found in this provenience except the burial and the candeleros.

C1-951	Level 6-B
B1-951	Level 6-B

Feature 7. These candeleros appear to have been associated with Feature 7, a large semicircular activity area. The area is demarcated by a flat section of cobbles and stones with large spots of ash and bits of charcoal. This could be a ritual activity area on a house floor. The candeleros may have been part of a ritual of rebuilding and covering an early floor or structure.

C1-972	Level 5-C
C1-1045	Level 6-C Special Find 47
B1-1057 (3)	Level 8-C

Miscellaneous Associations. We have no clear data of association for the candeleros listed below; they are simply part of the material obtained from the lower levels of Structure E2. Quite probably, they were associated with the other candeleros presented above.

C1-859	Level 2
C1-918 (2)	Level 3
B1-902	Level 4

Burials 18, 20, and 22 and Feature 14
Operation 102(A), trench through Structure E-1. These 15 Special Find candeleros and 14 other candeleros were all found within Level 4 or 5, and it is clear that they were associated with one of several burials or features; but specific associations cannot be identified. Three burials and a cache were found within this section of the excavations.

1. Burial 18 was located within a tomb (Feature 10). This burial had jade and pyrite dental inlays (Special Find 49), two jade earspools and a jade button (Special Finds 50, 51, and 171), a small shell pendant (Special Find 52), a small stone bead (Special Find 53), and two ceramic vessels (Special Finds 46 and 48) in association.
2. Burial 20, a tightly flexed individual, was in direct association with one vessel (Special Find 82), a miniature vessel (Special Find 84), and a cylindrical candelero (Cat. No. 1-1121,

Special Find 83). Burial was located in Level 5.

3. Burial 22 is a badly eroded burial located within a crypt (Feature 16). In direct association with the burial were two vessels (Special Finds 86 and 87) and two jade beads covered with red pigment (Special Finds 88 and 89).

4. A cache, Feature 14, was located within Level 5 of the trench. The cache is not demarcated by stones or other materials. It consists of three small groupings or artifacts:

a. a small Copador effigy (frog) vessel (Special Find 69) and several human teeth;

b. a small group of beads—two jade and one shell (Special Finds 70, 71, and 72);

c. another group of adornos—three jade beads, two shell beads, and a bone effigy (Special Finds 73, 74, 75, 76, 77, and 79).

C1-1078	Level 4 Special Find 58
C1-1077	Level 4 Special Find 59
B1-1066	Level 4 Special Find 60
C1-1070	Level 4 Special Find 61
C1-1067	Level 4 Special Find 62
B1-1069	Level 4 Special Find 63
B1-1068	Level 4 Special Find 64
C1-1085 (8)	Level 5
B1-1085 (6)	Level 5
B1-1124	Level 5 Special Find 65
B1-1123	Level 5 Special Find 66
C1-1137	Level 5 Special Find 67
B1-1135	Level 5 Special Find 68
C1-1119	Level 5 Special Find 78
C1-1138	Level 5 Special Find 81
C1-1190	Level 5 Special Find 85

The following candeleros were also found within Levels 4 and 5 of this excavation. There is no evidence of direct association, but they may have been associated originally with any of the burials or the cache listed above.

C1-953 (6)	Level 3
B1-953	Level 3
C1-1053 (2)	Level 4
B1-1053	Level 4

Burials 21 and 24
Operation 100(B), trench through Structure B, CV-43. These candeleros are possibly associated with Burials 21 and 24. Burial 21 consists only of a few fragments of skull recovered from the

northwest corner of the trench in Level 5-A. Burial 24 is a large tomb (Feature 13) that is located within Levels 8 and 9. A large number of artifacts were found within this well-constructed tomb.

C1-923	Level 1
M1-923	Level 1
C1-974	Level 2
C1-975 (4)	Level 3
B1-975	Level 3
M1-1020	Level 3
C1-1020	Level 3
B1-1027 (2)	Level 4
C1-1027	Level 4
M1-1027	Level 4
C1-1058 (5)	Level 5-A
B1-1058 (4)	Level 5-A
B1-1156	Level 9-B

Burial 23
Operation 105(A), test pit in Structure B, CV-44. These candeleros are possibly associated with Burial 23, which was located within the wall of this test excavation cut through Structure B. The burial was located within Level 7.

C1-1093	Level 4
C1-1106	Level 5

Burial 1
Operation 33(E), test excavation in the western portion of CV-43 plaza. These candeleros are possibly associated with Burial 1, a loosely flexed skeleton. A small eroded tripod vessel was also possibly in association (Special Find 7).

B1-472	Level 3
C1-477 (3)	Level 4
M1-477	Level 4
C1-474 (2)	Level 5
B1-474	Level 5
C1-487 (2)	Level 6
B1-493	Level 7

CV-43 Plaza Excavations: Within the western portion of the CV-43 plaza area, a small low platform was uncovered. This structure was completely cleared and then excavated. Three burials, all in small crypts, were found either under the structure, partially under the structure, or immediately next to the structure. It appears that the structure was constructed after the burials had been placed under the plaza floor. These burials are the following:

Burial 7, located within a crypt (Feature 5). This is a tightly flexed individual with jade-inlaid teeth (Special Find 26).

Burial 9, located within a crypt (Feature 2). This is a partially eroded burial found with a ceramic vessel (Special Find 28) and jade dental inlays (Special Find 30).

Burial 19, located within a crypt (Feature 12). No burial furniture was found with it.

Burial 9. The following candeleros were associated with Burial 9.

Operation 33(F), test excavation in the western portion of CV-43 plaza.

C1-467 (3)	Level 4
B1-467	Level 4
C1-479	Level 4 Special Find 2
C1-481	Level 4 Special Find 3
C1-483	Level 4 Special Find 4
C1-482	Level 4 Special Find 6

Operation 33(BB).

B1-517 (2)	Level 4
B1-512	Level 4 Special Find 9
B1-511	Level 4 Special Find 10

Operation 33 (DD).

C1-539	Level 1
B1-552	Level 2

Operation 33(GG).

C1-811	Special Find 27—associated with Feature 2

Operation 33(HH).

C1-856	Level 1

Burial 9 or 19. These candeleros were possibly associated with Burial 9 or Burial 19.

Operation 33(EE).

C1-555	Level 2

Burial 19. These candeleros were possibly associated with Burial 19.

Operation 33(II).

B1-879	Level 2
B1-891	Level 3

Operation 33(JJ).

C1-1063	Level 2

Burial 7. The following candeleros were possibly associated with Burial 7.

Operation 33(CC), excavation of small platform.

C1-542 (2)	Level 4
B1-553	Level 4 Special Find 14

Burial 6, Feature 1. We excavated a large section of the plaza in front of Structure A, CV-43. Burial 6, within a large tomb (Feature 1), was found here. Between this tomb and Structure A was Feature 4, a refilled hole. This fill was very rich in material, including a cache of obsidian blades (Special Find 23). Three other caches within this Operation 33(FF) area were clearly associated with Burial 6 and its tomb. They include two other caches of obsidian blades (Special Finds 24 and 25) and a lip-to-lip vessel cache (Special Finds 20 and 21). It is quite possible that all four of these caches were originally associated with the tomb, and it is even possible that the refilled hole area was, in some way, related to the tomb and its burial rituals.

The one candelero with full provenience information, Special Find 29, appears to be associated with the tomb. Also, the other candeleros found within Operation 33(Z), the excavation within which the tomb was uncovered, are directly associated with the burial/tomb. Finally, Operation 23(A) was a test excavation from 1976, and this candelero was probably also associated with the tomb.

Operation 33(FF).

B1-608	Level 1
C1-617	Level 2
M1-617	Level 2
M1-617	Level 2
B1-745	Level 4-B
B1-810	Level 4-B Special Find 29

Operation 33(Z).

C1-526	Level 4
C1-531	Level 5
B1-548	Level 5 Special Find 13

Operation 23(A).

C1-277	Level 4

Burial 16

Operation 50(A), trench through the CV-45 structure. Burial 16 is a badly disintegrated burial within this trench excavation, located within Level 6-A. It is definitely associated with candelero Special Find 44 and possibly the others found within the trench.

C1-954 (2)	Level 5
B1-1008	Level 6-A Special Find 44
B1-1024	Level 8
B1-1082	Level 10

Feature 18

Operation 104(A), trench through Structure A, CV-43. The following candeleros were possibly associated with a cache identified as Feature 18. This cache consisted of an ash- and charcoal-stained area with stingray spines and miscellaneous shells under some rocks. The cache/feature extended from Level 8 down to 10.

B1-970	Level 2
C1-1086	Level 6
M1-150	Level 7

Burials 13, 14, and 17

Operation 103(A), CV-46. Within this trench through Structure A, CV-46, three burials were uncovered. Burial 13 is located at the southern end of the trench within Level 1, Burial 14 is located at the northern end of the trench within Level 3, and Burial 17 is located about 0.8 to 1 meters below Burial 13 within Level 4. It is quite probable, although not definite, that the candeleros listed below were associated with one of these burials.

C1-920	Level 1
C1-905	Level 2

Burial 10. Burial 10 appears to be a secondary burial placed next to Structure A, CV-44, and between this structure and Structure A, CV-43. Two (possibly three) candeleros were found within excavation units, which may indicate a possible association between this burial and the candeleros.

C1-843	Op. 39(N), Level 1
C1-950	Op. 39(S), Level 1
M1-537	Op. 34(I), Level 1

CV-20
Burials 1, 2, and 3

Operations 2(B) and 2(C), test excavations within the plaza. These two test excavations at CV-20 uncovered three burials:

Burial 1 is a secondary burial within Operation 2(C), Level 3. This secondary burial was associated with Burial 3 (described below).

Burial 2 is a poorly preserved burial associated with a small, white sandstone rock—the only burial furniture (Special Find 7).

Burial 3 is a tightly flexed burial within a crypt (Feature 2). This burial was probably associated with a cache consisting of two chert leaf-shaped blades and several obsidian blades (Special Finds 1 and 2). It was also associated with two ceramic vessels (Special Finds 4 and 5) and two small jade pieces (Special Find 6).

It appears that the main burial is number 3 and that the candeleros from both excavation units were placed in association with this burial.

Operation 2(B).

C1-14 (3)	Level 3
C1-22 (7)	Level 4

Operation 2(C).

C1-17	Level 3
C1-27 (2)	Level 4

Burial 4

Operation 6(J) a clearing operation behind Structure A of CV-20. Within this operation, a tightly flexed burial (Burial 4) was uncovered next to the base of the exterior retaining wall of the structure. A candelero was found within this excavation unit, possibly associated with the burial.

C1-98

Burial 5

Operation 6(K) another clearing operation behind Structure A of CV-20. Another tightly flexed individual (Burial 5) was recovered in probable association with two candeleros.

C1-108
B1-108

Burials 10, 12, and 16

Operation 19(C), an excavation trench through Structure A, CV-20. Three burials were found within this trench:

Burial 10 was a flexed burial associated with two partial vessels (Special Finds 50 and 51).

Burial 12 was a poorly preserved burial with jade inlays (Special Find 55).

Burial 16 was a partially preserved burial associated with a vessel (Special Find 59) and jade inlays (Special Find 60).

A candelero may have been associated with one of these burials.

B1-260	Level 6

Burials 9 and 15

Operation 21(A), trench through Structure B, CV-20. Within Level 2 of this excavation, which included much of the fill of the structure, an elaborate burial (Burial 9) was uncovered. A candelero found may have been associated with Burial 15, which was in a crypt/tomb (Feature 13).

C1-254	

Burials 13 and 14

Operation 20(A), a trench through Structure D. Burials 13 and 14 were found in Level 5 and several caches in Levels 3 and 4. While there is no clear association between the burials and the caches or the one candelero found lower down, in Level 8, an association remains a possibility.

B1-270	Level 8

Test Excavations
CV-17

Operation 10(A), test excavation within the plaza of CV-17. Three burials (Burials 1, 2, and 3) were found in Level 2 of this test excavation. The one candelero found in this level may have been associated with one of these burials.

C1-105	Level 2

CV-22

Operation 14(A), test excavation within the plaza of CV-22. No burials were found in association with these candeleros, but they probably were associated with a series of caches that were placed immediately below the plaza floor.

C1-159	Level 3
B1-162	Level 3 Special Find 2
B1-164	Level 3 Special Find 4
C1-165 (2)	Level 4
B1-169	Level 4 Special Find 5
B1-173	Level 5 Special Find 6

B1-162 was found in direct association with a small jade pebble (Special Find 1). B1-164 was also part of a similar cache and also associated with a jade pebble (Special Find 3). The other candeleros are not directly associated with either of these small caches but appear to have been purposefully placed under this plaza floor.

CV-56

Operation 17(A), test excavation within the plaza of CV-56.

C1-190	Level 1
B1-191	Level 1 Special Find 1
M1-194	Level 3
C1-205	Level 4

There is no evidence of association of these candeleros with a cache or burial.

CV-94

Operation 54(A), test excavation within the plaza of CV-94. This test excavation found an early floor at Level 6. It is possible that part of the ritual of building over this floor involved the use of candeleros.

Within Level 7-A a large stone toad effigy was recovered—again, possibly part of a cache with the candeleros from this level.

Finally, there is a burial that intrudes into Level 8 from above, and the candeleros may have been associated with it.

C1-609	Level 2
C1-661 (2)	Level 6
B1-661	Level 6
C1-655 (2)	Level 7-A
C1-657 (2)	Level 7-B
C1-650	Level 8

Candelero Function—Summary Comments: The pottery candeleros, judging from their appearance, do not seem to have been highly valuable or prestigious items in ancient Copan society. They look to have been too hastily made, and they are too numerous. A religious or ritual purpose is certainly suggested by the fact that a great many of them show evidences of burning in their interiors, as though they may have held some combustible material, perhaps incense. Their frequent associations with human burials or with artifact caches further strengthens this ritual inference about the candeleros. R. M. Leventhal, who excavated most of them, observed that the candeleros were not, themselves, the center or focus of the ritual. Presumably, that focus was the dead person being interred or the artifact cache being placed beneath the floor of a building. Rather, the candeleros were sustaining paraphernalia, usually placed around the edges of the place where the burial or cache deposit was made. By a very general analogy, one thinks of the many candles lighted by worshippers in the Roman Catholic church: they are not central to the proceedings but merely accompany offerings placed by the faithful. Did the candeleros serve such a function?

Chronology of Candeleros: Unlike most of the other artifacts presented above, candeleros appear early in the chronology as defined from the settlement excavations. Table 23 provides the chronological placement of all the candeleros.

According to our data, both primary forms of the candelero, the cylindrical and the bottle-shaped, first appear in numbers during the Cueva phase at Copan, correlating to the early part of the Late Classic period. They both continue in quantity into the Coner phase. Cylindrical candeleros are more numerous, found within 40 per cent of the Coner proveniences, than bottle-shaped candeleros, found within 28 percent of these Coner proveniences.

This slight increased use of candeleros in the Coner phase may relate to the decrease in elaboration found within the burial contexts of the Coner phase. With the apparent disappearance of tomb architecture and complex burial furniture during the Coner phase, the increased usage of candeleros in rituals may indicate a resurgence of folk ritual activities.

At the present time, our data do not indicate whether candeleros were common within the Copan Main Center or were a ritual feature related primarily to the outlying residential groups. The excavations by the Carnegie Institution of Washington (Longyear 1952) do not pinpoint the context of the candeleros found during their excavations; however, the largest number came from Trench 1-46, located in the El Bosque section to the south of the Main Center. This trench was located within what appears to be an elite residential unit, comparable in many ways to CV-43.

TABLE 23

Distribution of candeleros by phase

	Phase 1	Phase 2	Phase 3	Phase 4	Phase 5	Phase 6	Unknown
Cylindrical	0 / 0%	0 / 0%	19 / 11%	17 / 10%	47 / 28%	66 / 40%	17 / 10%
Bottle-shaped	1 / 1%	0 / 0%	19 / 22%	9 / 10%	18 / 21%	24 / 28%	16 / 18%
Miscellaneous	0 / 0%	0 / 0%	1 / 6%	0 / 0%	4 / 24%	9 / 53%	3 / 18%
Total	1 / 0%	0 / 0%	39 / 14%	26 / 10%	69 / 26%	99 / 37%	36 / 13%

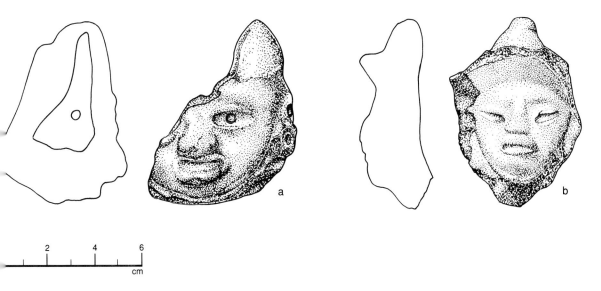

Figure 136a–b. Preclassic–Early Classic(?) figurines: a, 1-737; b, 1-777.

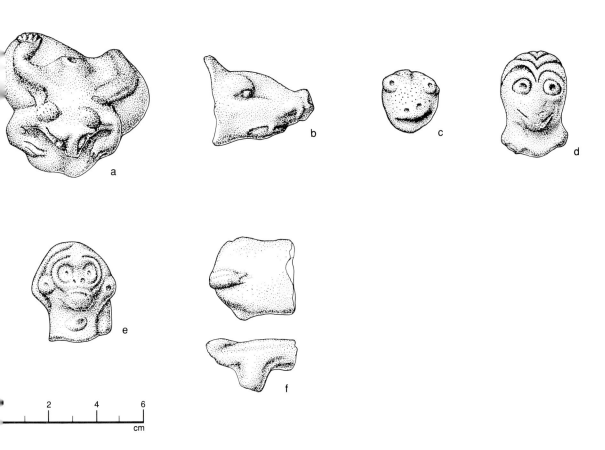

Figure 137a–f. Late Classic figurines and figurine whistles: a, 1-534; b, 1-522; c, 1-950; d, 1-540; e, 1-115; f, 1-1177.

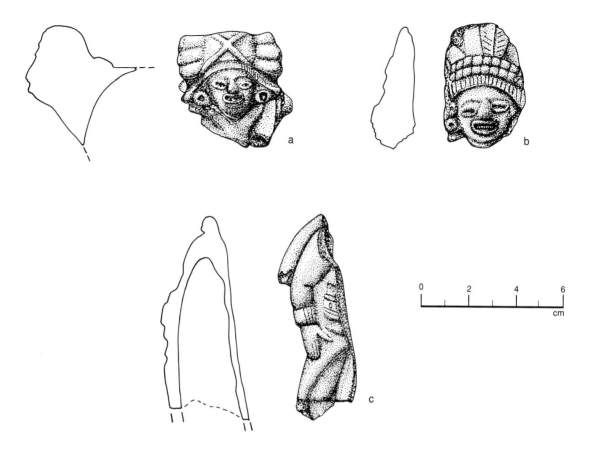

Figure 138a–c.   Elaborately attired Maya men: a, 1-196; b, no cat. number—8; c, 1-285.

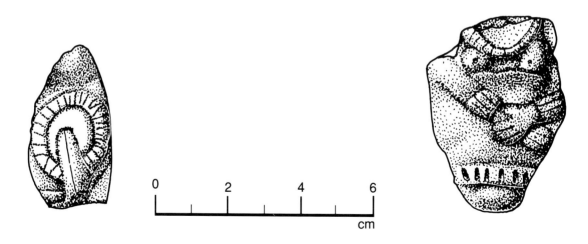

Figure 139.   Maya warrior 1-1025   **Figure 140.**   Maya woman 1-31

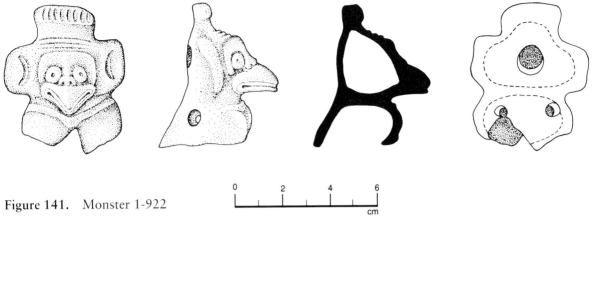

Figure 141. Monster 1-922

Figure 142a–b. Semi-solid, simply dressed figurines: a, 1-861; b, 1-1060.

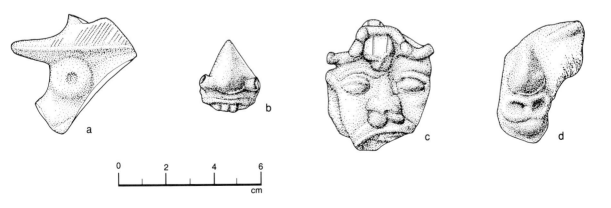

Figure 143a–d. Large human figurines: a, 1-115; b, 1-632; c, 1-895; d, 1-1085.

Figure 144a–e.   Unperforated potsherd disks

Figure 145a–g.   Perforated potsherds

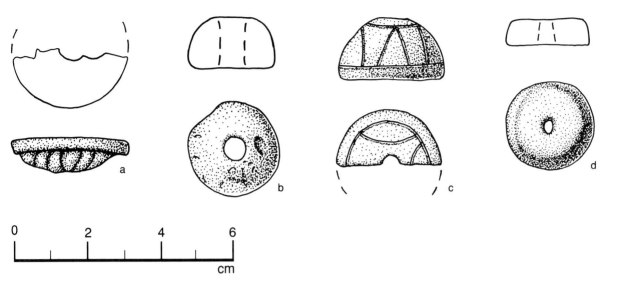

Figure 146a–d. Spindle whorls, specially manufactured: a, 1-98; b, 1-566; c, 1-602; d, 1-1086.

Figure 147. Potsherd pendant 1-954

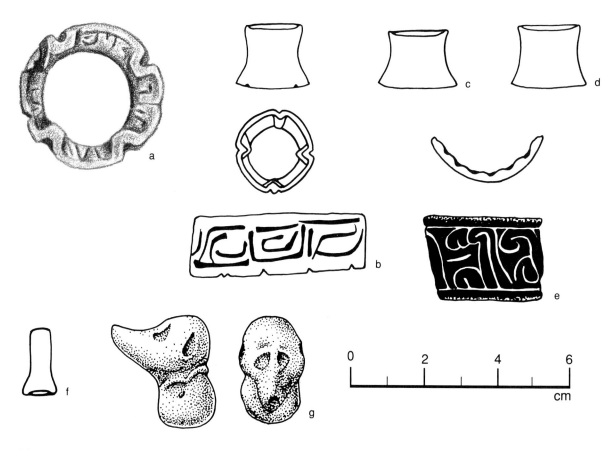

Figure 148a–g.   Ear ornaments: a, 1-110; b, 1-224; c, 1-313; d, 1-312; e, 1-316; f, 1-314; g, 1-1085.

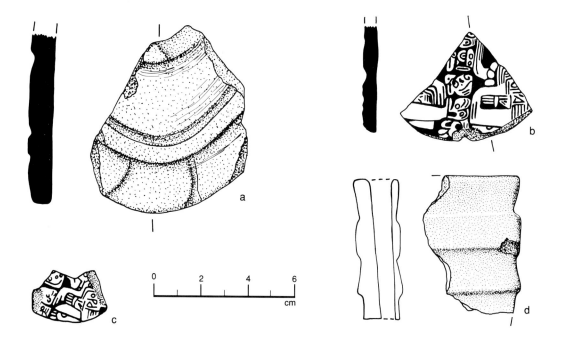

Figure 149a–d.   Ceramic ornaments or ritual objects: a, 1-238; b, 1-524; c, 1-524; d, 1-815.

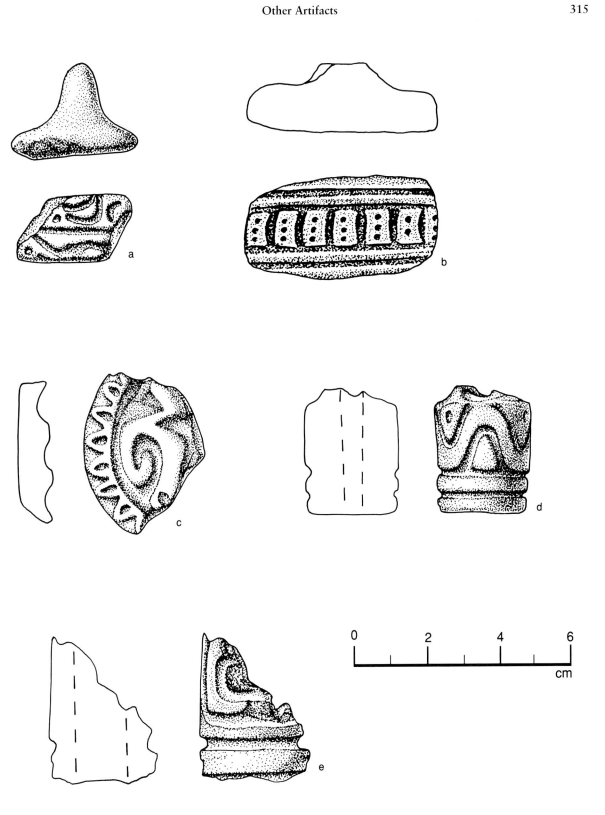

Figure 150a–e. Seals or stamps: a, 1-418; b, 1-561; c, 1-686; d, 1-595; e, 1-1024.

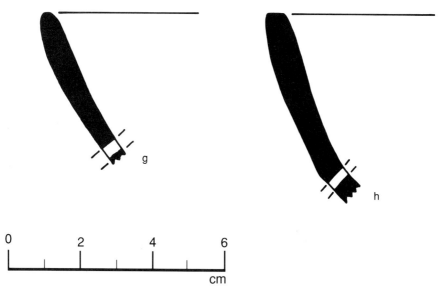

Figure 151a–h.   Collanders: a–f, fragments; g–h, rim profiles.

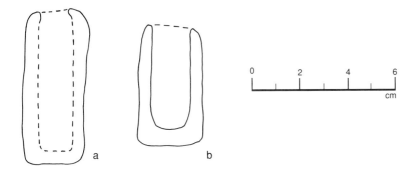

Figure 152a–b.   Candeleros, cylindrical, profiles

Figure 153a–g.   Candeleros, cylindrical

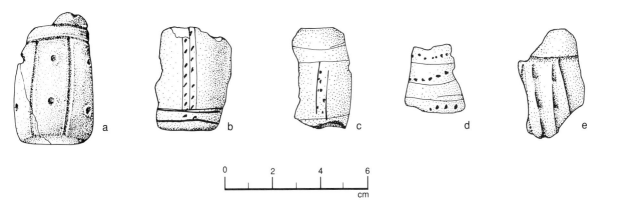

Figure 154a–e.   Candeleros, cylindrical, incised and punctated: a, 1-191; b, 1-543; c, 1-1020;
d, 1-975; e, 1-899.

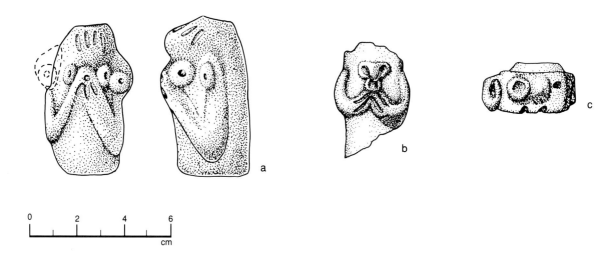

Figure 155a–c.   Candeleros, cylindrical, modeled: a, 1-1077; b, 1-953; c, 1-1085.

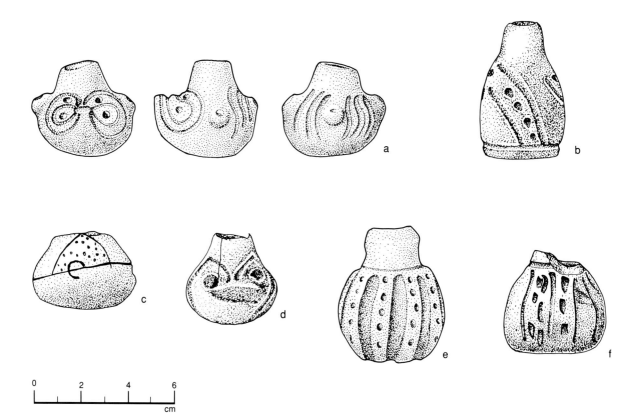

Figure 156a–f.   Candeleros, bottle-shaped, incised and punctated: a, 1-1135; b, 1-548; c, 1-108; d, 1-191; e, 1-1069; f, 1-1053.

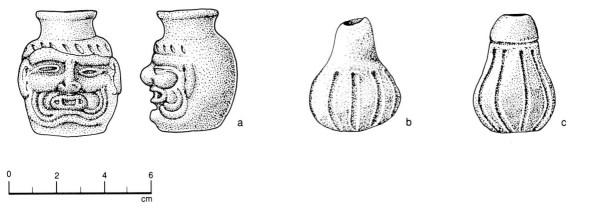

Figure 157a–c.   Candeleros, bottle-shaped, incised: a, 1-970; b, 1-173; c, 1-553.

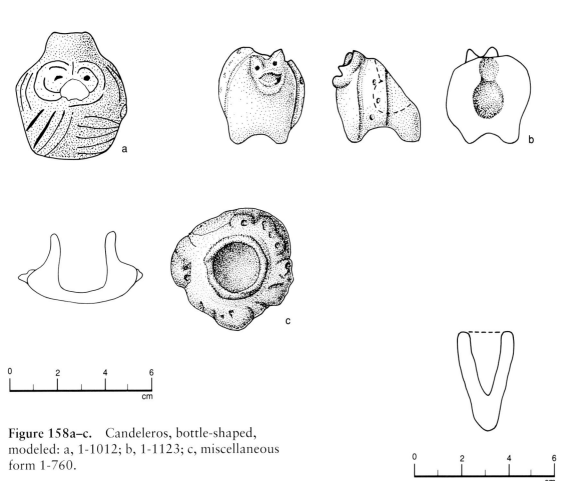

Figure 158a–c.   Candeleros, bottle-shaped, modeled: a, 1-1012; b, 1-1123; c, miscellaneous form 1-760.

Figure 159.   Candelero, conical 1-52

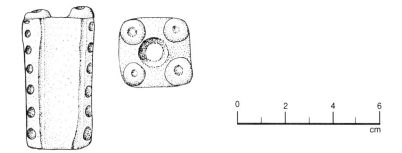

Figure 160. Candelero, rectangular 1-949

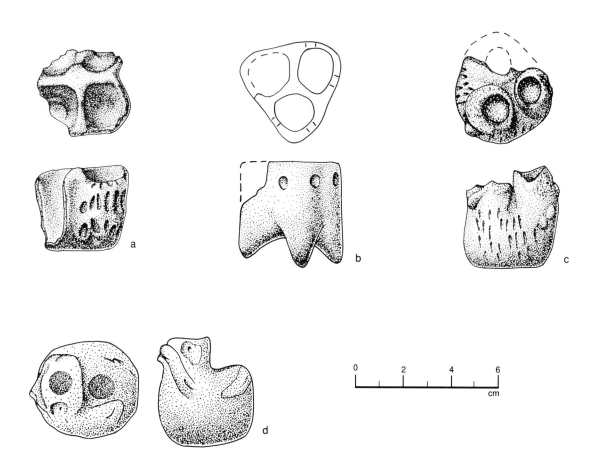

Figure 161a–d. Candeleros, multi-chambered: a, 1-638; b, 1-537; c, 1-1020; d, 1-1005.

Figure 162.   Miniature vessel 1-1214

Figure 163a–b.   Miniature vessels: a, 1-950; b, 1-1118.

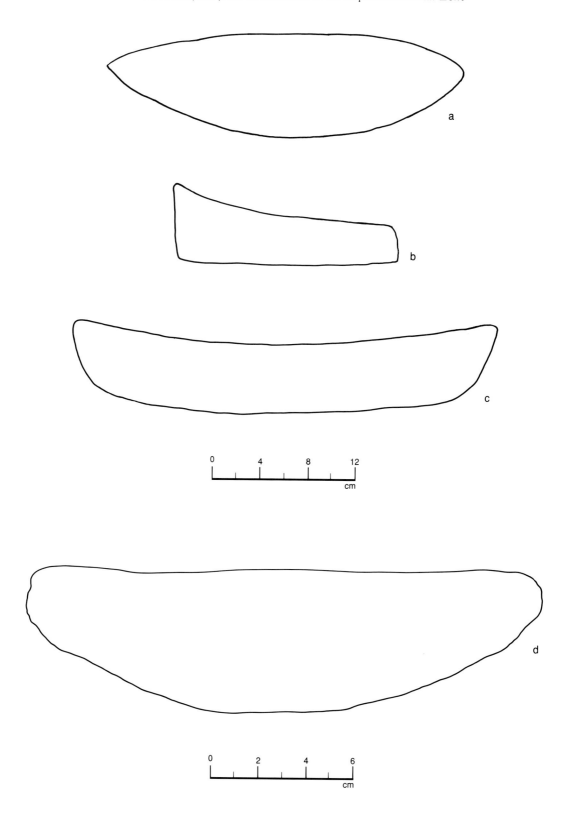

Figure 164a–d.   Metates, Type 1 cross sections (scale of a, b, and c: 1:2)

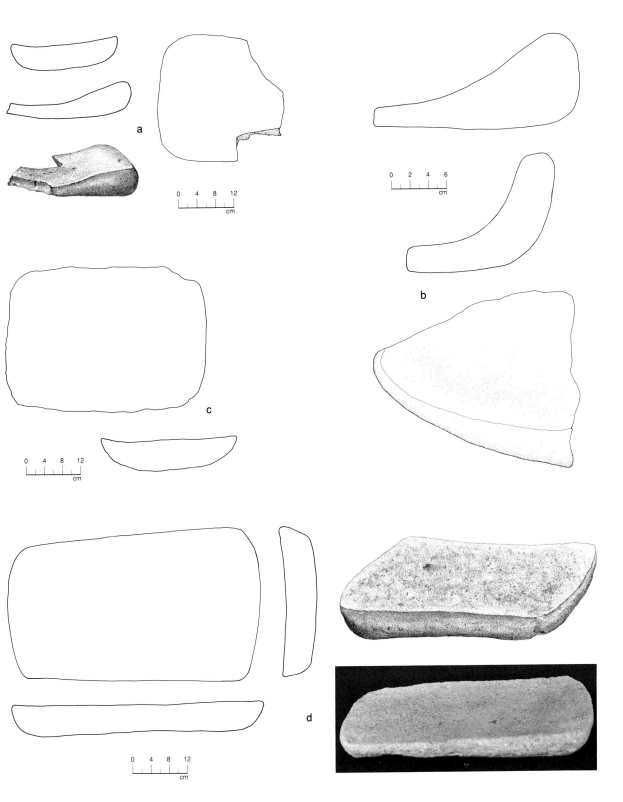

Figure 165a–d.   Metates, Type 1: a, 1-124 (scale: 1:2); b, 1-899;
c, 1-98 (scale: 1:2); d, 1-1023 (scale: 1:2).

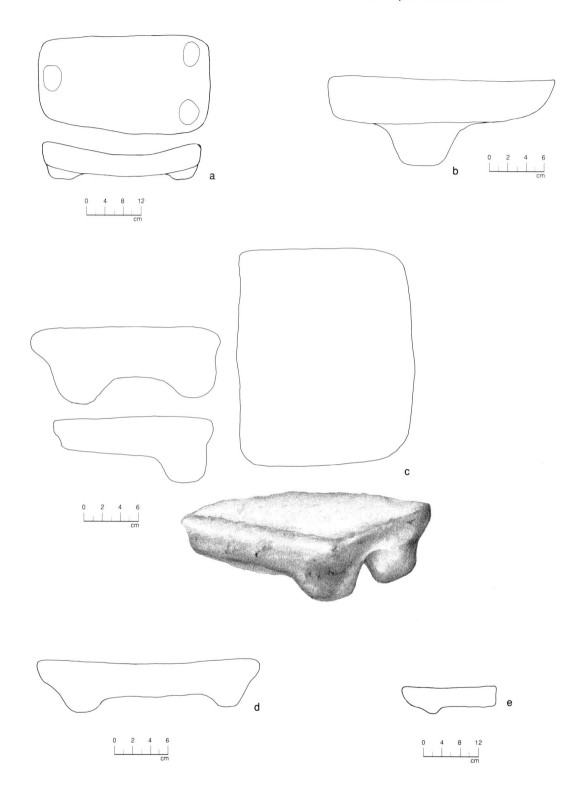

Figure 166a–e.   Metates, Type 2: a, 1-706 (scale: 1:2); b, 1-1084; c, 1-145; d, 1-867; e, 1-83 (scale: 1:2).

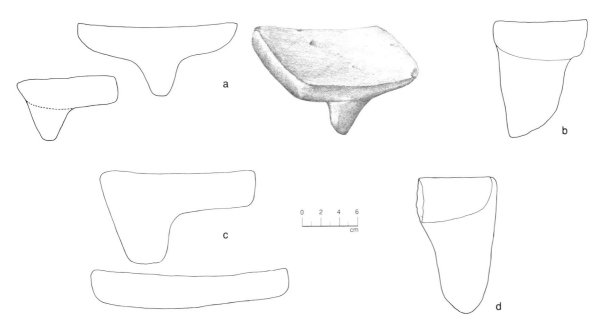

Figure 167a–d.   Metates, Type 3: a, 1-202; b, 1-206; c, 1-615; d, 1-68.

Figure 168a–b.   Metates, Type 4: a, 1-278 (scale: 1:2); b, left 1-841, right 1-631.

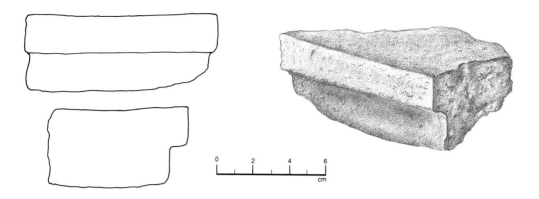

Figure 169.   Metate, Special 1-107

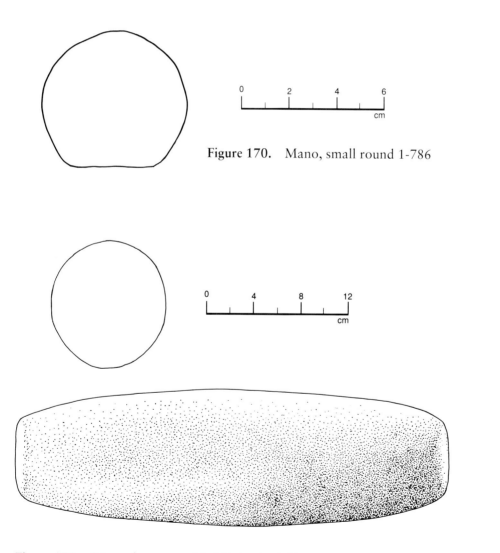

Figure 170.   Mano, small round 1-786

Figure 171.   Mano, large round 1-361 (scale: 1:2)

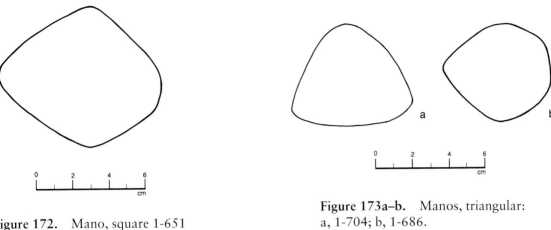

Figure 172.   Mano, square 1-651

Figure 173a–b.   Manos, triangular: a, 1-704; b, 1-686.

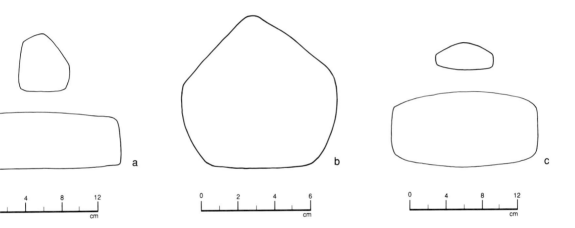

Figure 174a–c.   Manos, pentagonal: a, 1-52 (scale: 1:2); b, 1-615; c, 1-156 (scale: 1:2).

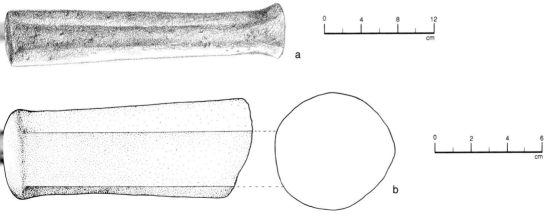

Figure 175a–b.   Manos, overhang: a, 1-98 (scale: 1:2); b, 1-451.

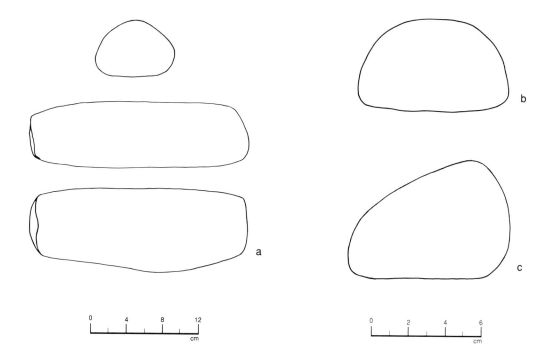

Figure 176a–c.   Manos, plano-convex: a, 1-361 (scale: 1:2); b, 1-841; c, 1-1020.

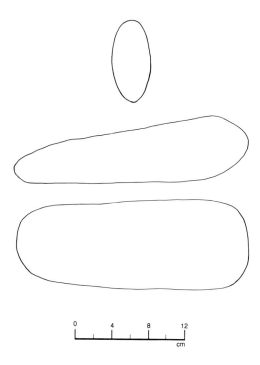

Figure 177.   Mano, thin ovate-rectangular 1-108 (scale: 1:2)

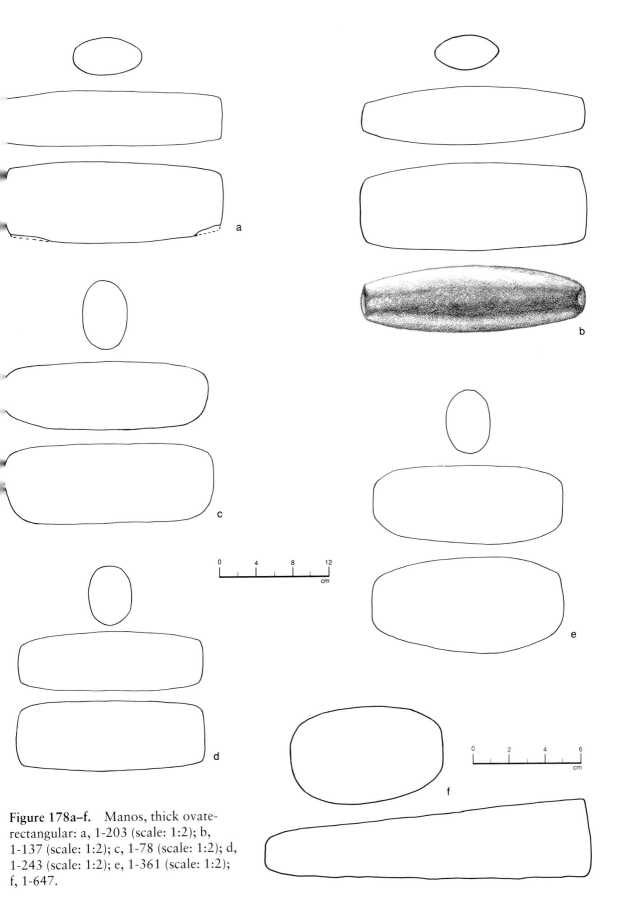

Figure 178a–f. Manos, thick ovate-rectangular: a, 1-203 (scale: 1:2); b, 1-137 (scale: 1:2); c, 1-78 (scale: 1:2); d, 1-243 (scale: 1:2); e, 1-361 (scale: 1:2); f, 1-647.

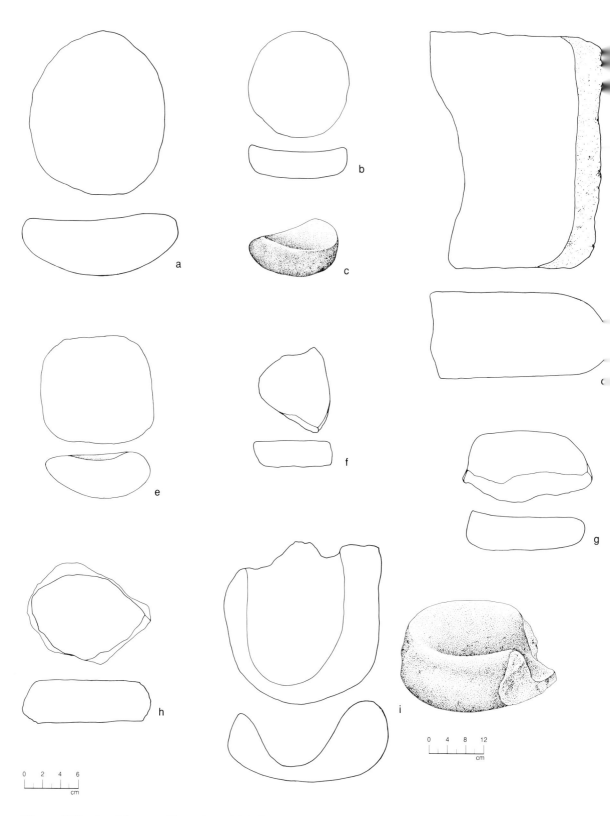

Figure 179a–i. Mortars, Type 1: a, 1-77; b, 1-108; c, 1-124; d, 1-633; e, 1-454; f, 1-68; g, 1-78; h, 1-271; i, 1-615 (scale: 1:2).

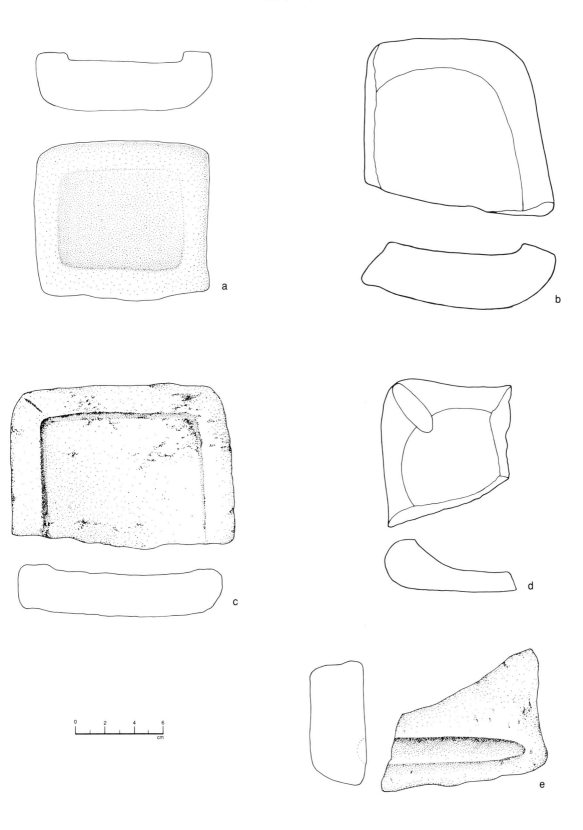

Figure 180a–e.   Mortars, Type 2: a, 1-569; b, 1-126; c, 1-1056; d, 1-107; e, 1-838.

Figure 181a–g.   Barkbeaters: a, 1-1183; b, 1-353; c, 1-242; d, 1-202; e, 1-220; f, 1-765; g, 1-1.

Figure 182a–f. Rubbing and pounding stones

Figure 183a–c. Pounders

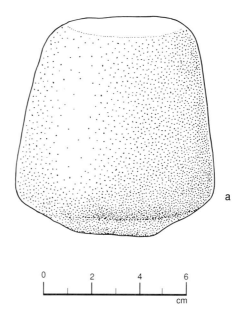

Figure 184a–b. Pounders: a, 1-821; b, 1-115.

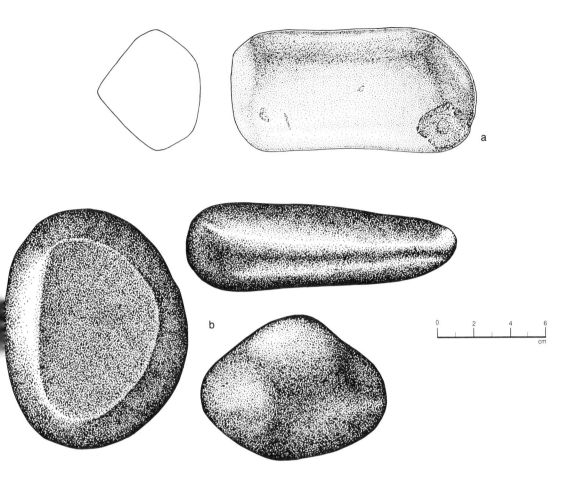

Figure 185a–b.   Polishing stones: a, 1-950; b, 1-215.

Figure 186.   Pestle

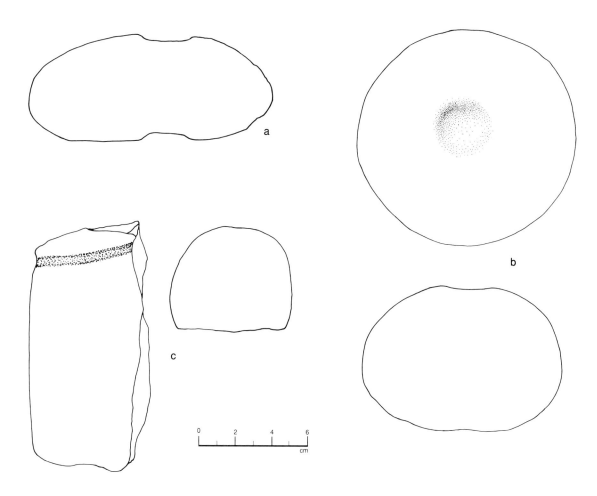

Figure 187a–c.   Anvils: a, 1-1; b, 1-451; c, 1-545.

Figure 188.   Anchor/weight 1-196

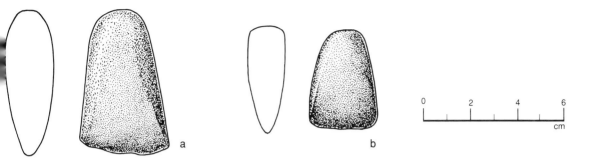

Figure 189a–b.　Celts: a, 1-58; b, 1-52.

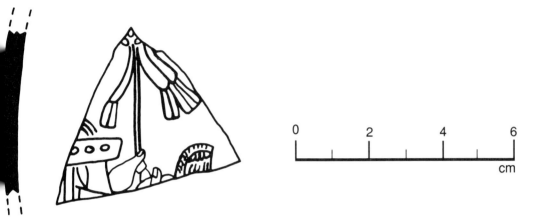

Figure 190.　Alabaster sherd 1-270

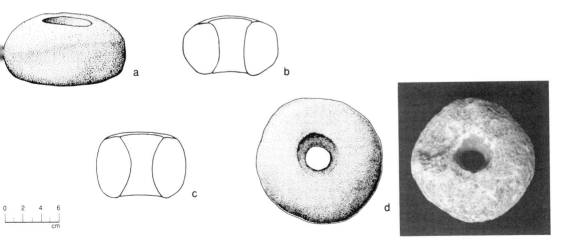

Figure 191a–d.　Ring stones: a, 1-86; b, 1-108; c, 1-138; d, 1-710.

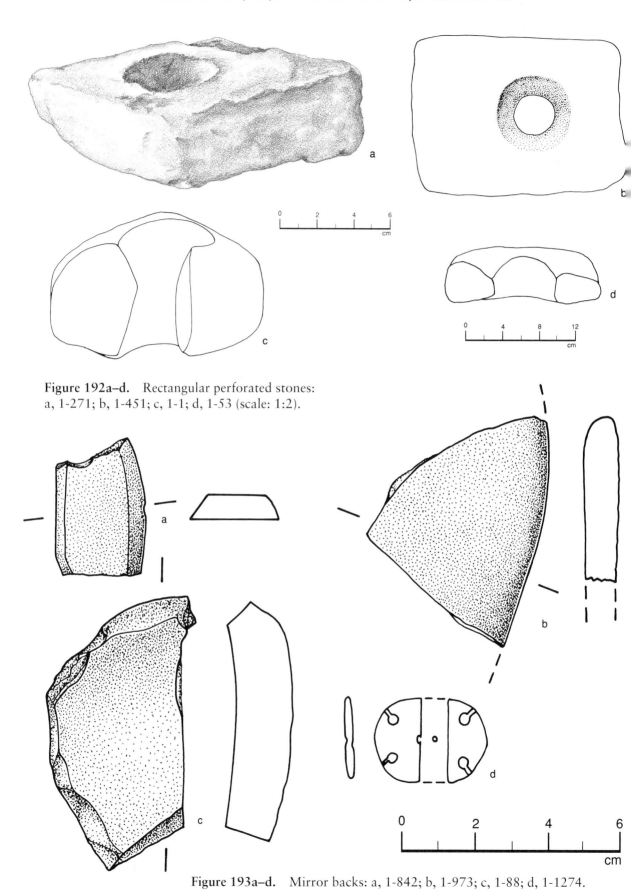

Figure 192a–d.   Rectangular perforated stones:
a, 1-271; b, 1-451; c, 1-1; d, 1-53 (scale: 1:2).

Figure 193a–d.   Mirror backs: a, 1-842; b, 1-973; c, 1-88; d, 1-1274.

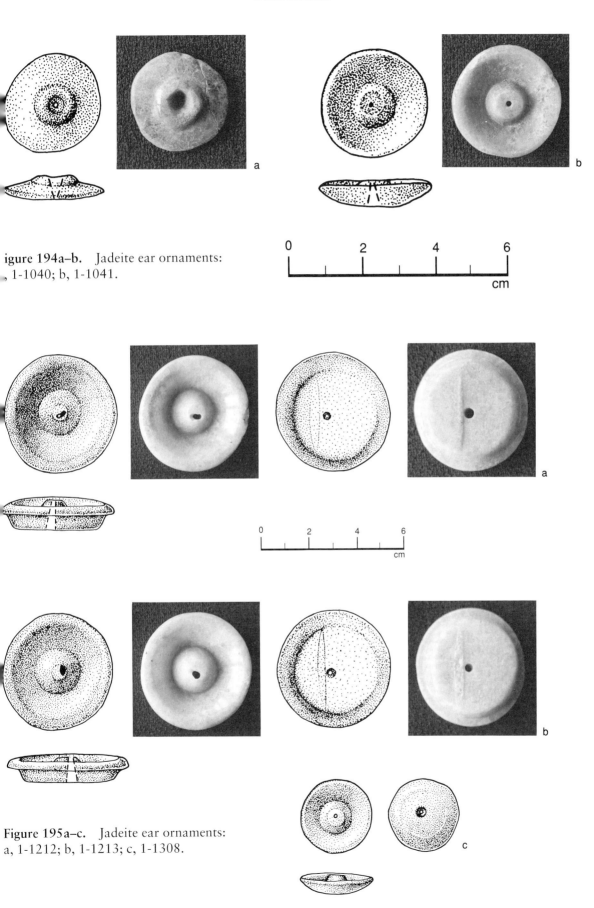

Figure 194a–b. Jadeite ear ornaments: a, 1-1040; b, 1-1041.

Figure 195a–c. Jadeite ear ornaments: a, 1-1212; b, 1-1213; c, 1-1308.

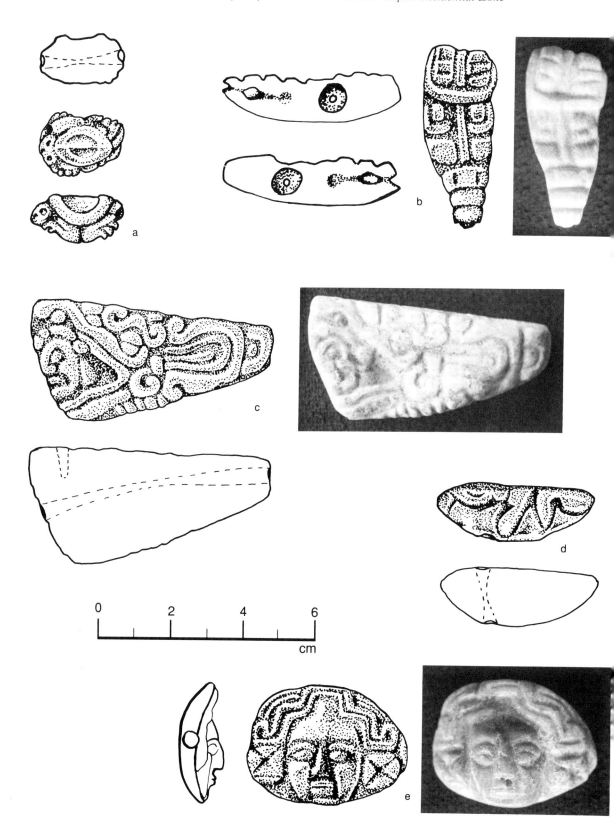

Figure 196a–e.   Jadeite pendants: a, 1-230; b, 1-335; c, 1-336; d, 1-337; e, 1-338.

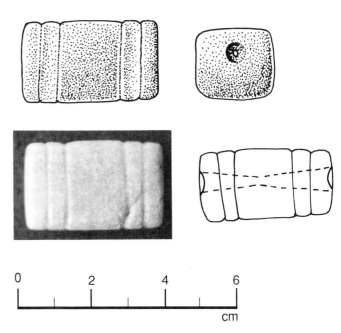

Figure 197. Large tubular jadeite beads   Figure 198.   Large tubular jadeite bead 1-1226

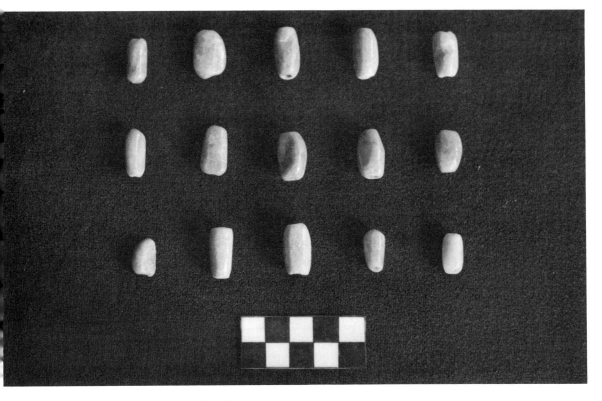

Figure 199.   Small tubular jadeite beads

Figure 200.   Subspherical jadeite beads

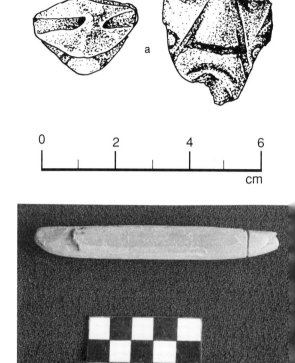

Figure 201a–b.   Stone ornaments:
a, 1-318; b, 1-1053.

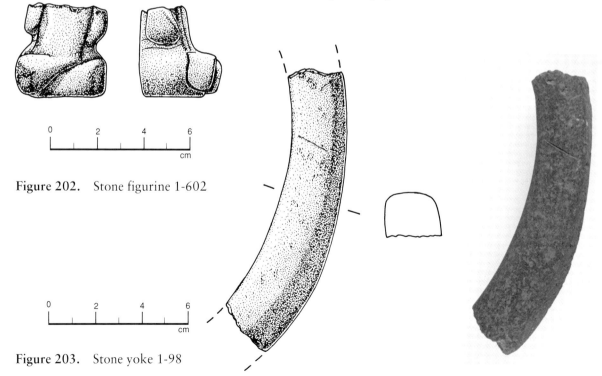

Figure 202.   Stone figurine 1-602

Figure 203.   Stone yoke 1-98

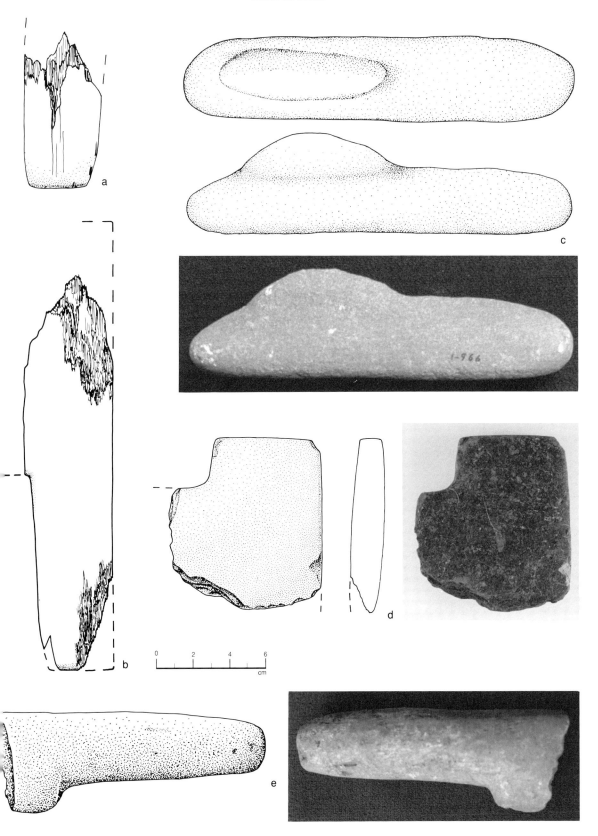

Figure 204a–e.   Maces: a, 1-901; b, 1-922; c, 1-966; d, 1-617; e, 1-206.

Figure 205.   Star-shaped stone

Figure 206a–c.   Stone disks:
a, 1-765; b, 1-1059; c, 1-754.

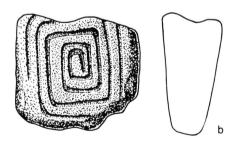

Figure 207a–b.   Incised stones: a, 1-540; b, 1-894.

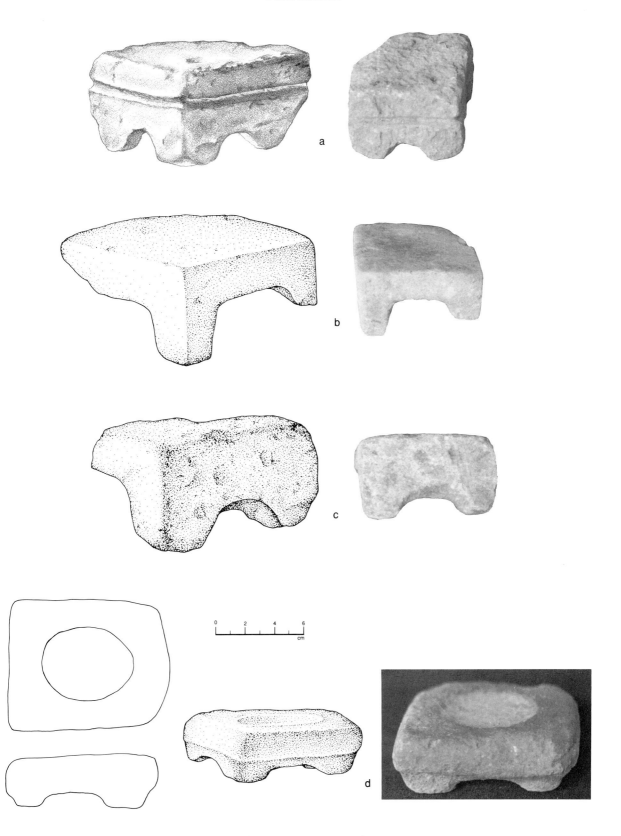

Figure 208a–d.   Miniature tables: a, 1-4; b, 1-215; c, 1-137; d, 1-279.

Figure 209. L-shaped stones

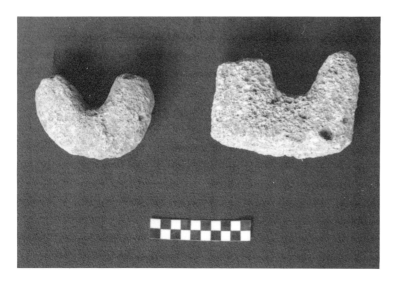

Figure 210. U-shaped stones

Figure 211. T-shaped stone

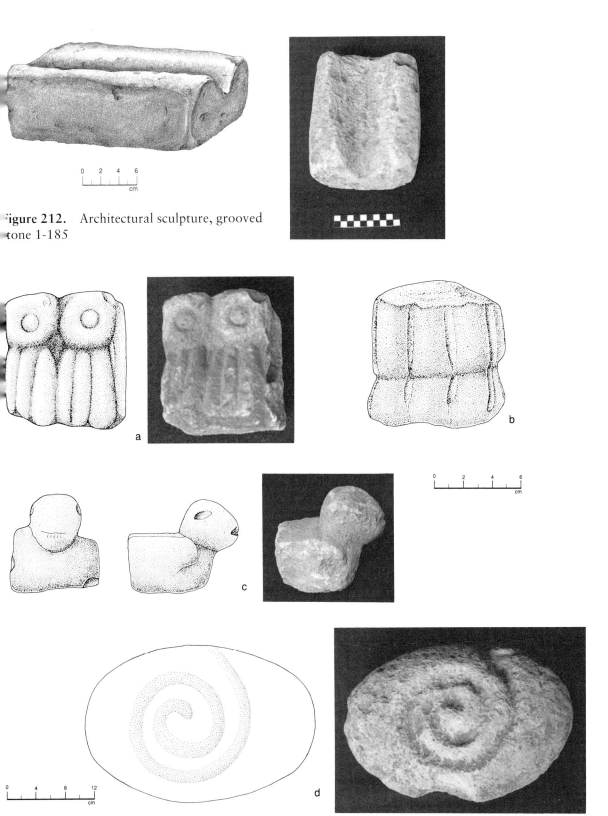

Figure 212. Architectural sculpture, grooved
stone 1-185

Figure 213a–d. Architectural sculpture: a, 1-449; b, 1-451; c, 1-619; d, 1-747 (drawing scale: 1:2).

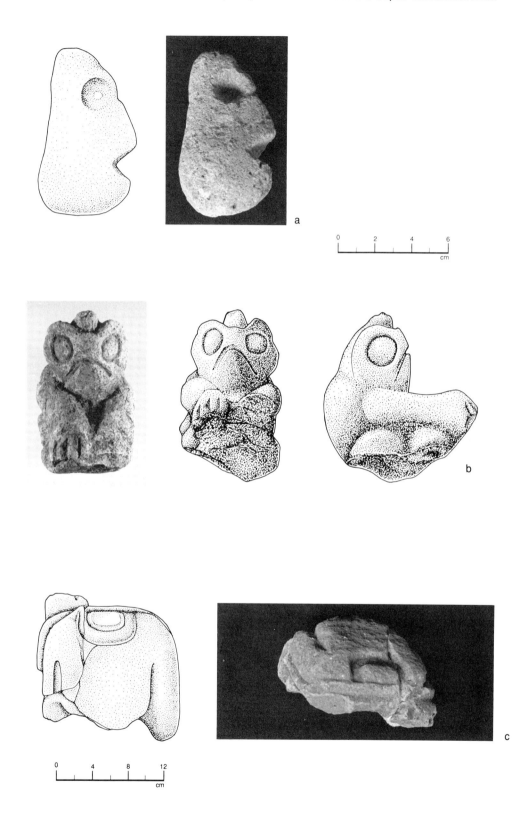

Figure 214a–c.   Sculpture: a, 1-451; b, 1-657; c, 1-864 (drawing scale: 1:2).

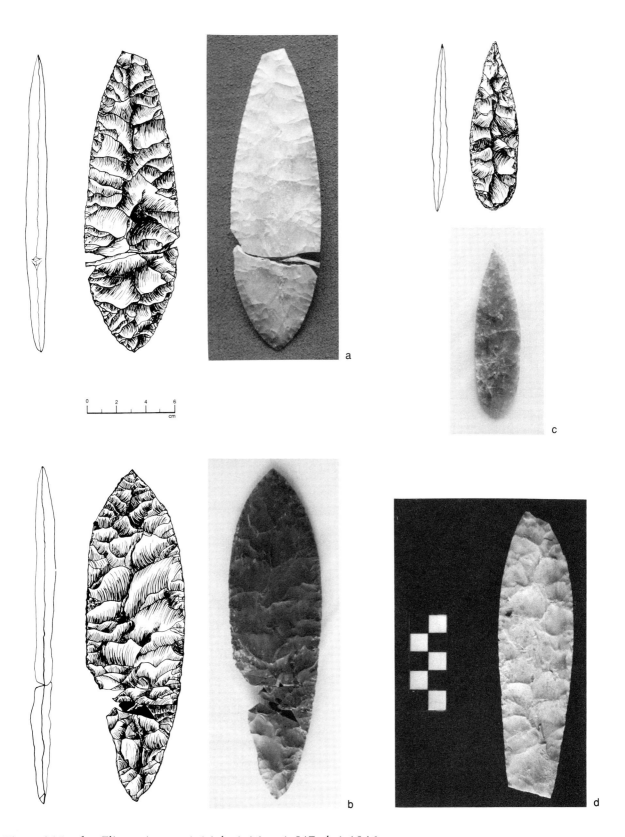

Figure 215a–d. Flint points: a, 1-16; b, 1-16; c, 1-547; d, 1-1046.

Figure 216.   Scrapers

Figure 217a–e.   Drills

Figure 218a–e.
Choppers

Figure 219a–b. Eccentrics: a, 1-206; b, 1-814.

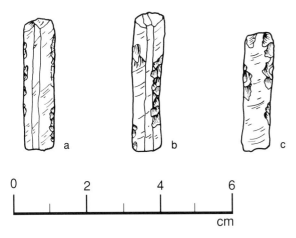

Figure 220a–f. Obsidian use-wear categories

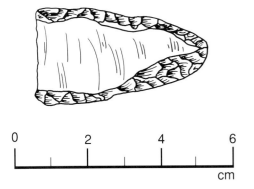

Figure 221. Obsidian macroblade

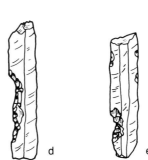
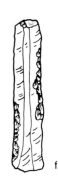
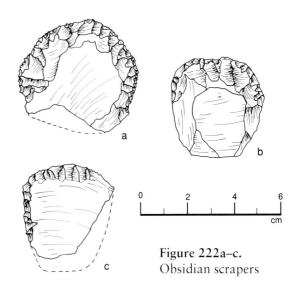

Figure 222a–c.
Obsidian scrapers

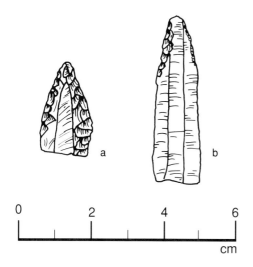

Figure 223a–b.   Obsidian pointed blades

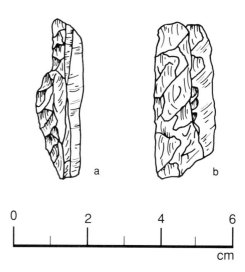

Figure 224a–b.   Obsidian ridge flakes

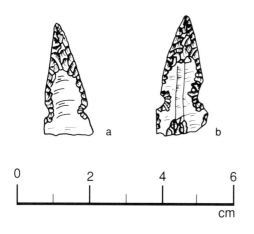

Figure 225a–b.   Obsidian arrow points

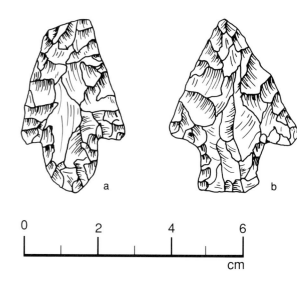

Figure 226a–b.   Obsidian dart points

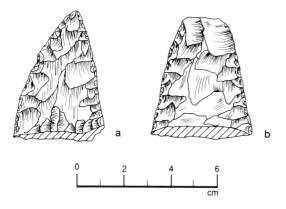

Figure 227a–b.   Obsidian large biface fragments

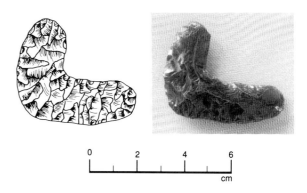

Figure 228.   Obsidian eccentric

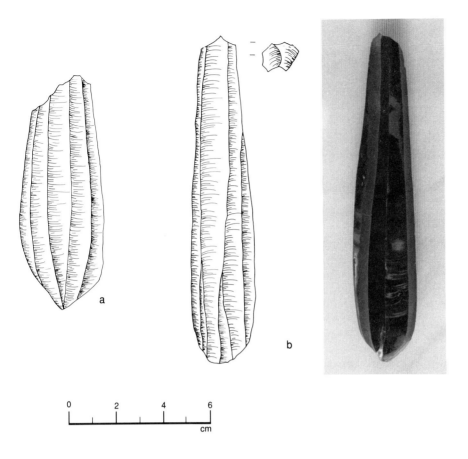

Figure 229a–c.   Obsidian cores

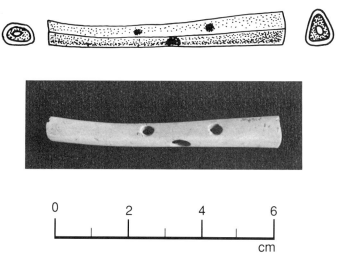

Figure 230. Bone whistle 1-918

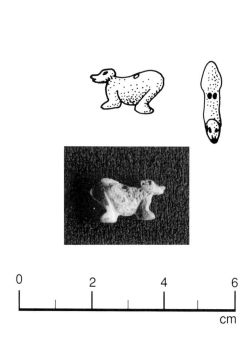

Figure 231. Effigy 1-1129

Figure 232. Bone tube 1-207

Figure 233a–k.   Awls

Figure 234a–b.   Shell pendants: a, 1-349;
b, 1-361.

Figure 235a–b.   Shell adornos: a, 1-333; b, 1-1275.

Figure 236a–i.   Shell, miscellaneous 1-1277

Figure 237. *Spondylus* shell 1-718

Figure 238a–b. Crab claw 1-953 (a) and stingray spine 1-1179 (b)

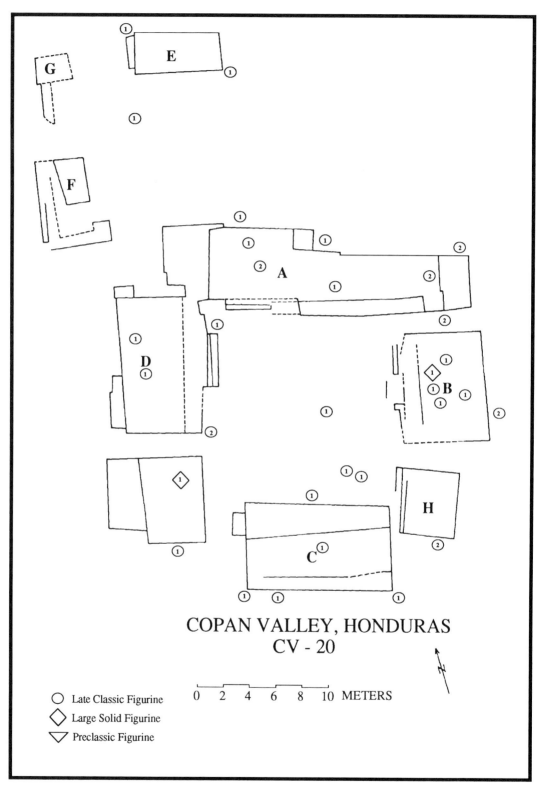

Figure 239a.   Distribution of figurines: CV-20.

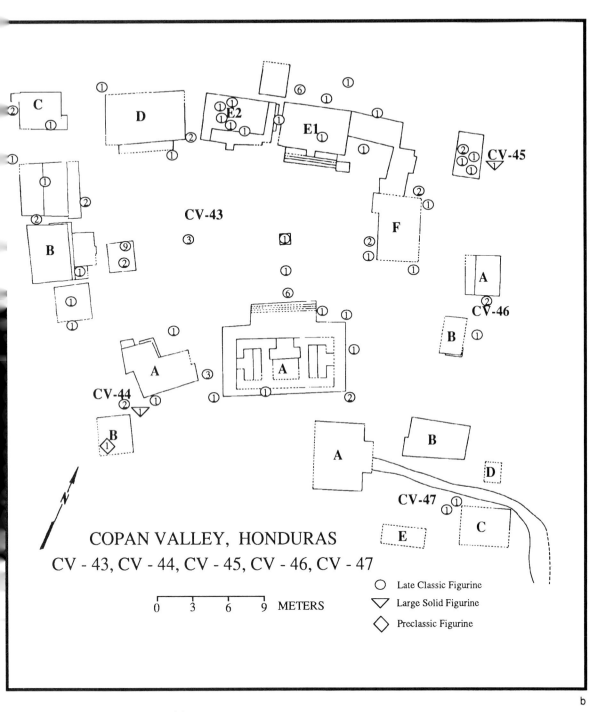

Figure 239b.   Distribution of figurines: CV-43.

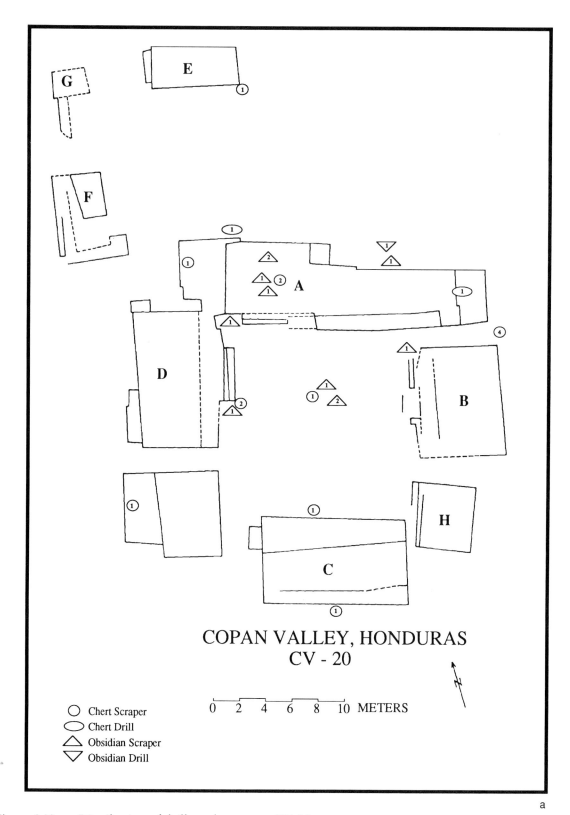

Figure 240a. Distribution of drills and scrapers: CV-20.

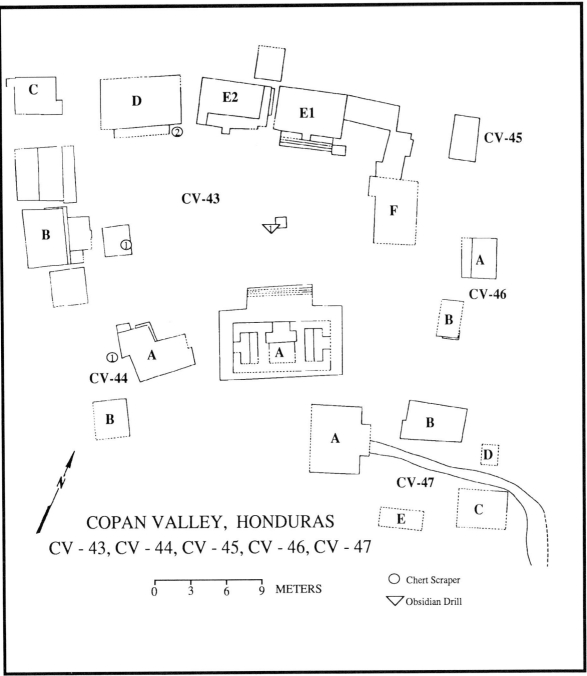

Figure 240b.   Distribution of drills and scrapers: CV-43.

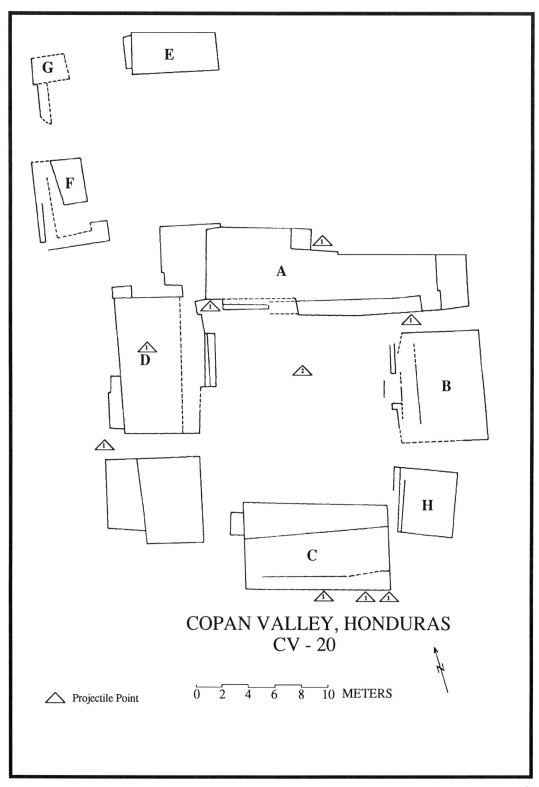

Figure 241a.   Distribution of projectile points and chert artifacts: CV-20.

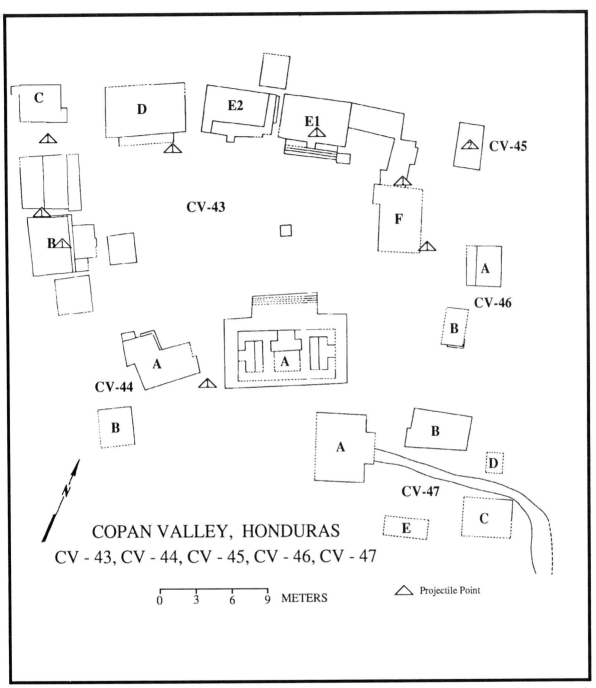

b

Figure 241b. Distribution of projectile points and chert artifacts: CV-43.

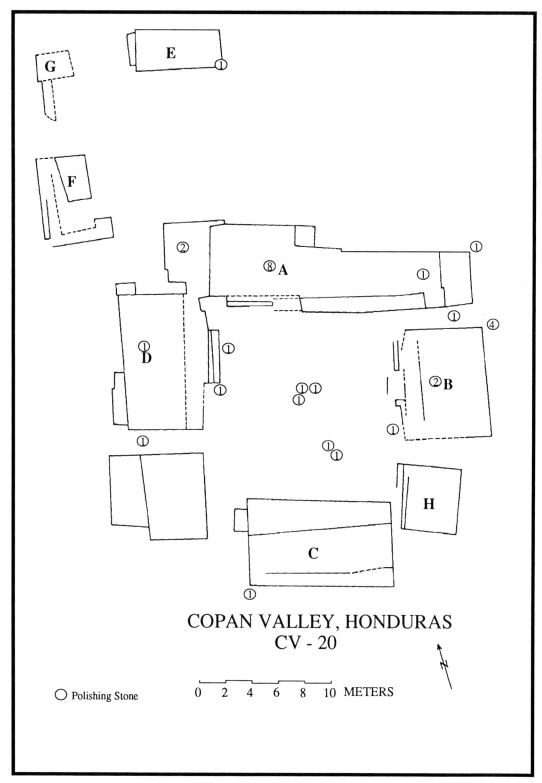

Figure 242a.   Distribution of polishing stones: CV-20.

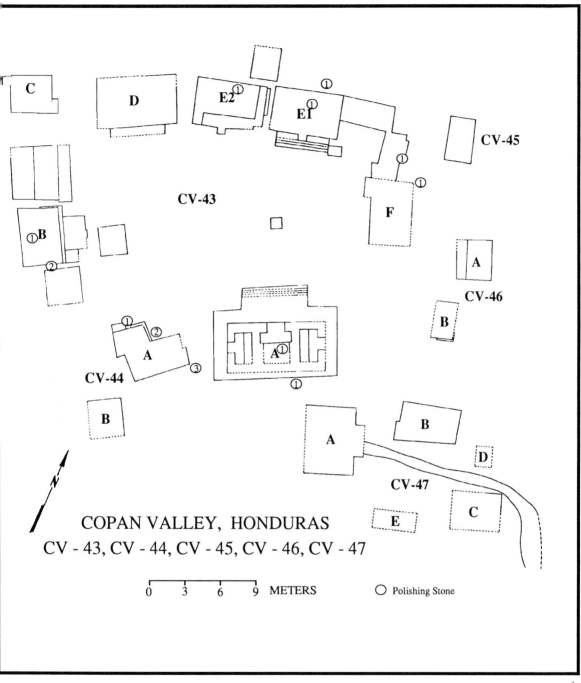

Figure 242b. Distribution of polishing stones: CV-43.

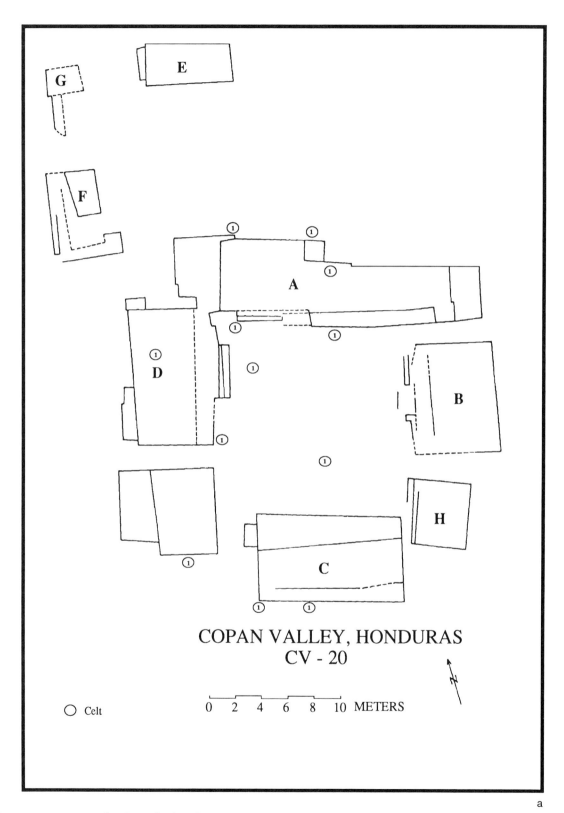

Figure 243a.   Distribution of celts: CV-20.

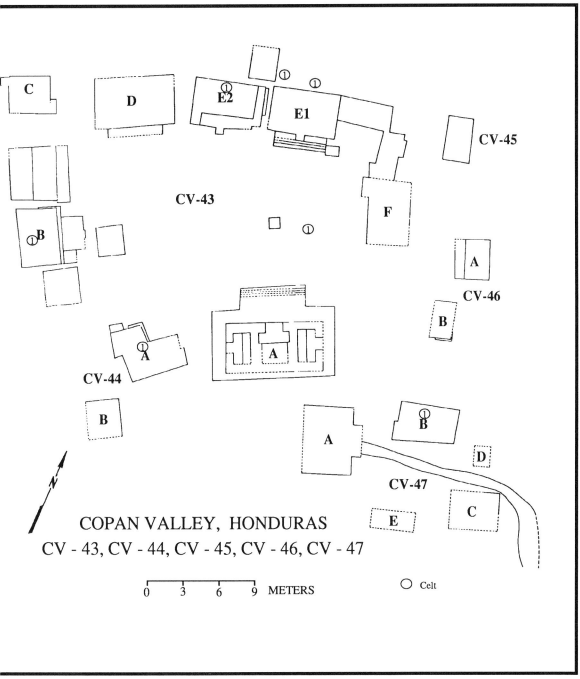

COPAN VALLEY, HONDURAS
CV - 43, CV - 44, CV - 45, CV - 46, CV - 47

0 3 6 9 METERS

○ Celt

b

Figure 243b. Distribution of celts: CV-43.

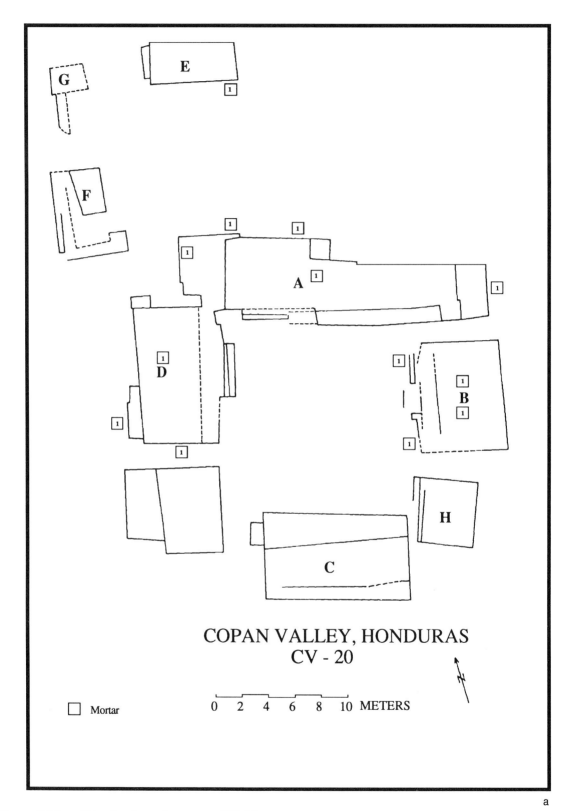

a

Figure 244a.   Distribution of mortars: CV-20.

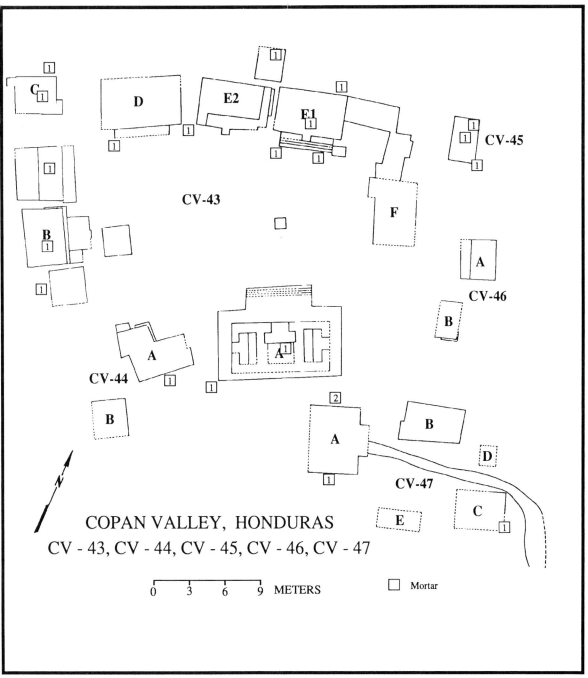

Figure 244b. Distribution of mortars: CV-43.

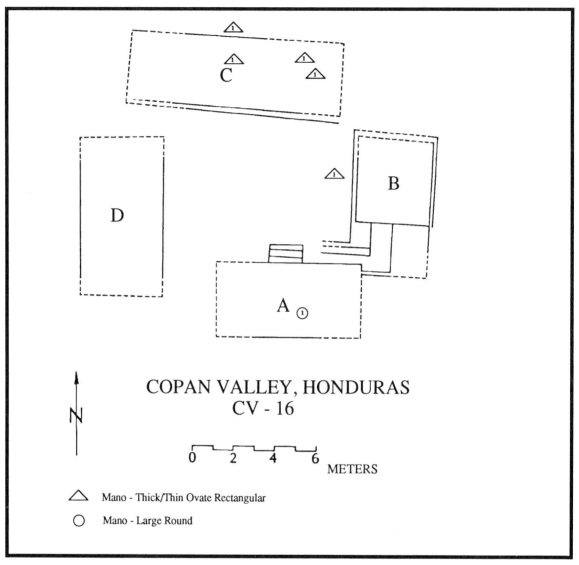

Figure 245a.   Distribution of manos: CV-16.

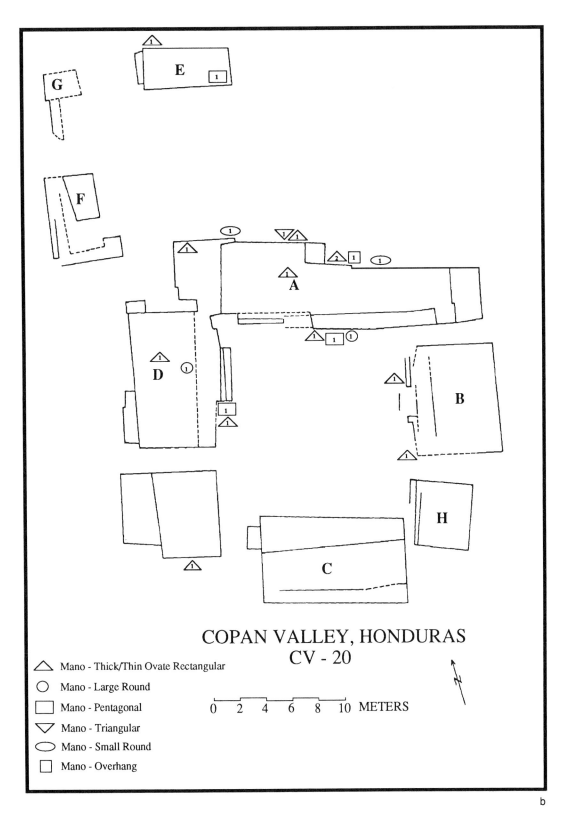

COPAN VALLEY, HONDURAS
CV - 20

△ Mano - Thick/Thin Ovate Rectangular

○ Mano - Large Round

□ Mano - Pentagonal

▽ Mano - Triangular

⬭ Mano - Small Round

▢ Mano - Overhang

0   2   4   6   8   10   METERS

b

Figure 245b.   Distribution of manos: CV-20.

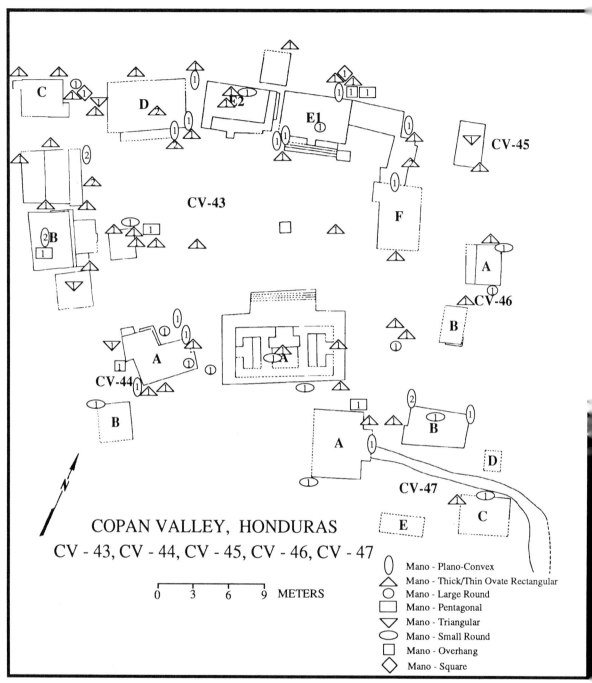

Figure 245c.   Distribution of manos: CV-43.

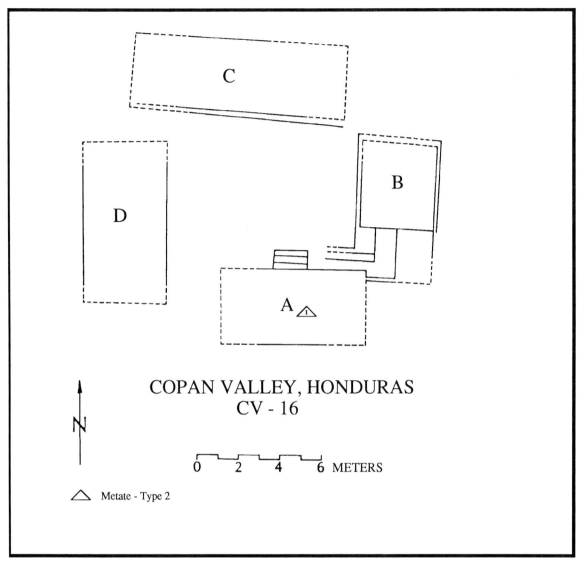

Figure 246a. Distribution of metates: CV-16.

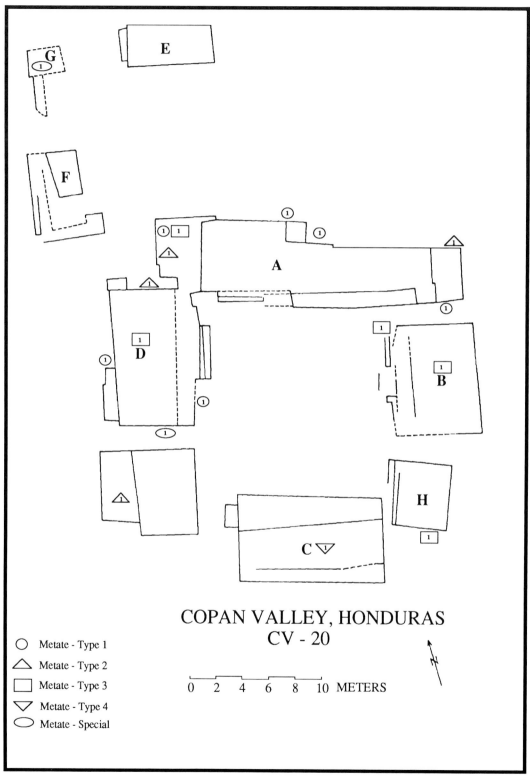

COPAN VALLEY, HONDURAS
CV - 20

○ Metate - Type 1
△ Metate - Type 2
□ Metate - Type 3
▽ Metate - Type 4
⬭ Metate - Special

0 2 4 6 8 10 METERS

b

Figure 246b. Distribution of metates: CV-20.

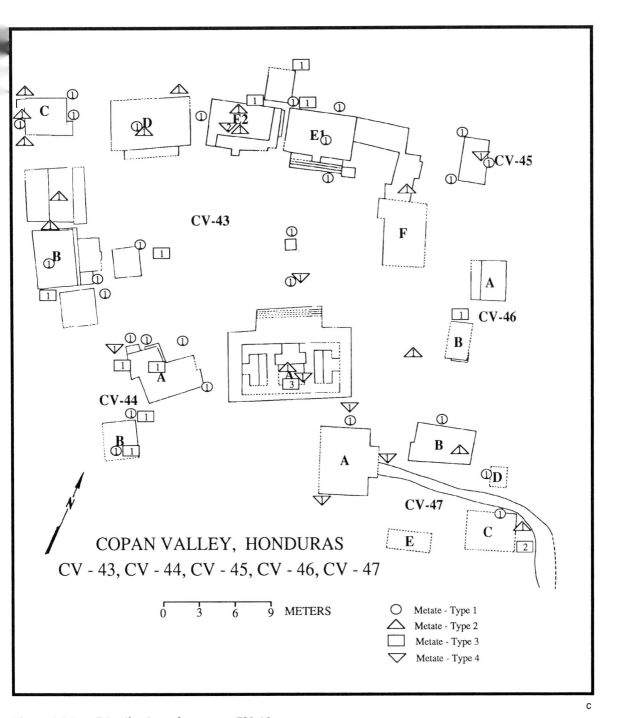

Figure 246c. Distribution of metates: CV-43.

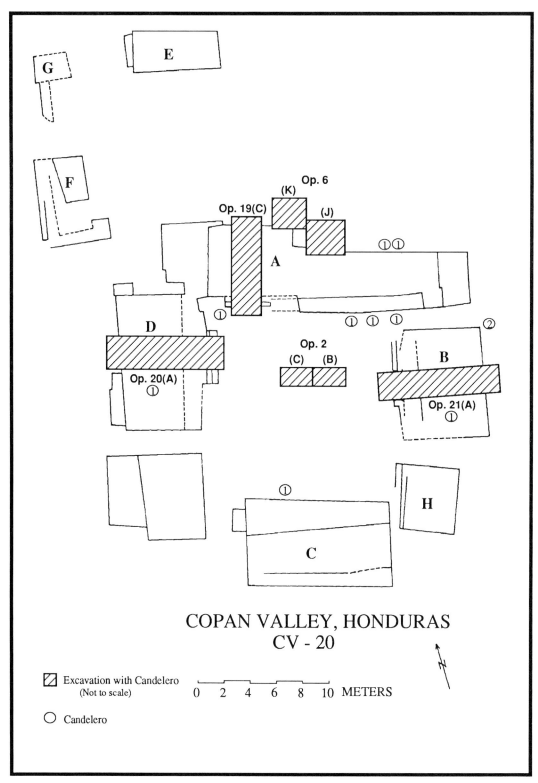

Figure 247a.   Location of excavations with candeleros: CV-20.

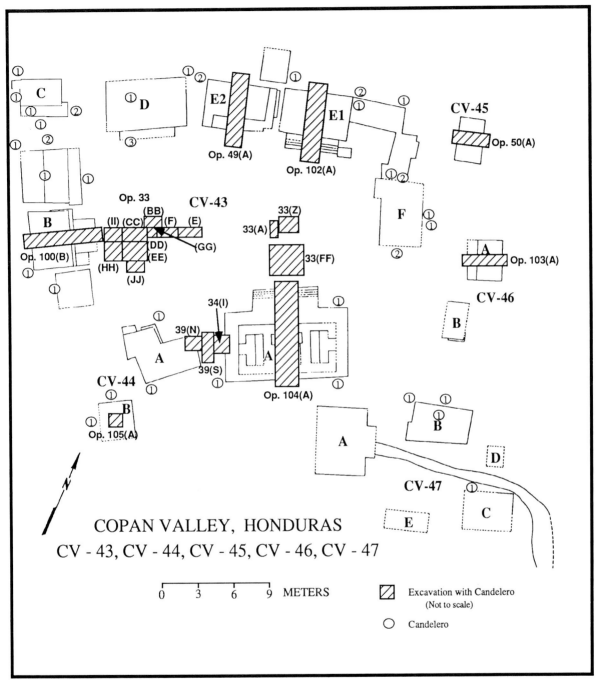

Figure 247b. Location of excavations with candeleros: CV-43.

4 Statistical Analyses and Interpretations

with assistance from

Kevin Baxter and Mary Bane Stevens

The analysis of the Copan Valley artifact and ceramic collections included a computerized statistical study. The large quantity of data was effectively controlled and managed in this manner. We had several basic goals in employing statistical tests.

One of the most important needs was to analyze the creation of our ceramic types. A potential problem in their identification, particularly with the unslipped types, is that different parts of a single vessel may have been placed within two or more type categories. We wanted to examine and test for the magnitude of such a problem. Second, we were interested in checking the relative chronological placement of the ceramic types. Rank-order correlation analyses of the ceramic types by excavation provenience was the focus of both the typological and chronological analyses. A third goal of this study was to examine the differential distribution of ceramic and artifact types in relation to excavated areas, individual structures, or plaza groups that would allow us to define activity areas and to speculate upon the functions of the different buildings.

The Data

All the ceramics and artifacts were classified following the standard type-variety system commonly used within the Maya area. This classificatory system is based primarily upon differences in ware and surface decoration.

The data set comprised locational information and ceramic and artifact type counts for each of the 812 excavation proveniences within our sample (including the sterile proveniences). Detailed provenience information provided a hierarchically flexible system to group and regroup the proveniences and recovered material. Along with this provenience information, the raw counts of each of the major ceramic and artifact types were utilized. Some of the ceramic and artifact types are very small in number or very specialized and we therefore grouped some of these types into broader, identifiable groups.

The variables (provenience, ceramic, and artifact) that were used for the coding are listed below.

Catalog Number
1. Operation Number
2. Sub-Operation Letter
3. Site Number
4. Location of Excavation
5. Associated Structure
6. Primary Structure or Plaza Designation
7. Type of Excavation
8. Level Number
9. Sub-level Letter
10. Excavation of Structure—Location
11. Trench Trough Structure—Type

12. Vertical Stratigraphic Trench—Context
13. Plaza and Test Excavations—Context
14. Number of Associated Tombs
15. Number of Associated Crypts
16. Number of Associated Plain Burials
17. Total Number of Burials
18. Number of Associated Caches
19. Number of Associated Features
20. Provenience—Sterile or with Cultural Material
21. Number of Associated Ceramic Vessels
22. Total Number of Sherds
23. Lysandro Unslipped
24. Sepultura Unslipped
25. Lorenzo Red
26. Casaca Striated
27. Switch Molina Striated
28. Antonio Buff
29. Arroyo Red
30. Raul Red: Raul Variety
31. Raul Red: Unspecified Variety
32. Raul Red (Total)
33. Eroded
34. Chilanga Red-painted: Osicala Variety
35. Chilanga Red-painted: Chilanga Variety
36. Chilanga Red-painted: Unspecified Variety
37. Arturo Incised and Cara Gorda Composite
38. Cementerio Incised and Mapache Grooved
39. Masica Incised
40. Reina Incised
41. Tipon Orange-brown
42. Don Gordon Modeled-carved
43. Tasu Fluted
44. Claudio Incised
45. Capulin Cream
46. Copador Polychrome: Copador and Geometric Varieties and Doric Composite
47. Gualpopa Polychrome
48. Caterpillar Polychrome
49. Babilonia Polychrome
50. Eroded Polychrome
51. Izalco Usulutan: A Variety
52. Izalco Usulutan: B Variety
53. Izalco Usulutan: C Variety
54. Izalco Usulutan: Unspecified Variety
55. Pacheco Zoned Bichrome
56. Unclassified
57. Polychrome—Unknown
58. Ardilla Group
59. Chalja Group
60. Melano Group
61. Capulin Group
62. Prospero Group: Ricardo Composite and Adan Red-on-buff
63. Prospero Group: Chitam Red-on-cream and Unspecified
64. Povmec Red-on-orange
65. Misc. Types
66. Uir Phase
67. Obsidian Bladelets
68. Obsidian Scrap
69. Obsidian Artifacts
70. Obsidian Cores
71. Chert Scrap
72. Chert Artifacts
73. Total—Metates
74. Total—Manos
75. Type 1 Metates
76. Type 2 and 3 Metates
77. Type 4 Metates
78. Misc. Metates
79. Thick Ovate-rectangular Manos
80. Thin Ovate-rectangular Manos
81. Large Round Manos
82. Small Round Manos
83. Plano-convex Manos
84. Pentagonal Manos
85. Triangular Manos
86. Square Manos
87. Overhang Manos
88. Misc. Manos
89. Total—Candeleros
90. Bottle-shaped Candeleros
91. Cylindrical Candeleros
92. Misc. Candeleros
93. Spindle Whorls
94. Worked Sherds
95. Ceramic Figurines
96. Briquettes
97. Misc. Ceramic Artifacts
98. Ring Stones
99. Misc. Perforated Stones
100. Stone Spheres
101. Miniature Stone Tables

An initial examination of the data—the raw counts of the ceramic types—indicated that the data are not normally distributed. This recognition comes from histograms of data frequencies in addition to tests of skewness. We attempted to normalize the data using logarithmic transformations (natural log and base ten log) along with square root and squared transformations. This attempt was not successful. The predominance of proveniences with low frequencies prevented the normalization of the data distribution. Even the elimination of the proveniences with less than 25 sherds did not help. We determined that we did not want to eliminate proveniences with more sherds, as we felt that we would begin to lose potentially interesting and important information. This lack of a normal distribution for the data did not prevent the use of many statistical tests, as can be seen below.

Correlation

In order to test the existence of ceramic types and the relative chronological structure of the types, a correlation matrix was generated comparing all pottery types by excavation provenience. Because the data are not normally distributed, we used Spearman's rank-order correlation (the equivalent of Pearson's correlation, which is used with normally distributed data). The large number of ceramic types or groups in the correlation (42) made it necessary for us to use Bonferoni's adjustment correction when assessing the significance of the correlation results. In all, 706 proveniences were utilized in this correlation; only the sterile proveniences were eliminated. This correlation matrix is presented in table 24.

Correlation Interpretation

The correlation did not force us to rethink our ceramic types or groupings. An extremely high correlation or even a 1.0 correlation between types would indicate the total correspondence of one type to another. Such a correspondence between types is not in evidence within the matrix, and we feel confident of the existence of our defined ceramic types.

We approached this test with several specific typological questions in mind. Let us present one as an example. We were uncertain about the relationship of Raul Red and Masica Incised. Masica Incised sherds had a red slip on the shoulder and a central portion of the vessel, below the area of the incision. Did Raul Red vessels exist or were we classifying the upper portions with the incis-

ing into the Masica Incised type and the lower portions into Raul Red? The correlation between Masica Incised and Raul Red: Raul Variety is .6194; between Masica Incised and Raul Red: Unspecified Variety, it is .5337. Both correlations are at an acceptable level of significance. These types, therefore, show evidence of a high correspondence but one that we interpret to be due to the similar chronological placement rather than confusion in the creation of the types themselves.

The correlation matrix also corroborated the late phases of our chronological sequence. The types that fall within the Coner phase showed a strong correlation with one another. These include, for example, Sepultura Unslipped, Lorenzo Red, Masica Incised, Casaca Striated, Tipon Orange-brown, Copador Polychrome. The Cueva phase is less clearly defined with correlating types, but types such as Antonio Buff, Arroyo Red, and Chilanga Red-painted do show a reasonably strong correlation with one another.

Most of the types within the earlier phases do not significantly correlate with other types in concise chronological phases. This may be due to the relative lack of earlier provenience units in our excavations. Much of the earlier material was from secondary deposition in the fill of Coner or Cueva phase architecture.

Structure Function

Understanding the function of buildings has always been a problem in Maya archaeology. There are questions of both the size, nature, and functions of cities as a whole and the identifications of individual buildings. Over the years, there has been considerable interest in defining and describing individual residential or family structures within the cities (Wauchope 1934, 1938; A. L. Smith 1962; Willey et al. 1965; Haviland 1963, 1981; Tourtellot 1982; Leventhal 1983). One matter has been the identification of a dwelling house and the relationship of this house to the household or the family unit. It has been known for some time that not all small structures in or around a Maya center or city were actual living houses; many may have been storage sheds, animal coops, religious shrines, sweat-bath huts, or other ancillary units. Not only archaeological exploration but also ethnographic investigations of modern Maya (Wauchope 1938; Vogt 1969) have confirmed this. The question of individual building functions in archaeology is also complicated by the fact that the modern, as well as ancient, Maya often used the same building for more than one purpose.

Copan Valley Excavations

Only a brief review of the architectural units (figs. 248, 249, 250) excavated is presented here (see Leventhal, in prep., for a detailed statement on these). Criteria for functional identifications of structures include size, interior features, location in relation to other structures, accretional growth, quality of construction, and associated cultural deposits (burials, caches). Utilizing these criteria, Leventhal (1983) has identified the structures of groups CV-20 and CV-43 as to function.

In CV-20, Structures A, C, and D all appear to have been of domestic function. Structure B, however, looks like a ceremonial building, perhaps a small family temple or shrine.

In the larger CV-43 group, Structure A was almost certainly of nondomestic function. It is the largest and most elaborate structure of the group and was not altered or added to after its original construction. It consists of three separate rooms, not interconnected, each having its separate doorway opening out on the mound platform terrace in different directions. Each of these rooms had a painted interior of a different color, corresponding to Maya directional colors: red for the eastern room, black for the western, white for the northern part of the central room, and green for the center of this room. Finally, a ceremonial deposit of stingray spines and marine shells was discovered within the building platform. A stone bench in the central room was carved with a hieroglyphic inscription. We assume this Structure A was the temple-shrine of the principal family living in CV-43.

Structures B and E1 of CV-43 appear to have been elite residences. Benches were constructed in each, and numerous burials were found beneath the floor platforms of each, including a prepared masonry tomb in each structure. All of these criteria signal an elite residence (see Tozzer 1941).

Finally, CV-45 and CV-46, small structure units situated just to the outside of the CV-43 plaza group, may have been the foundations for the dwellings of servants or retainers to the governing family of the CV-43 household. CV-45 and CV-46, Structure A, are very similar to each other, each consisting of a low platform surmounted by a higher C-shaped one.

Data Analysis

There are two general ways to approach the question of whether differential artifact distribution reflects different structure functions. The first, cluster analysis, begins with a set of unclassified objects and derives groupings. The second method begins with a number of predetermined structure types and uses a discriminant analysis to determine which artifact variables best discriminate between the groups. Since multivariate techniques have not been used for this particular research question in the Maya area, and because this research is very exploratory in nature, we used both methods.

The first step was to decide which set of data would be most appropriate for this analysis. It was important to consider only those variables which would best lend themselves to discussion of the function of structures. Otherwise, the results, while perhaps statistically significant, might not be meaningful. One of the problems in using the differential distribution of ceramics to determine the functions of buildings was the need to determine the function of the ceramic types. The ceramic types chosen for this analysis from the Copan Valley collection included Babilonia/Ulua Polychrome, Copador Polychrome, Raul Red, Sepultura Unslipped, Gualpopa Polychrome, Caterpillar Polychrome, Cementerio Incised, Casaca Striated, Masica Incised, and Lorenzo Red. These types were chosen for many reasons. First, all are contemporaneous, falling within the Coner complex, the final Late Classic ceramic phase at Copan. Second, they are types that represent large numbers of sherds. It was felt that small type collections would only add confusion to the distribution data. Finally, these ceramic types were chosen because a functional interpretation might be offered for each. For example, Sepultura Unslipped appears to represent incense burners. Babilonia/Ulua, Copador, Gualpopa, and Caterpillar are all polychrome types, which, because of their elaborate surface treatment, are assumed to have been elite wares, perhaps relating to both ceremonial and domestic activities; and the large jar forms of Raul Red, Lorenzo Red, Masica Incised, Cementerio Incised, and Casaca Striated are all assumed to have had a domestic function. It is perhaps too simplistic to argue that individual artifacts or pots represent only a single function; however, for the purposes of our analysis, the ceramics were divided into the three general functional categories.

Many artifacts with a more clearly demonstrable function, as derived from their appearance and abundance and from ethnohistoric and ethnographic data, such as manos and metates, were not present in large enough numbers in our sample for our statistical analyses. Other artifacts, such as obsidian and chert implements, while present in sufficient quantities, were difficult to identify as to function. In addition, the status of obsidian within Maya society is still uncertain. Was it an elite or common utilitarian item (Webster, personal communication 1988)?

The final consideration of data selection focused upon provenience. We assumed that the artifacts excavated from a structure were associated with the use of that structure in the past. For this reason, artifacts from the core construction fill of structures (recovered in the trenches) were excluded from consideration. These artifacts were placed in their archaeological context during the construction of the building, and therefore have less likelihood of being representative of that building's function.

Clustering Techniques

A cluster analysis was run on the data to see if the structures could be sorted into a sensible and coherent pattern without using predefined structure types. The process of cluster analysis is described in detail by Everitt (1974). Essentially, it entails the computation of a matrix of similarities or distances between each pair of cases (or structures, in this analysis). These measures are derived from the artifact variables of each case. This matrix then forms the basis upon which cas-

es are grouped together. The two cases that have the least distance between them are grouped (or linked) together. The next two closest cases are linked, and so on, until all cases are combined into a single group.

The three plaza groups (CV-16, CV-20, and CV-43) discussed in this volume cover a broad range of size and complexity, comprising respectively 4, 9, and 22 structures. We decided not to cluster all three of the plaza groups simultaneously because of the probable difference in the organization of activities at each plaza group. The difference in size and number of structures between plaza groups is probably due at least in part to the status and power of each plaza group's occupants. While a similar range of activities was probably performed at all these plazas, it cannot be assumed that the archaeological patterning of these activities at each group will be similar. For example, at CV-16, with only four structures, there may be a spatial overlap of activities, such that one structure was the locus of many activities. This same overlap may not be present at CV-43, with five times the number of structures. Because CV-43 had the largest number of structures, the initial analysis focused only on this plaza group.

Several computer programs are available for this analysis, from which the subprogram BMDP2M (Dixon 1983, 1982 version) was chosen. A total of 12 runs were attempted, using both single linkage and centroid methods of clustering, with sum-of-squares as the distance measurement (see table 25 for a summary of these runs). Some runs included only plain wares, some only polychromes, and others both general types. To take into account the different amounts of excavation at each structure, ceramic types were divided by the total ceramic count for that structure. On those runs where noted in table 25, the ceramic percentages are standardized using Z-scores.

Each computer run produced a dendrogram, or tree diagram, showing how the structures were grouped together (see fig. 251). One can see from the dendrogram the order in which pairs were linked. It is up to the researcher to determine at which point the clustering should cease, that is, how many clusters one wants to end with. The results of these analyses (of which two are shown in fig. 251) differed substantially from one run to

TABLE 25

Results of the cluster analysis

Run Number	Variables	Linkage	Standardized
1	9, 6, 7	single	yes
2	9, 6, 7	single	no
3	1, 3, 4	single	yes
4	1, 3, 4	single	no
5	1, 3, 4	centroid	no
6	11, 12, 13	single	no
7	11, 12, 13	centroid	no
8	5, 10, 14, 6, 7	single	no
9	9, 15, 16	single	yes
10	1, 2, 3, 4, 5, 6, 7, 8, 9, 10	single	yes
11	1, 2, 3, 4, 5, 6, 7, 8, 9	centroid	yes
12	5, 1	single	yes

KEY FOR VARIABLES:

1	Copador	9	Sepultura
2	Gualpopa	10	Cementerio
3	Caterpillar	11	Antonio
4	Babilonia	12	Arroyo
5	Raul	13	Chilanga
6	Casaca	14	Reina
7	Masica	15	Manos
8	Lorenzo	16	Metates

the next. We had hoped that some pattern would emerge from a number of runs, but this was not the case. In fact, the only runs with comparable results are those which used the same data set, and either single or centroid linkage.

None of the cluster runs produced a dendrogram that was easily interpreted. Although there may have been some grouping of similar structures in some runs, there was no consistency or patterning of the results. Moreover, there was no way to decide systematically on a cutoff point that would mark the end of the clustering into groups. If functional groups do exist, it became clear to us that cluster analysis was not the method with which to proceed with our data set.

Discriminant Analysis

The next option was to run a stepwise discriminant analysis. As mentioned above, discriminant analysis begins with a set of predetermined groups and then calculates which variables will best discriminate between them. This type of analysis has been used in projectile point typology, fossil taxonomy, and obsidian source determination (Baxter 1984; Gunn and Prewitt 1975), but not in this type of structure classification.

The mathematical procedure of discriminant analysis is somewhat complicated. Alice Benfer and Robert A. Benfer (1981) describe in understandable terms the details of the process, while Spencer Bennett and David Bowers (1976) and M. S. Srivastiva and E. M. Carter (1983) give a more mathematical discussion. The procedure will only be touched upon briefly here.

A stepwise discriminant analysis derives discriminant functions (also called classification functions and canonical functions) that are linear combinations of a set of variables that best distinguish each group from the others. These functions are in the form of

$$Y_i = g_{i1}X_1 + g_{i2}X_2 + \ldots + g_{ip}X_p$$

where Y_i is the score on the discriminant function i, the X's are values of the discriminating variables, and the g's are the weighting coefficients.

The stepwise procedure enters variables into this formula one at a time, beginning with that variable which best distinguishes between the groups. Subsequent variables are added into the function until those which remain cannot increase the separation between groups. The total number of discriminant functions is at most equal to the number of variables used in the analysis, or one less than the number of groups, whichever is smaller.

As discussed above, Leventhal (1983) has assigned with some confidence Structure A of CV-43 to a religious category, Structures B and E1 to a residential category (probably elite), and CV-46, Structure A, and CV-45 to the category of servants' quarters. These five structures form the base from which discriminant functions are to be derived. In the second part of the analysis, the discriminant functions were used to calculate the group to which each of the remaining structures is closest.

Following the BMDP7M program (Dixon 1983, 1983 version), the sherd counts are standardized by dividing each count by the total of the 10 ceramic types. Ideally, the ceramic count is divided by cubic volume of excavation, but these data were not available.

Only two pottery type variables entered into the analysis, Raul Red and Copador Polychrome, from which two discriminant functions were computed (see table 26). The remaining variables were unable to distinguish further between these groups. A test of significance for the functions treats the summation of the eigenvalues as an approximate chi-square, with p(k-1) degrees of freedom (where p is the number of variables and k is the number of groups). Thus, the two functions together have a chi-square value of 2100 with 4 degrees of freedom. This value is significant at p<1000. However, when the first eigenvalue is stripped off, we are left with a chi-square value of 1.4, with degrees of freedom equal to (p-1)(k-2), or 1. This second value is not significant, and therefore the second discriminant function does not add to the discriminating power of the first function.

Another test of the discriminant function is how well it reclassifies the members of each group used to derive the function. Particularly when group membership is large, members near the periphery of that group are sometimes reclas-

TABLE 26
Results of the discriminant analysis

Eigenvalues

	First Function	Second Function
	2168.6	1.4

Standardized Coefficients for Canonical Variables

Variable	First Function	Second Function
Raul	95.4	3.7
Copador	29.5	-4.1

sified into another group. In this analysis, with group membership at a minimum, this was not expected, nor did it occur. Using the standardized canonical coefficients in table 26, the discriminant function correctly reclassified each of the five preassigned structures.

Interpretations

The classification categories of the discriminant analysis assigned each of the excavated structures into one of the three predefined groups. The next step was to compare the structures within each group in order to ascertain whether other criteria (i.e., architectural features) are similar enough to warrant the placement of these structures into a type category. One fact should be reemphasized at this point: The excavated structures are from the three plaza groups mentioned above. Each of these plaza groups represents a different size unit and therefore, perhaps, a different organizational scheme. Even the Type 1 groups within the CV-43 compound cannot easily be compared to CV-16. CV-44, CV-45, and CV-46 are all oriented toward a larger compound, unlike CV-16, which is located, spatially, by itself. It would probably be best to attempt to examine like objects within such a functional study; however, our limited data set forced us to examine all the excavated structures of these three groups.

As mentioned, the discriminant analysis utilized three broad categories. The first one focused upon the known structures of CV-45 and CV-46, Structure A. Both of these buildings had been tentatively identified as servants' quarters. The graph in figure 252 clearly indicates that it is possible to break this group into two subgroups. The first includes CV-45 and CV-46, Structure A. In addition to these two, the following structures are included: CV-43, Structures I, D, and K; CV-44, Structure A; and CV-47, Structure B. Structures A, D, F, and H from CV-20 are part of this category. Finally, Structure C of CV-16 is included.

The above-listed structures from CV-43 appear to fit a general pattern. The architectural features of all these buildings are minimal. All are of small size, and all have a secondary location within the compound. When we turn to the CV-20 data, the results are not as consistent. Certainly, the small, secondary structures of F and H fit this general type; however, Structures A and D of CV-20 are probably domestic structures of the main occupants of the plaza group. Why have they been grouped with the possible servants' quarters? We again must return to the question of analyzing and comparing like objects. The servants' quarters from the Type 3 group may be similar to the domestic structures from the Type 2 group.

The second subcategory consists of the following structures: CV-44, Structure B; CV-47, Structures C and D; and CV-20, Structure G. These are even smaller and more peripheral in location than those buildings included above within the first subcategory. Although no specific function was initially defined for these latter buildings, ethnographic and ethnohistoric evidence shows the existence of small secondary buildings within household compounds.

The second major grouping from the discriminant analysis focuses upon Structures E1 and B of CV-43. These two structures, based upon their architectural features, have been identified as elite residences. It also appears as though Structures E2 and F of CV-43 fit into this same category. Although not architecturally impressive, these structures fit the category from the standpoint of their prominent location within the plaza group.

Within this same category is also Structure A of CV-47, the largest building of this secondary plaza attached to CV-43. Structure C of CV-20 and Structure A of CV-16 are also included.

The final grouping of structures, however, brings us into a situation that is more difficult to interpret, one in which tight cohesive architectural features are lacking. This group was defined by Structure A, CV-43, as a possible religious or special structure (nonresidential). In addition to this building, Structures C and G of CV-43 are also included. Both of the latter are small secondary buildings. Structures from CV-20 include B, E, and I. The one CV-20 building among these that fits this type on the basis of architectural criteria is Structure B. The other two CV-20 structures, E and I, are very small secondary ancillary structures. Finally, two small structures from CV-16, B and D, are included in the type.

How can we begin to explain this discrepancy between architectural and artifactual evidence? Four viable explanations come to mind. First, as mentioned above, there is the potential inability to create appropriate data sets for comparison. Second, it is clear that the concept of a single-function building is overly simplistic and therefore we should expect buildings of different architectural forms to be grouped together. Third, we should not exclude the possibility of this group being a viable functional category. Again, ethnohistoric and ethnographic evidence points to many buildings as being secondary structures to religious or special-function structures. These buildings may have served as storage facilities for ritual paraphernalia. Fourth, the ceramic types chosen may not be the best functional indicators. The strength of the type-variety system of ceramic classification is not in its functional identifications. In the end, this group of structures, which are now clustered with Structure A, CV-43, exists as a tentative entity but one to be tested by future excavations and research.

Therefore, the four broad groupings of structures discussed above present us with preliminary generalized functions for all the excavated buildings. Where architectural features are lacking we have been able to group structures in a preliminary way based upon ceramic type distribution.

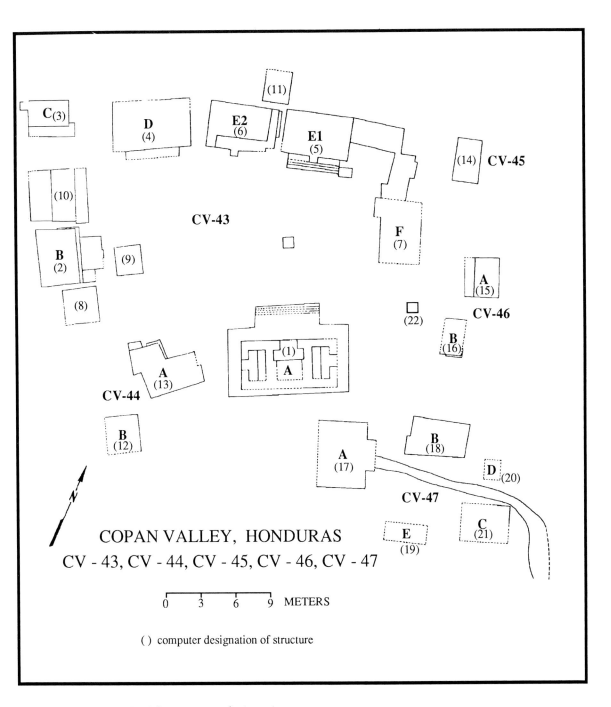

Figure 248. CV-43 with computer designations

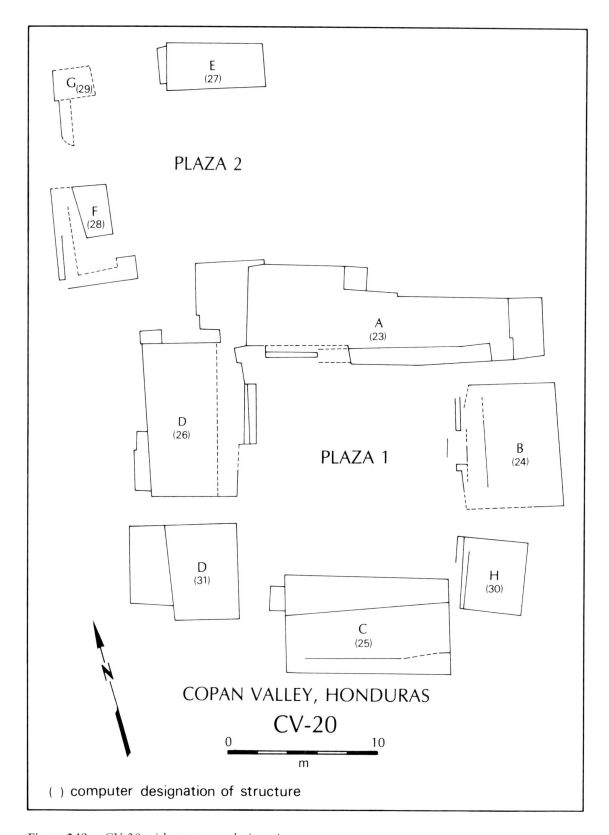

Figure 249. CV-20 with computer designations

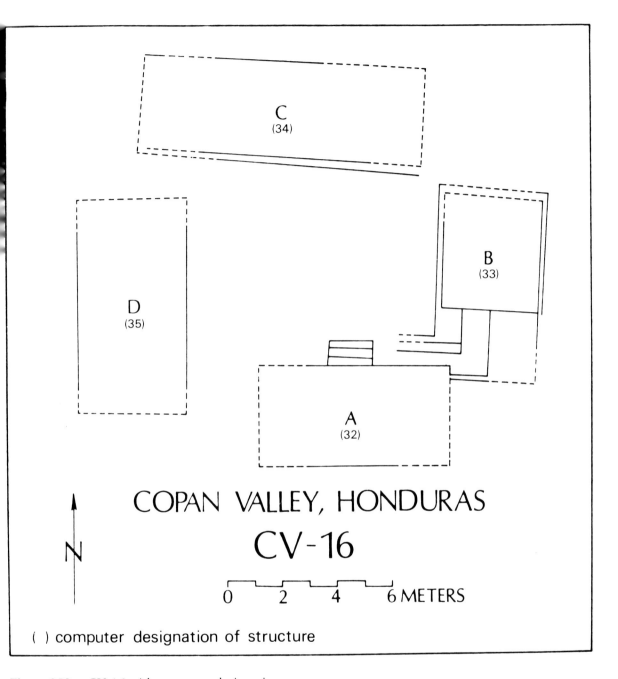

COPAN VALLEY, HONDURAS

CV-16

0   2   4   6 METERS

( ) computer designation of structure

Figure 250. CV-16 with computer designations

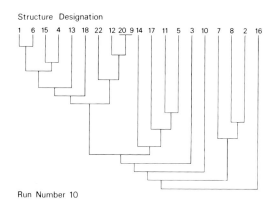

Run Number 10

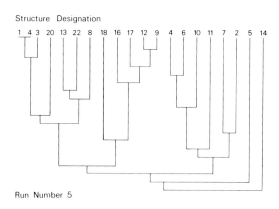

Run Number 5

Figure 251.   Results of the cluster analysis, runs 5 and 10

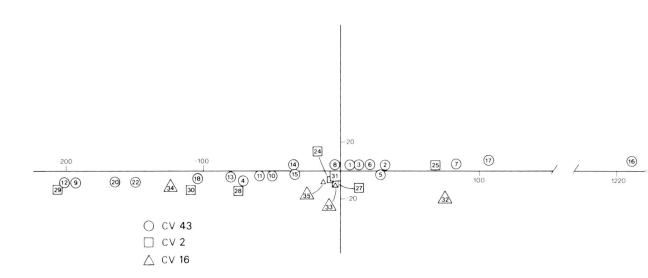

Figure 252.   Results of the discriminant analysis

5 General Summary and Conclusions

The Harvard University surveys and excavations of the 1975–77 seasons were concentrated in an outlying zone of the Copan Main Center (the location of the well-known Acropoli and the Great Plaza). This zone, known locally as Las Sepulturas, lies between a half-kilometer and a kilometer east of the Copan Main Center on an upper terrace of the Copan River. In ancient times it was a densely settled residential area, and today the remains of this former settlement are seen as clusters of numerous small to medium-sized mounds.

We excavated three of these mound clusters, which we interpret as residential site compounds, CV-16, CV-20, and CV-43, in considerable detail. In addition, we tested a number of other residential units. Unit CV-16 is a small courtyard arrangement of mound structures of the size class, or type, which we designated as a Type 1, the smallest of our residential type classes (see Willey, Leventhal, and Fash 1978; Willey and Leventhal 1979). Our scattered test excavations were also made in Type 1–sized units. CV-20 is somewhat larger than CV-16 and the units in which we made the test excavations and is representative of our Type 2 class unit. CV-43 is still larger and is classed as a Type 3. There is still a larger unit class, the Type 4. Although we did not excavate a unit of this class, one such, CV-36 (known as 9N-82 in the more recent Copan Valley survey identification system), was excavated

by W. T. Sanders, D. Webster, and their associates in the early 1980s (see Webster 1989).

A report of the Harvard excavation procedures, with particular attention to settlement arrangements and architectural detail, is now in preparation by R. M. Leventhal and will be presented in a later publication. This monograph is devoted to the ceramics and the artifacts from these excavations. Throughout the monograph we have taken some pains to summarize by section and topic; therefore, this chapter is not a lengthy one.

The ceramic history of Copan begins at the Early to Middle Preclassic period transition. Knowledge of these earlier ceramic phases comes largely from the work of others (Viel 1983; Webster 1988). In our own diggings we found only a few potsherds of the Middle Preclassic Uir phase (900–400 B.C.). These came from the refuse fill in some of the Las Sepulturas structures, and we suppose that they were simply incidental to materials used in later constructions. The Copan Uir pottery can be described as belonging to a Middle Preclassic Honduran and eastern Salvadoran plain ware and zoned bichrome tradition. This tradition, as it continued into the Late Preclassic, merged with an Usulutan negative-painted, or resist-painted, decorative tradition that had its origins in western El Salvador and the adjacent Guatemalan highlands. After this merger, it is sometimes referred to as the Uapala ceramic tradition or ceramic sphere, which brings us into the Late Preclassic Chabij phase (400 B.C.–A.D. 100) at Copan. Chabij, with its Uapala complex, is represented by a slightly larger collection of sherds from our excavations, although these still appear to be incidental to constructional fill. One might speculate that there had been Middle and Late Preclassic settlements in Las Sepulturas, but, except for the presence of these early sherds, we have no clue to such a settlement. Following Chabij, we have a few sherds of the succeeding Bijac phase (A.D. 100–400), a Copan phase corresponding to the Protoclassic and the earlier part of the Classic period, and one that also appears to pertain to the Uapala sphere or tradition.

It is with the succeeding Acbi phase (A.D. 400–600) of the middle to latter part of the Early Classic period that we have the first substantial pottery collections from our excavations, and it is likely that some architectural remnants encountered in the lower levels of our diggings date to this phase. Acbi encompasses a greater diversification in ceramic influences at Copan: types of a utilitarian appearance continue in the old local Honduran tradition; other types, such as Izalco Usulutan, continue and strengthen the ties to the Maya highlands; while still others, such as polished and carved fine wares, suggest contacts with the Maya lowlands of the Peten. We found very definite Cueva phase (A.D. 600–700) architecture in Las Sepulturas, with pottery coming out in abundance in our diggings. In Cueva, utilitarian monochromes (Arroyo Red, Antonio Buff) and various incised types are easily traced back to local Honduran roots, while Chilanga Red-painted Usulutan can be considered as a continuity out of Izalco Usulutan and a maintenance of the link with the Maya highlands. Maya lowland resemblances are seen in polished plain wares of the Tipon-Capulin groups and in the decoration of fine ware vessels with incised and carved pseudo-glyphs and other Classic Maya motifs. Importantly, a new polychrome type appears, Gualpopa Polychrome, which in its black-and-red-on-orange color scheme and its glyph-like, monkey, and human figure designs looks like a fusion of Maya highland and lowland ceramic traditions. Gualpopa looks like a Copan invention, and it is almost certainly the prototype for Copador Polychrome, the dominant decorated

painted pottery of the succeeding Coner phase (A.D. 700–1000).

Coner phase architecture is well defined in all of our residential group excavations, representing, in many cases, constructions built over or onto earlier Cueva, or Acbi-Cueva, buildings. The Coner phase marked the climax of Copan's greatness as revealed in the temple and palace architecture of the Main Center, the numerous stelae erected to the site's rulers, and the various hieroglyphic inscriptions on these and other monuments that relate the site's dynastic history. Coner was also the time of the Copan Valley's largest and most densely settled population. Las Sepulturas, with its numerous residential mounds, was but one section of such settlement. Coner was a time, too, of political rivalry. Glyphic texts tell us of the ruler of Quirigua's capture and sacrifice of a ruler of Copan, although this defeat and humiliation by no means put an end to Copan's prowess or independence (Culbert 1988; Fash 1988). Indeed, a subsequent ruler of Copan carried out one of the largest building programs in the city's history in the latter part of the eighth century.

But by A.D. 800/850 Copan's epoch of greatness—at least insofar as this can be measured by constructional and dedicatory activities in the Main Center—was over. There are now indications, though, that sizable, if somewhat reduced, populations continued to live in the residential sections of the valley until at least A.D. 1000 or, possibly, even as late as A.D. 1100/1200. Evidence for this has come from the hydration dating of hundreds of obsidian bladelets found in these residential units, such as the ones we excavated in Las Sepulturas (W. T. Sanders and D. Webster, personal communication 1989). As yet, the effects of this revised dating have not been fully appraised from within the context of ceramic phasing. It may be that the Coner complex continued through into these later centuries of the valley's history. Certainly, Coner pottery types were the last to be used and made in the site units that we excavated; however, D. Webster's (1988) Ejar complex, dated at A.D. 900 to 1000/1200, may constitute a phase that can be differentiated Coner. Ejar has not yet been defined ceramically, but we anticipate that it would be a direct development out of Coner.

To turn to Coner ceramics as we have described them, the marker type for the early-eighth-century inception of the phase is Copador Polychrome. The type is highly distinctive, being executed in black, specular hematite red, and orange positive-painting on a cream slip. The frequent life-form designs, while charmingly stylized, are recognizable as men, deities, monkeys, and Maya glyphs or pseudo-glyphs. Paste studies indicate a local manufacture of the type, and it is highly likely that Copan, or the immediate Copan Valley, was its place of origin (see Bishop and Beaudry, appendix B). Such an interpretation is, of course, consistent with our belief that the also locally made Cueva phase type, Gualpopa Polychrome, was the immediate forerunner of Copador.

Other Coner phase types include several that appear to be of Maya lowland inspiration, although made locally. Among these would be the luxury ware Don Gordon Modeled-carved, with its carved glyphic decoration; the incensario forms of Sepultura Unslipped, which look very much like incensarios of the Peten; and the utility water-jars of the type Casaca Striated, which are very like their lowland Maya counterparts. The old local Honduran tradition, which we have traced through several preceding phases, stays alive in Coner in such utility types as Masica Incised and Raul Red. Ulua Polychrome (or Babilonia Polychrome), which has its origins in northwestern Honduras through contacts with the lowland Maya, appears as a significant trade pottery at Copan (Bishop and Beaudry, appendix B). Although some trade contacts with the Maya highlands must have continued unabated during the phase, as witnessed by the abundant obsidian that came into Copan from this region (Harbottle, Neff, and Bishop, appendix C), there is little in the Coner ceramic complex that points in this direction.

The other artifacts that we found in our Copan residential zone excavations have the appearance of household items discarded, broken, or lost around living quarters. We found a good many pottery figurines and figurine fragments. A very few of these are typologically Preclassic, although we cannot demonstrate this dating by excavation provenience. The vast majority of the figurines were, however, moldmade figurine-whistles of human, animal, and various forms. These are all typically lowland Maya in aspect and are fully at home in their Late Classic (Tepeu 2 horizon) Coner contexts. While it is unlikely that such figurines were high-status goods, it is of interest that we found more of them in and around the principal buildings of CV-43, our Class 3 residential unit, than in our other, more modest proveniences. They occur in general refuse, not with burials or in special caches.

Chipped stone, both chert and obsidian, was found in all residential contexts; however, there was substantially more in CV-20, our Class 2 unit, than in CV-43, the Class 3 unit, a circumstance that may point toward some craft activities being carried out in CV-20 that were not so frequently performed in CV-43. The vast bulk of our chipped stone, both artifacts and scrap, dates to the Cueva and Coner phases. We assume this to be largely a function of our excavation sample, which drew heavily upon these later phases. Certainly, some trade in obsidian with the nearby Maya highlands must have been in progress since Preclassic times.

In ground stone, it is of interest to note that the flat, rectangular metate forms (our Metate Types 1, 2, and 3) all have some few occurrences as early as Cueva, while the turtle-back or basin-shaped metate form (our Metate Type 4) is essentially confined to the Coner phase. Metate Type 4 is a lowland Maya Peten form, while the flat, rectangular metate is at home in Honduras and lower Central America. Stone barkbeaters occur in pre-Cueva proveniences, as well as later.

The little pottery candeleros are the only other artifact deserving of mention in such a brief summary. These occurred in great numbers at Copan, and we are inclined to believe that they are a Honduran regional trait not shared with either the Maya highlands or lowlands. Indeed, more of them are known from Copan than from anywhere else. They are most numerous in Cueva and Coner contexts, but a few were found in pre-Cueva proveniences. In many instances, we found the candeleros placed, apparently purposefully, near or around burials or caches, suggesting a ritual function for them.

We have already referred to some of the ceramic and obsidian analyses that are presented in the several appendices to this monograph. In addition to their determinations on the production provenience of Copador Polychrome and the trade ware status of Ulua (Babilonia) Poly-chrome, R. Bishop and M. Beaudry (appendix B) find that the Tipon group fine wares, which have Maya lowland and even more distant Teotihua-canoid resemblances, were locally manufactured; and Garman Harbottle, Ronald Bishop, and Hector Neff (appendix C) tell us that the main highland obsidian source for Copan was the expectably nearest one, Ixtepeque.

Mary Pohl (appendix D) shows quite conclu-sively that there was a correlation between social status and the feasting on the meat of the white-tailed deer. The bones of such deer were much more frequent in the detritus around CV-43 than in that around CV-20 or CV-16. Not only did the more elite have more meat to eat, but they also had access to and possession of more species of animals than the less elite. These deer bones, like the bones of the ocelot, were placed in ritual caches, and, presumably, before their deaths their pelts were removed as status possessions.

The several site units we explored in the Las Sepulturas sector of the Copan Valley were surely residential quarters for Copanecos living on the outskirts of the Copan Main Center. The three principal units excavated in detail—CV-43, CV-20, and CV-16—present a gradient in social status, in the order in which they are listed, from higher to lower. The nature of the buildings, the associated graves and ritual deposits, and the ceramic and artifact contents found in the build-ings all follow this gradient; and our reading of this gradient is one of social status differentia-tion. As a particular mark of high status, we might note that unit CV-43 had within it a spe-cial building situated on the highest mound of the immediate group. This building appeared to have had functions other than domestic ones, presum-ably functions involving ritual, religion, and gov-ernance. This special building had three rooms, and in the center room there was an elaborate stone bench or throne carved with a hieroglyphic inscription. The interpretation is that of a famil-ial, or extended familial, shrine or office in which the elite leadership must have controlled CV-43 and, quite probably, those living in the lesser quarters surrounding it.

Viewed in wider perspective, Las Sepulturas was an elite-controlled neighborhood on the out-skirts of the Copan Main Center. Its upper class-es lived in Type 4 and Type 3 residential com-pounds. Persons of lesser status lived in those of the Type 2 and 1 classes. These latter may have been servants, but certainly in some way they were retainers of the elite. Our excavations in this neighborhood provide a sampling of some of the social complexity in ancient Maya society at Copan.

Bibliography

Adams, R. E. W.
  1971 *The Ceramics of Altar de Sacrificios, Guatemala.* Papers of the Peabody Museum, vol. 63, no. 1. Harvard University, Cambridge, Massachusetts.
Andrews V, E. W.
  1976 *The Archaeology of Quelepa, El Salvador.* Middle American Research Institute, Publication 42. Tulane University, New Orleans.
Bamforth, D.
  1986 "A Comment on 'Functional Variability in an Assemblage of End Scrapers.'" *Lithic Technology* 15(2).
Baudez, C. F.
  1966 "Niveaux ceramiques au Honduras: une reconsideration de l'évolution culturelle." *Journal de le Société des Americanistes* 4(2): 299–342.
  1967 Recherches archéologiques dans la vallée du Tempisque, Guanacaste, Costa Rica, no. 18. Paris.
Baudez, C. F., ed.
  1983 *Introduccion a la Arqueologia de Copan, Honduras.* Proyecto Arqueologico Copan, Secretaria de Estado en el Despacho de Cultura Y Turismo, Tegucigalpa, Honduras.
Baudez, C. F., and P. Becquelin
  1973 *Archéologie de Los Naranjos, Honduras.* Etudes mesoamericaines, Mission Archéologique et Ethnologique Française au Mexique, vol. 2. Mexico, D.F.
Baxter, K.
  1984 "Obsidian Source Analysis and the Economy of Tipu, Belize." Paper presented at the 24th annual meeting of the Northeast Anthropological Association, Hartford, Connecticut.
Beaudry, M. P.
  1983 "Production and Distribution of Painted Late Classic Maya Ceramics in the Southeastern Periphery." Ph.D. dissertation, University of California, Los Angeles.
Benfer, R. A., and A. N. Benfer
  1981 "Automatic Classification of Inspectional Categories: Multivariate Theories of Archaeological Data." *American Antiquity* 46:381–396.
Bennett, S., and D. Bowers
  1976 *Introduction to Multivariate Techniques.* Wiley Press, New York.
Benyo, J. C.
  1978 "Quirigua Censers, A Preliminary Report." Manuscript in the possession of the authors.
Bishop, R. L.
  1984 "El Analisis de Activacion de Neutronas de la Ceramica de El Mirador," in *Proyecto El Mirador de la Harvard University 1982–1983, Mesoamerica,* A. A. Demarest and W. Fowler, eds., vol. 7, pp. 148–159. CERMA, Antigua, Guatemala.
Bishop, R. L., M. P. Beaudry, R. M. Leventhal, and R. J. Sharer
  1986 "Compositional Analysis of Copador and Related Pottery in the Southeast Maya Area," in *The Southeast Maya Periphery,* P. A. Urban and E. M. Schortman, eds. University of Texas Press, Austin.

Boggs, S. H.
1945 "Archaeological Material from the Club Internacional, El Salvador." *Carnegie Institution of Washington Notes of Middle American Archaeology and Ethnology*, no. 94. Washington, D.C.

Borhegyi, S. F.
1950 "Rim-head Vessels and Cone-shaped Effigy Prongs of the Preclassic Period at Kaminaljuyu, Guatemala." *Carnegie Institution of Washington Notes of Middle American Archaeology and Ethnology*, no. 97. Washington, D.C.
1951a "A Study of Three-pronged Incense Burners from Guatemala and Adjacent Areas." *Carnegie Institution of Washington Notes of Middle American Archaeology and Ethnology*, no. 101. Washington, D.C.
1951b "Further Notes on Three-pronged Incense Burners and Rimhead Vessels in Guatemala." *Carnegie Institution of Washington Notes of Middle American Archaeology and Ethnology*, no. 105. Washington, D.C.
1951c "'Loop-nose' Incense Burners in the Guatemala National Museum." *Carnegie Institution of Washington Notes of Middle American Archaeology and Ethnology*, no. 103. Washington, D.C.

Bullard, W. R., Jr.
1973 "Postclassic Culture in Central Peten and Adjacent British Honduras," in *The Classic Maya Collapse*, T. P. Culbert, ed., pp. 221–242. University of New Mexico Press, Albuquerque.

Butler, M.
1935 *Piedras Negras Pottery*. Piedras Negras Preliminary Papers, no. 4. The University Museum, Philadelphia.

Canby, J. S.
1951 "Possible Chronological Implications of the Long Ceramic Sequence Recovered at Yarumela, Spanish Honduras." *Proceedings of the 29th International Congress of Americanists*, vol. 1, pp. 79–85. Chicago.

Clark, J.
1979 "A Method for the Analysis of Mesoamerican Lithic Industries: An Application to the Obsidian Industry of La Libertad, Chiapas, Mexico." M.A. thesis, Brigham Young University, Provo, Utah.

Clark, J., and T. Lee, Jr.
1979 "A Behavioral Model for the Obsidian Industry of Chiapa de Corzo." *Estudios de Cultura Maya* XII:33–51.

Coe, M. D.
1961 *La Victoria: An Early Site on the Pacifi Coast of Guatemala*. Papers of the Peabod Museum, vol. 53. Harvard University, Cambridge, Massachusetts.
1973 *The Maya Scribe and His World*. Grolie Club, New York.

Coe, W. R.
1959 *Piedras Negras Archaeology: Artifacts Caches, and Burials*. Museum Monographs The University Museum, Philadelphia.

Crabtree, D.
1968 "Mesoamerican Polyhedral Cores and Prismatic Blades." *American Antiquity* 33:446–478.

Culbert, T. P.
1988 "Political History and the Maya Glyphs." *Antiquity* 62(234):135–152.

Dahlin, B.
1978 "Figurines," in *The Prehistory of Chalchuapa, El Salvador*, vol. 2, R. J. Sharer, ed., pp. 134–178. University of Pennsylvania Press, Philadelphia.

Demarest, A. A.
1986 *The Archaeology of Santa Leticia and the Rise of Maya Civilization*. Middle American Research Institute, Publication 52. Tulane University, New Orleans.

Demarest, A. A., and R. J. Sharer
1982 "The Origins and Evolution of the Usulutan Ceramic Style." *American Antiquity* 47:810–822.
1986 "Late Preclassic Ceramic Spheres, Culture Areas, and Cultural Evolution in the Southeastern Highlands of Mesoamerica," in *The Southeast Maya Periphery*, P. A. Urban and E. M. Schortman, eds., pp. 194–223. University of Texas Press, Austin.

Dixon, W. J., ed.
1983 *BMDP: Biomedical Computer Program*. University of California Press, Berkeley.

Everitt, B.
1974 *Cluster Analysis*. Halsted Press, Berkeley.

Fash, W. L., Jr.
1988 "Maya Statecraft from Copan, Honduras." *Antiquity* 62(234):157–169.

Fowler, W. R., Jr.
1981 "The Pipil-Nicarao of Central America." Ph.D. dissertation, University of Calgary, Canada.

Garber, J. F.
1981 "Material Culture and Patterns of Artifact Consumption and Disposal at the Maya Site of Cerros in Northern Belize." Ph.D. dissertation, Southern Methodist University, Dallas.

Gifford, J. C.
1976   *Prehistoric Pottery Analysis and the Ceramics of Barton Ramie in the Belize Valley.* Memoirs of the Peabody Museum, vol. 18. Harvard University, Cambridge, Massachusetts.

Glass, J. B.
1966   "Archaeological Survey of Western Honduras," in *Handbook of Middle American Indians, Vol. 4, Archaeological Frontiers and External Connections,* G. F. Ekholm and G. R. Willey, eds., pp. 157–179. University of Texas Press, Austin.

Gonzalez, D. de, and R. K. Wetherington
1978   "Incensarios and Other Ceremonial Forms at Kaminaljuyu," in *The Ceramics of Kaminaljuyu, Guatemala,* R. K. Wetherington, ed., pp. 279–298. Pennsylvania State University Press, University Park.

Gordon, G. B.
1896   *Prehistoric Ruins of Copan, Honduras. A Preliminary Report of the Explorations of the Museum, 1891–1895.* Memoirs of the Peabody Museum, vol. 1, no. 1, pp. 1–48. Harvard University, Cambridge, Massachusetts.
1898   *Researches in the Uloa Valley. Report of the Expedition of 1896–1897.* Memoirs of the Peabody Museum, vol. 1, nos. 4, 5. Harvard University, Cambridge, Massachusetts.
1902   *The Hieroglyphic Stairway, Ruins of Copan. Report on Explorations by the Museum.* Memoirs of the Peabody Museum, vol. 1, no. 6. Harvard University, Cambridge, Massachusetts.

Gunn, J. E., and E. R. Prewitt
1975   "Automatic Classification: Projectile Points from West Texas." *Plains Anthropologist* 20:139–149.

Haberland, W.
1958   "A Preclassic Complex of Western El Salvador, Central America." *Proceedings of the 32nd International Congress of Americanists,* pp. 485–490. Copenhagen.

Haviland, W. A.
1963   "Excavations of Small Structures in the Northeast Quadrant of Tikal." Ph.D. dissertation, University of Pennsylvania, Philadelphia.
1981   "Dower Houses and Minor Centers at Tikal, Guatemala: An Investigation into the Identification of Valid Units in Settlement Hierarchies," in *Lowland Maya Settlement Patterns,* W. Ashmore, ed., pp. 89–117. University of New Mexico Press, Albuquerque.

Hayden, B.
1979   *Lithic Use Wear.* Academic Press, New York.
1986   "Use and Misuse: The Analysis of Endscrapers." *Lithic Technology* 15(2).

Healy, P. F.
1980   *Archaeology of the Rivas Region, Nicaragua.* Wilfred Laurier University Press, Waterloo, Ontario.

Henderson, J. S., I. Sterns, A. Wonderley, and P. Urban
1979   "Archaeological Investigations in the Valle de Naco, Northwestern Honduras." *Journal of Field Archaeology* 6:169–192.

Hester, T. R.
1972   "Notes on Large Blade Cores and Core-Blade Technology in Mesoamerica." *Contributions of the University of California Archaeological Research Facility* 14:95–105.
1975   "The Obsidian Industry of Beleh (Chinautla Viejo) Guatemala." *Actas del XLI Congreso Internacional de Americanistas* 1:473–488, Mexico.
1978   "Notes on Large Obsidian Blade Cores and Coreblade Technology in Mesoamerica," in *Archaeological Studies of Mesoamerican Obsidian,* T. R. Hester, ed., pp. 100–111. Balena Press, Socorro, New Mexico.

Hester, T. R., R. N. Jack, and R. F. Heizer
1978   "The Obsidian of Tres Zapotes, Veracruz, Mexico," in *Archaeological Studies of Mesoamerican Obsidian,* T. R. Hester, ed., pp. 37–99. Balena Press, Socorro, New Mexico.

Hester, T. R., H. Shafer, and J. D. Eaton
1982   *Archaeology at Colha Belize: The 1981 Interim Report.* Center for Archaeological Research, University of Texas, San Antonio.

Honea, K.
1965   "A Morphology of Scrapers and Their Production." *Southwestern Lore* 31:25–40.

Hopkins, Mary R.
1986   "Analyses of the Technique of Izalco-type Usulutan Decoration," in *The Archaeology of Santa Leticia and the Rise of Maya Civilization,* by A. A. Demarest, Appendix 9, pp. 239–249. Middle American Research Institute, Publication 52. Tulane University, New Orleans.

Keeley, L.
1980   *Experimental Determination of Stone Tool Uses.* University of Chicago Press, Chicago.

Kennedy, N. C.
1977   "On the Frontier at Playa de Los Muertos, Honduras." Manuscript in the possession of the authors.
1981   "The Formative Period Ceramic Sequence from Playa de Los Muertos, Honduras."

Ph.D. dissertation, University of Illinois, Urbana-Champaign.

Kennedy, N. C., P. E. Messenger, and J. Yonk
  1982 "A Preliminary Ceramic Sequence from Salitron, Honduras: A Report Submitted to El Proyecto Arqueologico El Cajon." Manuscript in the possession of the authors.

Kidder, A. V.
  1947 *The Artifacts of Uaxactun, Guatemala.* Carnegie Institution of Washington, Publication 576. Washington, D.C.

Kidder, A. V., J. D. Jennings, and E. M. Shook
  1946 *Excavations at Kaminaljuyu, Guatemala.* Carnegie Institution of Washington, Publication 561. Washington, D.C.

Leventhal, R. M.
  1983 "Household Groups and Classic Maya Religion," in *Prehistoric Settlement Patterns*, E. Z. Vogt and R. M. Leventhal, eds., pp. 55–76. University of New Mexico Press, Albuquerque; and Peabody Museum, Harvard University, Cambridge, Massachusetts.
  1986 "A Reexamination of Stela Caches at Copan: New Dates for Copador," in *The Southeast Maya Periphery*, P. A. Urban and E. M. Schortman, eds., pp. 138–142. University of Texas Press, Austin.
  In prep. *Excavations in the Copan Valley, Honduras.* Papers of the Peabody Museum. Harvard University, Cambridge, Massachusetts.

Leventhal, R. M., and K. H. Baxter
  1988 "The Use of Ceramics to Identify the Function of Copan Structures," in *Household and Community in the Mesoamerican Past*, R. R. Wilk and W. Ashmore, eds., pp. 51–72. University of New Mexico Press, Albuquerque.

Linares de Sapir, O.
  1968 *Cultural Chronology in the Gulf Coast of Chiriqui, Panama.* Smithsonian Contributions to Anthropology, no. 8. Smithsonian Institution, Washington, D.C.

Lischka, J. J.
  1978 "A Functional Analysis of Middle Classic Ceramics at Kaminaljuyu," in *The Ceramics of Kaminaljuyu*, R. K. Wetherington, ed., pp. 223–278. Pennsylvania State University Press, University Park.

Longyear, J. M., III
  1944 *Archaeological Investigations in El Salvador.* Memoirs of the Peabody Museum, vol. 9, no. 2. Harvard University, Cambridge, Massachusetts.
  1952 *Copan Ceramics: A Study of Southeastern Maya Pottery.* Carnegie Institution of Washington, Publication 597. Washington, D.C.

  1966 "Archaeological Survey of El Salvador," in *Handbook of Middle American Indians, Vol. 4, Archaeological Frontiers and External Connections*, G. F. Ekholm and G. R. Willey, eds., pp. 132–156. University of Texas Press, Austin.

Lothrop, S. K.
  1937 *Cocle: An Archaeological Study of Central Panama, Part I.* Memoirs of the Peabody Museum, vol. 7. Harvard University, Cambridge, Massachusetts.
  1963 *Archaeology of the Diquis Delta, Costa Rica.* Papers of the Peabody Museum, vol. 51. Harvard University, Cambridge, Massachusetts.

Mallory, J. D.
  1986 "'Workshops' and 'Specialized Production' in the Production of Maya Chert Tools: A Response to Shafer and Hester." *American Antiquity* 51(1):152–158.

McDonald, G. F.
  1968 *Debert: A Paleo-Indian Site in Central Nova Scotia.* Anthropology Papers, no. 16. National Museum of Canada, Ottawa.

McGuire, R. H., J. Whittaker, M. McCarthy, and R. McSwain
  1982 "A Consideration of Observational Error in Lithic Use Wear Analysis." *Lithic Technology* 11(3).

Merwin, R. E., and G. C. Vaillant
  1932 *The Ruins of Holmul, Guatemala.* Memoirs of the Peabody Museum, vol. 3, no. 2. Harvard University, Cambridge, Massachusetts.

Morley, S.
  1920 *The Inscriptions at Copan.* Carnegie Institution of Washington, Publication 219. Washington, D.C.

Oakley, K.
  1964 *Man the Tool-Maker.* University of Chicago Press, Chicago.

Parsons, L. A.
  1969 *Bilbao, Guatemala.* Publications in Anthropology, vol. 2, no. 12. Milwaukee Public Museum, Milwaukee.

Patterson, L.
  1979 "Limitations in Uses of Large Prismatic Blades." *Lithic Technology* 8(1).

Potter, D. R.
  1987 "Chichen Itza Lithics Project: Interim Report." Manuscript in the possession of the authors.

Proskouriakoff, T.
  1962 "The Artifacts of Mayapan," in *Mayapan, Yucatan, Mexico*, by H. E. D. Pollock, R. L. Roys, T. Proskouriakoff, and A. L. Smith, pp. 321–442. Carnegie Institution of Washing-

ton, Publication 619, part 4. Washington, D.C.

Rands, R. L., and B. C. Rands
1959   "The Incensario Complex of Palenque, Chiapas." *American Antiquity* 25:225–236.

Rice, P.
1978   "Ceramic Continuity and Change in the Valley of Guatemala: A Technological Analysis," in *The Ceramics of Kaminaljuyu,* R. K. Wetherington, ed., pp. 401–510. Pennsylvania State University Press, University Park.

Ricketson, O. G., Jr., and E. B. Ricketson
1937   *Uaxactun, Guatemala Group E—1926–1931.* Carnegie Institution of Washington, Publication 477. Washington, D.C.

Ruz Lhuillier, A.
1958   "Exploraciones Arqueologicas en Palenque: 1953–1956." *Anales Instituto Nacional de Antropologia e Historia,* vol. 10, pp. 69–299. Secretaria de Educacion Publica, Mexico D.F.

Sabloff, J. A.
1975   *Excavations at Seibal: Ceramics.* Memoirs of the Peabody Museum, vol. 13, no. 2. Harvard University, Cambridge, Massachusetts.

Sabloff, J. A., and R. E. Smith
1969   "The Importance of Both Analytical and Taxonomic Classification in the Type-Variety System." *American Antiquity* 34(3):278–285.
1972   "Ceramic Wares in the Maya Area: A Clarification of an Aspect of the Type-Variety System and Presentation of a Formal Model for Comparative Use." *Estudios de Cultura Maya* 8:97–115.

Sanders, W. T.
1960   *Prehistoric Ceramics and Settlement Patterns in Quintana Roo, Mexico.* Carnegie Institution of Washington, Publication 606, Contributions to American Anthropology and History, no. 606. Washington, D.C.

Sanders, W. T., ed.
1986   *Excavaciones en el Area Urbana de Copan.* Tomo I, Instituto Hondureno de Antropologia e Historia. Tegucigalpa, Honduras.

Sanger, D.
1968   "The High River Microblade Industry, Alberta." *Plains Anthropologist* 13(41): 190–208.

Schele, L., and P. Mathews
1979   *The "Bodega" of Palenque, Chiapas, Mexico.* Dumbarton Oaks, Trustees for Harvard University, Washington, D.C.

Schortman, E. M., P. A. Urban, and W. Ashmore
1983   "Santa Barbara Archaeological Project, 1983 Season. Instituto Hondureno de Antropolo-

gia e Historia." Manuscript in the possession of the authors.

Shafer, H. J.
1970   "Notes on Uniface Retouch Technology." *American Antiquity* 35(4):480–487.

Shafer, H. J., and T. R. Hester
1986   "Maya Stone-Tool Craft Specialization and Production at Colha, Belize: Reply to Mallory." *American Antiquity* 51(1):158–166.

Sharer, R. J.
1974   "The Prehistory of the Southeastern Maya Periphery." *Current Anthropology* 15(2):165–187.
1978   *The Prehistory of Chalchuapa, El Salvador, Vol. 3, Pottery and Conclusions,* R. J. Sharer, gen. ed. University of Pennsylvania Press, Philadelphia.

Sheehy, J.
n.d.   "Preliminary Observations on the Ceramics from Colonia Care (Choloma), Cortes, Honduras." Manuscript in the possession of the authors.

Sheets, P. D.
1978   "The Artifacts," in *The Prehistory of Chalchuapa, El Salvador,* vol. 2, R. J. Sharer, ed., pp. 2–107. University of Pennsylvania Press, Philadelphia.
1979   "Environmental and Cultural Effects of the Ilopongo Eruption in Central America," in *Volcanic Activity and Human Ecology,* P. Sheets and D. Grayson, eds., pp. 525–564. Academic Press, New York.

Shook, E. M.
1965   "Archaeological Survey of the Pacific Coast of Guatemala," in *Handbook of Middle American Indians, Vol. 2, Archaeology of Southern Mesoamerica,* part 1, R. Wauchope and G. R. Willey, eds., pp. 180–194. University of Texas Press, Austin.

Shook, E. M., and A. V. Kidder
1952   *Mound E-III-3, Kaminaljuyu, Guatemala.* Carnegie Institution of Washington, Publication 596. Washington, D.C.

Siegel, P.
1986   "More on Functional Variability Within an Assemblage of End Scrapers: A Reply to Hayden and Bamforth." *Lithic Technology* 15(2).

Smith, A. L.
1962   "Residential and Associated Structures at Mayapan." in *Mayapan, Yucatan, Mexico,* by H. E. D. Pollock, R. L. Roys, T. Proskouriakoff, and A. L. Smith, pp. 165–320. Carnegie Institution of Washington, Publication 619, part 4. Washington, D.C.

Smith, A. L., and A. V. Kidder
1943 *Explorations in the Motagua Valley, Guatemala.* Carnegie Institution of Washington, Publication 546, Contribution 41. Washington, D.C.

Smith, R. E.
1955 *Ceramic Sequence at Uaxactun, Guatemala.* Middle American Research Institute, Publication 20. Tulane University, New Orleans.

Smith, R. E., and J. Gifford
1966 "Maya Ceramic Varieties, Types and Wares at Uaxactun," supplement to *Ceramic Sequence at Uaxactun, Guatemala.* Middle American Research Institute, Publication 28, pp. 125–174. Tulane University, New Orleans.

Sollberger, J., and L. Patterson
1976 "Prismatic Blade Replication." *American Antiquity* 41:517–531.

Srivastiva, M. S., and E. M. Carter
1983 *An Introduction to Applied Multivariate Statistics.* North Holland, New York.

Stone, D.
1941 *Archaeology of the North Coast of Honduras.* Memoirs of the Peabody Museum, vol. 9, no. 1. Harvard University, Cambridge, Massachusetts.
1957 *The Archaeology of Central and Southern Honduras.* Papers of the Peabody Museum, vol. 49, no. 3. Harvard University, Cambridge, Massachusetts.

Stromsvik, G.
1931 *Notes on the Metates of Chichen Itza, Yucatan.* Carnegie Institution of Washington, Publication 403, Contribution 4. Washington, D.C.
1935 *Notes on the Metates from Calakmul, Campeche, and from the Mercado, Chichen Itza, Yucatan.* Carnegie Institution of Washington, Publication 456, Contributions to American Archaeology, no. 16. Washington, D.C.
1938 "Copan." *Carnegie Institution of Washington Yearbook* 37:147–152. Washington, D.C.
1950 "Las Ruinas de Asuncion Mita: Informe de su Reconocimiento." *Antropologia e Historia de Guatemala* 2:23–27.

Strong, W. D.
1935 *Archaeological Investigations in the Bay Islands, Spanish Honduras.* Smithsonian Miscellaneous Collection, vol. 92, no. 14. Washington, D.C.
1948 "The Archaeology of Honduras." *Handbook of South American Indians* 4:71–120.

Strong, W. D., A. Kidder, II, and J. D. Paul, Jr.
1938 *Preliminary Report on the Smithsonian Institution—Harvard University Archaeological Expedition to Northwestern Honduras.* Smithsonian Miscellaneous Collection, vol. 97, no. 1. Washington, D.C.

Stoltman, J. B.
1975 "An Analysis of Chipped Stone Artifacts from Becan, Campeche, Mexico: A Case Study of the Value of Detailed Lithic Analyses in Complex Societies." Manuscript in the possession of the authors.

Thompson, J. E. S.
1939 *Excavations at San Jose, British Honduras.* Carnegie Institution of Washington, Publication 506. Washington, D.C.

Tourtellot, G.
1982 "Ancient Maya Settlements at Seibal, Peten, Guatemala: Peripheral Survey and Excavation." Ph.D. dissertation, Harvard University, Cambridge, Massachusetts.

Tozzer, A. M.
1941 *Landa's Relación de las Cosas de Yucatan.* Papers of the Peabody Museum, no. 18. Harvard University, Cambridge, Massachusetts.

Tringham, R., G. Cooper, G. Odell, B. Voytek, and A. Whitman
1974 "Experimentation in the Formation of Edge Damage: A New Approach to Lithic Analysis." *Journal of Field Archaeology* 1:171–195.

Valdez, F.
1986 "The Santa Leticia Obsidian Assemblage: Form, Technology and Use Wear." *Santa Leticia and the Rise of Maya Civilization*, by Arthur Demarest. Middle American Research Institute, Publication 52. Tulane University, New Orleans.

Valdez, F., and D. R. Potter
1982 "The Chert Industry at Copan: A Preliminary Assessment." Paper presented at the Second Maya Lithics Conference, San Antonio, Texas.

Viel, R.
1978 "Etude de la Céramique Ulua-Yojoa (Nord-Ouest de Honduras)." Ph.D. dissertation, Université René Descartes, Paris.
1983 "Evolucion de la Ceramica en Copan. Resultados Preliminares." *Introduccion a la Arqueologia de Copan, Honduras*, Tomo I, Proyecto Arqueologico Copan, Secretaria de Estado en el Despacho de Cultura y Turismo, pp. 471–550. Tegucigalpa, Honduras.

Viel, R., and C. D. Cheek
1983 "Sepulturas." *Introduccion a la Arqueologia de Copan, Honduras*, Tomo I, Proyecto

Arqueologico Copan, Secretaria de Estado en el Despacho de Cultura y Turismo, pp. 551–610. Tegucigalpa, Honduras.

Vogt, E. Z.
1969 *Zinacantan: A Maya Community in the Highlands of Chiapas.* Harvard University Press, Cambridge, Massachusetts.

Wallace, I.
1977 "Polychrome Ceramics in the Valle de Naco and Their External Relationships." Paper presented at the 42nd Society for American Archaeology meetings, New Orleans.

Washington, H. S.
1921 "Obsidian from Copan and Chichen Itza." *Journal of the Washington Academy of Sciences* 11(2):481–487.

Wauchope, R.
1934 *House Mounds of Uaxactun, Guatemala.* Carnegie Institution of Washington, Publication 436, Contributions to American Archaeology 7:107–171. Washington, D.C.
1938 *Modern Maya Houses: A Study of Their Archaeological Significance.* Carnegie Institution of Washington, Publication 502. Washington, D.C.
1948 *Excavations at Zacualpa, Guatemala.* Middle American Research Institute, Publication 14. Tulane University, New Orleans.

Webster, D. L.
1988 "Copan as a Classic Maya Center," in *The Southeast Classic Maya Zone,* E. H. Boone and G. R. Willey, eds., pp. 5–30. Dumbarton Oaks, Washington, D.C.

Webster, D. L., ed.
1989 *House of the Bacabs, Copan, Honduras.* Dumbarton Oaks, Washington, D.C.

Wetherington, R. K.
1978a "Ceramic Analysis: The Methodology of the Kaminaljuyu Project," in *The Ceramics of Kaminaljuyu, Guatemala,* R. K. Wetherington, ed., pp. 3–51. Pennsylvania State University Press, University Park.
1978b "Descriptive Taxonomy of Kaminaljuyu Ceramics," in *The Ceramics of Kaminaljuyu, Guatemala,* R. K. Wetherington, ed., pp.

51–114. Pennsylvania State University Press, University Park.

Wilk, R.
1978 "Microscopic Analysis of Chipped Flint and Obsidian," in *Excavations at Seibal: Artifacts,* by Gordon R. Willey, pp. 139–145. Memoirs of the Peabody Museum, vol. 14, no. 1. Harvard University, Cambridge, Massachusetts.

Willey, G. R.
1972 *The Artifacts of Altar de Sacrificios.* Papers of the Peabody Museum, vol. 64, no. 1. Harvard University, Cambridge, Massachusetts.
1978 *Excavations at Seibal: Artifacts.* Memoirs of the Peabody Museum, vol. 14, no. 1. Harvard University, Cambridge, Massachusetts.
1988 "The Southeast Classic Maya Zone: A Summary," in *The Southeast Classic Maya Zone,* E. H. Boone and G. R. Willey, eds., pp. 395–408. Dumbarton Oaks, Washington, D.C.

Willey, G. R., W. R. Coe, and R. J. Sharer
1975 "A Proposal for the Development of Archaeological Research and Preservation at Copan (Honduras) and Vicinity: 1976–1981." Manuscript, Instituto Hondureño de Antropologia y Historia, Tegucigalpa, Honduras.

Willey, G. R. and C. R. McGimsey, III
1954 *The Monagrillo Culture of Panama.* Papers of the Peabody Museum, vol. 49, no. 2. Harvard University, Cambridge, Massachusetts.

Willey, G. R., and R. M. Leventhal
1979 "Prehistoric Settlement at Copan," in *Maya Archaeology and Ethnohistory,* N. Hammond and G. R. Willey, eds., pp. 75–102. University of Texas Press, Austin.

Willey, G. R., R. M. Leventhal, and W. L. Fash, Jr.
1978 "Maya Settlement in the Copan Valley." *Archaeology* 31:32–43.

Willey, G. R., W. R. Bullard, J. B. Glass, and J. C. Gifford
1965 *Prehistoric Maya Settlements in the Belize Valley.* Papers of the Peabody Museum, no. 54. Harvard University, Cambridge, Massachusetts.

Whole Vessels and Special Find Proveniences

CV-20

Plaza

Op. 2(E), 1-16, Sp. Fd. 1	Two flint leaf-shaped blades and seven obsidian blades, associated with Burials 1, 3
Op. 2(C), Level 3, Sp. Fd. 2	Cache of obsidian bladelets and scrap, associated with Burials 1, 3
Op. 2(B), Level 4, 1-15, Sp. Fd. 3	Jade pendant
Op. 2(C), Level 5, 1-20, Sp. Fd. 4	Tipon Orange-brown: Moni Variety cylinder vessel, associated with Burials 1, 3
Op. 2(C), Level 5, 1-19, Sp. Fd. 5	Copador Polychrome: Glyphic Varieties, associated with Burials 1, 3
Op. 2(C), Level 5, 1-34, Sp. Fd. 6	Two small jade pieces, associated with Burial 3
Op. 2(B), Level 6, 1-35, Sp. Fd. 7	Small white disk-like object—plaster, associated with Burial 2
Op. 2(C), Level 6, 1-37, Sp. Fd. 8	White limestone or plaster rock, associated with Burial 3
Op. 2(C), Level 6, 1-38, Sp. Fd. 9	Nine green pebbles, associated with Burial 3
Op. 2(C), Level 6, 1-36, Sp. Fd. 10	Pebble, associated with Burial 3

Structure A

Op. 6(I), 1-92, Sp. Fd. 13	Sepultura Unslipped exterior base of Structure A
Op. 6(I), 1-97, Sp. Fd. 14	Sepultura Unslipped exterior base of Structure A
Op. 6(I), 1-103, Sp. Fd. 15	Raul Red: Raul Variety exterior base of Structure A
Op. 6(J), 1-109, Sp. Fd. 16	Sepultura Unslipped exterior base of Structure A
Op. 6(K), 1-120, Sp. Fd. 18	Sepultura Unslipped exterior base of Structure A
Op. 6(J), 1-117, Sp. Fd. 19	Sepultura Unslipped surface of Structure A
Op. 6(M), 1-131, Sp. Fd. 20	Sepultura Unslipped exterior base of Structure A
Op. 6(K), 1-134, Sp. Fd. 2	One animal tooth pendant exterior base of Structure A
Op. 6(M), 1-140, Sp. Fd. 23	Sepultura Unslipped on terrace of Structure A
Op. 6(K), 1-108	Lorenzo Red
Op. 6(K), 1-108	Clearing up of Structure A, Casaca Striated
Op. 6(N), 1-137	Chalja Incised

Op. 6(N), 1-137	Don Gordon Modeled-carved
Op. 6(N), 1-137	Ardilla Gouged-incised

Structure A Trench

Op. 19(C), Level 2, 1-214, Sp. Fd. 24	Tipon Orange-brown: Moni Variety associated with Sp. Fd. 25 on paving below floor
Op. 19(C), Level 2, 1-213, Sp. Fd. 25	Sepultura Unslipped, associated with Sp. Fd. 24
Op. 19(C), Level 3, 1-215, Sp. Fd. 28	Cache—eight polishing stores of black diorite, one miniature table
Op. 19(C), Level 3, 1-207	Chilanga Red-painted Usulutan: Osicala Variety
Op. 19(C), Level 5, 1-251, Sp. Fd. 50	Copador Polychrome, associated with Sp. Fd. 51, Burial 10
Op. 19(C), Level 5, 1-249, Sp. Fd. 51	Sepultura Unslipped
Op. 19(C), Level 6, 1-319, Sp. Fd. 59	Melano Carved, associated with Burial 16
Op. 19(F), Level 2, 1-303, Sp. Fd. 66	Sepultura Unslipped
Op. 19(F), Level 2, 1-271	Lorenzo Red

Structure B

Op. 7(E), 1-86, Sp. Fd. 12	Ring stone—found around base of Structure B
Op. 7(H), 1-135, Sp. Fd. 22	Marine worm tubes and coral section

Structure B Trench

Op. 21(A), Level 2, 1-222, Sp. Fd. 30	Diorite polishing stone associated with Sp. Fd. 31, 33–41, Burial 9
Op. 21(A), Level 2, 1-223, Sp. Fd. 31	Chilanga Red-painted Usulutan: Osicala Variety, associated with Sp. Fd. 30, 33–41, Burial 9
Op. 21(A), Level 2, 1-225, Sp. Fd. 33	Chilanga Red-painted Usulutan: Chilanga Variety, associated with Sp. Fd. 30, 31, 34–41, Burial 9
Op. 21(A), Level 2, 1-226, Sp. Fd. 34	Chilanga Red-painted Usulutan: Osicala Variety, associated with Sp. Fd. 30, 31, 33, 35–41, Burial 9
Op. 21(A), Level 2, 1-227, Sp. Fd. 35	Lorenzo Red, associated with Sp. Fd. 30, 31, 33–34, 36–41, Burial 9
Op. 21(A), Level 2, 1-228, Sp. Fd. 36	Chilanga Red-painted Usulutan: Chilanga Variety, associated with Sp. Fd. 30, 31, 33–35, 37–41, Burial 9
Op. 21(A), Level 2, 1-229, Sp. Fd. 37	Caterpillar Polychrome, associated with Sp. Fd. 30, 31, 33–36, 38–41, Burial 9
Op. 21(A), Level 2, 1-230, Sp. Fd. 38	Carved jade bead associated with Sp. Fd. 30, 31, 33–37, 39–41, Burial 9
Op. 21(A), Level 2, 1-231, Sp. Fd. 39	Small jade bead associated with Sp. Fd. 30, 31, 33–38, 40–41, Burial 9
Op. 21(A), Level 2, 1-232, Sp. Fd. 40	Small jade bead associated with Sp. Fd. 30, 31, 33–39, 41, Burial 9
Op. 21(A), Level 2, 1-206	Copador Polychrome
Op. 21(A), Level 2, 1-206	Don Gordon Modeled-carved
Op. 21(A), Level 2, 1-224, Sp. Fd. 32	Ceramic ear ornament, associated with Burial 8
Op. 21(A), Level 3, 1-250, Sp. Fd. 52	Cache of obsidian bladelets
Op. 21(A), Level 4, 1-299, Sp. Fd. 58	Copador Polychrome, associated with Sp. Fd. 63
Op. 21(A), Level 4, 1-315, Sp. Fd. 63	Copador Polychrome, associated with Sp. Fd. 58

Structure C Trench

Op. 24(A), Level 4, 1-314, Sp. Fd. 64	Ceramic ear ornament, associated with Sp. Fd. 65, Burial 19
Op. 24(A), Level 4, i-322, Sp. Fd. 65	Copador Polychrome associated with Sp. Fd. 64, Burial 19

Structure D

Op. 4(K), 1-75, Sp. Fd. 11	Sepultura Unslipped on back terrace of Structure D
Op. 4(N), 1-106, Sp. Fd. 17	Pottery jar—unclassified/eroded

Structure D Trench

Op. 20(A), Level 3, 1-211, Sp. Fd. 26	Copador Polychrome, associated with Sp. Fd. 27
Op. 20(A), Level 3, 1-212, Sp. Fd. 27	Copador Polychrome, associated with Sp. Fd. 26
Op. 20(A), Level 5, 1-241, Sp. Fd. 42	Large round mano, associated with Sp. Fd. 43–49, 68
Op. 20(A), Level 5, 1-242, Sp. Fd. 43	Barkbeater part of cache, associated with Sp. Fd. 42, 44–49, 68
Op. 20(A), Level 5, 1-243, Sp. Fd. 44	Small round mano, associated with Sp. Fd. 42–43, 45–49, 68
Op. 20(A), Level 5, 1-244, Sp. Fd. 45	Diorite polishing stone, associated with Sp. Fd. 42–44, 46–49, 68
Op. 20(A), Level 5, 1-305, Sp. Fd. 46	Sopi Incised, associated with Sp. Fd. 42–45, 47–49, 68
Op. 20(A), Level 5, 1-306, Sp. Fd. 47	Cementerio Incised: Zigoto Variety, associated with Sp. Fd. 42–46, 48, 49, 68
Op. 20(A), Level 5, 1-307, Sp. Fd. 48	Mapache Grooved, associated with Sp. Fd. 42–47, 49, 68
Op. 20(A), Level 5, 1-253, Sp. Fd. 49	Arroyo Red, associated with Sp. Fd. 42–48, 68
Op. 20(A), Level 5, 1-450, Sp. Fd. 68	Mapache Grooved, associated with Sp. Fd. 42–49
Op. 20(A), Level 5, 1-256, Sp. Fd. 53	Sopi Incised
Op. 20(A), Level 5, 1-312, Sp. Fd. 56	Ceramic ear ornament, associated with Sp. Fd. 57, Burial 13
Op. 20(A), Level 5, 1-313, Sp. Fd. 57	Ceramic ear ornament, associated with Sp. Fd. 56, Burial 13
Op. 20(A), Level 6, 1-317, Sp. Fd. 61	Small celt
Op. 20(A), Level 6, 1-318, Sp. Fd. 62	Stone ornament
Op. 20(A), Level 6, 1-316, Sp. Fd. 67	Ceramic ear ornament
Op. 20(A), Level 5, 1-238	Two vessels—Chilanga Red-painted Usulutan: Osicala Variety

---
CV-17

Test Pit

Op. 10(A), Level 2, 1-110, Sp. Fd. 1	Ceramic ear ornament
Op. 10(A), Level 3, 1-123, Sp. Fd. 2	Small jade bead, associated with Burial 5
Op. 10(A), Level 4, 1-130, Sp. Fd. 3	Gualpopa Polychrome

CV-13

Test Pit

Op. 11(A), Level 3, 1-147, Sp. Fd. 1	Carved jade ornament

CV-22

Test Pit

Op. 14(A), Level 3, 1-161, Sp. Fd. 1	Jade pebble, associated with Sp. Fd. 2
Op. 14(A), Level 3, 1-162, Sp. Fd. 2	Bottle-shaped candelero, associated with Sp. Fd. 1
Op. 14(A), Level 3, 1-163, Sp. Fd. 3	Two small jade pebbles, associated with Sp. Fd. 4
Op. 14(A), Level 3, 1-164, Sp. Fd. 4	Bottle-shaped candelero, associated with Sp. Fd. 3
Op. 14(A), Level 14, 1-169, Sp. Fd. 5	Bottle-shaped candelero
Op. 14(A), Level 5, 1-173, Sp. Fd. 6	Bottle-shaped candelero

CV-56

Test Pit

Op. 17(A), Level 1, 1-191, Sp. Fd. 1	Bottle-shaped candelero

CV-48

Test Pit

Op. 22(B), Level 4, 1-252, Sp. Fd. 1	Fragment of pyrite mirror(?) associated with Burial 1

L11-93

Salvage Test Excavation

Op. 26(A), Level 2, 1-326, Sp. Fd. 1	Jade adorno, associated with Sp. Fd. 2, 3, 4
Op. 26(A), Level 2, 1-327, Sp. Fd. 2	Babilonia Polychrome, associated with Sp. Fd. 1, 3, 4
Op. 26(A), Level 2, 1-328, Sp. Fd. 3	Eroded Polychrome(?), associated with Sp. Fd. 1, 2, 4
Op. 26(A), Level 2, 1-329, Sp. Fd. 4	Melano Carved, associated with Sp. Fd. 1, 2, 3
Op. 26(A), Level 2, 1-333, Sp. Fd. 5	Shell adorno found within Sp. Fd. 2
Op. 26(A), Level 2, 1-334, Sp. Fd. 6	Large tubular jade bead found within Sp. Fd. 2
Op. 26(A), Level 2, 1-335, Sp. Fd. 7	Jade pendant found within Sp. Fd. 2
Op. 26(A), Level 2, 1-336, Sp. Fd. 8	Jade pendant found within Sp. Fd. 2
Op. 26(A), Level 2, 1-337, Sp. Fd. 9	Jade pendant found within Sp. Fd. 2
Op. 26(A), Level 2, 1-338, Sp. Fd. 10	Jade pendant found within Sp. Fd. 2
Op. 26(A), Level 5, 1-342, Sp. Fd. 11	Babilonia Polychrome
Op. 26(A), Level 5, 1-352	Copador Polychrome found within Sp. Fd. 11
Op. 26(A), Level 5, 1-343, Sp. Fd. 12	Spondylus shell
Op. 26(A), Level 5, 1-345, Sp. Fd. 13	Polished pebble found within Sp. Fd. 12
Op. 26(A), Level 5, 1-346, Sp. Fd. 14	Jade pebble found within Sp. Fd. 12
Op. 26(A), Level 5, 1-347, Sp. Fd. 15	Polished pebble found within Sp. Fd. 12
Op. 26(A), Level 5, 1-348, Sp. Fd. 16	Polished pebble found within Sp. Fd. 12
Op. 26(A), Level 5, 1-349, Sp. Fd. 17	Shell pendant found within Sp. Fd. 12
Op. 26(A), Level 5, 1-350, Sp. Fd. 18	Jade adorno found within Sp. Fd. 12
Op. 26(A), Level 5, 1-351, Sp. Fd. 19	Jade pendant found within Sp. Fd. 12
Op. 26 (A), destroyed provenience, 1-361	1. Antonio Buff: Antonio Variety 2. Chilanga Red-painted Usulutan: Osicala Variety 3. Tipon Orange-brown: Moni Variety

Santa Rita

Op. 27(B), Level 8, 1-382, Sp. Fd. 1	Chilanga Red-painted Usulutan: Osicala Variety associated with Sp. Fd. 2
Op. 27(B), Level 8, 1-383, Sp. Fd. 2	Copador Polychrome, associated with Sp. Fd. 1

Surface

Op. 3, 1-356	Sepultura Unslipped in Copan Village
Op. 3, 1-355	Tipon Orange-brown: Moni Variety

Chemical Compositional Analysis of Southeastern Maya Ceramics

Ronald L. Bishop and Marilyn P. Beaudry

Conservation Analytical Laboratory

Smithsonian Institution

Study of the chemical composition of ceramics from the southeastern Maya periphery was initiated in 1979 as an extension of the Maya Jade and Ceramic Project (MJCP) then in progress at Brookhaven National Laboratory.[1]

The MJCP staff had completed extensive analyses of materials from the central Peten region of the Maya lowlands and was interested in gathering empirical data from an area geographically distinct from but culturally affiliated with the Peten. This, in effect, would establish a boundary for the central Peten production zone by providing comparative regional profiles of chemical compositional patterning.

The Copan Valley was clearly outside of the central Peten zone and yet was part of the southern lowland Maya subarea. Thus, it fulfilled the requirements of the MJCP. Therefore, the MJCP trace elemental ceramic information could contribute to the Harvard project's database. Consequently, the original goal was to analyze a sample of Copan Valley ceramics that were considered local products, thereby establishing a ceramic paste composition reference (CPCR) group for the valley. Then the chemical composition of other ceramics that might have been either locally made or imported could be assessed against the reference group, and the probability of Copan Valley production could be determined.

As often happens with research projects, the original goal expanded gradually as sets of analyses were completed. The first expansion came about because of the interest of one of the investigators (Beaudry) in Copan's role in Late Classic Coner phase exchange systems. This resulted in more extensive sampling of the cream paste painted serving vessels (Chilanga, Gualpopa, and Copador) from the Copan Valley as well as from additional proveniences where these types had been recovered. Understanding Copan's role as an exporter meant getting to know chemically the complexes from possible importing areas. So samples from western El Salvador, the Motagua Valley of Guatemala, and western Honduras[2] were incorporated into the chemical compositional analysis.

Full-scale reference group development was not undertaken for each of the regions mentioned. A small sample of assumed local wares was analyzed to provide a comparative framework for the data derived from the trade ware analysis. In all cases the goal was to assess the likelihood of Copan Valley production against the probability of manufacture at the recovery location.

Copan's role as an importer of ceramic material was implicit in the original design whereby nonlocal ceramics would be distinguished by their deviation from the Copan Valley CPCR. This deviation did occur, as will be discussed in a subsequent section. In addition, as fieldwork in the Copan Valley has continued after the completion of the Harvard Copan Project, the frequency of occurrence of imported Ulua Polychrome has grown and questions about its distribution path have become more intriguing. Consequently, another extension of this project is in progress with samples of Ulua Polychrome from selected Copan Valley loci being compared with materials from other western Honduran proveniences, and from proveniences as far south as Costa Rica.

The southeast Maya ceramics considered in this work, therefore, stem from a Copan Valley perspective—as local products consumed in the valley, as local products exported to other areas or as imported products consumed in the valley. Table B-1 identifies by provenience and ceramic classification the 358 ceramic vessels analyzed in this project. The geographic area covered is shown in the map (fig. B-1).

TABLE B-1

Sample provenience and compositional classification

Reference group: Copan Domestic 1 (n = 40)

ID. No.	Provenience/Site	Location/Lot	Ceramic Classification
MSC003	Copan Valley, CV-20	Op. 19(C), Level 4	Antonio Buff
MSC005	Copan Valley, CV-20	Op. 19(C), Level 4	Antonio Buff
MSC007	Copan Valley, CV-20	Op. 19(C), Level 4	Lysandro Unslipped
MSC008	Copan Valley, CV-20	Op. 4(R), Level 1	Lysandro Unslipped
MSC010	Copan Valley, CV-20	Op. 6(I), Level 1	Lysandro Unslipped
MSC011	Copan Valley, CV-20	Op. 7(E), Level 1	Lysandro Unslipped
MSC012	Copan Valley, CV-20	Op. 5(B), Level 1	Lysandro Unslipped
MSC013	Copan Valley, CV-20	Op. 15(B), Level 1	Raul Red: Raul Variety
MSC014	Copan Valley, CV-20	Op. 19(B), Level 2	Raul Red: Raul Variety
MSC015	Copan Valley, CV-20	Op. 5(B), Level 1	Raul Red: Raul Variety
MSC016	Copan Valley, CV-20	Op. 19(B), Level 2	Raul Red: Raul Variety
MSC017	Copan Valley, CV-56	Op. 17(A), Level 6	Raul Red: Raul Variety
MSC034	Copan Valley, CV-20	Op. 19(C), Level 4	Cementerio Incised: Cementerio Variety
MSC040	Copan Valley, CV-20	Op. 6(C), Level 1	Masica Incised: Cruz Variety
MSC041	Copan Valley, CV-20	Op. 7(B), Level 1	Masica Incised: Cruz Variety
MSC042	Copan Valley, CV-20	Op. 6(J), Level 1	Masica Incised: Cruz Variety
MSC043	Copan Valley, CV-20	Op. 6(J), Level 1	Masica Incised: Cruz Variety
MSC044	Copan Valley, CV-20	Op. 6(A), Level 1	Masica Incised: Cruz Variety
MSC051	Copan Valley	Unknown	Casaca Striated: Casaca Variety
MSC052	Copan Valley	Unknown	Casaca Striated: Casaca Variety
MSC054	Copan Valley, CV-20	Op. 5(B), Level 1	Casaca Striated: Casaca Variety
MSC055	Copan Valley, CV-20	Op. 5(B), Level 1	Casaca Striated: Casaca Variety
MSC056	Copan Valley, CV-20	Op. 6(K), Level 1	Casaca Striated: Casaca Variety
MSC057	Copan Valley	Unknown	Masica Incised: Cruz Variety
MSC122	Copan Valley, CV-20	Op. 7(H), Level 1	Capulin Cream: Uogistus Variety
MSC126	Copan Valley, CV-20	Op. 19(C), Level 4	Cementerio Incised: Cementerio Variety
MSC128	Copan Valley, CV-20	Op. 19(C), Level 4	Cementerio Incised: Cementerio Variety
MSC174	Copan Valley, CV-43	Op. 49(A), Level 2	Caterpillar Polychrome
MSC175	Copan Valley, CV-43	Op. 36(H), Level 1	Caterpillar Polychrome
MSC176	Copan Valley, CV-43	Op. 104(A), Level 9-B	Caterpillar Polychrome
MSC177	Copan Valley	Unknown	Copador Polychrome

MSC192	Copan Valley, CV-43	Op. 102(A), Level 3	Caterpillar Polychrome
MSC193	Copan Valley, CV-43	Op. 102(A), Level 3	Caterpillar Polychrome
MSC213	Copan Valley, CV-20	Op. 20(A), Level 11	Capulin Cream: Uogistus Variety
MSC219	Copan Valley, CV-43	Op. 102(A), Level 3	Caterpillar: Caterpillar Variety
MSC244	Copan Valley, CV-43	Op. 49(A), Level 15B	Unclassified bichrome
MSM043	La Canteada, Honduras	D4-327	Unslipped domestic ware

Reference group: Copan Domestic 2 (n = 6)

ID. No.	Provenience/Site	Location/Lot	Ceramic Classification
MSC004	Copan Valley, CV-20	Op. 2(C), Level 3	Antonio Buff
MSC024	Copan Valley, CV-20	Op. 24(A), Level 4	Sepulturas Unslipped
MSC025	Copan Valley, CV-20	Op. 2(B), Level 1	Sepulturas Unslipped
MSC026	Copan Valley, CV-20	Op. 18(B), Level 1	Sepulturas Unslipped
MSC027	Copan Valley, CV-20	Op. 19(F), Level 2	Sepulturas (cacao pod from censer)
MSC038	Copan Valley, CV-20	Op. 4(J)	Cementerio Incised: Cementerio Variety

Reference group: Tipon A (n = 32)

ID. No.	Provenience/Site	Location/Lot	Ceramic Classification
MSC029	Copan Valley, CV-20	Op. 5(M), Level 1	Tipon Orange-brown
MSC030	Copan Valley, CV-20	Op. 6(I), Level 1	Tipon Orange-brown
MSC031	Copan Valley, CV-18	Op. 9(A), Level 1	Tipon Orange-brown
MSC032	Copan Valley, CV-20	Op. 6(I), Level 1	Tipon Orange-brown
MSC047	Copan Valley, CV-20	Op. 21(A), Level 3	Chilanga Red-painted Usulutan
MSC053	Copan Valley, CV-20	Op. 2(I), Level 1	Casaca Striated: Casaca Variety
MSC104	Copan Valley, CV-20	Op. 7(G), Level 1	Tipon Orange-brown
MSC106	Copan Valley, CV-20	Op. 7(E), Level 1	Tipon Orange-brown
MSC113	Copan Valley, CV-20	Op. 4(R), Level 1	Tipon Orange-brown
MSC114	Copan Valley, CV-20	Op. 7(E), Level 1	Tipon Orange-brown
MSC115	Copan Valley, CV-20	Op. 6(N), Level 1	Tipon Orange-brown
MSC117	Copan Valley, CV-22	Op. 14(A), Level 7	Capulin Cream: Uogistus
MSC120	Copan Valley, Sacbe	Op. 16(D), Level 6	Capulin Cream: Uogistus
MSC154	Copan Valley, CV-20	Op. 21(A), Level 4	Capulin Cream: Uogistus
MSC155	Copan Valley, CV-20	Op. 19(A), Level 2	Capulin Cream: Uogistus
MSC156	Copan Valley, Sacbe	Op. 16(O), Level 6	Capulin Cream: Uogistus
MSC157	Copan Valley, Sacbe	Op. 16(O), Level 6	Capulin Cream: Uogistus
MSC179	Copan Valley, CV-43	Op. 35(J), Level 1	Tipon Orange-brown
MSC181	Copan Valley, CV-43	Op. 35(O), Level 1	Tipon Orange-brown
MSC183	Copan Valley, CV-43	Op. 37(H), Level 1	Tipon Orange-brown
MSC184	Copan Valley, CV-45	Op. 50(A), Level 7	Daub
MSC185	Copan Valley, CV-45	Op. 50(A), Level 7	Daub
MSC186	Copan Valley, CV-43	Op. 33(M), Level 1	Daub
MSC194	Copan Valley, CV-20	Op. 5(O), Level 1	Tipon Orange-brown
MSC195	Copan Valley, CV-43	Op. 100(B), Level 3	Tipon Orange-brown
MSC199	Copan Valley, CV-20	Op. 20(A), Level 6	Capulin Cream: Uogistus Variety
MSC254	Copan Valley, CV-20	Op. 7(B), Level 1	Don Gordon Modeled-carved (Tipon group)

T ABLE B-1 *(continued)*

Sample provenience and compositional classification

Reference group: Tipon A (n = 32)

ID. No.	Provenience/Site	Location/Lot	Ceramic Classification
MSC255	Copan Valley, CV-20	Op. 6(J), Level 1	Don Gordon Modeled-carved (Tipon group)
MSC258	Copan Valley, CV-20	Op. 20(A), Level 6	Incised Red-on-white
MSLL12	Las Flores, Honduras	Peabody Museum col.	Ulua Polychrome
MSSB04	Santa Barbara Valley	9B/2	Santa Rosita Red-on-brown: Santa Rosita Variety
MSSB17	Santa Barbara Valley	3A/12	Guayabita Burnished Black (Early Classic)

Reference group: Tipon B (n = 12)

ID. No.	Provenience/Site	Location/Lot	Ceramic Classification
MSC033	Copan Valley, CV-20	Op. 20(A), Level 3	Tipon Orange-brown: Moni Variety
MSC097	Copan Valley, CV-20	Op. 1(A), surface, lg. plaza	Tipon Orange-brown: Moni Variety
MSC100	Copan Valley, CV-20	Plaza	Tipon Orange-brown: Moni Variety
MSC102	Copan Valley, CV-20	Plaza	Tipon Orange-brown: Moni Variety
MSC103	Copan Valley, CV-20	Op. 21(A), Level 3	Tipon Orange-brown: Moni Variety
MSC110	Copan Valley, CV-20	Op. 20(A), Level 3	Tipon Orange-brown: Moni Variety
MSC111	Copan Valley, CV-20	Op. 7(E), Level 1	Tipon Orange-brown: Moni Variety
MSC112	Copan Valley, CV-20	Op. 2(C), Level 3	Tipon Orange-brown: Moni Variety
MSC141	Central Copan	C 980	Ulua Polychrome
MSC180	Copan Valley, CV-20	Op. 4(P), Level 1	Tipon Orange-brown: Moni Variety
MSC182	Copan Valley, CV-20	Op. 1(A), surface, lg. plaza	Tipon Orange-brown: Moni Variety
MSC256	Copan Valley, CV-20	Op. 21(A), Level 3	Don Gordon Modeled-carved (Tipon group)

Reference group: Copan Fine Paste (n = 24)

ID. No.	Provenience/Site	Location/Lot	Ceramic Classification
MSC022	Copan Valley, CV-20	Op. 7(F), Level 1	Copador Polychrome
MSC039	Copan Valley, CV-20	Op. 4(O), Level 1	Cementerio Incised: Cementerio Variety
MSC046	Copan Valley, CV-20	Op. 20(A), Level 3	Chilanga Red-painted Usulutan
MSC048	Copan Valley, CV-20	Op. 21(A), Level 2	Chilanga Red-painted Usulutan
MSC050	Copan Valley, CV-20	Op. 21(A), Level 2	Chilanga Red-painted Usulutan
MSC059	Copan Valley, CV-20	Op. 20(A), Level 5	Chilanga Red-painted Usulutan
MSC061	Copan Valley	Unknown	Chilanga Red-painted Usulutan
MSC067	Copan Valley, CV-20	Op. 4(R), Level 1	Copador Polychrome
MSC070	Copan Valley, CV-20	Op. 21(A), Level 3	Copador Polychrome
MSC072	Copan Valley, CV-20	Op. 6(I), Level 1	Copador Polychrome
MSC116	Copan Valley, Sacbe	Op. 16(A), Level 1	Capulin Cream: Uogistus Variety
MSC118	Copan Valley, Sacbe	Op. 16(A), Level 1	Capulin Cream: Uogistus Variety

MSC119	Copan Valley, CV-20	Op. 21(A), Level 2	Capulin Cream: Uogistus Variety
MSC123	Copan Valley, CV-20	Op. 6(N), Level 1	Capulin Cream: Uogistus Variety
MSC147	Copan Valley, CV-20	Op. 6(B), Level 1	Claudio Incised (Tipon group)
MSC148	Copan Valley, CV-20	Op. 4(A), Level 1	Claudio Incised (Tipon group)
MSC149	Copan Valley, CV-20	Op. 6(A), Level 1	Claudio Incised (Tipon group)
MSC150	Copan Valley, CV-20	Op. 4(A), Level 1	Claudio Incised (Tipon group)
MSC151	Copan Valley, CV-20	Op. 4(A), Level 1	Claudio Incised (Tipon group)
MSC152	Copan Valley, CV-20	Op. 4(A), Level 1	Claudio Incised (Tipon group)
MSC153	Copan Valley, CV-20	Op. 6(M), Level 1	Copador Polychrome
MSC169	Copan Valley, CV-20	Op. 19(F), Level 2	Gualpopa Polychrome
MSC187	Copan Valley	Unknown	Gualpopa Polychrome
MSC242	Copan Valley, CV-20	Op. 6(M), Level 1	Caterpillar Polychrome

Reference group: Copan-focus Copador (*n* = 136)

ID. No.	*Provenience/Site*	*Location/Lot*	*Ceramic Classification*
MSC018	Copan Valley, CV-20	Op. 21(A), Level 2	Copador Polychrome
MSC019	Copan Valley, CV-20	Op. 24(A), Level 5	Copador Polychrome
MSC020	Copan Valley, CV-20	Op. 24(A), Level 5	Copador Polychrome
MSC021	Copan Valley, CV-48	Op. 22(B), Level 4 (Special Find 1)	Copador Polychrome
MSC023	Copan Valley, CV-20	Op. 7(E), Level 1	Copador Polychrome
MSC028	Copan Valley, CV-20	Op. 15(B), Level 1	Tipon Orange-brown
MSC049	Copan Valley, CV-20	Op. 21(A), Level 2	Chilanga Red-painted Usulutan
MSC060	Copan Valley, CV-20	Op. 19(C), Level 5	Chilanga Red-painted Usulutan
MSC062	Copan Valley, CV-20	Op. 19(C), Level 5	Chilanga Red-painted Usulutan
MSC063	Copan Valley, CV-20	Op. 21(A), Level 2 (Special Find 38)	Chilanga Red-painted Usulutan
MSC064	Copan Valley, CV-20	Op. 7(E), Level 1	Copador Polychrome
MSC065	Copan Valley, CV-20	Op. 7(E), Level 1	Copador Polychrome
MSC069	Copan Valley, CV-20	Op. 6(N), Level 1	Copador Polychrome
MSC071	Copan Valley, CV-20	RML 216, surface	Copador Polychrome
MSC073	Copan Valley, CV-20	Op. 6(K), Level 1	Copador Polychrome
MSC074	Copan Valley, CV-20	Op. 19(A), Level 2	Copador Polychrome
MSC075	Copan Valley, CV-20	Op. 6(J), Level 1	Copador Polychrome
MSC076	Copan Valley, CV-20	Op. 21(A), Level 3	Copador Polychrome
MSC077	Copan Valley, CV-20	Op. 24(A), Level 7	Copador Polychrome
MSC078	Copan Valley, CV-20	Op. 21(A), Level 3	Copador Polychrome
MSC079	Copan Valley, CV-20	Op. 4(N), Level 1	Copador Polychrome
MSC083	Copan Valley, CV-20	Op. 2(B), Level 6	Copador Polychrome
MSC084	Copan Valley, CV-20	Op. 21(A), Level 3	Copador Polychrome
MSC085	Copan Valley, CV-20	Op. 5(M), Level 1	Copador Polychrome
MSC086	Copan Valley, CV-20	Op. 5(A), Level 1	Copador Polychrome
MSC109	Copan Valley, CV-20	Op. 21(A), Level 3	Copador Polychrome
MSC138	Central Copan	C/986, Peabody Mus. col.	Copador Polychrome
MSC142	Central Copan	C/980, Peabody Mus. col.	Copador Polychrome

Sample provenience and compositional classification

Reference group: Copan-focus Copador (n = 136)

ID. No.	Provenience/Site	Location/Lot	Ceramic Classification
MSC143	Central Copan	C/980, Peabody Mus. col.	Copador Polychrome
MSC144	Central Copan	C/980, Peabody Mus. col.	Copador Polychrome
MSC145	Central Copan	C/980, Peabody Mus. col.	Copador Polychrome
MSC146	Central Copan	C/980, Peabody Mus. col.	Copador Polychrome
MSC165	Copan Valley, CV-20	Op. 20(A), Level 3	Gualpopa Polychrome
MSC166	Copan Valley, CV-20	Op. 20(A), Level 3	Gualpopa Polychrome
MSC167	Copan Valley, CV-20	Op. 20(A), Level 3	Gualpopa Polychrome
MSC168	Copan Valley, CV-20	Op. 20(A), Level 3	Gualpopa Polychrome
MSC170	Central Copan	Peabody Mus. col.	Copador Polychrome
MSC171	Central Copan	Peabody Mus. col.	Copador Polychrome
MSC172	Central Copan	Peabody Mus. col.	Copador Polychrome
MSC188	Central Copan	Peabody Mus. col.	Gualpopa Polychrome
MSC189	Central Copan	Peabody Mus. col.	Gualpopa Polychrome
MSC190	Central Copan	Peabody Mus. col.	Gualpopa Polychrome
MSC200	Copan Valley, CV-20	Op. 20(A), Level 5	Capulin Cream: Uogistus Variety
MSC214	Copan Valley, CV-20	Op. 7(E), Level 1	Capulin Cream: Uogistus Variety
MSC215	Central Copan	C/887, Peabody Mus. col.	Copador Polychrome
MSC217	Central Copan	C/980, Peabody Mus. col.	Copador Polychrome
MSC218	Central Copan	Peabody Mus. col.	Gualpopa Polychrome
MSC221	Copan Valley, CV-20	Op. 19(C), Level 3	Copador Polychrome
MSC222	Copan Valley, CV-43	Op. 35(O), Level 1	Copador Polychrome
MSC223	Copan Valley, CV-43	Op. 49(A), Level 8-C	Copador Polychrome
MSC224	Copan Valley, CV-20	Op. 7(G), Level 1	Copador Polychrome
MSC225	Central Copan	C/980, Peabody Mus. col.	Copador Polychrome
MSC226	Central Copan	C/980, Peabody Mus. col.	Copador Polychrome
MSC227	Central Copan	C/980, Peabody Mus. col.	Copador Polychrom
MSC228	Central Copan	C/980, Peabody Mus. col.	Copador Polychrome
MSC229	Central Copan	C/980, Peabody Mus. col.	Copador Polychrome
MSC240	Copan Valley, CV-43	Op. 49(A), Level 8-C	Copador Polychrome
MSC243	Copan Valley, CV-43	Op. 104(A), Level 7	Unclassified polychrome
MSCC06	Chalchuapa	LL-S/5b	Copador Polychrome
MSCC07	Chalchuapa	LL-S/6b	Copador Polychrome
MSCC17	Chalchuapa	LL-S/1a	Gualpopa Polychrome

MSCC18	Chalchuapa	LL-S/2a	Gualpopa Polychrome
MSCC21	Chalchuapa	67.8.12	Gualpopa Polychrome
MSCC25	Chalchuapa	SM.S	Copador Polychrome
MSCC26	Chalchuapa	67.8.14	Copador Polychrome
MSCC27	Chalchuapa	LL-5	Copador Polychrome
MSCC28	Chalchuapa	CH-S-13	Copador Polychrome
MSCC30	Chalchuapa	LL-5	Copador Polychrome
MSCC31	Chalchuapa	EC-51	Copador Polychrome
MSCC32	Chalchuapa	LL-5	Copador Polychrome
MSCC34	Chalchuapa	Unknown	Copador Polychrome
MSCC36	Chalchuapa	CH-S-13	Copador Polychrome
MSCC37	Chalchuapa	LL-5	Copador Polychrome
MSCC39	Chalchuapa	LC3-6-4	Chilanga Red-painted Usulutan
MSCC90	Chalchuapa	LL-5	Gualpopa Polychrome
MSCC95	Chalchuapa	Unknown	Gualpopa Polychrome
MSCC96	Chalchuapa	EC-51	Gualpopa Polychrome
MSCC97	Chalchuapa	CB3-2.S	Gualpopa Polychrome
MSC/16	Chalchuapa	LC3-6M	Copador Polychrome
MSC/18	Chalchuapa	CB3-27-3	Chilanga Red-painted Usulutan
MSC/19	Chalchuapa	LL-5	Chilanga Red-painted Usulutan
MSG300	Guaytan, Q15	GMNAE	Chilanga Red-painted Usulutan
MSG329	Asuncion Mita	GMNAE	Chilanga Red-painted Usulutan
MSG332	Asuncion Mita	GMNAE	Gualpopa Polychrome
MSG334	Asuncion Mita	GMNAE	Copador Polychrome
MSG335	Asuncion Mita	GMNAE	Copador Polychrome
MSG336	Guaytan	GMNAE	Gualpopa Polychrome
MSG337	Guaytan	GMNAE	Gualpopa Polychrome
MSG341	Tiquisate	GMNAE	Copador Polychrome
MSM001	La Canteada, Honduras	D4-444	Copador Polychrome
MSM004	La Canteada, Honduras	D4-320	Copador Polychrome
MSM005	La Canteada, Honduras	D4-327	Copador Polychrome
MSM008	La Canteada, Honduras	D4-327-1	Copador Polychrome
MSM009	La Canteada, Honduras	D4-496	Copador Polychrome
MSM015	La Canteada, Honduras	D4-329-4	Gualpopa Polychrome
MSM025	Cambio, El Salvador	336-1M2	Copador Polychrome
MSM026	Cambio, El Salvador	336-1R4	Copador Polychrome
MSM027	Cambio, El Salvador	336-1V4	Copador Polychrome
MSM028	Cambio, El Salvador	336-1S1	Copador Polychrome
MSM038	Cambio, El Salvador	336-1O4	Copador Polychrome
MSM041	La Canteada, Honduras	D4-638	Chilanga Red-painted Usulutan
MSM042	La Canteada, Honduras	D4-260-12	Chilanga Red-painted Usulutan
MSM047	La Canteada, Honduras	D4-260-6	Chilanga Red-painted Usulutan
MSM076	Cambio, El Salvador	336-1G2	Gualpopa Polychrome
MSM078	Cambio, El Salvador	336-1T6	Gualpopa Polychrome
MSM081	Cambio, El Salvador	336-1S2	Gualpopa Polychrome
MSM085	Cambio, El Salvador	336-1T6	Gualpopa Polychrome
MSM098	La Canteada, Honduras	D4-571-5	Chilanga Red-painted Usulutan
MSM099	La Canteada, Honduras	D4-630-1	Chilanga Red-painted Usulutan

TABLE B-1 (*continued*)

Sample provenience and compositional classification

Reference group: Copan-focus Copador (n = 136)

ID. No.	Provenience/Site	Location/Lot	Ceramic Classification
MSM108	Ceren, El Salvador	295-1B4	Gualpopa Polychrome
MSM109	Ceren, El Salvador	295-1A1	Gualpopa Polychrome
MSM115	Ceren, El Salvador	295-1A15	Copador Polychrome
MSM117	Ceren, El Salvador	295-1B12	Copador Polychrome
MSM123	La Canteada, Honduras	D4-630	Chilanga Red-painted Usulutan
MSM124	La Canteada, Honduras	D4-571	Chilanga Red-painted Usulutan
MSM125	La Canteada, Honduras	D4-571-13	Chilanga Red-painted Usulutan
MSM129	Acasaguastlan, Guatemala	Unknown	Gualpopa Polychrome
MSM130	Acasaguastlan, Guatemala	Unknown	Gualpopa Polychrome
MSM131	Acasaguastlan, Guatemala	Unknown	Gualpopa Polychrome
MSM132	Acasaguastlan, Guatemala	Unknown	Gualpopa Polychrome
MSQ046	Quirigua	18A/7, 3d	Chilanga Red-painted Usulutan
MSSB30	Santa Barbara, Honduras	4B/4	Chilanga Red-painted Usulutan
MSSB32	Santa Barbara, Honduras	2A/2	Copador Polychrome
MSW004	Acasaguastlan, Guatemala	Unknown	Gualpopa Polychrome
MSW031	Acasaguastlan, Guatemala	Unknown	Chilanga Red-painted Usulutan
MSO424	Pusilha, Belize	Unknown	Copador Polychrome
MSO425	Pusilha, Belize	Unknown	Copador Polychrome
MSO426	Pusilha, Belize	Unknown	Copador Polychrome
MSO427	Pusilha, Belize	Unknown	Copador Polychrome
MSO428	Pusilha, Belize	Unknown	Copador Polychrome
MSO430	Pusilha, Belize	Unknown	Copador Polychrome
MSO432	Pusilha, Belize	Unknown	Copador Polychrome
MSO433	Pusilha, Belize	Unknown	Copador Polychrome
MSO434	Pusilha, Belize	Unknown	Copador Polychrome
MSO436	Pusilha, Belize	Unknown	Copador Polychrome

Reference group: Western Honduras Domestic (n = 13)

ID. No.	Provenience/Site	Location/Lot	Ceramic Classification
MSLL04	Los Naranjos, Honduras	Peabody Mus. col.	Red and black on orange
MSLL05	Los Naranjos, Honduras	Peabody Mus. col.	Red and black on orange
MSLL06	Los Naranjos, Honduras	Peabody Mus. col.	Red and black on orange
MSNV13	Naco Valley, La Sierra	54a	Chilanga Usulutan
MSNV17	Naco Valley, Site 111	F/3 (lu)	Red-painted Usulutan
MSNV26	Naco Valley, Site 113	MIS-HP (31b)	Magdalena Tan
MSNV34	Naco Valley, Site 111	B/1 (55d)	Jicaro Unslipped: Variety unspecified
MSNV35	Naco Valley, Site 111	F/2 (55b)	Jicaro Unslipped: Variety unspecified
MSNV37	Naco Valley, La Sierra	(36a)	Cerro Azul Buff: Cerro Azul Variety
MSNV38	Naco Valley, Site 177	C/1 (36e)	Cerro Azul Buff: Cerro Azul Variety
MSNV39	Naco Valley, Site 123	A/1 (51c)	Montanitas Yellow-tan paste

MSNV47	Naco Valley, Site 123	B/1 (41a)	Calanar Cream Paste: Calanar Variety
MSSB46	Santa Barbara, Honduras	10G/3g	Aguagua Uneven Orange slip

Reference group: Western Honduras Painted (n = 41)

ID. No.	Provenience/Site	Location/Lot	Ceramic Classification
MSC081	Copan Valley, CV-20	Op. 21(A), Level 3	Ulua Polychrome
MSC087	Copan Valley, CV-20	Op. 7(E), Level 1	Ulua Polychrome
MSC088	Copan Valley	Unknown	Ulua Polychrome
MSC140	Central Copan	C/980, Peabody Mus. col.	Ulua Polychrome
MSC201	Copan Valley, CV-20	Op. 6(J), Level 1	Tipon Orange-brown
MSC205	Copan Valley, CV-20	Op. 7(E), Level 1	Ulua Polychrome
MSC206	Copan Valley, CV-43	Op. 35(O), Level 1	Ulua Polychrome
MSC208	Copan Valley, CV-43	Op. 37(N), Level 1	Ulua Polychrome
MSC209	Copan Valley, CV-43	Op. 35(O), Level 1	Ulua Polychrome
MSC211	Copan Valley, CV-43	Op. 35(O), Level 1	Ulua Polychrome
MSLL07	Santa Rita Farm, Honduras	Peabody Mus. col.	Ulua Polychrome
MSLL08	Santa Rita Farm, Honduras	Peabody Mus. col.	Ulua Polychrome
MSLL09	Santa Rita Farm, Honduras	Peabody Mus. col.	Ulua Polychrome
MSLL13	Las Flores, Honduras	Peabody Mus. col.	Ulua Polychrome
MSLL14	Santa Rita Farm, Honduras	Peabody Mus. col.	Ulua Polychrome
MSLL15	Santa Rita Farm, Honduras	Peabody Mus. col.	Geometric polychrome
MSLL21	Santa Ana, Honduras	Peabody Mus. col.	Carved polychrome (Ulua variant?)
MSNV01	Naco Valley, Site 120	F/6 (46a)	Animalistic polychrome
MSNV07	Naco Valley, Site 123	C-2/3 (42d)	Polychrome A
MSNV28	Naco Valley, Site 120	F/2 (42g)	Miscellaneous polychrome
MSNV31	Naco Valley, La Sierra	(43d)	Ulua Polychrome
MSNV32	Naco Valley, Site 120	f/6 (32n)	Chamelecon Orange-slipped: Chamelecon
MSNV36	Naco Valley, Site 111	F/1 (55a)	Jicaro: Variety unspecified
MSNV44	Naco Valley, Site 120	H/3 (45b)	Sloppy Geometric
MSNV45	Naco Valley, Site 120	F/H (45c)	Sloppy Geometric
MSNV49	Naco Valley, Site 111	F/2 (54d)	Chilanga (Usulutan: Variety unspecified)
MSNV50	Naco Valley, Site 120	F/6 (44g)	Ulua Polychrome
MSNV51	Naco Valley, Site 120	F/7 (44b)	Ulua Polychrome
MSNV52	Naco Valley, Site 159	C/2 (48b)	Miscellaneous polychrome
MSNV53	Naco Valley	Unknown	Ulua Polychrome
MSNV54	Naco Valley	Unknown	Ulua Polychrome
MSSB03	Santa Barbara, Gualjoquito	5A/5	Rosita Red-on-brown
MSSB05	Santa Barbara, Gualjoquito	3A/8	Taixiguat Blotchy Red
MSSB22	Santa Barbara, Gualjoquito	9B/8	Galeras Polychrome: Variety unspecified
MSSB27	Santa Barbara, Gualjoquito	2A/2	San Gaspar Soft Orange-slipped Polychrome
MSSB35	Santa Barbara, Gualjoquito	2A/2	Ulua Polychrome
MSSB36	Santa Barbara, Gualjoquito	9B/8	Ulua Polychrome
MSSB38	Santa Barbara, Gualjoquito	9B/5	Ulua Polychrome
MSSB40	Santa Barbara, Gualjoquito	9B/8	Ulua Polychrome

TABLE B-1 *(continued)*

Sample provenience and compositional classification

Reference group: Western Honduras Painted *(n = 41)*

ID. No.	Provenience/Site	Location/Lot	Ceramic Classification
MSSB41	Santa Barbara, Gualjoquito	9B/8	Ulua Polychrome
MSSB43	Santa Barbara, Gualjoquito	9A/2	Ulua Polychrome

Reference group: Quirigua *(n = 52)*

ID. No.	Provenience/Site	Location/Lot	Ceramic Classification
MSC080	Copan Valley, CV-20	Op. 19(C), Level 5	Basal flange polychrome
MSC089	Copan Valley, CV-20	Op. 20(A), Level 5	Basal flange polychrome
MSC099	Copan Valley, CV-20	Op. 4(R), Level 1	Tipon Orange-brown
MSC107	Copan Valley, CV-20	Op. 20(A), Level 7	Basal flange polychrome
MSC202	Copan Valley, CV-20	Op. 7(E), Level 1	Plano-relief model carved
MSC230	Copan Valley, CV-45	Op. 50(A), Level 7	Ring-base polychrome
MSC235	Copan Valley, CV-45	Op. 50(A), Level 6-B	Probable basal flange polychrome
MSC236	Copan Valley, CV-45	Op. 50(A), Level 5	Probable basal flange polychrome
MSC238	Copan Valley, CV-20	Op. 20(A), Level 6	Probable basal flange polychrome
MSLM24	Lower Motagua, Quebradas		Encantado
MSLM26	Lower Motagua, Playitas		Encantado
MSQ017	Quirigua		Chinok
MSQ025	Quirigua		Tipon
MSQ026	Quirigua		Tipon
MSQ027	Quirigua		Tipon
MSQ038	Quirigua		Tipon: Chalja Red-on-orange
MSQ039	Quirigua		Tipon: Chalja Red-on-orange
MSQ040	Quirigua		Tipon: Zarco Incised
MSQ041	Quirigua		Dartmouth: Sioux Polychrome
MSQ042	Quirigua		Dartmouth: Sioux Polychrome
MSQ043	Quirigua		Dartmouth: Sioux Polychrome
MSQ044	Quirigua		Dartmouth: Dartmouth
MSQ045	Quirigua		Dartmouth: Dartmouth
MSQ048	Quirigua		Chilanga
MSQ051	Quirigua		Oneida
MSQ052	Quirigua		Oneida
MSQ060	Quirigua		Chinok
MSQ061	Quirigua		Chinok
MSQ064	Quirigua		Seneca
MSQ072	Quirigua		Seminole: Hopi Red-on-cream
MSQ073	Quirigua		Seminole: Hopi Red-on-cream
MSQ075	Quirigua		Cylindrical tripod
MSQ088	Quirigua		Panama
MSQ089	Quirigua		Panama

MSQ094	Quirigua	Cacaguat
MSQ095	Quirigua	Cacaguat: fine paste variety
MSQ096	Quirigua	Tipon: Capulin
MSQ097	Quirigua	Tipon: Capulin
MSQ098	Quirigua	Tipon: Morja Bichrome
MSQ099	Quirigua	Tipon: Mariscos Trichrome
MSQ100	Quirigua	Tipon
MSQ101	Quirigua	Tipon
MSQ102	Quirigua	Tipon
MSQ103	Quirigua	Tipon
MSQ104	Quirigua	Dartmouth: Delicias
MSQ105	Quirigua	Dartmouth: Delicias
MSQ122	Quirigua	Quequexque
MSQ123	Quirigua	Dartmouth: Onandaga Polychrome
MSQ124	Quirigua	Dartmouth: Dartmouth

Ungrouped: directional affiliations found from search techniques (n = 25)

ID. No.	Provenience/Site	Location/Lot	Ceramic Classification
Set 1: Western Honduras and southern West Central Belize (noncarbonate temper)			
MSC108	Copan Valley, CV-20	Op. 7(E), Level 1	Ulua Polychrome (?)
MSC134	Central Copan	C/980, Peabody Mus. col.	Unclassified polychrome
MSC136	Central Copan	C/980, Peabody Mus. col.	Ulua Polychrome (?)
MSC137	Central Copan	C/980, Peabody Mus. col.	Ulua Polychrome (?)
MSC207	Copan Valley, CV-20	Op. 6(J), Level 1	Ulua Polychrome
MSC210	Copan Valley, CV-43	Op. 35(G), Level 1	Ulua Polychrome
Set 2: Southern Belize and the Maya Mountains (carbonate temper)			
MSC159	Central Copan	C/980, Peabody Mus. col.	Unclassified polychrome
MSC160	Central Copan	C/980, Peabody Mus. col.	Unclassified polychrome
MSC245	Copan Valley, CV-115	Op. 55(A), Level 2 (Special Feature 3)	Unclassified polychrome
MSC246	Copan Valley, CV-44	Op. 39(O), Level 1	Unclassified polychrome
MSC251	Copan Valley, CV-45	Op. 50(A), Level 5	Unclassified polychrome
Set 3: Belize–Eastern Peten–Southern Yucatan (carbonate temper)			
MSC161	Central Copan	C/980, Peabody Mus. col.	Unclassified polychrome
MSC164	Central Copan	C/980, Peabody Mus. col.	Unclassified polychrome
MSC233	Copan Valley, CV-43	Op. 49(A), Level 4	Unclassified polychrome
MSC252	Copan Valley, CV-43	Op. 49(A), Level 4	Unclassified polychrome
MSC257	Copan Valley	Unknown	Unclassified incised red-on-white

TABLE B-1 (*continued*)

Sample provenience and compositional classification

Ungrouped: directional affiliations found from search techniques (n = 25)

ID. No.	Provenience/Site	Location/Lot	Ceramic Classification
Set 4: Uaxactun-Tikal region (noncarbonate temper)			
MSC231	Copan Valley, CV-43	Op. 49(A), Level 4	Unclassified polychrome
MSC232	Copan Valley, CV-43	Op. 49(A), Level 4	Unclassified polychrome
Set 5: West Central Belize and Eastern Peten (noncarbonate temper)			
MSC178	Central Copan	C/980, Peabody Mus. col.	Unclassified polychrome
MSC239	Copan Valley, CV-43	Op. 49(A), Level 4	Unclassified polychrome
MSC247	Copan Valley, CV-43	Op. 102(A), Level 3	Unclassified polychrome
Set 6: Tikal vicinity (noncarbonate temper)			
MSC133	Central Copan	C/982, Peabody Mus. col.	Unclassified polychrome cylinder
MSC249	Copan Valley, CV-17	Op. 10(A), Level 4	Unclassified polychrome, basal ridge dish
MSC253	Copan Valley, CV-43	Op. 102(A), Level 3	Unclassified polychrome
Set 7: Northern lowlands (carbonate temper)			
MSC091	Central Copan, Tomb 2	Peabody Mus. col.	Quetzal Vase, Longyear 1952: fig. 108a

Ungrouped: no directional affiliations found from search techniques (n = 13)

ID. No.	Provenience/Site	Location/Lot	Ceramic Classification
MSC082	Copan Valley, CV-20	Op. 6(I), Level 1 (Special Feature 13)	Unclassified mold-made bottle
MSC090	Central Copan, Tomb 2	Peabody Mus. col.	Polychrome cylinder, Longyear 1952: fig. 107a
MSC092	Central Copan, Tomb 2	Peabody Mus. col.	Polychrome barrel, Longyear 1952: fig. 108b
MSC096	Central Copan, Tomb 1	Peabody Mus. col.	Brown wolf head vase, Longyear 1952: fig. 107d
MSC139	Central Copan	C/980, Peabody Mus. col.	Unclassified polychrome
MSC162	Central Copan	C/980, Peabody Mus. col.	Unclassified polychrome
MSC163	Central Copan	C/980, Peabody Mus. col.	Unclassified, cream incised
MSC220	Copan Valley, CV-43	Op. 49(A), Level 17c	Ulua Polychrome
MSC234	Copan Valley, CV-43	Op. 104(A), Level 8	Unclassified basal flange polychrome
MSC237	Copan Valley, CV-45	Op. 50(A), Level 5	Unclassified polychrome
MSC241	Copan Valley, CV-43	Op. 49(A), Level 2	Unclassified polychrome
MSC248	Copan Valley, CV-44	Op. 105(A), Level 6	Unclassified basal flange polychrome
MSC250	Copan Valley, CV-20	Op. 4(T), Level 1	Unclassified polychrome

Ungrouped: not subjected to search technique (n = 21)

ID. No.	Provenience/Site	Location/Lot	Ceramic Classification
MSC001	Copan Valley, CV-20	Op. 19(C), Level 4	Antonio Buff
MSC002	Copan Valley, CV-20	Op. 19(C), Level 4	Antonio Buff
MSC009	Copan Valley	Unknown	Lysandro Unslipped
MSC035	Copan Valley, CV-20	Op. 4(N), Level 1	Cementerio Incised: Cementerio Variety
MSC036	Copan Valley, CV-20	Op. 2(B), Level 7	Cementerio Incised: Cementerio Variety
MSC037	Copan Valley, CV-20	Op. 2(B), Level 1	Cementerio Incised: Cementerio Variety
MSC045	Copan Valley, CV-20	Op. 21(A), Level 2	Chilanga Red-painted Usulutan
MSC058	Copan Valley, CV-20	Op. 24(A), Level 6	Chilanga Red-painted Usulutan
MSC066	Copan Valley, CV-20	Op. 6(N), Level 1	Copador Polychrome
MSC068	Copan Valley, CV-20	Op. 6(K), Level 1	Copador Polychrome
MSC093	Central Copan, Stela M cache	Peabody Mus. col.	Copador Polychrome, Longyear 1952: fig. 114f
MSC094	Copan	Unknown	Gualpopa Polychrome
MSC095	Copan	Unknown	Gualpopa Polychrome
MSC124	Copan Valley, CV-20	Op. 19(C), Level 5	Capulin Cream: Uogistus Variety
MSC125	Copan Valley, CV-20	Op. 6(N), Level 1	Capulin Cream: Uogistus Variety
MSC127	Copan Valley, CV-20	Op. 20(A), Level 5	Cementerio Incised: Cementerio Variety
MSC131	Copan Valley, CV-20	Op. 20(A), Level 3	Cementerio Incised: Cementerio Variety
MSC132	Copan Valley, CV-20	Op. 19(C), Level 4	Cementerio Incised: Cementerio Variety
MSC191	Copan Valley, CV-43	Op. 104(A), Level 6	Caterpillar Polychrome
MSC196	Copan Valley, CV-20	Op. 6(H), Level 1	Tipon Orange-brown
MSC198	Copan Valley, CV-20	Op. 20(A), Level 5	Capulin Cream: Uogistus Variety

METHODOLOGY

Neutron Activation Analysis Procedures

Samples of the ceramic pastes were chemically analyzed by instrumental neutron activation analysis (INAA). INAA continues to be a technique preferred by many scholars for ceramic compositional investigations. Other chemical analytical techniques are available, including X-ray fluorescence, atomic absorption, and, with recent advances, emission spectrographic methods. INAA, however, combines quick sample preparation, high sensitivity for determining elemental concentrations (some as low as a few parts per billion), and extensive automation of the stages of data recording and reduction to final elemental concentrations (Bishop, Rands, and Holley 1982:288–293; Harbottle 1982:26).

Simply stated, neutron activation involves the exposure of nuclei of stable isotopes in a sample to a source of neutrons. Certain atomic nuclei capture neutrons and are elevated to a higher energetic state, producing radioactive isotopes. As these energetic radioisotopes decay to stable nuclei they emit radiation, including that of electromagnetic energy, as gamma rays. The emitted gamma rays may be detected, counted, and sorted by their respective energies, which are specific for the various radioisotopes. By comparing the emissions from the unknown sample with those of a sample of reference material containing known elemental concentrations, the amount of certain elemental constituents in the unknown ceramic paste can be calculated.

INAA has been applied to archaeological problems since the early 1950s (Sayre, Murrenhoff, and Weick 1958), and several extensive discussions of the technique as well as specific irradiation-counting configurations have been presented (Perlman and Asaro 1969; Blackman 1984). Since the present investigation generally followed the procedures discussed by Bishop, Harbottle, and Sayre (1982), only a brief statement of the analytical procedures will be given here.

Approximately 400 mg of powder were removed from each ceramic by drilling in a cleaned area with a tungsten carbide drill bit. The extracted sample was dried overnight at 100° C. Fifty milligrams of the dried sample were weighed out and sealed in ultra-high-purity quartz tubing. Ceramic samples and similarly prepared reference materials consisting of rocks analyzed by the U.S. Geological Survey, AGV-1, BCR-1, DTS-1, PCC-1, GSP-1, and G-2, were irradiated for six hours in the Brookhaven National Laboratory High Flux Beam Reactor at a neutron flux of 1.5 x 10^{13} neutrons/cm^2 sec. After a cooling period of nine days, samples were counted using a Princeton Gammatech 15 percent Ge-Li detector capable of 1.79 keV resolution on cobalt-60. The pulses from this detector were amplified and fed to a Nuclear Data ND66 8192 channel pulse height analyzer for subsequent gamma analysis by the Brookhaven gamma reduction programs.

For this project a single 100-minute count of a sample after a nine-day cooling period was used. This procedure deviated from the more standard Brookhaven procedures, which include an additional irradiation and two earlier counts to determine the concentrations of Mn, Na, and K. Our decision not to seek the concentrations of these elements was influenced by several factors. First of all, experience with numerous data sets of Maya area ceramic chemical analyses has suggested that concentrations of these elements are greatly influenced by moderate differences in environmental factors and in the amounts or kinds of temper, as well as by sampling errors (especially in the case of Mn; see Abscal, Harbottle, and Sayre 1974). Second, the elimination of handling and counting time would be advantageous in light of the large number of analyses involved in the overall MJCP. As in many analytical situations, a trade-off or compromise was necessary; in this case we opted for increased

numbers of analyzed samples in exchange for not determining these three additional elemental concentrations. Final concentrations were determined for Rb, Cs, Ba, Sc, La, Ce, Eu, Lu, Hf, Th, Ta, Cr, Fe, Co, Sm, Yb, and Ca.

Data Analysis

The search for meaningful structure in a data set is, at best, a tedious endeavor. This report presents only an outline of the actual steps that were taken during this investigation, because we assume the end result is of more interest to the majority of readers. However, this mode of presentation might give an erroneous impression of ceramic compositional analysis. Different techniques are applied to subsets of the data as well as to the entire set, often employing varying elemental suites. There is just too much noise in the ceramic system—natural, cultural, or analytical—for a single stepwise procedure to yield maximally informative partitions. No single dendrogram or other approach to pattern recognition captures the natural structure. In a similar way, no bivariate plot can illustrate adequately the multivariate relationships among the data points. This should not give the impression that the partitions presented here, and subsequently used as the basis of interpretation, are not reproducible; they are. However, it might be that two investigators would get to the groups in a different manner.

The accumulation of elemental concentrations is presumed to represent an individual sample's profile or fingerprint, which can be compared to a profile developed for a group of pottery or to the profiles of other individual samples. While no single approach to data reduction can be considered best, a basic objective is to group together samples that are considered to be similar according to some stated criteria. The cultural meaning of a group thus formed, however, is conjectural.

According to the Provenience Postulate (Weigand, Harbottle, and Sayre 1977), which provides a philosophical framework for compositional analysis, sufficient differences must exist between resources of raw materials so that those differences may be identified by an appropriate analytical technique. Yet, even in an area of chemically distinct clay resources suitable for ceramic production, the culturally imposed modification of the compositional profile during the production process (such as by the addition of clay, sand, chaff, etc., as temper) may blur the differences. In fact, the chemical profile of the finished ceramic—a weight combination of all constituents—need not resemble the composition of the original clay resource (Rice 1978; Bishop 1980).

Additional interpretive problems arise when a geological feature extends over a large geographical area, as might be the situation along a river drainage. For example, the Nile River alluvium has a characterizable pattern over much of its length, rendering difficult the differentiation of pottery-producing centers along its course (Tobia and Sayre 1974). Similar difficulties may be encountered in a valley setting.

Taking natural and cultural factors into consideration, compositional groups of pottery are often formed that match no specific material procurement source. In these situations, the decision as to whether or not a ceramic group is indicative of local or nonlocal manufacture lies not with chemistry but with archaeological interpretation.

The Criterion of Abundance has been frequently mentioned in the archaeological literature. This rule, as a matter of first approximation, considers pottery found frequently at one site, but more rarely at others, to have a strong likelihood of having been locally produced where it is more abundant. There are obvious weaknesses in the concept, several of which have been discussed by Shepard (1942). And, as has been noted elsewhere (Bishop, Rands, and Holley 1982:309), delineation of the ceramic production area is assumed by the Criterion of Abundance rather than demonstrated. Nevertheless, in ceramic paste compositional investigation, lacking direct linkage to specific raw material resources or to production loci by products such as wasters, relative abundance does provide an initial reference point.

The inference of local production may be strengthened when a given compositional profile is observed to have persisted through time and across multiple ceramic types. The delineation of the area of production depends on additional factors that are specific to each application. Among others, these include idiosyncratic potting behavior, social constraints on access to

resources, and functional considerations regarding the type of pottery produced, as well as the variation in the regional geology (Rands and Bishop 1980:19–20).

We wish to emphasize that inferring localized production, at the regional or finer level, requires the heuristic use of several assumptions regarding both cultural and natural factors. Some have been mentioned here; more detailed discussions are found in Rands and Bishop (1980) and Bishop, Rands, and Holley (1982). The additive effect of the various assumptions upon the final data interpretation in a large part depends upon the level at which an investigation is conducted. Investigational objectives differ. The close scrutiny of potential sources of variation in a compositional investigation is of critical importance for studies seeking patterned intraregional socioeconomic relationships among closely situated sites. Some assumptions may be relaxed, even ignored, when, on the other hand, the investigation is conducted at the interregional level, essentially involving the documentation of long distance trade (Arnold 1980; Hodder 1980; Rands and Bishop 1980; Fry and Cox 1974).

Different kinds of reference units can serve as the basis for cultural interpretation. The nature or utility of the units clearly is a function of how they are formed and refined as well as the level at which cultural interpretation is to take place. Bishop and Rands (1982) attempted to call attention to the variable character of compositional reference units by drawing a distinction between reference units defined according to chemistry alone and those units modified according to additional information (see also Bishop, Rands, and Holley 1982:302–306). A chemically defined group (chemical paste compositional reference unit, CPCRU) is just that—a chemical group. It provides a means for comparing chemically grouped data with other groups similarly derived.

The extent of archaeological applicability of compositional groups may vary depending on little more than the extent to which a group is subject to statistical refinement. For example, a 95 percent confidence interval about a group may be too encompassing; a more restricted interval may reveal stronger covariation between chemical composition and archaeological information, that is, form, provenience, and so on. "An acceptable level of probability, therefore, is relative to a particular research orientation and the amount of patterned similarities between chemical and nonchemical data" (Bishop and Rands 1982:287). Utility of the CPCRU lies in its formation, functionally independent of archaeological attribute manipulation. The groupings derived chemically may then be inspected for their makeup using archaeological attributes (e.g., time period, form, color, decoration). Strong patterned covariation among archaeological and chemical attributes argues for the validity and potential archaeological utility of the chemical groups.

A further step is usually undertaken: refinement and modification of the CPCRU based upon archaeological or other considerations. For example, the refinement may consist of removing members of the chemically defined group to strengthen mineralogical or archaeological attribute homogeneity within a group. Alternatively, it may result not from subtraction but from the fusion of two or more similar yet separable CPCRUs. For example, we might merge slightly separable chemically characterized reference units derived for locations along a river into a single unit, which heuristically would represent a compositional profile for the drainage. Such a group, polythetically formed, has been termed the paste compositional reference unit (PCRU) (Rands and Bishop 1982:290).

Compositional data also provide an opportunity for assessing by some measure the sample-to-sample similarity rather than maintaining a group perspective. Individual samples, not being members of a characterized group nor showing similarity to members of some other group, may reveal an acceptable level of compositional correspondence to other individual samples analyzed from a particular site or region. In this context, it is reasonable—within the limits of the sampling and analytical error—to suggest a potential location of production for the individual rather than grouped specimens.[3]

In our data processing not all available southeast Maya sample analyses were subjected to group formation and refinement at one time, as some had been reported on previously (Beaudry 1984). This large group of 127 samples of cream paste ceramics including Copador, Chilanga, and Gualpopa ceramic types was initially excluded. Proveniences within the group were heavily weighted toward Copan, but specimens were present from El Salvador, the Middle Motagua Valley, the Honduran–Guatemalan border area, and Belize. Quirigua samples were also omitted from the southeast Maya sample initially processed, as their chemically divergent composition from Honduran pottery could be observed in the listing of elemental concentrations. At a later step, the cream paste ceramic group and Quirigua specimens were rejoined with the southeast pottery in order to expand the interpretive perspective. Finally, within the southeast Maya area, but clearly of different composition, is the reddish paste pottery from Chalchuapa, El Salvador. This last group of specimens was not included in the current statistical analysis.

Of the 17 elemental determinations, 11, consisting of Sc, La, Ce, Eu, Lu, Hf, Th, Cr, Fe, Sm, and Yb, were utilized in the data analysis. Three of the other determinations, Rb, Cs, and Ba, were rejected because of their frequently large variability due to environmental or temper-related factors. Co was eliminated because of possible drill bit contamination during the sampling process; Ta and Ca were omitted because of relatively poor analytical determination.

Using all 11 variables, transformed to their log concentrations (Harbottle 1976), a cluster analysis was carried out. We utilized the average link procedure, which employed a matrix of Euclidean distances and resulted in a summary expression of the sample-to-sample relationships in the form of a dendrogram (cf. Doran and Hodson 1975:160). One group was especially well isolated from all others and consisted exclusively of domestic ceramic types that had a Copan provenience. This group was submitted to statistical evaluation and refinement through a process that utilized the group's interelemental correlational properties.

Many of the statistical procedures utilized in the synthesis of analytical data impose a particular structure on the outcome. For example, chemical analysis of pottery yields elemental concentration data that usually are highly correlated. If elemental pairs are plotted, the data points can be seen to be distributed in an elliptical fashion about a correlation line. Yet, if Euclidean distances between all pairs of samples are calculated and the matrix of distances is then clustered by the commonly employed unweighted pair group method, clusters will result and a natural hyperellipsoidal group of specimens may end up being divided into two groups.

If the coordinate axes are rotated so that they coincide with the directions of symmetry of the ellipse, the measurements relative to these rotated axes are no longer correlated. We also may normalize the coordinates so that the larger axis of the ellipse is shortened and the shorter axis is lengthened so that both axes have a variance equal to unity. In this manner, the ellipse has been transformed into a circle. Once we expand the two-variable example to fit the full multidimensional, 11-variable space, the standard Euclidean distance similarity measure is a more appropriate measure of similarity. An additional advantage in such data transformation is that one is no longer relying strictly on the absolute magnitude of concentration differences among samples. The available information pertaining to the pattern of elemental covariation is now part of the data modeling process. Rather than being a source of unnecessary redundancy, as some have claimed (Wilson 1978:223), it provides additional information that can be used to determine the directions of variation that underlie the data structure (cf. Sayre 1977).

Using the makeup of the Copan domestic ceramic group, as it was refined from its initial dendrogram membership, that group's variance-covariance properties were determined. In addition, the likelihood of a sample actually belonging to the group, given the sample's distance from the group's multivariate centroid, was calculated. This distance in the uncorrelated space is the Mahalanobis distance from which the probability of membership in the group is calculated as Hotelling's T^2, the multivariate extension of the Student's t (Sayre 1977; Bishop, Harbottle, and Sayre 1982:281). Samples not originally in the Copan domestic group but now found to have probabilities of membership exceeding 20 percent were added to the group, and the group's characteristics were then recalculated.

To compensate for the effect of variable correlation, all of the data were transformed to orthogonal, uncorrelated coordinates, relative to the variance-covariance properties of the refined Copan domestic group. Following this transformation, the data were reclustered and a new dendrogram summary of sample-to-sample relationships was produced.

Groups of samples that were found to be isolated on the normalized dendrogram were compared to group partitions determined by an iterative k-means cluster program, MIKCA (McRae 1971). The latter attempts to use the relationship of the within and among group variation matrices to form groups that are minimally variable yet maximally isolated from the others. The technique partitions a data matrix into a successively larger number of groups until one of several criteria is optimized. In this case we based group membership on the relationships expressed in the fundamental matrix relationship:

$$T = W + B$$

where T is the total sums of squares and cross products dispersion matrix, W is the "within groups" dispersion matrix, and B is the "between groups" dispersion matrix (Friedman and Rubin 1967). The criterion value we followed in this work was that obtained by the maximization of the ratio of the determinants of T divided by W (Marriot 1971). An indication of the best partition of the data was obtained by plotting the criterion value against the number of groups. A deflection in a curve drawn to connect the criterion values was taken to indicate that an optimum partition had been exceeded. Unlike the earlier employed Euclidean—hierarchical approach, groups need not be spherical, just similar in geometric shape.

Specimens were assembled into a group when there was notable overlap in sample membership occurring in the two clustering techniques. Once selected, a group was subjected to refinement or expansion as discussed above for the Copan domestic group. That is, the group variance-covariance properties were calculated and the probability of a given sample belonging to the group was determined, given that sample's Mahalanobis distance from the group's centroid. Samples originally in the group but found to lie outside of the 80 percent confidence interval were removed; those specimens not in the group but determined to have a greater than 20 percent chance of belonging to the group were added.

PRESENTATION OF RESULTS

Nine CPCRUs resulted from the multivariate statistical procedures already described. The relationships among these groups are illustrated by a number of vector plots. The numbered groups on these plots represent sets of samples that clustered together and that, by their content, suggest type-related or site-related production. The descriptive titles will be introduced as the plots are examined. One comment should be made about these titles, however.

A ceramic type name used in the title, such as Copador, means that the group is heavily weighted with that type, not made up exclusively of the type. Similarly, a site name in the title signifies a strong representation of material from that provenience or region. Throughout this work compositional patterning was investigated at a regional level. The objective was to distinguish the Copan Valley from other parts of western Honduras, from Quirigua and the Lower Motagua, from western El Salvador, and so on. Thus, the names of the groups are convenient rubrics for discussing the units rather than precise definitions of their contents.

Several factors should be kept in mind as the final reference groups are discussed:

1. As just mentioned, the purpose of the project was to distinguish regional patterns of chemical ceramic paste composition. Intraregional variability was not explored to the fullest possible extent.
2. Actual separation among the groups took place in multidimensional space; in the vector plots the separation is shown on two of the eleven dimensions. The vectors selected for the plots are those which illustrate most clearly in two-dimensional space the separation determined in the multidimensional procedures.

The distinctiveness of the main group of Copan domestic pottery (Group 1) is seen in its separation from other compositional groups in the upper right portion of figure B-2. This group of Copan domestic pottery served as the basis for normalization (see methodology section).

Figure B-3 shows the separation between two small Copan-area groups. These divisions can be seen on the left side of the plot with Copan Domestic 2 (Group 5) in the upper portion and Copan Tipon B (Group 6) in the lower area.

Figure B-4 illustrates other group separation: in the lower left the Copan-focus Copador group (Group 7) and Copan Fine Paste group (Group 8) overlap each other but separate from other units. The Quirigua regional group (Group 9) is quite distinct in its separation in the upper right section. The lower right contains samples from four groups: Copan Domestic 1 (Group 1), Western Honduras domestic (Group 2), Copan Tipon A (Group 3) and Western Honduras painted (Group 4). The separation of Copan Domestic 1 was already illustrated in figure B-2. The other three groups are distinguishable in the full multispace; this tendency is shown in figure B-5. In this representation, Tipon A (Group 3) appears in the upper center, Western Honduras painted (Group 4) toward the lower left, and Western Honduras domestic (Group 2) in the right section.

In summary, the nine reference groups resulting from the multivariate statistical procedures and illustrated by separation on vector plots are the following:

1. Copan Domestic 1: 40 cases
2. Western Honduras Domestic: 13 cases
3. Tipon A: 32 cases
4. Western Honduras Painted: 41 cases
5. Copan Domestic 2: 6 cases
6. Tipon B: 12 cases
7. Copan-focus Copador: 136 cases
8. Copan Fine Paste: 24 cases
9. Quirigua: 52 cases

In addition to these reference groups, 59 Copan samples remained ungrouped. These were evaluated using a different analytical approach to assess foreign directional affiliations.

Data Discussion

The compositional groups and their relationships will be discussed in more detail, organized in the following way. Copan Valley production and consumption will be reviewed from the standpoint of the two Copan domestic reference groups and the two Tipon groups and from the standpoint of the Copan fine paste group and the Copan-focus Copador group. Then the Copan Valley's external connections will be reviewed on the basis of (1) cream paste exports generally to the south and southwest of Copan; (2) imports from western Honduras; (3) changing interaction with the Quirigua region from the Early Classic to the Late Classic; (4) more distant associations.

Copan Valley Production and Consumption

Copan Domestic Groups and Tipon Groups. The
main Copan domestic group includes a variety of ceramic types from different proveniences within the valley. The inclusion of one unslipped plainware sherd from the nearby Rio Amarillo site probably reflects the geomorphological similarity of clay deposits in the adjacent valley pockets rather than production considerations.

The smaller domestic group, by contrast, contains materials only from CV-20. The compositional separation of these two groups results from differences in the Cr and Th concentrations.

The Tipon groups separate from the Copan Domestic groups as shown in figures B-2 and B-3. However, local Copan Valley production is inferred from several lines of evidence:

1. Included in the Tipon A group are three samples of fired daub, two recovered at CV-45 and one at CV-43. It is highly unlikely that material for house construction would come from a nonlocal source.
2. Tipon samples from Quirigua separate from the Copan Tipon specimens and group within a Quirigua regional group. Thus, this fine paste tradition seems to have been executed locally by potters at the different centers.
3. Although statistically separable, chemical compositional similarities between the Tipon groups and the Copan domestic groups do exist.

Three non-Copan provenience samples are included in the Tipon A group: one from Las Flores on the lower Ulua River and two from Santa Barbara in the Jicatuyo drainage. It is unlikely that these represent Copan Valley production or resource utilization. Multivariate statistical similarity was sufficient for them to cluster chemically with the Copan ceramics and so they are thus reported. This is an instance when archaeological common sense should override chemical analysis. Without strong independent evidence to support an inference that these particular isolated pieces came from the Copan Valley, the statistical association will be considered a fortuitous one.

Copan Fine Paste Group. This unit is not as well
defined as most of the other CPCR groups that emerged from the analytic work. It contains samples of ceramic types in which most specimens had clustered in type-related CPCR groups: Capulin Cream and Tipon Orange-brown in the Tipon group; Copador, Gualpopa, and Chilanga in the Copador group. Thus, this group of ceramics appears to be associated at the level of general paste characteristics—fine grain size, low elemental iron/light-colored paste firing, limited temper or inclusions. At this regional level of analysis, in fact, they do not separate from the Copan-focus Copador group. (See fig. B-4.) However, the earlier work with the cream paste ceramics, done on a finer scale of differentiation, did succeed in distinguishing the Copador group from these other fine paste materials (Beaudry 1984; Bishop et al. 1986).

The Copan Valley's External Connections

Cream Paste Exports: the Copan-focus Copador
Group. This very large CPCR group represents cream-colored, fine paste ceramics produced and used in the Copan Valley as well as those produced in the valley but distributed to other locations. The Copan Valley attribution for the clay resources does not derive from chemical compositional similarity to the Copan domestic group since there are statistically significant chemical differences between these two compositional units. In the earlier work (Beaudry 1984; Bishop et al. 1986) the hypothesis of a Copan Valley production locus was considered viable for two reasons. First of all, the percentage of Copan provenience pottery in the Copan-focus Copador CPCRU group argues for Copan Valley production on the basis of a Criterion of Abundance (Bishop, Rands, and Holley 1982). Second, clay

deposits in the Copan Valley as preliminarily described (Turner et al. 1980) appear to be diverse, resulting from different geological histories. Consequently, the geological possibility of Copador clay sources in the valley is realistic. Additional inferential support is now added from the finding that at a regional level the Copador CPCR blends with the Copan fine paste unit, reinforcing the Copan Valley provenience for the Copador reference group.

Analysis of the distribution of the Copan-produced Copador group ceramics shows a definite directionality to the south and southwest from Copan. Beyond a 50 km radius, distribution was sharply channeled toward settlements in western and central El Salvador. Two other areas were recipients of Copan's exported ceramics: the Middle Motagua near San Agustin Acasaguastlan and the mountainous Guatemalan–Honduras border area. This economic orientation away from the main Maya culture zone toward the outlying areas of El Salvador is interesting since Copan's political orientation during the Late Classic (as shown by architecture, sculpture, and epigraphy) associates it with other major Maya centers to the north and west of Copan.

Imports from Western Honduras. As mentioned, recent fieldwork in the Copan Valley has uncovered significantly more Ulua polychrome ceramics than had been known from earlier investigations. The production zone or zones of this widely distributed ceramic group have yet to be determined, but it has always been considered an import at Copan. This analysis supports that hypothesis. Fifteen Copan-provenience Ulua Polychrome samples were studied. Eight of those grouped with painted ceramics from other western Honduras sites, including Ulua Polychrome from Santa Rita Farm, Las Flores, Santa Ana, Naco Valley, and Santa Barbara Valley. (The other Copan-provenience Ulua Polychrome samples distributed as follows: four ungrouped but having directional affiliation with western Honduras; two ungrouped entirely; one grouped with Tipon B.)

Thus, at least some of the Ulua polychrome used at Copan came from the same production zone as the Ulua polychrome used at the above-mentioned sites. There also are suggestions in the data that the clay resources utilized for Ulua polychrome differ from those which characterize some of the western Honduras domestic wares. Figure B-5 shows the separation of these two groups, Western Honduras Painted and Western Honduras Domestic. However, the data are too limited at this time to draw even tentative conclusions about the Ulua polychrome production system. Its import status at Copan, nevertheless, seems secure.

Interaction with the Quirigua Region. An interesting set of ceramics makes up this CPCR group. The majority are of Quirigua provenience, with several from Lower Motagua sites as well. Also included, however, are nine Copan Valley pieces. With the exception of one Tipon sherd, the other Copan material consists of basal flange polychromes and several other pieces distinct from Copan's Coner phase complex. These ceramics seem to represent an Early Classic component of probable imports to Copan. It is not suggested that Quirigua itself was the source of these vessels; rather that the clay resources used in their production point to the region that includes Quirigua.

The cases are few, but the finding corroborates the previously observed tendency for Copan's orientation to shift from the north during Early Classic times to the south in Late Classic times. The chemical compositional separation of the Late Classic Tipon ceramics from Copan and Quirigua reinforces the point regarding a change in the relationship between these two centers around A.D. 737.

Copan's More Distant Associations

Once the nine CPCR groups had been determined, 59 Copan samples remained ungrouped. Nothing further was done with 21 cases, which included local domestic types as well as cream fine paste types, that had been explored so thoroughly. The rest of the 38 ungrouped Copan painted serving vessels were examined using a different analytical approach. The objective of this final stage of the work was to determine if the chemical compositional pattern of a Copan vessel associated with that of any other vessel in the data base containing over 10,000 analyses of the MJCP. The search of the data bank and calulation of similarity between individual Copan ungrouped specimens and data bank samples were carried out by a program written specially for use with ceramic compositional data.[4]

Following this search technique, 25 specimens showed directional affiliations in terms of other ceramics in the data base that associated at the preset level of probability. The associations of sets of ceramic specimens suggest production zones from where the Copan exotic imports came. Tables B-2 through B-8 present the details of this part of the analysis. A word about the form used in the tabular presentation.

The columns of each table list the Copan sherds that associated with other specimens in MJCP. The rows list the specimens in MJCP with which the Copan material showed association. The MJCP specimens are grouped according to their status in the data base: in the southeast Maya data set (analyzed in this report); in the larger data base and provenienced; in the larger data base, not provenienced. By looking down a column the reader can see with which specific MJCP specimens an ungrouped Copan sherd associated. By looking across a row, the reader can determine with what ungrouped Copan sherd(s) a MJCP specimen associated.

The following section will review briefly the data presented in the tables. A concluding summary will interpret the analytic results from the standpoint of Copan's interaction with other areas of the Maya lowlands.

Western Honduras–Southern West Central Belize Affiliations (table B-2). Six ungrouped sherds—five probable Ulua polychrome and one unclassified polychrome—associated with specimens from western Honduras and southern west central Belize proveniences. The stylistic types represented in the associated specimens reflect western Honduran ceramic traditions of relatively fine wares—Ulua and Copador Polychrome, Berlin Bichrome, and Tipon Orange-brown ware. Some of the associated specimens in the southeast Maya data set grouped with Tipon A or the Western Honduras Painted group.

Southern Belize–Maya Mountains Affiliations (table B-3). A group of five unclassified Copan sherds associated with each other and with two MJCP pieces, one from Lubantuun and the other from Naj Tunich.

Belize–Eastern Peten–Southern Yucatan Affiliations (table B-4). A set of sherds with carbonate temper showed associations with ceramics from this part of the lowlands. The five carbonate-tempered Copan specimens associated with each other and with provenienced pieces from Altun Ha, Porvenir, Seibal, and Becan as well as with a Saxche orange polychrome piece found at San Agustin Acasaguastlan. The nonprovenienced pieces associated with these Copan ceramics tend to have figural representations in the Holmul style. The three Codex style polychromes that associated are believed to have been made in the general El Mirador–Pacaya area (Reents-Budet and Bishop n.d.).

Uaxactun–Tikal Region Affiliations (table B-5). Two noncarbonate unclassified polychromes from Copan are affiliated with Tikal and Uaxactun specimens as well as with a number of nonprovenienced pieces. The nonprovenienced ceramics include tall round-sided bowls, basal flange dishes (two lidded), and a cylinder. The bottom half of a pair of cache vessels is intricately decorated with a high relief applique face of god g1. The styles of the associated vessels align with those identified for production zones in the northeast Peten, central Belize to the border, and southeast of Tikal (Yaxha, Nakum) (Reents-Budet, personal communication).

West Central Belize–Eastern Peten Affiliations (table B-6). Three unclassified polychrome ceramics from Copan associated with provenienced MJCP specimens from Holmul, Poptun, El Zotz, and Seibal. The nonprovenienced pieces that associated with these Copan sherds included several characterized as being in the Holmul style and produced near Naranjo (Reents 1985). Most of the nonprovenienced vessels were painted with human representations in various poses. Glyphs were present on a number of the pieces, sometimes as the only motif in a band around the rim, other times along with human figurative scenes. Stylistically, a number of the associated polychromes relate to ceramics produced in the Peten, close to the Belize border (Reents-Budet, personal communication).

TABLE B-2

Ungrouped sherds from Copan showing affiliations with Western Honduras
and southern West Central Belize (noncarbonate temper)

			COPAN SHERDS					
ID No.	Provenience	Type/ Description	MSC108 Ulua Poly.	MSC134 Unclass Poly.	MSC136 Ulua Poly.	MSC137 Ulua Poly.	MSC207 Ulua Poly.	MSC210 Ulua Poly.
SE Maya Data Set								
MSC184*	Copan	Daub						x
MSC185*	Copan	Daub			x			x
MSC186*	Copan	Daub						x
MSC195*	Copan	Tipon			x		x	
MSC208†	Copan	Ulua Poly.			x	x		
MSC210	Copan	Ulua Poly.				x		
MSC254*	Copan	Ulua Poly.	x					
MSCLAY	Copan	Raw Clay		x				
MSLL10	Santa Rita	Ulua Poly.			x		x	
MSLL12	Las Flores	Ulua Poly.			x	x		
MSLL16	Santa Rita	Ulua Poly.				x		
MSLL17	Santa Rita	Ulua Poly.	x		x			
MSLL19	Santa Rita	Ulua Poly.	x					
MSSB14	Santa Barbara	Masica Incised		x				
MSSB17	Santa Barbara	Guayabita			x			
MSSB27†	Santa Barbara	Eroded Ulua?				x		
MSSB42	Santa Barbara	Ulua Poly.			x			
MSNV04	Naco Valley	Chamelecon/ Chalma						x
MSNV15	Naco Valley	Berlin				x		
MSO420	Pusilha	Copador					x	
MSO436	Pusilha	Copador						x
MSA038	Altun Ha	Incensario lid				x		x
MSBV11	Benque Viejo	EC orange poly.				x		
MSYA16	Yaxox	Orange Poly.						x
MSO310	Unknown	Holmul style cyl.						x
MS1370	Unknown	Figure painted Orange poly.						x

*Grouped with Tipon A
†Grouped with Western Honduran Painted

Area Group (Tikal Vicinity) Affiliations (table B-7). Two unclassified polychrome sherds showed association with these characteristic Peten ceramics (Bishop et al. 1985). The associated provenienced pieces include vessels from Pop- tun, Santa Elena, Seibal, Tikal, and Baking Pot. The majority of the nonprovenienced pieces were cylinders painted with figural design elements including the area group "paddler program" (ibid.).

TABLE B-3

Ungrouped sherds from Copan showing affiliations with Southern Belize
and the Maya Mountains (carbonate temper)

			COPAN SHERDS				
ID No.	Provenience	Type/ Description	MSC159 Unclass. Poly.	MSC160 Unclass. Poly.	MSC245 Unclass. Poly.	MSC246 Unclass. Poly.	MSC251 Unclass. Poly.
SE Maya Data Set							
MSC159	Copan	Unclass.		x		x	
MSC160	Copan	Unclass.	x			x	
MSC246	Copan	Unclass.		x		x	
MSC251	Copan	Unclass.	x	x		x	
MJCP Data Base							
MSLU70	Lubaantun	Turniffe Unslipped	x		x	x	x
MSG760	Naj Tunich	Zacatel Cream Poly	x	x			

The nonprovenienced pieces include several typical dancer plates, a checkerboard design cylinder, and a Tau-shaped basal flange dish.

Northern Lowlands Affiliation (table B-8). The Quetzal vase from Copan (Longyear 1952; fig. 108a from Tomb 2) associated with two Yucatan peninsula specimens in MJCP.

Summary of Copan's Maya Lowlands Ceramic Associations

The foregoing review shows that the ungrouped Copan material associated with MJCP vessels whose proveniences extend away from Copan in somewhat of an arc. The sites are found to the northeast of Copan in Honduras,

TABLE B-4

Ungrouped sherds from Copan showing affiliations with Belize, Eastern Peten,
or Southern Yucatan (carbonate temper)

			COPAN SHERDS				
ID No.	Provenience	Type/ Description	MSC161 Unclass. Poly.	MSC164 Unclass. Poly.	MSC233 Unclass. Poly.	MSC252 Unclass. Poly.	MSC257 Unclass. Red-on-white
SE Maya Data Set							
MSC161	Copan	Unclass. poly.		x		x	x
MSC164	Copan	Unclass. poly.	x			x	x
MSC233	Copan	Unclass. poly.	x	x			
MSC252	Copan	Unclassified	x	x			x
MSC257	Copan	Unclassified	x	x		x	

TABLE B-4 *(continued)*

Ungrouped sherds from Copan showing affiliations with Belize, Eastern Peten, or Southern Yucatan (carbonate temper)

			COPAN SHERDS				
ID No.	Provenience	Type/ Description	MSC161 Unclass. Poly.	MSC164 Unclass. Poly.	MSC233 Unclass. Poly.	MSC252 Unclass. Poly.	MSC257 Unclass. Red-on-white
MJCP Data Base							
MSA045	Altun Ha	Basal Ridge poly.	x			x	x
MSPV04	El Porvenir	Palmar ceramic group	x				
MSS009	Seibal	Tinaja Red				x	x
MSY109	Becan	Saxche Orange Poly.				x	x
MSW016	San Agustin	Saxche Orange Poly.	x			x	x
MS0055	Unknown	Figural painted cylinder, water resurrection scene	x	x		x	x
MS0352	Unknown	Codex-style poly.	x	x			
MS0358	Unknown	Codex-style poly.	x				x
MS0403	Unknown	Basal flange poly.	x	x			
MS0444	Unknown	Poly. bowl with god N	x	x	x	x	x
MS0445	Unknown	Throne scene cylinder	x	x	x		
MS0450	Unknown	Cylinder with old deity blowing conch	x	x		x	x
MS0564	Unknown	Plate with seated figure		x		x	x
MS1039	Unknown	Codex-style poly.	x				

directly north in Belize, farther north into the eastern and central Peten, and finally to the northern lowlands.

This pathway is somewhat at odds with the reconstruction of Copan's interregional Late Classic period relationships proposed by Coggins (1984). She associates Copan most closely with the Alta Verapaz (Chama followed by Chajcar) from where influences reached into the Peten and thence to the Puuc region. Since her interpretation is based on evidence other than paste compositional data, the different conclusions cannot be reconciled at this time.

TABLE B-5

Ungrouped sherds from Copan showing affiliations with Uaxactun and the Tikal region
(noncarbonate temper)

| | | | COPAN SHERDS | |
| | | | --- | --- |
ID No.	Provenience	Type/Description	MSC231 Unclass. Poly.	MSC232 Unclass. Poly.
SE Maya Data Set				
MSC232	Copan	Polychrome	x	
MSC231	Copan	Polychrome		x
MJCP Data Base				
MSG128	Uaxactun	Palmar ceramic group	x	x
MSG145	Uaxactun	Saxche ceramic group	x	x
MSG455	Ramonal	Tau-shaped basal flange polychrome	x	x
MST085	Tikal	Imix Orange Polychrome	x	x
MST097	Tikal	Imix Orange Polychrome	x	x
MSU020	Uaxactun	Mono Orange	x	x
MSU047	Uaxactun	Saxche ceramic group	x	x
MS0197	Unknown	Tall bowl, polychrome with death head on serpent wing	x	x
MS0209	Unknown	Black basal flange carved lidded dish, with "winged" caiman	x	x
MS0404	Unknown	Shallow ring-based basal flange dish, intertwined water lily motif	x	x
MS0622	Unknown	Lidded basal flange dish, with stylized serpent head	x	
MS0903	Unknown	Footed barrel-shaped polychrome with throne scene	x	x
MS0991	Unknown	Outflared low cylinder, with curvilinear design	x	x
MS1017	Unknown	Round-sided bowl with single row of glyphs	x	x
MS1295	Unknown	Bottom half of cache pair with applique face of G1	x	x

TABLE B-6

Ungrouped sherds from Copan showing affiliations with West Central Belize
and the Eastern Peten (noncarbonate temper)

| | | | COPAN SHERDS | | |
| | | | MSC178 Unclass. Poly. | MSC239 Unclass. Poly. | MSC247 Unclass. Poly. |
ID No.	Provenience	Type/Description			
MJCP Data Base					
MSH033	Holmul		x		
MSG006*	Poptun	Saxche ceramic group			x
MSG122	Uaxactun	Saxche ceramic group			x
MSG272	El Zotz	Palmar ceramic group			x
MSS050*	Seibal	Saxche ceramic group			x
MS0067	Unknown	Round-sided bowl, glyph bands and kin signs			x
MS0205	Unknown	Lidded bowl, shell on lid, row of lamat glyphs at rim			x
MS0273	Unknown	Cylinder, standing and kneeling figures		x	
MS0380	Unknown	Figural painted Saxche polychrome cylinder		x	
MS0501	Unknown	Cylinder, modeled-carved, God K in cartouche		x	
MS0603	Unknown	Very tall cylinder with Holmul dancer program	x		
MS0736	Unknown	Glossware dancer plate		x	
MS0757	Unknown	Cylinder, dancing possum wearing a "vomit bib"		x	
MS0885	Unknown	Round-sided bowl with two rows of frog-insects			x
MS0843	Unknown	Plate with seated warrior figure		x	
MS0897	Unknown	Tall cylinder with seated figure on throne		x	
MS0972	Unknown	Round-sided bowl with seated God N and young lord		x	
MS1047	Unknown	Tall round-sided glossware bowl with pseudo-glyph band		x	
MS1170	Unknown	Plate with glyphs around rim			x
MS1311	Unknown	Cylinder with shells in floral shape		x	

*Also associated with MSC249, Area Group Affiliation

TABLE B-7

Ungrouped sherds from Copan showing affiliations with Tikal vicinity ceramics (noncarbonate temper)

| | | | COPAN SHERDS | | |
			MSC133 Unclass. Poly.	*MSC249 Poly. Basal Flange Dish*	*MSC253 Unclass Poly.*
ID No.	*Provenience*	*Type/Description*			
MJCP Data Base					
MSG046	Santa Elena	Saxche ceramic group	x		
MSG006*	Poptun	Saxche ceramic group		x	
MSG010	Poptun	Saxche ceramic group	x		x
MSG044	Santa Elena	Saxche ceramic group	x		
MSG047	Santa Elena	Saxche ceramic group	x		
MSG122	Uaxactun	Saxche ceramic group			x
MSG213	Uaxactun	Saxche ceramic group			x
MSS028	Seibal	Saxche ceramic group	x		
MSS050*	Seibal	Saxche ceramic group (Sabloff 1975: fig. 243a)			x
MSS056	Seibal	Saxche ceramic group			x
MST066	Tikal	Imix Orange Polychrome			x
MST067	Tikal	Imix Orange Polychrome			x
MST079	Tikal	Imix Orange Polychrome			x
MSBP16	Baking Pot	Dos Arroyos ceramic group	x		
MS0158	Unknown	Cylinder, Area Group "paddler program"			x
MS0161	Unknown	Cylinder with glyph band at rim, complex design, saurian with serpent-wing on one side, other side with bold curvilinear design			x
MS0200	Unknown	Cylinder, Area Group "paddler program"	x		x
MS0285	Unknown	Incurved bowl, Area Group "paddler program"	x		
MS0304	Unknown	Cylinder, Area Group God N with blowgun			x
MS0317	Unknown	Round-sided bowl, painted with vertical bands		x	
MS0327	Unknown	Round-sided bowl, lower band of repeated circular motif, upper glyph band		x	
MS0377	Unknown	Very tall cylinder, glyph band at rim, wide diagonal band of curvilinear designs	x		x
MS0639	Unknown	Cylinder, Tlaloc mask with muan feathers, mat motif on opposite side	x		
MS0759	Unknown	Cylinder, figure dressed as G3 with 2 large water symbols with death collar	x		x

Ungrouped sherds from Copan showing affiliations with Tikal vicinity ceramics (noncarbonate temper)

			COPAN SHERDS		
ID No.	Provenience	Type/Description	MSC133 Unclass. Poly.	MSC249 Poly. Basal Flange Dish	MSC253 Unclass Poly.
MJCP Data Base					
MS0808	Unknown	Cylinder, Area Group "paddler program"	x		x
MS0845	Unknown	Tripod basal flange dish with "tau shape" flange, stylized saurian mirror imaged on interior rim, dancer figure interior bottom		x	
MS0846	Unknown	Plate, standing profile figure, bold geometric rim band	x		x
MS0876	Unknown	Outflared wall bowl, vertical panels and large glyphs, saurian head		x	
MS0881	Unknown	Cylinder, checkerboard pattern		x	
MS0918	Unknown	Tall cylinder, throne scene	x		
MS0942	Unknown	Round-sided bowl, saurian with serpent-wing design, primary standard sequence glyphs		x	
MS1023	Unknown	Outflared wall bowl, vertical solid-painted stripes		x	
MS1082	Unknown	Round-sided bowl, seated figures enacting enema ritual	x		
MS1139	Unknown	Plate with dancing figure		x	
MS1156	Unknown	Footed cylinder, seated figure facing throne		x	
MS1158	Unknown	Cylinder, glyph band at rim, complex design, saurian with serpent-wing on one side, other side has bold curvilinear design			x

*Also associated with MSC247 (see table B-6)

TABLE B-8

Ungrouped sherds from Copan showing affiliations with
the northern lowlands (carbonate temper)

			COPAN SHERDS
ID No.	Provenience	Type/ Description	MSC091 Quetzal Vase
MJCP Data Base			
MSY117	Dzibilchaltun	Juleki Cream	x
MSY166	Uxmal	Orange monochrome	x

NOTES

1. The MJCP was sponsored between 1978 and 1983 by the Research Laboratory of the Museum of Fine Arts of Boston and by Mr. Landon T. Clay, also of Boston. It was carried out in collaboration with the Department of Chemistry at Brookhaven National Laboratory, where analytical work was conducted under the auspices of the U.S. Department of Energy. Work on the project is continuing at the Conservation Analytical Laboratory, Smithsonian Institution. All data referred to in the present paper have been entered into the Smithsonian Archaeometric Research Collections and Records Facility (SARCAR), located in the Conservation Analytical Laboratory.

2. The projects other than the Harvard Copan Project providing data for the chemical characterization analysis include in Honduras, the Rio Amarillo (La Canteada) Project at UCLA (Beaudry 1977, 1987; Pahl 1987) the Santa Barbara Project at Rutgers University and Kenyon College (Schortman et al. 1986); and the Naco Valley Project at Cornell University (Henderson et al. 1979; Urban 1986); in El Salvador, the Zapotitan Protoclassic Project at the University of Colorado (Sheets 1983) and the Chalchuapa Project at the University of Pennsylvania (Sharer 1978a); and in Guatemala, the Quirigua Project at the University of Pennsylvania (Sharer 1978b). Material from the Tiquisate region of Guatemala and from the sites of Asuncion Mita and Guaytan was made available through the courtesy of the Museo Nacional de Guatemala. Pottery from San Agustin Acasaguastlan was submitted by Gary R. Walters. Specimens from various sites in western Honduras were made available by the Peabody Museum, Harvard University.

3. Based upon their surface finish, stylistic decoration, and compositional profile, a number of specimens clearly were imports to Copan, some from outside of the southeast Maya area. With the exception of small groups of two or three, the analyzed exotics showed little tendency to link together meaningfully, suggesting that multiple regions were the sources for the pottery. Carbonate-tempered as well as volcanic ash-tempered pottery was present. The elemental profiles for exotic specimens were compared one at a time against the compositional background data provided by the MJCP data bank for almost 10,000 analyses of Maya pottery. Finding multiple matching specimens from a given subregion would inform about the directionality of ceramic movement thus yielding empirical data, albeit fragmentary, about Copan's external contacts.

   Working in a log concentration space, mean Euclidean distances were determined between each Copan exotic and all other Maya ceramic analyses. Samples lying within a given distance were noted for later inspection. The selected interobject distance is based upon distances among samples of compositional groups defined in the target area. In the present case, using 11 variables, a mean Euclidean distance of 0.08 was used. All samples lying within that region, however, might not be equally good matches. For example, a comparative sample might diverge on one or two well-determined elements that have been found to be less variable than others in a given area. Some control, or additional screening, may be employed by using allowable elemental deviations for each variable. If one treats each elemental concentration as being independent of the others (not really a valid assumption given the discussion of interelemental correlation in the text), and assuming that the reference specimen is a vector of mean values for a group of stated size, a value expressed in the form of a probability may be calculated. This value constitutes a flag to call attention to the situation that although a sample lies within the stated Euclidean distance of the ref-

erence specimen, it exceeds expected percent deviation ranges on one or more of the variables; it probably should not be considered as having a compositional profile that matches the one used as reference for the search.

4. As previously mentioned, this data base includes the neutron activation data of Maya pottery from sites throughout the Maya area. Intensity of sampling coverage is uneven; large sites such as Tikal or Copan are each represented by more than 150 analyses, but other sites may have as few as 20 samples analyzed. The majority of the analyses are of Late Classic pottery. They derive from an investigation of Maya ceramic art utilizing ceramic compositional data to study distributional patterns that might reflect subregional differentiation in Maya painting, iconographic, and epigraphic traditions (Bishop et al. 1985).

BIBLIOGRAPHY

Abscal, R., G. Harbottle, and E. V. Sayre
    1974   "Correlations Between Terra Cotta Figurines and Pottery from the Valley of Mexico and Source Clays by Neutron Activation Analysis," in *Archaeological Chemistry*, C. W. Beck, ed., pp. 81–99. American Chemical Society, Washington, D.C.

Arnold, D. E.
    1980   "Localized Exchange: An Ethnoarchaeological Perspective," in *Models and Methods in Regional Exchange*, R. E. Fry, ed., pp. 147–150. Society for American Archaeology, SAA Papers 1. Washington, D.C.

Beaudry, M. P.
    1977   "Classification and Analysis of Painted Ceramics from La Canteada, Copan, Honduras (D-4)." M.A. thesis, University of California, Los Angeles.
    1984   *Ceramic Production and Distribution in the Southeastern Maya Periphery. Late Classic Painted Serving Vessels.* BAR International Series 203, Oxford.
    1987   "La Canteada Ceramics in the Context of the Southeastern Maya Periphery."*The Periphery of the Southeastern Classic Maya Realm*. University of California at Los Angeles Latin American Studies vol. 61, pp. 263–280.

Bishop, R. L.
    1980   "Aspects of Compositional Modeling," in *Models and Methods in Regional Exchange*,

R. E. Fry, ed., pp. 47–66. Society for American Archaeology, SAA Papers 1. Washington, D.C.

Bishop, R. L., M. P. Beaudry, R. M. Leventhal, and R. J. Sharer
    1986   "Compositional Analysis of Copador and Related Pottery in the Southeast Maya Area," in *The Southeast Maya Periphery*, P. A. Urban and E. M. Schortman, eds. University of Texas Press, Austin.

Bishop, R. L., G. Harbottle, and E. V. Sayre
    1982   "Chemical and Mathematical Procedures Employed in the Maya Fine Paste Ceramics Project," in *Excavations at Seibal: Analyses of Fine Paste Ceramics*, J. A. Sabloff, ed., pp. 272–282. Memoirs of the Peabody Museum, vol. 15, no. 2. Cambridge, Massachusetts.

Bishop, R. L., and R. L. Rands
    1982   "Maya Fine Paste Ceramics: A Compositional Perspective," in *Excavations at Seibal: Analyses of Fine Paste Ceramics*, J. A. Sabloff, ed., pp. 283–314. Memoirs of the Peabody Museum, vol. 15, no. 2. Cambridge, Massachusetts.

Bishop, R. L., R. L. Rands, and G. R. Holley
    1982   "Ceramic Compositional Analysis in Archaeological Perspective," in *Advances in Archaeological Method and Theory*, vol. 5, M. B. Schiffer, ed., pp. 275–331. Academic Press, New York.

Bishop, R. L., D. J. Reents, G. Harbottle, E. V. Sayre, and L. van Zelst
1985 "The Area Group: An Example of Style and Paste Compositional Covariation in Maya Pottery," in *Fifth Palenque Roundtable, 1983*, M. G. Robertson and V. M. Fields, eds., pp. 79–84. Pre-Columbian Art Institute, Herald Printers, Monterey.

Blackman, M. J.
1984 "Provenance Studies of Middle Eastern Obsidian From Sites in Highland Iran," in *Archaeological Chemistry-III*, J. B. Lambert, ed., pp. 19–50. Advances in Chemistry Series 205. American Chemical Society, Washington, D.C.

Coggins, C. C.
1984 Decorated Ceramics at Copan and Quirigua in Their Relation to Other Classic Maya Regions: A Pot Can Look at a King. Paper presented at the Dumbarton Oaks Symposium on the Southeastern Classic Maya Zone, Washington, D.C.

Doran, J. E., and F. R. Hodson
1975 *Mathematics and Computers in Archaeology*. Edinburgh University Press, Edinburgh.

Friedman, H. P., and J. Rubin
1967 "On Some Invariant Criteria for Grouping Data," in *Journal of the American Statistical Association* 62:320.

Fry, R. E., and S. C. Cox
1974 "The Structure of Ceramic Exchange at Tikal, Guatemala." *World Archaeology* 6:209–225.

Harbottle, G.
1976 "Activation Analysis in Archaeology." *Radiochemistry* 3:33–72.
1982 "Chemical Characterization in Archaeology," in *Contexts for Prehistoric Exchange*, J. E. Ericson and T. K. Earle, eds., pp. 13–52. Academic Press, New York.

Henderson, J., J. Sterns, A. Wonderley, and P. Urban
1979 "Archaeological Investigations in the Valle de Naco, Northwestern Honduras: A Preliminary Report." *Journal of Field Archaeology* 6:169–192.

Hodder, I.
1980 "Trade and Exchange: Definitions, Identifications, and Functions," in *Models and Methods in Regional Exchange*, R. E. Fry, ed., pp. 151–156. Society for American Archaeology, SAA Papers 1. Washington, D.C.

Longyear, J. L., III
1952 *Copan Ceramics: A Study of Southeastern Maya Pottery*. Carnegie Institution of Washington, Publication 597. Washington, D.C.

Marriot, F. H. C.
1971 "Practical Problems in a Method of Cluster Analysis." *Biometrics* 27:501–514.

McRae, D. J.
1971 "MIKCA: A FORTRAN IV Iterative K-Means Cluster Analysis Program." *Behavioral Science* 16:423–424.

Pahl, G. W.
1987 "The Survey and Excavation of La Canteada, Copan, Honduras: Preliminary Report, 1975 Season." *The Periphery of the Southeastern Classic Maya Realm*. University of California at Los Angeles Latin American Studies vol. 61, pp. 227–261.

Perlman, I., and F. Asaro
1969 "Pottery Analysis by Neutron Activation." *Archaeometry* 11:21–52.

Rands, R. L., and R. L. Bishop
1980 "Resource Procurement Zones and Patterns of Ceramic Exchange in the Palenque Region, Mexico," in *Models and Methods in Regional Exchange*, R. E. Fry, ed., pp. 19–46. Society for American Archaeology, SAA Papers 1. Washington, D.C.

Reents, D. J.
1985 "The Late Classic Maya Holmul Style Polychrome Pottery." Ph.D. dissertation, University of Texas, Austin.

Reents-Budet, D. J., and R. L. Bishop
n.d. "The Late Classic Maya 'Codex Style' Pottery." Manuscript on file, Conservation Analytical Laboratory, Smithsonian Institution, Washington, D.C.

Rice, P. M.
1978 "Clear Answers to Vague Questions: Some Assumptions of Provenience Studies of Pottery," in *The Ceramics of Kaminaljuyu, Guatemala*, R. K. Wetherington, ed., pp. 401–510. The Pennsylvania State University Press, University Park.

Sayre, E. V.
1977 "Brookhaven Procedures of Statistical Analysis of Multivariate Archaeometric Data." Brookhaven National Laboratory Report, BNL-21693. Upton, New York.

Schortman, E. M., P. A. Urban, W. Ashmore, and J. C. Benyo
1986 "Interregional Interaction in the Southeast Maya Periphery: The Santa Barbara Archaeological Project 1983–1984 Season." *Journal of Field Archaeology* 13:259–272.

Sharer, R. J., ed.
1978a *The Prehistory of Chalchuapa, El Salvador*. (3 vols.) University Museum Monograph 36. University of Pennsylvania Press, Philadelphia.

Sharer, R. J.

1978b "Archaeology and History at Quirigua, Guatemala." *Journal of Field Archaeology* 5:51–71.

Sheets, P.

1983 *Volcanic Eruptions in Prehistoric Central America: The Zapotitan Valley of El Salvador.* University of Texas Press, Austin.

Shepard, A. O.

1942 *Rio Grande Glaze Paint Ware, a Study Illustrating the Place of Ceramic Technological Analyses in Archaeological Research.* Carnegie Institution of Washington, Publication 573, Contribution 30. Washington, D.C.

Tobia, S. K. and E. V. Sayre

1974 "An Analytical Comparison of Various Egyptian Soils, Clays, Shales and Some Ancient Pottery," in *Recent Advances in Science and Technology of Materials III,* A. Bishay, ed., pp. 99–128. Plemen Press, New York.

Turner, B. L., III, W. C. Johnson, G. Mahood, F. W. Wiseman, B. L. Turner, and J. Poole

1980 "Habitat and Agriculture in the Rio Copan Zone: Report to the Ecological Section of the Proyecto Arqueologico Copan, 1978–80." Manuscript in the possession of the authors.

Urban, P. A.

1986 "Systems of Settlement in the Naco Valley, Northwestern Honduras." Ph.D. dissertation, University of Pennsylvania, Philadelphia.

Weigand, P. C., G. Harbottle, and E. V. Sayre

1977 "Turquoise Sources and Source Analysis: Mesoamerica and the Southwestern U.S.A.," in *Exchange Systems in Prehistory,* T. K. Earle and J. E. Ericson, eds., pp. 15–34. Academic Press, New York.

Wilson, A. L.

1978 "Elemental Analysis of Pottery in the Study of Its Provenance: A Review." *Journal of Archaeological Science* 5:219–236.

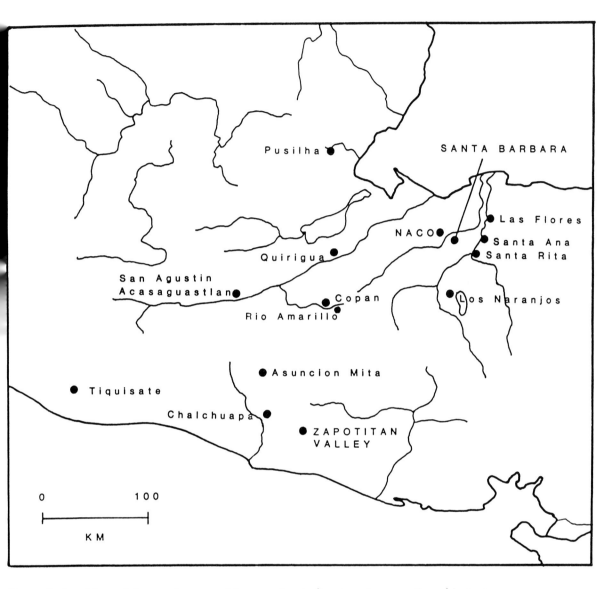

Figure B-1.   Map of the southeastern Maya region indicating sites mentioned in text

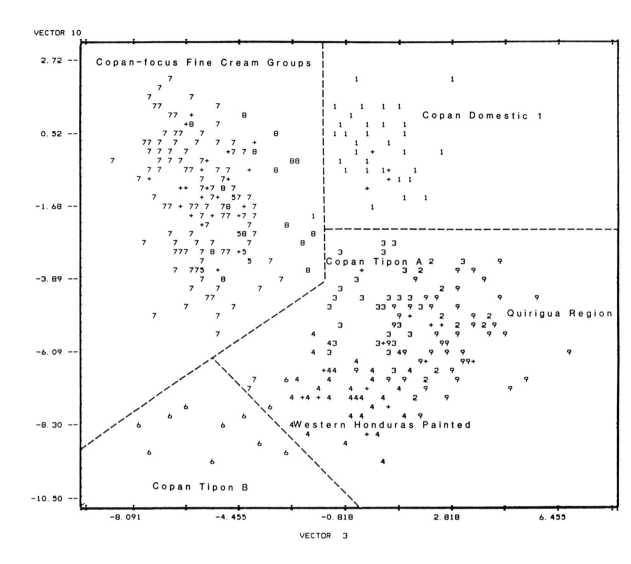

Figure B-2. Bivariate plot of Standardized Characteristic Vectors 3 and 10. In this and following plots, data points have been determined by projection onto the orthogonal axes obtained from the variance-covariance matrix of the Copan Domestic Chemical Paste Compositional Reference Unit (symbol group 1).

Group Symbols:
1   Copan Domestic 1
2   Western Honduras Domestic
3   Tipon A
4   Western Honduras Painted
5   Copan Domestic 2
6   Tipon B
7   Copan-focus Copador
8   Copan Fine Paste
9   Quirigua
+   indicates the overlap of two or more data points

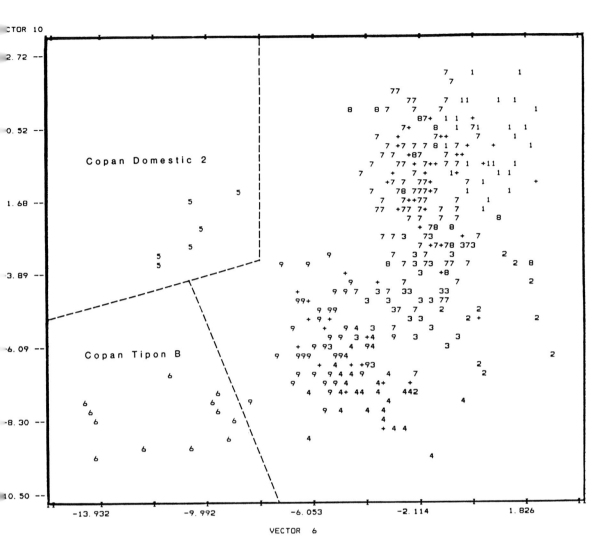

Figure B-3. Bivariate plot of Standardized Characteristic Vectors 6 and 10

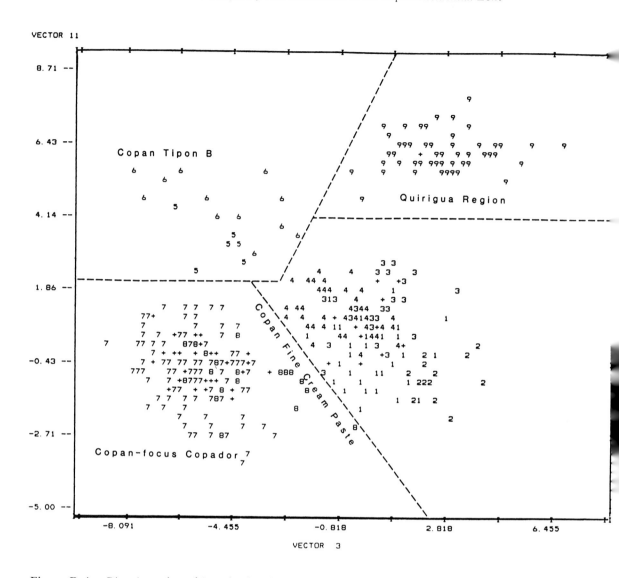

Figure B-4.   Bivariate plot of Standardized Characteristic Vectors 3 and 11

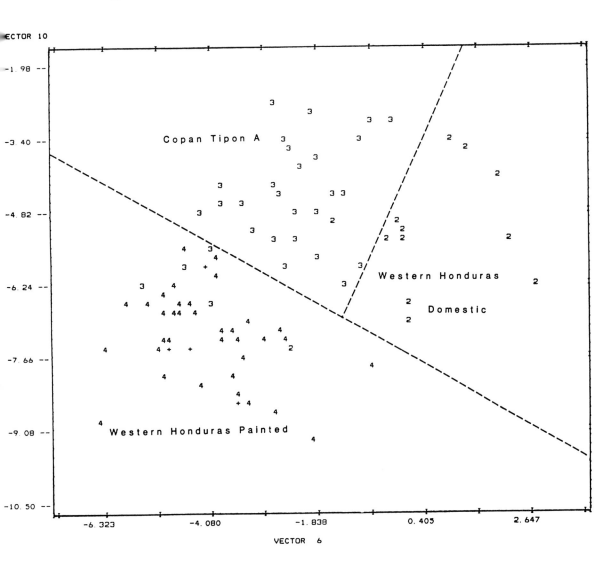

Figure B-5. Bivariate plot of Standardized Characteristic Vectors 6 and 10

APPENDIX C

The Sources of Copan Valley Obsidian

Garman Harbottle, Brookhaven National Laboratory; Hector Neff and Ronald L. Bishop, Conservation Analytical Laboratory, Smithsonian Institution

One hundred thirty-nine obsidian samples from the Copan Valley were subjected to neutron activation analysis at Brookhaven National Laboratory (BNL) (analyzed specimens are listed in table C-1).[1] The samples were prepared by cutting small wedges with a diamond saw, then labeling, washing, weighing, and packaging them in aluminum foil. Sixteen packages and six standards were included in each irradiation. Irradiation in the BNL High Flux Beam Reactor was for 7 1/2 hours (nominal) at a flux of 1.8×10^{14} n/cm^2 sec. Samples were allowed to decay for 16 days (nominal), after which gamma-ray counting for 2,000 seconds per sample was carried out using a Ge(Li) detector with 1.7 KeV resolution at 1332 KeV. The gamma spectra were reduced to elemental concentration data using standard BNL techniques (Abscal-M, Harbottle, and Sayre 1974; Harbottle 1976; Bieber Jr. et al. 1976).

Obsidian sources from Mesoamerica have been characterized by a number of different laboratories using several techniques (e.g., Hammond 1972). Over 1,800 samples from Mesoamerica have been analyzed by neutron activation at BNL (Boksenbaum et al. 1987; Hammond, Neivens, and Harbottle 1984; Spence, Kimberlin, and Harbottle 1984; Neivens, Harbottle, and Kimberlin 1983). These data are now housed both at BNL and in the Smithsonian Archaeometric Research Collections and Records (SARCAR) data base. Previous statistical analysis of the Mesoamerican obsidian artifacts and source samples has produced reference groups representing many of the sources, including Ixtepeque, San Martin Jilotepeque, and El Chayal, the three sources closest to the Copan Valley and therefore most likely to be represented in the analyzed sample (see map, fig. C-1).

Reference groups for most obsidian sources are characterized by extremely high correlations among the elements. Due to these extreme correlations, the dimensionality of the data can be reduced dramatically without significant loss of information. Thus, in a data set consisting of all reference group specimens from the three Guatemalan sources, nearly 90 percent of the total variation in the 14-dimensional data set can be represented in just two dimensions (the first two principal components). Furthermore, as shown in figure C-2, the reference groups are completely separable in these two dimensions alone. As indicated by the principal component coefficients listed in table C-2, component 1, which clearly separates the source groups, is attributable primarily to difference in Cs values, with moderate contributions from Fe, Gd, Hf, and Se. Component 2 is a positive interelemental correlation vector, on which all elements have positive coefficients of roughly the same magnitudes (see table C-2). The ellipses drawn on the plot (fig. C-2) enclose the 95 percent confidence region for each group in the two-dimensional principal components space, as calculated using Hotelling's T^2.

When the 139 obsidian samples from the Copan Valley are projected into the principal component space defined by the source reference groups (fig. C-3), the affiliations of all specimens are easily inferred by visual inspection alone. All but seven apparently pertain to the Ixtepeque source, the seven remaining showing El Chayal affiliation. A number of specimens fall outside the 95 percent confidence ellipse for the Ixtepeque source, but there is little doubt that they fall on the same correlational axis. When the full dimensionality of the data is taken into account by calculating Hotelling's T^2 based on all 14 dimensions of the data, all but 14 of the putative Ixtepeque specimens from the Copan Valley show above 5 percent probability of membership in the Ixtepeque reference group (table C-1). The low-probability specimens probably reflect a slight bias in the Ixtepeque reference group as

originally formulated. With the new Ixtepeque specimens from the Copan Valley, some of this bias in our reference group is eliminated.

Table C-3 lists the elemental concentration means and percent standard deviations for the three reference groups, along with those for the Copan Valley specimens attributed to El Chayal and Ixtepeque, respectively.

As anticipated, the overwhelming majority of obsidian recovered in the Copan Valley come from the closest source, Ixtepeque. Of the seven El Chayal specimens, four pertain to CV-43 and three pertain to CV-20. These data provide no evidence of a difference between the two localities in external obsidian exchange relations. Thus, we find no grounds for questioning the assumption that the minor quantities of El Chayal obsidian that reached the Copan Valley were distributed through the same channels responsible for distribution of the more common Ixtepeque obsidian.

NOTE

1. The authors wish to acknowledge the analytical work of Jerome Kimberlin and Mary Neivens. Neivens's work resulted in the original definition of reference groups for the three Guatemalan sources.

The neutron activation analyses were undertaken at BNL under the auspices of the U.S. Department of Energy.

BIBLIOGRAPHY

Abscal-M, R., G. Harbottle, and E. V. Sayre
  1974 "Correlations Between Terra Cotta Figurines and Pottery from the Valley of Mexico and Source Clays by Neutron Activation Analysis," in *Archaeological Chemistry,* C. W. Beck, ed., pp. 81–99. American Chemical Society, Washington, D.C.

Bieber, A. M., Jr., D. W. Brooks, G. Harbottle, and E. V. Sayre
  1976 "Application of Multivariate Techniques to Analytical Data on Aegean Ceramics." *Archaeometry* 1:59–74.

Boksenbaum, M. W., P. Tolstoy, G. Harbottle, J. Kimberlin, and M. Neivens

  1987 "Obsidian Industries and Cultural Evolution in the Basin of Mexico Before 500 b.c." *Journal of Field Archaeology* 14:65–75.
Hammond, N.
  1972 "Obsidian Trade Routes in the Mayan Area." *Science* 178:1092–1093.
Hammond, N., M. D. Neivens, and G. Harbottle
  1984 "Trace Element Analysis of Obsidian Artifacts from a Classic Maya Residential Group at Nohmul, Belize." *American Antiquity* 49: 815–820.
Harbottle, G.
  1976 "Activation Analysis in Archaeology." *Radiochemistry.* Chemical Society Specialist Periodical Report, vol. 3, pp. 33–72. London.

Neivens, M., G. Harbottle, and J. Kimberlin
1983 "Trace Element Analysis of Obsidian Arti-facts from Northern Belize," in *Archaeological Excavations in Northern Belize, Central America,* by Raymond V. Sidrys, pp. 321–339. Monograph XVII, Institute of Archaeology. University of California, Los Angeles.

Spence, M. W., J. Kimberlin, and G. Harbottle
1984 "State-Controlled Procurement and the Obsidian Workshops of Teotihuacan, Mexico," in *Prehistoric Quarries and Lithic Production,* J. E. Ericson and B. A. Purdy, eds., pp. 97–105. Cambridge University Press, Cambridge and New York.

TABLE C-1

Copan obsidian sources

Analytical I.D.	Context	Description	Probability of Membership in El Chayal Core	Probability of Membership in Ixtepeque Core	Source*
JK1571	CV-43	Bladelet	0.00000	74.77106	Ixtepeque
JK1572	CV-43	Bladelet	0.00000	90.19050	Ixtepeque
JK1573	CV-43	Bladelet	0.00000	72.23039	Ixtepeque
JK1574	CV-43	Bladelet, proximal end	0.00000	60.02236	Ixtepeque
JK1575	CV-43	Bladelet	0.00000	58.22679	Ixtepeque
JK1576	CV-43	Bladelet	0.50846	0.00000	El Chayal*
JK1577	CV-43	Core fragment	0.00000	92.18464	Ixtepeque
JK1578	CV-43	Bladelet	85.39511	0.00000	El Chayal
JK1579	CV-43	Bladelet, proximal end	0.00000	95.21930	Ixtepeque
JK1580	CV-43	Bladelet	0.00000	5.99356	Ixtepeque
JK1581	CV-43	Bladelet	0.00000	0.00325	Ixtepeque*
JK1582	CV-43	Bladelet	0.00000	0.00000	Ixtepeque*
JK1583	CV-43	Bladelet, flake	0.00000	0.00001	Ixtepeque*
JK1584	CV-43	Bladelet, proximal end	0.00000	84.32801	Ixtepeque
JK1585	CV-43	Bladelet, proximal end	0.00000	87.47293	Ixtepeque
JK1586	CV-43	Bladelet	0.00000	98.29251	Ixtepeque
JK1587	CV-43	Bladelet	0.00000	82.87660	Ixtepeque
JK1588	CV-43	Bladelet	0.00000	87.52565	Ixtepeque
JK1589	CV-43	Bladelet	0.00000	68.68499	Ixtepeque
JK1590	CV-43	Bladelet, proximal end	0.00000	0.00000	Ixtepeque*
JK1591	CV-43	Bladelet	0.00000	95.85444	Ixtepeque
JK1592	CV-43	Bladelet	0.00000	96.18010	Ixtepeque
JK1593	CV-43	Bladelet	0.00000	40.82624	Ixtepeque
JK1594	CV-43	Bladelet	0.00000	97.85866	Ixtepeque
JK1595	CV-43	Bladelet	0.00000	78.90781	Ixtepeque
JK1596	CV-43	Bladelet	79.45616	0.00000	El Chayal

*Asterisk following entry for "source" indicates that specimen showed lower than 5% probability of membership in all source reference groups. In these cases, specimens are assigned to the reference group for which Mahalanobis distance from specimen to centroid is minimized.

TABLE C-1 *(continued)*

Copan obsidian sources

Analytical I.D.	Context	Description	Probability of Membership in El Chayal Core	Probability of Membership in Ixtepeque Core	Source*
JK1597	CV-43	Bladelet, proximal end	0.00000	79.93271	Ixtepeque
JK1598	CV-43	Bladelet, flake	0.00000	54.87824	Ixtepeque
JK1599	CV-43	Bladelet	0.00000	12.62694	Ixtepeque
JK1600	CV-43	Bladelet	0.00000	61.96738	Ixtepeque
JK1601	CV-43	Flake	0.00000	0.40591	Ixtepeque*
JK1602	CV-40	Debris	0.00000	82.16896	Ixtepeque
JK1603	CV-43	Flake	0.00000	48.15933	Ixtepeque
JK1604	CV-43	Flake	0.00000	15.09087	Ixtepeque
JK1605	CV-43	Flake	0.00000	42.64914	Ixtepeque
JK1606	CV-43	Flake	0.00000	0.00000	Ixtepeque*
JK1607	CV-43	Flake	0.00000	72.35548	Ixtepeque
JK1608	CV-43	Flake	0.00000	86.28487	Ixtepeque
JK1609	CV-43	Flake	0.00000	77.86607	Ixtepeque
JK1610	CV-43	Flake	0.00000	0.00000	???—bad data
JK1659	CV-43	Exhausted? Broken core	0.00000	0.00000	Ixtepeque*
JK1660	CV-43	Broken exhausted core, distal end	0.00000	33.01946	Ixtepeque
JK1661	CV-43	Broken exhausted core	0.00000	73.20115	Ixtepeque
JK1662	CV-43	Exhausted core, distal end	0.00000	85.22125	Ixtepeque
JK1663	CV-43	Bladelet, proximal end	0.00000	45.87993	Ixtepeque
JK1664	CV-43	Bladelet, proximal end	0.00000	70.78660	Ixtepeque
JK1665	CV-43	Bladelet, proximal end	0.00000	14.87786	Ixtepeque
JK1666	CV-43	Bladelet	67.90371	0.00000	El Chayal
JK1667	CV-43	Bladelet	0.00000	26.00464	Ixtepeque
JK1668	CV-43	Bladelet, flake	0.00000	0.25296	Ixtepeque*
JKW472	CV-20, Op. 19(C), Level 2, Structure A	Bladelet, distal end	0.00000	62.13664	Ixtepeque
JKW473	CV-20, Op. 19(B)	Bladelet, proximal end	0.00000	81.63631	Ixtepeque
JKW474	CV-20	Bladelet, proximal end	0.00000	93.42985	Ixtepeque
JKW475	CV-20, Op. 19(A), Structure A	Bladelet clearing structure addition	0.00000	82.79619	Ixtepeque
JKW476	CV-20, Op. 20(A), Level 5, Structure D	Bladelet	0.00000	27.69419	Ixtepeque
JKW477	CV-20, Op. 5(B)	Bladelet, proximal end	0.00000	8.59598	Ixtepeque

*Asterisk following entry for "source" indicates that specimen showed lower than 5% probability of membership in all source reference groups. In these cases, specimens are assigned to the reference group for which Mahalanobis distance from specimen to centroid is minimized.

JKW478	CV-20, Op. 20(A), Level 5, Structure D	Bladelet, proximal end	0.00000	98.20371	Ixtepeque
JKW479	CV-20, Op. 19(C), Level 3, Structure A	Bladelet, proximal end	0.00000	95.58413	Ixtepeque
JKW480	CV-20, Op. 4(R)	Bladelet, proximal end	0.00000	22.62532	Ixtepeque
JKW481	CV-22, Op. 14(A), Level 2	Bladelet, proximal end	0.00000	56.65648	Ixtepeque
JKW482	CV-20, Op. 4(F)	Bladelet, proximal end	0.00000	71.43965	Ixtepeque
JKW483	CV-20, Op. 6(C)	Bladelet, distal end	0.00000	99.38989	Ixtepeque
JKW484	CV-20, Op. 6(N)	Bladelet	0.00000	13.56430	Ixtepeque
JKW485	CV-20, Op. 19(C), Level 5, Structure A	Bladelet, proximal end	0.00000	99.99820	Ixtepeque
JKW486	CV-20, Op. 6(M)	Bladelet, proximal end	0.00000	68.74116	Ixtepeque
JKW487	CV-20, Op. 19(B)	Bladelet	0.00000	89.10064	Ixtepeque
JKW488	CV-20, Op. 2(H)	Bladelet	0.00000	20.98605	Ixtepeque
JKW489	CV-20, Op. 19(C), Level 4, Structure A	Bladelet, proximal end	0.00000	11.92953	Ixtepeque
JKW490	CV-20, Op. 1(A), surface	Bladelet, proximal end	0.00000	96.93866	Ixtepeque
JKW491	CV-20, Op. 2(C)	Bladelet	0.00000	6.51298	Ixtepeque
JKW492	CV-20, Op. 6(J)	Bladelet	0.00000	1.02498	Ixtepeque*
JKW493	CV-20, Op. 19(B)	Bladelet, proximal end	0.00000	0.00013	Ixtepeque*
JKW494	CV-20, Op. 6(H)	Bladelet, proximal end	0.00000	56.18511	Ixtepeque
JKW495	CV-20, Op. 4(D)	Bladelet	0.00000	93.76178	Ixtepeque
JKW496	CV-20, Op. 20(A), Level 3, Structure D	Bladelet	0.00000	49.18015	Ixtepeque
JKW497	CV-20, Op. 6(C)	Bladelet	0.00000	92.16227	Ixtepeque

*Asterisk following entry for "source" indicates that specimen showed lower than 5% probability of membership in all source reference groups. In these cases, specimens are assigned to the reference group for which Mahalanobis distance from specimen to centroid is minimized.

TABLE C-1 *(continued)*

Copan obsidian sources

Analytical I.D.	Context	Description	Probability of Membership in El Chayal Core	Probability of Membership in Ixtepeque Core	Source*
JKW498	CV-20, Op. 1(B), surface	Bladelet, proximal end	0.00000	87.71144	Ixtepeque
JKW499	CV-20, Op. 19(C), Level 4, Structure A	Bladelet, proximal end	0.00000	23.91326	Ixtepeque
JKW500	CV-20, Op. 4(L)	Bladelet, proximal end	0.00000	99.29378	Ixtepeque
JKW501	CV-20, Op. 19(C), Level 4, Structure A	Bladelet, proximal end	0.00000	99.00968	Ixtepeque
JKW502	CV-20, Op. 19(C), Level 4, Structure A	Bladelet	0.00000	93.64178	Ixtepeque
JKW503	CV-20, Op. 18(A)	Bladelet, proximal end	0.00000	55.40459	Ixtepeque
JKW504	CV-20, Op. 2(B)	Bladelet	0.00000	26.54039	Ixtepeque
JKW505	CV-20, Op. 4(N)	Bladelet	0.00000	14.79697	Ixtepeque
JKW506	CV-20, Op. 7(F), Structure B	Bladelet, proximal end	0.00000	58.58039	Ixtepeque
JKW507	CV-20, Op. 6(I), Structure A	Bladelet, proximal end	0.00000	6.71915	Ixtepeque
JKW508	CV-20, Op. 18(A)	Bladelet	0.00000	57.98833	Ixtepeque
JKW509	CV-20, Op. 21(A), Level 2, Structure B	Bladelet	0.00000	69.81519	Ixtepeque
JKW510	CV-20, Op. 12(B), Structure H	Bladelet, proximal end	0.00000	47.23931	Ixtepeque
JKW511	CV-20, Op. 19(H), Structure A	Almost whole bladelet, proximal end	0.00000	99.01902	Ixtepeque
JKW512	CV-20, Op. 6(M), Structure A	Whole bladelet, proximal end	0.00000	74.99703	Ixtepeque

*Asterisk following entry for "source" indicates that specimen showed lower than 5% probability of membership in all source reference groups. In these cases, specimens are assigned to the reference group for which Mahalanobis distance from specimen to centroid is minimized.

JKW513	CV-56, Op. 17(A)	Whole bladelet, proximal end	0.00000	10.29276	Ixtepeque
JKW514	CV-20, Op. 19(A), Structure A	Bladelet, proximal end	0.00000	30.12034	Ixtepeque
JKW515	CV-13, Op. 11(A), Level 2	Bladelet, proximal end	0.00000	1.73081	Ixtepeque*
JKW516	CV-13, Op. 11(A), Level 3	Bladelet, proximal end	0.00000	59.16899	Ixtepeque
JKW517	CV-20, Op. 1(A), surface	Bladelet, proximal end	0.00000	3.29805	Ixtepeque*
JKW518	CV-20, Op. 4(M), Structure D	Bladelet	0.00000	19.49713	Ixtepeque
JKW519	CV-20, Op. 5(O), Structure C	Bladelet	0.00000	40.19181	Ixtepeque
JKW520	CV-20, Op. 7(F), Structure B	Bladelet, proximal end	0.00000	84.81014	Ixtepeque
JKW521	CV-20, Op. 1(A), surface	Bladelet	0.00000	59.09388	Ixtepeque
JKW522	CV-20, Op. 5(M), Structure C	Bladelet	0.00000	81.09756	Ixtepeque
JKW523	CV-20, Op. 20(A), Level 5, Structure D	Bladelet, proximal end	0.00000	61.98290	Ixtepeque
JKW524	CV-20, Op. 6(J), Structure A	Bladelet	0.00000	79.63562	Ixtepeque
JKW525	CV-20, Op. 4(M), Structure D	Bladelet, proximal end	0.00000	98.87136	Ixtepeque
JKW526	CV-20, Op. 19(C) Level 3, Structure A	Bladelet, proximal end	0.00000	99.13959	Ixtepeque
JKW527	CV-20, Op. 20(A), Level 4, Structure D	Bladelet	0.00000	62.91702	Ixtepeque
JKW528	CV-20, Op. 5(H), Structure A	Bladelet, proximal end	0.00000	60.14785	Ixtepeque
JKW529	CV-20, Op. 19(D), Structure A	Bladelet, proximal end	0.00000	59.42862	Ixtepeque

*Asterisk following entry for "source" indicates that specimen showed lower than 5% probability of membership in all source reference groups. In these cases, specimens are assigned to the reference group for which Mahalanobis distance from specimen to centroid is minimized.

TABLE C-1 *(continued)*

Copan obsidian sources

Analytical I.D.	Context	Description	Probability of Membership in El Chayal Core	Probability of Membership in Ixtepeque Core	Source*
JKW530	CV-20, Op. 19(C) Level 4, Structure A	Bladelet	0.00000	64.94624	Ixtepeque
JKW531	CV-17, Op. 10(A), Level 3	Bladelet, proximal end	0.00000	97.27954	Ixtepeque
JKW532	CV-48, Op. 22(A), Level 1	Bladelet	0.00000	38.59661	Ixtepeque
JKW533	CV-20, Op. 19(C) Level 5, Structure A	Bladelet	0.00000	4.68300	Ixtepeque*
JKW534	CV-20, Op. 2(B), Level 2	Bladelet, proximal end	0.00000	3.03079	Ixtepeque*
JKW535	CV-20, Op. 12(A), Structure H	Bladelet	0.00000	30.87996	Ixtepeque
JKW536	CV-20, Op. 6(H), Structure A	Bladelet, proximal end	0.00000	17.81888	Ixtepeque
JKW537	CV-20, Op. 5(J), Structure C	Bladelet	0.00000	98.66329	Ixtepeque
JKW538	CV-20, Op. 24(A) Level 7, Structure C	Bladelet	0.00000	23.61385	Ixtepeque
JKW539	CV-20, Op. 6(K), Structure A	Bladelet, proximal end	0.00000	86.37277	Ixtepeque
JKW540	CV-20, Op. 2(C), Level 3	Bladelet	0.00000	88.64724	Ixtepeque
JKW541	CV-20, Op. 4(O), Structure D	Bladelet	0.00000	98.00695	Ixtepeque
JKW542	CV-20, Op. 19(A), Structure A	Bladelet, proximal end	0.00000	93.73450	Ixtepeque
JKW543	CV-20, Op. 15(A), Structure B	Bladelet, proximal end	0.00000	81.83134	Ixtepeque
JKW544	CV-20, Op. 5(H), Structure A	Bladelet, proximal end	0.00000	13.24560	Ixtepeque

*Asterisk following entry for "source" indicates that specimen showed lower than 5% probability of membership in all source reference groups. In these cases, specimens are assigned to the reference group for which Mahalanobis distance from specimen to centroid is minimized.

JKW545	CV-20, Op. 19(B), Structure A	Bladelet	36.54703	0.00000	El Chayal
JKW546	CV-17, Op. 10(A), Level 2	Bladelet	0.00000	39.70660	Ixtepeque
JKW547	CV-20, Op. 7(F), Structure B	Bladelet	0.00000	17.30260	Ixtepeque
JKW548	CV-20, Op. 2(L), Level 1	Bladelet	0.00000	99.83344	Ixtepeque
JKW549	CV-20, Op. 5(A)	Bladelet	0.00000	82.04976	Ixtepeque
JKW550	CV-20, Op. 1(A), surface	Bladelet	0.00000	29.86172	Ixtepeque
JKW551	CV-18, Op. 9(A), Level 3	Bladelet, proximal end	91.58026	0.00000	El Chayal
JKW552	CV-20, Op. 6(K), Structure A	Bladelet	0.00000	92.92833	Ixtepeque
JKW561	CV-20, Op. 13(C), Structure F	Core	0.00000	94.83098	Ixtepeque
JKW562	CV-20, Op. 4(H), Structure D	Core	0.00000	69.55615	Ixtepeque
JKW563	CV-20, Op. 20(A), Structure D	Core	0.00000	78.08021	Ixtepeque
JKW564	CV-20, Op. 8(B)	Core	0.00000	96.70832	Ixtepeque
JKW565	CV-20, Op. 1(A), surface	Core	0.00000	97.73327	Ixtepeque
JKW566	CV-20, Op. 2(A), Level 2	Bladelet	49.14712	0.00000	El Chayal
JKW567	CV-20, Op. 2(C), Level 5	Bladelet	0.00000	43.01041	Ixtepeque
JKW568	CV-20, Op. 2(C), Level 5	Bladelet	0.00000	81.13376	Ixtepeque

*Asterisk following entry for "source" indicates that specimen showed lower than 5% probability of membership in all source reference groups. In these cases, specimens are assigned to the reference group for which Mahalanobis distance from specimen to centroid is minimized.

TABLE C-2

The first two principal components of the data set
consisting of members of the Ixtepeque, El
Chayal, and San Martin Jilotepeque
reference groups

Element	Principal Component #1	Principal Component #2
Rb	-0.2851	0.1741
Cs	-0.7790	0.1524
Ba	0.0782	0.2250
Sc	0.0921	0.2049
Fe	0.3011	0.3056
Ce	-0.0749	0.2128
Nd	-0.1014	0.2435
Eu	-0.0614	0.2137
Gd	-0.2737	0.2323
Yb	-0.0595	0.3047
Zr	0.1236	0.3825
Hf	0.2055	0.3015
Os	-0.0660	0.2730
Se	0.2159	0.3895
Eigenvalue	0.0730	0.1012
% Variance Explained	77.8892	10.9142
Cumulative % Variance	77.8892	88.8034

TABLE C-3

Means and percent standard deviations for three reference groups and Copan specimens

	IXTEPEQUE REFERENCE GROUP			EL CHAYAL REFERENCE GROUP			SAN MARTIN JILOTEPEQUE REFERENCE GROUP			COPAN SPECIMENS ASSIGNED TO IXTEPEQUE			COPAN SPECIMENS ASSIGNED TO EL CHAYAL		
	Mean	St. Dev. (%)	N	Mean	St. Dev. (%)	N	Mean	St. Dev. (%)	N	Mean	St. Dev. (%)	N	Mean	St. Dev. (%)	N
Rb	103.425	6.458	142	146.971	8.232	469	118.763	9.949	22	98.897	10.545	131	142.890	8.279	7
Cs	2.804	6.455	141	7.684	10.133	468	3.635	22.428	22	2.703	10.827	131	7.531	8.118	7
Ba	1146.149	7.129	141	1010.142	9.146	468	1080.529	63.492	22	1111.458	10.972	131	1010.582	7.821	7
Sc	2.237	6.469	142	1.918	8.770	469	2.140	8.770	22	2.196	13.024	131	1.869	7.433	7
Fe	9681.209	9.005	142	6280.924	10.874	467	6937.888	8.412	22	9263.575	11.918	131	5984.117	7.414	7
Ce	40.699	7.598	142	43.382	8.985	469	45.252	8.991	22	37.793	11.562	130	41.020	8.071	7
Nd	22.742	11.963	141	25.486	10.614	468	24.006	11.671	22	20.653	12.723	131	23.659	6.976	7
Eu	0.616	6.624	142	0.650	8.619	469	0.577	35.434	22	0.593	10.907	131	0.650	5.102	7
Gd	1.598	9.721	141	2.228	10.266	468	2.017	18.705	22	1.474	12.420	130	2.080	7.576	7
Yb	2.257	8.712	140	2.320	9.799	468	1.864	14.205	22	2.095	12.692	131	2.178	9.628	7
Zr	161.311	11.978	140	132.459	14.217	469	120.352	13.684	22	145.953	14.262	131	115.649	6.245	7
Hf	4.298	6.191	140	3.115	8.351	469	3.159	8.877	22	4.094	10.632	131	3.006	8.217	7
Os	0.425	8.970	141	0.439	9.747	469	0.344	16.803	22	0.397	12.019	130	0.414	10.317	7
Se	2.852	8.941	141	2.038	10.468	469	2.043	9.926	22	2.623	11.402	130	1.858	9.073	7

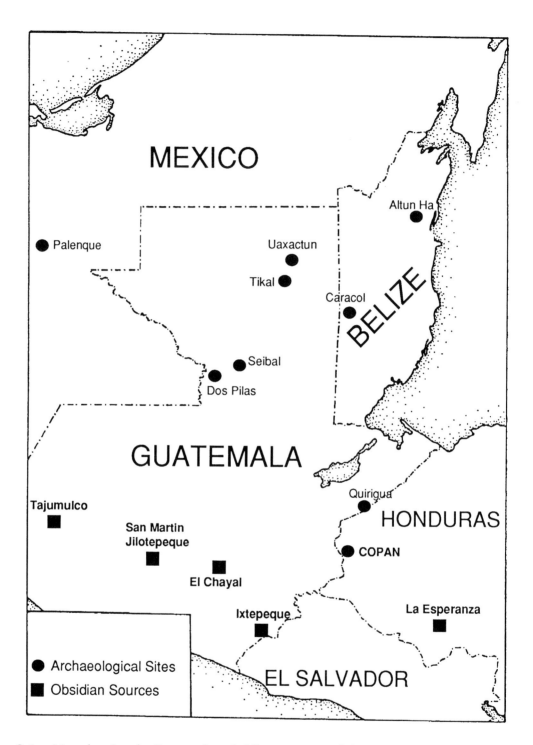

Figure C-1. Map showing the Guatemalan obsidian sources and Copan

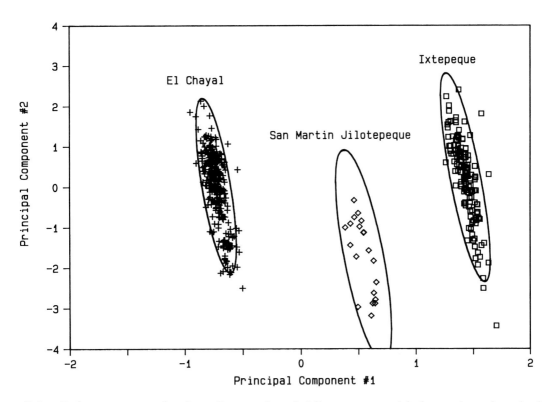

Figure C-2. Reference groups for three Guatemalan obsidian sources, with data points plotted relative to the first two principal components calculated for the data set consisting of specimens in all three reference groups. Ellipses indicate 95% confidence levels for each group in the two dimensions shown. Principal component coefficients, eigenvalues, and percentage of variance are explained in table C-2.

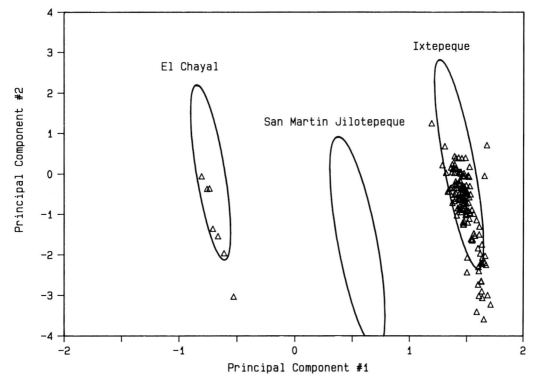

Figure C-3. One hundred thirty-nine obsidian artifacts from the Copan Valley plotted in the same principal component space shown in figure C-2. Ellipses are the 95% confidence levels for the three reference groups.

Late Classic Maya Fauna from Settlement in the Copan Valley, Honduras: Assertion of Social Status Through Animal Consumption

Mary D. Pohl

Florida State University

This report describes animal bones recovered by G. R. Willey and R. M. Leventhal (1979) in the Harvard Copan Project (see table D-1). One of the principal objectives of the project was to investigate plaza groups of differing social status on the periphery of the Copan Main Center, and how faunal remains contributed to consumption patterns. My conclusions pertain only to larger animal species preserved since ancient times and recovered through excavation techniques used.

The analysis of fauna showed that the primary animal consumed at all social levels was white-tailed deer. This finding reflects a strong food preference among residents of Copan, and they may have raised deer in their house compounds to meet demand for venison, as well as for deer sacrifices, dance headdresses, skins, and bone tool blanks.

Dogs were the second most frequent vertebrate in the faunal collection, and the Maya used them for food and for sacrifices in addition to hunting. The incidence of healed trauma and pathology in the dog bones is noteworthy because it shows that the Copan Maya nurtured dogs.

Evidence for dedicatory offerings of animals complements earlier archaeological findings at Copan and other sites, and places Copan in the competitive sphere of Classic Maya ritual. Of particular significance was a left deer haunch found beside the remains of an early Late Classic period house, an immature ocelot skeleton below a Terminal Late Classic (Coner phase) plaza floor, and a cache that included two ferruginous pygmy owls from the same period.

Ethnohistoric data indicate that animal consumption was closely linked to social status and often occurred in the context of public feasts and private (i.e., elite only) rituals. Eating high status meat, the caching of spotted cats, and the conspicuous display of their skins were not just a reflection of status, they were a means by which the elite asserted their political position (Douglas and Isherwood 1979).

I looked for evidence of the connection between animals and status in the archaeological record at Copan. Analysis of faunal distribution by mound group status indicated that the more elite the group, the higher the number of bones of larger animal species. A spotted cat cache also occurred in a high-status context. Thus, I conclude that animal consumption was an important means by which the Maya elite achieved privileged social rank in Late Classic times.

TABLE D-1

Context of Copan fauna

Excavations

I. CV-43: Type 3 group. Groups 43–47 have been
interpreted as an extended family compound with
possible servant quarters.

  A. CV-43: Coner phase

    1. Structure A:

      Odocoileus virginianus
        phalange, second 1

    2. Structure B:

      Odocoileus virginianus
        ulna, L 1
        tibia, R 1
        humerus, R 2; both grooved on
          posterior side

      Unidentified large mammal (probably
      Odocoileus virginianus)
        long bone fragments 5

    3. Structure C:

      Odocoileus virginianus
        humerus, R 1

      Unidentified large mammal 5

    4. Structure D:

      Bos taurus
        molar, 3rd lower 1

    5. Structure E1:

      Odocoileus virginianus
        humerus, R 2, L 1
        femur, R, immature 2
        antler, 2: one pedicle and beam of a
          yearling, one (?shed) beam with burr
          removed

      Unidentified large mammal 19:
      1 immature

      Unidentified very large mammal 1

      Canis familiaris
        axis 1
        mandible, R, immature 1
        *single adult individual:
          humerus, L 1
          ulna, R 1, L 1
          radius, R 1, L 1
          femur, R 1, L 1
          tibia, L 1
          innominate, L 1
          calcaneus, R 1, L 1
          astragalus, R 1, L 1: both fused with
            calcaneus
          metapodial, complete 2, fragments 19
          phalange, first 9, second 11, third 3

      Procyonidae, possible *Nasua narica*
        humerus, R 1

Dasyproctidae cf. *Cuniculus paca*
  femur, L distal 1, proximal 1, probably
    one bone

Unidentified small mammal 2

Unidentified bird
  coracoid L 1, R 1: medium sized,
    probably same individual
  shaft fragments 2

    6. Structure E2:

      Odocoileus virginianus
        radius, L 1
        scapula R 1
        metatarsal
        vertebra fragment 1
        antler 1 shed beam

      Unidentified large mammal 12

      Didelphis spp.
        femur, R 1
        ulna, R 1
        scapula 1
        caudal vertebrae 1

      Unidentified medium mammal 1

      Unidentified small mammal 2

    7. Structure F:

      Odocoileus virginianus
        antler tine and base with cut mark 1

      Unidentified large mammal 2

  B. CV-43: Fill

    Odocoileus virginianus
      antler, 2
      humerus, L 3; 1 immature
      ulna, R 4, L 1
      radius, L 3
      scapula, R 1, L 2
      tibia, R 2
      metacarpal, R 1
      calcaneus, R 1, L 2
      astragalus, L 1
      molar, R m2 (upper)
      vertebra 2

    Unidentified large mammal 32

    Dicotyles tayacu
      cranium 1

    Tapirus bairdi
      humerus R 1

    Canis familiaris: probably single individual
      tibia, R 1, L 1
      metapodial 7
      caudal vertebra 1
      long bone fragments 4

    Unidentified small mammal 2

*Counted as one for modified NISP

Unidentified turtle 3

Pseudemys scripta
hyoplastron, R 1

Unidentified bird
shaft fragments 2: immature, possibly one
individual

II. CV-44: Type 1 group associated with CV-43.

A. CV-44: Coner phase

Odocoileus virginianus
scapula R 1
antler 2: one with part of frontal and cut
marks

Unidentified large mammal 6

B. CV-44: Fill

Unidentified large mammal 7

III. CV-45: Type 1 group.

A. CV-45: Coner phase, beside early house floor
or remains of early house.

Odocoileus virginianus: one individual
innominate, L 1
femur, L 2: probably one bone
tibia, L 1
calcaneus, L 1
long bone fragments 4
small bone fragments ca. 75

B. CV-45: Fill

Odocoileus virginianus
humerus, L 1
radius, L 1
ulna, L 1
tibia, R 1
innominate R 1
astragalus, L 2
molar, R M1 (upper)
antler tine 2: one fire darkened
vertebra 1

Unidentified large mammal 20

Canis familiaris
humerus, L 1
ulna, R 1, L 1: R is from a smaller
individual

IV. CV-47: Plaza group adjacent to CV-43. Type 2
group.

CV-47: Coner phase:

Odocoileus virginianus
antler 2: one shed beam and tine, one cut off
at proximal end

V. CV-20: Type 2 group.

A. CV-20: Coner phase

1. Structure A:

Didelphis spp.
mandible, R 1

Unidentified large mammal 4: 1 long
bone fragment with use marks, very
smooth

Unidentified very large mammal 1

2. Structure B:

Odocoileus virginianus
scapula, R 1

Unidentified large mammal 4: 2 shaft
fragments with grooving

3. Structure D:

Unidentified large mammal 10

B. CV-20: Fill

Odocoileus virginianus
humerus, R 1: immature
ulna, L 1
radius, L 1
innominate, R 1
femur, R 1
tibia, R 1
metatarsal 1: grooved
astragalus, L 2

Unidentified large mammal 11

Dicotyles spp.
metapodial 1

Didelphis spp.
mandible, L 1

Bos taurus
molar m3 (lower)

VI. CV-17: Type 3 group.

A. CV-17: Probably Coner phase. Test excavation in plaza, level 2, below plaza floor.

Felis pardalis: one immature individual
mandible (includes 2 deciduous premolars) 1
skull fragments 16
hyoid 1
innominate fragments
ulna, R 1, L 1
radius, R 1
femur, R 1, L 1: with proximal head
fragments unfused
long bone shaft fragments 8
metapodial, complete 2, fragments 8
phalanges, first 8, second 4

B. CV-17: Fill

Unidentified large mammal 3

VII. CV-68: Type 4 group.

A. CV-68: Coner phase; excavation in middle of
plaza; level 3 below plaza floor.

Canis familiaris: one individual
mandible, R 1 with M1
maxilla, R 1 with M1
teeth: incisors 3; L lower M1 1
humerus, R 1, L 1

*Counted as one for modified NISP

TABLE D-1 (*continued*)

Context of Copan fauna

radius, R 1, L 1
ulna, R 1, L 1
scapula, L 1
tibia, R 1, L 1
calcaneus, R 1
astragalus, R 1
vertebrae, caudal 3, fragments 20
metapodials, complete 6, fragments 10:
 right metacarpals II and III with evidence of exotoses; metacarpals IV and V
 fused
phalanges, first 7, second 2, third 1

B. CV-68: Fill
 Odocoileus virginianus
  metacarpal, R 1
  phalange, first 1: immature
 Unidentified large mammal 2

VIII. CV-125: Cueva/Coner phase. Type 1 group.
 Odocoileus virginianus
  antler tine 1

Test pits. All test pits are located in the center of the plaza of each group.

I. CV-91: Type 1 group.
  CV-91: Fill
   Unidentified large mammal 1

II. CV-94: Type 2 group.
  CV-94: Fill
   Odocoileus virginianus
    antler tine 1
   Unidentified large mammal 3

*Counted as one for modified NISP

III. CV-115: Type 2 group.
  A. CV-115: Coner phase cache below plaza floor.
   Glaucidium brasilianum: 2 male sized individuals in a single cache
   1. Within Spondylus shell
     femur, L 1
     tibiotarsus, L 1
     vertebra, dorsal 1
     pedal phalange 2
   2. Within carved, polished brown ceramic vessel
     humerus, R 1, L 1
     ulna, R 1
     femur, R 1
     tibiotarsus, R 1
     tarsometatarsus, L 1
  B. CV-115: Fill
   Unidentified large mammal 1

IV. CV-190: Type 1 group.
  A. CV-190: Fill
   Odocoileus virginianus
    antler tine 1
   Dicotyles spp.
    canine fragments 3

V. CV-204: Type 2 group.
  A. CV-204: Fill or Coner phase
   Odocoileus virginianus
    scapula, L 1
    astragalus, L 1
   Unidentified large mammal 3

BACKGROUND

Copan is in western Honduras on the southeastern periphery of the Maya lowlands, and the ecology (Willey and Leventhal 1979; Rue 1987; Fash 1983) differs from that of other southern lowland Maya sites such as Seibal, which is located to the northwest in Peten, Guatemala. The terrain, climate, and vegetation of western Honduras are transitional to the highlands, and the Copan Valley lies 2,000 ft above sea level amidst rugged hills that rise 1,300 to 2,000 m. Mesic deciduous tropical forest covers valley bottoms, lower hills have upland deciduous forest, and pine-oak montane forest covers higher ridges. The Río Copan, a smallish stream, cuts through the hills forming small valleys or pockets. The "Copan Pocket" has the largest expanse of bottomlands (both floodplain and low terraces), which are well drained and constantly renewed, and the largest expanse of foothills. These ecological advantages must account for the antiquity and density of settlement here despite the fact that rainfall is relatively low (610 m, 1,300 mm).

Seibal, also excavated as a Harvard University project with Willey as principal investigator, provides a good comparison for Copan. Seibal is a more typical lowland site situated on the sizable Pasion River, which is part of the Usumacinta drainage. Vegetation is true tropical rainforest (Lundell 1938), with apparently heavier rainfall, although no specific figures on precipitation are available (Furley 1968).

Tourtellot (1982) investigated settlement in the zone peripheral to the main center at Seibal. At Copan more attention was given to complete clearing of structures, following updated approaches to excavation. The recovery techniques used at Copan and Seibal were similar, however. Excavators did not screen, so the fauna represents primarily larger vertebrates.

Research has revealed differences between archaeological groups at Copan and those at Seibal (Fash 1983). At Copan groups tend to be more agglutinated and to have more than one shared patio space. Fash suggests that the settlement pattern at Copan may reflect a tendency toward larger extended family units than elsewhere in the Maya lowlands.

The Copan Valley settlement survey revealed two major phases of Late Classic occupation: the Cueva phase representing the first half of the Late Classic period and the Coner phase representing the Terminal Late Classic period. The Coner (or Copador) phase dating to between A.D. 700 and 850 contained in situ refuse deposits that excavators could assign to this time period exclusively. A limited amount of in situ refuse with bones dated to the Late Classic Cueva/Coner phase overlap (A.D. 600–700). Other bones of mixed Cueva and Coner phase occurred in construction fill, and I have made use of these data by creating a category labeled All Late Classic Contexts. Seibal was also a prominent center during the Late Classic period, and I shall compare Seibal fauna with all Late Classic contexts at Copan.

The percentages of individual bones (number of individual specimens preserved or NISP) in the Copan faunal sample appear in table D-2 in unmodified and modified form. The unmodified version lists all bones present. In the modified version, I counted multiple bones from one individual animal only once. (The individuals in question are marked by an asterisk in the complete list of bones appearing in table D-1.)

TABLE D-2

Total number of bones for Coner Phase and all Late Classic contexts

	UNMODIFIED				MODIFIED			
Species	Coner Phase Total Bones	%	Late Classic Total Bones	%	Coner Phase Total Bones	%	Late Classic Total Bones	%
Odocoileus virginianus	35	11.1	86	18.2	27	22.5	78	28.2
Dicotyles tayacu	0	0.0	1	0.2	0	0.0	1	0.4
Dicotyles spp.	0	0.0	4	0.8	0	0.0	4	1.4
Tapirus bairdi	0	0.0	1	0.2	0	0.0	1	0.4
Canis familiaris	124	39.2	131	27.7	2	1.7	9	3.2
Procyonidae cf. *Nasua narica*	1	0.3	1	0.2	1	0.8	1	0.4
Felis pardalis	58	18.4	58	12.3	1	0.8	1	0.4
Dasyproctidae cf. *Cuniculus paca*	2	0.6	2	0.4	2	1.7	2	0.7
Didelphis spp.	6	1.9	7	1.5	6	5.0	7	2.5

Total number of bones for Coner Phase and all Late Classic contexts

	UNMODIFIED				MODIFIED			
Species	Coner Phase Total Bones	%	Late Classic Total Bones	%	Coner Phase Total Bones	%	Late Classic Total Bones	%
Bos taurus	1	0.3	2	0.4	1	0.8	2	0.7
Unidentified small mammal	4	1.3	6	1.3	4	3.3	6	2.2
Unidentified medium mammal	1	0.3	1	0.2	1	0.8	1	0.4
Unidentified large mammal	67	21.2	150	31.7	67	55.8	150	54.2
Unidentified very large mammal	2	0.6	2	0.4	2	1.7	2	0.7
Total Mammals	**301**	**95.2**	**452**	**95.5**	**114**	**95.0**	**265**	**95.7**
Glaucidium brasilianum	11	3.5	11	2.3	2	1.7	2	0.7
Unidentified bird	4	1.3	6	1.3	4	3.3	6	2.2
Total Birds	**15**	**4.8**	**17**	**3.6**	**6**	**5.0**	**8**	**2.9**
Pseudemys scripta	0	0.0	1	0.2	0	0.0	1	0.4
Unidentified turtle	0	0.0	3	0.6	0	0.0	3	1.1
Total Turtles	**0**	**0.0**	**4**	**0.8**	**0**	**0.0**	**4**	**1.4**
Total Vertebrates	**316**		**473**		**120**		**277**	

Many of the bones were fragmentary, and I could not identify them as to species. The Unidentified Large Mammal category is probably white-tailed deer *(Odocoileus virginianus)*. The Unidentified Very Large Mammal category may be tapir *(Tapirus bairdi)* or cattle *(Bos taurus)* introduced by the Spaniards. The sample did not consist exclusively of closed prehistoric contexts.

Table D-3 presents the minimum number of individuals (MNI) at Copan according to maximal and minimal methods. In the maximal method, the minimum numbers are calculated for each structure and the results totaled. In the minimal method, the minimum numbers are calculated for the sample as a whole. Both minimum numbers counts include only those bones that I identified as to species.

The MNI method of calculating bone frequencies gets around the problem of bone inflation when more than one bone from an individual animal occurs. Nevertheless, in a sample as small as this, the MNI method overrepresents infrequently occurring species. Thus, the discussion below is based on both the NISP and MNI data.

TABLE D-3

Total number of MNI for Coner Phase and all Late Classic contexts

| | MAXIMAL METHOD | | | | MINIMAL METHOD | | | |
| | Coner Phase | | Late Classic | | Coner Phase | | Late Classic | |
Species	MNI	%	MNI	%	MNI	%	MNI	%
Odocoileus virginianus	8	47.1	16	47.1	5	35.7	6	28.6
Dicotyles tayacu	0	0.0	1	2.9	0	0.0	1	
4.8Dicotyles spp.	0	0.0	1	2.9	0	0.0	1	4.8
Tapirus bairdi	0	0.0	1	2.9	0	0.0	1	4.8
Canis familiaris	2	11.8	5	14.7	2	14.3	3	14.3
Procyonidae cf. Nasua narica	1	5.9	1	2.9	1	7.1	1	4.8
Felis pardalis	1	5.9	1	2.9	1	7.1	1	4.8
Dasyproctidae cf. Cuniculus paca	1	5.9	1	2.9	1	7.1	1	4.8
Didelphis spp.	2	11.8	3	8.8	1	7.1	1	4.8
Bos taurus	0	0.0	1	2.9	1	7.1	2	9.5
Total Mammals	15	88.2	31	91.2	12	85.7	18	85.7
Glaucidium brasilianum	2	11.8	2	5.9	2	14.3	2	9.5
Pseudemys scripta	0	0.0	1	2.9	0	0.0	1	4.8
Total Vertebrates	17		34		14		21	

RESULTS OF FAUNAL ANALYSIS

White-tailed Deer

All methods for calculating frequencies indicate that the overwhelming majority of bones were those of white-tailed deer (*Odocoileus virginianus*). The total white-tailed deer count is probably much higher because most of the Unidentified Large Mammals undoubtedly also belong to this species. The modified NISP for these two categories combined (table D-2) is 78 percent for the Coner phase and 82 percent for all Late Classic contexts.

This Copan fauna contrasts sharply with fauna from Longyear's (1948) Sub-Pottery Deposit at the site, where burned and broken bones of small animals were associated with plant charcoal and blackened river stones that perhaps formed a hearth. Longyear never published faunal iden-tifications, but an exhibit at the Peabody Museum displayed a few bones of paca-agouti-rabbit-sized small game as well as a tapir bone. No one has ever dated the Sub-Pottery Deposit, although the fauna appears consistent with a heavily forested environment.

Deer are browsers, and their populations rise sharply with the introduction of agriculture, which provides a maximum of forest edge habitat. Most Maya agricultural sites have deer bones, although the degree to which the Copanecos focused on this species is unusual. This difference is evident in a comparison between Late Classic fauna from settlement at Copan and that from the peripheral zone at Seibal. White-tailed deer compose 36 percent of the Coner phase minimum numbers and 29 percent of the minimum numbers (both calculated according to the minimal method) of all Late Classic contexts at Copan (table D-3). Deer made up 19 percent of the minimum numbers in the Late Classic peripheral zone at Seibal (Pohl 1985).

Small sample size cannot account for the low species diversity at Copan entirely. The peripheral plain and peripheral fancy structures at Seibal produced only a slightly larger faunal sample— 43 total minimum numbers.

I expected to find higher percentages of deer bones at Seibal than at Copan. Seibal has access to the savanna region of central Peten, Guatemala, a habitat with a maximum of the forest edge environment that deer love. The Maya appear to have settled the central Peten savannas sparsely in the Late Classic period (Rice and Rice 1979), and deer might well have been plentiful there.

The high percentages of deer in the Copan settlement must reflect strong food preferences. This conclusion is consistent with the very low representation of turtle bones at Copan—only 3 percent of the total minimum numbers (calculated by the minimal method) for all Late Classic contexts. Turtles are very abundant in most Classic period refuse from sites of the southern lowlands (Pohl 1976, in press). For example, turtles comprise 33 percent of minimum numbers in all Late Classic peripheral zone contexts at Seibal. Even though the residents of Seibal may have had more turtles available to them in the Pasion River, Copanecos could have taken turtles from the Copan River had they wanted to.

The low species diversity, and perhaps the low total bone count, undoubtedly also reflect human destruction of animal habitats around Copan. The pollen sequence from a core in Petapilla Swamp near Copan (Rue 1987) has revealed that by the end of the Classic period the Maya had completely cleared the valley floor and foothills, and even montane forest may have been partially stripped judging from the low percentages of pine *(Pinus)* pollen.

The extent of deforestation raises the question of where the Copanecos got their venison and whether they might have managed herds of deer or raised the animals around their house compounds (Pohl 1976, in press). Bishop Landa (Tozzer 1941:127) observed Maya women raising deer in sixteenth-century Yucatan: "they raise

other domestic animals, and let the deer suck their breasts, by which means they raise them and make them so tame that they never go into the woods." We have two other historic period references to this practice, one from the lowlands (Martínez Hernández 1929) and one from the highlands (Ximénez 1967). There is no specific proof that the Copan Maya also nurtured deer in the Late Classic period. The deer bones from CV-43 to 47, a high-status (Type 3) extended family compound with servants' quarters, did include three antler fragments that had been shed. This evidence is inconclusive, however, because residents might have brought shed antlers home for some utilitarian use.

The Copan Maya elite might have raised deer because they needed them for ceremonial offerings as well as for general consumption. The Maya looked on deer as animal supernaturals linked to agricultural fertility (Pohl 1981), and a deer offering was required in many rituals. Palacio (Tozzer and Allen 1910:349) described a deer sacrifice that may have taken place near ancient Copan in a report to King Philip II of Spain. Celebrants took a live deer to the courtyard of their temple, where they cut up the animal and cooked it while they danced. The priest and his attendants burned the heart in a brazier and offered the head and legs to their idol, and then repaired to the priest's house, where they feasted on the venison and blood before the statue of the deity.

An examination of the elements of white-tailed deer represented in the Copan faunal sample (table D-4) reveals a skewed distribution of body parts. Antler fragments were especially numerous, and the majority occurred in CV-43 and associated structures. Most antler fragments were very weathered, and a rodent had chewed one, indicating that the Maya had left them lying around the house compound for some time. Although I noted no use-wear because of the poor and fragmentary condition of the antlers, their presence suggests that the Maya might have had them in the residential area CV-43 to -47 for use in some sort of craft activity. Two antlers showed traces of having been cut from the skull, and one was modified by having the burr removed. One fragment was burned, perhaps to harden it. If the Maya did use the antler fragments in craft production, the other artifacts do not provide a clue as to what that activity might

TABLE D-4

Elements of white-tailed deer

Element	Right	Left	Undetermined	Total Elemental Bones	Corrected Frequency*	Percent
Antler			15	15	7.50	20.7
Vertebrae			4	4	0.13	0.4
Scapula	4	3		7	3.50	9.7
Humerus	6	5		11	5.50	15.2
Ulna	4	4		8	4.00	11.0
Radius	3	3		6	3.00	8.3
Innominate	2	1		3	1.50	4.1
Femur	3	2		5	2.50	6.9
Tibia	5	1		6	3.00	8.3
Astragalus		6		6	3.00	8.3
Calcaneum	1	2		3	1.50	4.1
Metapodial	2		2	4	1.00	2.8
Phalanges (1, 2, 3)			2	2	0.08	0.2
Total Deer Bones				80	36.21	

*Total bones divided by number of elements of that type in the body

have been. Leventhal (personal communication 1988) reports no unusual distribution of ceramics, flint, or obsidian from the CV-43 to -47 area.

Other explanations may account for the antlers. The deer antlers in CV-43 to 47 might represent remains of ceremonialism that the elite would have directed. For example, Bishop Landa (Tozzer 1941:155-156) tells us that at an important ceremony in the month of Zip, celebrants assembled at the house of one of their number and performed a dance holding a deer skull and an arrow. Representations of deer on Classic period pots and in the Postclassic codices are often males without antlers (Pohl 1981), possibly because the removal of the antlers, as shown in the Calcehtok Vase, signified regeneration (Coe 1975; Pohl 1981). Maya gods (Pohl 1981: fig. 5) and ball game players frequently appear with deer headdresses minus the antlers (fig. D-1). The Maya probably fashioned these antlerless headdresses from real deer skulls, and this practice might have resulted in antlers being discarded in domestic compounds.

Other parts of the white-tailed deer are underrepresented: the innominate, calcaneum, metapodials, and particularly the phalanges and vertebrae. These elements may have been destroyed in the cooking process or chewed up by dogs. The phalanges may have been taken away with the skin, which was probably tanned.

Previous research on Maya fauna has indicated that left animal elements may occur in frequencies greater than one might expect by chance (e.g., Pendergast 1971). The Seibal fauna had a statistically significant bias toward left deer bones (Pohl 1985). At Copan I discerned no real trend in the deer fauna as a whole, although there was a predominance of right tibiae and left astragali (table D-4). Since the haunch is the prize piece of meat, one might expect to find directional bias in the hind limb. The faunal sample is small, however, and this evidence alone does not confirm a pattern in the bones. Nevertheless, excavators did find an offering of the complete left hind limb of a deer next to an early floor or remains of an early house in CV-45.

Other evidence for offerings of left deer limbs has been appearing. One example comes from western Belize at the Guerra locality, a settlement zone located about 1 km south of the Buenavista del Cayo organizational center on the east bank of the Lower Mopan River. There excavators uncovered two left deer haunches in a Late Early Classic (ca. A.D. 450) dedicatory cache beneath the stair block on the north side of a suburban, middle-status, residential platform. Smashed pottery vessels, obsidian blades, and abundant carbonized organic material accompanied the faunal remains (Ball, personal communication 1986). At the prominent center of Caracol in South Central Belize, the remains of at least four left deer limbs occurred in the hallway bordering high status palace rooms in the Late to Terminal Classic (post A.D. 750) Caana range structures (Diane and Arlen Chase, personal communication 1989).

In many areas of aboriginal Mesoamerica directional symbolism is pervasive, and the side of an animal seems to have held special significance (Pohl 1985:142). Traditionally the Maya have recognized left as the direction of the underworld, the place where the sun sets. Left is of course also the side of the heart, the source of life. Unfortunately, we have no surviving ethnographic or ethnohistoric practices that allow us to decipher the meaning of left deer haunches. Nevertheless, the heart offering did figure prominently in the deer sacrifice that Palacio witnessed (Tozzer and Allen 1910:349).

Domestic Animals

Domestic dog *(Canis familiaris)* was the second most abundant animal in the Copan settlement fauna. Two or perhaps three individuals are represented by partial skeletons, and the two most complete ones had pathologies. One of these came from the middle of the plaza of CV-68, a Type 4 group and one of the largest sites in the Copan Valley outside of the Copan Main Center. The right front paw of this dog had been injured, resulting in new bone formation (exotoses) on metacarpals II and III and the fusion (ankylosis) of metacarpals IV and V (fig. D-2).

The same individual had an unusual characteristic in the mandible. The lower right mandible (the only one we have) lacked premolars anterior to the molars (fig. D-3). Because the mandible was broken, we do not know exactly how many teeth the dog was missing. This excavation lot

yielded three incisors, but canines were absent. The mandible may represent a pathology or abnormality. Alternatively, the dog may be our first tangible evidence for the Mexican hairless breed, *xoloitzcuintli* or *sholo,* known as *ixbil ahbil* in the Maya language (Lejón 1625).

The Mexican hairless dog is medium-sized, as this specimen is, and today has the osteological peculiarity of an "almost invariable absence of teeth between the foremost molars and the incisors" (Wright 1970:39). The Spaniards saw the Maya using hairless dogs to hunt deer and birds in Yucatan (Roys 1931:328). The absence of canines and premolars might have been an advantage to hunters (perhaps even selected for in breeding) because the dogs would theoretically have caused less damage to game before the hunter himself could reach the prey.

Why are there not more dogs lacking premolars and canines—even in a sizable (93 MNIs) Late Postclassic population that lived on Cozumel Island (Hamblin 1984) shortly before the Spaniards noted the presence of the hairless breed in Yucatan? The high frequency of this dental peculiarity in present-day animals may be due to the fact that the breed nearly died out and has only recently been revived from a very limited gene pool. This speculation about the presence of the Mexican hairless must await verification through study of larger populations of ancient Maya dogs.

Archaeologists uncovered another skeleton of a crippled dog in refuse that was piled up along the back wall of a terrace to the east of Structure E1 in CV-43. This dog would have had particular difficulty walking because the calcanea were completely fused to the astragali in both hind feet (fig. D-4).

This skeleton lacked a head. The Maya might have used the head for a sacrificial offering, as illustrated in a Late Classic polychrome vase from Nebaj (Pohl and Pohl 1983: fig. 3.5). Further evidence for the use of dog crania for sacrifices comes from Late Postclassic bones taken from the cenotes at Mayapan (Pohl 1983).

Another excavation lot from Structure E1 yielded a dog axis deformed in such a way that the animal's head was twisted to the side (fig. D-5). The presence of these handicapped dogs, all of which had been reared to adulthood, and the occurrence of much of the skeleton in two instances suggests sentimental attachment to the animals beyond use for hunting or food and purposeful burial.

Women probably raised dogs in their Copan house compounds (Pohl and Feldman 1982). A number of Classic period pottery figurines (fig. D-6) show women nurturing small animals that are probably dogs or coatis (see below). Ethnohistoric accounts tell us that the Maya raised dogs in their houses (Ximénez 1967:167) and that these compounds were the domain of women (Tozzer 1949:127). Women undoubtedly raised dogs as they raise pigs today (Pohl and Feldman 1982; Nimis 1982).

Procyonids are rare at lowland Maya sites (Pohl 1990), with the exception of Late Postclassic Cozumel Island (Hamblin 1984). The fragmentary procyonid humerus from Structure E1 in CV-43 at Copan was large and has therefore been tentatively identified as coati (Nasua narica) rather than raccoon (Procyon lotor) following Leopold's (1972) reports of representative weights of these two animals in Mexico. Bishop Landa (Tozzer 1941:204–205) tells us that Maya women raised coatis as pets and for food. Among the modern Lacandon Maya, coati is a food reserved exclusively for women (Baer 1971).

Ritual Offerings

The two most likely remains of ritual offerings are the bones of an ocelot (identified by staff in the Mammal Department of Harvard University's Museum of Comparative Zoology) and two ferruginous pygmy owls (identified by Pierce Brodkorb of the University of Florida). The partial pygmy owl skeletons (Glaucidium brasilianum) were part of a small Coner phase cache below the plaza floor in CV-115, a Type 2 group. One individual was covered with red pigment and lay within a Spondylus shell, which itself was within a carved, polished brown vessel containing the other owl. The owls' heads were missing, and the Maya may have removed them as part of the ceremony, as illustrated in codices such as the Dresden (Villacorta and Villacorta 1930).

The Maya liked to use pygmy owls in caches. Another example is the headless owl inside a limestone vessel containing remnants of textile

and a spectacular turquoise mosaic-backed mirror at Chichen Itza (Morris, Charlot, and Morris 1931:189), which also dates to the Terminal Late Classic period.

We can only guess why the pygmy owl attracted the Maya. The Copan owls in the CV-115 cache were males, the smaller of the two sexes. Cave 3 at Copan contained three jars with the charred remains of small rodents as well as the bones of children (Gordon 1898:11). The Maya often used small animals for ritual.

The pygmy owl's habitat may also account for the use of these birds. They fly about the entrances to caves (Fisher 1953), which the Maya believed to be sources of life-giving water and avenues of communication with the gods (Pohl and Pohl 1983).

The Maya left evidence of the sacredness of caves at the Copan Main Center (Longyear 1952). For example, Stelae I and N had caches containing 24 stalactites, along with evidence for the rain cult known as the Cult of the Sea consisting of a stingray spine, two lumps of coral, and two marine shells with traces of red pigment. Girard (1962:197–205) suggests that elaborate cruciform substela vaults at Copan represented caves, and he draws parallels with the present-day Chorti, perhaps the descendants of the prehistoric Copanecos, whose foliated cross and altar have a pit or cave in front said to represent the umbilical cord of the world.

The other special deposit was the burial, probably during the Coner phase, of an immature ocelot (Felis pardalis) below the plaza floor in CV-17, a Type 3 group. The absence of any vertebrae or third phalanges suggests that the Maya had removed the prized spotted skin before burying the animal.

The Maya frequently cached whole or partial skeletons of ocelot as well as puma and jaguar in high-status contexts (Pohl 1983:73–74), and Copan has produced more such burials than any other site to date. Under the main mound in the Great Plaza of the Copan Main Center, the Maya buried the teeth and some bones of one feline said to be a jaguar and covered them first with red pigment and then with a layer of charcoal. In a smaller mound, 100 yards to the south, another cat skeleton occurred along with fragments of human bones and dog teeth (Maudslay 1889–1902:20). The disposition of Copan felines is consistent with that at Seibal (Pohl 1985), where cat bones occur only in very high status contexts.

Deforestation in the Copan Valley (Rue 1987) by the end of the Classic period must have meant that Copanecos went to some trouble to procure felines. Jaguars and ocelots are forest dwellers; jaguars reside primarily in undisturbed *monte*. The presence of spotted cat offerings at Copan is a measure of the high position of the site in the Maya political hierarchy.

Fauna and Social Status

The sixteenth- and seventeenth-century historic data indicate that meat consumption was closely tied to social status. The elite ate meat more frequently than did commoners, and animal consumption frequently occurred in the context of public or private ritual feasting (Relaciones de Yucatán 1898–1900:244, 271: López de Cogolludo 1688, I:228, 235, 296; Roys 1943). These reports probably refer to prestigious meat of larger animals. Bones of larger animals are the only ones available to me from prehistoric Copan given the problems of preservation and recovery (i.e., use of one-half-inch screen).

Table D-5 presents the distribution of Copan fauna by type of group. The higher the group number, the higher the status. The counts include only bones from the Coner phase, which represents in situ refuse. The figures (NISP) are modified so that the bones from a single individual were counted only once. The highest-status Type 4 group was only test pitted, but structures in group Types 1 through 3 were completely excavated.

TABLE D-5

Total bone counts for group types in Coner Phase*

Species	Type 1 Total Bones	%	Type 2 Total Bones	%	Type 3 Total Bones	%	Type 4 Total Bones	%
Odocoileus virginianus	5	45.5	3	12.0	19	23.2	0	0.0
Dicotyles tayacu	0	0.0	0	0.0	0	0.0	0	0.0
Dicotyles spp.	0	0.0	0	0.0	0	0.0	0	0.0
Tapirus bairdi	0	0.0	0	0.0	0	0.0	0	0.0
Canis familiaris	0	0.0	0	0.0	1	1.2	1	100.0
Procyonidae cf. *Nasua narica*	0	0.0	0	0.0	1	1.2	0	0.0
Felis pardalis	0	0.0	0	0.0	1	1.2	0	0.0
Dasyproctidae cf. *Cuniculus paca*	0	0.0	0	0.0	2	2.4	0	0.0
Didelphis spp.	0	0.0	1	4.0	5	6.1	0	0.0
Bos taurus	0	0.0	0	0.0	0	0.0	0	0.0
Unidentified small mammal	0	0.0	0	0.0	4	4.9	0	0.0
Unidentified medium mammal	0	0.0	0	0.0	1	1.2	0	0.0
Unidentified large mammal	6	54.5	18	72.0	43	52.4	0	0.0
Unidentified very large mammal	0	0.0	1	4.0	1	1.2	0	0.0
Total Mammals	11	100.0	23	92.0	78	95.0	1	100.0
Glaucidium brasilianum	0	0.0	2	8.0	0	0.0	0	0.0
Unidentified bird	0	0.0	0	0.0	4	4.9	0	0.0
Total Birds	0	0.0	2	8.0	4	4.9	0	0.0
Pseudemys scripta	0	0.0	0	0.0	0	0.0	0	0.0
Unidentified turtle	0	0.0	0	0.0	0	0.0	0	0.0

Total Turtles	0	0.0	0	0.0	0	0.0	0	0.0
Total Vertebrates	11		25		82		1	

*Modified counts

The data show that the higher-status Type 3 group had more large animal bones and greater diversity of species than Type 1 or 2. Type 3 contexts had deer, dog, birds, coati, ocelot, opossum, and probably paca relished today for its fat, in addition to unidentified small, medium, and large mammals. Since excavators cleared structures completely, this finding is real and not the result of greater sampling in larger, higher-status buildings. Elites in Type 3 groups may have shared their high-status food with kin or clients living in Type 1 and 2 groups in the context of feasting.

CONCLUSIONS

The fauna from Late Classic period settlement in the "Copan Pocket" reveals that Copanecos had a strong preference for venison, as did many lowland Maya (Pohl 1976, 1990). The percentages of white-tailed deer bones are particularly high at Copan, however, while pollen data suggest that the Maya had virtually eliminated the forests of the region late in the Classic period. In view of the evidence for demand for animals together with habitat destruction, I have suggested that women might have raised deer for food, ritual offerings, dance headdresses, skins, and bone blanks for tools.

Women did raise dogs for sacrifices, for sustenance, and for such hunting that was possible given animal habitat destruction. Women nurtured at least three crippled dogs into adulthood. One dog had a dental peculiarity—lack of premolars and possibly also canines—and may provide evidence for the prehistoric presence of the Mexican hairless breed (known as *ixbil ahbil* in Mayan) that hunters used to track down deer and birds in the early historic period.

Copanecos mirrored other lowland Maya in their use of left deer haunches, pygmy owls, whole felines, and perhaps also dogs' heads in ceremonial offerings. Various probes into the Copan Main Center and now the surrounding settlement have revealed that Copanecos performed an unusual number of feline burials. Before burial of the young ocelot described here, the elite may have removed the spotted pelt to fashion high-status paraphernalia for themselves. The fact that they were able to procure these animals, which inhabit forested areas, testifies to the political power of the Copan center.

Habitat destruction may account for the low overall bone counts of mammals at Copan, but the virtual absence of turtles, a common food elsewhere (Pohl 1990) in the lowlands, is puzzling. One would expect that more turtles would have been available in spite of hypothetical increased sediment loads in the rivers due to deforestation and erosion.

Although the total number of bones in the excavated plaza was low, I found that distribution of fauna was unequal. Higher-status residential compounds had more bones of larger animals and more species represented than lower-status houses.

In sum, this faunal sample from Late Classic period settlement in the "Copan Pocket" shows that animal consumption is a very good indicator of consumption patterns among residents of different social status. Indeed, animal consumption in the form of meat-eating, display of spotted skins, and caches was one of the ways the elite asserted their privileged positions.

ACKNOWLEDGMENTS

Mary LePoer and Bridget Beers helped with tabulation of the fauna. Richard Brunck produced the photographs.

BIBLIOGRAPHY

Baer, P.
1971 "Lacandone Subsistence," in *Two Studies on the Lacandones of Mexico,* by P. Baer and W. R. Merrifield. Summer Institute of Linguistics, Publication 33. University of Oklahoma, Norman.

Coe, M.
1975 *Classic Maya Pottery at Dumbarton Oaks.* Dumbarton Oaks, Washington, D.C.

Douglas, M., and B. Isherwood
1979 *The World of Goods.* Basic Books, New York.

Fash, W.
1983 "Deducing Social Organization from Classic Maya Settlement Patterns: A Case Study from the Copan Valley," in *Civilization in the Ancient Americas,* R. Leventhal and A. Kolata, eds., pp. 261–288. University of New Mexico Press, Albuquerque, and Peabody Museum Press, Cambridge, Massachusetts.

Fisher, H.
1953 "The Birds," in *Faunal and Archaeological Researches in Yucatan Caves,* R. Hatt, H. Fisher, D. Langebartel, and G. Brainerd, eds. Cranbrook Institute of Science, Bulletin no. 33.

Furley, P.
1968 "The University of Edinburgh, British Honduras–Yucatan Expedition." *Geographical Journal* 134:38–54.

Girard, R.
1962 *Los Mayas Eternos.* Antigua Libreria Robredo, Mexico City.

Gordon, G. B.
1898 *Caverns of Copan, Honduras.* Memoirs of the Peabody Museum, vol. 1, no. 5. Cambridge, Massachusetts.

Hamblin, N. L.
1984 *Animal Use by the Cozumel Maya.* University of Arizona Press, Tucson.

Joyce, T. A.
1933 "The Pottery Whistle-Figurines at Lubaantun." *Journal of the Royal Anthropological Institute* 63:XV–XXV.

Lejón, D.
1625 Bocabulario de Mayathan por su Abesario (Vienna Dictionary). Manuscript in the National Library in Vienna, Austria. From microfilm in the Library of Pomona College, Claremont, California.

Leopold, A. S.
1972 *Wildlife of Mexico.* University of California Press, Berkeley.

Longyear, John M.
1948 "A Sub-Pottery Deposit at Copan, Honduras." *American Antiquity* 13:248–249.
1952 *Copan Ceramics: A Study of Southeastern Maya Pottery.* Carnegie Institution of Washington, Publication 597. Washington, D.C.

López, de Cogolludo, D.
1688 Los tres Siglos de la Dominacion Española en Yucatan o sea Historia de esta Provincia. 2 vols. Akademische Druk-u. Verlangsanstalt, Graz (1971).

Lundell, C. L.
1938 "Plants Probably Utilized by the Old Empire Maya of Peten and Adjacent Lowlands." *Michigan Academy of Science, Arts and Letters* 24:37–56.

Martínez, Hernández, J., ed.
1929 Diccionario de Motul: Maya–Español. Atribuido a Fray Antonio Ciudad Real y Arte de Lengua Maya par Fray Juan Coronel. Mérida, Companía Tipográphia Yucateca, S.A.

Maudslay, Alfred P.
1889– "Archaeology," *Biologia Centrali-Americana,*
1902 4 vols. R. H. Porter, London.

Morris, E. H., J. Charlot, and A. A. Morris
1931 *The Temple of the Warriors at Chichen Itza.* Carnegie Institution of Washington, Publication 406. Washington, D.C.

Morris, W., and L. Schele
1980 Commentary. Palenque Round Table Conference. Palenque, Mexico.

Nimis, M. M.
1982 "The Contemporary Role of Women in Lowland Maya Livestock Production," in *Maya Subsistence*, K. Flannery, ed., pp. 313–326. Academic Press, New York.

Pendergast, D. M.
1971 *Excavations at Eduardo Quiroz Cave, British Honduras.* Royal Ontario Museum of Art and Archaeology, Occasional Papers, no. 21. Toronto.

Pohl, Mary
1976 "The Ethnozoology of the Maya: An Analysis of Faunal Remains from Five Sites in Peten, Guatemala." Ph.D. dissertation, Harvard University, Cambridge, Massachusetts.
1981 "Ritual Continuity and Transformation in Mesoamerica: Reconstructing the Ancient Maya *Cuch* Ritual." *American Antiquity* 46:513–529.
1983 "Maya Ritual Faunas: Vertebrate Remains from Burials, Caches, Caves, and Cenotes in the Maya Lowlands," in *Civilization in the Ancient Americas*, R. M. Leventhal and A. L. Kolata, eds., pp. 55–104. University of New Mexico Press, Albuquerque, and Peabody Museum Press, Cambridge, Massachusetts.
1985 "The Privileges of Maya Elites: Prehistoric Vertebrate Fauna from Seibal," in *Prehistoric Lowland Maya Environment and Subsistence Economy*, Mary Pohl, ed., pp. 133–145. Peabody Museum Papers, vol. 77. Harvard University, Cambridge, Massachusetts.
1990 *Excavations at Seibal: The Ethnozoology of the Maya: Faunal Remains from Five Sites in Peten, Guatemala*, G. R. Willey, ed., pp. 143–174. Memoirs of the Peabody Museum, vol. 17, no. 3. Cambridge, Massachusetts.

Pohl, M., and L. Feldman
1982 "The Traditional Role of Women and Animals in Lowland Maya Economy," in *Maya Subsistence*, K. Flannery, ed., pp. 295–312. Academic Press, New York.

Pohl, M., and J. Pohl
1983 "Ancient Maya Cave Rituals." *Archaeology* 36:28–32, 50–51.

Relaciones de Yucatán
1898– *Colección de Documentos Inéditos Relativos*
1900 *al Descubrimiento Conquista y Organización de las Antiguas Posesiones Españolas de Ultramar.* 2nd series, vols. 11 and 13, Madrid.

Rice, P., and D. Rice
1979 "Home on the Range." *Archaeology* 32:16–25.

Roys, R. L.
1931 *The Ethnobotany of the Maya*, Middle American Research Institute, Publication 2. Tulane University, New Orleans.
1943 *The Indian Background of Colonial Yucatan.* Carnegie Institution of Washington, Publication 548. Washington, D.C.

Rue, D.
1987 "Early Agriculture and Early Postclassic Maya Occupation in Western Honduras." *Nature* 326:285–286.

Tourtellot, G., III
1982 "Ancient Maya Settlement at Seibal, Peten, Guatemala: Peripheral Survey and Excavation." Ph.D. dissertation, Harvard University, Cambridge, Massachusetts.

Tozzer, A. M.
1941 *Landa's Relación de las Cosas de Yucatan.* Papers of the Peabody Museum, vol. 18. Cambridge, Massachusetts.

Tozzer, A. M., and G. Allen
1910 *Animal Figures in the Maya Codices.* Papers of the Peabody Museum, vol. 4. Cambridge, Massachusetts.

Villacorta C., J. A., and C. A. Villacorta R.
1930 *Codices Maya: Dresdensis-Peresianus-Tro-Cortesianus.* Tipografía Nacional, Guatemala.

Willey, G. R.
1972 *The Artifacts of Altar de Sacrificios*, Papers of the Peabody Museum, vol. 64. Cambridge, Massachusetts.

Willey, G. R., and R. M. Leventhal
1979 "Prehistoric Settlement at Copan," in *Maya Archaeology and Ethnohistory*, N. Hammond and G. R. Willey, eds., pp. 75–102. University of Texas Press, Austin.

Wright, N. P.
1970 *A Guide to Mexican Mammals and Reptiles.* Minutiae Mexicana, Mexico.

Ximénez, F.
1967 *Historia Natural del Reino de Guatemala.* Socieded de Geographía e Historia de Guatemala, Special Publication, 14.

Figure D-1. God L, the Underworld Deity, dances with a deer headdress and a spear in the Madrid Codex (Villacorta and Villacorta 1930).

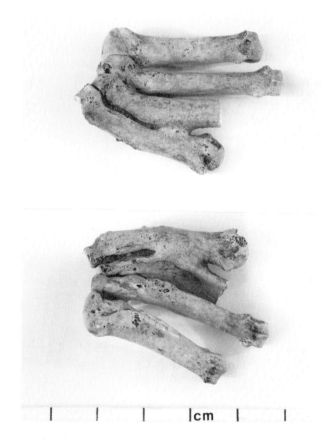

Figure D-2. Volar (top) and palmar (bottom) views of a wounded dog paw with new bone formation on metacarpals II and III and fusion of metacarpals IV and V.

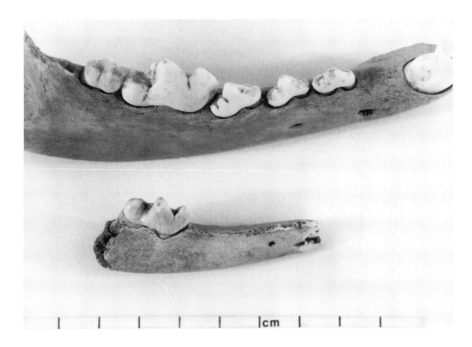

Figure D-3. Modern dog mandible (top) compared with mandible of Copan dog (below) illustrating the lack of premolars in the prehistoric specimen. Is this an ancient Mexican hairless?

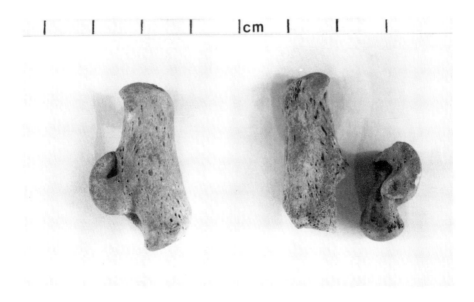

Figure D-4. One of the two fused calcanea and astragali (left) belonging to an ancient crippled dog. The normal bones from the dog shown in figures D-2 and D-3 appear at right.

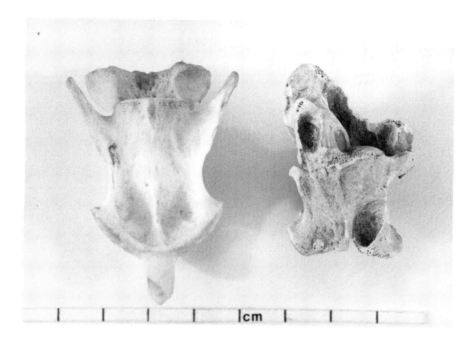

Figure D-5.   Modern dog axis (left) and a severely deformed Copan dog axis (right) resulting in a crooked head.

Figure D-6.   Late Classic Maya pottery figurines depicting a woman nurturing dogs or coatis: a, Altar de Sacrificios (Willey 1972); b–d, Lubaantun (Joyce 1933).

The Mollusks of Copan

Lawrence H. Feldman

Museum of Anthropology,

University of Missouri

This report, completed in July 1982, is based upon the analysis of shells obtained as a result of the early G. B. Gordon and H. J. Spinden expeditions to Copan and the recent Harvard Copan Project excavations in or near Copan, Honduras, that are now in storage at the Peabody Museum. This must be considered a preliminary report on Copan mollusks, as it does not include material obtained by Baudez or Sanders or the reports of Stromsvik (1942) and Longyear (1952).

Ten Pacific (Tropical West American), six Caribbean, one that may be either Pacific or Caribbean, six freshwater, and four land species were present in the available sample and reports (table E-1). Copan is an unusual lowland Maya site in having so many Pacific species represented (cf. Feldman 1970), even more so in having species representing such a wide range of environments (e.g., rocky shore, mangrove swamps, sandy beaches). All of these species are potentially available from the shores of either Guatemala or El Salvador. Of the Caribbean species, one (*S. gigas*) almost certainly came from the east coast of the Yucatan peninsula (or the Bay Islands), one (known from the literature) has not actually been seen in the inspected Copan material (*P. apicina*), and one has the unique distinction (*P. erectus*) of not being known from any other Mesoamerican site.

Of the four land species, two (*O. princep* and *N. dysoni*) deserve special attention. *O. princeps* appears to be associated elsewhere (e.g., at Seibal [Feldman 1978] and in Belize [Feldman 1979]) with ultimate phases, probably being more indicative of second growth vegetation than human occupation. This may also be true at Copan. *N. dysoni* has a converse implication, representing disturbed areas (e. g., swiddening). Its minor presence in the caches, assuming as is true elsewhere, that the mollusk never had any cultural function, indicates that the caches were to some extent not totally sealed off from outside access.

Freshwater species number six. One, *P. flagellata,* may be omitted from the discussion since the specimen in the Peabody collections came from the Ulua Valley, where it was a common food resource in sites of all periods (Howard Lynn, personal communication). *N. goascoranensis,* also common in the Ulua Valley (and at Naco [cf. Wonderley 1981]), is exceedingly rare at Copan. The presence of *Succinea* and the Hydrobidae is something of an enigma since it is hard to visualize their being noticed by the local inhabitants, much less serving any useful function. One possible explanation for their presence is in association with a water plant that did serve some purpose. This seems to be the case at Cuello Belize, where such very small freshwater shells are found with utilized reeds (Charles Mikucek, personal communication). Another, which, given the known climatic conditions in the area, is by

TABLE E-1
List of mollusks

Tropical West American

Spondylus calcifer (Carpenter 1856)   R
Spondylus princeps (Broderip 1833)   R
Ostrea palmula (Carpenter 1856)   R
Chama buddiana (C. B. Adams 1852)   R
Anadara grandis (Broderip and Sowerby 1829)   B
Melongena patula (Broderip and Sowerby 1829)   Sa
Muricanthus callidinus (Berry 1958)
Pinctada mazatlanica (Hanley 1856)   R
Oliva porphyria (Linnaeus 1758)   Sa
Oliva spicata (Rodding 1798)   Sa

Caribbean

Spondylus americanus (Hermann 1781)   R
Lyropecten nodosus (Linnaeus 1758)   Sa
Conus spurius (Gmelin 1791)
Strombus gigas (Linnaeus 1758)   Sa
Petaloconchus erectus (Dall 1888)   R
Prunum apicina (Menke 1828)   Sa

Either Tropical West American or Caribbean

Strombus gracilior (Sowerby 1825) or *Strombus pugilis* (Linnaeus 1758)

Freshwater

Pachychilus corvinus (Morelet 1849)
Pachychilus largillierti (Phillipi 1843)
Nephronais goascoranensis (Lea 1858)
Succinea sp.
Pomacea flagellata (Say 1829)
Hydrobidae

Land

Orthalicus princeps (Broderip 1833)
Neocyclotus dysoni (Pfeiffer 1852)
Bulimulus unicolor (Sowerby 1833)
Lamellaxis micra (D'Orbigny 1835)

KEY TO MARINE ENVIRONMENT CODE:
R   Rocky shore
B   Brackish water/mangrove swamp
Sa Sandy shore to 10 meters

no means impossible, is that they denote the presence of temporary bodies of water, perhaps due to exceptionally heavy rainfall.

The most common freshwater genus, *Pachychilus*, is the edible snail known as the jute in highland Guatemala. It is divided into several different species, the boundaries between which have yet to be established in a completely satisfactory manner in the literature. At Copan there are two separate species (*P. corvinus* and *P. largillierti*). Significant differences exist in their distribution (cf. tables E-2 and E-3). In addition, there was one in function since none of the *P. largillierti* was modified and all were encrusted with limy deposits. Usage of *P. corvinus* as a snack food, the shell being broken and the live animal sucked out and consumed raw, is still common in the Guatemalan highlands (personal observation). This practice is attested to by the most common modification, tipping (removal of the tip of the spire). At other localities in Mesoamerica, even at Naco in Honduras (where the animal was boiled in its shell [Wonderley 1981]), different procedures were used to process this food resource. Nor was it only a food resource, some lowland Maya processed freshwater shells for lime (Nations 1979; Hellmuth 1977). One wonders if the *P. largillierti* were not intentionally being mined from some natural deposit of discarded shell with this aim in mind. Still the very few on the site, plus their presence in late deposits, suggests another possibility: that they, like the very small freshwater snails, somehow arrived on the site naturally (after abandonment?) during periods of extreme wetness.

TABLE E-2
Mollusks per ceramic complex, a partial listing

	Coner	Mixed	Late Acbi
O. princeps	1		
P. corvinus:	10	61	24
tipped	3	44	16
broken	4	8	6
limy	3	1	0
unmodified	0	8	2
P. largillierti	10	3	
Marine	6	4	2
Total	27	68	26

TABLE E-3

Mollusks per archaeological context,
a partial listing

	Structural	Plaza	Cache	
O. princeps	1			
P. corvinus	38	39		
tipped	26	28		
broken	7	8		
limy	1	0		
unmodified	4	3		
P. largillierti	4	7		
Marine	6	1	44	
Very small shells			346	
Neocyclotus			58	(17%)
Bulimulus			9	(3%)
Lamellaxis			248	(71%)
Succinea			25	(7%)
Hydrobidae			6	(2%)
Total	49	47	390	

Whatever the use may be, the presence of two different *Pachychilus* species, each with a different archaeological distribution and cultural function, demonstrates once more how important it is to systematically collect all remains, even every example of the common jute.

BIBLIOGRAPHY

Feldman, L. H.
1970   "Moluscos Mayas, Especies y Origenes." *Estudios de Cultura Maya* 8:117–183.
1978   "Seibal and the Mollusks of the Usumacinta Valley," in *Excavations at Seibal: Artifacts,* by Gordon R. Willey, pp. 166–167. Memoirs of the Peabody Museum, vol. 14, no. 1. Harvard University, Cambridge, Massachusetts.
1979   "Invertebrados Arquelogicos," *Antropologicos de la Universidad de Yucatan, Boletin* 6:33-2-23.

Hellmuth, N.
1977   "Cholti-Lacandon (Chiapas) and Peten-Ytza Agriculture, Settlement Pattern and Population," in *Social Process in Maya Prehistory,* N. Hammond, ed., pp. 421–448. Academic Press, New York.

Longyear, J. M.
1952   *Copan Ceramics.* Carnegie Institution of Washington, No. 597. Washington, D.C.

Nations, J. D.
1979   "Snail Shells and Maize Preparation: A Lacandon Maya Analogy." *American Antiquity* 44:568–571.

Stromsvik, G.
1942   "Substela Caches and Stela Foundations at Copan and Quirigua." *Contributions to American Anthropology and History,* vol. 7, no. 37, pp. 65–96. Carnegie Institution of Washington, Publication 528. Washington, D.C.

Wonderley, A. W.
1981   *Late Postclassic Excavations at Naco, Honduras.* Latin American Studies Program, Dissertation Series. Cornell University.